Corporate Justice

Corporate Justice

Todd J. Clark
Professor of Law
North Carolina Central University School of Law

andré douglas pond cummings
Associate Dean and Professor of Law
Indiana Tech Law School

Carolina Academic Press
Durham, North Carolina

Print ISBN: 978-1-61163-358-0
eBook ISBN: 978-1-5310-0193-3
LCCN: 2016935733

Carolina Academic Press, LLC
700 Kent Street
Durham, North Carolina 27701
Telephone (919) 489-7486
Fax (919) 493-5668
www.cap-press.com

Printed in the United States of America

Contents

Table of Cases

Primary cases are in bold.

Acknowledgments

Todd J. Clark

First, I would like to thank God for putting me in a position to write about and shed light on issues that I find compelling. I would also like to thank my mother, Dora L. Clark, my father, Sherwood Hill, and my aunt, Selena Comer for all of their love and support. Additionally, I would like to thank my son, Jordan K. Clark, for serving as part of my motivation for writing. Hopefully, my writings and work as a professor will one day inspire him to achieve his greatest potential.

Second, working on this project with Dean andré douglas pond cummings has been amazing. Dean cummings was instrumental in helping me to enter the academy and his mentorship and friendship has helped me to become the professor I am today. Moreover, our work on this book has inspired me to think about the world from a different and more informed vantage point that has inured to the benefit of my classroom teaching and student mentorship.

In addition, I would like to thank Dean Angela Gilmore and Professors Reggie Momburn and Kimberly Cogdell for motivating and encouraging me to write this book. But for their inspiration and consistent support I would not have written it and for that I am forever in their debt.

I am also extremely grateful to have the honor of teaching at North Carolina Central University School of Law. Professor cummings and I have taught "Corporate Justice" since 2012 and the students that have participated in our past classes have substantially influenced these materials. Their passion, previous experiences, and classroom contributions challenged us to think more critically about the law. While we were listed as the instructors for the course, we were the true beneficiaries of the course experience. Many times, after class, we spent numerous hours reflecting and debating about the classroom commentary.

I also extend my sincere gratitude to Dean cummings and Professors Reggie Mombrun, Grace Wigal, and Mary Wright for all of the time they dedicated to helping me improve as both a scholar and a law professor. Anything that I have managed to do well as a member of the academy is largely a function of their dedication and vested interest in my success.

I am also grateful to Professors Atiba Ellis, Kevin Foy, Joseph Grant, Jena Martin, Steven Ramirez, and Cheryl Wade for reading drafts of our book. Their feedback and review was invaluable and substantially enhanced the quality of this book.

I also appreciate the scholarship grant provided by North Carolina Central University School of Law that supported the production of this book. Moreover, I am extremely grateful to the IT and administrative staff at North Carolina Central University School of Law in supporting the facilitation of the "Corporate Justice" course.

Last but not least, I am extremely grateful for the assistance provided by my research assistants Lauren McKoy and Raven Tyndall who worked diligently to help me organize this book.

andré douglas pond cummings

No book or manuscript makes it to publication without a talented team of contributors and supporters. I gratefully acknowledge that team of talented individuals here. First, I am extraordinarily grateful to my co-author and friend Todd J. Clark, who led us into this Corporate Justice journey with passion, innovation, and perseverance. This book would never have seen the light of day without Todd's vision, intellect, and persistence. Second, both Todd and I owe a debt of gratitude to the North Carolina Central University School of Law administration, staff, and students, particularly those four classes of students who signed-up to take a summer certificate course entitled "Corporate Justice." The NCCU Law students that engaged in the following material with us were sharp, hard-working, smart, and they challenged us consistently on the materials that follow. This coursebook has been shaped and sharpened by the excellent NCCU Law students that have taken our course. Thank you. Futher, I have been very impressed with the administration at NCCU Law and the staff, particularly the technical and IT staff as we have offered this course through distance education technology that mirrors an in-class experience in very real ways. Thank you to the Deans that had the vision to approve this course along with the Social Justice Lawyering summer certificate program, the staff who have assisted and supported our delivery of these materials, and again the students who have tackled this material with zeal and forward-thinking precision.

I am deeply indebted to the staff, student research assistants and faculty at Indiana Tech Law School and West Virgnia University College of Law who have worked side-by-side with me in compiling, editing, and drafting this book. To those administrative assistants, student research assistants, and faculty members who have supported my efforts, either by editing, organizing, assisting in drafting, or proofreading, I offer sincere appreciation and respect: Lydia LaMont, Michael Nissim-Sabat, Ruth de Wit, Jennifer Hitchcock, Kim Landis-Savieo, Noah Moore, Katrese Reeves, Prosper Batinge, Guadalupe Luna, Justin McKinzie, Celia Garza, and Phebe Poydras. Thank you.

Prior to going to press, Todd and I reached out to our friends in the Corporate Law professoriate and asked them to give a rigorous reading to our manuscript. I am so grateful to the following law professors and legal practitioners that provided incisive commentary and constructive criticism that improved our book immeasurably: Jena Martin, Steven Ramirez, Cheryl Wade, Atiba Ellis, Joseph Grant, and Kevin Foy. Thank you.

To our editorial team at the Carolina Academic Press, we express gratitude, particularly to Jefferson Moors who first saw potential in this project and offered us a book contract, Ryland Bowman who shepherded the project, and Grace Pledger who took us to the finish line with editing suggestions and assistance. Thank you.

Finally, I am personally grateful to my own little family that continues to sacrifice along with me as we created a new book in a never-before-offered subject matter while building a brand new law school in Fort Wayne, IN, the Indiana Tech Law School. Thank you to my forever partner Lavinia Mann Cummings and our babies, Cole Kaianuanu, Malia Ao-ilagi, and Maxwell Keavé. I cannot imagine the past four year journey, in creating, building, and bringing to accreditation an innovative and cutting-edge new law school while also drafting this coursebook, without the support, sunshine, and reality check that Luvie, Cole, Malia, and Max have provided. In addition, to the extended cummings and Mann families, I will always be grateful for the support, love and kindness that we can always count on.

Todd and I hope that all who read and study this book will be inspired and empowered to believe that a better and more just system of corporate law and capitalism can be pursued and achieved.

Introduction

Lawyers play a critical role in designing the social fabric of morality and justice. The following quote from Charles Hamilton Houston, Civil Rights activist, architect of the *Brown v. Board of Education* strategy, and former Dean of Howard Law School, eloquently highlights the ethos of this idea.

> [The] Negro lawyer must be trained as a social engineer and group interpreter. Due to the Negro's social and political condition ... the Negro lawyer must be prepared to anticipate, guide and interpret his group advancement.... [Moreover, he must act as] business advisor ... for the protection of the scattered resources possessed or controlled by the group.... He must provide more ways and means for holding within the group the income now flowing through it.[1]

In penning these words, Houston was endeavoring to inspire black lawyers to actively engage in the process of social and legal change. Houston famously proclaimed further that lawyers have a choice, to either become social engineers or parasites on society. Houston's efforts during the Civil Rights movement embody the essence of the type of training that is absent from most law school classrooms today. Houston's leadership during the Civil Rights movement consisted of much more than a discussion about the evils of segregation. Instead, his efforts were defined by his concerted activism as exemplified by his promulgation of the plan for overturning *Plessy v. Ferguson*, as well as his inspiration and mentoring of individuals like Thurgood Marshall, James Nabrit, Spottswood Robinson, A. Leon Higginbotham, Constance Baker Motley, Robert Carter and William Hastie to execute his ideas of social justice.

In an effort to capture the essence of Houston's charge to inspire students to get involved in the Civil Rights movement, beyond the walls of the classroom—it is our hope that this book will motivate students of all races to move beyond a preliminary discussion and investigation of what we call "corporate justice." More specifically, we endeavor to inspire students to become involved as activists and to promote real change toward equality and social justice in America's corporate boardrooms and on Wall Street.

In some business law textbooks, there is some, although inadequate, discussion regarding issues of corporate justice; however, there is little to no discussion concerning the tools

---

1. Genna Rae McNeil, Groundwork: Charles Hamilton Houston and the Struggle for Civil Rights (1983) (quoting Charles Hamilton Houston, *Personal Observations on the Summary of Studies in Legal Education as Applied to the Howard University School of Law,* (May 28, 1929)).

and processes by which future lawyers can actually engineer change. In essence, there is some talk, but little practical development of the skills needed or the pedagogical methods necessary to move students from the essence of the discussion of corporate justice to an existence as corporate justice activist.

The impetus behind this book is to get students to think more critically about the business world around them and to inspire them to get actively involved as agents of change. Through the readings and exercises included in this text, we are confident that you will walk away enlightened and will have a greater sense of your personal obligation to make a difference as well as the power you possess to effectuate change.

To develop our view of creating engineers of corporate justice, this book will place particular emphasis on how the law, and lawyers in their practice of the law, interact with corporations and other business enterprises. To facilitate this objective, this book will explore the following issues: foundational aspects of corporate governance; how issues of gender and racial diversity affect the corporate decision making processes; the causes and effects of the financial market crisis of 2008; regulation, or lack thereof, of credit default swaps and other derivative instruments; director/officer fiduciary duties; the Dodd-Frank Act; *Citizens United*, the prison industrial complex; and finally, we will explore the impact and effect of social movements on financial reform.

Furthermore, to aid in our discussion about the role of corporations in a just society, we will also look at how corporations are governed, and what responsibilities board members and officers have in their governance. We will ask how it is possible that companies like Enron, Lehman Brothers, AIG, and WorldCom so recently functioned in a manner that apparently defrauded investors and the general public. We will seek to understand the stabilizing influence that good corporate governance brings to society, and how it is possible for shareholders and others to benefit from the positive influences that corporations can have on society.

We hope that after reading and studying this book you will have a better understanding of the role that business plays in American life, and of the ways in which the law is an integral part of business. And more importantly, we hope that you will come to appreciate the role that you can have in helping to create a more justice oriented economic structure.

A. What Is Corporate Justice?

Corporate Justice is an elusive term — easily stated, but not easily defined. At its core, Corporate Justice refers to a responsibility, even a moral obligation, which businesses and corporations have to engage fairly, civilly and responsibly in the world and community that they do business and from which they derive profits. More than that, the concept of Corporate Justice also focuses on the roles that shareholders, policy makers, other stakeholders and the community at large have in fostering a more just and responsible business community.

Corporate Justice requires that corporations do no harm in their pursuit of profits. Corporate Justice acknowledges the exciting and important role that a successful corporation can play in the lives of the founders, stakeholders and communities with which that business intersects. While recognizing this exciting role, Corporate Justice expects that founders, stakeholders and executives in a business will honor human potential and eschew profits when those profits are derived from unfairness, inequality, danger, and damage.

Corporate Justice recognizes the value, even beauty, of capitalism and free enterprise, as an economic system that when intelligently, effectively and lightly regulated enables beneficiaries the opportunity to realize their best potential. Human capital is successfully harnessed when an efficient Corporate Justice regime exists. Corporate Justice rejects the Law and Economics and free market fundamentalist approaches to capital markets, recognizing that the weaknesses in Law and Economics and unfettered capital markets is the failure of these approaches to appropriately account for inequality, social injustice, entrenched elitism, and continuing discrimination that pervades global capital markets, perpetrated both by its market makers and market players. Corporate Justice embraces capitalism and free enterprise while simultaneously demanding that corporate law and corporate citizens eliminate inequities, discrimination, and entrenchment of the elite.

Corporate Justice challenges the assumption that a corporation is a fictional person imbued with free speech protections under the First Amendment to the United States Constitution. Corporate Justice advocates for Shareholder Activism as a valuable method in challenging the socially dysfunctional corporation. Corporate Justice identifies the perverse incentives inherent in the privatization of certain industries including detention and prison regimes and challenges those corporations that pursue these perverse ends. Corporate Justice recognizes that only when human capital is fully exercised, rather than the elite protected, will true capitalism emerge.[2] To that end, Corporate Justice challenges the Board of Director model where only elite, primarily white male executives, dominate the corporate world in the United States.

B. Corporate Justice Is Not Corporate Social Responsibility or Economic Justice

Corporate Justice is not the same as Corporate Social Responsibility (CSR). In fact, CSR can properly be viewed as a subset of Corporate Justice. While CSR focuses on the corporation and its decision makers, as noted above, Corporate Justice focuses on these individuals as well as the corporation's shareholders, policy makers, other stakeholders, and the community at large.

CSR has gained great popularity in recent years and much has been written and said about a corporation's responsibility to engage in socially responsible behavior. CSR is often defined as a company operating in a manner that respects and accounts for its social and environmental impact on the citizens and communities in which it engages its business. A corporation engaging in CSR will be committed to enacting policies that integrate responsible practices into its daily operations, and with great transparency, monitoring these policies and reporting on the progress made toward its socially responsible goals.[3] The publication *Making Good Business Sense* defines CSR as "the continuing commitment by business to behave ethically and contribute to economic development while improving the quality of life of the workforce and their families as well as of the local community and society at large."[4]

---

2. STEVEN RAMIREZ, LAWLESS CAPITALISM (NYU Press 2013).

3. *Corporate Social Responsibility*, AsYOUSOW.ORG, (last visited Nov. 10, 2015), http://www.asyousow.org/about-us/theory-of-change/corporate-social-responsibility/.

4. Lord Holme & Richard Watt, *Making Good Business Sense*, THE WORLD BUSINESS COUNCIL FOR SUSTAINABLE DEVELOPMENT (last visited May 15, 2016), http://www.wbcsd.org/work-program/business-role/previous-work/corporate-social-responsibility.aspx.

Today, CSR includes a broad commitment by businesses to improve the lives of its employees and to improve the conditions of the communities in which they do business. These objectives are most often met by companies adopting fair policies and developing cultures that include governance and ethics, employee hiring, opportunity and training, responsible supply chain and purchasing policies, and responsible energy and environmental impacts.[5] Of course, CSR is not without its critics.[6]

Corporate Justice encompasses much more than CSR. While Corporate Justice embraces the ethos and goals of CSR, it requires much more than good citizenship by a corporation. Corporate Justice seeks to hold corporate leaders, shareholders, politicians and the community at large responsible for ensuring that financial markets operate in a manner that promotes the financial well-being of more than a corporation's own shareholders or the corporation's own decision makers. While Corporate Justice does not reject the idea of generating profit, it does mandate that profit maximization cannot be a corporation's only objective. Unlike CSR, Corporate Justice recognizes that a corporation's obligation to promote this responsibility is a responsibility that is shared by groups in and outside of the corporation.

Similarly, Corporate Justice is not the same as Economic Justice. Economic Justice can properly be viewed as a subset of or corollary to Corporate Justice. Economic Justice encompasses the moral principles which guide the design of economic institutions. These institutions all differently determine how each person earns a living, enters into contracts, exchanges goods and services with others and otherwise produces an independent material foundation for his or her economic sustenance. The ultimate purpose of economic justice is to free each person to engage creatively in the unlimited work beyond economics, that of the mind and the spirit.[7]

C. Shareholder Activism

One of the ways in which Corporate Justice seeks to proactively engage corporate law, particularly in challenging the dysfunctional corporate citizen, is through shareholder activism. Examples of shareholder activism abound and will be covered in great detail in later sections of this book. Because shareholders of a corporation are imbued with certain rights, a solitary, committed shareholder can wield great power when she recognizes that a corporation is potentially injuring society. As you study the material in this book, and think deeply about the arguments and cases presented herein, consider the statements above made by Charles Hamilton Houston in connection with social engineering and the financial condition of people of color in the United States and across the world. A lawyer can play a significant role in seeking and pursuing justice locally, nationally and globally. As you read about shareholder power and corporate leadership, contemplate on the avenues that are available to forward-thinking, socially conscious practitioners of the law, to seek and to perpetuate economic equality and social justice. We believe that a solitary,

---

5. *Corporate Social Responsibility, supra* note 3.

6. Aneen Karnani, *The Case Against Corporate Social Responsibility,* Wall St. J. (Aug. 23, 2010), *available at* http://online.wsj.com/article/SB10001424052748703338004575230112664504890.html.

7. *Defining Economic Justice and Social Justice,* Center for Economic and Social Justice CESJ.org, (last visited May 14, 2016), http://www.cesj.org/learn/definitions/defining-economic-justice-and-social-justice/.

committed attorney, who is also a corporate leader or shareholder can become a dynamic social engineer. In the prescient words of Margaret Mead "[N]ever doubt that a small group of thoughtful, committed citizens can change the world; indeed, it's the only thing that ever has."

Authors' Note

All cases, law review articles, and newspaper stories that follow have been reproduced with permission (where required) and have been edited by the authors for relevance, scope, and space. In all of the edited material, original footnotes have been omitted and most references eliminated. While quotation marks have been retained in many places to indicate direct quotation from a source other than the author, we have omitted those references as well. In order to view all citations, footnotes and references, a reader must pull-up and review the original article at the place of first publication. The place of original publication appears prominently at the beginning of or in the first footnote of each edited and re-printed piece.

Corporate Justice

Chapter One

Corporate Law Basics

A. Structure of a Corporation

1. What Is a Corporation and How Does It Come into Existence?

A corporation is a business entity that allows its owners, also known as shareholders or stockholders, to invest money into the business without incurring personal liability for the business's debts and obligations. This legal structure is of significant importance to the facilitation of commerce and wealth development because the limited liability protection offered through the corporation increases the likelihood that potential investors will be willing to invest. The corporation is not the only choice of business entity that an owner may select. Contingent upon the state in which the business plans to operate, many of the following entities may be available: a general partnership, a limited partnership ("LP"), a limited liability partnership ("LLP"), an S corporation ("S corp"), a limited liability company ("LLC"), a professional corporation ("PC") or a professional LLC. While each of the aforementioned business entities offers different tax and limitation of liability benefits, the sole focus of this book is on corporations, also known as "C corporations."

A corporation comes into existence once its articles of incorporation are filed with the state in which the corporation is formed. A corporation's articles of incorporation are analogous to an individual's birth certificate. The articles signify that the corporation is "alive" and able to transact business. What must be included in a corporation's articles of incorporation vary by state. Typically, the following things must be included regardless of the state in which the corporation is incorporated:

(1) Name of the corporation;

(2) Name of the registered agent: This item is often required because the person listed as the registered agent is the person to whom all legal notices and official corporate documentation will be sent;

(3) Duration: Many states will not require that a specific duration be included. Instead, most states allow for a company to comply with this requirement by indicating that it will operate "perpetually" (for as long as it is engaged in business);

(4) Number of authorized shares: The number of authorized shares refers to the maximum number of shares that a corporation can "issue";[1]

(5) Name and address of the directors;

(6) Name and address of the incorporators: An incorporator is a person that has assisted the corporation in getting started; and

(7) Purpose of the corporation: Normally, a corporation's purpose is stated very broadly to avoid having to amend its articles in the event that the corporation decides to change the nature of its business. Therefore, most articles merely state the corporate purpose is to "engage in any lawful business activity."

2. Corporate Logistics

Undergraduate students who are interested in law school often major in political science because there is a belief that majoring in this discipline provides a measurable substantive benefit to law school preparation. While this seems to be a fundamental tenet, we have yet to observe its benefit in any meaningful way. However, there is at least one place where a political science degree can be useful in the law school environment—in helping students to understand the relationship between shareholders, board members and officers in a corporation. The relationship between these parties operates much like the federal government's checks and balances system. The primary purpose of the checks and balances system is to prevent tyranny by ensuring that no one branch of government becomes too powerful and that power in each branch remains separate. To accomplish this goal, each of the three branches of government (Legislative, Executive, and Judicial) has a check on the other. For example, the central power of the legislative branch is to "make laws." If the legislative branch introduces and votes to approve a new bill it does not become law unless the executive branch approves it. If the executive branch does not veto the bill, and it becomes law, the judicial branch may determine that the law is unenforceable because it is unconstitutional. This is a basic example of how the checks and balances system operates between governmental branches in the United States.

The structure of a corporation is similar to the government's system of checks and balances. While the central purpose of the checks and balances system is to prevent tyranny, the central purpose of the corporate structure is multifaceted. It can be used to generate profit, to limit liability, to provide tax benefits or to serve a social or public benefit. The purpose is largely determined by a corporation's articles of incorporation, state and federal law as well as the relevant case law.

In a corporation, the three primary parties internal to the organization are the shareholders, the officers, and the board of directors. The shareholders are the owners of a corporation, the officers are the day-to-day executives that run the corporation, and the directors are the supervisors or pace setters of a corporation who establish its goals and policies. In terms of checks and balances in a corporation, let's start with the shareholders since they are the "owners" of the business. In a basic corporation, shareholders have a check on the board in that the shareholders have the power to elect and remove board members. In addition, unless otherwise stated in a corporation's articles of incorporation, bylaws, or in a State statute or rule, the shareholders approve any fundamental

---

1. In the context of corporations, the word issue means to sell. Once a corporation "issues" shares, those shares are considered to "issued and outstanding."

corporate change. Typical fundamental corporate changes include a sale of substantially all of a corporation's assets, a merger, modification of the articles of incorporation, or dissolution of the corporation (terminating the corporation's existence). Shareholders also have an indirect check on the officers because it is the board that hires the officers. As such, in theory, the shareholders have the power to influence who will serve as the officers of the corporation because the shareholders appoint the directors.

Boards have a check on the shareholders in that it is the board that sets the long term strategic plan for the corporation. Essentially, it is the board's vision that determines whether the corporation earns a profit and if so, how much of that profit the shareholders will receive. Shareholders delegate this decision-making function to the board of directors. Again, the board of directors have a check on the officers in that it is the board that hires and fires the officers.

To see how the officers have the power to check the shareholders and the directors, we must revisit our previous comment that it is the shareholders "who determine who will serve as the officers of the corporation because the shareholders appoint the directors." Interestingly, this is not entirely true. To adequately understand why this statement is not wholly accurate, one must understand shareholder voting. Shareholders vote in two situations, fundamental corporate changes and for the election and removal of directors (shareholders may also have the power to vote on non-fundamental corporate changes; if the articles of incorporation, bylaws or State law provide). Shareholder voting takes place at the annual meeting, the meeting that the corporation holds every year to update the investing public and the shareholders about the corporation's past and future performance, or the special meeting, any meeting other than the annual meeting. Prior to that meeting, the officers of the corporation send out a proxy statement[2] explaining what actions the shareholders will vote on at the meeting and more importantly, a list of directors for election. Based on this practice, the officers set the agenda for what issues the shareholders will consider as well as identify the candidates from which the shareholders will vote to elect. Accordingly, it is the officers who decide who will serve as their superiors because the officers control what names make the ballot for shareholder consideration. Through this practice, it is likely that the officers will identify directorial candidates who will maximize the officers' power in the corporation.

a. The Board of Directors

Board members are voted into service by the shareholders. Once in position, board members owe fiduciary duties to the corporation to act in the corporation's best interests. The primary purpose of the board is to set the long term strategic vision of the corporation and to hire officers to effectuate that vision. It is the board that sets the course of action for the corporation. Once the board makes this determination, the board empowers the corporation's officers to carry out the corporation's vision.

b. Executive Officers

The executive officers are those persons that run the day to day operations of the corporation. For those of you that remember George Lucas's 1970's Star Wars movies, the board's relationship with a corporation's officers is analogous to Senator Palpatine's relationship with Darth Vader.

---

2. The proxy statement is essentially a newsletter that contains information about the corporation.

Palpatine was the evil leader of the Galactic Empire (the "Empire") who set into action a plan to eliminate the Jedi Order in order to expand his rule, without opposition, throughout the universe. While Palpatine was clearly the leader of the Empire, it was Darth Vader who Palpatine empowered to carry out the day to day aspects of his maniacal vision. Similarly, the board appoints the corporation's executive officers to execute the board's directives. The board of directors are analagous to Palpatine and the executive officers are more closely aligned with Darth Vader.

c. Shareholders

The shareholders are effectively the owners of a corporation. Shareholders own the outstanding shares of a company and hold rights which allow them to elect the directors of a corporation and vote on important company matters, as discussed above. The owners of a corporation hold shares with an eye toward an increase in share value and to have some say in how the corporation is run.

As corporations have gained power and influence in U.S. and global markets, the individuals that run corporations have concomitantly grown to wield great power. Today's corporations control vast wealth and some multinational corporations employ thousands and thousands of people. We will consider the power of the modern corporation in later chapters, but seeing how powerful corporations have become, an important question becomes who really runs these corporations?

d. Who "Really" Runs America's Corporate Boardrooms?

According to a study published by Alliance for Board Diversity ("ABD") entitled "Missing Pieces: Women and Minorities on Fortune 500 Boards—2010 Alliance for Board Diversity Census" Fortune 500 companies are dominated by white males. ABD determined that of all the board seats of the companies listed on the fortune 500 list:

- 77.6% were held by White men
- 12.7% were held by White women
- 2.7% were held by Black men
- 2.3% were held by Hispanic men
- 1.9% were held by Black women
- 1.8% were held by Asian and Pacific Islander men
- 0.7% were held by Hispanic women
- 0.3% were held by Asian and Pacific Islander women

In regards to board leadership positions, 94.9% were held by white men. These statistics highlight a reality that America's wealth centers are largely controlled by one class of people, wealthy white men.

While we will discuss this issue in much greater detail in chapter six, consider the following questions:

(1) Should we care about whether America's corporate boards are diverse?

(2) Are these statistics the function of an underlying ethos of discrimination or are these statistics representative of the fact that white males tend to be the most experienced and knowledgeable candidates for the position?

(3) If you were a shareholder of a Fortune 500 company, would board diversity matter to you if the company's financial performance was exceptional?

(4) Are the concepts of board diversity and positive financial performance mutually exclusive? More specifically, does a mandate for diversity increase the possibility that financial performance may increase? Or decline?

(5) Should the law mandate greater levels of diversity?

In an effort to explain the lack of diversity in America's corporate boardrooms, Professor Steven Ramirez, in a very compelling piece entitled "Games CEOs Play and Interest Convergence Theory: Why Diversity Lags in America's Boardrooms and What To Do About It," advances the idea that a lack of diversity occurs because it is actually the executive officers who select the board, not the shareholders. According to Ramirez, this method of selection inhibits corporations from obtaining any meaningful amount of board diversity because CEOs typically select board members that mirror themselves.

> Of course, this being America at the turn of the twenty-first century, many still do believe in race. Because many of these maleducated denizens of our racialized society are shareholders or board members, the pressure to insist upon culturally diverse boards is diluted. Similarly, it is clear that our racialized society fails to invest in the human capital of minority groups at the same rate it invests in whites. Economists also have shown that minority groups generally do not have access to the same social capital—or social networks—that are accessible to whites. Proportionately, this means an artificial shortage of elite people of color throughout our society in general, and for board service in particular. Thus, CEOs may be tempted, under cover of these facts, to avoid any compulsion for diversifying their boards. Instead, studies have demonstrated that executives will seek to fill boards with demographic and cultural reproductions of themselves. This conclusion enjoys empirical support from abroad suggesting that the selection of board members and senior management teams are naturally subject to homosocial reproduction. It is no accident that boards are not diverse.

> After all, most people do not get to pick their bosses. Yet in America, even today after much heralded reforms, CEOs of publicly held companies get to pick their bosses—the board of directors. As I have previously demonstrated, in corporate America director elections resemble elections in Soviet Russia—there is only one candidate to vote for because generally only management solicits proxies and SEC rules do not require the inclusion of candidates running against management's nominees. Given this power, it would be natural for a CEO to select a board of directors comprised of the CEO's clones. Certainly this would be a formula that would encourage maximum, even excessive, pay and benefits for the CEO. Instead, CEOs do the next best thing—they select their cultural and demographic clones. This effectively achieves the same outcome: CEO power over board selection leads to enhanced compensation of CEOs. Recent history confirms that American CEOs have received excessive, even outrageous, compensation. Homosocial reproduction is likely a prime cause of this malady.

> Another outcome that could be expected from allowing CEOs to select their boards would be that boards reflect the cultural background of the selecting CEO. Again, this is exactly the longstanding reality in corporate America. CEOs and boards demographically mirror each other. Quite frequently CEOs select other CEOs for their boards, and even place them on the all-important compensation committee. It is only natural that a CEO would prefer someone that is culturally proximate to himself; nevertheless, it effectively perpetuates yesteryear's tradition of racial apartheid. I have previously referred to this dynamic

as a "racial half-life," meaning an entrenched social convention that leads to racially disparate results with no prospect of disruption or violation of law. If directors select CEOs and CEOs select directors, a preexisting apartheid tradition can deteriorate very slowly before giving way to a racially equitable process. Indeed, at today's rate of board diversification, the arrival of racial equity at this level may be measured in centuries rather than decades.

(1) Is Professor Ramirez right, do executive officers hire their own bosses?

(2) Technically, in many corporations, the directors are selected by the Corporate Governance and Nominating Committee; however, this committee often consists of corporate officers or is often largely influenced by the corporation's officers. For an example of how the process typically operates, consider the following "Corporate Governance Guidelines" from Ingersoll Rand, a publicly traded company that specializes in enhancing "the quality and comfort of air in homes and buildings; transporting and protecting food and perishables; and increasing industrial productivity and efficiency":

> Under the Articles of Association, the Board of Directors has authority to fill vacancies in the Board and appoint additional directors (in each case subject to their re-election at the next annual general meeting) and to nominate candidates for election by the shareholders. The screening process is done by the Corporate Governance and Nominating Committee with direct input from the Chairman and CEO and from the other directors and from time to time with the assistance of director search firms. In considering candidates for director, the Corporate Governance and Nominating Committee will take into account all factors it considers appropriate, including, among other things, breadth of experience, understanding of business and financial issues, ability to exercise sound judgment, diversity, leadership, and achievements and experience in matters affecting business and industry. The Corporate Governance and Nominating Committee considers the entirety of each candidate's credentials and believes that at a minimum each nominee should satisfy the following criteria: highest character and integrity, experience and understanding of strategy and policy-setting, sufficient time to devote to Board matters, and no conflict of interest that would interfere with performance as a director. Shareholders may recommend candidates for Board membership for consideration by the Corporate Governance and Nominating Committee. Such recommendations should be sent to the Committee, care of the Secretary of the Company. Candidates recommended by shareholders are evaluated in the same manner as director candidates identified by any other means.

(3) Is a lack of board diversity happening because of a conscious racist agenda, or do people merely select whom they know or other people with whom they feel most comfortable?

B. Stock Ownership and Rights

1. Issuance of Stock

When a corporation needs to raise capital for expenses and expansion, the management of the company has several options. One option is to procure cash from management's or owner's personal funds as provided through a loan to the corporation (often to be repaid when the company is profitable). Another option is to seek small business loans and other types of loans from local or national banks (which often comes with high interest rates attached). A common alternative for raising capital is through issuance of equity or debt through the corporation itself. In issuing equity, management of a company offers shares of ownership (also called "stock") to investors that will provide working capital for the company and a share of ownership and profit for those that purchase equity shares in the company. The sale of equity or shared ownership in the company is primarily done through an issuance either of common stock or preferred shares (and sometimes both) in the company.

Common stock is a class of stock that entitles its owner to vote on fundamental corporate changes. The holder of a share a common stock hopes to buy low and sell high, thereby allowing the owner to take advantage of market appreciation. In addition, the owner may receive a special type of distribution from a share of a corporation's profits called a dividend, at the corporation's discretion if the corporation is profitable, for each share of common stock that the owner owns. The key point here is that common stock holders are not "entitled" to receive a dividend—instead, whether to distribute a dividend is within the board's discretion.

Preferred stock is any share that has a right or rights not provided to the holders of common stock. The most typical type of preference is a contractual right to receive a dividend. While the holders of common stock "may" receive a dividend, the holders of preferred stock are contractually entitled to receive a dividend. Therefore, preferred stock is considered a hybrid of debt and equity. Preferred stock has attributes of "debt" because the corporation is required to pay the dividend much like the corporation is required to pay back a loan to a creditor. Preferred stock has attributes of "equity" because the owner of preferred stock is also considered an owner of the business and a share of preferred stock can experience market appreciation much like common stock. Also, preferred shares are essentially negotiated contracts, meaning that one contractual right might include voting for some or all members of the board of directors.

In addition to the right to receive a dividend, preferred stock can also confer one of the following types of preferences: redemption (the right to force the corporation to buy back the stock at a certain time or for a specific price), conversion (the right to trade in the preferred stock for some other form of consideration, such as common stock), and liquidation (the right to receive a greater benefit upon the occurrence of some condition such as the merger of the corporation). The disadvantage of preferred stock is that it generally does not have voting rights unless provided for in the articles of incorporation, and is typically not entitled to an unlimited upside in the share of profits.

In sum, when an investor purchases equity ownership in a company, the purchaser becomes a shareholder and is entitled to specific rights as an owner in the company, as enumerated below. The shareholder, depending on the amount of ownership purchased, will have some decision making power and will also have a stake in the profits (and losses) of the company.

Stock can be purchased from one of two entities. First, it can be purchased from the corporation. If stock is purchased from the corporation, such transaction is effectively referred to as an "issuance" and the consideration given by the investor in exchange for the share goes directly to the corporation. The corporation can then use this money to make more money by purchasing additional equipment, buying additional materials or by investing the funds. If the company is able to make more money and increase profits, then it is possible that the value of the shareholder's share will increase which is known as "market appreciation." If this happens, the shareholder is very pleased because the share is now worth more than the price that the shareholder paid.

Second stock can also be sold by a current shareholder. If a current shareholder sells a share to a third party, the current shareholder will provide the third party with a share of stock and the third party will give any consideration directly to the shareholder. In this transaction, the corporation does not make any money from the sale. Instead, any financial gain goes directly to the current shareholder. If the current shareholder sells all of the shares that the current shareholder owns, the current shareholder ceases to be a shareholder.

In issuing debt, management of a company seeks a "loan" from investors where the company receives a finite amount of money from an investor, pays interest on that amount for a designated period of time, and then returns the corpus of the money to the investor once the time period has run. The sale of debt is typically accomplished through issuance of notes or debentures to the investing public that the company is obligated to repay (also referred to as "bonds").

When an investor purchases debt in a company, the purchaser does not become an owner of the company, but becomes a creditor of the company. The investor holds a "note" or "debenture" similar to a bond or an IOU. An investor does not receive rights as a shareholder or part owner, rather the investor receives interest payments at an agreed upon percentage, and expects full repayment of the borrowed amount upon a date certain in the future. Issuing debt allows a company to receive much needed capital, but rather than giving up ownership in return, simply obligates itself to repay the amount received when the company becomes more profitable.

2. Basic Shareholder Rights

Ownership of a corporation is vested in those that hold or own equity shares of stock in a particular company. Corporate law dictates that when a company is incorporated that it vests ownership of the company in stockholders. Other business entity types, such as LLCs or S corps also vest ownership in shareholders or "members." Shares of stock represent an ownership stake in a company and the value of those shares loosely interpreted captures the value of a particular corporation. Though many disagree, United States lawmakers accept the efficient market hypothesis as a baseline for initiating laws that regulate the sale and re-sale of stock. The efficient market hypothesis essentially posits that the actual market value of a particular share of company ownership reflects the true value of the company, as multiplied by the number of outstanding shares (also known as "market capitalization" or "market cap").

Shareholders as owners are imbued with particular rights and responsibilities based on their ownership of shares in the company. In a general sense, shareholders have several primary rights that ownership of shares vests in them, including (1) the ability to vote on major issues that impact a company; these include voting to approve modifications of a corporation's articles of incorporation or bylaws, a merger, a sale of substantially all of a corporation's assets, or dissolution; (2) ownership of a portion of the assets of a company (but no individual claim on those assets); (3) the right to elect a board of directors that will shepherd the company on a going forward basis; (4) a right to inspect some corporate books and records; (5) an ability to sue the company for wrongful acts or abuse of power; (6) an entitlement to dividends if given; and (7) the right to transfer ownership if desired. These rights provide shareholders a stake in the company and invite the fiction that shareholders are the "owners" of a particular company. In small companies or corporations that are not public, including those called "closely held" corporations, it can be true that ownership of stock provides power and "ownership" in the stockholders. In large public companies, stock ownership is typically spread across millions of shareholders, thus making the power of the board of directors and that of the day-to-day executive officers much broader than in small or non-public corporations. That is to say, that in large public companies, great power is wielded by members of the board of directors and even more so by primary day-to-day executives, including the Chief Executive Officer (CEO), Chief Financial Officer (CFO), Chief Operating Officer (COO) and so on.

3. Primary and Secondary Markets

Shares in a corporation are referred to as "securities." The sale of a security occurs in many ways and can happen on multiple markets. A security encompasses many types of investment vehicles besides shares, but the primary securities that are sold to the general public and institutional investors include stock, bonds, notes, debentures, and investment contracts. As introduced briefly above, the two principal markets where securities are sold are the primary market and the secondary market. The primary market consists of issuers and investors where a corporation, as issuer, offers securities, either in the form of equity or debt, to purchasers or investors who buy the security with an eye toward investment and gain. In a primary market scenario, the issuer is literally selling ownership shares or debt instruments to an investor whose purchase of those shares provides capital directly to the issuing company. The primary market is the entry point for companies seeking new or additional capital and often makes use of the underwriting services of investment banks to secure capital up front with the responsibility of actually selling the securities left to the underwriter. While the primary market enables an issuing corporation to raise capital, it is important to note that a security may be resold, perhaps hundreds of times, but the first and primary sale is the one where the issuing company receives capital in exchange for the purchase.[3] This is what was described above as purchasing stock from a corporation.

The secondary securities market is distinct from the primary market because the secondary market consists of investors trading securities with other investors with an expectation that market share price will increase. Once capital has been raised by the issuing corporation in the primary market sale, a secondary trading market develops as investors hold a corporation's shares expecting the market price to increase and then look to sell that security to a secondary investor who looks to purchase the share with the hope that it will continue to increase in market price or yield attractive dividends. Corporate disclosures are extraordinarily important for secondary market traders so that investors can monitor the health and vitality of a particular company before deciding whether to purchase shares of that company from a similarly situated seller who has decided to sell shares in order to realize gains or avoid future losses. Nearly all buying and selling of stock, conducted by average citizens on various trading mechanisms like E*Trade and ScottTrade, occurs on the secondary market where, for example, a buy order to purchase 100 shares of Disney actually requires a current Disney shareholder who wants to sell 100 shares. This is what was described above as purchasing stock from a current shareholder.

Thus, an initial public offering (IPO) by a corporation occurs on the primary market, and represents the first public capital raising effort of a formerly private company. The

---

3. *A Look at Primary and Secondary Markets*, Investopedia (last visited May 15, 2016), http://www.investopedia.com/articles/02/101102.asp.

IPO is where offering prices are established.[4] Following an IPO, with the issuing company no longer involved, shares in that corporation are traded amongst individual traders (or entities) on the secondary market, where these previously sold IPO shares are traded for a second, and third time, and so on. The New York Stock Exchange, and other major exchanges around the world represent examples of organized structures of investors trading amongst themselves on the secondary market.

When the United States Congress passed federal law to regulate capital markets in the aftermath of the Great Depression, it enacted the Securities Act of 1933 (the "1933 Act") to regulate the primary market and the Securities Exchange Act of 1934 (the "Exchange Act") to regulate the secondary market. The 1933 Act was adopted during an era where investor confidence and capital market stability in the U.S. was at a devastating low. In the years leading up to the Great Depression, it has been estimated that 50% of all companies offering stock investments were defrauding the investing public. This motivated the government to pass legislation that was meant to bring light and disclosure to the U.S. capital markets. Thus, the 1933 Act, sometimes referred to as the "truth in securities" law, became the nation's first federal legislation regulating companies that issue securities to the public. The 1933 Act requires that issuers of securities provide voluminous disclosure of company information to the investing public and to the Securities and Exchange Commission ("SEC"). This public disclosure, called a "registration statement" serves the purpose of the 1933 Act's objectives: requiring that investors have significant information on securities for sale, and prohibiting misrepresentations and fraud on the part of the issuing company.[5] Ultimately, by disclosing important financial information through registration, including disclosure of the company's property, details regarding the security being offered, information on the management of the company, and independently audited financial statements, investors can make more informed decisions in their trading.

In contrast to the 1933 Act, the Exchange Act regulates transactions of securities on the secondary market, and it created the SEC, which regulates the securities industry. The Exchange Act was designed to protect investors by requiring mandatory disclosures to investors allowing them to make informed investment decisions. Additionally, the Exchange Act regulates both the secondary markets (stock exchanges) and their participants (i.e., brokers and issuers).[6] The Exchange Act requires that companies file periodic reports, produce proxy materials for shareholder votes, disclose information regarding tender offers, restricts insider trading (trading while in possession of material nonpublic information), and requires certain market participants to file disclosure documents with the SEC.

4. The Facebook Example

To understand the importance of why disclosure matters to a potential investor who is selling stock, consider the first page of the prospectus that Facebook released prior to its IPO in May of 2012.[7]

---

4. David C. Mauer and Lemma W. Senbet, *The Effect of the Secondary Market on the Pricing of Initial Public Offerings: Theory and Evidence*, 27 J. Fin. Quant. Analysis 55, 58 (1992).

5. *The Laws that Govern the Securities Industry*, SEC.gov (October 1, 2013), http://www.sec.gov/about/laws.shtml.

6. *Securities Exchange Act of 1934*, Legal Information Institute (last visited Nov. 11, 2015) https://www.law.cornell.edu/wex/securities_exchange_act_of_1934.

7. A prospectus is a document that a corporation must file with the SEC, the governmental entity that regulates the purchase and sell of stock, in the event that a corporation desires to offer its shares for sale to the investing public. The prospectus provides material information about the corporation

"Facebook, Inc. is offering 180,000,000 shares of its Class A common stock and the selling stockholders are offering 241,233,615 shares of Class A common stock. We will not receive any proceeds from the sale of shares by the selling stockholders. This is our initial public offering and no public market currently exists for our shares of Class A common stock. We anticipate that the initial public offering price will be between $34.00 and $38.00 per share."[8]

(1) Why would it be important that Facebook explain who is selling the shares as part of the offering?

(2) Do potential investors care? If so, why?

(3) If Facebook's prospectus had indicated that all of the Class A common stock shares were being offered by the corporation would you have any concerns about acquiring Facebook's stock if you were an investor?

C. Fiduciary Duties

The "business judgment rule" protects the decisions of corporate leaders from subsequent challenge by shareholders or stakeholders who may ultimately disagree with the decisions of the board of directors or day-to-day executives. Essentially, the business judgment rule is based on an assumption that board members and executives have acted on an informed basis, in good faith, and in the best interest of the corporation and its shareholders. When the business judgment rule is applicable, courts will not challenge or second-guess the decisions made by corporate leaders and will not hold them personally liable even if the decision turns out to be wrong or results in a catastrophic loss for the corporation. Fiduciary duties attach to corporate board members and executives upon assumption of responsibility and those duties can be enumerated as the duty of care, the duty of loyalty, and the obligation to act in good faith.

1. Duty of Care

A corporation's board of directors and day-to-day executives are legally responsible to the corporation and its shareholders in a number of ways. Once an individual becomes a member of a company's board of directors s/he must exercise a duty of care toward the corporation and its shareholders. The duty of care can be likened to a standard akin to gross negligence in the torts context where a board member and an executive must act in the best interest of the corporation and its shareholders by fully informing themselves before making important corporate decisions. A failure to fully inform oneself before making certain business decisions or acting with reckless disregard toward the corporation's and shareholders best interest can end up in a board member or executive breaching their duty of care obligation. Cases like *Van Gorkom*, *Dodge v. Ford*, and *Wrigley v. Shlensky*

---

to ensure that the investing public is adequately informed prior to investing. Material information may include, but is not limited to financial statements, business projections, contingent liabilities, information about the directors and officers, who is selling stock, and background information about the business.

8. *Understanding the Facebook Prospectus*, N.Y. TIMES, May 16, 2012, *available at* http://www.nytimes.com/interactive/2012/05/04/business/dealbook/20120504_dbdoc-facebook-ipo.html.

(all covered in Chapter 2) define this duty of care responsibility that requires board members to act on full information, in good faith, and to place the best interest of the corporation at the forefront of all business decisions.

The board of directors, in informing themselves and considering all relevant information before making a decision should consider the following in order to adhere to its care obligation: (a) obtain all relevant information; (b) take the necessary time to consider all relevant information; (c) come to an understanding as to the terms and depth of proposed transactions; (d) monitor the corporation's finances and performance; (e) hire experts and professionals when necessary, including financial analysts, lawyers, accountants, compensation experts, etc.; (f) monitor the effectiveness of day-to-day executives and leaders; and (g) devise and monitor policies that ensure compliance with regulations and laws that affect the corporation's business.

While board members and day-to-day executives are often emboldened and incentivized by a motivation to maximize shareholder profits, these efforts to increase profits for shareholders (and for themselves) should never cause a board member or executive to ignore their duty of care obligation to shareholders or to act illegally or in bad faith. The question as to whether a "duty" exists to maximize shareholder profits has been passionately debated in recent years by scholars and practitioners alike with many concluding that there is no duty or affirmative responsibility that corporate leaders maximize profits, rather to holistically act in the best interest of the corporation and its shareholders. There can be no doubt however, that a strong incentive exists for all corporate leaders to seek to maximize profit to ensure shareholder satisfaction.

2. Duty of Loyalty

Board members and company executives owe a duty of loyalty to the corporation and its shareholders. The duty of loyalty is akin to a conflict of interest standard, where board members and those with a fiduciary duty to a corporation must avoid self-dealing and instances where the board member or executive enriches themselves at the expense of the corporation and its shareholders. While duty of care obligations are contested under a gross negligence type standard, when a duty of loyalty breach allegation is considered the protection of the business judgment rule yields. The business judgment rule gives way when a duty of loyalty breach occurs because in instances where loyalty has been compromised through a conflict of interest, self-dealing, or by competing with the corporation, such transactions are not in the best interest of the corporation.

Duty of loyalty breaches can occur in a number of circumstances, including when an executive engages in behavior that is a clear conflict of interest, when an executive or board members takes a corporate opportunity for himself rather than allowing the corporation to take advantage of it, and also when a corporate executive refuses to act when he knows he has an affirmative duty to act.

3. Obligation to Act in Good Faith

Most states conflate the obligation to act in good faith as a corollary to or subset of the duty of loyalty. Whether a third responsibility exists in a particular state to act in good faith, the obligation essentially requires corporate leaders to act if they are aware of a distinct obligation or responsibility to act rather than standing idly and refusing to engage in required action. A failure to act when a known obligation to act mandates action is akin to bad faith. At one point, Delaware courts seemed to be carving out a third triad duty requiring a new duty to act in good faith (see *Disney* in chapter two), but Chancery Court judges have recently pulled back and now describe the obligation to act in good faith as a subset of the duty of loyalty. Therefore, the duty of loyalty in Delaware requires a corporate leader to avoid self-dealing, usurping corporate opportunities, conflicts of interest, and failing to act when an affirmative obligation requires action (bad faith).

4. Bank of America — Countrywide Example

While cases in chapter two will illustrate what constitutes a breach under the duty of care, a modern example exists in the case of Bank of America's acquisition of Countrywide Financial during the mortgage crisis era. Countrywide Financial, under the leadership of then CEO Angelo Mozilo, aggressively wrote irresponsible loans to hundreds of thousands of borrowers in the period between 2000 and 2007. Due to relaxed lending standards and a voracious appetite by Wall Street to securitize home loans, Countrywide began extending thousands of loans to borrowers that simply could not ever repay the obligation that they undertook. At one point, CEO Mozilo described the loans that Countrywide was routinely extending as "toxic" because he understood that the many loans that he sold to Wall Street banks for purposes of packaging into investments, would ultimately fail.

When the mortgage crisis of 2008 befell Wall Street, Countrywide Financial, because of its predatory and fraudulent lending behavior, stood on the precipice of collapse. At that point, Bank of America's board of directors began considering whether to purchase Countrywide Financial and its portfolio of loans and clients. During the chaos of the financial market crisis of 2008, Bank of America finalized its acquisition of Countryside and agreed to absorb all of Countrywide's assets and liabilities. Since acquiring Countrywide, Bank of America has been hit with dozens of lawsuits brought by various investors and homeowners based on the behavior of Countrywide in the run-up to the financial market crisis. Bank of America has absorbed billions of dollars of liability as the board of directors of the bank has settled case after case brought against Countrywide, its new subsidiary bank.[9]

(1) Do you believe that the Bank of America board of directors fully informed themselves of Countrywide Financial's precarious position prior to agreeing to acquire Countrywide's banking portfolio?

(2) Could a Bank of America shareholder successfully establish a duty of care breach claim against Bank of America's board of directors for its acquisition of Countrywide Financial?

---

9. Sophia Pearson & Edvard Pettersson, *BofA's Countrywide Agrees to $500 Million MBS Settlement*, Bloomberg (April 7, 2013, 4:42P.M.) http://www.bloomberg.com/news/2013-04-17/bofa-s-country-wide-agrees-to-500-million-mbs-settlement.html.

Chapter Two

Duty of Care

Former Supreme Court Justice Sandra Day O'Connor, while visiting Howard University School of Law in 1995, was asked about her time on the Court with Howard Law alum Justice Thurgood Marshall. Justice O'Connor thoughtfully responded that whenever the Supreme Court was grappling with a particularly difficult case, and the discussion turned to Justice Marshall, he would lean back in his chair and tell a story. Sometimes the story was about the litigants in the case before the Court. Other times, the story was about Justice Marshall's experiences growing up in the United States as an African American during the days of Jim Crow and the Civil Rights Movement. Justice Marshall would purposefully slow down the Supreme Court machine to discuss real people and real lives. Justice O'Connor's point, of course, was that she deeply appreciated Justice Marshall's ability to remind the Court and his fellow justices, that in the final analysis, the cases they were deciding were about real people and that their decisions impacted the lives of the litigants before them and the lives of the hundreds of millions of U.S. citizens that would be impacted by the case outcome.

Inspired by Justice Marshall and Justice O'Connor, the following cases and material contain an explicit focus on the facts before the courts. While crucially important case law is developed in the following cases, the law always develops around the lives of real people embroiled in human drama. Corporate Justice examines the evolution of the law while remembering that the lives of citizens and constituents will always be important in the final analysis.

A. Action Cases

In what has become one of the more controversial cases in corporate law, *Dodge v. Ford* introduces us to several important concepts that must be considered in thinking about Corporate Justice. To begin, *Dodge v. Ford* introduces the idea that has long held sway in corporate law of "profit maximization," or the concept that corporations exist solely or primarily to increase profits for shareholders. Second, this case introduces the concept of the "business judgment rule" which essentially forbids courts from second guessing the business judgment of corporate executives, so long as those decisions are informed, made in good faith and in the best interest of the corporation and its shareholders.

The concept of profit maximization, that corporations exist primarily to enrich shareholders, has been challenged in recent years by those that argue the corporations operate for purposes beyond that of profit maximization. Further, while infamous, the *Dodge v. Ford* case was decided in 1919 by the Supreme Court of Michigan, hardly a court or state that carries great corporate precedential value. Still, the fact remains that many corporate executives and board members are highly motivated by the pressure to increase profits for shareholders and many corporate law teachers continue to put forward the construct that corporations exist primarily to increase profits for both the shareholders and the leadership through executive compensation. We will return to the concept of profit maximization and how it operates within our conception of corporate justice.

profit maximization

Dodge et al. v. Ford Motor Co. et al.

204 Mich. 459, 170 N.W. 668, 3 A.L.R. 413
Supreme Court of Michigan

Feb. 7, 1919.

Appeal from Circuit Court, Wayne County, in Chancery; George S. Hosmer, judge.

Action by John F. Dodge and Horace E. Dodge against the Ford Motor Company and others. Decree for plaintiffs, and defendants appeal. Affirmed in part and reversed in part.

Article II of the articles of association reads:

'The purpose or purposes of this corporation are as follows: To purchase, manufacture and placing on the market for sale of automobiles or the purchase, manufacture and placing on the market for sale of motors and of devices and appliances incident to their construction and operation.'

The parties in the first instance associating, who signed the articles, included Henry Ford, whose subscription was for 255 shares, John F. Dodge, Horace E. Dodge, the plaintiffs, Horace H. Rackham and James Couzens, who each subscribed for 50 shares, and several other persons. The company began business in the month of June, 1903.

The business of the company continued to expand. The cars it manufactured met a public demand, and were profitably marketed, so that, in addition to regular quarterly dividends equal to 5 per cent. monthly on the capital stock of $2,000,000, its board of directors declared and the company paid special dividends [totaling $41,000,000 from December 1911 to October 1915]. [During approximately the same period, sales and profits increased from 18,644 cars for a total profit of $4,521,509 up to 1,272,986 cars for a total profit of $173, 895,416. Essentially, over a five year period of time, car sales increased by 6,828% and total profit increased by 3,846%. Needless to say, the Ford Motor Company was making a lot of money.]

Originally, the car made by the Ford Motor Company sold for more than $900; however, from time to time, the selling price was lowered and by August 1916 the car was selling for $360.

No special dividend having been paid after October, 1915 (a special dividend of $2,000,000 was declared in November, 1916, before the filing of the answers), the plaintiffs, who together own 2,000 shares, or one-tenth of the entire capital stock of the Ford Motor Company, on the 2d of November, 1916, filed in the circuit court for the county of Wayne, in chancery, their bill of complaint, which bill was later, upon leave granted, on April 26, 1917, amended, in which bill they charge that since 1914 they have not been represented on the board of directors of the Ford Motor Company, and that since that time the policy of the board of directors has been dominated and controlled absolutely by Henry Ford, the president of the company, who owns and for several years has owned 58 per cent. of the entire capital stock of the company; that the directors of the company are Henry Ford, David H. Gray, Horace H. Rackham, F. L. Klingensmith, and James Couzens, and the executive officers Henry Ford, president, F. L. Klingensmith, treasurer, and Edsel B. Ford, son of Henry Ford, secretary. On the 31st of July, 1916, the end of its last fiscal year, the said Henry Ford gave out for publication a statement of the financial condition of the company:

> 'And the said Henry Ford, president of the company, has declared it to be the settled policy of the company not to pay in the future any special dividends, but to put back into the business for the future all of the earnings of the company, other than the regular dividend of five per cent. (5%) monthly upon the authorized capital stock of the company—two million dollars ($2,000,000).'

This declaration of the future policy, it is charged in the bill, was published in the public press in the city of Detroit and throughout the United States in substantially the following language:

"'My ambition,' declared Mr. Ford, 'is to employ still more men; to spread the benefits of this industrial system to the greatest possible number, to help them build up their lives and their homes. To do this, we are putting the greatest share of our profits back into the business.'"

It is charged further that the said Henry Ford stated to plaintiffs personally, in substance, that as all the stockholders had received back in dividends more than they had invested they were not entitled to receive anything additional to the regular dividend of 5 per cent. a month, and that it was not his policy to have larger dividends declared in the future, and that the profits and earnings of the company would be put back into the business for the purpose of extending its operations and increasing the number of its employees, and that, inasmuch as the profits were to be represented by investment in plants and capital investment, the stockholders would have no right to complain. It is charged (paragraph 16) that—

The said Henry Ford, 'dominating and controlling the policy of said company, has declared it to be his purpose—and he has actually engaged in negotiations looking to carrying such purposes into effect—to invest millions of dollars of the company's money in the purchase of iron ore mines in the Northern Peninsula of Michigan or state of Minnesota; to acquire by purchase or have built ships for the purpose of transporting such ore to smelters to be erected on the River Rouge adjacent to Detroit in the county of Wayne and state of Michigan; and to construct and install steel manufacturing plants to produce steel products to be used in the manufacture of cars at the factory of said company; and by this means to deprive the stockholders of the company of the fair and reasonable returns upon their investment by way of dividends to be declared upon their stockholding interest in said company.'

Setting up that the present invested assets of the company, exclusive of cash on hand, as of July 31, 1916, represented more than 30 times the present authorized capital of the company, and 2 ½ times the maximum limit ($25,000,000) fixed by the laws of the state of Michigan for capitalization of such companies (now $50,000,000), it is charged that the present investment in capital and assets constitutes an unlawful investment of the earnings, and that the continued investment of earnings would be a continuation of such unlawful policy. Setting up unsuccessful efforts to secure a conference with Mr. Ford for the purpose of discussing the question and asking that there be a distribution of a part of the accumulations, it is charged: That on September 28, 1916, plaintiffs addressed to him, and had delivered to him by registered letter, the following communication:

'We have for some time, as you know, been endeavoring to make an appointment to see you, for the purpose—as you assumed and informed one of your associates—of discussing the affairs of the Ford Motor Company from the standpoint of our interest as stockholders and with a view to securing action by the board of directors looking to a very substantial distribution from its cash surplus as dividends.

'Not having been able to make an appointment to discuss the matter with you personally, as we very much desired to do, we write you this letter upon the subject.

'The conditions shown by your recent financial statement—showing approximately $60,000,000 of net profits for the past year and cash surplus in bank exceeding $50,000,000—it seems to us would suggest, without the action being requested, the propriety of the board taking prompt action to distribute a large part of the accumulated cash surplus as dividends to the stockholders to whom it belongs.'

Plaintiffs ask for an injunction to restrain the carrying out of the alleged declared policy of Mr. Ford and the company, for a decree requiring the distribution to stockholders of at least 75 per cent of the accumulated cash surplus, and for the future that they be required to distribute all of the earnings of the company except such as may be reasonably required for emergency purposes in the conduct of the business.

The answer of the Ford Motor Company, denies that Henry Ford forced upon the board of directors his policy of reducing the price of cars by $80, and says that the action of the board in that behalf was unanimous and made after careful consideration. It admits that it has decided to increase the output of the company and is engaged in practically duplicating its plan at Highland Park; that plans therefor have been under consideration and practically agreed upon for a year and the lands necessary for the expansion acquired a year before this suit was begun and their acquisition laid before the board on the 28th of January, 1916, and ratified; that these plans were made public as early as December, 1915; and, upon information and belief, it is alleged that the plaintiffs knew all about it and never made any complaint until they filed their bill in this cause, unless the letter set forth in the bill of complaint can be called a complaint; that it has been the policy of the company and its practice for eight or ten years to cut the price of cars and increase the output, a plan which has been productive of great prosperity, and that what was done the 1st of August, 1916, was strictly in accordance with this policy; that it was not carried out by cutting the price of cars August 1, 1915, because after full discussion it was determined that the proposed expansions of business were necessary to secure the continued success of the company and that a considerable additional sum ought to be accumulated for the purpose of extensions and making the improvements complained of; that this policy for the year ending July 31, 1916, was understood by all the directors and the management and, it is believed, by all of the stockholders, including the plaintiffs; that the expansion is well under way, building operations are being carried on; that there is a great demand for Ford trucks which could not be supplied without such expansion; that only such extensions and expansions are contemplated as are shown in the estimates found in the minutes of the directors' meeting. It is denied that the proposed expansions jeopardize the interests of the plaintiffs and asserted that they are in accordance with the best interests of the company and in pursuance of their past policy. It is denied that the policy continued would destroy competition, and any idea of creating a monopoly is denied. The allegations in regard to mining, shipping, and transporting iron ore are denied, or that anything is being done or contemplated which will result in disaster. Any plan or purpose or thought to injure or impair the value of plaintiffs' capital stock is denied, while it is asserted that their interests will be improved. The minutes attached to this answer showing action of the board of directors at meetings held in October and November, 1916, are voluminous. They show, among other things, approval of a purchase of property in the city of New York costing $560,052.40. They show discussion of plans regarding a building to be erected on such property, and deferred action.

'Defendant denies that he has declared it to be his purpose to invest millions of dollars of the company's money in the purchase of iron ore mines anywhere or to acquire by purchase or have built ships for the purpose of transporting ore. He admits that he caused an investigation to be made relative to obtaining the necessary ore for the proposed blast furnaces hereinafter referred to, but upon having such investigation made several months ago he found that there was abundant competition in the iron ore market and that it was wholly unnecessary and undesirable to acquire ore in any other way than by purchase, and therefore all thought in that direction was abandoned. The same is true with respect to the acquisition of ships for the transportation of ore. This defendant says that the Ford Motor Company has for more than a year past been laying plans publicly and openly for the building of blast furnaces, stoves, blowing engines, coke ovens, foundry buildings and equipment, malleable foundries and equipment and the necessary accompaniments therefor, for the purpose of producing the iron used in the construction of the cars of the Ford Motor Company. That some contracts have been entered into by the company to that end and some substantial amounts paid out upon the preliminary work. He shows that such blast furnaces and the works above described will be for the great benefit and advantage of the company, not only in the direct saving of cost of iron parts, but in the improvement of the quality thereof. He further shows that the present plans do not contemplate the manufacture of steel but that in the future it is hoped to be able to produce at comparatively small increased expense the steel required by the Ford Motor Company in the manufacture of its cars. This defendant denies absolutely the allegation of the sixteenth subdivision that by the means stated in said subdivision sixteen or in any other way, that this defendant proposed to deprive the stockholders of the company of the fair and reasonable return upon their investments.'

The cause came on for hearing in open court on the 21st of May, 1917. A large volume of testimony was taken, with the result that a decree was entered December 5, 1917, in and by which it is decreed that within 30 days from the entry thereof the directors of the Ford Motor Company declare a dividend upon all of the shares of stock in an amount equivalent to one-half of, and payable out of, the accumulated cash surplus of said Ford Motor Company, on hand at the close of the fiscal year ending July 31, 1916, less the aggregate amount of the special dividends declared and paid after the filing of the bill and during the year ending July 31, 1917; the amount to be declared being $19,275,385.96. It was further decreed:

Third. The owning, holding or operating by the defendant, Ford Motor Company, of, and the using or appropriating or incurring obligations which might require or necessitate the using or appropriating of any funds or other property of said defendant, Ford Motor Company, for a smelting plant or blast furnace or furnaces of the kind or character which the proofs adduced herein show to be contemplated and now in course of construction on or near the River Rouge, and of any lands, buildings, machinery or equipment therefor, and other incident thereof, is without authority of law and is permanently and absolutely restrained and enjoined.

Defendants have appealed, plaintiffs have not appealed, from the decree. In the briefs, appellants state and discuss the following propositions:

'(1) The claim of plaintiffs' counsel that a manufacturing corporation in Michigan may not have more than twenty-five millions (now fifty million) of capital assets, is without merit.

'(2) Monopoly. There is nothing in the antitrust laws which affects this case. Mere bigness of a corporation is not unlawful.

'(3) It is lawful for the Ford Motor Company to build blast furnaces at the Rouge.

   '(a) No claim in this regard is made by plaintiffs in the bill of complaint.

   '(b) The plaintiffs are estopped by their conduct to raise the question.

   '(c) The work is not ultra vires the corporation.

'(4) The management of the corporation and its affairs rests in the board of directors, and no court will interfere or substitute its judgment so long as the proposed actions are not ultra vires or fraudulent. They may be ill advised, in the opinion of the court, but this is no ground for exercise of jurisdiction.

'(5) The board has full power over the matter of investing the surplus and as to dividends so long as they act in good faith.

'(6) Such rights of management and control over investments and dividends are not only rules of law, they are rights fixed by the contract between the parties in the formation of the corporation.

'(7) These things are so although the majority of the stock is held by one man.

'It is the right and the duty of the majority to control. This duty must be exercised, and the responsibility cannot be shifted or evaded.

'(8) Motives of the board members are not material and will not be inquired into by the court so long as the acts are within their lawful powers.

'(9) Motives of a humanitarian character will not invalidate or form the basis of any relief so long as the acts are within the lawful powers of the board, if believed to be for the permanent welfare of the company.

'(10) The court will not entertain a bill to enforce unconscionable demands, no matter what the legal rights of plaintiffs may be.'

In the brief for plaintiffs, the grounds for relief are stated as follows:

'(1) The proposed scheme of expansion is not for the financial advantage of the corporation, either mediate or immediate, and is not to be prosecuted with that intent, but for the purpose of increasing the number of employés and of the cars produced, to the end of giving employment and low-priced cars to a greater number of people.

'(These are ends worthy in themselves but not within the scope of an ordinary business corporation—ends which, if prosecuted, should be by individuals associated for such purposes.)

'(2) If the proposed scheme of expansion were for the proper and legitimate uses and needs of the corporation and a cash surplus equivalent to that accumulated and now on hand were necessary for the business of the corporation, nevertheless, a proper dividend ought to be required to be declared and paid out of such accumulated cash surplus, because the only reason there would not be ample cash on hand for all purposes, including proper dividends, is that the price of the cars and of the parts therefor, has been arbitrarily fixed at a figure which it is intended shall not produce a net profit sufficient to fulfill all those requirements, including the payment of proper dividends, and the requiring of the payment of dividends will force, and it is the only way by which can be forced the fixing of prices which will produce the requisite amount of net profits.

'(The whole scheme is to bring about such a relation of wages, revenue and cash requirements of the business as to preclude dividends of a reasonable return upon the fair value of the capital stock.)

'(4) A smelting plant for the manufacture from the ore of iron for use in the manufacture of automobiles is not within the power of a corporation organized under Act 232 of the Public Acts of 1903.'

Argued before OSTRANDER, C. J., and BIRD, MOORE, STEERE, BROOKE, FELLOWS, STONE, and KUHN, JJ.

OSTRANDER, C. J. (after stating the facts as above).

There is little, if anything, in the bill of complaint which suggests the contention that the smelting of iron ore as a part of the process of manufacturing motors is, or will be, an activity ultra vires the defendant corporation. On the contrary, the bill charges that the erection of smelters and such other buildings, machinery, and appliances as are intended to go along with the business of smelting ore, is part of a general plan of expansion of the business of defendant corporation which is in itself unwise and which is put into operation for the purpose of absorbing profits which ought to be distributed to shareholders. Restraint is asked, not because the smelting business is ultra vires the corporation, but because the whole plan of expansion is inimical to shareholders' rights and was formulated and will be carried out in defiance of those rights.

The smelter proposition involves, of course, much more than the initial expenditure for a plant. It involves the use of a large amount of capital to secure the finished product for the cars. Quantities of iron ore must be purchased and carried in stock; coal for the coke ovens must be purchased; the plant must be maintained. If the plant produces the necessary iron, and 800,00[0] car[s] are made in a year, something more than 270,000,000 pounds of iron ore will be produced, and if, as is claimed by Mr. Ford, the cost is reduced to the company by one-half and better iron made, a saving of $9 or $10 on the cost of each car will be the result. Presumably, this saving will also be reflected in the profits made from sales of parts. Ultimately, the result will be, either a considerable additional profit upon each car sold, or it will permit a reduction in the selling price of cars and parts. The process proposed to be used has not been used commercially.

Strictly, upon the pleadings, the question of ultra vires is not for decision, and this is not seriously denied. Assuming, however, in view of the course taken at the hearing, it is proper to express an opinion upon the point, it must be said that to make castings from iron ore, rather than to make them from pig iron, as defendant is now doing, eliminating one usual process, is not beyond the power of the corporation. In its relation to the finished product, iron ore, an article of commerce, is not very different from lumber. It is admitted that the defendant company may not undertake to smelt ore except for its own uses. Defendant corporation is organized to manufacture motors and automobiles and their parts. To manufacture implies the use of means of manufacturing as well as the material. No good reason is perceived for saying that as matter of power it may not manufacture all of an automobile. In doing so, it need not rely upon the statute grant of incidental powers. Extreme cases may be put; as, for example, if it may make castings from iron ore, may it invest in mines which produce the ore and in means for transporting the ore from mine to factory? Or, if it may make the rubber tires for cars, may it own and exploit a rubber plantation in Brazil, or elsewhere? No such case is presented, and until presented need not be considered.

As we regard the testimony as failing to prove any violation of anti-trust laws or that the alleged policy of the company, if successfully carried out, will involve a monopoly other than such as accrues to a concern which makes what the public demands and sells it at a price which the public regards as cheap or reasonable, the case for plaintiffs must rest upon the claim, and the proof in support of it, that the proposed expansion of the business of the corporation, involving the further use of profits as capital, ought to be enjoined because inimical to the best interests of the company and its shareholders, and upon the further claim that in any event the withholding of the special dividend asked for by plaintiffs is arbitrary action of the directors requiring judicial interference.

The rule which will govern courts in deciding these questions is not in dispute. It is, of course, differently phrased by judges and by authors, and, as the phrasing in a particular instance may seem to lean for or against the exercise of the right of judicial interference with the actions of corporate directors, the context, or the facts before the court, must be considered. This court, in *Hunter v. Roberts, Throp & Co.*, 83 Mich. 63, 71, 47 N. W. 131, 134, recognized the rule in the following language:

'It is a well-recognized principle of law that the directors of a corporation, and they alone, have the power to declare a dividend of the earnings of the corporation, and to determine its amount. 5 Amer. & Eng. Enc. Law, 725. Courts of equity will not interfere in the management of the directors unless it is clearly made to appear that they are guilty of fraud or misappropriation of the corporate funds, or refuse to declare a dividend when the corporation has a surplus of net profits which it can, without detriment to its business, divide among its stockholders, and when a refusal to do so would amount to such an abuse of discretion as would constitute a fraud, or breach of that good faith which they are bound to exercise towards the stockholders.'

In Cook on Corporations (7th Ed.) § 545, it is expressed as follows:

'The board of directors declare the dividends, and it is for the directors, and not the stockholders, to determine whether or not a dividend shall be declared.

'When, therefore, the directors have exercised this discretion and refused to declare a dividend, there will be no interference by the courts with their decision, unless they are guilty of a willful abuse of their discretionary powers, or of bad faith or of a neglect of duty. It requires a very strong case to induce a court of equity to order the directors to declare a dividend, inasmuch as equity has no jurisdiction, unless fraud or a breach of trust is involved. There have been many attempts to sustain such a suit, yet, although the courts do not disclaim jurisdiction, they have quite uniformly refused to interfere. The discretion of the directors will not be interfered with by the courts, unless there has been bad faith, willful neglect, or abuse of discretion.

'Accordingly, the directors may, in the fair exercise of their discretion, invest profits to extend and develop the business, and a reasonable use of the profits to provide additional facilities for the business cannot be objected to or enjoined by the stockholders.'

In Morawetz on Corporations (2d Ed.) § 447, it is stated:

'Profits earned by a corporation may be divided among its shareholders, but it is not a violation of the charter if they are allowed to accumulate and remain invested in the company's business. The managing agents of a corporation are impliedly invested with a discretionary power with regard to the time and manner of distributing its profits. They may apply profits in payment of floating or funded debts, or in development of the company's business; and so long as they do not abuse their discretionary powers, or violate the company's charter, the courts cannot interfere.

'But it is clear that the agents of a corporation, and even the majority, cannot arbitrarily withhold profits earned by the company, or apply them to any use which is not authorized by the company's charter. The nominal capital of a company does not necessarily limit the scope of its operations; a corporation may borrow money for the purpose of enlarging its business, and in many instances it may use profits for the same purpose. But the amount of the capital contributed by the shareholders is an important element in determining the limit beyond which the company's business cannot be extended by the investment of profits. If a corporation is formed with a capital of $100,000 in order to carry on a certain business, no one would hesitate to say that it would be a departure from the intention of the founders to withhold profits, in order to develop the company's business, until the sum of $500,000 had been amassed, unless the company was formed mainly for the purpose of accumulating the profits from year to year. The question in each case depends upon the use to which the capital is put and the meaning of the company's charter. If a majority of the shareholders or the directors of a corporation wrongfully refuse to declare a dividend and distribute profits earned by the company, any shareholder feeling aggrieved may obtain relief in a court of equity.

'It may often be reasonable to withhold part of the earnings of a corporation in order to increase its surplus fund, when it would not be reasonable to withhold all the earnings for that purpose. The shareholders forming an ordinary business corporation expect to obtain the profits of their investment in the form of regular dividends. To withhold the entire profits merely to enlarge the capacity of the company's business would defeat their just expectations. After the business of a corporation has been brought to a prosperous condition, and necessary provision has been made for future prosperity, a reasonable share of the profits should be applied in the payment of regular dividends, though a part may be reserved to increase the surplus and enlarge the business itself.'

One other statement may be given from *Park v. Grant Locomotive Works*, 40 N. J. Eq. 114, 3 Atl. 162 (45 N. J. Eq. 244, 19 Atl. 621):

'In cases where the power of the directors of a corporation is without limitation, and free from restraint, they are at liberty to exercise a very liberal discretion as to what disposition shall be made of the gains of the business of the corporation. Their power over them is absolute so long as they act in the exercise of their honest judgment. They may reserve of them whatever their judgment approves as necessary or judicious for repairs or improvements, and to meet contingencies, both present and prospective. And their determination in respect of these matters, if made in good faith and for honest ends, though the result may show that it was injudicious, is final, and not subject to judicial revision.'

To develop the points now discussed, and to a considerable extent they may be developed together as a single point, it is necessary to refer with some particularity to the facts.

When plaintiffs made their complaint and demand for further dividends, the Ford Motor Company had concluded its most prosperous year of business. The demand for its cars at the price of the preceding year continued. It could make and could market in the year beginning August 1, 1916, more than 500,000 cars. Sales of parts and repairs would necessarily increase. The cost of materials was likely to advance, and perhaps the price of labor; but it reasonably might have expected a profit for the year of upwards of $60,000,000. It had assets of more than $132,000,000, a surplus of almost $112,000,000, and its cash on hand and municipal bonds were nearly $54,000,000. Its total liabilities, including capital stock, was a little over $20,000,000. It had declared no special dividend during the business year except the October, 1915, dividend. It had been the practice, under similar circumstances, to declare larger dividends. Considering only these facts, a refusal to declare and pay further dividends appears to be not an exercise of discretion on the part of the directors, but an arbitrary refusal to do what the circumstances required to be done. These facts and others call upon the directors to justify their action, or failure or refusal to act. In justification, the defendants have offered testimony tending to prove, and which does prove, the following facts: It had been the policy of the corporation for a considerable time to annually reduce the selling price of cars, while keeping up, or improving, their quality. As early as in June, 1915, a general plan for the expansion of the productive capacity of the concern by a practical duplication of its plant had been talked over by the executive officers and directors and agreed upon; not all of the details having been settled, and no formal action of directors having been taken. The erection of a smelter was considered, and engineering and other data in connection therewith secured. In consequence, it was determined not to reduce the selling price of cars for the year beginning August 1, 1915, but to maintain the price and to accumulate a large surplus to pay for the proposed expansion of plant and equipment, and perhaps to build a plant for smelting ore. It is hoped, by Mr. Ford, that eventually 1,000,000 cars will be annually produced. The contemplated changes will permit the increased output.

The plan, as affecting the profits of the business for the year beginning August 1, 1916, and thereafter, calls for a reduction in the selling price of the cars. It is true that this price might be at any time increased, but the plan called for the reduction in price of $80 a car. The capacity of the plant, without the additions thereto voted to be made (without a part of them at least), would produce more than 600,000 cars annually. This number, and more, could have been sold for $440 instead of $360, a difference in the return for capital, labor, and materials employed of at least $48,000,000. In short, the plan does not call for and is not intended to produce immediately a more profitable business, but a less profitable one; not only less profitable than formerly, but less profitable than it is admitted it might be made. The apparent immediate effect will be to diminish the value of shares and the returns to shareholders.

It is the contention of plaintiffs that the apparent effect of the plan is intended to be the continued and continuing effect of it, and that it is deliberately proposed, not of record and not by official corporate declaration, but nevertheless proposed, to continue the corporation henceforth as a semi-eleemosynary institution and not as a business institution. In support of this contention, they point to the attitude and to the expressions of Mr. Henry Ford.

Mr. Henry Ford is the dominant force in the business of the Ford Motor Company. No plan of operations could be adopted unless he consented, and no board of directors can be elected whom he does not favor. One of the directors of the company has no stock. One share was assigned to him to qualify him for the position, but it is not claimed that he owns it. A business, one of the largest in the world, and one of the most profitable, has been built up. It employs many men, at good pay.

'My ambition,' said Mr. Ford, 'is to employ still more men, to spread the benefits of this industrial system to the greatest possible number, to help them build up their lives and their homes. To do this we are putting the greatest share of our profits back in the business.'

'With regard to dividends, the company paid sixty per cent. on its capitalization of two million dollars, or $1,200,000, leaving $58,000,000 to reinvest for the growth of the company. This is Mr. Ford's policy at present, and it is understood that the other stockholders cheerfully accede to this plan.'

He had made up his mind in the summer of 1916 that no dividends other than the regular dividends should be paid, 'for the present.'

'Q. For how long? Had you fixed in your mind any time in the future, when you were going to pay — A. No.

'Q. That was indefinite in the future? A. That was indefinite; yes, sir.'

The record, and especially the testimony of Mr. Ford, convinces that he has to some extent the attitude towards shareholders of one who has dispensed and distributed to them large gains and that they should be content to take what he chooses to give. His testimony creates the impression, also, that he thinks the Ford Motor Company has made too much money, has had too large profits, and that, although large profits might be still earned, a sharing of them with the public, by reducing the price of the output of the company, ought to be undertaken. We have no doubt that certain sentiments, philanthropic and altruistic, creditable to Mr. Ford, had large influence in determining the policy to be pursued by the Ford Motor Company — the policy which has been herein referred to.

It is said by his counsel that —

'Although a manufacturing corporation cannot engage in humanitarian works as its principal business, the fact that it is organized for profit does not prevent the existence of implied powers to carry on with humanitarian motives such charitable works as are incidental to the main business of the corporation.'

And again:

'As the expenditures complained of are being made in an expansion of the business which the company is organized to carry on, and for purposes within the powers of the corporation as hereinbefore shown, the question is as to whether such expenditures are rendered illegal because influenced to some extent by humanitarian motives and purposes on the part of the members of the board of directors.'

After all, like all others in which the subject is treated, turn finally upon the point, the question, whether it appears that the directors were not acting for the best interests of the corporation. The difference between an incidental humanitarian expenditure of corporate funds for the benefit of the employés, like the building of a hospital for their use and the employment of agencies for the betterment of their condition, and a general purpose and plan to benefit mankind at the expense of others, is obvious. There should be no confusion (of which there is evidence) of the duties which Mr. Ford conceives that he and the stockholders owe to the general public and the duties which in law he and his codirectors owe to protesting, minority stockholders. A business corporation is organized and carried on primarily for the profit of the stockholders. The powers of the directors are to be employed for that end. The discretion of directors is to be exercised in the choice of means to attain that end, and does not extend to a change in the end itself, to the reduction of profits, or to the nondistribution of profits among stockholders in order to devote them to other purposes.

There is committed to the discretion of directors, a discretion to be exercised in good faith, the infinite details of business, including the wages which shall be paid to employés, the number of hours they shall work, the conditions under which labor shall be carried on, and the price for which products shall be offered to the public.

It is said by appellants that the motives of the board members are not material and will not be inquired into by the court so long as their acts are within their lawful powers. As we have pointed out, and the proposition does not require argument to sustain it, it is not within the lawful powers of a board of directors to shape and conduct the affairs of a corporation for the merely incidental benefit of shareholders and for the primary purpose of benefiting others, and no one will contend that, if the avowed purpose of the defendant directors was to sacrifice the interests of shareholders, it would not be the duty of the courts to interfere.

We are not, however, persuaded that we should interfere with the proposed expansion of the business of the Ford Motor Company. In view of the fact that the selling price of products may be increased at any time, the ultimate results of the larger business cannot be certainly estimated. The judges are not business experts. It is recognized that plans must often be made for a long future, for expected competition, for a continuing as well as an immediately profitable venture. The experience of the Ford Motor Company is evidence of capable management of its affairs. It may be noticed, incidentally, that it took from the public the money required for the execution of its plan, and that the very considerable salaries paid to Mr. Ford and to certain executive officers and employés were not diminished. We are not satisfied that the alleged motives of the directors, in so far as they are reflected in the conduct of the business, menace the interests of shareholders. It is enough to say, perhaps, that the court of equity is at all times open to complaining shareholders having a just grievance.

Defendants say, and it is true, that a considerable cash balance must be at all times carried by such a concern. But, as has been stated, there was a large daily, weekly, monthly, receipt of cash. The output was practically continuous and was continuously, and within a few days, turned into cash. Moreover, the contemplated expenditures were not to be immediately made. The large sum appropriated for the smelter plant was payable over a considerable period of time. So that, without going further, it would appear that, accepting and approving the plan of the directors, it was their duty to distribute on or near the 1st of August, 1916, a very large sum of money to stockholders.

The decree of the court below fixing and determining the specific amount to be distributed to stockholders is affirmed. In other respects, except as to the allowance of costs, the said decree is reversed. Plaintiffs will recover interest at 5 per cent. per annum upon their proportional share of said dividend from the date of the decree of the lower court. Appellants will tax the costs of their appeal, and two-thirds of the amount thereof will be paid by plaintiffs. No other costs are allowed.

Notes

(1) What were the two major issues that the court considered in this case? Why did the court hold that Ford could build the smelting plant but that it could not withhold the special dividend payments to its shareholders? Does this case stand for the

proposition that a corporation is always required to give shareholders dividends when the company is making substantial profits?

(2) Apple, Inc. has long had a deeply rooted practice against paying dividends. While the company's stock price has experienced substantial market appreciation, and it has been extremely profitable, Apple rarely pays dividends. Instead, it has preferred to keep large cash reserves within its own corporate coffers. In fact, in 2011, Apple had approximately 76 billion dollars in cash on hand.[1] During this time, Apple had approximately one billion shares outstanding. Accordingly, Apple could have given a dividend of 26 dollars per share and it would have still had 50 billion dollars in cash. If you were an Apple shareholder, is it likely that you would have been able to compel Apple to issue a dividend like the Dodge brothers did to Ford? Why would you want to own stock in a company that refused to issue dividends?

(3) What is the relationship between the plaintiffs/minority shareholders in this case (the Dodge brothers) and the defendant (Henry Ford/Ford Motor Co.)? Why is the relationship important?

(4) Is one principle that can be pulled from this case the requirement that corporations concern themselves only with increasing profits for shareholders?

(5) Was Henry Ford the philanthropist and humanist that he appears to be in this case? What does Henry Ford's life and history seem to indicate in connection with his "everyman" claim?

The truth is that Henry Ford, while a very successful businessman, had a nefarious side that tends to garner little attention. Ford was an anti-semite who was known to have collected Nazi memorabilia and was a supporter of Adolf Hitler. *See* Ford's Anti-Semitism, PBS.org, available at: http://www.pbs.org/wgbh/americanexperience/features/interview/henryford-antisemitism/

(6) Pursuant to Act No. 232 of the Public Acts of 1903, Ford was authorized by the state of Michigan to carry "on any other lawful business, except such as are precluded from organization under this act by its express provisions, and to prescribe the powers and fix the duties and liabilities of such corporations." Given this express grant of authority by the State, could Ford have reasonably argued that it could operate for any purpose it desired, even if that purpose was not to maximize profit, as long as the purpose was lawful?

(7) Could Ford have successfully argued that the Dodge brothers breached their fiduciary duty of loyalty by attempting to start a competing business?

(8) Do you think that Ford's lawyers advised him to connect his purpose for failing to pay the special dividend to a legitimate business purpose? If so, why do you think that he instead focused on his own personal desire to create an affordable car?

(9) Why might Ford have believed that a Michigan court would not rule against him?

(10) Some have speculated that Ford resented the Dodge brothers because they were Jewish and that it was this resentment that led to the feud. However, the Dodge brothers were not Jewish. The rumor was likely created because the original Dodge emblem contained a six-point star, a symbol that is often associated with Jewish faith.

According to the Dodge Brothers Club website:

---

1. In 2015, Apple reported having approximately 203 billion dollars in cash on hand!

John and Horace Dodge died before they publically told anyone how they arrived at this symbol. If any family members knew the reasons behind this, nothing was ever revealed or discovered. Apparently no one thought to ask them!

Among the possibilities:

- These are two interlocking Greek letter "deltas" or "Ds" for the two Dodge brothers
- A medieval symbol of mysticism and the joining of mind and body, also possibly the joining of two brothers, who were known to be personally very close, in this business venture.
- An abstraction of the square and compass of the Freemasons.
- Nothing more or less than a badge with six pointed star similar to those used for law-enforcement officer's badges, some outlined with triangles. Sheriff, Marshall, and police badges frequently were and are six pointed stars. The old-west Dodge City badge had six points. Horace Dodge was said to enjoy accompanying local law-enforcement officers on their runs.
- There are other instances of a company "logo" selected for no particular deep meaning other than that it suited the fancy of those who selected it. The Chevrolet "bowtie" is a classic example, as it was copied from the wall paper of a hotel room.
- At the time the emblem was selected (most likely 1912–1914) it's likely that the Dodge brothers were unaware of its use in Judaism. In fact, at this time, that symbol was not used universally in this context.

Rumors that are wrong include:

- They chose the "Star of David" as a Jewish symbol to anger Henry Ford.

  Fact: The brothers were actually friends with Ford at the time the emblem was selected. They were business partners with Ford and even were guests at Edsel Ford's wedding.
- They chose the "Star of David" as a Jewish symbol to appease Jewish bankers who financed the business.

  Fact: There were no outside investors.
- The Dodge Brothers were Jewish

  Fact: They were not.[2]

Fifty years following the "profit maximization" case of *Dodge v. Ford*, disgruntled Chicago Cubs fan and shareholder William Shlensky attempted to sue the Wrigley family, owners of the Chicago Cubs, for their failure to install lights at Wrigley field for evening baseball games. Shlensky attempted to get the Illinois courts to follow the theme established in *Dodge v. Ford* by arguing that the Wrigley family was not maximizing its profit potential by refusing to install lights thereby blocking the Cubs from playing evening games at their home field. Shlensky theorized that more fans would be able to attend Cubs home games if the weekday games were played at night, like all of the other Major League Baseball teams during this period, including the cross-town Chicago White Sox.

---

2. *Club Information: F.A.Q.,* Dodge Brothers Club, (Oct. 29, 2015), http://www.dodge brothersclub.org/faq.

In the fifty years that passed since the *Ford* holding, the business judgment rule had become a very powerful consideration for U.S. courts, particularly when shareholders sued derivatively seeking to second guess decisions made by corporate executives and board members.

William Shlensky v. Philip K. Wrigley

95 Ill.App.2d 173, 237 N.E.2d 776 (1968)
Appellate Court of Illinois, First District, Third Division

SULLIVAN, Justice.

This is an appeal from a dismissal of plaintiff's amended complaint on motion of the defendants. The action was a stockholders' derivative suit against the directors for negligence and mismanagement. The corporation was also made a defendant. Plaintiff sought damages and an order that defendants cause the installation of lights in Wrigley Field and the scheduling of night baseball games.

Plaintiff is a minority stockholder of defendant corporation, Chicago National League Ball Club (Inc.), a Delaware corporation with its principal place of business in Chicago, Illinois. Defendant corporation owns and operates the major league professional baseball team known as the Chicago Cubs. The corporation also engages in the operation of Wrigley Field, the Cubs' home park, the concessionaire sales during Cubs' home games, television and radio broadcasts of Cubs' home games, the leasing of the field for football games and other events and receives its share, as visiting team, of admission moneys from games played in other National League stadia. The individual defendants are directors of the Cubs and have served for varying periods of years. Defendant Philip K. Wrigley is also president of the corporation and owner of approximately 80% of the stock therein.

Plaintiff alleges that since night baseball was first played in 1935 nineteen of the twenty major league teams have scheduled night games. In 1966, out of a total of 1620 games in the major leagues, 932 were played at night. Plaintiff alleges that every member of the major leagues, other than the Cubs, scheduled substantially all of its home games in 1966 at night, exclusive of opening days, Saturdays, Sundays, holidays and days prohibited by league rules. Allegedly this has been done for the specific purpose of maximizing attendance and thereby maximizing revenue and income.

The Cubs, in the years 1961–65, sustained operating losses from its direct baseball operations. Plaintiff attributes those losses to inadequate attendance at Cubs' home games. He concludes that if the directors continue to refuse to install lights at Wrigley Field and schedule night baseball games, the Cubs will continue to sustain comparable losses and its financial condition will continue to deteriorate.

Plaintiff alleges that, except for the year 1963, attendance at Cubs' home games has been substantially below that at their road games, many of which were played at night.

Plaintiff compares attendance at Cubs' games with that of the Chicago White Sox, an American League club, whose weekday games were generally played at night. The weekend attendance figures for the two teams was similar; however, the White Sox week-night games drew many more patrons than did the Cubs' weekday games.

Plaintiff alleges that the funds for the installation of lights can be readily obtained through financing and the cost of installation would be far more than offset and recaptured by increased revenues and incomes resulting from the increased attendance.

Plaintiff further alleges that defendant Wrigley has refused to install lights, not because of interest in the welfare of the corporation but because of his personal opinions 'that baseball is a "daytime sport" and that the installation of lights and night baseball games will have a deteriorating effect upon the surrounding neighborhood.' It is alleged that he has admitted that he is not interested in whether the Cubs would benefit financially from such action because of his concern for the neighborhood, and that he would be willing for the team to play night games if a new stadium were built in Chicago.

Plaintiff alleges that the other defendant directors, with full knowledge of the foregoing matters, have acquiesced in the policy laid down by Wrigley and have permitted him to dominate the board of directors in matters involving the installation of lights and scheduling of night games, even though they knew he was not motivated by a good faith concern as to the best interests of defendant corporation, but solely by his personal views set forth above. It is charged that the directors are acting for a reason or reasons contrary and wholly unrelated to the business interests of the corporation; that such arbitrary and capricious acts constitute mismanagement and waste of corporate assets, and that the directors have been negligent in failing to exercise reasonable care and prudence in the management of the corporate affairs.

The question on appeal is whether plaintiff's amended complaint states a cause of action. It is plaintiff's position that fraud, illegality and conflict of interest are not the only bases for a stockholder's derivative action against the directors. Contrariwise, defendants argue that the courts will not step in and interfere with honest business judgment of the directors unless there is a showing of fraud, illegality or conflict of interest.

The cases in this area are numerous and each differs from the others on a factual basis. However, the courts have pronounced certain ground rules which appear in all cases and which are then applied to the given factual situation. The court in *Wheeler v. Pullman Iron and Steel Company*, 143 Ill. 197, 207, 32 N.E. 420, 423, said:

> 'It is, however, fundamental in the law of corporations, that the majority of its stockholders shall control the policy of the corporation, and regulate and govern the lawful exercise of its franchise and business. * * * Every one purchasing or subscribing for stock in a corporation impliedly agrees that he will be bound by the acts and proceedings done or sanctioned by a majority of the shareholders, or by the agents of the corporation duly chosen by such majority, within the scope of the powers conferred by the charter, and courts of equity will not undertake to control the policy or business methods of a corporation, although it may be seen that a wiser policy might be adopted and the business more successful if other methods were pursued. The majority of shares of its stock, or the agents by the holders thereof lawfully chosen, must be permitted to control the business of the corporation in their discretion, when not in violation of its charter or some public law, or corruptly and fraudulently subversive of the rights and interests of the corporation or of a shareholder.'

The standards set in Delaware are also clearly stated in the cases. The court in *Toebelman v. Missouri-Kansas Pipe Line Co.*, D.C., 41 F.Supp. 334, said at page 339:

> The general legal principle involved is familiar. Citation of authorities is of limited value because the facts of each case differ so widely. Reference may be made to the statement of the rule in *Helfman v. American Light & Traction Company*, 121 N.J.Eq. 1, 187 A. 540, 550, in which the Court stated the law as follows: 'In a purely business corporation * * * the authority of the directors in the conduct

of the business of the corporation must be regarded as absolute when they act within the law, and the court is without authority to substitute its judgment for that of the directors.'

Plaintiff argues that the allegations of his amended complaint are sufficient to set forth a cause of action under the principles set out in *Dodge v. Ford Motor Co.*, 204 Mich. 459, 170 N.W. 668. In that case plaintiff, owner of about 10% of the outstanding stock, brought suit against the directors seeking payment of additional dividends and the enjoining of further business expansion. In ruling on the request for dividends the court indicated that the motives of Ford in keeping so much money in the corporation for expansion and security were to benefit the public generally and spread the profits out by means of more jobs, etc. The court felt that these were not only far from related to the good of the stockholders, but amounted to a change in the ends of the corporation and that this was not a purpose contemplated or allowed by the corporate charter. The court relied on language found in *Hunter v. Roberts, Throp & Co.*, 83 Mich. 63, 47 N.W. 131, 134, wherein it was said:

> Courts of equity will not interfere in the management of the directors unless it is clearly made to appear that they are guilty of fraud or misappropriation of the corporate funds, or refuse to declare a dividend when the corporation has a surplus of net profits which it can, without detriment to its business, divide among its stockholders, and when a refusal to do so would amount to such an abuse of discretion as would constitute a fraud or breach of that good faith which they are bound to exercise toward the stockholders.

From the authority relied upon in that case it is clear that the court felt that there must be fraud or a breach of that good faith which directors are bound to exercise toward the stockholders in order to justify the courts entering into the internal affairs of corporations. This is made clear when the court refused to interfere with the directors decision to expand the business.

> We are not, however, persuaded that we should interfere with the proposed expansion of the business of the Ford Motor Company. In view of the fact that the selling price of products may be increased at any time, the ultimate results of the larger business cannot be certainly estimated. The judges are not business experts. It is recognized that plans must often be made for a long future, for expected competition, for a continuing as well as an immediately profitable venture. * * * We are not satisfied that the alleged motives of the directors, in so far as they are reflected in the conduct of business, menace the interests of the shareholders.

Plaintiff in the instant case argues that the directors are acting for reasons unrelated to the financial interest and welfare of the Cubs. However, we are not satisfied that the motives assigned to Philip K. Wrigley, and through him to the other directors, are contrary to the best interests of the corporation and the stockholders. For example, it appears to us that the effect on the surrounding neighborhood might well be considered by a director who was considering the patrons who would or would not attend the games if the park were in a poor neighborhood. Furthermore, the long run interest of the corporation in its property value at Wrigley Field might demand all efforts to keep the neighborhood from deteriorating. By these thoughts we do not mean to say that we have decided that the decision of the directors was a correct one. That is beyond our jurisdiction and ability. We are merely saying that the decision is one properly before directors and the motives alleged in the amended complaint showed no fraud, illegality or conflict of interest in their making of that decision.

While all the courts do not insist that one or more of the three elements must be present for a stockholder's derivative action to lie, nevertheless we feel that unless the conduct of the defendants at least borders on one of the elements, the courts should not interfere. The trial court in the instant case acted properly in dismissing plaintiff's amended complaint.

We feel that plaintiff's amended complaint was also defective in failing to allege damage to the corporation.

There is no allegation that the night games played by the other nineteen teams enhanced their financial position or that the profits, if any, of those teams were directly related to the number of night games scheduled. There is an allegation that the installation of lights and scheduling of night games in Wrigley Field would have resulted in large amounts of additional revenues and incomes from increased attendance and related sources of income. Further, the cost of installation of lights, funds for which are allegedly readily available by financing, would be more than offset and recaptured by increased revenues. However, no allegation is made that there will be a net benefit to the corporation from such action, considering all increased costs.

Plaintiff claims that the losses of defendant corporation are due to poor attendance at home games. However, it appears from the amended complaint, taken as a whole, that factors other than attendance affect the net earnings or losses. For example, in 1962, attendance at home and road games decreased appreciably as compared with 1961, and yet the loss from direct baseball operation and of the whole corporation was considerably less.

The record shows that plaintiff did not feel he could allege that the increased revenues would be sufficient to cure the corporate deficit. The only cost plaintiff was at all concerned with was that of installation of lights. No mention was made of operation and maintenance of the lights or other possible increases in operating costs of night games and we cannot speculate as to what other factors might influence the increase or decrease of profits if the Cubs were to play night home games.

[I]n the instant case, plaintiff's allegation that the minority stockholders and the corporation have been seriously and irreparably damaged by the wrongful conduct of the defendant directors is a mere conclusion and not based on well pleaded facts in the amended complaint.

Finally, we do not agree with plaintiff's contention that failure to follow the example of the other major league clubs in scheduling night games constituted negligence. Plaintiff made no allegation that these teams' night schedules were profitable or that the purpose for which night baseball had been undertaken was fulfilled. Furthermore, it cannot be said that directors, even those of corporations that are losing money, must follow the lead of the other corporations in the field. Directors are elected for their business capabilities and judgment and the courts cannot require them to forego their judgment because of the decisions of directors of other companies. Courts may not decide these questions in the absence of a clear showing of dereliction of duty on the part of the specific directors and mere failure to 'follow the crowd' is not such a dereliction.

For the foregoing reasons the order of dismissal entered by the trial court is affirmed.

Affirmed.

Notes

(1) What role does the business judgment rule play in this case?

(2) Did the court in Wrigley focus on the "profit maximization" concept?

(3) How can the cases of *Dodge v. Ford* and *Shlensky v. Wrigley* be reconciled? If the Plaintiff's allegations were correct that Wrigley refused to install the lights because of his personal opinion that baseball is a daytime sport and that night games would have a deteriorating effect on the surrounding neighborhood, why did the court still provide the board's decision with business judgment rule protection? Is there a legitimate argument that Wrigley was not concerned with the corporation but instead in his own philosophical beliefs about baseball and the neighborhood? Were Wrigley's motivations similar to Ford's motivation wherein Ford wanted to ensure that everyone could afford a car, or is there a way that you can distinguish the cases?

Smith v. Van Gorkom is one of the most well known cases in corporate law jurisprudence. The Court's opinion in *Van Gorkom* is rather long and somewhat complex. To clarify why Trans Union decided to allow itself to be merged into another company, consider the following introduction. Trans Union operated a successful rail car leasing business. At the time of the merger, Trans Union was generating hundreds of millions of dollars in cash flows. To offset its cash flows and to reduce its taxable income, Trans Union deducted large amounts of depreciation expense from its revenue.[3] However, after Trans Union took its depreciation expense, Trans Union's income was too low to enable it to take advantage of government issued investment tax credits ("ITC"). The government prohibited a corporation from claiming the ITCs unless the corporation generated sufficient taxable income. To resolve this issue, Trans Union considered acquiring other companies but this strategy was unsuccessful. As a result, Trans Union's management, led by 65-year-old, Chairman and Chief Executive Officer, Jerome W. Van Gorkom, approved a triangle merger[4] that merged Trans Union into New T Company ("New T"), a wholly-owned subsidiary of Marmon Group, Inc. ("Marmon"), a company that was principally owned by named defendant Jay Pritzker, to ensure that the ITCs would not be wasted. After the merger was approved, New T would have enough cash flow, combined with that of Trans Union's, to claim the ITCs.

Alden Smith v. W. Van Gorkom

488 A.2d 858 (1985)
Supreme Court of Delaware

Following trial, the former Chancellor granted judgment for the defendant directors ... based on two findings: (1) that the Board of Directors had acted in an informed manner so as to be entitled to protection of the business judgment rule in approving the cash-

---

3. By lowering its taxable income, Trans Union would be able to keep more money in the business or to pay out that money to shareholders in the form of dividends. For example, assume that an individual tax payer grosses $100,000 in the current year. Hypothetically, if the tax payer is in a 40% tax bracket, the tax payer will pay $40,000 in taxes. If, however, the tax payer has income deductions in the form of depreciation in the amount of $20,000, the tax payer will now have $80,000 in taxable income. Again, if the tax payer's income is taxed at 40%, the tax payer will only pay $32,000 in income tax.

4. A triangle merger is a special type of merger wherein one company, the surviving company, creates a new company, a wholly owned subsidiary of surviving company, for the purposes of merging with another company ("disappearing corporation"). The primary reason that the surviving company structures the transaction as a triangle merger is because such transaction allows surviving company to facilitate the merger without having to get approval from its own shareholders.

out merger; and (2) that the shareholder vote approving the merger should not be set aside because the stockholders had been "fairly informed" by the Board of Directors before voting thereon.

Speaking for the majority of the Court, we hold: (1) that the Board's decision, reached September 20, 1980, to approve the proposed cash-out merger was not the product of an informed business judgment; (2) that the Board's subsequent efforts to amend the Merger Agreement and take other curative action were ineffectual, both legally and factually; and (3) that the Board did not deal with complete candor with the stockholders by failing to disclose all material facts, which they knew or should have known, before securing the stockholders' approval of the merger.

I.

The nature of this case requires a detailed factual statement. The following facts are essentially uncontradicted:

−A−

Beginning in the late 1960's, and continuing through the 1970's, Trans Union pursued a program of acquiring small companies in order to increase available taxable income. In July 1980, Trans Union Management prepared the annual revision of the Company's Five Year Forecast. This report was presented to the Board of Directors at its July, 1980 meeting. The report projected an annual income growth of about 20%. The report also concluded that Trans Union would have about $195 million in spare cash between 1980 and 1985, "with the surplus growing rapidly from 1982 onward." The report referred to the ITC situation as a "nagging problem" and, given that problem, the leasing company "would still appear to be constrained to a tax breakeven."

Donald Romans, Chief Financial Officer of Trans Union, stated that his department had done a "very brief bit of work on the possibility of a leveraged buy-out." This work had been prompted by a media article which Romans had seen regarding a leveraged buy-out by management. The work consisted of a "preliminary study" of the cash which could be generated by the Company if it participated in a leveraged buy-out. As Romans stated, this analysis "was very first and rough cut at seeing whether a cash flow would support what might be considered a high price for this type of transaction."

On September 5, at another Senior Management meeting which Van Gorkom attended, Romans again brought up the idea of a leveraged buy-out as a "possible strategic alternative" to the Company's acquisition program. Romans and Bruce S. Chelberg, President and Chief Operating Officer of Trans Union, had been working on the matter in preparation for the meeting. According to Romans: They did not "come up" with a price for the Company. They merely "ran the numbers" at $50 a share and at $60 a share with the "rough form" of their cash figures at the time. Their "figures indicated that $50 would be very easy to do but $60 would be very difficult to do under those figures." This work did not purport to establish a fair price for either the Company or 100% of the stock. It was intended to determine the cash flow needed to service the debt that would "probably" be incurred in a leveraged buy-out, based on "rough calculations" without "any benefit of experts to identify what the limits were to that, and so forth." These computations were not considered extensive and no conclusion was reached.

At this meeting, Van Gorkom stated that he would be willing to take $55 per share for his own 75,000 shares. Van Gorkom, a certified public accountant and lawyer, had been an officer of Trans Union for 24 years, its Chief Executive Officer for more than 17 years, and Chairman of its Board for 2 years. It is noteworthy in this connection that he was then approaching 65 years of age and mandatory retirement.

Van Gorkom decided to meet with Jay A. Pritzker, a well-known corporate takeover specialist and a social acquaintance. However, rather than approaching Pritzker simply to determine his interest in acquiring Trans Union, Van Gorkom assembled a proposed per share price for sale of the Company and a financing structure by which to accomplish the sale. Van Gorkom did so without consulting either his Board or any members of Senior Management except one: Carl Peterson, Trans Union's Controller. Telling Peterson that he wanted no other person on his staff to know what he was doing, but without telling him why, Van Gorkom directed Peterson to calculate the feasibility of a leveraged buy-out at an assumed price per share of $55. Apart from the Company's historic stock market price, and Van Gorkom's long association with Trans Union, the record is devoid of any competent evidence that $55 represented the per share intrinsic value of the Company.

Having thus chosen the $55 figure, based solely on the availability of a leveraged buy-out, Van Gorkom multiplied the price per share by the number of shares outstanding to reach a total value of the Company of $690 million. Van Gorkom told Peterson to use this $690 million figure and to assume a $200 million equity contribution by the buyer. Based on these assumptions, Van Gorkom directed Peterson to determine whether the debt portion of the purchase price could be paid off in five years or less if financed by Trans Union's cash flow as projected in the Five Year Forecast, and by the sale of certain weaker divisions identified in a study done for Trans Union by the Boston Consulting Group ("BCG study"). Peterson reported that, of the purchase price, approximately $50–80 million would remain outstanding after five years. Van Gorkom was disappointed, but decided to meet with Pritzker nevertheless.

Van Gorkom arranged a meeting with Pritzker at the latter's home on Saturday, September 13, 1980. Van Gorkom prefaced his presentation by stating to Pritzker: "Now as far as you are concerned, I can, I think, show how you can pay a substantial premium over the present stock price and pay off most of the loan in the first five years. * * * If you could pay $55 for this Company, here is a way in which I think it can be financed."

Van Gorkom then reviewed with Pritzker his calculations based upon his proposed price of $55 per share. Although Pritzker mentioned $50 as a more attractive figure, no other price was mentioned. However, Van Gorkom stated that to be sure that $55 was the best price obtainable, Trans Union should be free to accept any better offer. Pritzker demurred, stating that his organization would serve as a "stalking horse" for an "auction contest" only if Trans Union would permit Pritzker to buy 1,750,000 shares of Trans Union stock at market price which Pritzker could then sell to any higher bidder. After further discussion on this point, Pritzker told Van Gorkom that he would give him a more definite reaction soon.

On Monday, September 15, Pritzker advised Van Gorkom that he was interested in the $55 cash-out merger proposal and requested more information on Trans Union. Van Gorkom agreed to meet privately with Pritzker, accompanied by Peterson, Chelberg, and Michael Carpenter, Trans Union's consultant from the Boston Consulting Group. The meetings took place on September 16 and 17. Van Gorkom was "astounded that events were moving with such amazing rapidity."

On Thursday, September 18, Van Gorkom met again with Pritzker. At that time, Van Gorkom knew that Pritzker intended to make a cash-out merger offer at Van Gorkom's proposed $55 per share. Pritzker instructed his attorney, a merger and acquisition specialist, to begin drafting merger documents. There was no further discussion of the $55 price.

At this point, Pritzker insisted that the Trans Union Board act on his merger proposal within the next three days, stating to Van Gorkom: "We have to have a decision by no later than Sunday [evening, September 21] before the opening of the English stock exchange on Monday morning." Pritzker's lawyer was then instructed to draft the merger documents, to be reviewed by Van Gorkom's lawyer, "sometimes with discussion and sometimes not, in the haste to get it finished."

On Friday, September 19, Van Gorkom, Chelberg, and Pritzker consulted with Trans Union's lead bank regarding the financing of Pritzker's purchase of Trans Union. On the same day, Van Gorkom retained James Brennan, Esquire, to advise Trans Union on the legal aspects of the merger. Van Gorkom did not consult with William Browder, a Vice-President and director of Trans Union and former head of its legal department, or with William Moore, then the head of Trans Union's legal staff.

On Friday, September 19, Van Gorkom called a special meeting of the Trans Union Board for noon the following day. He also called a meeting of the Company's Senior Management to convene at 11:00 a.m., prior to the meeting of the Board. No one, except Chelberg and Peterson, was told the purpose of the meetings. Van Gorkom did not invite Trans Union's investment banker, Salomon Brothers or its Chicago-based partner, to attend.

Of those present at the Senior Management meeting on September 20, only Chelberg and Peterson had prior knowledge of Pritzker's offer. Van Gorkom disclosed the offer and described its terms, but he furnished no copies of the proposed Merger Agreement. Romans announced that his department had done a second study which showed that, for a leveraged buy-out, the price range for Trans Union stock was between $55 and $65 per share. Van Gorkom neither saw the study nor asked Romans to make it available for the Board meeting.

Senior Management's reaction to the Pritzker proposal was completely negative. No member of Management, except Chelberg and Peterson, supported the proposal. Romans objected to the price as being too low; he was critical of the timing and suggested that consideration should be given to the adverse tax consequences of an all-cash deal for low-basis shareholders; and he took the position that the agreement to sell Pritzker one million newly-issued shares at market price would inhibit other offers, as would the prohibitions against soliciting bids and furnishing inside information to other bidders. Romans argued that the Pritzker proposal was a "lock up" and amounted to "an agreed merger as opposed to an offer." Nevertheless, Van Gorkom proceeded to the Board meeting as scheduled without further delay.

Ten directors served on the Trans Union Board, five inside (defendants Bonser, O'Boyle, Browder, Chelberg, and Van Gorkom) and five outside (defendants Wallis, Johnson, Lanterman, Morgan and Reneker). All directors were present at the meeting, except O'Boyle who was ill. Of the outside directors, four were corporate chief executive officers and one was the former Dean of the University of Chicago Business School. None was an investment banker or trained financial analyst. All members of the Board were well informed about the Company and its operations as a going concern. They were familiar with the current financial condition of the Company, as well as operating and earnings projections reported in the recent Five Year Forecast. The Board generally received regular and detailed reports and was kept abreast of the accumulated investment tax credit and accelerated depreciation problem.

Van Gorkom began the Special Meeting of the Board with a twenty-minute oral presentation. Copies of the proposed Merger Agreement were delivered too late for study

before or during the meeting. Van Gorkom did not disclose to the Board, however, the
methodology by which he alone had arrived at the $55 figure, or the fact that he first
proposed the $55 price in his negotiations with Pritzker.

Van Gorkom outlined the terms of the Pritzker offer as follows: Pritzker would pay
$55 in cash for all outstanding shares of Trans Union stock upon completion of which
Trans Union would be merged into New T Company, a subsidiary wholly-owned by
Pritzker and formed to implement the merger; for a period of 90 days, Trans Union could
receive, but could not actively solicit, competing offers; the offer had to be acted on by
the next evening, Sunday, September 21; Trans Union could only furnish to competing
bidders published information, and not proprietary information; the offer was subject
to Pritzker obtaining the necessary financing by October 10, 1980; if the financing
contingency were met or waived by Pritzker, Trans Union was required to sell to Pritzker
one million newly-issued shares of Trans Union at $38 per share.

Van Gorkom took the position that putting Trans Union "up for auction" through a
90-day market test would validate a decision by the Board that $55 was a fair price. He
told the Board that the "free market will have an opportunity to judge whether $55 is a
fair price." Van Gorkom framed the decision before the Board not as whether $55 per
share was the highest price that could be obtained, but as whether the $55 price was a
fair price that the stockholders should be given the opportunity to accept or reject.

Attorney Brennan advised the members of the Board that they might be sued if they
failed to accept the offer and that a fairness opinion was not required as a matter of law.

Romans attended the meeting as chief financial officer of the Company. He told the
Board that he had not been involved in the negotiations with Pritzker and knew nothing
about the merger proposal until the morning of the meeting; that his studies did not
indicate either a fair price for the stock or a valuation of the Company; that he did not
see his role as directly addressing the fairness issue; and that he and his people "were
trying to search for ways to justify a price in connection with such a [leveraged buy-out]
transaction, rather than to say what the shares are worth."

Romans told the Board that, in his opinion, $55 was "in the range of a fair price," but
"at the beginning of the range."

The Board meeting of September 20 lasted about two hours. Based solely upon Van
Gorkom's oral presentation, Chelberg's supporting representations, Romans' oral statement,
Brennan's legal advice, and their knowledge of the market history of the Company's stock,
the directors approved the proposed Merger Agreement. However, the Board later claimed
to have attached two conditions to its acceptance: (1) that Trans Union reserved the right
to accept any better offer that was made during the market test period; and (2) that Trans
Union could share its proprietary information with any other potential bidders. While
the Board now claims to have reserved the right to accept any better offer received after
the announcement of the Pritzker agreement (even though the minutes of the meeting
do not reflect this), it is undisputed that the Board did not reserve the right to actively
solicit alternate offers.

The Merger Agreement was executed by Van Gorkom during the evening of September
20 at a formal social event that he hosted for the opening of the Chicago Lyric Opera. Neither
he nor any other director read the agreement prior to its signing and delivery to Pritzker.

On February 10, the stockholders of Trans Union approved the Pritzker merger proposal.
Of the outstanding shares, 69.9% were voted in favor of the merger; 7.25% were voted
against the merger; and 22.85% were not voted.

II.

We turn to the issue of the application of the business judgment rule to the September 20 meeting of the Board.

The Court of Chancery concluded from the evidence that the Board of Directors' approval of the Pritzker merger proposal fell within the protection of the business judgment rule. The Court found that the Board had given sufficient time and attention to the transaction, since the directors had considered the Pritzker proposal on three different occasions, on September 20, and on October 8, 1980 and finally on January 26, 1981. On that basis, the Court reasoned that the Board had acquired, over the four-month period, sufficient information to reach an informed business judgment on the cash-out merger proposal. The Court ruled:

> … that given the market value of Trans Union's stock, the business acumen of the members of the board of Trans Union, the substantial premium over market offered by the Pritzkers and the ultimate effect on the merger price provided by the prospect of other bids for the stock in question, that the board of directors of Trans Union did not act recklessly or improvidently in determining on a course of action which they believed to be in the best interest of the stockholders of Trans Union.

The Court of Chancery made but one finding; i.e., that the Board's conduct over the entire period from September 20 through January 26, 1981 was not reckless or improvident, but informed. We conclude that the Court's ultimate finding that the Board's conduct was not "reckless or imprudent" is contrary to the record and not the product of a logical and deductive reasoning process.

Under Delaware law, the business judgment rule is the offspring of the fundamental principle, codified in 8 *Del.C.* § 141(a), that the business and affairs of a Delaware corporation are managed by or under its board of directors. In carrying out their managerial roles, directors are charged with an unyielding fiduciary duty to the corporation and its shareholders. The business judgment rule exists to protect and promote the full and free exercise of the managerial power granted to Delaware directors. The rule itself "is a presumption that in making a business decision, the directors of a corporation acted on an informed basis, in good faith and in the honest belief that the action taken was in the best interests of the company." Thus, the party attacking a board decision as uninformed must rebut the presumption that its business judgment was an informed one.

The determination of whether a business judgment is an informed one turns on whether the directors have informed themselves "prior to making a business decision, of all material information reasonably available to them."

Under the business judgment rule there is no protection for directors who have made "an unintelligent or unadvised judgment." *Mitchell v. Highland-Western Glass,* Del.Ch., 167 A. 831, 833 (1933). A director's duty to inform himself in preparation for a decision derives from the fiduciary capacity in which he serves the corporation and its stockholders. Since a director is vested with the responsibility for the management of the affairs of the corporation, he must execute that duty with the recognition that he acts on behalf of others. Such obligation does not tolerate faithlessness or self-dealing. But fulfillment of the fiduciary function requires more than the mere absence of bad faith or fraud. Representation of the financial interests of others imposes on a director an affirmative duty to protect those interests and to proceed with a critical eye in assessing information of the type and under the circumstances present here.

Thus, a director's duty to exercise an informed business judgment is in the nature of a duty of care, as distinguished from a duty of loyalty. Here, there were no allegations of fraud, bad faith, or self-dealing, or proof thereof. Hence, it is presumed that the directors reached their business judgment in good faith, and considerations of motive are irrelevant to the issue before us.

The standard of care applicable to a director's duty of care has also been recently restated by this Court. In *Aronson, supra,* we stated:

> While the Delaware cases use a variety of terms to describe the applicable standard of care, our analysis satisfies us that under the business judgment rule director liability is predicated upon concepts of gross negligence.

We again confirm that view. We think the concept of gross negligence is also the proper standard for determining whether a business judgment reached by a board of directors was an informed one.

In the specific context of a proposed merger of domestic corporations, a director has a duty under 8 *Del.C.* § 251(b), along with his fellow directors, to act in an informed and deliberate manner in determining whether to approve an agreement of merger before submitting the proposal to the stockholders. Certainly in the merger context, a director may not abdicate that duty by leaving to the shareholders alone the decision to approve or disapprove the agreement. Only an agreement of merger satisfying the requirements of 8 *Del.C.* § 251(b) may be submitted to the shareholders under § 251(c).

It is against those standards that the conduct of the directors of Trans Union must be tested, as a matter of law and as a matter of fact, regarding their exercise of an informed business judgment in voting to approve the Pritzker merger proposal.

III.

The issue of whether the directors reached an informed decision to "sell" the Company on September 20, 1980 must be determined only upon the basis of the information then reasonably available to the directors and relevant to their decision to accept the Pritzker merger proposal. This is not to say that the directors were precluded from altering their original plan of action, had they done so in an informed manner. What we do say is that the question of whether the directors reached an informed business judgment in agreeing to sell the Company, pursuant to the terms of the September 20 Agreement presents, in reality, two questions: (A) whether the directors reached an informed business judgment on September 20, 1980; and (B) if they did not, whether the directors' actions taken subsequent to September 20 were adequate to cure any infirmity in their action taken on September 20. We first consider the directors' September 20 action in terms of their reaching an informed business judgment.

–A–

On the record before us, we must conclude that the Board of Directors did not reach an informed business judgment on September 20, 1980 in voting to "sell" the Company for $55 per share pursuant to the Pritzker cash-out merger proposal. Our reasons, in summary, are as follows:

The directors (1) did not adequately inform themselves as to Van Gorkom's role in forcing the "sale" of the Company and in establishing the per share purchase price; (2) were uninformed as to the intrinsic value of the Company; and (3) given these circumstances, at a minimum, were grossly negligent in approving the "sale" of the

Company upon two hours' consideration, without prior notice, and without the exigency of a crisis or emergency.

As has been noted, the Board based its September 20 decision to approve the cash-out merger primarily on Van Gorkom's representations. None of the directors, other than Van Gorkom and Chelberg, had any prior knowledge that the purpose of the meeting was to propose a cash-out merger of Trans Union. No members of Senior Management were present, other than Chelberg, Romans and Peterson; and the latter two had only learned of the proposed sale an hour earlier. Both general counsel Moore and former general counsel Browder attended the meeting, but were equally uninformed as to the purpose of the meeting and the documents to be acted upon.

Without any documents before them concerning the proposed transaction, the members of the Board were required to rely entirely upon Van Gorkom's 20-minute oral presentation of the proposal. No written summary of the terms of the merger was presented; the directors were given no documentation to support the adequacy of $55 price per share for sale of the Company; and the Board had before it nothing more than Van Gorkom's statement of his understanding of the substance of an agreement which he admittedly had never read, nor which any member of the Board had ever seen.

Under 8 *Del.C.* § 141(e), "directors are fully protected in relying in good faith on reports made by officers." The term "report" has been liberally construed to include reports of informal personal investigations by corporate officers. However, there is no evidence that any "report," as defined under § 141(e), concerning the Pritzker proposal, was presented to the Board on September 20. Van Gorkom's oral presentation of his understanding of the terms of the proposed Merger Agreement, which he had not seen, and Romans' brief oral statement of his preliminary study regarding the feasibility of a leveraged buy-out of Trans Union do not qualify as § 141(e) "reports" for these reasons: The former lacked substance because Van Gorkom was basically uninformed as to the essential provisions of the very document about which he was talking. Romans' statement was irrelevant to the issues before the Board since it did not purport to be a valuation study. At a minimum for a report to enjoy the status conferred by § 141(e), it must be pertinent to the subject matter upon which a board is called to act, and otherwise be entitled to good faith, not blind, reliance. Considering all of the surrounding circumstances—hastily calling the meeting without prior notice of its subject matter, the proposed sale of the Company without any prior consideration of the issue or necessity therefor, the urgent time constraints imposed by Pritzker, and the total absence of any documentation whatsoever—the directors were duty bound to make reasonable inquiry of Van Gorkom and Romans, and if they had done so, the inadequacy of that upon which they now claim to have relied would have been apparent.

The defendants rely on the following factors to sustain the Trial Court's finding that the Board's decision was an informed one: (1) the magnitude of the premium or spread between the $55 Pritzker offering price and Trans Union's current market price of $38 per share; (2) the amendment of the Agreement as submitted on September 20 to permit the Board to accept any better offer during the "market test" period; (3) the collective experience and expertise of the Board's "inside" and "outside" directors; and (4) their reliance on Brennan's legal advice that the directors might be sued if they rejected the Pritzker proposal. We discuss each of these grounds *seriatim:*

(1)

A substantial premium may provide one reason to recommend a merger, but in the absence of other sound valuation information, the fact of a premium alone does not provide an adequate basis upon which to assess the fairness of an offering price. Here, the judgment reached as to the adequacy of the premium was based on a comparison between the historically depressed Trans Union market price and the amount of the Pritzker offer. Using market price as a basis for concluding that the premium adequately reflected the true value of the Company was a clearly faulty, indeed fallacious, premise, as the defendants' own evidence demonstrates.

We do not say that the Board of Directors was not entitled to give some credence to Van Gorkom's representation that $55 was an adequate or fair price. Under § 141(e), the directors were entitled to rely upon their chairman's opinion of value and adequacy, provided that such opinion was reached on a sound basis. Here, the issue is whether the directors informed themselves as to all information that was reasonably available to them. Had they done so, they would have learned of the source and derivation of the $55 price and could not reasonably have relied thereupon in good faith.

None of the directors, Management or outside, were investment bankers or financial analysts. Yet the Board did not consider recessing the meeting until a later hour that day (or requesting an extension of Pritzker's Sunday evening deadline) to give it time to elicit more information as to the sufficiency of the offer, either from inside Management (in particular Romans) or from Trans Union's own investment banker, Salomon Brothers, whose Chicago specialist in merger and acquisitions was known to the Board and familiar with Trans Union's affairs.

Thus, the record compels the conclusion that on September 20 the Board lacked valuation information adequate to reach an informed business judgment as to the fairness of $55 per share for sale of the Company.

(2)

This brings us to the post-September 20 "market test" upon which the defendants ultimately rely to confirm the reasonableness of their September 20 decision to accept the Pritzker proposal. In this connection, the directors present a two-part argument: (a) that by making a "market test" of Pritzker's $55 per share offer a condition of their September 20 decision to accept his offer, they cannot be found to have acted impulsively or in an uninformed manner on September 20; and (b) that the adequacy of the $17 premium for sale of the Company was conclusively established over the following 90 to 120 days by the most reliable evidence available — the marketplace. Thus, the defendants impliedly contend that the "market test" eliminated the need for the Board to perform any other form of fairness test either on September 20, or thereafter.

Again, the facts of record do not support the defendants' argument. There is no evidence: (a) that the Merger Agreement was effectively amended to give the Board freedom to put Trans Union up for auction sale to the highest bidder; or (b) that a public auction was in fact permitted to occur. The minutes of the Board meeting make no reference to any of this. Indeed, the record compels the conclusion that the directors had no rational basis for expecting that a market test was attainable, given the terms of the Agreement as executed during the evening of September 20.

Van Gorkom states that the Agreement as submitted incorporated the ingredients for a market test by authorizing Trans Union to receive competing offers over the next 90-day period. However, he concedes that the Agreement barred Trans Union from actively soliciting such offers and from furnishing to interested parties any information about the Company other than that already in the public domain.

The defendant directors assert that they "insisted" upon including two amendments to the Agreement, thereby permitting a market test: (1) to give Trans Union the right to accept a better offer; and (2) to reserve to Trans Union the right to distribute proprietary information on the Company to alternative bidders. Yet, the defendants concede that they did not seek to amend the Agreement to permit Trans Union to solicit competing offers.

(3)

The directors' unfounded reliance on both the premium and the market test as the basis for accepting the Pritzker proposal undermines the defendants' remaining contention that the Board's collective experience and sophistication was a sufficient basis for finding that it reached its September 20 decision with informed, reasonable deliberation.

(4)

Part of the defense is based on a claim that the directors relied on legal advice rendered at the September 20 meeting by James Brennan, Esquire, who was present at Van Gorkom's request. Unfortunately, Brennan did not appear and testify at trial even though his firm participated in the defense of this action.

Several defendants testified that Brennan advised them that Delaware law did not require a fairness opinion or an outside valuation of the Company before the Board could act on the Pritzker proposal. If given, the advice was correct. However, that did not end the matter. Unless the directors had before them adequate information regarding the intrinsic value of the Company, upon which a proper exercise of business judgment could be made, mere advice of this type is meaningless; and, given this record of the defendants' failures, it constitutes no defense here.

We conclude that Trans Union's Board was grossly negligent in that it failed to act with informed reasonable deliberation in agreeing to the Pritzker merger proposal on September 20; and we further conclude that the Trial Court erred as a matter of law in failing to address that question before determining whether the directors' later conduct was sufficient to cure its initial error.

A second claim is that counsel advised the Board it would be subject to lawsuits if it rejected the $55 per share offer. It is, of course, a fact of corporate life that today when faced with difficult or sensitive issues, directors often are subject to suit, irrespective of the decisions they make. However, counsel's mere acknowledgement of this circumstance cannot be rationally translated into a justification for a board permitting itself to be stampeded into a patently unadvised act. While suit might result from the rejection of a merger or tender offer, Delaware law makes clear that a board acting within the ambit of the business judgment rule faces no ultimate liability. *Pogostin v. Rice, supra.* Thus, we cannot conclude that the mere threat of litigation, acknowledged by counsel, constitutes either legal advice or any valid basis upon which to pursue an uninformed course.

–B–

We now examine the Board's post-September 20 conduct for the purpose of determining first, whether it was informed and not grossly negligent; and second, if informed, whether it was sufficient to legally rectify and cure the Board's derelictions of September 20.

(1)

The public announcement of the Pritzker merger resulted in an "en masse" revolt of Trans Union's Senior Management. The head of Trans Union's tank car operations (its most profitable division) informed Van Gorkom that unless the merger were called off, fifteen key personnel would resign.

Instead of reconvening the Board, Van Gorkom again privately met with Pritzker, informed him of the developments, and sought his advice. Pritzker then made the following suggestions for overcoming Management's dissatisfaction: (1) that the Agreement be amended to permit Trans Union to solicit, as well as receive, higher offers; and (2) that the shareholder meeting be postponed from early January to February 10, 1981. In return, Pritzker asked Van Gorkom to obtain a commitment from Senior Management to remain at Trans Union for at least six months after the merger was consummated.

Van Gorkom then advised Senior Management that the Agreement would be amended to give Trans Union the right to solicit competing offers through January, 1981, if they would agree to remain with Trans Union. Senior Management was temporarily mollified; and Van Gorkom then called a special meeting of Trans Union's Board for October 8.

Thus, the primary purpose of the October 8 Board meeting was to amend the Merger Agreement, in a manner agreeable to Pritzker, to permit Trans Union to conduct a "market test." Van Gorkom understood that the proposed amendments were intended to give the Company an unfettered "right to openly solicit offers down through January 31." Van Gorkom presumably so represented the amendments to Trans Union's Board members on October 8. In a brief session, the directors approved Van Gorkom's oral presentation of the substance of the proposed amendments, the terms of which were not reduced to writing until October 10. But rather than waiting to review the amendments, the Board again approved them sight unseen and adjourned, giving Van Gorkom authority to execute the papers when he received them.

Thus, the Court of Chancery's finding that the October 8 Board meeting was convened to *reconsider* the Pritzker "proposal" is clearly erroneous. Further, the consequence of the Board's faulty conduct on October 8, in approving amendments to the Agreement which had not even been drafted, will become apparent when the actual amendments to the Agreement are hereafter examined.

The next day, October 9, and before the Agreement was amended, Pritzker moved swiftly to off-set the proposed market test amendment. First, Pritzker informed Trans Union that he had completed arrangements for financing its acquisition and that the parties were thereby mutually bound to a firm purchase and sale arrangement. Second, Pritzker announced the exercise of his option to purchase one million shares of Trans Union's treasury stock at $38 per share — 75 cents above the current market price.

The next day, October 10, Pritzker delivered to Trans Union the proposed amendments to the September 20 Merger Agreement. Van Gorkom promptly proceeded to countersign all the instruments on behalf of Trans Union without reviewing the instruments to determine if they were consistent with the authority previously granted him by the Board.

In our view, the record compels the conclusion that the directors' conduct on October 8 exhibited the same deficiencies as did their conduct on September 20. The Board permitted its Merger Agreement with Pritzker to be amended in a manner it had neither authorized nor intended.

We conclude that the Board acted in a grossly negligent manner on October 8; and that Van Gorkom's representations on which the Board based its actions do not constitute "reports" under § 141(e) on which the directors could reasonably have relied

The October 9 press release, coupled with the October 10 amendments, had the clear effect of locking Trans Union's Board into the Pritzker Agreement. Pritzker had thereby foreclosed Trans Union's Board from negotiating any better "definitive" agreement over the remaining eight weeks before Trans Union was required to clear the Proxy Statement submitting the Pritzker proposal to its shareholders.

(2)

Next, as to the "curative" effects of the Board's post-September 20 conduct, we review in more detail the reaction of Van Gorkom to the KKR proposal and the results of the Board-sponsored "market test."

The KKR proposal was the first and only offer received subsequent to the Pritzker Merger Agreement. The offer resulted primarily from the efforts of Romans and other senior officers to propose an alternative to Pritzker's acquisition of Trans Union. In late September, Romans' group contacted KKR about the possibility of a leveraged buy-out by all members of Management, except Van Gorkom. By early October, Henry R. Kravis of KKR gave Romans written notice of KKR's "interest in making an offer to purchase 100%" of Trans Union's common stock.

Thereafter, and until early December, Romans' group worked with KKR to develop a proposal. It did so with Van Gorkom's knowledge and apparently grudging consent. On December 2, Kravis and Romans hand-delivered to Van Gorkom a formal letter-offer to purchase all of Trans Union's assets and to assume all of its liabilities for an aggregate cash consideration equivalent to $60 per share. The offer was contingent upon completing equity and bank financing of $650 million, which Kravis represented as 80% complete.

Van Gorkom's reaction to the KKR proposal was completely negative; he did not view the offer as being firm because of its financing condition. It was pointed out, to no avail, that Pritzker's offer had not only been similarly conditioned, but accepted on an expedited basis. Van Gorkom refused Kravis' request that Trans Union issue a press release announcing KKR's offer, on the ground that it might "chill" any other offer. Romans and Kravis left with the understanding that their proposal would be presented to Trans Union's Board that afternoon.

Within a matter of hours and shortly before the scheduled Board meeting, Kravis withdrew his letter-offer. He gave as his reason a sudden decision by the Chief Officer of Trans Union's rail car leasing operation to withdraw from the KKR purchasing group. Van Gorkom had spoken to that officer about his participation in the KKR proposal immediately after his meeting with Romans and Kravis. However, Van Gorkom denied any responsibility for the officer's change of mind.

At the Board meeting later that afternoon, Van Gorkom did not inform the directors of the KKR proposal because he considered it "dead."

GE Credit Corporation's interest in Trans Union did not develop until November; and it made no written proposal until mid-January. Even then, its proposal was not in the form of an offer. Had there been time to do so, GE Credit was prepared to offer between $2 and $5 per share above the $55 per share price which Pritzker offered. But GE Credit needed an additional 60 to 90 days; and it was unwilling to make a formal offer without a concession from Pritzker extending the February 10 "deadline" for Trans Union's stockholder meeting. As previously stated, Pritzker refused to grant such extension; and on January 21, GE Credit terminated further negotiations with Trans Union. Its stated reasons, among others, were its "unwillingness to become involved in a bidding contest with Pritzker in the absence of the willingness of [the Pritzker interests] to terminate the proposed $55 cash merger."

V.

The defendants ultimately rely on the stockholder vote of February 10 for exoneration. The defendants contend that the stockholders' "overwhelming" vote approving the Pritzker Merger Agreement had the legal effect of curing any failure of the Board to reach an informed business judgment in its approval of the merger.

The parties tacitly agree that a discovered failure of the Board to reach an informed business judgment in approving the merger constitutes a voidable, rather than a void, act. Hence, the merger can be sustained, notwithstanding the infirmity of the Board's action, if its approval by majority vote of the shareholders is found to have been based on an informed electorate.

The settled rule in Delaware is that "where a majority of fully informed stockholders ratify action of even interested directors, an attack on the ratified transaction normally must fail." *Gerlach v. Gillam,* Del.Ch., 139 A.2d 591, 593 (1958). The question of whether shareholders have been fully informed such that their vote can be said to ratify director action, "turns on the fairness and completeness of the proxy materials submitted by the management to the ... shareholders." *Michelson v. Duncan, supra* at 220. As this Court stated in *Gottlieb v. Heyden Chemical Corp.,* Del.Supr., 91 A.2d 57, 59 (1952): "[T]he entire atmosphere is freshened and a new set of rules invoked where a formal approval has been given by a majority of independent, fully informed stockholders...."

Applying this standard to the record before us, we find that Trans Union's stockholders were not fully informed of all facts material to their vote on the Pritzker Merger and that the Trial Court's ruling to the contrary is clearly erroneous. We list the material deficiencies in the proxy materials:

(1) The fact that the Board had no reasonably adequate information indicative of the intrinsic value of the Company, other than a concededly depressed market price, was without question material to the shareholders voting on the merger. Accordingly, the Board's lack of valuation information should have been disclosed. Instead, the directors cloaked the absence of such information in both the Proxy Statement and the Supplemental Proxy Statement. Through artful drafting, noticeably absent at the September 20 meeting, both documents create the impression that the Board knew the intrinsic worth of the Company.

What the Board failed to disclose to its stockholders was that the Board had not made any study of the intrinsic or inherent worth of the Company; nor had the Board even discussed the inherent value of the Company prior to approving the merger on September 20, or at either of the subsequent meetings on October 8 or January 26.

(3) We find misleading the Board's references to the "substantial" premium offered. The Board gave as their primary reason in support of the merger the "substantial premium" shareholders would receive. But the Board did not disclose its failure to assess the premium offered in terms of other relevant valuation techniques, thereby rendering questionable its determination as to the substantiality of the premium over an admittedly depressed stock market price.

(4) We find the Board's recital in the Supplemental Proxy of certain events preceding the September 20 meeting to be incomplete and misleading. It is beyond dispute that a reasonable stockholder would have considered material the fact that Van Gorkom not only suggested the $55 price to Pritzker, but also that he chose the figure because it made feasible a leveraged buy-out.

The burden must fall on defendants who claim ratification based on shareholder vote to establish that the shareholder approval resulted from a fully informed electorate. On the record before us, it is clear that the Board failed to meet that burden.

VI.

To summarize: we hold that the directors of Trans Union breached their fiduciary duty to their stockholders (1) by their failure to inform themselves of all information reasonably available to them and relevant to their decision to recommend the Pritzker merger; and (2) by their failure to disclose all material information such as a reasonable stockholder would consider important in deciding whether to approve the Pritzker offer.

We hold, therefore, that the Trial Court committed reversible error in applying the business judgment rule in favor of the director defendants in this case.

On remand, the Court of Chancery shall conduct an evidentiary hearing to determine the fair value of the shares represented by the plaintiffs' class, based on the intrinsic value of Trans Union on September 20, 1980. Thereafter, an award of damages may be entered to the extent that the fair value of Trans Union exceeds $55 per share.

REVERSED and REMANDED for proceedings consistent herewith.

McNEILLY, Justice, dissenting:

The majority opinion reads like an advocate's closing address to a hostile jury. And I say that not lightly. Throughout the opinion great emphasis is directed only to the negative, with nothing more than lip service granted the positive aspects of this case. Because of my diametrical opposition to all evidentiary conclusions of the majority, I respectfully dissent.

The majority has spoken and has effectively said that Trans Union's Directors have been the victims of a "fast shuffle" by Van Gorkom and Pritzker. That is the beginning of the majority's comedy of errors. The first and most important error made is the majority's assessment of the directors' knowledge of the affairs of Trans Union and their combined ability to act in this situation under the protection of the business judgment rule.

Trans Union's Board of Directors consisted of ten men, five of whom were "inside" directors and five of whom were "outside" directors. The "inside" directors were Van Gorkom, Chelberg, Bonser, William B. Browder, Senior Vice-President-Law, and Thomas P. O'Boyle, Senior Vice-President-Administration. At the time the merger was proposed the inside five directors had collectively been employed by the Company for 116 years and had 68 years of combined experience as directors. The "outside" directors were A.W. Wallis, William B. Johnson, Joseph B. Lanterman, Graham J. Morgan and Robert W. Reneker. With the exception of Wallis, these were all chief executive officers of Chicago based corporations that were at least as large as Trans Union. The five "outside" directors had 78 years of combined experience as chief executive officers, and 53 years cumulative service as Trans Union directors.

The inside directors wear their badge of expertise in the corporate affairs of Trans Union on their sleeves. But what about the outsiders? Dr. Wallis is or was an economist and math statistician, a professor of economics at Yale University, dean of the graduate school of business at the University of Chicago, and Chancellor of the University of Rochester. Dr. Wallis had been on the Board of Trans Union since 1962. He also was on the Board of Bausch & Lomb, Kodak, Metropolitan Life Insurance Company, Standard Oil and others.

William B. Johnson is a University of Pennsylvania law graduate, President of Railway Express until 1966, Chairman and Chief Executive of I.C. Industries Holding Company, and member of Trans Union's Board since 1968.

Joseph Lanterman, a Certified Public Accountant, is or was President and Chief Executive of American Steel, on the Board of International Harvester, Peoples Energy, Illinois Bell Telephone, Harris Bank and Trust Company, Kemper Insurance Company and a director of Trans Union for four years.

Graham Morgan is a chemist, was Chairman and Chief Executive Officer of U.S. Gypsum, and in the 17 and 18 years prior to the Trans Union transaction had been involved in 31 or 32 corporate takeovers.

Robert Reneker attended University of Chicago and Harvard Business Schools. He was President and Chief Executive of Swift and Company, director of Trans Union since 1971, and member of the Boards of seven other corporations including U.S. Gypsum and the Chicago Tribune.

Directors of this caliber are not ordinarily taken in by a "fast shuffle." I submit they were not taken into this multi-million dollar corporate transaction without being fully informed and aware of the state of the art as it pertained to the entire corporate panorama of Trans Union. True, even directors such as these, with their business acumen, interest and expertise, can go astray. I do not believe that to be the case here. These men knew Trans Union like the back of their hands and were more than well qualified to make on the spot informed business judgments concerning the affairs of Trans Union including a 100% sale of the corporation. Lest we forget, the corporate world of then and now operates on what is so aptly referred to as "the fast track." These men were at the time an integral part of that world, all professional business men, not intellectual figureheads.

Notes

(1) Why would Pritzker insist that the deal close before the opening of the English stock exchange on a Monday morning?

(2) What is a stalking horse? What is an "auction contest"?

(3) In the actual case, the market price per share of Trans Union was $38. Since the board approved a deal in excess of the market price at the time of the merger, why wasn't that fact alone sufficient to establish that the board met its applicable duty of care? Does the current market price always reflect the fair market value?

(4) What is a leveraged buyout? In the case, the board attempted to establish that it was adequately informed in making the decision to approve the cash out merger by introducing Roman's report that $55 per share was a "fair price" within the context of a leveraged buyout. Specifically, the court opined that the report "was not designed to determine the fair value of the Company, but rather to assess the feasibility of a leveraged buy-out financed by the Company's projected cash flow, making certain assumptions as to the purchaser's borrowing needs." Why did the court disregard this evidence? What is the difference between a leveraged buyout and an all cash merger? In a leveraged buyout what is the primary motivation behind setting the price per share? Is it to determine shareholder value or to ensure that there are sufficient assets to pay back the creditor?

(5) Assume that you are chief counsel for a corporation facing the same decision that was presented to the board in *Van Gorkom*. Given what you have learned from this case, how would you advise?

(6) Why do you think that the following facts failed to influence the court to rule in the board's favor?

- The $55 Pritzker offering price was $17 above Trans Unions then market share price of $38.

- The board was permitted to accept a better offer from another entity during the "market test" period.

- The collective experience and expertise of the Board's "inside" and "outside" directors.

- That Trans Union's legal counsel advised the board that failure to approve the Pritzker deal might result in litigation.

(7) Is *Van Gorkom* a case that expanded or lessened directorial liability?

(8) While Van Gorkom was an extremely educated and successful businessman, it was obvious that his knowledge of mergers and acquisitions was grossly disproportionate to Pritzker's knowledge. Van Gorkom's expertise was in running companies, Pritzker's expertise was in taking them over! Pritzker was a known corporate raider.[5] As evidence of Pritzker's takeover savvy consider the following:

- The preliminary merger negotiation took place at Pritzker's house. It was as if Van Gorkom voluntarily decided to walk into a lion's den.

- Second, there was little to no dickering over the price. Pritzker made his offer and did not offer a penny more. Once Van Gorkom approached Pritzker from such a disadvantaged and uninformed position, Pritzker knew that he had him.

- Third, after the merger was announced, several key management figures, in one of Trans Union's most successful business units, decided that they would quit unless the merger was abandoned. Instead of speaking with Trans Union's management, Van Gorkom immediately contacted Pritzker and sought his advice regarding the situation. In response, Pritzker told Van Gorkom to request that the dissatisfied managers remain at Trans Union for at least six months after the merger was approved in exchange for a promise to modify the merger agreement to (1) provide a market test amendment by permitting "Trans Union to solicit, as well as receive, higher offers"; and (2) postpone the scheduled shareholder meeting to approve the merger. However, immediately after advising Van Gorkom, the very next day, Pritzker undermined his own advice and exploited the situation by offsetting the market test amendment. "First, Pritzker informed Trans Union that he had completed arrangements for financing its acquisition and that the parties were thereby mutually bound to a firm purchase and sale arrangement. Second, Pritzker announced the exercise of his option to purchase one million shares of Trans Union's treasury stock at $38 per share—75 cents above the current market price. Trans Union's management responded the same day by issuing a press release announcing: (1) that all financing arrangements for Pritzker's acquisition of Trans Union had been completed; and (2) Pritzker's purchase of one million shares of Trans Union's treasury stock at $38 per share."

(9) What do you think about the dissenting opinion? Should the majority have given more consideration to the credentials of the board members?

(10) When Directors and/or Officers are held liable for breaching their duty of care like Van Gorkom and the Board of Directors here, who pays the damages to the

---

5. A corporate raider is an investor that buys enough shares of a corporation to take control of it without the approval of the target company's board.

shareholders? Often, it is insurance companies that end up paying damages as all well informed corporate leaders carry malpractice insurance, often paid for by the corporation. So, most times, directors who breach their duties are not out-of-pocket when facing a damages payment. Additionally, many states have passed protective laws that allow corporations to indemnify their directors against liability exposure by employment contract ensuring that the corporation pays legal fees and potential damages for corporate duty breaches. As we have learned, when a corporation pays for the grossly negligent behavior of its leaders, it is the shareholders that are footing the bill for corporate wrongdoing or negligence.

(11) In response to *Van Gorkom*, the Delaware State legislature enacted 8 Delaware Code Section 102(b)(7) that limited personal director liability. Pursuant to 102(b)(7), in relevant part, directors will be liable for breach only when directors act intentionally or in bad faith. To establish either one of these, the shareholders carry a substantial burden of proof that is unlikely to be established as you will see from the case below.

After seeing that corporate directors can be held liable when grossly negligent for a duty of care breach, many shareholders began bringing duty of care breach challenges against corporate executives for decisions that purportedly ended in corporate waste. Perhaps the most compelling and infamous example of corporate waste occurred when the Walt Disney Corporation hired and fired Hollywood superagent Michael Ovitz after only 14 months of service to Disney. When Ovitz walked out the door with his pink slip, he also carried with him a severance package of over $140 million dollars, negotiated as part of his employment contract when hired. Disney shareholders were incensed to learn that Ovitz earned more money fired than he would have earned had he served out the terms of his employment contract. Shareholders brought suit alleging that the Disney board had been grossly negligent in hiring and firing Ovitz, just as Van Gorkom had violated his care duties when selling Trans Union to Jay Pritzker.

As you read *Disney*, consider how 102(b)(7) influences the way the shareholders plead and argue their case.

In re The Walt Disney Company Derivative Litigation
907 A.2d 693, 31 Del. J. Corp. L. 349 (2005)
Court of Chancery of Delaware

OPINION, CHANDLER, J.

INTRODUCTION

This is the Court's decision after trial in this long running dispute over an executive compensation and severance package. The stockholder plaintiffs have alleged that the director defendants breached their fiduciary duties in connection with the 1995 hiring and 1996 termination of Michael Ovitz as President of The Walt Disney Company. The trial consumed thirty-seven days (between October 20, 2004 and January 19, 2005) and generated 9,360 pages of transcript from twenty-four witnesses. The Court also reviewed thousands of pages of deposition transcripts and 1,033 trial exhibits that filled more than twenty-two 3 ½-inch binders. Extensive post-trial memoranda also were submitted and considered. After carefully considering all of the evidence and arguments, and for the reasons set forth in this Opinion, I conclude that the director defendants did not breach their fiduciary duties or commit waste. Therefore, I will enter judgment in favor of the defendants as to all claims in the amended complaint.

Because this matter, by its very nature, has become something of a public spectacle — commencing as it did with the spectacular hiring of one of the entertainment industry's best-known personalities to help run one of its iconic businesses, and ending with a spectacular failure of that union, with breathtaking amounts of severance pay the consequence — it is, I think, worth noting what the role of this Court must be in evaluating decision-makers' performance with respect to decisions gone awry, spectacularly or otherwise.

Even where decision-makers act as faithful servants, however, their ability and the wisdom of their judgments will vary. The redress for failures that arise from faithful management must come from the markets, through the action of shareholders and the free flow of capital, and not from this Court. Should the Court apportion liability based on the ultimate outcome of decisions taken in good faith by faithful directors or officers, those decision-makers would necessarily take decisions that minimize risk, not maximize value. The entire advantage of the risk-taking, innovative, wealth-creating engine that is the Delaware corporation would cease to exist, with disastrous results for shareholders and society alike. That is why, under our corporate law, corporate decision-makers are held strictly to their fiduciary duties, but within the boundaries of those duties are free to act as their judgment and abilities dictate, free of *post hoc* penalties from a reviewing court using perfect hindsight. Corporate decisions are made, risks are taken, the results become apparent, capital flows accordingly, and shareholder value is increased.

I. FACTS

A. Michael Ovitz Joins The Walt Disney Company

1. Background

The story of Michael Ovitz's rise and fall at The Walt Disney Company ("Disney" or the "Company") begins with the unfortunate and untimely demise of Frank Wells. Before his death, Wells served as Disney's President and Chief Operating Officer, and both he and Michael Eisner, Disney's Chairman and CEO, enjoyed ten years of remarkable success at the Company's helm. In April 1994, a fatal helicopter crash ended Wells' tenure at Disney and forced the company to consider a decision it was not properly prepared or ready to make.

Disney's short list of potential internal successors produced, for one reason or another, no viable candidates. Instead, Eisner assumed Disney's presidency, and for a brief moment, the Company was able to stave off the need to replace Wells. Within three months, however, misfortune again struck the Company when Eisner was unexpectedly diagnosed with heart disease and underwent quadruple bypass surgery. The unfortunate timing of Eisner's illness and operation set off an "enormous amount of speculation" concerning Eisner's health and convinced Eisner of the need to "protect[ ] the company and get [ ] help." Over the next year, Eisner and Disney's board of directors discussed the need to identify Eisner's successor. These events were the springboard from which Eisner intensified his longstanding desire to bring Michael Ovitz within the Disney fold.

By the summer of 1995, Michael Ovitz and Michael Eisner had been friends for nearly twenty-five years. These men were very well acquainted, both socially and professionally. Over time, this relationship engendered numerous overtures, by which Eisner and Ovitz flirted with the idea of joining ranks and doing something together. As Eisner put it: "I had been trying to hire him forever.... I couldn't do business with him ... he was too tough, so I thought he would be better … on our side." But until Eisner had offered Ovitz Disney's presidency, Ovitz had never seriously considered any of Eisner's offers.

After graduating college, Ovitz left the studios and gained employment in the mailroom of the William Morris Agency. At that time, William Morris was well regarded as the oldest and largest theatrical talent agency in the world. Ovitz worked for William Morris for six years, and had worked his way up to become a talent agent within the agency's television department. Here, Ovitz began to question the company's direction and its approach to representing its clients. Despite several colleagues' attempts to address their discontent with management, their efforts were not well received and, eventually, these philosophical disagreements led to an impasse. Ovitz and four other William Morris agents left, and Creative Artist Agency ("CAA") was born.

Ovitz attributes CAA's rise, in part, to a business model that he dubbed: "packaging." As Ovitz explained, before CAA, it was Hollywood studios, distributors or networks that controlled the talent "either contractually or by virtue of the fact that they had all of the distribution capability." CAA revolutionized this system by grouping various talents, whether they were actors, directors or writers. These "packaged" talents could then coordinate their efforts to best exploit their leverage and maximize the economics of any given deal. The effect of Ovitz's business model was clear. By 1995, CAA had reshaped an entire industry and had grown from five men sitting around a card table to the premier Hollywood talent agency. When Ovitz joined Disney, he left behind 550 employees and an impressive roster of about 1400 of Hollywood's top actors, directors, writers and musicians—a roster that earned CAA approximately $150 million in annual revenues. In turn, this success translated into an annual income of $20 million for Ovitz and, for his part, he was regarded as one of the most powerful figures in Hollywood.

Michael Eisner had been following Ovitz's [career] closely and believed that now was the time to either talk to Ovitz seriously about joining Disney or face the possibility of having Ovitz at the helm of a major Disney competitor.

Eisner's renewed efforts to recruit Ovitz received support from Sid Bass and Roy Disney (Roy Disney was also a director of the Company), two of the company's largest individual shareholders. Eisner's efforts to hire Ovitz were in full swing by mid-July 1995. Russell, per Eisner's direction, assumed the lead role in negotiating the financial terms of the contract. These efforts took on significant import in the face of Disney's recent announcement of the acquisition of CapCities/ABC, a transaction that would double the size of Disney, place even greater demands on Eisner, and exacerbate the need for someone else to shoulder some of the load. Russell, in his negotiations with Bob Goldman, Ovitz's attorney, learned that Ovitz was making approximately $20 to $25 million a year from CAA and owned fifty-five percent of the company. From the start, Ovitz made it clear that he would not give up his fifty-five percent interest in CAA without downside protection

By the beginning of August 1995, the non-contentious terms of Ovitz's employment agreement (the "OEA") were $1 million in annual salary and a performance-based, discretionary bonus. The remaining terms were not as easily agreed to and related primarily to stock options and Ovitz's insistence for downside protection. Ovitz, using Eisner's contract as a yardstick, was asking for options on eight million shares of Disney's stock. Both Russell and Eisner, however, refused to offer eight million options and believed that no options should be offered within the first five years of Ovitz's contract. This was a non-starter, since Ovitz would not leave CAA without downside protection and Disney had a policy against front-loading contracts with signing bonuses. Using both Eisner's and Wells' original employment contracts as a template, the parties reached a compromise.

Under the proposed OEA, Ovitz would receive a five-year contract with two tranches of options. The first tranche consisted of three million options vesting in equal parts in the third, fourth and fifth years, and if the value of those options at the end of the five years had not appreciated to $50 million, Disney would make up the difference. The second tranche consisted of two million options that would vest immediately if Disney and Ovitz opted to renew the contract.

The proposed OEA sought to protect both parties in the event that Ovitz's employment ended prematurely and provided that absent defined causes, neither party could terminate the agreement without penalty. If Ovitz, for example, walked away, for any reason other than those permitted under the OEA, he would forfeit any benefits remaining under the OEA and could be enjoined from working for a competitor. Likewise, if Disney fired Ovitz for any reason other than gross negligence or malfeasance, Ovitz would be entitled to a non-fault payment (Non-Fault Termination or "NFT"), which consisted of his remaining salary, $7.5 million a year for any unaccrued bonuses, the immediate vesting of his first tranche of options and a $10 million cash out payment for the second tranche of options.

stock options

As the basic terms of the OEA were coming together, Russell authored and provided Eisner and Ovitz with a "Case Study" outlining the OEA parameters and Russell's commentary on what he believed was an extraordinary level of executive compensation. Specifically, Russell noted that it was appropriate to provide Ovitz with "downside protection and upside opportunity" and to assist Ovitz with "the adjustment in life style resulting from the lower level of cash compensation from a public company in contrast to the availability of cash distributions and perquisites from a privately held enterprise." According to Russell, Ovitz was an "exceptional corporate executive" who was a "highly successful and unique entrepreneur." Nevertheless, Russell cautioned that Ovitz's salary under the OEA was at the top level for any corporate officer and significantly above that of the CEO and that the number of stock options granted under the OEA was far beyond the standards applied within Disney and corporate America "and will raise very strong criticism." Russell rounded out his analysis by recommending an additional study so that he and Eisner could answer questions should they arise. Russell did not provide this Case Study to any other member of Disney's board of directors.

With the various financial terms of the OEA sufficiently concrete, Russell enlisted the aid of two people who could help with the final financial analysis: Raymond Watson, a current member of Disney's compensation committee and the past chairman of Disney's board of directors (and one of the men who designed the original pay structure behind Wells' and Eisner's compensation packages); and Graef Crystal, an executive compensation consultant, who is particularly well known within the industry for lambasting the extravagant compensation paid to America's top executives. The three men were set to meet on August 10. Before the meeting, Crystal prepared, on a laptop computer, a comprehensive executive compensation database that would accept various inputs and run Black-Scholes* analyses to output a range of values for the options. At the meeting, the three men worked with various assumptions and manipulated inputs in order to generate a series of values that could be attributed to the OEA. In addition to Crystal's work,

---

* The Black-Scholes' method is a formula for option valuation, widely used and accepted by industry figures and regulators, that determines option value based upon a complex calculation involving the exercise price and term of the options, the price of the underlying stock, its dividend history and volatility, and the risk-free interest rate. Tr. 764:20–765:13.

Watson had prepared several spreadsheets presenting similar assessments, but these spreadsheets did not use the Black-Scholes valuation method. At the end of the day, the men made their conclusions, discussed them, and agreed that Crystal would memorialize his findings and fax the report to Russell.

Two days later, Crystal faxed his memorandum to Russell. In the memo, Crystal concluded that the OEA would provide Ovitz with approximately $23.6 million per year for the first five years of the deal. Crystal estimated that the contract was worth $23.9 million a year, over a seven-year period, if Disney and Ovitz exercised the two-year renewal option. Crystal opined that those figures would approximate Ovitz's present compensation with CAA. Crystal contended that the current language of the OEA, if he was reading it correctly, would allow Ovitz to hold the first tranche of options, wait until his five-year term was up, collect the $50 million guarantee and then exercise in-the-money options for an additional windfall. In light of this, Crystal was philosophically opposed to a pay package that would give Ovitz the best of both worlds—*i.e.*, low risk and high return. Crystal's letter was never circulated to any board member other than Eisner. Rather, Russell addressed Crystal's concerns and clarified that the guarantee would not function in the manner Crystal believed. Up until this point, only three members of Disney's board of directors were in the know concerning the status of the negotiations with Ovitz or the particulars of the OEA—Eisner, Russell and Watson.

While Russell, Watson and Crystal were finalizing their analysis of the OEA, Eisner and Ovitz were coming to terms of their own. Eisner, having recently conferred with Russell concerning his ongoing research, gave Ovitz a take-it-or-leave-it offer: If Ovitz joined Disney as its new President, he would not assume the duties or title of COO. After short deliberation, Ovitz accepted Eisner's terms.

Ovitz and Eisner signed the letter agreement ("OLA") that outlined the basic terms of Ovitz's employment. The OLA specified that Ovitz's hiring was subject to approval of Disney's compensation committee and board of directors. As for communications with the other board members, Eisner contacted each of them by phone to inform them of the impending deal. During these calls, Eisner described his friendship with Ovitz, and Ovitz's background and qualifications.

On the same day that Eisner and Ovitz signed the OLA, the news of Ovitz's hiring was made public via a press release. Public reaction was extremely positive. Disney was applauded for the decision, and Disney's stock price increased 4.4 percent in a single day —increasing Disney's market capitalization by more than $1 billion.

On September 26, 1995, the compensation committee met *for one hour* to consider the proposed terms of the OEA. The discussion concerning the OEA focused on a term sheet (the actual draft of the OEA was not distributed), from which Russell and Watson outlined the process they had followed and described Crystal's analysis. Russell testified that the topics discussed were historical comparables such as Eisner's and Wells' option grants, and the factors that he, Watson and Crystal had considered in setting the size of the option grants and the termination provisions of the contract. Watson testified that he provided the committee with the spreadsheet analysis he had performed back in August and discussed his findings. Crystal, however, did not attend the meeting and his work product was not distributed to the Committee. At trial, Crystal testified that he was available via telephone to respond to questions if needed, but no one from the committee in fact called. Poitier and Lozano testified that they believed they had received sufficient information from Russell's and Watson's presentations to enable them to exercise their judgment in the best interest of the Company. When the discussions concluded, the Committee unanimously voted to approve the terms of the OEA subject to "reasonable further negotiations within the framework of the terms and conditions" described in the OEA.

An executive meeting of Disney's board immediately followed the compensation committee's meeting. Upon resuming the regular session, the board deliberated further, then voted unanimously to elect Ovitz as President.

Ovitz's tenure as President of The Walt Disney Company officially began on October 1, 1995. As late as the end of 1995, Eisner's attitude with respect to Ovitz was positive. Eisner opined that Ovitz performed well during 1995, notwithstanding the difficulties Ovitz was experiencing assimilating to Disney's culture.

In 1996, however, the tenor of the comments surrounding Ovitz's performance and his transition to The Walt Disney Company changed. In short, Ovitz "was a little elitist for the egalitarian Walt Disney World cast members [employees]," and a poor fit with his fellow executives.

As 1996 wore on, it became apparent that the difficulties Ovitz was having at the Company were less and less likely to be resolved. By the summer of 1996, Eisner had spoken with several directors about Ovitz's failure to adapt to the Company's culture.

By the fall of 1996, directors began discussing that the disconnect between Ovitz and the Company was likely irreparable, and that Ovitz would have to be terminated.

4. *Specific Examples of Ovitz's Performance as President of The Walt Disney Company*

There are three competing theories as to why Ovitz was not successful. First, plaintiffs argue that Ovitz failed to follow Eisner's directives, especially in regard to acquisitions, and that generally, Ovitz did very little. Second, Ovitz contends that Eisner's micromanaging prevented Ovitz from having the authority necessary to make the changes that Ovitz thought were appropriate. In addition, Ovitz believes he was not given enough time for his efforts to bear fruit. Third, the remaining defendants simply posit that Ovitz failed to transition from a private to public company, from the "sell side to the buy side," and otherwise did not adapt to the Company culture or fit in with other executives. In the end, however, it makes no difference why Ovitz was not as successful as his reputation would have led many to expect, so long as he was not grossly negligent or malfeasant.

Many of Ovitz's efforts failed to produce results, often because his efforts reflected an opposite philosophy than that held by Eisner, Iger, and Roth. This does not mean that Ovitz intentionally failed to follow Eisner's directives or that he was insubordinate. To the contrary, it demonstrates that Ovitz was attempting to use his knowledge and experience, which was fundamentally different from Eisner's, Iger's, and Roth's, to benefit the Company. But different does not mean wrong. Total agreement within an organization is often a far greater threat than diversity of opinion. Unfortunately, the philosophical divide between Eisner and Ovitz was greater than both believed, and as two proud and stubborn individuals, neither of them was willing to consider the possibility that their point of view might be incorrect, leading to their inevitable falling out.

Ovitz's relationship with Eisner, and with other Disney executives and directors, continued to deteriorate through September 1996.

Eisner and Ovitz had several meetings on or around September 21, 1996, during which they discussed Ovitz's future (or lack thereof) at Disney, and the possibility that Ovitz would seek employment at Sony. Eisner believed that Sony would be both willing and excited to take Ovitz in "trade" from Disney because Ovitz had a very positive longstanding relationship with many of Sony's top executives. Eisner favored the Sony "trade" because, not only would it remove Ovitz and his personality from the halls of Disney, but it would also relieve Disney of having to pay Ovitz under the OEA and would hopefully bring a valuable return to Disney in the form of licensing rights for *The Young and the Restless*.

On November 1, Ovitz wrote a letter to Eisner notifying Eisner that things had failed to work out with Sony and that Ovitz had instead decided to recommit himself to Disney.

Although Eisner never sat down at a full board meeting to discuss the persistent and growing Ovitz problem, it is clear that he made an effort to notify and talk with a large majority, if not all, of the directors.

Eisner met with Ovitz personally on November 13 and they discussed Ovitz's alleged management and ethics problems. Eisner believed that Ovitz just would not listen to what he was trying to tell him and instead, Ovitz insisted that he would stay at Disney, going so far as to state that he would chain himself to his desk.

Since the Sony option was discussed in early September, Eisner and Litvack had also been discussing whether Ovitz could be terminated, and more importantly, whether he could be terminated for cause. Eisner hoped to obtain a termination for cause because he believed that although Ovitz "had not done the job that would warrant [the NFT] payment" Disney was obliged to honor the OEA. Honoring the OEA meant that if Ovitz was terminated without cause, he would receive the NFT payment that the OEA called for, which consisted of the balance of Ovitz's salary, an imputed amount of bonuses, a $10 million termination fee and the immediate vesting of his three million stock options at the time. Litvack advised Eisner from the very beginning that he did not believe that there was cause to terminate Ovitz under the OEA.

Litvack reviewed the OEA, refreshed himself on the meaning of gross negligence and malfeasance and reviewed all of the facts concerning Ovitz's performance of which he was aware. After taking these steps, Litvack, for the second time, concluded that there was no cause to terminate Ovitz. Litvack, however, produced no written work product or notes to show to the board that would explain or defend his conclusion, and because he did not ask for an outside opinion to be authored, there was no written work product at all.

In a perfect, more responsible world, both Litvack and Eisner would have had sufficient documentation not only to back up their conclusion that Ovitz could not be terminated for cause, but they would have also had sufficient evidence of the research and legwork they did to arrive at that conclusion. Despite the paucity of evidence, it is clear to the Court that both Eisner and Litvack wanted to fire Ovitz for cause to avoid the costly NFT payment, The Court is convinced, that Eisner and Litvack did in fact make a concerted effort to determine if Ovitz could be terminated for cause, and that despite these efforts, they were unable to manufacture the desired result.

In addition to determining that there was no cause to fire Ovitz as defined in the OEA, Litvack also testified that it would be inappropriate and unethical for Disney to try to bluff Ovitz into accepting an amount less than agreed to in the OEA in case of an NFT.

4. *The November 25, 1996 Board Meeting*

The Disney board held its next meeting on November 25, and Ovitz was present. Although there was no mention of Ovitz's impending termination at the board meeting, it is apparent, despite the lack of a written record, that directly following the board meeting, there was some discussion concerning Ovitz at the executive session. Eisner testified that, in addition to the other items, he informed those in attendance of what the NFT would cost Disney.

Disney, and more accurately, Eisner, rejected every request that Ovitz had made, informing him that all he would receive is what he had contracted for in the OEA and nothing more. Other than the extra benefits which Ovitz requested and Disney summarily denied, there seems to have been no negotiation between anyone in Ovitz's camp and anyone at Disney concerning whether there would be a for cause termination or an NFT, and nobody seems to have even mentioned to Ovitz or his representatives the possibility of a for cause termination.

On December 10, the Executive Performance Plan Committee ("EPPC") met to consider annual bonuses for Disney's most highly-compensated executive officers. Russell informed all those in attendance of his conversations with Ovitz's representatives and that Ovitz was going to be terminated, but that he was not going to be terminated for cause. At this meeting, Russell recommended that Ovitz, despite his poor performance and imminent termination, should receive a $7.5 million bonus for his services during the 1996 fiscal year because Disney had done so well during the fiscal year and because Disney had a large bonus pool. The EPPC approved this recommendation and it appears that Russell may have even advised the EPPC (despite the *clear* language in the OEA stating that the *bonus was discretionary*) that Disney was contractually obligated to pay Ovitz his bonus. Despite the fact that all of those in attendance should have known better, nobody spoke up to correct the mistaken perception that Ovitz had to receive a bonus, let alone a $7.5 million bonus.

Ovitz's termination was memorialized in a letter signed by Litvack and dated December 12. Litvack testified that Russell negotiated the terms in the letter, but Litvack signed this document on Eisner's instructions. The board was not shown the December 12 letter, nor did it meet to approve its terms.

That same day, Eisner at least attempted to contact each of the Board members by phone before the issuance of the press release in order to notify them that Ovitz had been officially terminated. None of the board members at that time, or at any other time before or during trial, ever objected to Ovitz's termination; in fact, most if not all thought it was the appropriate move for Eisner to make. Also on December 12, copies of the press release along with a letter from Eisner were sent to each of the directors. The letters contained no more information regarding the termination than was contained in the press release.

Thus, as of December 12, Ovitz was officially terminated without cause. Up to this point, however, the Disney board had never met in order to vote on, or even discuss, the termination at a full session, and few if any directors did an independent investigation of whether Ovitz could be terminated for cause. As a result, the Disney directors had been taken for a wild ride, and most of it was in the dark. Additionally neither the EPPC nor the compensation committee had a vote on the matter, and it seems as though they had yet to have a substantive discussion of whether Ovitz could be terminated for cause. Many directors believed that Eisner had the power to fire Ovitz on his own and that he did not need to convene a board meeting to do so. Other directors believed that if a meeting was required to terminate Ovitz, that Litvack, serving as corporate counsel, would have advised them that was the case and he would have made sure one was called. Litvack believed that Eisner had the power to fire Ovitz on his own accord and, therefore, did not believe it was necessary to convene a meeting. Litvack also stated that he did not call a meeting because not only did he believe that Eisner was empowered to fire Ovitz on his own, but Litvack believed that all the directors were up to speed and in agreement that Ovitz should be terminated. Although there was no meeting called to vote on or even discuss Ovitz's termination, it is clear that most, if not all, directors trusted Eisner's and Litvack's conclusion that there was no cause and that Ovitz should still be terminated without cause even though this entailed making the costly NFT payment.

Following the official termination, the EPPC met on December 20 with the sole purpose of rescinding Ovitz's $7.5 million bonus.

The full board next met on January 27, 1997. By this time, the board was aware of the negative publicity that the Ovitz termination and NFT payment had received. There was an extensive discussion of Ovitz's termination at this meeting and the pending lawsuit. Litvack, addressing the full board for the first time concerning the cause issue, notified the board that in his opinion there had been no gross negligence or malfeasance and, thus, Ovitz could not be terminated for cause.

II. LEGAL STANDARDS

The outcome of this case is determined by whether the defendants complied with their fiduciary duties in connection with the hiring and termination of Michael Ovitz. At the outset, the Court emphasizes that the best practices of corporate governance include compliance with fiduciary duties. Compliance with fiduciary duties, however, is not always enough to meet or to satisfy what is expected by the best practices of corporate governance.

The fiduciary duties owed by directors of a Delaware corporation are the duties of due care and loyalty. Of late, much discussion among the bench, bar, and academics alike, has surrounded a so-called third fiduciary duty, that of good faith. Of primary importance in this case are the fiduciary duty of due care and the duty of a director to act in good faith. Other than to the extent that the duty of loyalty is implicated by a lack of good faith, the only remaining issues to be decided herein with respect to the duty of loyalty are those relating to Ovitz's actions in connection with his own termination. These considerations will be addressed *seriatim,* although issues of good faith are (to a certain degree) inseparably and necessarily intertwined with the duties of care and loyalty, as well as a principal reason the distinctness of these duties make a difference—namely § 102(b)(7) of the Delaware General Corporation Law.**

** Perhaps these categories of care and loyalty, so rigidly defined and categorized in Delaware for many years, are really just different ways of analyzing the same issue. Professor Sean Griffith said it best when he recently wrote:

At first glance, the duties of care and loyalty appear quite distinctive....

A bit of digging beneath these surface differences, however, reveals the richly interconnected roots of the two doctrinal paradigms. Start with the duty of care: directors must conduct themselves as ordinarily prudent persons managing their own affairs. So far so good, but a moment's reflection reveals that an ordinarily prudent person becomes an ordinarily prudent director only once we assume an element of loyalty. How do ordinarily prudent directors conduct their affairs? A decision is taken with due care, when from an array of alternatives, the directors employ a procedure to pick the one that best advances *the interests of the corporation.* Now pause for a moment to consider what a funny way this is of conceiving what an ordinarily prudent person would do *in the conduct of her own affairs.* We might typically assume that an ordinarily prudent person, in evaluating a set of alternatives, picks the one that provides the most benefit and least cost to *herself.* A director's decision-making process, however, can be evaluated only by changing the referent from herself to the corporation. The question of prudence, in other words, is framed with a tacit element of loyalty....

[Shareholders and courts] are worried about the directors' loyalty because we are concerned that their disloyalty will result in a poor bargain for the corporation. We are concerned, in other words, that conflicted directors will strike bargains for the corporation that an ordinarily prudent person would not strike for herself. This can be seen most clearly if the non-arms-

A. The Business Judgment Rule

A comprehensive review of the history of the business judgment rule is not necessary here, but a brief discussion of its boundaries and proper use is appropriate. Delaware law is clear that the business and affairs of a corporation are managed by or under the direction of its board of directors. The business judgment rule serves to protect and promote the role of the board as the ultimate manager of the corporation. Because courts are ill equipped to engage in *post hoc* substantive review of business decisions, the business judgment rule "operates to preclude a court from imposing itself unreasonably on the business and affairs of a corporation."

The business judgment rule is not actually a substantive rule of law, but instead it is a presumption that "in making a business decision the directors of a corporation acted on an informed basis, ... and in the honest belief that the action taken was in the best interests of the company [and its shareholders]." This presumption applies when there is no evidence of "fraud, bad faith, or self-dealing in the usual sense of personal profit or betterment" on the part of the directors.*** In the absence of this evidence, the board's decision will be upheld unless it cannot be "attributed to any rational business purpose." When a plaintiff fails to rebut the presumption of the business judgment rule, she is not entitled to any remedy, be it legal or equitable, unless the transaction constitutes waste.

This presumption can be rebutted by a showing that the board violated one of its fiduciary duties in connection with the challenged transaction. In that event, the burden

---

length transactions that raise duty of loyalty concerns are imagined as arms-length transactions with third parties. Would an ordinarily prudent person lease a corporate asset to a third party on exceedingly generous terms? Would an ordinarily prudent person lavish compensation on a third party and permit the third party to divert investment opportunities that would otherwise come her way? These are duty of loyalty concerns framed as duty of care questions. The phrasing is natural because, at its core, the duty of loyalty is just a bet that some situations are likely to lead to careless or imprudent transactions for the corporation, which is to say that the duty of care is a motivating concern for the duty of loyalty. Here again the duties overlap.

Sean J. Griffith, *Good Faith Business Judgment: A Theory of Rhetoric in Corporate Law Jurisprudence,* 55 Duke L.J. (forthcoming 2005) (manuscript of May 25, 2005 at 39–42 available at http://papers. ssrn.com/sol3/papers.cfm?abstract_id=728431) (emphasis in original, citations omitted).

*** *Grobow v. Perot,* 539 A.2d 180, 187 (Del.1988); *Cede III,* 634 A.2d at 360. In *Gagliardi,* Chancellor Allen described the policy rationale for the business judgment rule in the paragraph quoted below. Although this statement, made in 1996, may at first appear to be undercut by the increased incentive compensation of the dot-com era, the rationale still applies because of the relatively small percentages of stock held by officers and directors of public companies.

Corporate directors of public companies typically have a very small proportionate ownership interest in their corporations and little or no incentive compensation. Thus, they enjoy (as residual owners) only a very small proportion of any "upside" gains earned by the corporation on risky investment projects. If, however, corporate directors were to be found liable for a corporate loss from a risky project on the ground that the investment was too risky (foolishly risky! stupidly risky! egregiously risky—you supply the adverb), their liability would be joint and several for the whole loss (with I suppose a right of contribution). Given the scale of operation of modern public corporations, this stupefying disjunction between risk and reward for corporate directors threatens undesirable effects. Given this disjunction, only a very small probability of director liability based on "negligence", "inattention", "waste", etc. could induce a board to avoid authorizing risky investment projects to any extent! Obviously, it is in the shareholders' economic interest to offer sufficient protection to directors from liability for negligence, etc., to allow directors to conclude that, as a practical matter, there is no risk that, if they act in good faith and meet minimalist proceduralist standards of attention, they can face liability as a result of a business loss.

Gagliardi v. TriFoods Int'l Inc., 683 A.2d 1049, 1052 (Del.Ch.1996).

shifts to the director defendants to demonstrate that the challenged transaction was "entirely fair" to the corporation and its shareholders.

Even if the directors have exercised their business judgment, the protections of the business judgment rule will not apply if the directors have made an "unintelligent or unadvised judgment." Furthermore, in instances where directors have not exercised business judgment, that is, in the event of director inaction, the protections of the business judgment rule do not apply. Under those circumstances, the appropriate standard for determining liability is widely believed to be gross negligence, but a single Delaware case has held that ordinary negligence would be the appropriate standard.

B. Waste

Corporate waste is very rarely found in Delaware courts because the applicable test imposes such an onerous burden upon a plaintiff-proving "an exchange that is so one sided that no business person of ordinary, sound judgment could conclude that the corporation has received adequate consideration." In other words, waste is a rare, "unconscionable case where directors irrationally squander or give away corporate assets."

The Delaware Supreme Court has implicitly held that committing waste is an act of bad faith. It is not necessarily true, however, that every act of bad faith by a director constitutes waste. For example, if a director acts in bad faith (for whatever reason), but the transaction is one in which a businessperson of ordinary, sound judgment concludes that the corporation received adequate consideration, the transaction would not constitute waste.

C. The Fiduciary Duty of Due Care

The fiduciary duty of due care requires that directors of a Delaware corporation "use that amount of care which ordinarily careful and prudent men would use in similar circumstances," and "consider all material information reasonably available" in making business decisions, and that deficiencies in the directors' process are actionable only if the directors' actions are grossly negligent. Chancellor Allen described the two contexts in which liability for a breach of the duty of care can arise:

> First, such liability may be said to follow *from a board decision* that results in a loss because that decision was ill advised or "negligent". Second, liability to the corporation for a loss may be said to arise from an *unconsidered failure of the board to act* in circumstances in which due attention would, arguably, have prevented the loss.

Chancellor Allen then explained with respect to board decisions:

> [These] cases will typically be subject to review under the director-protective business judgment rule, assuming the decision made was the product of *a process* that was *either* deliberately considered in good faith or was otherwise rational. What should be understood, but may not widely be understood by courts or commentators who are not often required to face such questions, is that compliance with a director's duty of care can never appropriately be judicially determined by reference to *the content of the board decision* that leads to a corporate loss, apart from consideration of the good faith or rationality of the process employed. That is, whether a judge or jury considering the matter after the fact, believes a decision substantively wrong, or degrees of wrong extending through "stupid" to "egregious" or "irrational", provides no ground for director liability, so long as the court determines that the process employed was either rational or employed in *a good faith* effort to advance corporate interests. To employ a different rule —

one that permitted an "objective" evaluation of the decision—would expose directors to substantive second guessing by ill-equipped judges or juries, which would, in the long-run, be injurious to investor interests. Thus, the business judgment rule is process oriented and informed by a deep respect for all *good faith* board decisions.

Indeed, one wonders on what moral basis might shareholders attack a *good faith* business decision of a director as "unreasonable" or "irrational". Where a director *in fact exercises a good faith effort to be informed and to exercise appropriate judgment*, he or she should be deemed to satisfy fully the duty of attention.

With respect to liability for director inaction, Chancellor Allen wrote that in order for the inaction to be so great as to constitute a breach of the director's duty of care, a plaintiff must show a "lack of good faith as evidenced by sustained or systematic failure of a director to exercise reasonable oversight."

In the duty of care context with respect to corporate fiduciaries, gross negligence has been defined as a "'reckless indifference to or a deliberate disregard of the whole body of stockholders' or actions which are 'without the bounds of reason.'" Because duty of care violations are actionable only if the directors acted with gross negligence, and because in most instances money damages are unavailable to a plaintiff who could theoretically prove a duty of care violation, duty of care violations are rarely found.

D. The Fiduciary Duty of Loyalty

The fiduciary duty of loyalty was described in the seminal case of *Guth v. Loft, Inc.*, in these strict and unyielding terms:

> Corporate officers and directors are not permitted to use their position of trust and confidence to further their private interests.... A public policy, existing through the years, and derived from a profound knowledge of human characteristics and motives, has established a rule that demands of a corporate officer or director, peremptorily and inexorably, the most scrupulous observance of his duty, not only affirmatively to protect the interests of the corporation committed to his charge, but also to refrain from doing anything that would work injury to the corporation, or to deprive it of profit or advantage which his skill and ability might properly bring to it, or to enable it to make in the reasonable and lawful exercise of its powers. The rule that requires an undivided and unselfish loyalty to the corporation demands that there be no conflict between duty and self-interest.

In the specific context at issue here with respect to a classic duty of loyalty claim, Ovitz, as a fiduciary of Disney, was required to act in an "adversarial and arms-length manner" when negotiating his termination and not abuse or manipulate the corporate process by which that termination was granted. He was obligated to act in good faith and "not advantage himself at the expense of the Disney shareholders."

E. Section 102(b)(7)

Following the Delaware Supreme Court's landmark decision in *Van Gorkom*, the Delaware General Assembly acted swiftly to enact 8 *Del. C.* § 102(b)(7).

The purpose of Section 102(b)(7) was to *permit shareholders*—who are entitled to rely upon directors to discharge their fiduciary duties at all times—to adopt a provision in the certificate of incorporation to exculpate directors from any personal liability for the payment of monetary damages for breaches of their duty of care, but not for duty of loyalty violations, good faith violations and certain other conduct.

Recently, Vice Chancellor Strine wrote that, "[o]ne of the primary purposes of § 102(b)(7) is to encourage directors to undertake risky, but potentially value-maximizing, business strategies, so long as they do so in good faith." Or in other words, § 102(b)(7) is most useful "when, despite the directors' good intentions, [the challenged transaction] did not generate financial success and ... the possibility of hindsight bias about the directors' prior ability to foresee that their business plans would not pan out" could improperly influence a *post hoc* judicial evaluation of the directors' actions.

The vast majority of Delaware corporations have a provision in their certificate of incorporation that permits exculpation to the extent provided for by § 102(b)(7). This provision prohibits recovery of monetary damages from directors for a successful shareholder claim, either direct or derivative, that is exclusively based upon establishing a violation of the duty of due care. The existence of an exculpation provision authorized by § 102(b)(7) does not, however, eliminate a director's fiduciary duty of care, because a court may still grant injunctive relief for violations of that duty.

An exculpation provision such as that authorized by § 102(b)(7) is in the nature of an affirmative defense. As a result, it is the burden of the director defendants to demonstrate that they are entitled to the protections of the relevant charter provision.

F. Acting in Good Faith

Decisions from the Delaware Supreme Court and the Court of Chancery are far from clear with respect to whether there is a separate fiduciary duty of good faith. Good faith has been said to require an "honesty of purpose," and a genuine care for the fiduciary's constituents, but, at least in the corporate fiduciary context, it is probably easier to define bad faith rather than good faith. This may be so because Delaware law presumes that directors act in good faith when making business judgments. Bad faith has been defined as authorizing a transaction "for some purpose *other than* a genuine attempt to advance corporate welfare or [when the transaction] is *known to constitute* a violation of applicable positive law." In other words, an action taken with the intent to harm the corporation is a disloyal act in bad faith. A similar definition was used seven years earlier, when Chancellor Allen wrote that bad faith (or lack of good faith) is when a director acts in a manner "unrelated to a pursuit of the corporation's best interests." It makes no difference the reason why the director intentionally fails to pursue the best interests of the corporation.

Shrouded in the fog of this hazy jurisprudence, the defendants' motion to dismiss this action was denied because I concluded that the complaint, together with all reasonable inferences drawn from the well-plead allegations contained therein, could be held to state a non-exculpated breach of fiduciary duty claim, insofar as it alleged that Disney's directors *"consciously and intentionally disregarded their responsibilities,* adopting a 'we don't care about the risks' attitude concerning a material corporate decision."

Upon long and careful consideration, I am of the opinion that the concept of *intentional dereliction of duty,* a *conscious disregard for one's responsibilities,* is an appropriate (although not the only) standard for determining whether fiduciaries have acted in good faith. Deliberate indifference and inaction *in the face of a duty to act* is, in my mind, conduct that is clearly disloyal to the corporation. It is the epitome of faithless conduct.

To act in good faith, a director must act at all times with an honesty of purpose and in the best interests and welfare of the corporation. The presumption of the business judgment rule creates a presumption that a director acted in good faith. In order to overcome that presumption, a plaintiff must prove an act of bad faith by a preponderance of the evidence. To create a definitive and categorical definition of the universe of acts that would constitute bad faith would be difficult, if not impossible. And it would misconceive how, in my judgment, the concept of good faith operates in our common law of corporations. Fundamentally, the duties traditionally analyzed as belonging to corporate fiduciaries, loyalty and care, are but constituent elements of the overarching concepts of allegiance, devotion and faithfulness that must guide the conduct of every fiduciary. The good faith required of a corporate fiduciary includes not simply the duties of care and loyalty, in the narrow sense that I have discussed them above, but all actions required by a true faithfulness and devotion to the interests of the corporation and its shareholders. A failure to act in good faith may be shown, for instance, where the fiduciary intentionally acts with a purpose other than that of advancing the best interests of the corporation, where the fiduciary acts with the intent to violate applicable positive law, or where the fiduciary intentionally fails to act in the face of a known duty to act, demonstrating a conscious disregard for his duties. There may be other examples of bad faith yet to be proven or alleged, but these three are the most salient. As evidenced by previous rulings in this case both from this Court and the Delaware Supreme Court, issues of the Disney directors' good faith (or lack thereof) are central to the outcome of this action. With this background, I now turn to applying the appropriate standards to defendants' conduct.

III. ANALYSIS

Stripped of the presumptions in their favor that have carried them to trial, plaintiffs must now rely on the evidence presented at trial to demonstrate by a preponderance of the evidence that the defendants violated their fiduciary duties and/or committed waste. More specifically, in the area of director action, plaintiffs must prove by a preponderance of the evidence that the presumption of the business judgment rule does not apply either because the directors breached their fiduciary duties, acted in bad faith or that the directors made an "unintelligent or unadvised judgment," by failing to inform themselves of all material information reasonably available to them before making a business decision.

If plaintiffs cannot rebut the presumption of the business judgment rule, the defendants will prevail. If plaintiffs succeed in rebutting the presumption of the business judgment rule, the burden then shifts to the defendants to prove by a preponderance of the evidence that the challenged transactions were entirely fair to the corporation.

As it relates to director inaction, plaintiffs will prevail upon proving by a preponderance of the evidence that the defendants breached their fiduciary duties by not acting. In order to invoke the protections of the provision in the Company's certificate of incorporation authorized by 8 *Del. C.* § 102(b)(7), the defendants must prove by a preponderance of the evidence that they are entitled to the protections of that provision.

B. Defendants Did Not Commit Waste

Plaintiffs pursued a claim for waste at trial and argued in their briefs that they have proven this claim. As stated above, the standard for waste is a very high one that is difficult to meet.

The record does not support these assertions in any conceivable way. Apart from his job performance, Ovitz was never in a position to determine if he would be terminated, and if so, whether it would be with or without cause. As it relates to job performance, I find it patently unreasonable to assume that Ovitz intended to perform just poorly enough to be fired quickly, but not so poorly that he could be terminated for cause. First, based upon my personal observations of Ovitz, he possesses such an ego, and enjoyed such a towering reputation before his employment at the Company, that he is not the type of person that would intentionally perform poorly. Ovitz did not build Hollywood's premier talent agency by performing poorly. Second, nothing in the trial record indicates to me that Ovitz intended to bring anything less than his best efforts to the Company. Additionally, I have found and concluded above that Eisner believed Ovitz would be an excellent addition to the company throughout 1995, a far cry from plaintiffs' accusations of deciding to hire him for the purpose of firing him shortly thereafter with a spectacular severance payoff.

More importantly, however, I conclude that given his performance, Ovitz could not have been fired for cause under the OEA. Any early termination of his employment, therefore, had to be in the form of an NFT. Nevertheless, by applying the myriad of definitions for gross negligence and malfeasance, I also independently conclude, based upon the facts as I have found them, that Ovitz did not commit gross negligence or malfeasance while serving as the Company's President.

As a result, terminating Ovitz and paying the NFT did not constitute waste because he could not be terminated for cause and because many of the defendants gave credible testimony that the Company would be better off without Ovitz, meaning that it would be impossible for me to conclude that the termination and receipt of NFT benefits resulted in "an exchange that is so one sided that no business person of ordinary, sound judgment could conclude that the corporation has received adequate consideration," or a situation where the defendants have "irrationally squander[ed] or give[n] away corporate assets." In other words, defendants did not commit waste.

C. The Old Board's Decision to Hire Ovitz and the Compensation Committee's Approval of the OEA Was Not Grossly Negligent and Not in Bad Faith

The members of the "Old Board" (Eisner, Bollenbach, Litvack, Russell, Roy Disney, Gold, Nunis, Poitier, Stern, Walker, Watson, Wilson, Bowers, Lozano and Mitchell) were required to comply with their fiduciary duties on behalf of the Company's shareholders while taking the actions that brought Ovitz to the Company. For the future, many lessons of what not to do can be learned from defendants' conduct here. Nevertheless, I conclude that the only reasonable application of the law to the facts as I have found them, is that the defendants did not act in bad faith, and were at most ordinarily negligent, in connection with the hiring of Ovitz and the approval of the OEA. In accordance with the business judgment rule, ordinary negligence is insufficient to constitute a violation of the fiduciary duty of care. I shall elaborate upon this conclusion as to each defendant.

1. Eisner

Eisner was clearly the person most heavily involved in bringing Ovitz to the Company and negotiating the OEA. He was a long-time friend of Ovitz and the instigator and mastermind behind the machinations that resulted in Ovitz's hiring and the concomitant approval of the OEA. On the other hand, at least as the duty of care is typically defined in the context of a business judgment, of all the defendants, he was certainly the most informed of all reasonably available material information, making him the least culpable in that regard.

Eisner to a large extent is responsible for the failings in process that infected and handicapped the board's decisionmaking abilities. Eisner stacked his board of directors with friends and other acquaintances who, though not necessarily beholden to him in a legal sense, were certainly more willing to accede to his wishes and support him unconditionally than truly independent directors. On the other hand, I do not believe that the evidence, considered fairly, demonstrates that Eisner actively took steps to defeat or short-circuit a decisionmaking process that would otherwise have occurred.

Eisner obtained no consent or authorization from the board before agreeing to hire Ovitz, before agreeing to the substantive terms of the OLA, or before issuing the press release. Indeed, outside of his small circle of confidantes, it appears that Eisner made no effort to inform the board of his discussions with Ovitz until after they were essentially completed and an agreement in principle had been reached.

As a general rule, a CEO has no obligation to continuously inform the board of his actions as CEO, or to receive prior authorization for those actions. Nevertheless, a reasonably prudent CEO would not have acted in as unilateral a manner as did Eisner when essentially committing the corporation to hire a second-in-command, appoint that person to the board, and provide him with one of the largest and richest employment contracts ever enjoyed by a non-CEO.

Because considerations of improper motive are no longer present in this case, the decision to hire Ovitz and enter into the OEA is one of business judgment, to which the presumptions of the business judgment rule apply. In order to prevail, therefore, plaintiffs must demonstrate by a preponderance of the evidence that Eisner was either grossly negligent or acted in bad faith in connection with Ovitz's hiring and the approval of the OEA.

As I mentioned earlier, Eisner was very much aware of what was going on as the situation developed. In the limited instances where he was not the primary source of information relating to Ovitz, Russell kept Eisner informed of negotiations with Ovitz. Eisner knew Ovitz; he was familiar with the career Ovitz had built at CAA and he knew that the Company was in need of a senior executive, especially in light of the upcoming CapCities/ABC merger. In light of this knowledge, I cannot find that plaintiffs have demonstrated by a preponderance of the evidence that Eisner failed to inform himself of all material information reasonably available or that he acted in a grossly negligent manner.

Notwithstanding the foregoing, Eisner's actions in connection with Ovitz's hiring should not serve as a model for fellow executives and fiduciaries to follow. His lapses were many. He failed to keep the board as informed as he should have. He stretched the outer boundaries of his authority as CEO by acting without specific board direction or involvement. He prematurely issued a press release that placed significant pressure on the board to accept Ovitz and approve his compensation package in accordance with the press release. To my mind, these actions fall far short of what shareholders expect and demand from those entrusted with a fiduciary position. Eisner's failure to better involve the board in the process of Ovitz's hiring, usurping that role for himself, although not in violation of law, does not comport with how fiduciaries of Delaware corporations are expected to act.

Despite all of the legitimate criticisms that may be leveled at Eisner, especially at having enthroned himself as the omnipotent and infallible monarch of his personal Magic Kingdom, I nonetheless conclude, after carefully considering and weighing all the evidence, that Eisner's actions were taken in good faith. That is, Eisner's actions were taken with the subjective belief that those actions were in the best interests of the Company—he believed that his taking charge and acting swiftly and decisively to hire Ovitz would serve the best interests of the Company notwithstanding the high cost of Ovitz's hiring and notwithstanding that two experienced executives who had arguably been passed over for the position (Litvack and Bollenbach) were not completely supportive. Those actions do not represent a knowing violation of law or evidence a conscious and intentional disregard of duty. In conclusion, Eisner acted in good faith and did not breach his fiduciary duty of care because he was not grossly negligent.

4. *Poitier and Lozano*

this is nothing like Van Gorkom

Poitier and Lozano were the remaining members of the compensation committee that considered the economic terms of the OEA. It is not disputed that they were far less involved in the genesis of the OEA than were Russell, and to a lesser extent, Watson. The question in dispute is whether their level of involvement in the OEA was so low as to constitute gross negligence and, therefore, a breach of their fiduciary duty of care, or whether their actions evidence a lack of good faith. As will be shown, I conclude that neither of these men acted in a grossly negligent manner or in bad faith.

There is no question that Poitier and Lozano's involvement in the process of Ovitz's hiring came very late in the game. As found above, Poitier received a call from Russell on August 13 (and another the next day), during which they discussed the terms of the proposed OLA. Lozano spoke with Watson regarding this same subject. It appears that neither Poitier nor Lozano had any further involvement with the hiring process, apart from these phone calls, until the September 26, 1995 compensation committee meeting.

At that meeting, both Poitier and Lozano received the term sheet that explained the key terms of Ovitz's contract, and they were present for and participated in the discussion that occurred. Both then voted to approve the terms of the OEA, and both credibly testified that they believed they possessed sufficient information at that time to make an informed decision. Plaintiffs largely point to two perceived inadequacies in this meeting first, that insufficient time was spent reviewing the terms of Ovitz's contract and, second, that Poitier and Lozano were not provided with sufficient documentation, including Crystal's correspondence, Watson's calculations, and a draft of the OEA. These arguments understandably hearken back to *Van Gorkom*, where the Supreme Court condemned the Trans Union board for agreeing to a material transaction after a board meeting of about two hours and without so much as a term sheet of the transaction as contemplated. Although the parallels between *Van Gorkom* and this case at first appear striking, a more careful consideration will reveal several important distinctions between the two.

First and foremost, the nature of the transaction in *Van Gorkom* is fundamentally different, and orders of magnitude more important, than the transaction at issue here. In *Van Gorkom,* the Trans Union board was called into a special meeting on less than a day's notice, without notice of the reason for the meeting, to consider a merger agreement that would result in the sale of the entire company. As footnoted above, Delaware law, *as a matter of statute,* requires directors to take certain actions in connection with a merger of the corporation, as was being contemplated by Trans Union. No statute required the Company's board to take action in connection with Ovitz's hiring. The Company's governing documents provide that the officers of the corporation will be selected by the board of directors, and the charter of the compensation committee states that the committee is responsible for establishing and approving the salary of the Company's President. That is exactly what happened. The board meeting was not called on short notice, and the directors were well aware that Ovitz's hiring would be discussed at the meeting as a result of the August 14 press release more than a month before. Furthermore, analyzing the transactions in terms of monetary value, and even accepting plaintiffs' experts' bloated valuations for comparison purposes, it is beyond question that the $734 million sale of

Trans Union was material and significantly larger than the financial ramifications to the Company of Ovitz's hiring.

Second, the Trans Union board met for about two hours to discuss and deliberate on this monumental transaction in the life of Trans Union. A precise amount of time for the length of the compensation committee meeting, and more specifically, the length of the discussion regarding the OEA, is difficult to establish.

I am persuaded by Russell and Lozano's recollection that the OEA was discussed for a not insignificant length of time. Is that length of time markedly less than the attention given by the Trans Union board to the merger agreement they were statutorily charged with approving or rejecting? Yes. Is that difference probative on the issue of whether the compensation committee adequately discussed the OEA? Not in the least. When the Trans Union board met for those two hours, it was the very first time any of those directors had discussed a sale of the company. Here, all the members of the committee were aware in advance that Ovitz's hiring would be discussed, and the members of the committee had also previously had more than minimal informal discussions amongst themselves as to the *bona fides* of the OEA before the meeting ever occurred. Furthermore, as mentioned above, the nature and scope of the transactions are fundamentally different.

Third, the Trans Union board had absolutely no documentation before it when it considered the merger agreement. The board was completely reliant on the misleading and uninformed presentations given by Trans Union's officers (Van Gorkom and Romans). In contrast, the compensation committee was provided with a term sheet of the key terms of the OEA and a presentation was made by Russell (assisted by Watson), who had personal knowledge of the relevant information by virtue of his negotiations with Ovitz and discussions with Crystal.

Fourth, Trans Union's senior management completely opposed the merger. In contrast, the Company's senior management generally saw Ovitz's hiring as a boon for the Company. In sum, although Poitier and Lozano did very little in connection with Ovitz's hiring and the compensation committee's approval of the OEA, they did not breach their fiduciary duties. I conclude that they were informed by Russell and Watson of all *material* information reasonably available, even though they were not privy to every conversation or document exchanged amongst Russell, Watson, Crystal and Ovitz's representatives.

Much has been made throughout the various procedural iterations of this case about Crystal's involvement in the compensation committee's deliberations and decisionmaking. Although there are many criticisms that could and have been made regarding Crystal's failure to calculate *ex ante* the cost of a potential NFT, nothing in the record leads me to conclude that any member of the compensation committee had actual knowledge that would lead them to believe that Crystal's analysis was inaccurate or incomplete. Without that knowledge, I conclude that the compensation committee acted in good faith.

The compensation committee reasonably believed that the analysis of the terms of the OEA was within Crystal's professional or expert competence, and together with Russell and Watson's professional competence in those same areas, the committee relied on the information, opinions, reports and statements made by Crystal, even if Crystal did not relay the information, opinions, reports and statements in person to the committee as a whole. Crystal's analysis was not so deficient that the compensation committee would have reason to question it. Furthermore, Crystal appears to have been selected with reasonable care, especially in light of his previous engagements with the Company in connection with past executive compensation contracts that were structurally, at least, similar to the OEA. For all these reasons, the compensation committee also is entitled to the protections of 8 *Del. C.* § 141(e) in relying upon Crystal.

Poitier and Lozano did not intentionally disregard a duty to act, nor did they bury their heads in the sand knowing a decision had to be made. They acted in a manner that they believed was in the best interests of the corporation. Delaware law does not require (nor does it prohibit) directors to take as active a role as Russell and Watson took in connection with Ovitz's hiring. There is no question that in comparison to those two, the actions of Poitier and Lozano may appear casual or uninformed, but I conclude that they did not breach their fiduciary duties and that they acted in good faith in connection with Ovitz's hiring.

5. *The Remaining Members of the Old Board*

In accordance with the compensation committee's charter, it was that committee's responsibility to establish and approve Ovitz's compensation arrangements. In accordance with the OLA and the Company's certificate of incorporation, it was the full board's responsibility to elect (or reject) Ovitz as President of the Company. Plaintiffs' argument that the full board had a duty and responsibility to independently analyze and approve the OEA is simply not supported by the record. As a result, the directors' actions must be analyzed in the context of whether they properly exercised their business judgment and acted in accordance with their fiduciary duties when they elected Ovitz to the Company's presidency.

The record gives adequate support to my conclusion that the directors, before voting, were informed of who Ovitz was, the reporting structure that Ovitz had agreed to and the key terms of the OEA. Again, plaintiffs have failed to meet their burden to demonstrate that the directors acted in a grossly negligent manner or that they failed to inform themselves of all material information reasonably available when making a decision. They did not intentionally shirk or ignore their duty, but acted in good faith, believing they were acting in the best interests of the Company.

D. Eisner and Litvack Did Not Act in Bad Faith in Connection With Ovitz's Termination, and the Remainder of the New Board Had No Duties in Connection Therewith

The New Board was likewise charged with complying with their fiduciary duties in connection with any actions taken, or required to be taken, in connection with Ovitz's termination. The key question here becomes whether the board was under a duty to act in connection with Ovitz's termination, because if the directors were under no duty to act, then they could not have acted in bad faith by not acting, nor would they have failed to inform themselves of all material information reasonably available before making a decision, because no decision was required to be made. Furthermore, the actions taken by the Company's officers (namely Eisner and Litvack) in connection with Ovitz's termination must be viewed through the lens of whether the board was under a duty to act. If the board was under no such duty, then the officers are justified in acting alone. If the board was under a duty to act and the officers improperly usurped that authority, the analysis would obviously be different.

1. *The New Board Was Not Under a Duty to Act*

Determining whether the New Board was required to discuss and approve Ovitz's termination requires careful consideration of the Company's governing instruments. The parties largely agree on the relevant language from the Company's certificate of incorporation and bylaws, but as would be expected, they disagree as to the meaning of that language.

Having considered these documents, I come to the following conclusions: 1) the board of directors has the sole power to elect the officers of the Company; 2) the board of directors has the sole power to determine the "duties" of the officers of the Company (either through board resolutions or bylaws); 3) the Chairman/CEO has "general and active management, direction, and supervision over the business of the Corporation and over its officers," and that such management, direction and supervision is subject to the control of the board of directors; 4) the Chairman/CEO has the power to manage, direct and supervise the lesser officers and employees of the Company; 5) the board has the *right,* but not the *duty* to remove the officers of the Company with or without cause, and that right is non-exclusive; and 6) because that right is non-exclusive, and because the Chairman/CEO is affirmatively charged with the management, direction and supervision of the officers of the Company, together with the powers and duties incident to the office of chief executive, the Chairman/CEO, subject to the control of the board of directors, also possesses the *right* to remove the inferior officers and employees of the corporation.

The New Board unanimously believed that Eisner, as Chairman and CEO, possessed the power to terminate Ovitz without board approval or intervention. Nonetheless, the board was informed of and supported Eisner's decision. The board's simultaneous power to terminate Ovitz, reserved to the board by the certificate of incorporation, did not divest Eisner of the authority to do so, or vice-versa. Eisner used that authority, and terminated Ovitz—a decision, coupled with the decision to honor the OEA, that resulted in the Company's obligation to pay the NFT. Because Eisner unilaterally terminated Ovitz, as was his right, the New Board was not required to act in connection with Ovitz's termination.

Therefore, the fact that no formal board action was taken with respect to Ovitz's termination is of no import. Because the board was under no duty to act, they did not violate their fiduciary duty of care, and they also individually acted in good faith. For these reasons, the members of the New Board (other than Eisner and Litvack, who will be discussed individually below) did not breach their fiduciary duties and did not act in bad faith in connection with Ovitz's termination and his receipt of the NFT benefits included in the OEA.

2. *Litvack*

Litvack, as an officer of the corporation and as its general counsel, consulted with, and gave advice to, Eisner, on two questions relevant to Ovitz's termination. They are, first, whether Ovitz could or should have been terminated for cause and, second, whether a board meeting was required to ratify or effectuate Ovitz's termination or the payment of his NFT benefits. For the reasons I have already stated, Litvack properly concluded that the Company did not have good cause under the OEA to terminate Ovitz. He also properly concluded that no board action was necessary in connection with the termination. Litvack was familiar with the relevant factual information and legal standards regarding these decisions. Litvack made a determination in good faith that a formal opinion from outside counsel would not be helpful and that involving more people in the termination process increased the potential for news of the impending termination to leak out.

In conclusion, Litvack gave the proper advice and came to the proper conclusions when it was necessary. He was adequately informed in his decisions, and he acted in good faith for what he believed were the best interests of the Company.

3. *Eisner*

Having concluded that Eisner alone possessed the authority to terminate Ovitz and grant him the NFT, I turn to whether Eisner acted in accordance with his fiduciary duties and in good faith when he terminated Ovitz. As will be shown hereafter, I conclude that Eisner did not breach his fiduciary duties and did act in good faith in connection with Ovitz's termination and concomitant receipt of the NFT.

Eisner was unable to work well with Ovitz, and Eisner refused to let Ovitz work without close and constant supervision. Faced with that situation, Eisner essentially had three options: 1) keep Ovitz as President and continue trying to make things work; 2) keep Ovitz at Disney, but in a role other than President; or 3) terminate Ovitz.

In deciding which route to take, Eisner, consistent with his discretion as CEO, considered keeping Ovitz as the Company's President an unacceptable solution. Shunting Ovitz to a different role within the Company would have almost certainly entitled Ovitz to the NFT, or at the very least, a costly lawsuit to determine whether Ovitz was so entitled. Eisner would have also rightly questioned whether there was another position within the Company where Ovitz could be of use. Eisner was then left with the only alternative he considered feasible—termination. Faced with the knowledge that termination was the best alternative and knowing that Ovitz had not performed to the high expectations placed upon him when he was hired, Eisner inquired of Litvack on several occasions as to whether a for-cause termination was possible such that the NFT payment could be avoided, and then relied in good faith on the opinion of the Company's general counsel. Eisner also considered the novel alternative of whether a "trade" of Ovitz to Sony would solve the problem by both getting rid of Ovitz and simultaneously relieving the Company of the financial obligations of the OEA. In the end, however, he bit the bullet and decided that the best decision would be to terminate Ovitz and pay the NFT.

I conclude that Eisner's actions in connection with the termination are, for the most part, consistent with what is expected of a faithful fiduciary. Eisner unexpectedly found himself confronted with a situation that did not have an easy solution. He weighed the alternatives, received advice from counsel and then exercised his business judgment in the manner he thought best for the corporation. Eisner knew all the material information reasonably available when making the decision, he did not neglect an affirmative duty to act (or fail to cause the board to act) and he acted in what he believed were the best interests of the Company, taking into account the cost to the Company of the decision and the potential alternatives. Eisner was not personally interested in the transaction in any way that would make him incapable of exercising business judgment, and I conclude that plaintiffs have not demonstrated by a preponderance of the evidence that Eisner breached his fiduciary duties or acted in bad faith in connection with Ovitz's termination and receipt of the NFT.

IV. CONCLUSION

Based on the findings of fact and conclusions of law made herein, judgment is hereby entered in favor of the defendants on all counts.

IT IS SO ORDERED.

Notes

(1) What would have been the outcome for Disney if Eisner and Litvack had terminated Ovitz for cause? In your view, did grounds exist for a termination for cause?

(2) Why did the Disney Compensation Committee, even with a report from compensation expert Crystal, fail to recognize that Ovitz would reap a greater windfall if terminated than if he served out the terms of his employment contract?

(3) What are we to make of the Judge's determination that Disney made many mistakes that did not measure up to "best practices" for corporate governance, but at the end of the day, did not rise to the level of fiduciary duty breaches?

(4) In Delaware, does there exist a triad of duties for corporate officers? Is there now a duty of care, a duty of loyalty, and a duty to act in good faith, three separate duties or are there only two, the duty of care and the duty of loyalty? What does the *Disney* court seem to indicate?

(5) How does the court differentiate the gross negligence of the Trans Union board in *Van Gorkom* from the care exercised by the Disney board?

B. Inaction Cases

Graham: Foundation of the Failure to Monitor

The previous cases focused on a specific type of duty of care case—cases where a corporate director or officer made a decision. This section, while still focusing on the duty of care, focuses on cases involving inaction—cases where a corporate decision maker failed to stop or prevent some harm to the corporation. The seminal case in modern corporate law on this issue is *In re Caremark International Inc. Derivative Litigation*, 698 A.2d 959 (Del. Ch. 1996). However, before discussing *Caremark*, we begin with *Graham v. Allis-Chalmers Manufacturing Company* because it is the first case wherein the Delaware courts addressed director liability for failure to monitor.

In *Graham*, the shareholders of Allis-Chalmers Manufacturing brought a derivative action against the company's board of directors for failure to properly monitor after the company and several non-director employees were indicted for violating Federal Antitrust laws. The indictments were issued after the government learned that the non-director employees "conspired with other manufacturers and their employees to fix prices and to rig bids to private electric utilities and governmental agencies in violation of the anti-trust laws of the United States." As a result of these indictments, the shareholders claimed that the corporation suffered financial harm because of the fees, expenses and reputational injury to the corporation. The shareholders based their argument for directorial liability on two theories: (1) that the directors possessed actual knowledge of the employees' anti-trust conduct and/or (2) that the directors had sufficient knowledge that should have put them on notice of such conduct. The Delaware Court of Chancery dismissed the action and held that there was no "evidence that any director had any actual knowledge of the anti-trust activity, or had actual knowledge of any facts which should have put them on notice that anti-trust activity was being carried on by some of their company's employees." The court of appeals affirmed the lower court's decision and held that:

> directors are entitled to rely on the honesty and integrity of their subordinates until something occurs to put them on suspicion that something is wrong. If such occurs and goes unheeded, then liability of the directors might well follow, but absent cause for suspicion there is no duty upon the directors to install and operate a corporate system of espionage to ferret out wrongdoing which they have no reason to suspect exists.

The court reached this conclusion for several reasons. First, the court easily dismissed the notion that the directors had actual knowledge of any wrongdoing because the record contained no facts that could support such proposition. Second, the court also dismissed the notion that the directors should have known about the price fixing for the following reasons:

- In the board's oversight capacity, it only considered general questions concerning price levels and because of the complexity of the company's business operations, did not participate in the fixing of prices for specific products.

- Because of the sheer size of the company, it was not practicable for the board to know that low level employees were engaging in price fixing.

- Although the company entered into consent decrees, relating to a similar price fixing issue, approximately 25 years ago, none of the current board members were members of the board at the time the consent decrees were entered. In addition, the consent decrees did not acknowledge any fault and according to the language of the decrees, were only "consented to for the sole purpose of avoiding the trouble and expense of the proceeding."

After *Graham*, there was some opinion that board members had no obligation to set up monitoring systems and could meet their duty of care by simply assuming the integrity of the company's employees unless something miraculous happened to put the board on notice of some wrongdoing. As a result of this confusion, the Delaware court below clarified a board's obligation to monitor in *Caremark*.

In re Caremark International Inc. Derivative Litigation

698 A.2d 959 (1996)
Court of Chancery of Delaware

OPINION

ALLEN, Chancellor.

Pending is a motion pursuant to Chancery Rule 23.1 to approve as fair and reasonable a proposed settlement of a consolidated derivative action on behalf of Caremark International, Inc. ("Caremark"). The suit involves claims that the members of Caremark's board of directors (the "Board") breached their fiduciary duty of care to Caremark in connection with alleged violations by Caremark employees of federal and state laws and regulations applicable to health care providers. As a result of the alleged violations, Caremark was subject to an extensive four year investigation by the United States Department of Health and Human Services and the Department of Justice. In 1994 Caremark was charged in an indictment with multiple felonies. It thereafter entered into a number of agreements with the Department of Justice and others. Those agreements included a plea agreement in which Caremark pleaded guilty to a single felony of mail fraud and agreed to pay civil and criminal fines. Subsequently, Caremark agreed to make reimbursements to various private and public parties. In all, the payments that Caremark has been required to make total approximately $250 million.

This suit was filed in 1994, purporting to seek on behalf of the company recovery of these losses from the individual defendants who constitute the board of directors of Caremark. The parties now propose that it be settled and, after notice to Caremark shareholders, a hearing on the fairness of the proposal was held on August 16, 1996.

Legally, evaluation of the central claim made entails consideration of the legal standard governing a board of directors' obligation to supervise or monitor corporate performance. For the reasons set forth below I conclude, in light of the discovery record, that there is a very low probability that it would be determined that the directors of Caremark breached any duty to appropriately monitor and supervise the enterprise. Indeed the record tends to show an active consideration by Caremark management and its Board of the Caremark structures and programs that ultimately led to the company's indictment and to the large financial losses incurred in the settlement of those claims. It does not tend to show knowing or intentional violation of law. Neither the fact that the Board, although advised by lawyers and accountants, did not accurately predict the severe consequences to the company that would ultimately follow from the deployment by the company of the strategies and practices that ultimately led to this liability, nor the scale of the liability, gives rise to an inference of breach of any duty imposed by corporation law upon the directors of Caremark.

I. BACKGROUND

Caremark, a Delaware corporation with its headquarters in Northbrook, Illinois, was created in November 1992 when it was [a] spin-off from Baxter International, Inc. ("Baxter") and became a publicly held company listed on the New York Stock Exchange. The business practices that created the problem pre-dated the spin-off. During the relevant period Caremark was involved in two main health care business segments, providing patient care and managed care services. As part of its patient care business, which accounted for the majority of Caremark's revenues, Caremark provided alternative site health care services.

A. Events Prior to the Government Investigation

A substantial part of the revenues generated by Caremark's businesses is derived from third party payments, insurers, and Medicare and Medicaid reimbursement programs. The latter source of payments are subject to the terms of the Anti–Referral Payments Law ("ARPL") which prohibits health care providers from paying any form of remuneration to induce the referral of Medicare or Medicaid patients. From its inception, Caremark entered into a variety of agreements with hospitals, physicians, and health care providers for advice and services, as well as distribution agreements with drug manufacturers. Specifically, Caremark did have a practice of entering into contracts for services (*e.g.,* consultation agreements and research grants) with physicians at least some of whom prescribed or recommended services or products that Caremark provided to Medicare recipients and other patients. Such contracts were not prohibited by the ARPL but they obviously raised a possibility of unlawful "kickbacks."

As early as 1989, Caremark's predecessor issued an internal "Guide to Contractual Relationships" ("Guide") to govern its employees in entering into contracts with physicians and hospitals. The Guide tended to be reviewed annually by lawyers and updated. Each version of the Guide stated as Caremark's policy that no payments would be made in exchange for or to induce patient referrals. But what one might deem a prohibited *quid pro quo* was not always clear. Due to a scarcity of court decisions interpreting the ARPL, however, Caremark repeatedly publicly stated that there was uncertainty concerning Caremark's interpretation of the law.

B. Government Investigation and Related Litigation

In August 1991, the HHS Office of the Inspector General ("OIG") initiated an investigation of Caremark's predecessor. Caremark's predecessor was served with a subpoena requiring the production of documents, including contracts between Caremark's predecessor and physicians (Quality Service Agreements ("QSAs")). Under the QSAs, Caremark's predecessor appears to have paid physicians fees for monitoring patients under Caremark's predecessor's care, including Medicare and Medicaid recipients. Sometimes apparently those monitoring patients were referring physicians, which raised ARPL concerns.

In March 1992, the Department of Justice ("DOJ") joined the OIG investigation and separate investigations were commenced by several additional federal and state agencies.

C. Caremark's Response to the Investigation

During the relevant period, Caremark had approximately 7,000 employees and ninety branch operations. It had a decentralized management structure. By May 1991, however, Caremark asserts that it had begun making attempts to centralize its management structure in order to increase supervision over its branch operations.

The first action taken by management, as a result of the initiation of the OIG investigation, was an announcement that as of October 1, 1991, Caremark's predecessor would no longer pay management fees to physicians for services to Medicare and Medicaid patients. Despite this decision, Caremark asserts that its management, pursuant to advice, did not believe that such payments were illegal under the existing laws and regulations.

During this period, Caremark's Board took several additional steps consistent with an effort to assure compliance with company policies concerning the ARPL and the contractual forms in the Guide. In April 1992, Caremark published a fourth revised version of its Guide apparently designed to assure that its agreements either complied with the ARPL and regulations or excluded Medicare and Medicaid patients altogether. In addition, in September 1992, Caremark instituted a policy requiring its regional officers, Zone Presidents, to approve each contractual relationship entered into by Caremark with a physician.

Although there is evidence that inside and outside counsel had advised Caremark's directors that their contracts were in accord with the law, Caremark recognized that some uncertainty respecting the correct interpretation of the law existed. In its 1992 annual report, Caremark disclosed the ongoing government investigations, acknowledged that if penalties were imposed on the company they could have a material adverse effect on Caremark's business, and stated that no assurance could be given that its interpretation of the ARPL would prevail if challenged.

Throughout the period of the government investigations, Caremark had an internal audit plan designed to assure compliance with business and ethics policies. In addition, Caremark employed Price Waterhouse as its outside auditor. On February 8, 1993, the Ethics Committee of Caremark's Board received and reviewed an outside auditors report by Price Waterhouse which concluded that there were no material weaknesses in Caremark's control structure. Despite the positive findings of Price Waterhouse, however, on April 20, 1993, the Audit & Ethics Committee adopted a new internal audit charter requiring a comprehensive review of compliance policies and the compilation of an employee ethics handbook concerning such policies.

The Board appears to have been informed about this project and other efforts to assure compliance with the law. For example, Caremark's management reported to the Board that Caremark's sales force was receiving an ongoing education regarding the ARPL and the proper use of Caremark's form contracts which had been approved by in-house counsel. On July 27, 1993, the new ethics manual, expressly prohibiting payments in exchange for referrals and requiring employees to report all illegal conduct to a toll free confidential ethics hotline, was approved and allegedly disseminated. The record suggests that Caremark continued these policies in subsequent years, causing employees to be given revised versions of the ethics manual and requiring them to participate in training sessions concerning compliance with the law.

During 1993, Caremark took several additional steps which appear to have been aimed at increasing management supervision. These steps included new policies requiring local branch managers to secure home office approval for all disbursements under agreements with health care providers and to certify compliance with the ethics program. In addition, the chief financial officer was appointed to serve as Caremark's compliance officer. In 1994, a fifth revised Guide was published.

D. Federal Indictments Against Caremark and Officers

On August 4, 1994, a federal grand jury in Minnesota issued a 47 page indictment charging Caremark, two of its officers (not the firm's chief officer), an individual who had been a sales employee of Genentech, Inc., and David R. Brown, a physician practicing in Minneapolis, with violating the ARPL over a lengthy period. According to the indictment, over $1.1 million had been paid to Brown to induce him to distribute Protropin, a human growth hormone drug marketed by Caremark. The substantial payments involved started, according to the allegations of the indictment, in 1986 and continued through 1993. Some payments were "in the guise of research grants," and others were "consulting agreements." The indictment charged, for example, that Dr. Brown performed virtually none of the consulting functions described in his 1991 agreement with Caremark, but was nevertheless neither required to return the money he had received nor precluded from receiving future funding from Caremark. In addition the indictment charged that Brown received from Caremark payments of staff and office expenses, including telephone answering services and fax rental expenses.

Subsequently, five stockholder derivative actions were filed in this court and consolidated into this action.

After each complaint was filed, defendants filed a motion to dismiss. According to defendants, if a settlement had not been reached in this action, the case would have been dismissed on two grounds. First, they contend that the complaints fail to allege particularized facts sufficient to excuse the demand requirement under Delaware Chancery Court Rule 23.1. Second, defendants assert that plaintiffs had failed to state a cause of action due to the fact that Caremark's charter eliminates directors' personal liability for money damages, to the extent permitted by law.

F. The Proposed Settlement of this Litigation

In relevant part the terms upon which these claims asserted are proposed to be settled are as follows:

1. That Caremark, undertakes that it and its employees, and agents not pay any form of compensation to a third party in exchange for the referral of a patient to a Caremark facility or service or the prescription of drugs marketed or distributed by Caremark for which reimbursement may be sought from Medicare, Medicaid, or a similar state reimbursement program;

2. That Caremark, undertakes for itself and its employees, and agents not to pay to or split fees with physicians, joint ventures, any business combination in which Caremark maintains a direct financial interest, or other health care providers with whom Caremark has a financial relationship or interest, in exchange for the referral of a patient to a Caremark facility or service or the prescription of

drugs marketed or distributed by Caremark for which reimbursement may be sought from Medicare, Medicaid, or a similar state reimbursement program;

3. That the full Board shall discuss all relevant material changes in government health care regulations and their effect on relationships with health care providers on a semi-annual basis;

4. That Caremark's officers will remove all personnel from health care facilities or hospitals who have been placed in such facility for the purpose of providing remuneration in exchange for a patient referral for which reimbursement may be sought from Medicare, Medicaid, or a similar state reimbursement program;

5. That every patient will receive written disclosure of any financial relationship between Caremark and the health care professional or provider who made the referral;

6. That the Board will establish a Compliance and Ethics Committee of four directors, two of which will be non-management directors, to meet at least four times a year to effectuate these policies and monitor business segment compliance with the ARPL, and to report to the Board semi-annually concerning compliance by each business segment; and

7. That corporate officers responsible for business segments shall serve as compliance officers who must report semi-annually to the Compliance and Ethics Committee and, with the assistance of outside counsel, review existing contracts and get advanced approval of any new contract forms.

II. LEGAL PRINCIPLES

B. Directors' Duties To Monitor Corporate Operations

The complaint charges the director defendants with breach of their duty of attention or care in connection with the on-going operation of the corporation's business. The claim is that the directors allowed a situation to develop and continue which exposed the corporation to enormous legal liability and that in so doing they violated a duty to be active monitors of corporate performance. The complaint thus does not charge either director self-dealing or the more difficult loyalty-type problems arising from cases of suspect director motivation, such as entrenchment or sale of control contexts. The theory here advanced is possibly the most difficult theory in corporation law upon which a plaintiff might hope to win a judgment. The good policy reasons why it is so difficult to charge directors with responsibility for corporate losses for an alleged breach of care, where there is no conflict of interest or no facts suggesting suspect motivation involved, were recently described in *Gagliardi v. TriFoods Int'l, Inc.,* Del.Ch., 683 A.2d 1049, 1051 (1996) (1996 Del.Ch. LEXIS 87 at p. 20).

1. *Potential liability for directoral decisions:* Director liability for a breach of the duty to exercise appropriate attention may, in theory, arise in two distinct contexts. First, such liability may be said to follow *from a board decision* that results in a loss because that decision was ill advised or "negligent". Second, liability to the corporation for a loss may be said to arise from an *unconsidered failure of the board to act* in circumstances in which due attention would, arguably, have prevented the loss. The first class of cases will typically be subject to review under the director-protective business judgment rule, assuming the decision made was the product of *a process* that was *either* deliberately considered in good faith or was otherwise rational. What should be understood, but may not widely be understood by courts or commentators who are not often required to face such questions,

is that compliance with a director's duty of care can never appropriately be judicially determined by reference to *the content of the board decision* that leads to a corporate loss, apart from consideration of the good faith *or* rationality of the process employed. That is, whether a judge or jury considering the matter after the fact, believes a decision substantively wrong, or degrees of wrong extending through "stupid" to "egregious" or "irrational", provides no ground for director liability, so long as the court determines that the process employed was either rational or employed in *a good faith* effort to advance corporate interests. To employ a different rule—one that permitted an "objective" evaluation of the decision—would expose directors to substantive second guessing by ill-equipped judges or juries, which would, in the long-run, be injurious to investor interests. Thus, the business judgment rule is process oriented and informed by a deep respect for all *good faith* board decisions.

Indeed, one wonders on what moral basis might shareholders attack a *good faith* business decision of a director as "unreasonable" or "irrational." Where a director *in fact exercises a good faith effort to be informed and to exercise appropriate judgment,* he or she should be deemed to satisfy fully the duty of attention. If the shareholders thought themselves entitled to some other quality of judgment than such a director produces in the good faith exercise of the powers of office, then the shareholders should have elected other directors. Judge Learned Hand made the point rather better than can I. In speaking of the passive director defendant Mr. Andrews in *Barnes v. Andrews,* Judge Hand said:

> True, he was not very suited by experience for the job he had undertaken, but I cannot hold him on that account. After all it is the same corporation that chose him that now seeks to charge him.... Directors are not specialists like lawyers or doctors.... They are the general advisors of the business and if they faithfully give such ability as they have to their charge, it would not be lawful to hold them liable. Must a director guarantee that his judgment is good? Can a shareholder call him to account for deficiencies that their votes assured him did not disqualify him for his office? While he may not have been the Cromwell for that Civil War, Andrews did not engage to play any such role.

In this formulation Learned Hand correctly identifies, in my opinion, the core element of any corporate law duty of care inquiry: whether there was good faith effort to be informed and exercise judgment.

2. *Liability for failure to monitor:* The second class of cases in which director liability for inattention is theoretically possible entail circumstances in which a loss eventuates not from a decision but, from unconsidered inaction. Most of the decisions that a corporation, acting through its human agents, makes are, of course, not the subject of director attention. Legally, the board itself will be required only to authorize the most significant corporate acts or transactions: mergers, changes in capital structure, fundamental changes in business, appointment and compensation of the CEO, etc. As the facts of this case graphically demonstrate, ordinary business decisions that are made by officers and employees deeper in the interior of the organization can, however, vitally affect the welfare of the corporation and its ability to achieve its various strategic and financial goals. If this case did not prove the point itself, recent business history would. Recall for example the displacement of senior management and much of the board of Salomon, Inc.; the replacement of senior management of Kidder, Peabody following the discovery of large trading losses resulting from phantom trades by a highly compensated trader; or the extensive financial loss and reputational injury suffered by Prudential Insurance as a result its junior officers misrepresentations in connection with the distribution of limited

partnership interests. Financial and organizational disasters such as these raise the question, what is the board's responsibility with respect to the organization and monitoring of the enterprise to assure that the corporation functions within the law to achieve its purposes?

Modernly this question has been given special importance by an increasing tendency, especially under federal law, to employ the criminal law to assure corporate compliance with external legal requirements, including environmental, financial, employee and product safety as well as assorted other health and safety regulations. In 1991, pursuant to the Sentencing Reform Act of 1984, the United States Sentencing Commission adopted Organizational Sentencing Guidelines which impact importantly on the prospective effect these criminal sanctions might have on business corporations. The Guidelines set forth a uniform sentencing structure for organizations to be sentenced for violation of federal criminal statutes and provide for penalties that equal or often massively exceed those previously imposed on corporations. The Guidelines offer powerful incentives for corporations today to have in place compliance programs to detect violations of law, promptly to report violations to appropriate public officials when discovered, and to take prompt, voluntary remedial efforts.

In 1963, the Delaware Supreme Court in *Graham v. Allis-Chalmers Mfg. Co.*, addressed the question of potential liability of board members for losses experienced by the corporation as a result of the corporation having violated the anti-trust laws of the United States. There was no claim in that case that the directors knew about the behavior of subordinate employees of the corporation that had resulted in the liability. Rather, as in this case, the claim asserted was that the directors *ought to have known* of it and if they had known they would have been under a duty to bring the corporation into compliance with the law and thus save the corporation from the loss. The Delaware Supreme Court concluded that, under the facts as they appeared, there was no basis to find that the directors had breached a duty to be informed of the ongoing operations of the firm. In notably colorful terms, the court stated that "absent cause for suspicion there is no duty upon the directors to install and operate a corporate system of espionage to ferret out wrongdoing which they have no reason to suspect exists." The Court found that there were no grounds for suspicion in that case and, thus, concluded that the directors were blamelessly unaware of the conduct leading to the corporate liability.

How does one generalize this holding today? Can it be said today that, absent some ground giving rise to suspicion of violation of law, that corporate directors have no duty to assure that a corporate information gathering and reporting systems exists which represents a good faith attempt to provide senior management and the Board with information respecting material acts, events or conditions within the corporation, including compliance with applicable statutes and regulations? I certainly do not believe so. I doubt that such a broad generalization of the *Graham* holding would have been accepted by the Supreme Court in 1963. The case can be more narrowly interpreted as standing for the proposition that, absent grounds to suspect deception, neither corporate boards nor senior officers can be charged with wrongdoing simply for assuming the integrity of employees and the honesty of their dealings on the company's behalf.

A broader interpretation of *Graham v. Allis-Chalmers*—that it means that a corporate board has no responsibility to assure that appropriate information and reporting systems are established by management—would not, in any event, be accepted by the Delaware Supreme Court in 1996, in my opinion. In stating the basis for this view, I start with the recognition that in recent years the Delaware Supreme Court has made it clear—especially in its jurisprudence concerning takeovers, from *Smith v. Van Gorkom* through *Paramount*

Communications v. QVC—the seriousness with which the corporation law views the role of the corporate board. Secondly, I note the elementary fact that relevant and timely *information* is an essential predicate for satisfaction of the board's supervisory and monitoring role under Section 141 of the Delaware General Corporation Law. Thirdly, I note the potential impact of the federal organizational sentencing guidelines on any business organization. Any rational person attempting in good faith to meet an organizational governance responsibility would be bound to take into account this development and the enhanced penalties and the opportunities for reduced sanctions that it offers.

In light of these developments, it would, in my opinion, be a mistake to conclude that our Supreme Court's statement in *Graham* concerning "espionage" means that corporate boards may satisfy their obligation to be reasonably informed concerning the corporation, without assuring themselves that information and reporting systems exist in the organization that are reasonably designed to provide to senior management and to the board itself timely, accurate information sufficient to allow management and the board, each within its scope, to reach informed judgments concerning both the corporation's compliance with law and its business performance.

Obviously the level of detail that is appropriate for such an information system is a question of business judgment. And obviously too, no rationally designed information and reporting system will remove the possibility that the corporation will violate laws or regulations, or that senior officers or directors may nevertheless sometimes be misled or otherwise fail reasonably to detect acts material to the corporation's compliance with the law. But it is important that the board exercise a good faith judgment that the corporation's information and reporting system is in concept and design adequate to assure the board that appropriate information will come to its attention in a timely manner as a matter of ordinary operations, so that it may satisfy its responsibility.

Thus, I am of the view that a director's obligation includes a duty to attempt in good faith to assure that a corporate information and reporting system, which the board concludes is adequate, exists, and that failure to do so under some circumstances may, in theory at least, render a director liable for losses caused by non-compliance with applicable legal standards. I now turn to an analysis of the claims asserted with this concept of the directors duty of care, as a duty satisfied in part by assurance of adequate information flows to the board, in mind.

III. ANALYSIS OF THIRD AMENDED COMPLAINT AND SETTLEMENT

A. The Claims

On balance, after reviewing an extensive record in this case, including numerous documents and three depositions, I conclude that this settlement is fair and reasonable. In light of the fact that the Caremark Board already has a functioning committee charged with overseeing corporate compliance, the changes in corporate practice that are presented as consideration for the settlement do not impress one as very significant. Nonetheless, that consideration appears fully adequate to support dismissal of the derivative claims of director fault asserted, because those claims find no substantial evidentiary support in the record and quite likely were susceptible to a motion to dismiss in all events.

In order to show that the Caremark directors breached their duty of care by failing adequately to control Caremark's employees, plaintiffs would have to show either (1) that the directors knew or (2) should have known that violations of law were occurring and, in either event, (3) that the directors took no steps in a good faith effort to prevent or remedy that situation, and (4) that such failure proximately resulted in the losses complained of, although under *Cede & Co. v. Technicolor, Inc.*, Del.Supr., 636 A.2d 956 (1994) this last element may be thought to constitute an affirmative defense.

1. *Knowing violation for statute:* Concerning the possibility that the Caremark directors knew of violations of law, none of the documents submitted for review, nor any of the deposition transcripts appear to provide evidence of it. Certainly the Board understood that the company had entered into a variety of contracts with physicians, researchers, and health care providers and it was understood that some of these contracts were with persons who had prescribed treatments that Caremark participated in providing. The board was informed that the company's reimbursement for patient care was frequently from government funded sources and that such services were subject to the ARPL. But the Board appears to have been informed by experts that the company's practices while contestable, were lawful. There is no evidence that reliance on such reports was not reasonable. Thus, this case presents no occasion to apply a principle to the effect that knowingly causing the corporation to violate a criminal statute constitutes a breach of a director's fiduciary duty. It is not clear that the Board knew the detail found, for example, in the indictments arising from the Company's payments. But, of course, the duty to act in good faith to be informed cannot be thought to require directors to possess detailed information about all aspects of the operation of the enterprise. Such a requirement would simple be inconsistent with the scale and scope of efficient organization size in this technological age.

2. *Failure to monitor:* Since it does appears that the Board was to some extent unaware of the activities that led to liability, I turn to a consideration of the other potential avenue to director liability that the pleadings take: director inattention or "negligence". Generally where a claim of directorial liability for corporate loss is predicated upon ignorance of liability creating activities within the corporation, as in *Graham* or in this case, in my opinion only a sustained or systematic failure of the board to exercise oversight—such as an utter failure to attempt to assure a reasonable information and reporting system exists—will establish the lack of good faith that is a necessary condition to liability. Such a test of liability—lack of good faith as evidenced by sustained or systematic failure of a director to exercise reasonable oversight—is quite high. But, a demanding test of liability in the oversight context is probably beneficial to corporate shareholders as a class, as it is in the board decision context, since it makes board service by qualified persons more likely, while continuing to act as a stimulus to *good faith performance of duty* by such directors.

Here the record supplies essentially no evidence that the director defendants were guilty of a sustained failure to exercise their oversight function. To the contrary, insofar as I am able to tell on this record, the corporation's information systems appear to have represented a good faith attempt to be informed of relevant facts. If the directors did not know the specifics of the activities that lead to the indictments, they cannot be faulted.

The liability that eventuated in this instance was huge. But the fact that it resulted from a violation of criminal law alone does not create a breach of fiduciary duty by directors. The record at this stage does not support the conclusion that the defendants either lacked good faith in the exercise of their monitoring responsibilities or conscientiously permitted a known violation of law by the corporation to occur. The claims asserted against them must be viewed at this stage as extremely weak.

Notes

(1) What did the court clarify in *Caremark* that it had left unclear in *Graham*?

(2) Approximately 10 years after *Caremark*, in *Stone v. Ritter*, the Delaware court affirmed the rule that it laid out in *Caremark* regarding directorial liability for failure to monitor. The facts of *Stone* are somewhat similar to the facts of both *Caremark* and *Graham*. In *Stone*, a bank paid 50 million dollars in fines and civil penalties after the government learned that the bank's employees had failed to file "suspicious activity reports" ("SARS"). Pursuant to the federal Bank Secrecy Act ("BSA") and various anti-money-laundering regulations passed in the wake of 9/11, bank employees were required to file a SAR for any banking transaction that involved at least $5,000 and for which the bank knew, should have known, suspected or had reason to suspect involved funds from illegal conduct. The Delaware Supreme reaffirmed the rule from *Caremark* and held that:

> *Caremark* articulates the necessary conditions predicate for director oversight liability: (a) the directors utterly failed to implement any reporting or information system or controls; or (b) having implemented such a system or controls, consciously failed to monitor or oversee its operations thus disabling themselves from being informed of risks or problems requiring their attention. In either case, imposition of liability requires a showing that the directors knew that they were not discharging their fiduciary obligations. Where directors fail to act in the face of a known duty to act, thereby demonstrating a conscious disregard for their responsibilities, they breach their duty of loyalty by failing to discharge that fiduciary obligation in good faith.

Based on this holding, the *Stone* court affirmed the Chancery Court's decision that the plaintiffs were unable to plead the existence of "red flags"—facts that would have established: (1) that the bank's board was aware that its internal controls for discovering the SAR violations were inadequate, or (2) that such inadequacies would result in illegal activity, or (3) that the board knew these problems existed and decided to do nothing. The plaintiffs could not establish any of the aforementioned red flags because there was sufficient evidence in the record to show that the bank's board reasonably attempted to set up a monitoring system to catch improper conduct. In fact, the record established that the board had created committees and assigned employees the responsibility to oversee compliance and to report any SAR violations to the board. Moreover, the board wrote policies and provided training to ensure compliance with the federal law. Because of these efforts, there was no evidence that the board acted in bad faith by failing to set up a monitoring system or by failing to monitor such system.

(3) According to the court in *Caremark*, failure to monitor is "possibly the most difficult theory in corporation law upon which a plaintiff might hope to win a judgment." Why is this statement true?

(4) What degree of knowledge should we expect corporate leaders to possess regarding the work and actions of company employees? Should board members and/or corporate executives be held responsible for bad conduct or illegal actions of mid-level management or low-level employees?

Chapter Three

Corporate Power

A. Evolution of the C Corporation

The concept of the corporate form as a mechanism to facilitate business grew substantially in the early part of the 1800s. This period of rapid economic growth, also known as the industrial revolution, served as the foundation of power for the corporate form. Eli Whitney was one of the central individuals in helping to usher in the industrial revolution. Whitney is most widely known for inventing the cotton gin. Prior to his invention, southern plantation owners used slaves to remove the seeds from the harvested cotton. This process was tedious and time consuming. More importantly, it was highly inefficient. In fact, some scholars argue that this process was so inefficient that slavery may have ended much earlier in the south but for Whitney's invention. Whitney's cotton gin made the seed extraction process much more efficient—it could extract more seeds in a few hours than several slaves could extract in an entire day of work. Because of this invention, slavery became more critical to southern economies. Although Whitney's invention modernized and improved the cotton seed extraction process, it did not prove as profitable as one might think. Because the basic idea behind the machine was rather simple, many farmers built their own cotton gins in violation of Whitney's patent. As a result, Whitney spent more time initiating patent suits than collecting profits. Because of Whitney's success in developing the cotton gin, he turned his attention to the idea of "interchangeable parts." Prior to the entrenchment of this concept in American commerce, goods were manufactured by one person in their entirety. While this process allowed for individual uniqueness, and to some extent higher levels of quality, it was inefficient and time consuming. The idea of interchangeable parts focused on breaking down goods into their component parts, manufacturing the component parts in large quantities, via an assembly line, and then organizing the component parts into finished goods.

Whitney used this process to manufacture large quantities of weapons for the American government. As a result of his success, it was evident that the idea of interchangeable parts could revolutionize commerce.

At the same time, transportation in America was also expanding. Because of the railway system and the steamboat, it was easier to move people as well as goods from place to place. The developments in transportation enabled goods to be sold to more people in more places, which heightened a need for increased amounts of goods. To do this, businesses needed more labor, materials, and machines. Most importantly, business needed money to facilitate expansion. Before the proliferation of corporations, sole proprietorships (businesses owned by one person), and small general partnerships (businesses owned by two or more people), used the limited resources of their individual owners to expand. However, the limited resources of a few owners were not sufficient to meet the needs of the market. Businesses needed a way to capture significant infusions of capital. This gave rise to the corporation. The corporate form enabled business owners to sell shares of ownership in the business in exchange for cash or other consideration. In addition, unlike the owners in a sole proprietorship or general partnership, a corporation's shareholders were protected by the "corporate veil" and were not liable for the debts and obligations of the corporation. This allowed shareholders to freely invest without the fear of liability.

B. Corporations as Fictional Persons

The corporate entity has not always possessed the widespread wealth and power that it currently enjoys. Unlike today, where corporations operate for their own personal interest and the interest of the corporation's shareholders, in the early 1800s, corporations were largely operated for the benefit of the public at large.

Early corporate law was largely characterized by the charter system. Pursuant to the charter system, corporations did not have an inherent right to conduct business. Instead, a corporation's existence was predicated upon a State's decision to grant the corporation a charter. As a further restraint on corporate power, a corporation was only authorized to operate for a limited period of time and at the expiration of the initial time period, the corporation needed to obtain legislative approval for the continuation of its charter. This system gave States a substantial ability to regulate corporations in a manner that best served the public utility because the States retained authority to consistently exercise oversight over corporate affairs through the award, revocation and modification of corporate charters.

During its infancy, the corporation was not conceptualized as a "person." A corporation did not possess an inherent right to make charitable or political contributions, own stock in another corporation, or keep its financial records private. These limitations were primarily aimed at curbing the power of private corporations so as to protect against an upset in the balance of wealth and democracy in America.

An 1809 decision by the Virginia Supreme Court, *Currie's Adm'rs v. Mut. Assurance Soc'y*, affirming the legislature's decision to affirm a corporate charter, is indicative of the States' view of corporate power at its infancy. In this case, the court opined that:

> They ought never to be passed, but in consideration of services to be rendered to the public.... It may be often convenient for a set of associated individuals, to have the privileges of a corporation bestowed upon them; but if their object is merely private or selfish; if it is detrimental to, or not promotive of, the public good, they have no adequate claim upon the legislature for the privileges.[1]

Interestingly, according to the court, the primary purpose of the corporation was to facilitate social utility—not shareholder or corporate wealth. As further evidence of the lack of corporate power and personhood, in 1832, President Andrew Jackson declined to renew the Second Bank of the United State's ("Second Bank") corporate charter. Second Bank's president, Nicholas Biddle, had earned the ire of President Jackson after Biddle failed to investigate alleged misconduct by the bank. Instead of working with President

---

1. Currie's Adm'rs v. Mut. Assurance Soc'y, 14 Va. (4 Hen. & M.) 315, 437–48 (1809).

Jackson to reach a resolution regarding the misconduct, Biddle used the bank as a means of attacking President Jackson and threatened to withhold financial support from Jackson. Ultimately, Jackson declined to extend Second Bank's charter and it closed when its charter expired in 1836. As evidence of the very evil that concerned Jackson, once Jackson declined to extend the charter, Biddle, in response, quickly limited the amount of available credit causing business to substantially decline.

While this limited view of corporate power was largely followed in the early 1800's, today corporations have much greater power as we will discuss in this chapter.

(1) Why is this historical context relevant? What does it tell us about corporations today?

(2) Was the government's fear of corporate power justified?

(3) What do you think that President Jackson would say if he were to see a snapshot of corporate power today?

C. The Power of the Modern Corporation

1. Corporate Charitable Contributions

Making charitable contributions is strongly encouraged under United States business law. That said, a corporation must be wary when gifting contributions from the corporate treasury. Ultimately, a charitable contribution from the company coffers is a gifting of shareholder value and should be undertaken carefully and with purpose. *A.P. Smith v. Barlow* is an old New Jersey case that sets the parameters corporate leadership must follow in order to commit shareholder funds to charitable organizations.[2] In fact, funds can be charitably expended, even in cases where the shareholders stridently disagree, if established guidelines are met. The case is about a modest contribution of corporate money to Princeton University. While no mention is made as to why the shareholders were against the donation to Princeton, perhaps we can speculate that these aggrieved shareholders were graduates of Penn, Yale, or Rutgers. Look specifically to identify the factors established by this court that enable legal charitable contributions from the corporate treasury.

A. P. Smith Mfg. Co. v. Barlow et al.

13 N.J. 145, 98 A.2d 581, 39 A.L.R.2d 1179 (1953)
Supreme Court of New Jersey

The opinion of the court was delivered by

Jacobs, Justice

The Chancery Division determined that a donation by the plaintiff The A. P. Smith Manufacturing Company to Princeton University was intra vires.

The company was incorporated in 1896 and is engaged in the manufacture and sale of valves, fire hydrants and special equipment, mainly for water and gas industries. Its

---

2. *See* andré douglas pond cummings, *Procuring "Justice"?: Citizens United, Caperton, and Partisan Judicial Elections*, 95 Iowa L. Rev. Bull. 89 (2010), http://www.uiowa.edu/~ilr/bulletin/ILRB_95_cummings.pdf (describing the gifting of "other people's money" and the concept of "elephant bumping" by corporate executives and board members who stand in a fiduciary relationship to the true owners of the funds being committed, the shareholders).

plant is located in East Orange and Bloomfield and it has approximately 300 employees. Over the years the company has contributed regularly to the local community chest and on occasions to Upsala College in East Orange and Newark University, now part of Rutgers, the State University. On July 24, 1951 the board of directors adopted a resolution which set forth that it was in the corporation's best interests to join with others in the 1951 Annual Giving to Princeton University, and appropriated the sum of $1,500 to be transferred by the corporation's treasurer to the university as a contribution towards its maintenance. When this action was questioned by stockholders the corporation instituted a declaratory judgment action in the Chancery Division and trial was had in due course.

Mr. Hubert F. O'Brien, the president of the company, testified that he considered the contribution to be a sound investment, that the public expects corporations to aid philanthropic and benevolent institutions, that they obtain good will in the community by so doing, and that their charitable donations create a favorable environment for their business operations. In addition, he expressed the thought that in contributing to liberal arts institutions, corporations were furthering their self-interest in assuring the free flow of properly trained personnel for administrative and other corporate employment. Mr. Frank W. Abrams, chairman of the board of the Standard Oil Company of New Jersey, testified that corporations are expected to acknowledge their public responsibilities in support of the essential elements of our free enterprise system. He indicated that it was not 'good business' to disappoint 'this reasonable and justified public expectation,' nor was it good business for corporations 'to take substantial benefits from their membership in the economic community while avoiding the normally accepted obligations of citizenship in the social community.' Mr. Irving S. Olds, former chairman of the board of the United States Steel Corporation, pointed out that corporations have a self-interest in the maintenance of liberal education as the bulwark of good government. He stated that 'Capitalism and free enterprise owe their survival in no small degree to the existence of our private, independent universities' and that if American business does not aid in their maintenance it is not 'properly protecting the long-range interest of its stockholders, its employees and its customers.' Similarly, Dr. Harold W. Dodds, President of Princeton University, suggested that if private institutions of higher learning were replaced by governmental institutions our society would be vastly different and private enterprise in other fields would fade out rather promptly. Further on he stated that 'democratic society will not long endure if it does not nourish within itself strong centers of non-governmental fountains of knowledge, opinions of all sorts not governmentally or politically originated. If the time comes when all these centers are absorbed into government, then freedom as we know it, I submit, is at an end.'

The objecting stockholders have not disputed any of the foregoing testimony nor the showing of great need by Princeton and other private institutions of higher learning and the important public service being rendered by them for democratic government and industry alike. Similarly, they have acknowledged that for over two decades there has been state legislation on our books which expresses a strong public policy in favor of corporate contributions such as that being questioned by them. Nevertheless, they have taken the position that (1) the plaintiff's certificate of incorporation does not expressly authorize the contribution and under common-law principles the company does not possess any implied or incidental power to make it, and (2) the New Jersey statutes which expressly authorize the contribution may not constitutionally be applied to the plaintiff, a corporation created long before their enactment.

In his discussion of the early history of business corporations Professor Williston refers to a 1702 publication where the author stated flatly that 'The general intent and end of all civil incorporations is for better government.' And he points out that the early corporate charters, particularly their recitals, furnish additional support for the notion that the corporate object was the public one of managing and ordering the trade as well as the private one of profit for the members. However, with later economic and social developments and the free availability of the corporate device for all trades, the end of private profit became generally accepted as the controlling one in all businesses other than those classed broadly as public utilities. As a concomitant the common-law rule developed that those who managed the corporation could not disburse any corporate funds for philanthropic or other worthy public cause unless the expenditure would benefit the corporation. During the 19th Century when corporations were relatively few and small and did not dominate the country's wealth, the common-law rule did not significantly interfere with the public interest. But the 20th Century has presented a different climate. Control of economic wealth has passed largely from individual entrepreneurs to dominating corporations, and calls upon the corporations for reasonable philanthropic donations have come to be made with increased public support. In many instances such contributions have been sustained by the courts within the common-law doctrine upon liberal findings that the donations tended reasonably to promote the corporate objectives.

Thus, in the leading case of *Evans v. Brunner, Mond & Company, Ltd.* (1921) 1 Ch. 359, the court held that it was within the incidental power of a chemical company to grant 100,000 to universities or other scientific institutions selected by the directors 'for the furtherance of scientific education and research.' The testimony indicated that the company desired to encourage and assist men who would devote their time and abilities to scientific study and research generally, a class of men for whom the company was constantly on the lookout. This benefit was not considered by the court to be so remote as to bring it outside the common-law rule.

And in *Greene County Nat. Farm Loan Ass'n v. Federal Land Bank of Louisville*, 57 F.Supp. 783, 789 (D.C.W.D.Ky.1944) the court in dealing with a comparable problem said:

> But it is equally well established that corporations are permitted to make substantial contributions to have the outward form of gifts where the activity being promoted by the so-called gift tends reasonably to promote the good-will of the business of the contributing corporation. Courts recognize in such cases that although there is no dollar and cent supporting consideration, yet there is often substantial indirect benefit accruing to the corporation which supports such action. So-called contributions by corporations to churches, schools, hospitals, and civic improvement funds, and the establishment of bonus and pension plans with the payment of large sums flowing therefrom have been upheld many times as reasonable business expenditures rather than being classified as charitable gifts.

The foregoing authorities illustrate how courts, while adhering to the terms of the common-law rule, have applied it very broadly to enable worthy corporate donations with indirect benefits to the corporations. In *State ex rel. Sorensen v. Chicago B. & Q.R.Co.*, 112 Neb. 248, 199 N.W. 534, 537 (1924), the Supreme Court of Nebraska, through Justice Letton, went even further and without referring to any limitation based on economic benefits to the corporation said that it saw 'no reason why if a railroad company desires to foster, encourage and contribute to a charitable enterprise, or to one designed for the public weal and welfare, it may not do so'; later in its opinion it repeated this view with the expression that it saw 'no reason why a railroad corporation may not, to a reasonable extent, donate funds or services to aid in good works.'

When the wealth of the nation was primarily in the hands of individuals they discharged their responsibilities as citizens by donating freely for charitable purposes. With the transfer of most of the wealth to corporate hands and the imposition of heavy burdens of individual taxation, they have been unable to keep pace with increased philanthropic needs. They have therefore, with justification, turned to corporations to assume the modern obligations of good citizenship in the same manner as humans do. Congress and state legislatures have enacted laws which encourage corporate contributions, and much has recently been written to indicate the crying need and adequate legal basis therefor. In actual practice corporate giving has correspondingly increased. It is estimated that local community chests receive well over 40% of their contributions from corporations; these contributions and those made by corporations to the American Red Cross, to Boy Scouts and Girl Scouts, to 4-H Clubs and similar organizations have almost invariably been unquestioned.

During the first world war corporations loaned their personnel and contributed substantial corporate funds in order to insure survival; during the depression of the '30s they made contributions to alleviate the desperate hardships of the millions of unemployed; and during the second world war they again contributed to insure survival. More and more they have come to recognize that their salvation rests upon sound economic and social environment which in turn rests in no insignificant part upon free and vigorous nongovernmental institutions of learning. It seems to us that just as the conditions prevailing when corporations were originally created required that they serve public as well as private interests, modern conditions require that corporations acknowledge and discharge social as well as private responsibilities as members of the communities within which they operate. Within this broad concept there is no difficulty in sustaining, as incidental to their proper objects and in aid of the public welfare, the power of corporations to contribute corporate funds within reasonable limits in support of academic institutions. But even if we confine ourselves to the terms of the common-law rule in its application to current conditions, such expenditures may likewise readily be justified as being for the benefit of the corporation; indeed, if need be the matter may be viewed strictly in terms of actual survival of the corporation in a free enterprise system.

In 1930 a statute was enacted in our State which expressly provided that any corporation could cooperate with other corporations and natural persons in the creation and maintenance of community funds and charitable, philanthropic or benevolent instrumentalities conducive to public welfare, and could for such purposes expend such corporate sums as the directors 'deem expedient and as in their judgment will contribute to the protection of the corporate interests.' Under the terms of the statute donations in excess of 1% of the capital stock required 10 days' notice to stockholders and approval at a stockholders' meeting if written objections were made by the holders of more than 25% of the stock; in 1949 the statute was amended to increase the limitation to 1% of capital and surplus. In 1950 a more comprehensive statute was enacted. In this enactment the Legislature declared that it shall be the public policy of our State and in furtherance of the public interest and welfare that encouragement be given to the creation and maintenance of institutions engaged in community fund, hospital, charitable, philanthropic, educational, scientific or benevolent activities or patriotic or civic activities conducive to the betterment of social and economic conditions; and it expressly empowered corporations acting singly or with others to contribute reasonable sums to such institutions, provided, however, that the contribution shall not be permissible if the donee institution owns more than 10% of the voting stock of the donor and provided, further, that the contribution shall not exceed 1% of capital and surplus unless the excess is authorized by the stockholders at a regular or special meeting. To insure that the grant of express power in the 1950 statute would not displace pre-existing power at common law or otherwise, the Legislature provided that the 'act shall not be construed as directly or indirectly minimizing or interpreting the rights and powers of corporations, as heretofore existing, with reference to appropriations, expenditures or contributions of the nature above specified.' It may be noted that statutes relating to charitable contributions by corporations have now been passed in 29 states.

The appellants contend that the foregoing New Jersey statutes may not be applied to corporations created before their passage. Fifty years before the incorporation of The A. P. Smith Manufacturing Company our Legislature provided that every corporate charter thereafter granted 'shall be subject to alteration, suspension and repeal, in the discretion of the legislature.' A similar reserved power was placed into our State Constitution in 1875, and is found in our present Constitution.

State legislation adopted in the public interest and applied to pre-existing corporations under the reserved power has repeatedly been sustained by the United States Supreme Court above the contention that it impairs the rights of stockholders and violates constitutional guarantees under the Federal Constitution. We are entirely satisfied that the legislative enactments found in R.S. 14:3-13, N.J.S.A., and N.J.S.A. 14:3-13.1 et seq. and applied to pre-existing corporations do not violate any constitutional guarantees afforded to their stockholders.

In encouraging and expressly authorizing reasonable charitable contributions by corporations, our State has not only joined with other states in advancing the national interest but has also specially furthered the interests of its own people who must bear the burdens of taxation resulting from increased state and federal aid upon default in voluntary giving. It is significant that in its enactments the State has not in anywise sought to impose any compulsory obligations or alter the corporate objectives. And since in our view the corporate power to make reasonable charitable contributions exists under modern conditions, even apart from express statutory provision, its enactments simply constitute helpful and confirmatory declarations of such power, accompanied by limiting safeguards.

In the light of all of the foregoing we have no hesitancy in sustaining the validity of the donation by the plaintiff. There is no suggestion that it was made indiscriminately or to a pet charity of the corporate directors in furtherance of personal rather than corporate ends. On the contrary, it was made to a preeminent institution of higher learning, was modest in amount and well within the limitations imposed by the statutory enactments, and was voluntarily made in the reasonable belief that it would aid the public welfare and advance the interests of the plaintiff as a private corporation and as part of the community in which it operates. We find that it was a lawful exercise of the corporation's implied and incidental powers under common-law principles and that it came within the express authority of the pertinent state legislation. As has been indicated, there is now widespread belief throughout the nation that free and vigorous non-governmental institutions of learning are vital to our democracy and the system of free enterprise and that withdrawal of corporate authority to make such contributions within reasonable limits would seriously threaten their continuance. Corporations have come to recognize this and with their enlightenment have sought in varying measures, as has the plaintiff by its contribution, to insure and strengthen the society which gives them existence and the means of aiding themselves and their fellow citizens. Clearly then, the appellants, as individual stockholders whose private interests rest entirely upon the well-being of the plaintiff corporation, ought not be permitted to close their eyes to present-day realities and thwart the long-visioned corporate action in recognizing and voluntarily discharging its high obligations as a constituent of our modern social structure.

The judgment entered in the Chancery Division is in all respects

Affirmed.

Notes

(1) Before World War I, World War II and the rise of the corporation, where did most charitable contributions come from that supported philanthropic entities?

(2) With a new reliance on corporate contributions to support the arts, universities, and charitable organizations, what specifically must corporations do to make legal contributions from the corporate treasury?

(3) Why should corporations want to contribute generously to philanthropic causes?

(4) Recognizing the tension between the profit motive at the forefront of the minds of most corporate leaders and a desire to support charities, several states have begun to allow hybrid corporate organizations to exist in their states that combine a philanthropic purpose with a profit motive. The Benefit Corporation and the Low-profit Limited Liability Company ("L3C") are but two examples of newly emerging business entities that combine charitable purpose with limited profit expectation.[3] Prior to the Benefit Corporation and the L3C, individuals interested in running charitable organizations had to file to become a 501(c)(3) non-profit with the IRS. Now, entrepreneurs can combine philanthropic purposes with for-profit business, so long as shareholders, members, and affiliates understand that profit is not the primary motivation for leaders of these new hybrid businesses.

(5) Keeping in mind that general corporate treasury funds represent shareholders ownership interest in a corporation, should corporations be allowed to make charitable contributions to not-for-profit organizations that as an express part of their mission lobby legislatures and politic for specific causes? Should corporations be permitted to use corporate treasury fund to contribute to the campaigns of politicians or political causes?

2. Free Speech Rights and the Corporate Entity

We see now that corporations as fictional persons can freely give to charitable causes from the corporate treasury. What other rights do corporations possess? *Citizens United* may historically come to be viewed as one of the most significant decisions of the 21st century. Controversial from the moment it was announced, the case divided the country over the question of whether a corporation, a fictional person, has First Amendment Free Speech rights, such that its electioneering and politicking efforts cannot be legislatively restricted. While the 124 page opinion spends the bulk of its energy analyzing Election Law and Constitutional Law, the important portions of the opinion we include below implicate Corporate Law and the new ability of corporations (and labor unions) to straightforwardly influence elections and policymaking simply by contributing unrestricted

---

3. For background on the advent of and potential effectiveness of the Benefit Corporation, *see* Joseph Grant, *When Making Money and Making a Sustainable and Societal Difference Collide: Will Benefit Corporations Succeed or Fail?* 46 IND. L. REV. 581 (2013).

corporate funds from the corporate treasury of the company to politicians and propositions that it favors.

Citizens United v. Federal Election Commission
558 U.S. 310, 130 S.Ct. 876 (2010)
Supreme Court of the United States

Justice Kennedy

Affirmed in part, reversed in part, and remanded.

Federal law prohibits corporations and unions from using their general treasury funds to make independent expenditures for speech defined as an "electioneering communication" or for speech expressly advocating the election or defeat of a candidate. 2 U.S.C. §441b. Limits on electioneering communications were upheld in *McConnell v. Federal Election Comm'n,* 540 U.S. 93, 203–209, 124 S.Ct. 619, 157 L.Ed.2d 491 (2003). The holding of *McConnell* rested to a large extent on an earlier case, *Austin v. Michigan Chamber of Commerce,* 494 U.S. 652, 110 S.Ct. 1391, 108 L.Ed.2d 652 (1990). *Austin* had held that political speech may be banned based on the speaker's corporate identity.

In this case we are asked to reconsider *Austin* and, in effect, *McConnell.* It has been noted that "*Austin* was a significant departure from ancient First Amendment principles," *Federal Election Comm'n v. Wisconsin Right to Life, Inc.,* 551 U.S. 449, 490, 127 S.Ct. 2652, 168 L.Ed.2d 329 (2007). We agree with that conclusion and hold that *stare decisis* does not compel the continued acceptance of *Austin.* The Government may regulate corporate political speech through disclaimer and disclosure requirements, but it may not suppress that speech altogether. We turn to the case now before us.

I

A

Citizens United is a nonprofit corporation. Citizens United has an annual budget of about $12 million. Most of its funds are from donations by individuals; but, in addition, it accepts a small portion of its funds from for-profit corporations.

In January 2008, Citizens United released a film entitled *Hillary: The Movie.* We refer to the film as *Hillary.* It is a 90-minute documentary about then-Senator Hillary Clinton, who was a candidate in the Democratic Party's 2008 Presidential primary elections. *Hillary* mentions Senator Clinton by name and depicts interviews with political commentators and other persons, most of them quite critical of Senator Clinton. *Hillary* was released in theaters and on DVD, but Citizens United wanted to increase distribution by making it available through video-on-demand.

To implement the proposal, Citizens United was prepared to pay for the video-on-demand; and to promote the film, it produced two 10-second ads and one 30-second ad for *Hillary.* Citizens United desired to promote the video-on-demand offering by running advertisements on broadcast and cable television.

B

Before the Bipartisan Campaign Reform Act of 2002 (BCRA), federal law prohibited—and still does prohibit—corporations and unions from using general treasury funds to make direct contributions to candidates or independent expenditures that expressly advocate the election or defeat of a candidate, through any form of media, in connection with certain qualified federal elections. 2 U.S.C. § 441b (2000 ed.). BCRA § 203 amended § 441b to prohibit any "electioneering communication" as well. 2 U.S.C. § 441b(b)(2) (2006 ed.). An electioneering communication is defined as "any broadcast, cable, or satellite communication" that "refers to a clearly identified candidate for Federal office" and is made within 30 days of a primary or 60 days of a general election. § 434(f)(3)(A). The Federal Election Commission's (FEC) regulations further define an electioneering communication as a communication that is "publicly distributed." "In the case of a candidate for nomination for President ... *publicly distributed* means" that the communication "[c]an be received by 50,000 or more persons in a State where a primary election ... is being held within 30 days." Corporations and unions are barred from using their general treasury funds for express advocacy or electioneering communications. They may establish, however, a "separate segregated fund" (known as a political action committee, or PAC) for these purposes. The moneys received by the segregated fund are limited to donations from stockholders and employees of the corporation or, in the case of unions, members of the union.

C

Citizens United wanted to make *Hillary* available through video-on-demand within 30 days of the 2008 primary elections. It feared, however, that both the film and the ads would be covered by § 441b's ban on corporate-funded independent expenditures, thus subjecting the corporation to civil and criminal penalties under § 437g. In December 2007, Citizens United sought declaratory and injunctive relief against the FEC. It argued that (1) § 441b is unconstitutional as applied to *Hillary;* and (2) BCRA's disclaimer and disclosure requirements are unconstitutional as applied to *Hillary* and to the three ads for the movie.

The District Court denied Citizens United's motion for a preliminary injunction and then granted the FEC's motion for summary judgment.

The case was reargued in this Court after the Court asked the parties to file supplemental briefs addressing whether we should overrule either or both *Austin* and the part of *McConnell* which addresses the facial validity of 2 U.S.C. § 441b.

II

Before considering whether *Austin* should be overruled, we first address whether Citizens United's claim that § 441b cannot be applied to *Hillary* may be resolved on other, narrower grounds.

A

Citizens United contends that § 441b does not cover *Hillary,* as a matter of statutory interpretation, because the film does not qualify as an "electioneering communication." § 441b(b)(2). In our view the statute cannot be saved by limiting the reach of 2 U.S.C. § 441b through this suggested interpretation. Section 441b covers *Hillary.*

B

Citizens United next argues that § 441b may not be applied to *Hillary* under the approach taken in *WRTL. McConnell* decided that § 441b(b)(2)'s definition of an "electioneering communication" was facially constitutional insofar as it restricted speech that was "the functional equivalent of express advocacy" for or against a specific candidate. *WRTL* then found an unconstitutional application of § 441b where the speech was not "express advocacy or its functional equivalent."

Hillary is equivalent to express advocacy. The movie, in essence, is a feature-length negative advertisement that urges viewers to vote against Senator Clinton for President.

As the District Court found, there is no reasonable interpretation of *Hillary* other than as an appeal to vote against Senator Clinton. Under the standard stated in *McConnell* and further elaborated in *WRTL*, the film qualifies as the functional equivalent of express advocacy.

C

Citizens United further contends that § 441b should be invalidated as applied to movies shown through video-on-demand, arguing that this delivery system has a lower risk of distorting the political process than do television ads.

While some means of communication may be less effective than others at influencing the public in different contexts, any effort by the Judiciary to decide which means of communications are to be preferred for the particular type of message and speaker would raise questions as to the courts' own lawful authority. Substantial questions would arise if courts were to begin saying what means of speech should be preferred or disfavored.

Courts, too, are bound by the First Amendment. We must decline to draw, and then redraw, constitutional lines based on the particular media or technology used to disseminate political speech from a particular speaker.

D

Citizens United also asks us to carve out an exception to § 441b's expenditure ban for nonprofit corporate political speech funded overwhelmingly by individuals.

Citizens United does not qualify for the *MCFL* or for the Snowe-Jeffords exemption, under its terms as written, because *Hillary* was funded in part with donations from for-profit corporations.

E

As the foregoing analysis confirms, the Court cannot resolve this case on a narrower ground without chilling political speech, speech that is central to the meaning and purpose of the First Amendment. Here, the lack of a valid basis for an alternative ruling requires full consideration of the continuing effect of the speech suppression upheld in *Austin*.

Citizens United stipulated to dismissing count 5 of its complaint, which raised a facial challenge to § 441b, even though count 3 raised an as-applied challenge. The Government argues that Citizens United waived its challenge to *Austin* by dismissing count 5. We disagree.

First, even if a party could somehow waive a facial challenge while preserving an as-applied challenge, that would not prevent the Court from reconsidering *Austin* or addressing the facial validity of § 441b in this case. Second, throughout the litigation, Citizens United has asserted a claim that the FEC has violated its First Amendment right to free speech. Third, the distinction between facial and as-applied challenges is not so well defined that it has some automatic effect or that it must always control the pleadings and disposition in every case involving a constitutional challenge.

Consideration of the facial validity of § 441b is further supported by the following reasons.

First, when the Government holds out the possibility of ruling for Citizens United on a narrow ground yet refrains from adopting that position, the added uncertainty demonstrates the necessity to address the question of statutory validity.

Second, substantial time would be required to bring clarity to the application of the statutory provision on these points in order to avoid any chilling effect caused by some improper interpretation.

Third is the primary importance of speech itself to the integrity of the election process. As a practical matter, given the complexity of the regulations and the deference courts show to administrative determinations, a speaker who wants to avoid threats of criminal liability and the heavy costs of defending against FEC enforcement must ask a governmental agency for prior permission to speak. These onerous restrictions thus function as the equivalent of prior restraint by giving the FEC power analogous to licensing laws implemented in 16th- and 17th-century England, laws and governmental practices of the sort that the First Amendment was drawn to prohibit.

The FEC has created a regime that allows it to select what political speech is safe for public consumption by applying ambiguous tests. If parties want to avoid litigation and the possibility of civil and criminal penalties, they must either refrain from speaking or ask the FEC to issue an advisory opinion approving of the political speech in question. Government officials pore over each word of a text to see if, in their judgment, it accords with the 11-factor test they have promulgated. This is an unprecedented governmental intervention into the realm of speech.

The ongoing chill upon speech that is beyond all doubt protected makes it necessary in this case to invoke the earlier precedents that a statute which chills speech can and must be invalidated where its facial invalidity has been demonstrated. For these reasons we find it necessary to reconsider *Austin*.

III

The First Amendment provides that "Congress shall make no law ... abridging the freedom of speech." Laws enacted to control or suppress speech may operate at different points in the speech process.

The law before us is an outright ban, backed by criminal sanctions. Section 441b makes it a felony for all corporations—including nonprofit advocacy corporations—either to expressly advocate the election or defeat of candidates or to broadcast electioneering communications within 30 days of a primary election and 60 days of a general election.

Section 441b is a ban on corporate speech notwithstanding the fact that a PAC created by a corporation can still speak. A PAC is a separate association from the corporation. So the PAC exemption from § 441b's expenditure ban, § 441b(b)(2), does not allow corporations to speak. Even if a PAC could somehow allow a corporation to speak—and it does not—the option to form PACs does not alleviate the First Amendment problems with § 441b. PACs are burdensome alternatives; they are expensive to administer and subject to extensive regulations. For example, every PAC must appoint a treasurer, forward donations to the treasurer promptly, keep detailed records of the identities of the persons making donations, preserve receipts for three years, and file an organization statement and report changes to this information within 10 days.

And that is just the beginning. PACs must file detailed monthly reports with the FEC, which are due at different times depending on the type of election that is about to occur. Given the onerous restrictions, a corporation may not be able to establish a PAC in time to make its views known regarding candidates and issues in a current campaign.

Section 441b's prohibition on corporate independent expenditures is thus a ban on speech. As a "restriction on the amount of money a person or group can spend on political communication during a campaign," that statute "necessarily reduces the quantity of expression by restricting the number of issues discussed, the depth of their exploration, and the size of the audience reached." *Buckley v. Valeo,* 424 U.S. 1, 19, 96 S.Ct. 612, 46 L.Ed.2d 659 (1976) *(per curiam)*. Were the Court to uphold these restrictions, the Government could repress speech by silencing certain voices at any of the various points in the speech process. If §441b applied to individuals, no one would believe that it is merely a time, place, or manner restriction on speech. Its purpose and effect are to silence entities whose voices the Government deems to be suspect.

Speech is an essential mechanism of democracy, for it is the means to hold officials accountable to the people. The right of citizens to inquire, to hear, to speak, and to use information to reach consensus is a precondition to enlightened self-government and a necessary means to protect it. For these reasons, political speech must prevail against laws that would suppress it, whether by design or inadvertence. Laws that burden political speech are "subject to strict scrutiny," which requires the Government to prove that the restriction "furthers a compelling interest and is narrowly tailored to achieve that interest." *WRTL,* 551 U.S., at 464, 127 S.Ct. 2652 (opinion of ROBERTS, C.J.).

Premised on mistrust of governmental power, the First Amendment stands against attempts to disfavor certain subjects or viewpoints. Prohibited, too, are restrictions distinguishing among different speakers, allowing speech by some but not others. As instruments to censor, these categories are interrelated: Speech restrictions based on the identity of the speaker are all too often simply a means to control content.

The Court has upheld a narrow class of speech restrictions that operate to the disadvantage of certain persons, but these rulings were based on an interest in allowing governmental entities to perform their functions. The corporate independent expenditures at issue in this case, however, would not interfere with governmental functions, so these cases are inapposite.

We find no basis for the proposition that, in the context of political speech, the Government may impose restrictions on certain disfavored speakers.

A

1

The Court has recognized that First Amendment protection extends to corporations.

This protection has been extended by explicit holdings to the context of political speech. Under the rationale of these precedents, political speech does not lose First Amendment protection "simply because its source is a corporation." The Court has thus rejected the argument that political speech of corporations or other associations should be treated differently under the First Amendment simply because such associations are not "natural persons."

2

In *Buckley,* 424 U.S. 1, 96 S.Ct. 612, 46 L.Ed.2d 659, [the Court invalidated §608(e)'s, of the Federal Election Campaign Act of 1971's (FECA), as amended in 1974, ban on independent expenditures].

Less than two years after *Buckley, Bellotti,* 435 U.S. 765, 98 S.Ct. 1407, 55 L.Ed.2d 707, reaffirmed the First Amendment principle that the Government cannot restrict political speech based on the speaker's corporate identity by [reasoning that] that the Government lacks the power to ban corporations from speaking.

3

Austin "uph[eld] a direct restriction on the independent expenditure of funds for political speech for the first time in [this Court's] history." There, the Michigan Chamber of Commerce sought to use general treasury funds to run a newspaper ad supporting a specific candidate. Michigan law, however, prohibited corporate independent expenditures that supported or opposed any candidate for state office. A violation of the law was punishable as a felony. The Court sustained the speech prohibition.

The *Austin* Court identified a new governmental interest in limiting political speech: an antidistortion interest. *Austin* found a compelling governmental interest in preventing "the corrosive and distorting effects of immense aggregations of wealth that are accumulated with the help of the corporate form and that have little or no correlation to the public's support for the corporation's political ideas."

B

No case before *Austin* had held that Congress could prohibit independent expenditures for political speech based on the speaker's corporate identity.

In its defense of the corporate-speech restrictions in § 441b, the Government notes the antidistortion rationale on which *Austin* and its progeny rest. It [also] argues that two other compelling interests support *Austin*'s holding that corporate expenditure restrictions are constitutional: an anticorruption interest, and a shareholder-protection interest. We consider the three points in turn.

1

Austin's antidistortion rationale cannot support § 441b.

If the antidistortion rationale were to be accepted, it would permit Government to ban political speech simply because the speaker is an association that has taken on the corporate form.

The rule that political speech cannot be limited based on a speaker's wealth is a necessary consequence of the premise that the First Amendment generally prohibits the suppression of political speech based on the speaker's identity.

It is irrelevant for purposes of the First Amendment that corporate funds may "have little or no correlation to the public's support for the corporation's political ideas." All speakers, including individuals and the media, use money amassed from the economic marketplace to fund their speech. The First Amendment protects the resulting speech, even if it was enabled by economic transactions with persons or entities who disagree with the speaker's ideas.

Austin's antidistortion rationale would produce the dangerous, and unacceptable, consequence that Congress could ban political speech of media corporations. Media corporations are now exempt from § 441b's ban on corporate expenditures.

The law's exception for media corporations is, on its own terms, all but an admission of the invalidity of the antidistortion rationale. And the exemption results in a further, separate reason for finding this law invalid: Again by its own terms, the law exempts some corporations but covers others, even though both have the need or the motive to communicate their views. The exemption applies to media corporations owned or controlled by corporations that have diverse and substantial investments and participate in endeavors other than news. So even assuming the most doubtful proposition that a news organization has a right to speak when others do not, the exemption would allow a conglomerate that owns both a media business and an unrelated business to influence or control the media in order to advance its overall business interest. At the same time, some other corporation, with an identical business interest but no media outlet in its ownership structure, would be forbidden to speak or inform the public about the same issue. This differential treatment cannot be squared with the First Amendment.

By suppressing the speech of manifold corporations, both for-profit and nonprofit, the Government prevents their voices and viewpoints from reaching the public and advising voters on which persons or entities are hostile to their interests. Factions will necessarily form in our Republic, but the remedy of "destroying the liberty" of some factions is "worse than the disease." The Federalist No. 10, p. 130 (B. Wright ed.1961) (J. Madison). Factions should be checked by permitting them all to speak and by entrusting the people to judge what is true and what is false.

Even if §441b's expenditure ban were constitutional, wealthy corporations could still lobby elected officials, although smaller corporations may not have the resources to do so. And wealthy individuals and unincorporated associations can spend unlimited amounts on independent expenditures. Yet certain disfavored associations of citizens—those that have taken on the corporate form—are penalized for engaging in the same political speech.

When Government seeks to use its full power, including the criminal law, to command where a person may get his or her information or what distrusted source he or she may not hear, it uses censorship to control thought. This is unlawful. The First Amendment confirms the freedom to think for ourselves.

2

The Government falls back on the argument that corporate political speech can be banned in order to prevent corruption or its appearance. The *Buckley* Court, sustained limits on direct contributions in order to ensure against the reality or appearance of corruption. That case did not extend this rationale to independent expenditures, and the Court does not do so here.

Limits on independent expenditures, such as §441b, have a chilling effect extending well beyond the Government's interest in preventing *quid pro quo* corruption. The anti-corruption interest is not sufficient to displace the speech here in question. We now conclude that independent expenditures, including those made by corporations, do not give rise to corruption or the appearance of corruption.

Citizens United has not made direct contributions to candidates, and it has not suggested that the Court should reconsider whether contribution limits should be subjected to rigorous First Amendment scrutiny.

When *Buckley* identified a sufficiently important governmental interest in preventing corruption or the appearance of corruption, that interest was limited to *quid pro quo* corruption. The fact that speakers may have influence over or access to elected officials does not mean that these officials are corrupt.

The appearance of influence or access, furthermore, will not cause the electorate to lose faith in our democracy. By definition, an independent expenditure is political speech presented to the electorate that is not coordinated with a candidate. The fact that a corporation, or any other speaker, is willing to spend money to try to persuade voters presupposes that the people have the ultimate influence over elected officials. This is inconsistent with any suggestion that the electorate will refuse " 'to take part in democratic governance'" because of additional political speech made by a corporation or any other speaker.

Caperton v. A.T. Massey Coal Co., 556 U.S. 868 (2009), is not to the contrary. *Caperton* held that a judge was required to recuse himself "when a person with a personal stake in a particular case had a significant and disproportionate influence in placing the judge on the case by raising funds or directing the judge's election campaign when the case was pending or imminent." The remedy of recusal was based on a litigant's due process right to a fair trial before an unbiased judge. *Caperton* 's holding was limited to the rule that the judge must be recused, not that the litigant's political speech could be banned.

This case is about independent expenditures. Here Congress has created categorical bans on speech that are asymmetrical to preventing *quid pro quo* corruption.

3

The Government contends further that corporate independent expenditures can be limited because of its interest in protecting dissenting shareholders from being compelled to fund corporate political speech. This asserted interest, like *Austin*'s antidistortion rationale, would allow the Government to ban the political speech even of media corporations. Assume, for example, that a shareholder of a corporation that owns a newspaper disagrees with the political views the newspaper expresses. Under the Government's view, that potential disagreement could give the Government the authority to restrict the media corporation's political speech. The First Amendment does not allow that power.

Those reasons are sufficient to reject this shareholder-protection interest; and, moreover, the statute is both underinclusive and overinclusive. As to the first, if Congress had been seeking to protect dissenting shareholders, it would not have banned corporate speech in only certain media within 30 or 60 days before an election. A dissenting shareholder's interests would be implicated by speech in any media at any time. As to the second, the statute is overinclusive because it covers all corporations, including nonprofit corporations and for-profit corporations with only single shareholders. As to other corporations, the remedy is not to restrict speech but to consider and explore other regulatory mechanisms. The regulatory mechanism here, based on speech, contravenes the First Amendment.

C

Our precedent is to be respected unless the most convincing of reasons demonstrates that adherence to it puts us on a course that is sure error. "Beyond workability, the relevant factors in deciding whether to adhere to the principle of *stare decisis* include the antiquity of the precedent, the reliance interests at stake, and of course whether the decision was well reasoned."

These considerations counsel in favor of rejecting *Austin.* "This Court has not hesitated to overrule decisions offensive to the First Amendment."

For the reasons above, it must be concluded that *Austin* was not well reasoned. The Government defends *Austin,* relying almost entirely on "the quid pro quo interest, the corruption interest or the shareholder interest," and not *Austin*'s expressed antidistortion rationale. When neither party defends the reasoning of a precedent, the principle of adhering to that precedent through *stare decisis* is diminished.

Austin is undermined by experience since its announcement. Our Nation's speech dynamic is changing, and informative voices should not have to circumvent onerous restrictions to exercise their First Amendment rights.

Due consideration leads to this conclusion: *Austin*, 494 U.S. 652, 110 S.Ct. 1391, 108 L.Ed.2d 652, should be and now is overruled. We return to the principle established in *Buckley* and *Bellotti* that the Government may not suppress political speech on the basis of the speaker's corporate identity. No sufficient governmental interest justifies limits on the political speech of nonprofit or for-profit corporations.

D

Austin is overruled, so it provides no basis for allowing the Government to limit corporate independent expenditures. Section 441b's restrictions on corporate independent expenditures are therefore invalid and cannot be applied to *Hillary*.

Given our conclusion we are further required to overrule the part of *McConnell* that upheld BCRA § 203's extension of § 441b's restrictions on corporate independent expenditures.

It is so ordered.

Chief Justice Roberts, with whom Justice Alito joins, concurring.

The Government urges us in this case to uphold a direct prohibition on political speech. It asks us to embrace a theory of the First Amendment that would allow censorship not only of television and radio broadcasts, but of pamphlets, posters, the Internet, and virtually any other medium that corporations and unions might find useful in expressing their views on matters of public concern. Its theory, if accepted, would empower the Government to prohibit newspapers from running editorials or opinion pieces supporting or opposing candidates for office, so long as the newspapers were owned by corporations—as the major ones are. First Amendment rights could be confined to individuals, subverting the vibrant public discourse that is at the foundation of our democracy.

The Court properly rejects that theory, and I join its opinion in full. The First Amendment protects more than just the individual on a soapbox and the lonely pamphleteer. I write separately to address the important principles of judicial restraint and *stare decisis* implicated in this case.

[The remainder of Chief Justice Roberts concurrence is omitted wherein he argues chiefly that the principle of *stare decisis* is an important one, but should not be followed as to *Austin* in this particular instance. More specifically, Justice Roberts argues that the Government's "two new and potentially expansive interests—the need to prevent actual or apparent *quid pro quo* corruption, and the need to protect corporate shareholders," are not valid interests to uphold the result in Austin, because these interests were not part of the reasoning that the Court used to reach its holding in *Austin*. Eds.]

Justice Scalia, with whom Justice Alito joins, and with whom Justice Thomas joins in part, concurring.

I join the opinion of the Court.

I write separately to address Justice STEVENS' discussion of "*Original Understandings,*" (opinion concurring in part and dissenting in part) (hereinafter referred to as the dissent). This section of the dissent purports to show that today's decision is not supported by the original understanding of the First Amendment. The dissent attempts this demonstration, however, in splendid isolation from the text of the First Amendment. It never shows why "the freedom of speech" that was the right of Englishmen did not include the freedom to speak in association with other individuals, including association in the corporate form. To be sure, in 1791 (as now) corporations could pursue only the objectives set forth in their charters; but the dissent provides no evidence that their speech in the pursuit of those objectives could be censored.

Instead of taking this straightforward approach to determining the Amendment's meaning, the dissent embarks on a detailed exploration of the Framers' views about the "role of corporations in society." The Framers didn't like corporations, the dissent concludes, and therefore it follows (as night the day) that corporations had no rights of free speech. Of course the Framers' personal affection or disaffection for corporations is relevant only insofar as it can be thought to be reflected in the understood meaning of the text they enacted — not, as the dissent suggests, as a freestanding substitute for that text. But the dissent's distortion of proper analysis is even worse than that. Though faced with a constitutional text that makes no distinction between types of speakers, the dissent feels no necessity to provide even an isolated statement from the founding era to the effect that corporations are *not* covered, but places the burden on petitioners to bring forward statements showing that they *are* ("there is not a scintilla of evidence to support the notion that anyone believed [the First Amendment] would preclude regulatory distinctions based on the corporate form.").

Despite the corporation-hating quotations the dissent has dredged up, it is far from clear that by the end of the 18th century corporations were despised. If so, how came there to be so many of them? The dissent's statement that there were few business corporations during the eighteenth century — "only a few hundred during all of the 18th century" — is misleading. There were approximately 335 charters issued to business corporations in the United States by the end of the 18th century. This was a "considerable extension of corporate enterprise in the field of business," and represented "unprecedented growth." Moreover, what seems like a small number by today's standards surely does not indicate the relative importance of corporations when the Nation was considerably smaller. As I have previously noted, "[b]y the end of the eighteenth century the corporation was a familiar figure in American economic life." *McConnell v. Federal Election Comm'n*, 540 U.S. 93, 256, 124 S.Ct. 619, 157 L.Ed.2d 491 (2003) (SCALIA, J., concurring in part, concurring in judgment in part, and dissenting in part) (quoting C. Cooke, Corporation Trust and Company 92 (1951) (hereinafter Cooke)).

Even if we thought it proper to apply the dissent's approach of excluding from First Amendment coverage what the Founders disliked, and even if we agreed that the Founders disliked founding-era corporations; modern corporations might not qualify for exclusion. Most of the Founders' resentment towards corporations was directed at the state-granted monopoly privileges that individually chartered corporations enjoyed. Modern corporations do not have such privileges, and would probably have been favored by most of our enterprising Founders — excluding, perhaps, Thomas Jefferson and others favoring perpetuation of an agrarian society.

The lack of a textual exception for speech by corporations cannot be explained on the ground that such organizations did not exist or did not speak. Both corporations and voluntary associations actively petitioned the Government and expressed their views in newspapers and pamphlets. The dissent offers no evidence — none whatever — that the First Amendment's unqualified text was originally understood to exclude such associational speech from its protection....

The dissent says that when the Framers "constitutionalized the right to free speech in the First Amendment, it was the free speech of individual Americans that they had in mind." That is no doubt true. All the provisions of the Bill of Rights set forth the rights of individual men and women—not, for example, of trees or polar bears. But the individual person's right to speak includes the right to speak *in association with other individual persons.* Surely the dissent does not believe that speech by the Republican Party or the Democratic Party can be censored because it is not the speech of "an individual American." It is the speech of many individual Americans, who have associated in a common cause, giving the leadership of the party the right to speak on their behalf. The association of individuals in a business corporation is no different—or at least it cannot be denied the right to speak on the simplistic ground that it is not "an individual American."

The First Amendment is written in terms of "speech," not speakers. Its text offers no foothold for excluding any category of speaker, from single individuals to partnerships of individuals, to unincorporated associations of individuals, to incorporated associations of individuals—and the dissent offers no evidence about the original meaning of the text to support any such exclusion. We are therefore simply left with the question whether the speech at issue in this case is "speech" covered by the First Amendment. No one says otherwise. A documentary film critical of a potential Presidential candidate is core political speech, and its nature as such does not change simply because it was funded by a corporation. Nor does the character of that funding produce any reduction whatever in the "inherent worth of the speech" and "its capacity for informing the public," *First Nat. Bank of Boston v. Bellotti,* 435 U.S. 765, 777, 98 S.Ct. 1407, 55 L.Ed.2d 707 (1978). Indeed, to exclude or impede corporate speech is to muzzle the principal agents of the modern free economy. We should celebrate rather than condemn the addition of this speech to the public debate.

Justice Stevens, with whom Justice Ginsburg, Justice Breyer, and Justice Sotomayor join, concurring in part and dissenting in part.

The real issue in this case concerns how, not if, the appellant may finance its electioneering. Citizens United is a wealthy nonprofit corporation that runs a political action committee (PAC) with millions of dollars in assets. Under the Bipartisan Campaign Reform Act of 2002 (BCRA), it could have used those assets to televise and promote *Hillary: The Movie* wherever and whenever it wanted to. It also could have spent unrestricted sums to broadcast *Hillary* at any time other than the 30 days before the last primary election. Neither Citizens United's nor any other corporation's speech has been "banned." All that the parties dispute is whether Citizens United had a right to use the funds in its general treasury to pay for broadcasts during the 30-day period. The notion that the First Amendment dictates an affirmative answer to that question is, in my judgment, profoundly misguided. Even more misguided is the notion that the Court must rewrite the law relating to campaign expenditures by *for-profit* corporations and unions to decide this case.

The basic premise underlying the Court's ruling is its iteration, and constant reiteration, of the proposition that the First Amendment bars regulatory distinctions based on a speaker's identity, including its "identity" as a corporation. While that glittering generality has rhetorical appeal, it is not a correct statement of the law. Nor does it tell us when a corporation may engage in electioneering that some of its shareholders oppose. It does not even resolve the specific question whether Citizens United may be required to finance some of its messages with the money in its PAC. The conceit that corporations must be treated identically to natural persons in the political sphere is not only inaccurate but also inadequate to justify the Court's disposition of this case.

In the context of election to public office, the distinction between corporate and human speakers is significant. Although they make enormous contributions to our society, corporations are not actually members of it. They cannot vote or run for office. Because they may be managed and controlled by nonresidents, their interests may conflict in fundamental respects with the interests of eligible voters. The financial resources, legal structure, and instrumental orientation of corporations raise legitimate concerns about their role in the electoral process. Our lawmakers have a compelling constitutional basis, if not also a democratic duty, to take measures designed to guard against the potentially deleterious effects of corporate spending in local and national races.

The majority's approach to corporate electioneering marks a dramatic break from our past. Congress has placed special limitations on campaign spending by corporations ever since the passage of the Tillman Act in 1907. We have unanimously concluded that this "reflects a permissible assessment of the dangers posed by those entities to the electoral process," *FEC v. National Right to Work Comm.*, 459 U.S. 197, 209, 103 S.Ct. 552, 74 L.Ed.2d 364 (1982) *(NRWC),* and have accepted the "legislative judgment that the special characteristics of the corporate structure require particularly careful regulation," *id.,* at 209–210, 103 S.Ct. 552. The Court today rejects a century of history when it treats the distinction between corporate and individual campaign spending as an invidious novelty born of *Austin v. Michigan Chamber of Commerce.* Relying largely on individual dissenting opinions, the majority blazes through our precedents, overruling or disavowing a body of case law.

Although I concur in the Court's decision to sustain BCRA's disclosure provisions and join Part IV of its opinion, I emphatically dissent from its principal holding.

I

The Court's ruling threatens to undermine the integrity of elected institutions across the Nation. The path it has taken to reach its outcome will, I fear, do damage to this institution. Before turning to the question whether to overrule *Austin* and part of *McConnell,* it is important to explain why the Court should not be deciding that question.

Scope of the Case

[According to Justice Stevens, the following three grounds could have been used by the Court to reach the same holding:

(1) First, "the Court could have ruled, on statutory grounds, that a feature-length film distributed through video-on-demand does not qualify as an 'electioneering communication' under § 203 of BCRA."

(2) Second, "the Court could have expanded the *MCFL* exemption to cover § 501(c)(4) nonprofits that accept only a *de minimis* amount of money from for-profit corporations."

(3) Finally, "the Court could have easily limited the breadth of its constitutional holding had it declined to adopt the novel notion that speakers and speech acts must always be treated identically — and always spared expenditures restrictions — in the political realm." — Eds.]

III

The novelty of the Court's procedural dereliction and its approach to *stare decisis* is matched by the novelty of its ruling on the merits. The ruling rests on several premises. First, the Court claims that *Austin* and *McConnell* have "banned" corporate speech. Second, it claims that the First Amendment precludes regulatory distinctions based on speaker identity, including the speaker's identity as a corporation. Third, it claims that *Austin* and *McConnell* were radical outliers in our First Amendment tradition and our campaign finance jurisprudence. Each of these claims is wrong.

The So-Called "Ban"

Pervading the Court's analysis is the ominous image of a "categorical ba[n]" on corporate speech. Indeed, the majority invokes the specter of a "ban" on nearly every page of its opinion. This characterization is highly misleading, and needs to be corrected.

In fact it already has been. Our cases have repeatedly pointed out that, "[c]ontrary to the [majority's] critical assumptions," the statutes upheld in *Austin* and *McConnell* do "not impose an *absolute* ban on all forms of corporate political spending." *Austin*, 494 U.S., at 660, 110 S.Ct. 1391; see also *McConnell*, 540 U.S., at 203–204, 124 S.Ct. 619; *Beaumont*, 539 U.S., at 162–163, 123 S.Ct. 2200. For starters, both statutes provide exemptions for PACs, separate segregated funds established by a corporation for political purposes. "The ability to form and administer separate segregated funds," we observed in *McConnell*, "has provided corporations and unions with a constitutionally sufficient opportunity to engage in express advocacy. That has been this Court's unanimous view."

Under BCRA, any corporation's "stockholders and their families and its executive or administrative personnel and their families" can pool their resources to finance electioneering communications. A significant and growing number of corporations avail themselves of this option; during the most recent election cycle, corporate and union PACs raised nearly a billion dollars. Administering a PAC entails some administrative burden, but so does complying with the disclaimer, disclosure, and reporting requirements that the Court today upholds and no one has suggested that the burden is severe for a sophisticated for-profit corporation. To the extent the majority is worried about this issue, it is important to keep in mind that we have no record to show how substantial the burden really is, just the majority's own unsupported factfinding. Like all other natural persons, every shareholder of every corporation remains entirely free under *Austin* and *McConnell* to do however much electioneering she pleases outside of the corporate form. The owners of a "mom & pop" store can simply place ads in their own names, rather than the store's.

The laws upheld in *Austin* and *McConnell* leave open many additional avenues for corporations' political speech. Consider the statutory provision we are ostensibly evaluating in this case, BCRA § 203. It has no application to genuine issue advertising—a category of corporate speech Congress found to be far more substantial than election-related advertising—or to Internet, telephone, and print advocacy. Like numerous statutes, it exempts media companies' news stories, commentaries, and editorials from its electioneering restrictions, in recognition of the unique role played by the institutional press in sustaining public debate. It also allows corporations to spend unlimited sums on political communications with their executives and shareholders, to fund additional PAC activity through trade associations, to distribute voting guides and voting records, to underwrite voter registration and voter turnout activities, to host fundraising events for candidates within certain limits, and to publicly endorse candidates through a press release and press conference.

At the time Citizens United brought this lawsuit, the only types of speech that could be regulated under § 203 were: (1) broadcast, cable, or satellite communications; (2) capable of reaching at least 50,000 persons in the relevant electorate; (3) made within 30 days of a primary or 60 days of a general federal election; (4) by a labor union or a non-*MCFL*, nonmedia corporation; (5) paid for with general treasury funds; and (6) "susceptible of no reasonable interpretation other than as an appeal to vote for or against a specific candidate."

In many ways, § 203 functions as a source restriction or a time, place, and manner restriction. It applies in a viewpoint-neutral fashion to a narrow subset of advocacy messages about clearly identified candidates for federal office, made during discrete time periods through discrete channels. In the case at hand, all Citizens United needed to do to broadcast *Hillary* right before the primary was to abjure business contributions or use the funds in its PAC, which by its own account is "one of the most active conservative PACs in America."

Laws such as § 203 target a class of communications that is especially likely to corrupt the political process, that is at least one degree removed from the views of individual citizens, and that may not even reflect the views of those who pay for it. Such laws burden political speech, and that is always a serious matter, demanding careful scrutiny. But the majority's incessant talk of a "ban" aims at a straw man.

Identity-Based Distinctions

The second pillar of the Court's opinion is its assertion that "the Government cannot restrict political speech based on the speaker's ... identity." The case on which it relies for this proposition is *First Nat. Bank of Boston v. Bellotti*, 435 U.S. 765, 98 S.Ct. 1407, 55 L.Ed.2d 707 (1978). As I shall explain, the holding in that case was far narrower than the Court implies. Like its paeans to unfettered discourse, the Court's denunciation of identity-based distinctions may have rhetorical appeal but it obscures reality.

"Our jurisprudence over the past 216 years has rejected an absolutist interpretation" of the First Amendment. The First Amendment provides that "Congress shall make no law ... abridging the freedom of speech, or of the press." Apart perhaps from measures designed to protect the press, that text might seem to permit no distinctions of any kind. Yet in a variety of contexts, we have held that speech can be regulated differentially on account of the speaker's identity, when identity is understood in categorical or institutional terms. The Government routinely places special restrictions on the speech rights of students, prisoners, members of the Armed Forces, foreigners, and its own employees. When such restrictions are justified by a legitimate governmental interest they do not necessarily raise constitutional problems. In contrast to the blanket rule that the majority espouses, our cases recognize that the Government's interests may be more or less compelling with respect to different classes of speakers.

The free speech guarantee thus does not render every other public interest an illegitimate basis for qualifying a speaker's autonomy; society could scarcely function if it did. It is fair to say that our First Amendment doctrine has "frowned on" certain identity-based distinctions, particularly those that may reflect invidious discrimination or preferential treatment of a politically powerful group. But it is simply incorrect to suggest that we have prohibited all legislative distinctions based on identity or content. Not even close.

The election context is distinctive in many ways, and the Court, of course, is right that the First Amendment closely guards political speech. But in this context, too, the authority of legislatures to enact viewpoint-neutral regulations based on content and identity is well settled. We have, for example, allowed state-run broadcasters to exclude independent candidates from televised debates. We have upheld statutes that prohibit the distribution or display of campaign materials near a polling place. Although we have not reviewed them directly, we have never cast doubt on laws that place special restrictions on campaign spending by foreign nationals. And we have consistently approved laws that bar Government employees, but not others, from contributing to or participating in political activities. These statutes burden the political expression of one class of speakers, namely, civil servants. Yet we have sustained them on the basis of longstanding practice and Congress' reasoned judgment that certain regulations which leave "untouched full participation … in political decisions at the ballot box," *Civil Service Comm'n v. Letter Carriers,* 413 U.S. 548, 556, 93 S.Ct. 2880, 37 L.Ed.2d 796 (1973) (internal quotation marks omitted), help ensure that public officials are "sufficiently free from improper influences," *id.,* at 564, 93 S.Ct. 2880, and that "confidence in the system of representative Government is not … eroded to a disastrous extent," *id.,* at 565, 93 S.Ct. 2880.

The same logic applies to this case with additional force because it is the identity of corporations, rather than individuals, that the Legislature has taken into account. As we have unanimously observed, legislatures are entitled to decide "that the special characteristics of the corporate structure require particularly careful regulation" in an electoral context. *NRWC,* 459 U.S., at 209–210, 103 S.Ct. 552. Not only has the distinctive potential of corporations to corrupt the electoral process long been recognized, but within the area of campaign finance, corporate spending is also "furthest from the core of political expression, since corporations' First Amendment speech and association interests are derived largely from those of their members and of the public in receiving information," *Beaumont,* 539 U.S., at 161, n. 8, 123 S.Ct. 2200. Campaign finance distinctions based on corporate identity tend to be less worrisome, in other words, because the "speakers" are not natural persons, much less members of our political community, and the governmental interests are of the highest order. Furthermore, when corporations, as a class, are distinguished from noncorporations, as a class, there is a lesser risk that regulatory distinctions will reflect invidious discrimination or political favoritism.

In short, the Court dramatically overstates its critique of identity-based distinctions, without ever explaining why corporate identity demands the same treatment as individual identity. Only the most wooden approach to the First Amendment could justify the unprecedented line it seeks to draw.

Our First Amendment Tradition

A third fulcrum of the Court's opinion is the idea that *Austin* and *McConnell* are radical outliers, "aberration[s]," in our First Amendment tradition. The Court has it exactly backwards. It is today's holding that is the radical departure from what had been settled First Amendment law.

1. *Original Understandings*

Let us start from the beginning. The Court invokes "ancient First Amendment principles," and original understandings, to defend today's ruling, yet it makes only a perfunctory attempt to ground its analysis in the principles or understandings of those who drafted and ratified the Amendment. Perhaps this is because there is not a scintilla of evidence to support the notion that anyone believed it would preclude regulatory distinctions based on the corporate form. To the extent that the Framers' views are discernible and relevant to the disposition of this case, they would appear to cut strongly against the majority's position.

This is not only because the Framers and their contemporaries conceived of speech more narrowly than we now think of it, but also because they held very different views about the nature of the First Amendment right and the role of corporations in society. Those few corporations that existed at the founding were authorized by grant of a special legislative charter. Corporate sponsors would petition the legislature, and the legislature, if amenable, would issue a charter that specified the corporation's powers and purposes and "authoritatively fixed the scope and content of corporate organization," including "the internal structure of the corporation." J. Hurst, The Legitimacy of the Business Corporation in the Law of the United States 1780–1970, pp. 15–16 (1970) (reprint 2004). Corporations were created, supervised, and conceptualized as quasi-public entities, "designed to serve a social function for the state." Handlin & Handlin, Origin of the American Business Corporation, 5 J. Econ. Hist. 1, 22 (1945). It was "assumed that [they] were legally privileged organizations that had to be closely scrutinized by the legislature because their purposes had to be made consistent with public welfare." R. Seavoy, Origins of the American Business Corporation, 1784–1855, p. 5 (1982).

The Framers thus took it as a given that corporations could be comprehensively regulated in the service of the public welfare. Unlike our colleagues, they had little trouble distinguishing corporations from human beings, and when they constitutionalized the right to free speech in the First Amendment, it was the free speech of individual Americans that they had in mind. While individuals might join together to exercise their speech rights, business corporations, at least, were plainly not seen as facilitating such associational or expressive ends. Even "the notion that business corporations could invoke the First Amendment would probably have been quite a novelty," given that "at the time, the legitimacy of every corporate activity was thought to rest entirely in a concession of the sovereign." Shelledy, Autonomy, Debate, and Corporate Speech, 18 Hastings Const. L.Q. 541, 578 (1991); cf. *Trustees of Dartmouth College v. Woodward,* 4 Wheat. 518, 636, 4 L.Ed. 629 (1819) (Marshall, C.J.) ("A corporation is an artificial being, invisible, intangible, and existing only in contemplation of law. Being the mere creature of law, it possesses only those properties which the charter of its creation confers upon it"); Eule, Promoting Speaker Diversity: Austin and Metro Broadcasting, 1990 S.Ct. Rev. 105, 129 ("The framers of the First Amendment could scarcely have anticipated its application to the corporation form. That, of course, ought not to be dispositive. What is compelling, however, is an understanding of who was supposed to be the beneficiary of the free speech guaranty—the individual"). In light of these background practices and understandings, it seems to me implausible that the Framers believed "the freedom of speech" would extend equally to all corporate speakers, much less that it would preclude legislatures from taking limited measures to guard against corporate capture of elections.

The Court observes that the Framers drew on diverse intellectual sources, communicated through newspapers, and aimed to provide greater freedom of speech than had existed in England. From these (accurate) observations, the Court concludes that "[t]he First Amendment was certainly not understood to condone the suppression of political speech in society's most salient media." This conclusion is far from certain, given that many historians believe the Framers were focused on prior restraints on publication and did not understand the First Amendment to "prevent the subsequent punishment of such [publications] as may be deemed contrary to the public welfare." Yet, even if the majority's conclusion were correct, it would tell us only that the First Amendment was understood to protect political speech *in* certain media. It would tell us little about whether the Amendment was understood to protect general treasury electioneering expenditures *by* corporations, *and to what extent.*

Justice Scalia criticizes the foregoing discussion for failing to adduce statements from the founding era showing that corporations were understood to be excluded from the First Amendment's free speech guarantee. Of course, Justice Scalia adduces no statements to suggest the contrary proposition, or even to suggest that the contrary proposition better reflects the kind of right that the drafters and ratifiers of the Free Speech Clause thought they were enshrining. Although Justice Scalia makes a perfectly sensible argument that an individual's right to speak entails a right to speak with others for a common cause, he does not explain why those two rights must be precisely identical, or why that principle applies to electioneering by corporations that serve no "common cause." Nothing in his account dislodges my basic point that members of the founding generation held a cautious view of corporate power and a narrow view of corporate rights (not that they "despised" corporations), and that they conceptualized speech in individualistic terms. If no prominent Framer bothered to articulate that corporate speech would have lesser status than individual speech, that may well be because the contrary proposition—if not also the very notion of "corporate speech"—was inconceivable.

In any event, the text only leads us back to the questions who or what is guaranteed "the freedom of speech," and, just as critically, what that freedom consists of and under what circumstances it may be limited. Justice Scalia appears to believe that because corporations are created and utilized by individuals, it follows (as night the day) that their electioneering must be equally protected by the First Amendment and equally immunized from expenditure limits. That conclusion certainly does not follow as a logical matter, and Justice Scalia fails to explain why the original public meaning leads it to follow as a matter of interpretation.

2. Legislative and Judicial Interpretation

A century of more recent history puts to rest any notion that today's ruling is faithful to our First Amendment tradition. At the federal level, the express distinction between corporate and individual political spending on elections stretches back to 1907, when Congress passed the Tillman Act, banning all corporate contributions to candidates. The Senate Report on the legislation observed that "[t]he evils of the use of [corporate] money in connection with political elections are so generally recognized that the committee deems it unnecessary to make any argument in favor of the general purpose of this measure. It is in the interest of good government and calculated to promote purity in the selection of public officials." S.Rep. No. 3056, 59th Cong., 1st Sess., 2 (1906). President Roosevelt, in his 1905 annual message to Congress, declared:

" 'All contributions by corporations to any political committee or for any political purpose should be forbidden by law; directors should not be permitted to use stockholders' money for such purposes; and, moreover, a prohibition of this kind would be, as far as it went, an effective method of stopping the evils aimed at in corrupt practices acts.' " *United States v. Automobile Workers*, 352 U.S. 567, 572, 77 S.Ct. 529, 1 L.Ed.2d 563 (1957) (quoting 40 Cong. Rec. 96).

The Court has surveyed the history leading up to the Tillman Act several times, and I will refrain from doing so again. It is enough to say that the Act was primarily driven by two pressing concerns: first, the enormous power corporations had come to wield in federal elections, with the accompanying threat of both actual corruption and a public perception of corruption; and second, a respect for the interest of shareholders and members in preventing the use of their money to support candidates they opposed.

Buckley famously (or infamously) distinguished direct contributions from independent expenditures, *id.,* at 58–59, 96 S.Ct. 612, but its silence on corporations only reinforced the understanding that corporate expenditures could be treated differently from individual expenditures. "Since our decision in *Buckley,* Congress' power to prohibit corporations and unions from using funds in their treasuries to finance advertisements expressly advocating the election or defeat of candidates in federal elections has been firmly embedded in our law." *McConnell,* 540 U.S., at 203, 124 S.Ct. 619.

When we asked in *McConnell* "whether a compelling governmental interest justifie[d]" § 203, we found the question "easily answered": "We have repeatedly sustained legislation aimed at 'the corrosive and distorting effects of immense aggregations of wealth that are accumulated with the help of the corporate form and that have little or no correlation to the public's support for the corporation's political ideas.'" 540 U.S., at 205, 124 S.Ct. 619 (quoting *Austin*, 494 U.S., at 660, 110 S.Ct. 1391). These precedents "represent respect for the legislative judgment that the special characteristics of the corporate structure require particularly careful regulation." 540 U.S., at 205, 124 S.Ct. 619. BCRA, we found, is faithful to the compelling governmental interests in " 'preserving the integrity of the electoral process, preventing corruption, … sustaining the active, alert responsibility of the individual citizen in a democracy for the wise conduct of the government,'" and maintaining " 'the individual citizen's confidence in government.'" 540 U.S., at 206–207, n. 88, 124 S.Ct. 619 (quoting *Bellotti*, 435 U.S., at 788–789, 98 S.Ct. 1407. What made the answer even easier than it might have been otherwise was the option to form PACs, which give corporations, at the least, "a constitutionally sufficient opportunity to engage in" independent expenditures. 540 U.S., at 203, 124 S.Ct. 619.

3. *Buckley and Bellotti*

Over the course of the past century Congress has demonstrated a recurrent need to regulate corporate participation in candidate elections to " '[p]reserv[e] the integrity of the electoral process, preven[t] corruption, … sustai[n] the active, alert responsibility of the individual citizen,'" protect the expressive interests of shareholders, and " '[p]reserv [e] … the individual citizen's confidence in government.'" *McConnell*, 540 U.S., at 206–207, n. 88, 124 S.Ct. 619 (quoting *Bellotti*, 435 U.S., at 788–789, 98 S.Ct. 1407. These understandings provided the combined impetus behind the Tillman Act in 1907, the Taft-Hartley Act in 1947, FECA in 1971 and BCRA in 2002. Continuously for over 100 years, this line of "[c]ampaign finance reform has been a series of reactions to documented threats to electoral integrity obvious to any voter, posed by large sums of money from corporate or union treasuries." *WRTL*, 551 U.S., at 522, 127 S.Ct. 2652 (Souter, J., dissenting). Time and again, we have recognized these realities in approving measures that Congress and the States have taken. None of the cases the majority cites is to the contrary. The only thing new about *Austin* was the dissent, with its stunning failure to appreciate the legitimacy of interests recognized in the name of democratic integrity.

IV

Having explained why this is not an appropriate case in which to revisit *Austin* and *McConnell* and why these decisions sit perfectly well with "First Amendment principles," I come at last to the interests that are at stake. The majority recognizes that *Austin* and *McConnell* may be defended on anticorruption, antidistortion, and shareholder protection rationales. It badly errs both in explaining the nature of these rationales, which overlap and complement each other, and in applying them to the case at hand.

1. *The Anticorruption Interest*

Undergirding the majority's approach to the merits is the claim that the only "sufficiently important governmental interest in preventing corruption or the appearance of corruption" is one that is "limited to *quid pro quo* corruption." *Ante*, at 909–910. This is the same "crabbed view of corruption" that was espoused by Justice Kennedy in *McConnell* and squarely rejected by the Court in that case. While it is true that we have not always spoken about corruption in a clear or consistent voice, the approach taken by the majority cannot be right, in my judgment. It disregards our constitutional history and the fundamental demands of a democratic society.

On numerous occasions we have recognized Congress' legitimate interest in preventing the money that is spent on elections from exerting an " 'undue influence on an officeholder's judgment' " and from creating " 'the appearance of such influence,' " beyond the sphere of *quid pro quo* relationships. Corruption can take many forms. Bribery may be the paradigm case. But the difference between selling a vote and selling access is a matter of degree, not kind. And selling access is not qualitatively different from giving special preference to those who spent money on one's behalf. Corruption operates along a spectrum, and the majority's apparent belief that *quid pro quo* arrangements can be neatly demarcated from other improper influences does not accord with the theory or reality of politics. It certainly does not accord with the record Congress developed in passing BCRA, a record that stands as a remarkable testament to the energy and ingenuity with which corporations, unions, lobbyists, and politicians may go about scratching each other's backs—and which amply supported Congress' determination to target a limited set of especially destructive practices.

The District Court that adjudicated the initial challenge to BCRA pored over this record. In a careful analysis, Judge Kollar-Kotelly made numerous findings about the corrupting consequences of corporate and union independent expenditures in the years preceding BCRA's passage. See *McConnell*, 251 F.Supp.2d, at 555–560, 622–625; see also *id.*, at 804–805, 813, n. 143 (Leon, J.) (indicating agreement). As summarized in her own words:

> "The factual findings of the Court illustrate that corporations and labor unions routinely notify Members of Congress as soon as they air electioneering communications relevant to the Members' elections. The record also indicates that Members express appreciation to organizations for the airing of these election-related advertisements. Indeed, Members of Congress are particularly grateful when negative issue advertisements are run by these organizations, leaving the candidates free to run positive advertisements and be seen as 'above the fray.' Political consultants testify that campaigns are quite aware of who is running advertisements on the candidate's behalf, when they are being run, and where they are being run. Likewise, a prominent lobbyist testifies that these organizations use issue advocacy as a means to influence various Members of Congress.

> "The Findings also demonstrate that Members of Congress seek to have corporations and unions run these advertisements on their behalf. The Findings show that Members suggest that corporations or individuals make donations to interest groups with the understanding that the money contributed to these groups will assist the Member in a campaign. After the election, these organizations often seek credit for their support.... Finally, a large majority of Americans (80%) are of the view that corporations and other organizations that engage in electioneering communications, which benefit specific elected officials, receive special consideration from those officials when matters arise that affect these corporations and organizations." *Id.*, at 623–624.

Many of the relationships of dependency found by Judge Kollar-Kotelly seemed to have a *quid pro quo* basis, but other arrangements were more subtle. Her analysis shows the great difficulty in delimiting the precise scope of the *quid pro quo* category, as well as the adverse consequences that *all* such arrangements may have. There are threats of corruption that are far more destructive to a democratic society than the odd bribe. Yet the majority's understanding of corruption would leave lawmakers impotent to address all but the most discrete abuses.

Our "undue influence" cases have allowed the American people to cast a wider net through legislative experiments designed to ensure, to some minimal extent, "that officeholders will decide issues ... on the merits or the desires of their constituencies," and not "according to the wishes of those who have made large financial contributions"— or expenditures—"valued by the officeholder." *McConnell,* 540 U.S., at 153, 124 S.Ct. 619. When private interests are seen TO EXERT OUTSIZED CONTROL OVER officeholders solely on account of the money spent on their campaigns, the result can depart so thoroughly "from what is pure or correct" in the conduct of Government, that it amounts to a "subversion ... of the electoral process," *Automobile Workers,* 352 U.S., at 575, 77 S.Ct. 529. At stake in the legislative efforts to address this threat is therefore not only the legitimacy and quality of Government but also the public's faith therein, not only "the capacity of this democracy to represent its constituents [but also] the confidence of its citizens in their capacity to govern themselves," *WRTL,* 551 U.S., at 507, 127 S.Ct. 2652 (Souter, J., dissenting). "Take away Congress' authority to regulate the appearance of undue influence and 'the cynical assumption that large donors call the tune could jeopardize the willingness of voters to take part in democratic governance.'" *McConnell,* 540 U.S., at 144, 124 S.Ct. 619 (quoting *Shrink Missouri,* 528 U.S., at 390, 120 S.Ct. 897).

The cluster of interrelated interests threatened by such undue influence and its appearance has been well captured under the rubric of "democratic integrity." *WRTL,* 551 U.S., at 522, 127 S.Ct. 2652 (Souter, J., dissenting). This value has underlined a century of state and federal efforts to regulate the role of corporations in the electoral process.

Unlike the majority's myopic focus on *quid pro quo* scenarios and the free-floating "First Amendment principles" on which it rests so much weight this broader understanding of corruption has deep roots in the Nation's history. "During debates on the earliest [campaign finance] reform acts, the terms 'corruption' and 'undue influence' were used nearly interchangeably." Pasquale, Reclaiming Egalitarianism in the Political Theory of Campaign Finance Reform, 2008 U. Ill. L.Rev. 599, 601. Long before *Buckley,* we appreciated that "[t]o say that Congress is without power to pass appropriate legislation to safeguard ... an election from the improper use of money to influence the result is to deny to the nation in a vital particular the power of self protection." *Burroughs v. United States,* 290 U.S. 534, 545, 54 S.Ct. 287, 78 L.Ed. 484 (1934). And whereas we have no evidence to support the notion that the Framers would have wanted corporations to have the same rights as natural persons in the electoral context, we have ample evidence to suggest that they would have been appalled by the evidence of corruption that Congress unearthed in developing BCRA and that the Court today discounts to irrelevance. It is fair to say that "[t]he Framers were obsessed with corruption," Teachout 348, which they understood to encompass the dependency of public officeholders on private interests, They discussed corruption "more often in the Constitutional Convention than factions, violence, or instability." When they brought our constitutional order into being, the Framers had their minds trained on a threat to republican self-government that this Court has lost sight of.

Quid Pro Quo *Corruption*

A democracy cannot function effectively when its constituent members believe laws are being bought and sold.

In theory, our colleagues accept this much. As applied to BCRA § 203, however, they conclude "[t]he anticorruption interest is not sufficient to displace the speech here in question."

Business corporations must engage the political process in instrumental terms if they are to maximize shareholder value. The unparalleled resources, professional lobbyists, and single-minded focus they bring to this effort, I believed, make *quid pro quo* corruption and its appearance inherently more likely when they (or their conduits or trade groups) spend unrestricted sums on elections.

It is with regret rather than satisfaction that I can now say that time has borne out my concerns. The legislative and judicial proceedings relating to BCRA generated a substantial body of evidence suggesting that, as corporations grew more and more adept at crafting "issue ads" to help or harm a particular candidate, these nominally independent expenditures began to corrupt the political process in a very direct sense. The sponsors of these ads were routinely granted special access after the campaign was over; "candidates and officials knew who their friends were," *McConnell*, 540 U.S., at 129, 124 S.Ct. 619. Many corporate independent expenditures, it seemed, had become essentially interchangeable with direct contributions in their capacity to generate *quid pro quo* arrangements. In an age in which money and television ads are the coin of the campaign realm, it is hardly surprising that corporations deployed these ads to curry favor with, and to gain influence over, public officials.

The majority appears to think it decisive that the BCRA record does not contain "direct examples of votes being exchanged for ... expenditures." It would have been quite remarkable if Congress had created a record detailing such behavior by its own Members. Proving that a specific vote was exchanged for a specific expenditure has always been next to impossible: Elected officials have diverse motivations, and no one will acknowledge that he sold a vote. Yet, even if "[i]ngratiation and access ... are not corruption" themselves, *ibid.*, they are necessary prerequisites to it; they can create both the opportunity for, and the appearance of, *quid pro quo* arrangements. The influx of unlimited corporate money into the electoral realm also creates new opportunities for the mirror image of *quid pro quo* deals: threats, both explicit and implicit. Starting today, corporations with large war chests to deploy on electioneering may find democratically elected bodies becoming much more attuned to their interests. The majority both misreads the facts and draws the wrong conclusions when it suggests that the BCRA record provides "only scant evidence that independent expenditures ... ingratiate," and that, "in any event," none of it matters.

In sum, Judge Kollar-Kotelly found, "[t]he record powerfully demonstrates that electioneering communications paid for with the general treasury funds of labor unions and corporations endears those entities to elected officials in a way that could be perceived by the public as corrupting." *Id.*, at 622–623. She concluded that the Government's interest in preventing the appearance of corruption, as that concept was defined in *Buckley*, was itself sufficient to uphold BCRA § 203.

When the *McConnell* Court affirmed the judgment of the District Court regarding § 203, we did not rest our holding on a narrow notion of *quid pro quo* corruption. Instead we relied on the governmental interest in combating the unique forms of corruption threatened by corporations, as recognized in *Austin*'s antidistortion and shareholder protection rationales, 540 U.S., at 205, 124 S.Ct. 619 (citing *Austin*, 494 U.S., at 660, 110 S.Ct. 1391), as well as the interest in preventing circumvention of contribution limits, 540 U.S., at 128–129, 205, 206, n. 88, 124 S.Ct. 619. Had we felt constrained by the view of today's Court that *quid pro quo* corruption and its appearance are the only interests that count in this field, *ante*, at 903–911, we of course would have looked closely at that issue. And as the analysis by Judge Kollar-Kotelly reflects, it is a very real possibility that we would have found one or both of those interests satisfied and appropriately tailored to them.

The majority's rejection of the *Buckley* anticorruption rationale on the ground that independent corporate expenditures "do not give rise to [*quid pro quo*] corruption or the appearance of corruption," is thus unfair as well as unreasonable. Congress and outside experts have generated significant evidence corroborating this rationale, and the only reason we do not have any of the relevant materials before us is that the Government had no reason to develop a record at trial for a facial challenge the plaintiff had abandoned. The Court cannot both *sua sponte* choose to relitigate *McConnell* on appeal and then complain that the Government has failed to substantiate its case. If our colleagues were really serious about the interest in preventing *quid pro quo* corruption, they would remand to the District Court with instructions to commence evidentiary proceedings.

The insight that even technically independent expenditures can be corrupting in much the same way as direct contributions is bolstered by our decision last year in *Caperton v. A.T. Massey Coal Co.,* 556 U.S. 868, 129 S.Ct. 2252, 173 L.Ed.2d 1208 (2009). In that case, Don Blankenship, the chief executive officer of a corporation with a lawsuit pending before the West Virginia high court, spent large sums on behalf of a particular candidate, Brent Benjamin, running for a seat on that court. "In addition to contributing the $1,000 statutory maximum to Benjamin's campaign committee, Blankenship donated almost $2.5 million to 'And For The Sake Of The Kids,'" a corporation that ran ads targeting Benjamin's opponent. *Id.,* at ——, 129 S.Ct., at 2257. "This was not all. Blankenship spent, in addition, just over $500,000 on independent expenditures ... '"to support ... Brent Benjamin."'" *Id.,* at ——, 129 S.Ct., at 2257 (second alteration in original). Applying its common sense, this Court accepted petitioners' argument that Blankenship's "pivotal role in getting Justice Benjamin elected created a constitutionally intolerable probability of actual bias" when Benjamin later declined to recuse himself from the appeal by Blankenship's corporation. *Id.,* at ——, 129 S.Ct., at 2262. "Though n[o] ... bribe or criminal influence" was involved, we recognized that "Justice Benjamin would nevertheless feel a debt of gratitude to Blankenship for his extraordinary efforts to get him elected." *Ibid.* "The difficulties of inquiring into actual bias," we further noted, "simply underscore the need for objective rules," *id.,* at ——, 129 S.Ct., at 2263—rules which will perforce turn on the appearance of bias rather than its actual existence.

In *Caperton,* then, we accepted the premise that, at least in some circumstances, independent expenditures on candidate elections will raise an intolerable specter of *quid pro quo* corruption. Indeed, this premise struck the Court as so intuitive that it repeatedly referred to Blankenship's spending on behalf of Benjamin—spending that consisted of 99.97% independent expenditures ($3 million) and 0.03% direct contributions ($1,000)— as a "contribution." See, *e.g., id.,* at ——, 129 S.Ct., at 2257 ("The basis for the [recusal] motion was that the justice had received campaign contributions in an extraordinary amount from" Blankenship); *id.,* at ——, 129 S.Ct., at 2258 (referencing "Blankenship's $3 million in contributions"); *id.,* at ——, 129 S.Ct., at 2264 ("Blankenship contributed some $3 million to unseat the incumbent and replace him with Benjamin"); *id.,* at ——, 129 S.Ct., at 2264 ("Blankenship's campaign contributions ... had a significant and disproportionate influence on the electoral outcome"). The reason the Court so thoroughly conflated expenditures and contributions, one assumes, is that it realized that some expenditures may be functionally equivalent to contributions in the way they influence the outcome of a race, the way they are interpreted by the candidates and the public, and the way they taint the decisions that the officeholder thereafter takes.

Caperton is illuminating in several additional respects. It underscores the old insight that, on account of the extreme difficulty of proving corruption, "prophylactic measures, reaching some [campaign spending] not corrupt in purpose or effect, [may be] nonetheless required to guard against corruption." It underscores that "certain restrictions on corporate electoral involvement" may likewise be needed to "hedge against circumvention of valid contribution limits." It underscores that for-profit corporations associated with electioneering communications will often prefer to use nonprofit conduits with "misleading names," such as And For The Sake Of The Kids, "to conceal their identity" as the sponsor of those communications, thereby frustrating the utility of disclosure laws. *McConnell*, 540 U.S., at 128, 124 S.Ct. 619.

And it underscores that the consequences of today's holding will not be limited to the legislative or executive context. The majority of the States select their judges through popular elections. At a time when concerns about the conduct of judicial elections have reached a fever pitch, see, *e.g.*, O'Connor, Justice for Sale, Wall St. Journal, Nov. 15, 2007, p. A25, the Court today unleashes the floodgates of corporate and union general treasury spending in these races. Perhaps "*Caperton* motions" will catch some of the worst abuses. This will be small comfort to those States that, after today, may no longer have the ability to place modest limits on corporate electioneering even if they believe such limits to be critical to maintaining the integrity of their judicial systems.

Deference and Incumbent Self-Protection

Rather than show any deference to a coordinate branch of Government, the majority thus rejects the anticorruption rationale without serious analysis. Today's opinion provides no clear rationale for being so dismissive of Congress, but the prior individual opinions on which it relies have offered one: the incentives of the legislators who passed BCRA. Section 203, our colleagues have suggested, may be little more than "an incumbency protection plan," a disreputable attempt at legislative self-dealing rather than an earnest effort to facilitate First Amendment values and safeguard the legitimacy of our political system. This possibility, the Court apparently believes, licenses it to run roughshod over Congress' handiwork.

Austin and Corporate Expenditures

Just as the majority gives short shrift to the general societal interests at stake in campaign finance regulation, it also overlooks the distinctive considerations raised by the regulation of *corporate* expenditures. The majority fails to appreciate that *Austin*'s antidistortion rationale is itself an anticorruption rationale, see 494 U.S., at 660, 110 S.Ct. 1391 (describing "a different type of corruption"), tied to the special concerns raised by corporations. Understood properly, "antidistortion" is simply a variant on the classic governmental interest in protecting against improper influences on officeholders that debilitate the democratic process. It is manifestly not just an " 'equalizing' " ideal in disguise.

1. Antidistortion

The fact that corporations are different from human beings might seem to need no elaboration, except that the majority opinion almost completely elides it. *Austin* set forth some of the basic differences. Unlike natural persons, corporations have "limited liability" for their owners and managers, "perpetual life," separation of ownership and control, "and favorable treatment of the accumulation and distribution of assets ... that enhance their ability to attract capital and to deploy their resources in ways that maximize the return on their shareholders' investments." 494 U.S., at 658–659, 110 S.Ct. 1391. Unlike voters in U.S. elections, corporations may be foreign controlled. Unlike other interest groups, business corporations have been "effectively delegated responsibility for ensuring society's economic welfare"; they inescapably structure the life of every citizen. " '[T]he resources in the treasury of a business corporation,' " furthermore, " 'are not an indication of popular support for the corporation's political ideas.' " *Id.*, at 659, 110 S.Ct. 1391 (quoting *MCFL,* 479 U.S., at 258, 107 S.Ct. 616). " 'They reflect instead the economically motivated decisions of investors and customers. The availability of these resources may make a corporation a formidable political presence, even though the power of the corporation may be no reflection of the power of its ideas.' " 494 U.S., at 659, 110 S.Ct. 1391 (quoting *MCFL,* 479 U.S., at 258, 107 S.Ct. 616).

It might also be added that corporations have no consciences, no beliefs, no feelings, no thoughts, no desires. Corporations help structure and facilitate the activities of human beings, to be sure, and their "personhood" often serves as a useful legal fiction. But they are not themselves members of "We the People" by whom and for whom our Constitution was established.

These basic points help explain why corporate electioneering is not only more likely to impair compelling governmental interests, but also why restrictions on that electioneering are less likely to encroach upon First Amendment freedoms. One fundamental concern of the First Amendment is to "protec[t] the individual's interest in self-expression." *Consolidated Edison Co. of N.Y. v. Public Serv. Comm'n of N. Y.,* 447 U.S. 530, 534, n. 2, 100 S.Ct. 2326, 65 L.Ed.2d 319 (1980); see also *Bellotti,* 435 U.S., at 777, n. 12, 98 S.Ct. 1407. Freedom of speech helps "make men free to develop their faculties," *Whitney v. California,* 274 U.S. 357, 375, 47 S.Ct. 641, 71 L.Ed. 1095 (1927) (Brandeis, J., concurring), it respects their "dignity and choice," *Cohen v. California,* 403 U.S. 15, 24, 91 S.Ct. 1780, 29 L.Ed.2d 284 (1971), and it facilitates the value of "individual self-realization," Redish, The Value of Free Speech, 130 U. Pa. L.Rev. 591, 594 (1982). Corporate speech, however, is derivative speech, speech by proxy. A regulation such as BCRA § 203 may affect the way in which individuals disseminate certain messages through the corporate form, but it does not prevent anyone from speaking in his or her own voice. "Within the realm of [campaign spending] generally," corporate spending is "furthest from the core of political expression." *Beaumont,* 539 U.S., at 161, n. 8, 123 S.Ct. 2200.

It is an interesting question "who" is even speaking when a business corporation places an advertisement that endorses or attacks a particular candidate. Presumably it is not the customers or employees, who typically have no say in such matters. It cannot realistically be said to be the shareholders, who tend to be far removed from the day-to-day decisions of the firm and whose political preferences may be opaque to management. Perhaps the officers or directors of the corporation have the best claim to be the ones speaking, except their fiduciary duties generally prohibit them from using corporate funds for personal ends. Some individuals associated with the corporation must make the decision to place the ad, but the idea that these individuals are thereby fostering their self-expression or cultivating their critical faculties is fanciful. It is entirely possible that the corporation's electoral message will *conflict* with their personal convictions. Take away the ability to use general treasury funds for some of those ads, and no one's autonomy, dignity, or political equality has been impinged upon in the least.

Corporate expenditures are distinguishable from individual expenditures in this respect. I have taken the view that a legislature may place reasonable restrictions on individuals' electioneering expenditures in the service of the governmental interests explained above, and in recognition of the fact that such restrictions are not direct restraints on speech but rather on its financing. But those restrictions concededly present a tougher case, because the primary conduct of actual, flesh-and-blood persons is involved. Some of those individuals might feel that they need to spend large sums of money on behalf of a particular candidate to vindicate the intensity of their electoral preferences. This is obviously not the situation with business corporations, as their routine practice of giving "substantial sums to *both* major national parties" makes pellucidly clear. *McConnell*, 540 U.S., at 148, 124 S.Ct. 619. "[C]orporate participation" in elections, any business executive will tell you, "is more transactional than ideological."

In this transactional spirit, some corporations have affirmatively urged Congress to place limits on their electioneering communications. These corporations fear that officeholders will shake them down for supportive ads, that they will have to spend increasing sums on elections in an ever-escalating arms race with their competitors, and that public trust in business will be eroded. A system that effectively forces corporations to use their shareholders' money both to maintain access to, and to avoid retribution from, elected officials may ultimately prove more harmful than beneficial to many corporations. It can impose a kind of implicit tax.

In short, regulations such as § 203 and the statute upheld in *Austin* impose only a limited burden on First Amendment freedoms not only because they target a narrow subset of expenditures and leave untouched the broader "public dialogue," but also because they leave untouched the speech of natural persons. Recognizing the weakness of a speaker-based critique of *Austin,* the Court places primary emphasis not on the corporation's right to electioneer, but rather on the listener's interest in hearing what every possible speaker may have to say.

There are many flaws in this argument. If the overriding concern depends on the interests of the audience, surely the public's perception of the value of corporate speech should be given important weight. The distinctive threat to democratic integrity posed by corporate domination of politics was recognized at "the inception of the republic" and "has been a persistent theme in American political life" ever since. It is only certain Members of this Court, not the listeners themselves, who have agitated for more corporate electioneering.

Austin recognized that there are substantial reasons why a legislature might conclude that unregulated general treasury expenditures will give corporations "unfai[r] influence" in the electoral process, 494 U.S., at 660, 110 S.Ct. 1391, and distort public debate in ways that undermine rather than advance the interests of listeners. The legal structure of corporations allows them to amass and deploy financial resources on a scale few natural persons can match. The structure of a business corporation, furthermore, draws a line between the corporation's economic interests and the political preferences of the individuals associated with the corporation; the corporation must engage the electoral process with the aim "to enhance the profitability of the company, no matter how persuasive the arguments for a broader or conflicting set of priorities."

In addition to this immediate drowning out of noncorporate voices, there may be deleterious effects that follow soon thereafter. Corporate "domination" of electioneering, *Austin,* 494 U.S., at 659, 110 S.Ct. 1391, can generate the impression that corporations dominate our democracy. When citizens turn on their televisions and radios before an election and hear only corporate electioneering, they may lose faith in their capacity, as citizens, to influence public policy. A Government captured by corporate interests, they may come to believe, will be neither responsive to their needs nor willing to give their views a fair hearing. The predictable result is cynicism and disenchantment: an increased perception that large spenders " 'call the tune' " and a reduced " 'willingness of voters to take part in democratic governance.' " To the extent that corporations are allowed to exert undue influence in electoral races, the speech of the eventual winners of those races may also be chilled. Politicians who fear that a certain corporation can make or break their reelection chances may be cowed into silence about that corporation. On a variety of levels, unregulated corporate electioneering might diminish the ability of citizens to "hold officials accountable to the people," *ante,* at 898, and disserve the goal of a public debate that is "uninhibited, robust, and wide-open," *New York Times Co. v. Sullivan,* 376 U.S. 254, 270, 84 S.Ct. 710, 11 L.Ed.2d 686 (1964). At the least, I stress again, a legislature is entitled to credit these concerns and to take tailored measures in response.

In the real world, we have seen, corporate domination of the airwaves prior to an election may decrease the average listener's exposure to relevant viewpoints, and it may diminish citizens' willingness and capacity to participate in the democratic process.

The Court's blinkered and aphoristic approach to the First Amendment may well promote corporate power at the cost of the individual and collective self-expression the Amendment was meant to serve. It will undoubtedly cripple the ability of ordinary citizens, Congress, and the States to adopt even limited measures to protect against corporate domination of the electoral process. Americans may be forgiven if they do not feel the Court has advanced the cause of self-government today.

Shareholder Protection

There is yet another way in which laws such as § 203 can serve First Amendment values. Interwoven with *Austin*'s concern to protect the integrity of the electoral process is a concern to protect the rights of shareholders from a kind of coerced speech: electioneering expenditures that do not "reflec[t] [their] support." 494 U.S., at 660–661, 110 S.Ct. 1391. When corporations use general treasury funds to praise or attack a particular candidate for office, it is the shareholders, as the residual claimants, who are effectively footing the bill. Those shareholders who disagree with the corporation's electoral message may find their financial investments being used to undermine their political convictions.

The PAC mechanism, by contrast, helps ensure that those who pay for an electioneering communication actually support its content and that managers do not use general treasuries to advance personal agendas. *Ibid.* It " 'allows corporate political participation without the temptation to use corporate funds for political influence, quite possibly at odds with the sentiments of some shareholders or members.' " *McConnell,* 540 U.S., at 204, 124 S.Ct. 619 (quoting *Beaumont,* 539 U.S., at 163, 123 S.Ct. 2200). A rule that privileges the use of PACs thus does more than facilitate the political speech of like-minded shareholders; it also curbs the rent seeking behavior of executives and respects the views of dissenters. *Austin*'s acceptance of restrictions on general treasury spending "simply allows people who have invested in the business corporation for purely economic reasons"—the vast majority of investors, one assumes—"to avoid being taken advantage of, without sacrificing their economic objectives." Winkler, Beyond *Bellotti,* 32 Loyola (LA) L.Rev. 133, 201 (1998).

The Court dismisses this interest on the ground that abuses of shareholder money can be corrected "through the procedures of corporate democracy," and, it seems, through Internet-based disclosures. I fail to understand how this addresses the concerns of dissenting union members, who will also be affected by today's ruling, and I fail to understand why the Court is so confident in these mechanisms. By "corporate democracy," presumably the Court means the rights of shareholders to vote and to bring derivative suits for breach of fiduciary duty. In practice, however, many corporate lawyers will tell you that "these rights are so limited as to be almost nonexistent," given the internal authority wielded by boards and managers and the expansive protections afforded by the business judgment rule. Modern technology may help make it easier to track corporate activity, including electoral advocacy, but it is utopian to believe that it solves the problem. Most American households that own stock do so through intermediaries such as mutual funds and pension plans, which makes it more difficult both to monitor and to alter particular holdings.

Studies show that a majority of individual investors make no trades at all during a given year. Moreover, if the corporation in question operates a PAC, an investor who sees the company's ads may not know whether they are being funded through the PAC or through the general treasury.

If and when shareholders learn that a corporation has been spending general treasury money on objectionable electioneering, they can divest. Even assuming that they reliably learn as much, however, this solution is only partial. The injury to the shareholders' expressive rights has already occurred; they might have preferred to keep that corporation's stock in their portfolio for any number of economic reasons; and they may incur a capital gains tax or other penalty from selling their shares, changing their pension plan, or the like. The shareholder protection rationale has been criticized as underinclusive, in that corporations also spend money on lobbying and charitable contributions in ways that any particular shareholder might disapprove. But those expenditures do not implicate the selection of public officials, an area in which "the interests of unwilling ... corporate shareholders [in not being] forced to subsidize that speech" "are at their zenith." *Austin,* 494 U.S., at 677, 110 S.Ct. 1391 (Brennan, J., concurring). And in any event, the question is whether shareholder protection provides a basis for regulating expenditures in the weeks before an election, not whether additional types of corporate communications might similarly be conditioned on voluntariness.

Recognizing the limits of the shareholder protection rationale, the *Austin* Court did not hold it out as an adequate and independent ground for sustaining the statute in question. Rather, the Court applied it to reinforce the antidistortion rationale, in two main ways. First, the problem of dissenting shareholders shows that even if electioneering expenditures can advance the political views of some members of a corporation, they will often compromise the views of others. Second, it provides an additional reason, beyond the distinctive legal attributes of the corporate form, for doubting that these "expenditures reflect actual public support for the political ideas espoused." The shareholder protection rationale, in other words, bolsters the conclusion that restrictions on corporate electioneering can serve both speakers' and listeners' interests, as well as the anticorruption interest. And it supplies yet another reason why corporate expenditures merit less protection than individual expenditures.

V

Today's decision is backwards in many senses. It elevates the majority's agenda over the litigants' submissions, facial attacks over as-applied claims, broad constitutional theories over narrow statutory grounds, individual dissenting opinions over precedential holdings, assertion over tradition, absolutism over empiricism, rhetoric over reality. Our colleagues have arrived at the conclusion that *Austin* must be overruled and that §203 is facially unconstitutional only after mischaracterizing both the reach and rationale of those authorities, and after bypassing or ignoring rules of judicial restraint used to cabin the Court's lawmaking power. Their conclusion that the societal interest in avoiding corruption and the appearance of corruption does not provide an adequate justification for regulating corporate expenditures on candidate elections relies on an incorrect description of that interest, along with a failure to acknowledge the relevance of established facts and the considered judgments of state and federal legislatures over many decades.

In a democratic society, the longstanding consensus on the need to limit corporate campaign spending should outweigh the wooden application of judge-made rules. The majority's rejection of this principle "elevate[s] corporations to a level of deference which has not been seen at least since the days when substantive due process was regularly used to invalidate regulatory legislation thought to unfairly impinge upon established economic interests." *Bellotti*, 435 U.S., at 817, n. 13, 98 S.Ct. 1407 (White, J., dissenting). At bottom, the Court's opinion is thus a rejection of the common sense of the American people, who have recognized a need to prevent corporations from undermining self-government since the founding, and who have fought against the distinctive corrupting potential of corporate electioneering since the days of Theodore Roosevelt. It is a strange time to repudiate that common sense. While American democracy is imperfect, few outside the majority of this Court would have thought its flaws included a dearth of corporate money in politics.

I would affirm the judgment of the District Court.

Notes

(1) In the aftermath of *Citizens United*, what might some of the consequences be of that seminal decision?

(2) The majority opinion in *Citizens United* rejects the shareholder protection rationale as argued for pointedly in the dissent. What is "coerced speech" and how does the shareholder protection rationale interface with it?

(3) What is the anti-distortion principle as enumerated originally in *Austin*? Why was it rejected in *Citizens United*?

(4) When contemplating the consequences of *Citizens United*, think about the following: Whose money is being committed to political causes? Who is making the decisions as to how these contributions are made and toward what ends and goals?

In the article that follows, *Procuring "Justice"?*, Dean cummings discusses the uncomfortable reality that the *Citizens United* case presents when largely unfettered contributions from corporate treasuries are used to elect politicians and influence policy outcomes. Ultimately, cummings concludes that *Citizens United* enables a very small group of powerful elite white males (corporate executives) to spend "other people's money" to influence legislation, law, and policy in their favor. Shareholders and "Main Street" citizens are largely left without recourse when corporate elites are granted an outright ability to spend corporate dollars to ensure that election outcomes meet their needs.

Procuring "Justice"?: *Citizens United, Caperton,* and Partisan Judicial Elections

andré douglas pond cummings
95 Iowa L. Rev. Bull. 89 (2010)

I. Introduction

In recent years, two inextricably connected issues have received a great deal of attention in both U.S. political discourse and in the legal academic literature. One issue of intense legal debate and frustration has been that of judicial recusal, including an examination of the appropriate standards that should necessarily apply to judges that seem *conflicted* or *biased* in their role as neutral arbiter. A second issue that has spawned heated commentary and great dispute over the past decade is that of campaign-finance law, including examination of the role that powerful and wealthy benefactors play in American electioneering. Both issues came to a head in the past year as the U.S. Supreme Court decided two landmark cases that will have far-reaching implications and consequences, *Caperton v. A.T. Massey Coal* and *Citizens United v. Federal Election Commission.* The moment that these decisions were announced, their connection undoubtedly crystallized for many observers. As *Caperton* and *Citizens United* shed new light on judicial recusal and campaign finance in an interconnected manner, Professor Michael LeRoy delivers an important empirical study, *Do Partisan Elections of Judges Produce Unequal Justice When Courts Review Employment Arbitrations?*, that provides evidence that we as a nation have reason to fear this potentially pernicious interconnectedness.

In a confluence of circumstance, what has been historically controversial now puts in present peril the concept of "justice" and whether it can be "equal" in U.S. courts. *Citizens United, Caperton* and *Do Partisan Elections of Judges Produce Unequal Justice When Courts Review Employment Arbitrations?* together pose a troubling question: will judges who are elected in a partisan manner, where corporations can now more directly influence the result of judicial elections by contributing large cash electioneering outflows, manufacture outcomes that are biased toward those contributing corporations? The early returns are not good.

That is to say, contemporary empirical evidence suggests that the answer to the inquiry posed above is "yes." Apparently partisan elected judges are unable to sit neutrally when large corporate expenditure ushered them to the bench. Or stated differently, when corporations are able to manipulate the judicial election process through significant cash disbursement, a judge that is unfriendly, if not hostile, to employee rights will be the likely result. The Supreme Court's decisions in *Citizens United* and *Caperton* stand poised to exacerbate this disheartening empirical implication.

The Supreme Court's acrimonious 5–4 decision in *Citizens United* struck down federal law that had prohibited U.S. corporations, in specific and narrow circumstances, from making direct election expenditures on behalf of politicians or judges running for public office. In a carefully circumscribed way, federal law before *Citizens United* had prohibited corporations from using general treasury funds to make direct electioneering appeal to voters through visual media thirty or sixty days in advance of an election. The Supreme Court viewed this prohibition as violative of the First Amendment free speech rights of corporations and struck down the federal law as unconstitutional. This decision has generated much controversy and derision. At bottom, many commentators believe that corporations are now free to powerfully influence the assortment of individuals that will sit in Congress, the White House, and on the judicial bench, selecting those who will warmly embrace their specific corporate interests.

In *Caperton*, an equally rancorous Supreme Court, divided again 5–4, decided that under specific and narrow circumstances, due process requires that a judge recuse herself from cases where a financial donor is a party before the court and that donor played a significant monetary role in the judge assuming her seat on the very bench before which the case is pending. As judicial recusal standards are notoriously loose and open to individual judicial divination, *Caperton* attempts to place slight parameters around judges who have accepted generous financial support in gaining the judicial post by requiring recusal in situations where that generous financial benefactor appears before the court in which the individual, corporation, or Political Action Committee ("PAC") sought to insert the judge. The *Caperton* majority in announcing this narrow due process benchmark was very careful to state, repeatedly, that the circumstances that gave birth to this new recusal standard were "exceptional," "extreme," "rare," and "extraordinary," signaling that the Court believes its new rule will impact only an exceedingly narrow sliver of cases and judges.

Professor LeRoy's empirical study, *Do Partisan Elections of Judges Produce Unequal Justice When Courts Review Employment Arbitrations?*, finds that judges who are elected in partisan races are significantly more likely to rule in favor of corporations and against employees when confronted with employment law disputes than are those judges who are either appointed or elected to their judicial posts in nonpartisan elections. Through the lens of mandatory employment arbitration appeals, LeRoy's data shows that when partisan-elected judges review arbitration decisions, employees win only 32.1% of the cases compared to arbitration appeals in front of appointed or nonpartisan elected judges where employees win 52.7% of the time. This large gap in the data suggests troubling inferences for judges who are selected in partisan elections where corporations are now free, per *Citizens United*, to engage in largely unfettered free speech electioneering and where, per *Caperton*, recusal parameters are tightly constrained to very limited circumstances.

This Essay seeks to make sense of this confluence of Supreme Court decision making and recent empirical evidence. In examining this intermingling and its potential repercussions, Part II briefly considers several of Professor LeRoy's more disquieting findings in *Do Partisan Elections of Judges Produce Unequal Justice When Courts Review Employment Arbitrations?* Part III reviews the holding of the controversial *Citizens United* in light of LeRoy's empirical report. Part IV examines the *Caperton* decision and queries whether it will have any protective effects in connection with corporate influence over the partisan judicial election process. Part V interrogates the consequences of LeRoy's study, *Citizens United*, and *Caperton*, views each through a corporate law prism, and seeks to offer forward-looking conclusions and recommendations.

II. Do Partisan Elections of Judges Produce Unequal Justice When Courts Review Employment Arbitrations?

Professor Michael LeRoy begins his empirical study with the question "Do partisan elections of judges contribute to unequal justice in court decisions?" Though LeRoy is careful to cabin his answer and the implications of his empirical analysis, the answer to his query appears to be most probably "yes." Through a pointed analysis of appealed employment dispute arbitration cases, LeRoy is able to quantify the number of appeals appearing before partisan-elected judges and track the outcomes of those arbitration appeals. Similarly, the empirical data examines those employment arbitration appeals that come before appointed judges and those elected in nonpartisan elections and tracks those results. In front of partisan-elected judges, employees are successful in the appeal outcome only 32% of the time. Conversely, before appointed judges and nonpartisan elected judges, employees are successful in the appeal outcome 53% of the time. This single differentiation is significant and demands further examination. These results suggest that partisan-elected judges empirically favor corporate interests and disfavor employee interests at an alarming rate.

[A]s LeRoy is swift to acknowledge, empirically examining appeal outcomes proves little aside from uncovering a startling disparity and beginning the debate by asking why such significant inequality exists between partisan-elected judges and appointed or nonpartisan elected judges in employment arbitration appeal outcomes. Still, the data leads one to a likely conclusion that partisan-elected judges are much friendlier to corporate interests than are appointed judges. The data tends to show that partisan-elected judges are less likely to approve reasoned arbitration decisions that come down in favor of employees. The empirical analysis supports LeRoy's initial hypothesis that "judges selected in partisan elections where corporate political contributions are likely prevalent tend to decide cases in favor of corporate employers." While limited, LeRoy's findings are potentially explosive. The station of judge in the United States is roundly considered to be one of a dispassionate, respected, unbiased, neutral, and fair arbiter of equal justice before the law. LeRoy's findings undermine our judicial ideal.

Professor LeRoy points to two trends in his analysis that tend to support the argument that our nation's courts and judges have grown more hostile toward employees and their rights under the law. First, LeRoy carefully breaks down the employment arbitration process as it has evolved in the United States for the past several decades. Second, LeRoy provides a brief description of the meteoric rise of campaign contributions, particularly those made by corporations in the context of judicial elections across those states that engage partisan judicial elections. In reviewing both, LeRoy connects the litigation avoidance strategy employed by corporations through adopting the mandatory arbitration process and the trend toward challenging adverse decisions in the state courts, while simultaneously employing a stratagem of significantly influencing the judicial election process with large campaign contributions on behalf of those judges that embrace an employer friendly view of employment disputes.

The legal development of workplace disputes in America, under any fair observation, reveals a trending toward favoring employers and corporations and away from protecting the rights of employees. During the past decade, corporations began carefully selecting, imposing, and manipulating the mandatory arbitration process and embracing it as a strategic tactic employed to avoid liability, courts, and costs. By imposing mandatory arbitration upon its employees, corporations sought to bar individual employees from suing them, thus limiting litigation risks and costs and further specifying arbitral forums and arbitration-process rules. As corporations were securing judicial approval of the mandatory arbitration process and busying themselves with writing mandatory arbitration clauses that favored their interests in every conceivable way, something unexpected happened: employees began winning their arbitration hearings. This untenable result from the perspective of employers forced corporations to either abandon the mandatory arbitration process, or more often, begin seeking state court review of the "final and binding" arbitration proceedings it had forced upon its employee in the first instance. Corporations, in demanding to have it both ways, forced their employees into mandatory arbitration, but then upon discovery that the sought-after protections against employee claims were not forthcoming at the hoped-for percentages, began challenging the arbitration awards in the state courts—those very same courts that corporations had sought to avoid by forcing mandatory arbitration. As challenging arbitration awards in courts has become commonplace, the need to have a "certain" kind of judge on the bench has become imperative to corporations and their human executives.

The rise of campaign contributions in state judicial elections is breathtaking. LeRoy reports that state judicial campaign contributions have skyrocketed in the past decade. "Thirty-nine states hold judicial elections. Between 2000 and 2009, State Supreme Court candidates raised $205.8 million, according to the Justice at Stake Campaign, a watchdog group that monitors money in court races. That was more than double the $84.9 million raised the previous decade." [A] sitting judge and his opponent in an Illinois state court race raised $9.3 million between them, "an amount that exceeded expenditures that year in eighteen of thirty-four U.S. Senate campaigns." Spending for state supreme court seats in fourteen states increased 167% from 2000 to 2002 and increased another 163% from 2002 to 2004. Of course, the primary concern with this skyrocketing spending on state judicial elections is the threat posed to the ideal of judicial independence. Can a judge be truly independent when he or she has received extraordinary financial support from various interest groups and owes his or her seat on the bench to a particular benefactor or group?

Further, recent trends in judicial campaign finance indicate that out-of-state special interest groups are now taking particular issue interest in judicial candidates that meet their campaign contribution "criteria." Corporations and special interest groups, whose own states do not conduct partisan judicial elections, are now identifying judicial candidates that run in partisan election states and are directing their out-of-state funding toward election of particular candidates that have expressed a favored judicial viewpoint. Additionally, the Supreme Court has recently struck down state laws aimed at prohibiting particular political speech in judicial elections, thereby making it possible for judicial candidates running for election to make statements about abortion, rape, capital punishment, and gun control, amongst others. This, of course, allows candidates to curry favor with special interest groups that will provide campaign contributions to that judicial candidate that best promises to support a particular issue of interest. These trends continue to exist in an environment that claims to prize judicial independence and fair and impartial arbiters. LeRoy's empirical analysis prods the thoughtful reader to consider whether judicial independence remains a possibility in the new world of *Citizens United* and current campaign funding trends.

III. *Citizens United*

Citizens United created a firestorm upon its release. Condemned by a sitting president in a State of the Union address, the case explicitly overruled a line of judicial precedent that effectively outlawed direct corporate electioneering under specific circumstances and declared carefully crafted campaign-finance law as enacted by Congress unconstitutional. The holding of *Citizens United* makes permissible a corporation's direct expenditure of general treasury funds to explicitly endorse or malign a candidate for public office immediately prior to an election. According to the Supreme Court, the free speech rights of corporations, fictional persons under the law, simply cannot be infringed. The implications of this holding are enormous.

Prior to *Citizens United*, corporate electioneering had to be done through a PAC, which required corporations or individuals to make specific contributions that were carefully tracked and registered with the Federal Election Commission ("FEC"). The "whole point of the PAC mechanism" was to initiate a separate and distinct entity from the corporation wherein corporate executives would be forbidden from funneling general treasury funds into the PAC or from forcing shareholders to support the PAC's explicit political purpose. The PAC allowed a corporation to engage in electioneering without holding shareholder funds hostage to the political whims or goals of corporate leadership. Congress viewed this separation as a necessary protection of both the political process and of the ability of shareholders to engage in politicking on their own terms.

Citizens United turns this seemingly sensible separation upon its head. Today, corporations, through their human executives and boards of directors, may now, in a mostly unfettered manner, engage in politicking and electioneering with other people's money. Under the guise of free speech, general treasury funds of any corporation may now be used to campaign for or against candidates for the White House, the U.S. Senate, the U.S. House of Representatives, state governors, state legislators, state officers, and state judges. Prior to *Citizens United*, PACs could engage in the same electioneering activity, but the critical difference now is that personal and corporate contributions to a

PAC, tracked and registered, are no longer mandatory as a corporation can now spend its shareholders' value, from its general treasury, in campaigning and electioneering.

This is a subtle change of massive proportions. *Caperton* fully displayed the potential mischief this subtle shift created.

IV. *CAPERTON*

Ironically, just months before handing down *Citizens United*, the Supreme Court decided *Caperton*, a case where political campaign contributions played a significant role in the election of a judge that would later sit in judgment over the wealthy benefactor that provided the necessary campaign contributions and PAC television advertising to see the preferred candidate seated. In *Caperton*, Don Blankenship, then president and Chief Executive Officer ("CEO") of A.T. Massey Coal, contributed more than $3 million to support the candidacy of Brent Benjamin for the West Virginia Supreme Court in a partisan judicial election race. A majority of the $3 million contribution was to a PAC called "For the Sake of the Kids" which aired anti-incumbent Warren McGraw commercials on a constant loop for weeks prior to the supreme court election, asking citizens to reject "Radical" McGraw as a supreme court judge. Amazingly, during this harsh electioneering activity, Massey Coal had been hit with a $50 million adverse jury verdict for tortiously injuring the business of a competitor, an appeal that was pending before the West Virginia Supreme Court. The judges elected in the very cycle wherein Blankenship contributed the $3 million toward electing Benjamin would determine the fate of the sizable verdict against Massey, including whether the award would stand. One can imagine a scenario where Blankenship weighed the costs and benefits of supporting a corporate-friendly candidate for the state supreme court and decided that $3 million was a wise investment if it could make a $50 million verdict disappear.

The bitterly contested partisan election, complete with vicious attack ads and charges of misrepresentation flying, resulted in the incumbent McGraw's defeat and Benjamin's assumption of a seat on the West Virginia Supreme Court. Predictably, when *Caperton* came before that state supreme court months later, now-Justice Benjamin cast the deciding vote that reversed the jury verdict against Massey Coal and Blankenship, the company and man that were primarily responsible for ushering Benjamin onto the court. Plaintiff Caperton moved before the appeal "to disqualify now-Justice Benjamin under the Due Process Clause and the West Virginia Code of Judicial Conduct, based on the conflict caused by Blankenship's campaign involvement." Benjamin denied this motion. Throughout the machinations of the appeal and subsequent rehearings, Caperton moved to disqualify Benjamin three times as incapable of being fair and impartial; Benjamin rejected each of those motions. Thereafter, on appeal and again on rehearing, Benjamin cast the deciding vote in favor of Massey Coal and reversed the $50 million jury verdict on disparate grounds, albeit acknowledging that Massy had engaged in tortious business activity deserving of sanction.

When the U.S. Supreme Court decided *Caperton*, it waded into the normally amorphous arena of judicial recusal and disqualification standards. Long left to the discretion of a challenged judge, the Supreme Court offered a new standard for those judges who owe their judicial post to generous campaign contributors. In evaluating whether a probability of bias exists to the extent that it violates a party's due process rights to a fair trial, the Supreme Court held:

> Not every campaign contribution by a litigant or attorney creates a probability of bias that requires a judge's recusal, but this is an exceptional case. We conclude that there is a serious risk of actual bias—based on objective and reasonable perceptions—when a person with a personal stake in a particular case had a sig-

nificant and disproportionate influence in placing the judge on the case by raising funds or directing the judge's election campaign when the case was pending or imminent. The inquiry centers on the contribution's relative size in comparison to the total amount of money contributed to the campaign, the total amount spent in the election, and the apparent effect such contribution had on the outcome of the election.

In announcing this new standard, the Supreme Court extended its long held due process recusal standard—that the due process clause requires a judge to recuse herself when she "has 'a direct, personal, substantial, pecuniary interest' in a case"—to include scenarios where significant campaign contributions are bestowed upon a particular judge by interested parties before the court. The Court opined that "[t]his rule reflects the maxim that '[n]o man is allowed to be a judge in his own cause; because his interest would certainly bias his judgment, and, not improbably, corrupt his integrity.'" In analyzing the Caperton scenario against its new standard, the Court had little trouble finding that Benjamin should have recused himself and avoided the actual bias that informed his vote in the Massey appeal. The *Caperton* Court found that Blankenship's contributions "had a significant and disproportionate influence" in placing Benjamin on the case that posed the conflict.

While the Supreme Court acted boldly in recognizing the influence of campaign contributions on the ability of elected judges to act impartially and free from bias or to refuse the "possible temptation ... to ... lead him not to hold the balance nice, clear and true," the Court was careful, almost manic, in limiting the reach of its holding to the "extreme," "rare," and "exceptional" facts of the *Caperton* case. As pointed out in the biting dissent, the majority "over and over" limited its holding to the very extraordinary circumstance where a campaign contributor donates disproportionate and significant amounts of money to a judicial candidate at the same time that a case is or will be pending before the very court in which the judge seeks election. Truly, this recusal guidance will likely have very little impact because of its excruciatingly narrow holding.

In light of the *Caperton* holding, one might logically presume that the majority author actually had a prescient sense that *Citizens United* was forthcoming and that the floodgates of corporate campaign contributions would soon be flung open. Little comfort can be taken from *Caperton*'s conclusions in connection with LeRoy's empirical evidence described above, where partisan-elected judges are more likely to be biased against employees and biased in favor of corporate interests, simply because mandating recusal in scenarios of manipulating corporate contributions must be "extreme" and significantly disproportionate. Corporate leaders, having clear guidance from the case, will be much too savvy to get caught up in the *Caperton* net when placing preferred judges on the nation's courts.

V. An Emerging Corporatocracy

Caperton acknowledges the bias-inducing potential of massive campaign contributions to elected judges who are duty bound to act without bias. *Do Partisan Elections of Judges Produce Unequal Justice When Courts Review Employment Arbitrations?* provides emerging empirical evidence that judges who are elected in partisan races, where campaign contributions are significant, trend strongly toward favoring employers and corporate interests while disfavoring employees. *Citizens United* strips back the protections Congress provided the American election process from unfettered corporate bankrolling and electioneering. This combination of events is potentially toxic.

Simply stated, *Caperton* reveals a reality wherein targeted judicial positions are nearly, if not fully, bought and paid for by powerful corporate interests intent on influencing judicial outcome. Professor LeRoy's empirical study infers that when corporate interests are successful in positioning judges as pawns, their moves are predictably and strongly in favor of those corporate interests that positioned them. Finally, *Citizen United* literally invites corporate interests inside the electioneering process and enables corporations to seize an even more intimate position in U.S. elections going forward. Some argue that this powerful new ability to control elections moves our nation from a democracy toward an emerging corporatocracy.

While this potentially toxic prescription may sound intoxicating to some, most likely those whose interests will be furthered in this new era of corporate electioneering, others may simply agree with the *Citizens United* majority in holding that American corporations should have their ability to speak freely within the election context protected—what harm can be done? Those favoring the *Citizens United* outcome suggest that U.S. citizens should hear from all relevant voices, including corporations, and then freely choose from amongst all competing messages which ring particularly true when deciding upon whom to elect. In principle, this view is attractive and convincing. However, several doctrines of corporate law and recent trends in its practice should be examined before determining that corporations, and their newly actuated election voices, should be considered harmless.

A. OTHER PEOPLE'S MONEY

The most basic principle in corporate law is that corporations exist primarily to maximize profits for its shareholders. Limited exceptions exist that allow corporations to make meaningful but reasonable contributions to charitable organizations and public institutions for the purpose of increasing goodwill and contributing to the communities in which the corporations do business. A corporation is viewed as a fictional person under the law and as such, has the right to sue and be sued and after *Citizens United*, has the right to exercise its free speech at all times and in all places, particularly during election cycles. Of course, as a fictional person, the corporation cannot function without human management, so corporate law provides a management mechanism of shareholder ownership of a corporation with voting rights, an elected Board of Directors oversight regime where shareholders elect board members, and day-to-day business management by executives selected by the overseeing board. The CEO is the primary leader of the corporation and is tasked with managing the daily operations and also typically sits on the Board of Directors.

Corporate law has evolved to the point where the CEO has become an almost invincible corporate character. The model of shareholder democracy has been ameliorated to the point that the CEO and his pursuit of personal fortune is the primary driver behind most corporate positioning. The CEO dominates American corporations to the extent that he is held to very few standards of responsibility and is able to stave off all shareholder dissent through careful calculation. According to Professor Steven Ramirez, "CEOs of public companies have the unique privilege of picking their own nominal supervisors—the board of directors."

Today, the CEO in the United States has the power to appoint the board of directors that "oversees" his performance, to maneuver board members off of the board if they challenge his decisions, to establish his compensation through the board committee that he appoints, to make reckless decisions that are primarily protected by the business judgment rule, to exercise nearly unfettered power as the fiduciary duties of care and loyalty have been judicially emasculated to the point of near nonexistence, and to escape private shareholder lawsuits as class action securities fraud actions have been congressionally neutered to a near terminal state. U.S. corporate law has empowered CEOs and corporate management to generate personal short-term profit and gain at the expense of long-term vitality and shareholder profit maximization in astounding ways.

At base, CEOs and corporate boards are charged with overseeing the value of corporate wealth that belongs primarily to shareholders and only nominally to them as corporate leaders. Corporate executives and board members stand in a fiduciary relation to shareholders and are trusted to make sound decisions on behalf of the shareholders who have entrusted them with their wealth. Unfortunately, corporations, or more accurately, the human beings that actuate and lead a corporation, have proven repeatedly and consistently over the past several decades that they will act recklessly when spending other people's money. The financial market crisis of 2008 provides ample evidence that reckless pursuit of profit often prevails when executive leadership is taking risks with other people's money. Further, corporate executives are often careless when deciding upon what charitable contributions to make, again, when deciding how to spend the shareholders' money. Perhaps the most egregious example of irresponsible corporate caretaking occurred in the wake of the Troubled Asset Relief Program ("TARP") bailout where funds were dispersed to major corporations to save the economy from collapse. Corporate leaders' determination of how to spend and shepherd taxpayer funds provided through the largess of the U.S. government, particularly in light of the irresponsible decision making that necessitated the TARP disbursements, highlights the recklessness and harm that corporate decision makers can cause when dealing with other people's money.

First, in connection with the financial market crisis of 2008, recent reports, newspaper accounts, and congressional testimony reveal that from the very top of Wall Street corporate leadership all the way down to the trenches of unregulated mortgage brokering, corporations, through their human leaders, acted with reckless disregard for the value of shareholders, the life savings of employees and investors, and the mortgage burdens of clients and average citizen homeowners. This market was based primarily on a housing bubble that collapsed causing nearly every important U.S. investment bank and commercial bank to face certain collapse if not for the taxpayer bailout. The wild risk-taking adopted by nearly every corporate executive prior to the market collapse was breathtaking. Despite warning signs, signals, and contrary risk modeling, corporate executives intentionally ignored these signs and gambled with and lost billions of dollars of shareholder value.

Second, famed investor Warren Buffett, in recognizing the incredible phenomenon of corporate executives spending other people's money, originated a term he called "elephant bumping." Corporate law, while holding sacrosanct its primary principle of "maximizing shareholder profits," carves out an exception allowing modest charitable contributions from corporate coffers. Buffett describes the process of elephant bumping as one where a primary fundraiser who is seeking a generous charitable contribution from a targeted corporate executive will invite a very important celebrity or superstar executive to accompany the fundraiser to the pitch meeting. Once the fundraiser is sitting in the office of the targeted corporate executive with an elephant (very important executive or celebrity) beside him, nodding approvingly whenever the fundraiser asks for the large corporate contribution, Buffett reports that the fundraiser is successful 100% of the time in receiving the large contribution the fundraiser seeks. Thus, elephant bumping occurs by stroking the ego of a sitting executive by bringing an elephant into the meeting causing the targeted corporate executive, careless and self-important, to view himself as important enough to host elephants and thus capable of pledging shareholder value as a contribution that affirms his importance. Buffett muses that never has the fundraiser seen a corporate executive take out his own personal checkbook and contribute to the charity personally;

rather, each and every targeted executive, feeling his own importance, commits shareholder value to the particular charity of interest.

Finally, in considering how corporate executives spend other people's money, the TARP bailout funds were used primarily to prop up Wall Street titans at a cost to U.S. taxpayers of more than $3 trillion dollars. Rather than liberating (or freeing up) lending, which was a portion of the stated purpose of the infusion of TARP funds, the corporate executives hoarded the taxpayer gifted capital to improve their balance sheet performance. With massive infusion of taxpayer capital and huge loans made available to Wall Street firms from the Federal Reserve Bank, Wall Street responded almost immediately by paying near record executive compensation bonuses for 2009 "performance." Additionally, Wall Street leadership chose to use millions of dollars of TARP funds, provided by U.S. taxpayers, to pay lobbyists to fiercely lobby against new financial services regulations Congress was considering in light of the reckless behavior of those same executives.

When charged with caretaking either shareholder wealth or taxpayer funds, corporate executives historically make very bizarre decisions. Whether elephant bumping is motivating corporate donations or executives are leading their companies to near bankruptcy (requiring taxpayer bailout), it is to this group of leaders, with proven reckless and negligent leadership records, that the Supreme Court through *Citizens United* confers unfettered ability to spend shareholder funds in campaigning for preferred politicians and judges. To those that tend to view this new power as harmless, a potential result of *Citizens United* is that corporations are now positioned to exercise the same irresponsible disdain for fundamental principles of risk assessment, fairness, equity, and duty in the election process that was exercised in the run-up to the global financial crisis. How this newly unfettered voice is used, and in what kind of attack ads and candidate hijacking results, remains to be seen.

B. WHO LEADS?

Who is leading America's corporations? If *Citizens United* stands to transform American politicking and elections as we know them, it seems prudent to examine who leads the American corporations today that have gained this additional power. Of all Fortune 100 board of director seats, 83% are held by men, primarily white men. Amongst the Fortune 500, only five CEOs are African-American, and only one of those is an African-American woman. Only four Latinos are CEOs of Fortune 500 companies. Just fourteen women currently lead a Fortune 500 company. The most dominant corporate positions in the world, CEOs of Fortune 500 corporations, are overwhelmingly white male.

Of the Fortune 500 board of director seats, women hold only 15% of those seats, Latinos hold only 3% of directorships, whereas there are fewer African American directors, and the number is declining. It is fair to say that white men continue to dominate leadership in America's corporations despite the increasing voting power and representation of minorities and women in the workplace and the nation generally. "To the extent that *Citizens United* shifts political power to corporations, fundamentally, it shifts power away from communities of color (and women) notwithstanding their increased voting power."

Nearly every corporate leader that drove the global economy to the point of collapse, those men that led Lehman Brothers, Bear Stearns, Citigroup, Goldman Sachs, Merrill Lynch, Washington Mutual, Countrywide, and Bank of America, were a "precise" kind of corporate leader, specifically male, white, wealthy, privileged, disconnected, and possessing a voracious appetite for risky profiteering. Despite repeated calls for Wall Street to diversify and for corporate America to adopt a leadership paradigm that embraces a different kind of worldview perspective, these calls have gone largely unheeded.

In the pre-*Citizens United* election scheme, PACs were the primary electioneering arm of a corporation. Crucially, PACs could only accept individual contributions and corporations were unable to fund PAC activity out of their general treasuries. Corporate executives were forced to bring out their own checkbooks and spend their own money, reducing their own personal wealth, when electioneering and campaigning. *Citizens United* radically changes this conceptualization. Now, corporate executives, who have proven reckless and negligent repeatedly, are now able to freely assign corporate funds and shareholder value to campaigning and electioneering. There is little evidence to suggest that these executives will be careful, thoughtful, or responsible with the new ability to spend shareholder funds at their disposal.

VI. CONCLUSION

A five-member activist Supreme Court has delivered the future of American elections into the hands of America's corporate leadership, described above as reckless and myopic. U.S. corporate leadership in 2010 is simply a band of profit-driven, often careless, narrow, non-diverse group of leaders that seemingly holds a particular *laissez faire* mindset that represents only a miniscule percentage of U.S. citizens and interests. In light of this deliverance, a follow-up empirical study five or ten years from now to update campaign contribution impact on partisan-elected judges may very well find even more dismal results than what has been uncovered in 2010. Any inquiry into how electioneering funds will be spent has been signaled already through an examination of how TARP funds were exhausted. Following a highly politicized and controversial bailout, Wall Street banks and firms used the taxpayer bailout funds to shore up their balance sheets (rather than lending the funds to consumers), pay enormous 2009 bonuses claiming record profitability (rather than acknowledging the profits being gleaned on the back of Federal Reserve Bank loans and taxpayers bailout funds), and lobby intensely against new financial sector reform that would regulate away the ability of corporate executives to recklessly trade in or gamble their corporate funds to the point of bankruptcy (rather than humbly assisting the Government in conceptualizing moderate, common sense regulation that would prohibit too big to fail institutions). Little question remains, post-*Caperton* and *Do Partisan Elections of Judges Produce Unequal Justice When Courts Review Employment Arbitrations?*, as to where or how corporations will spend their new *Citizens United* allowance.

Seating judges that are hostile to workers and cozy to corporate interests will surely be a byproduct of *Citizens United*. Electing legislators that are passionate *laissez faire* capitalists and antagonistic toward common sense corporate regulation will surely be a byproduct of *Citizens United*, despite a clear failure of capitalism in the recent financial market crisis. To reverse the trend toward an emerging corporatocracy, radical corporate law reform is necessary. The first step is embracing a completely different corporate leadership paradigm. Is America ready to strip the CEO of his preeminence? Will Congress and the courts be willing to return power to the true corporation owners, the shareholders? Might Congress be willing to return private lawsuit power to shareholders that have been methodically stripped over the past two decades? Whether Wall Street and corporate America are willing to embrace diverse leadership and a genuine change in corporate culture is a question to which *Citizens United* will require an answer.

Notes

(1) What is the concept of "elephant bumping" and how does it relate to corporate justice?

(2) Who leads in America's corporate boardrooms? And how does *Citizens United* impact those that do lead?

(3) When considering how Wall Street executives spent TARP bailout funds, how do you predict these same executives will spend corporate treasury funds for political electioneering purposes?

In the following article, Professor Atiba Ellis provides an insightful hypothesis about the potential effect that *Citizens United* will have on corporate power. In summary, he postulates that *Citizens United* will stratify personhood in America and expand white America's dominance over disenfranchised minority groups. According to Professor Ellis, this is plausible because of the power that *Citizens United* has conferred upon corporate decisionmakers to exert greater influence over the political process.

Citizens United and Tiered Personhood

Atiba R. Ellis

44 J. Marshall L. Rev. 717 (2011)

I. Introduction

Citizens United v. FEC is, arguably, the most important campaign finance judicial decision of this century thus far and will likely be remembered as the most significant — and controversial — decision of the Roberts Court. At least one commentator has claimed that *Citizens United* rearranged the political landscape of the United States. The decision has certainly been the subject of much praise and even more criticism. The praise comes from pundits and opinion makers that have claimed that *Citizens United* finally made the law of politics more consistent with core free speech principles. Critics of the opinion have ranged from President Barack Obama; Senator Russ Feingold, with whom Senator John McCain disagreed; media analysts; election activists; and the American public themselves, who have called the opinion inconsistent with American democracy.

The debate concerning the ramifications of *Citizens United* has been equally robust. Scholars discussing *Citizens United* have focused on its impact within a variety of contexts: how *Citizens United* made First Amendment free speech doctrine more consistent, whether and to what extent the case will impact election spending, whether this case impacts the integrity of the campaign finance system, and the consistency or inconsistency of the idea of corporate personhood underlying the case.

The debate that has occurred since *Citizens United* has failed to pay full attention to the ramifications of the Court's analysis of "personhood." This is not to say that the topic of "corporate personhood" has not been given attention in the scholarly literature prior to *Citizens United*, that the way in which *Citizens United* has defined corporate personhood has not been explored, or that there is not a substantial literature concerning personhood as it pertains to natural persons. However, nowhere in this growing literature has anyone called attention to the theoretical intersection between the considerations of the larger literature of personhood, the shift in the idea of personhood created by *Citizens United*, and its ramifications for the jurisprudence on defining who is a person for purposes of distributing constitutional rights. This Article claims to present an initial effort to articulate this view.

Within the *Citizens United* context, the conventional starting point is to discuss the issue of corporate personhood. Indeed, the personhood issue seems to be a problem particular to the corporate form of artificial persons, and this Article will limit its discussion to corporations as artificial persons. The corporate person is traditionally conceived of as an artificial entity that exists by sufferance of the state and thus may be limited by the state. However, the *Citizens United* decision relied not merely on the conventional view of corporate personhood; it sought justification for its decision with the idea that a corporation is an "association of persons." At least part of the core justification for the decision is the view that an association of persons, whether a corporation or labor union or some other "association," ought to be imbued with the same rights as the rights the persons themselves possess. In other words, these "associations" should be wholly equated to natural persons in regards to constitutional rights.

This plausible reading of *Citizens United* continues to blur the distinction between artificial persons and natural persons. This blurring suggests that we ought not only look at *Citizens United* as merely a case that resolves a conflict about the First Amendment, or that pushes the boundaries of corporate personhood; we should recognize that *Citizens United* forces us to look at our assumptions about how legal personhood—for both natural and artificial persons—is constructed in the law. This shift raises the question of what the ramifications of our legal norms are if we accept this assumption.

The question of who was—and who was not—a legal person framed American society from its founding to today. Although the three-fifths compromise of the 1787 Constitution, and the Founders' and states' legal treatment of race shaped the fact that African Americans were treated as chattel or as noncitizens, the Court's jurisprudence had a direct hand in shaping this notion of personhood. The Court, in cases like *Dred Scott v. Sanford* and *Plessy v. Ferguson*, drew—and then redrew—the boundaries of political personhood in relation to race in our society. Similarly, in *Minor v. Happersett* the Court confirmed the boundaries of political personhood in regards to gender. These cases served to grant rights as well as legal and social privilege to certain persons in our society, usually at the expense of others. Similarly, during the early nineteenth century, the law and society maintained the notion that women had no social standing and thus were less than citizens. This also framed societal conceptions of personhood.

This way of thinking about legal personhood created what Professor Henry Chambers called (in the context of *Dred Scott*) "tiered personhood." The legal history discussed below illustrates the point that this process of granting personhood categorizes and makes separate levels of legal personhood by excluding some, giving others some rights, and giving the most privileged full rights—or full political personhood. Additionally, the forms of wealth and power that those privileged persons received through their status and which they used to re-enforce their status were also given prominence.

The question of personhood was (and is) imbedded in a related question, "who is a citizen?" As the post-Civil War amendments and their application sought to delete the distinction between legal persons and nonpersons—and as this shift towards equality was resisted at every turn—the citizenship question took prominence.

Though conceptually distinct, the citizenship question revolves around the same issue as the question of personhood: What entities are entitled to the range of constitutional rights as distinct from other entities? Cases like *Brown v. Board of Education* and *Roe v. Wade*, as well as passage of the Nineteenth Amendment, the Civil Rights Act of 1964, and the Voting Rights Act of 1965 ultimately expanded the boundaries of personhood to include people formerly excluded or subordinated by American society. Put another way, these cases were efforts to erase the tiers of personhood. As a whole, these personhood decisions confirmed or removed privilege and reset the political boundaries that restricted access to American democracy for their era.

This Article argues that *Citizens United* is the latest in this line of cases because it set wide open the category of personhood from simply natural persons—that is, human beings—to corporations, unions, and other legal entities. Put another way, *Citizens United* forces us to once again ask, "what is a person?"

The Court has expanded the boundaries of what I am calling "political personhood." I define political personhood as both a status and a framework. As a status, political personhood allows a natural person to exercise the range of constitutional rights and entitles a person to receive constitutional protections. The political personhood process is where the Court—as well as lawmakers, enforcers, and society generally—establishes a norm of who is recognized as a person for purposes of the legal privilege. In addition to being a grant of rights, political personhood provides privilege and status, allowing it to amass and affect capital in a manner that best enables and enforces the privilege of those who possess political personhood. In this way, granting political personhood reinforces status and separates some with greater status and power from others. The process creates tiers of personhood.

Now, after *Citizens United*, political personhood includes not only natural persons but also artificial persons—whose sole purpose is to amass capital and generate profit—to participate in political discourse. And arguably, the artificial person of the corporation may become more significant, and may have the power to exercise rights to a greater extent and on a greater tier, than the natural person.

This Article makes an initial effort to support the argument that the Court is engaged in an ongoing process of defining political personhood and *Citizens United* is the latest opinion to this end. Towards this goal, this Article will illustrate how the breadth and scope of the reasoning of *Citizens United* suggest that it more appropriately fits within the political personhood line of cases. This Article will argue that this expansion of the idea of personhood represents a fundamental shift in the idea of political personhood, yet at the same time represents the underlying operation of the political personhood idea as expressed during the nineteenth and twentieth centuries. Finally, this Article will conclude by offering thoughts on the effects of *Citizen United* if it is interpreted from this perspective. As I discuss below, the main effect of the new conception of personhood in *Citizens United* will be twofold: First, it will allow for corporate interests to obtain an unprecedented level of dominance over the American political discourse. Second, this corporate dominance will reaffirm an old form of supremacy: the power of the mostly white and mostly male class that controls corporations. This new era of corporate rights dominating the rights of natural persons may lead to a new period of tiered legal personhood in our democracy, an outcome that is inconsistent with the vision of rights under our modern Constitution.

III. Corporations: The Special Case of Political Personhood

The process of determining political personhood relates to the rights to be granted to natural persons as part of the polity of the United States. With the rise of the corporate form in the nineteenth and twentieth centuries, the Court had to confront the question of what rights corporations should be granted within the constitutional scheme. This issue of corporate personhood became a vexing intellectual and legal dilemma. *Citizens United* puts it squarely in relief once again.

The theoretical approach of this Article does not start with the ongoing debate about corporate personhood. It focuses instead on the transformation in the idea of political personhood that the Court has adopted in the past and is now revising via *Citizens United*. However, to effectively complete this commentary about *Citizens United*, it is necessary to make some observations about the corporate personhood dilemma. The Court's own decisions prior to *Citizens United* and the literature concerning corporate personhood suggest that though corporations have been granted certain legal rights depending on how the nature of the corporation was viewed, corporate artificial personhood nonetheless is wholly different than the personhood conceived of for natural persons.

Demonstrating this difference requires a brief discussion of the predominant models of corporate personhood. Thereafter, this next section observes how, pre-*Citizens United*, an artificial person model of corporate personhood was applied to the question of whether corporations were entitled First Amendment speech rights, and how this set up the problem in *Citizens United*. Additionally, the section will discuss the problematic compromise created by *Austin v. Michigan Chamber of Commerce*. Then, [the Article] will address how *Citizens United* shifted the paradigm of personhood to place corporations within the realm of objects of political personhood.

A. Political Personhood and the Theory of the Corporation

The personhood of corporations has been a longstanding topic of debate in both judicial and academic circles. Arguments about corporate personhood have generally revolved around three different theories of corporate personhood.

The earliest theory of the corporation is that it is merely a creation of the state. This "artificial person" or "concession" theory rested on the view that a corporation effectively exists at the sufferance of the state and, therefore, is not entitled to any rights or protections not granted to it by statute. Importantly, the corporation, as a creation of the state, could not assert rights against its benefactor, the state itself.

During the early part of the nineteenth century, political leaders and the courts took this view of the corporation. Corporations depended on legislative approval for their creation — i.e., corporations were a concession provided by the government — and were thus dependent on the legislature for their existence, regulation, and the scope of their powers. Underlying this theory is the idea that corporations were publically oriented. The corporation was created for a public purpose and thus the state could regulate its operations for the good of the public.

However, this view shifted with *County of Santa Clara v. Southern Pacific Rail Co.* from one of mere artificial personhood to a view that corporations held the status of personhood for purposes of the Fourteenth Amendment. In *Santa Clara*, the Court held that a corporation is a person for purposes of the Fourteenth Amendment, and accordingly, it cannot be taxed differently than natural persons. Within this model, it was argued that a corporation is an amalgamation of the people who stood behind the corporation. Thus, according to the amalgamation model, it was appropriate to grant the corporation rights in order to protect the rights of the people behind it.

This model was in ascendancy during the Lochner era of Supreme Court jurisprudence. Lochner jurisprudence allowed corporations to receive the benefits of the deregulation that took place during that period of the Court's jurisprudence. Indeed, this view is premised on the view that the corporation is not a creation of the state but the product of the free market and of economic forces, and exists for the benefit of the persons who constitute it. Accordingly, the state should support the rights of the persons who constitute corporations and not interfere with their consensual actions.

Indeed, at the turn of the twentieth century, a third model emerged among scholars and the Court for how to conceptualize the corporation: the "natural person" or "real entity" model. This model rests on the premise that the corporation is an entity that emerged separate and apart from the sanction or authorization of the state. Also, it exists separate and apart from the natural persons who might at any particular time control it. In this sense, a corporation is a person—an entity with status and rights that should be recognized under the constitution and laws.

The important implication of this real entity theory is that the corporation has a life completely separate and apart from the state; the state merely records the combination of the private parties and plays only observer of the corporation's formation. Accordingly, the corporation has a "collective consciousness" or a "collective will" that is separate and apart from those who may run the corporation at any given time. Thus, under this view, a corporation may be considered to be fully a "person" under the law and entitled to the legal rights and responsibilities that would attend to any natural person. A slightly different understanding of the natural person view of corporations is the view that there should be a public law of corporations, which seeks to regulate corporations to ensure that they use their powers not merely to generate profit for their shareholders, but that they benefit those affected by the corporation and advance the public good.

What this theoretical debate about how to conceptualize the corporation indicates is that there is a range of positions about whether corporations should or should not be granted political personhood. The concession model would suggest that there is no such thing as political personhood for corporations. As entities regulated and controlled by the state, statute defines the corporation's legal boundaries. Thus, a corporation would not be entitled any constitutional rights that would trump statutory control.

The aggregation or amalgamation model suggests that the corporation would be entitled a type of political personhood to the extent that its incorporators would be entitled political personhood status. Political personhood status for the corporation would derive from the personhood of the people who compose it, which would leave room to distinguish between the persons who organize the corporation and the corporation itself. Similarly, the real entity model suggests that the corporation is a political person entitled all of the protections within the Constitution. The distinction between it and the aggregation model is that the corporation is entitled political personhood as a right intrinsic to the corporation itself.

This brief discussion also suggests that it is plausible to read the conception of personhood in *Citizens United* as adopting a position relating to political personhood—the kind of personhood this article previously suggested was ordinarily applicable to human beings solely. This represents a substantial shift from the jurisprudence of the Court concerning the ability of corporations to spend in elections, where the Court upheld limits consistent with placing the interests of citizens ahead of those of corporations. To this prior jurisprudence this Article will now turn.

B. Political Speech and Corporations: The *Bellotti* and *Austin* Thicket

The jurisprudence of the Court within the realm of corporate political speech prior to *Citizens United* struck an uneasy balance between what appears to be an aggregation approach to the corporation and the desire to prevent the appearance of corruption within the political process. The Court recognized that corporations may have had First Amendment free speech rights when it came to ballot initiatives about which a corporation might wish to speak, but until *Citizens United*, a corporation's speech rights—i.e., its own direct spending on elections—were curtailed as to campaigns to elect political officials. These regulations had been upheld—until *Citizens United*. This suggests that the Court thought of corporations as political persons of a sort as they pertained to the First Amendment, but only to the extent that their interests did not interfere with the interests of citizens in their democracy. To explain this proposition, this part will briefly discuss the Court's campaign finance corporate spending jurisprudence.

The seminal case which defines modern campaign finance law is the 1976 case of *Buckley v. Valeo*. There, the Court struck down a number of spending limits under the Federal Election Campaign Act Amendments of 1974. *Buckley*, however, did not address legislatively-imposed spending limits imposed on corporations and labor unions. In the period between *Buckley* and *Citizens United*, the Court at times possessed skepticism about such limits and at times deferred to legislative judgments that such limits were necessary. Under this jurisprudence, the political personhood of the corporation was limited at best. The Court recognized that a corporation could exercise free speech rights, but the Court limited this right in recognition of the fact that the corporation's ability to amass wealth made it fundamentally different than the natural (political) person. Its influence could corrupt the political process.

The first case to effectively recognize the political personhood of corporations—at least as it relates to First Amendment free speech—was the 1978 case of *First National Bank of Boston v. Bellotti*. There, the Court ruled that corporations had a First Amendment right to make contributions in order to attempt to influence political processes. The corporation in question sought to spend money to influence a ballot initiative; however, the Massachusetts law prohibited corporations from making expenditures that would affect elections.

The *Bellotti* court reasoned that a speaker could not be prohibited from political speech simply because the speaker was a corporation. In particular, the Court rejected as an impermissible constraint on First Amendment rights the notion that its speech interests were restricted to topics that "materially impact[ed]" the corporation's business interests. This reasoning suggests the Court had in mind the notion that a corporation possessed political personhood—that it represented an entity entitled to absolute protection due to its status as an entity entitled to rights of speech.

Yet, this recognition was tempered by the Court in 1982 when it recognized, in *FEC v. National Right to Work Committee*, that the government had a compelling interest in limiting corporate spending to prevent corruption. *National Right to Work Committee* raised the constitutionality of section 441(b) of the Federal Election Campaign Act which limited corporate direct spending in campaigns. The Court upheld Section 441(b) as narrowly tailored to meet the government's interests in insuring that "substantial aggregations of wealth amassed by the special advantages which go with the corporate form of organization should not be converted into political 'war chests' which could be used to incur political debts from legislators who were aided by the contributions." The Court also reasoned that Congress had incentive "to protect the individuals who have paid money into a corporation or union for purposes other than the support of candidates from having that money used to support political candidates to who they may be opposed."

Subsequently, in 1990, the Court heard *Austin v. Michigan Chamber of Commerce*, where it reaffirmed this limitation on corporate rights of political speech. The Court ruled that a state statute that prohibited corporations from spending money to support or oppose candidates in elections was constitutional. There, the corporation in question litigated against the constitutionality of the Michigan statute that prohibited corporations from spending on behalf of candidates in elections.

The *Austin* court continued to afford corporations First Amendment protection as to speech, but it found that this particular campaign spending restriction passed constitutional muster. The *Austin* court again recognized that the state had an interest in preventing the corrosive influences that the massive wealth which could be infused into an election by corporate spending would have to distort an election. This view, often called the "antidistortion rationale" of *Austin*, swayed the Court to uphold the limits on campaign spending by corporations. The *Austin* majority worried that direct corporate spending in elections would have the effect of distorting the messages in the elections due to the impact that massive amounts of spending by corporations could have.

The Court also noted that the restriction was narrowly tailored to the state's interest in preventing corruption because "the Act does not impose an absolute ban on all forms of corporate political spending but permits corporations to make independent political expenditures through separate segregated funds." The Court noted that contributors who know the funds will be used for political speech can pay into the segregated fund so that the speech would accurately "reflect[] contributors' support for the corporation's political views." In other words, the *Austin* Court suggested that the interests in political speech — and the spending therefrom — were the province of natural persons — actual citizens who had the greatest stake in the electoral process. Speech via the corporate form (through, e.g., political action committee funds) that accommodated their views and still allowed their contributions to enable the corporate person to speak was acceptable.

Arguably, then, *Austin* balanced the risks of absolute corporate political free speech created by *Bellotti* if *Bellotti* were taken to its extreme: the balance sought to enable actual persons acting through the corporate form to have political free speech through that form. Though *Austin* was roundly criticized for creating this carve out in the ideal of the First Amendment, it did distinguish between the interest of natural persons and the interest of corporate persons. That uneasy balance continued until the Court handed down *Citizens United*.

IV. The Categorical Change Wrought by *Citizens United*

Seen from the lens of political personhood, *Citizens United* can be reasoned in this way: the *Citizens United* majority made a judgment as to what rights corporations are entitled to and then granted those rights. Arguably, the *Citizens United* Court could have shown judicial restraint by just invalidating the portions of the Bipartisan Campaign Reform Act that were directly at issue. However, the Court pushed forward to find a broad constitutional right of corporate political freedom of speech.

In its analysis, the *Citizens United* majority recognized that for purposes of the First Amendment, corporations were persons entitled to unlimited speech rights. The Court, through Chief Justice Roberts, arrived there by determining that corporations were merely associations of persons, citizens who then take the corporate form in order to act. As an "association of persons" the Court argued that a corporation — like any organization of people — should be entitled to rights of speech.

In this we see the political personhood process at work. The majority decided to first find a constitutional issue relating to free speech (when it had the option to decide the case on far narrower grounds). Second, the Court categorized corporations as persons by making a decision as to whether corporations fit into the notion of a political person, and then once a corporation was deemed to be sufficiently like a political person, the Court decided to imbue it with rights. Thus, both of the "process" criteria of political personhood have been met.

Indeed, it is clear from this that the Court adopted the amalgamation model of the corporation as its way of categorizing the corporation. The judgment of the majority was that the corporation merely was a proxy for the persons behind it and thus held political personhood to function for them. Accordingly, it was entitled the full panoply of First Amendment rights in relation to spending in elections. This sweeping theoretical choice locates the Court as viewing the corporation as possessing political personhood without limits.

As such an entity, the substantive concerns raised by the idea of political personhood come into play. Granting this privilege of absolute First Amendment freedom of speech creates a right that the holders of the right—the corporations themselves—may use to inculcate and replicate their privilege. As we saw with the slaveholders in *Dred Scott*, the white male political establishment in *Minor*, and the apartheid white society in *Plessy*, the Court's ruling has the effect of providing a means for corporations—who are organized by, controlled by, and provide profits to a privileged group of mostly straight, white men—to ensure their dominance over society through insuring their privilege through the political process. Just like *Dred Scott* made slavery constitutional and *Plessy* made segregation legally acceptable, the potential now exists for corporations to distort the political process for their own ends and dominate politics through unlimited spending. By allowing corporations an unfettered voice in the political marketplace, they have the potential through their amassed capital to dominate ordinary citizens. By their sheer power, and their ability to replicate and enforce that power, corporations can, arguably, operate on a different tier of political personhood than ordinary citizens and political parties.

This engagement of the political process to an end separate and apart from natural persons drove the concerns of the *Citizens United* dissent. Where the majority thought of the corporation as an association of persons—qualifying as close to being a political person—Justice Stevens in dissent saw corporations as state-created entities that "differ from natural persons in fundamental ways"; "have no consciences, no beliefs, no feelings, no thoughts, no desires"; and "must engage the political process in instrumental terms if they are to maximize shareholder value." Of particular note, the dissent asserted, "corporations have been 'effectively delegated responsibility for ensuring society's economic welfare.'" This differs markedly from the idea of political personhood espoused by the majority. Indeed, the majority clearly relies on shoehorning corporations into traditional bounds of personhood, an association of persons entitled to rights based on their natural status. However, the Stevens dissent points out the conflicting view, that corporations are better thought of as lacking the attributes of persons and thus may be limited as legal—but not real-person-like—entities.

As Justice Stevens observed, "corporations," those state sanctioned entities now granted political personhood, "have been 'effectively delegated responsibility for ensuring society's economic welfare.'" This observation that the corporation is the dominant form of capital in our modern society points us back to our recognition of the effects of political personhood, that these choices made by the Court are instrumental in the sense that they privilege some class, group, or new entity (a group that, as I will discuss shortly, is almost entirely white, straight, and male). Now, for First Amendment purposes, political persons—whether real persons or state-created entities—may participate in the political process. A class of entities is now privileged, so the question becomes: "At whose expense does this privilege come?"

V. *Citizens United*, Personhood, and the Political Person of the Future

Citizens United has expanded the category of persons for purposes of the First Amendment. By implication, this case has now included within the realm of political personhood the "person" of the corporation. What are the ramifications of this choice for the law of politics and for the philosophy of American law? This is a broad question that will be dealt with for years to come.

First, *Citizens United* at its most basic level seems to confirm the ascendancy of corporate interests as the dominant form of capital within our society. This will have a number of substantive ramifications for our Republic. The first of those is that corporate spending now has the great potential to dominate the elective process. Professor Dale Rubin explicitly argued that corporations can now "buy and sell" candidates. Professor andre cummings has pointed out that given the track record of corporate leaders prior to the financial crisis of 2008, there is no reason to believe that in a post-*Citizens United* world that they would not spend recklessly to the end of effectively hijacking the political process. There are others, like Professor Bradley Smith, who have observed that *Citizens United* was really an anti-incumbency decision. Smith argued that *Citizens United* provides an opportunity for either political party to receive support, and thus would frustrate only the interests of incumbents.

As a possible progressive reply to Professor Smith, Professor Stefan Padfield commented that corporate interests have already purchased candidates through the 2010 election and that the candidates elected by these corporate interests are supporting their backers. Professor Padfield commented:

> Against this backdrop, what have the newly-elected set out to do? They have set their sights on abolishing Dodd-Frank for the recently bailed-out Wall Street bankers who have recovered very nicely indeed to rake in record profits this year while Main Street continues to deal with unemployment and foreclosures. They have set their sights on repealing universal health care, a result much appreciated by the free-spending health-care industry. They plan on cutting much of the social safety net so they can continue to give tax breaks to the wealthy. (Moody's recently estimated that the House Republicans' proposed cuts would cost 700,000 jobs by 2012.) And they have set their sights on busting the unions that serve so much of Main Street.

It is an open question as to whether the ascendancy of corporate interests will be confirmed by future elections, but it would seem that this question, which raises serious issues about the integrity of our democratic process, will need to be addressed for years to come.

A second ramification that should be seriously considered and which was abandoned in *Citizens United* is the anti-distortion rationale of *Austin*. It follows from this rationale that direct corporate spending in elections at all, and especially at a level above and beyond what an individual could spend would, arguably, create a perception that the electoral system and ultimately the government itself are corrupt because they are beholden to corporate interests. It has been argued that the abandonment of the anti-distortion rational should be reconsidered.

To add to this concern, there exists the fear that corporate political personhood, which is now protected within terms of the speech rights of the First Amendment, can grow into an unpredictable trump on the political process. To be clear, this process was designed by citizens to be run for citizens. But now it may end up being dominated by artificial persons, corporations whose only interest in political outcomes stems from how those outcomes may maximize profit, a desire unrelated to that which Americans actually want. The anti-distortion rationale protects individuals from distorted communications during elections; it also creates a semblance of independence for political candidates. If both of these are lost, the voters may lose the faith in the political system, what of it there is that remains. Elections may become, in the words of Alexander Keyssar, "a pro forma ritual designed to ratify the selection of candidates who have already won the fund-raising contests." In a post-*Citizens United* world, these contests—and perhaps the candidates themselves—will be brought to the people by corporations.

Third, the ramifications of the process of political personhood ought to raise concern for us about who the privileged classes are in our society and how that privilege currently manifests. It can be argued that the potential exists to shift control of the American democratic process absolutely from individuals to corporations. The political, economic, and social concerns of individuals may then be ignored because corporate concerns will rate as more important. The more important political person after *Citizens United*—indeed, the now-privileged class—is apparently the corporation and the people who control it.

As *Dred Scott* empowered slaveholders, and *Plessy* privileged the separate white society over African American society, perhaps the ramification of the Court's latest personhood analysis is the privileging of corporate power over the traditional political power curried by parties and individuals. As evident in those periods, a stratification of political personhood existed between landed white men on the one hand, and women and people of color on the other; perhaps *Citizens United* now confirms that the corporate person possesses a greater political personhood status than the individual person.

Perhaps a third era of tiered personhood has manifested where corporate interests are superior to individual interests, which is ironic given that the Constitution and its amendments were designed to protect the natural person. The Founders undoubtedly believed in this protection, and perhaps this explains the outcry from the general public regarding *Citizens United*. Intuitively, this tiered personhood does not fit the reality of what people think of when they think of a "right." The ramifications of this turn—if it holds out to be true—will irrevocably change society in the twenty-first century.

Finally, and beyond mere analytical analogy to the personhood cases, maybe this story is, once again, explicitly about race, gender and class stratification. In the immediate aftermath of *Citizens United*, Steven Ramirez on the Corporate Justice Blog noted the following:

> [T]here has been one female of color who has ever served as the CEO of a Fortune 500 company—and that happened only last summer [2009]. That appears to bring the total number of African American CEOs to five. As of November, 2007, there were four Latino CEOs and fourteen women.

> With respect to board seats, men hold 83% of all Fortune 100 directorships. Latinos and African Americans hold 14% of such positions and Asian Americans hold 1%. For Fortune 500 companies the reality is bleaker—there are even fewer African American directors and the number is declining. Only 3% of all Fortune 500 board positions are held by Hispanics.

> To the extent that *Citizens United* shifts political power to corporations, fundamentally, it shifts power away from communities of color (and women) notwithstanding their increased voting power.

This shift in power to the corporate form appears to raise the question of legitimizing not only corporate form as the dominant form of capital but also affirming a new form of political power that will control the traditional political hierarchies. The blunt fact is that those who control these hierarchies are mostly white and mostly male. Further, this group is a substantial minority in American society, given that those who run corporations and own corporations are small in number in relation to the rest of diverse America. What we face is the possibility of a few who could represent a stratified, homogeneous class in America that holds the power to dominate elections and to tilt the democratic process in its favor. Put another way, the question to be asked is whether *Citizens United* marks the beginning of an era where this country makes plain the existence of tiered political personhood, where the individual citizens' interests are sublimated to the interests of corporate artificial persons (and the minority of upper-class, mostly white male persons who own the corporations).

This appears to be a consequence of the Court's granting political personhood to corporations. This choice—like that in *Dred Scott* and *Plessy*—may alter our society for years to come, especially given that by 2050 ethnic minorities may become the majority in this country. By 2050, political, economic, and social power may be concentrated in the hands of a minority of mostly white, mostly male powerbrokers who may effectively be an oligarchy in relation to the majority-minority population of the United States. Such a scenario certainly warrants concern.

VI. Conclusion

Corporate speech is only one piece of a larger puzzle that has to do with race, class, the distribution of wealth, and the manifestations of privilege in American society. But in this era of unfettered political speech by corporations, if we are not critical of the policies of democracy going forward, and if we do not look at the possibility of corporate dominance of the electoral system with a cynical and proactive eye, the generations that follow us may count *Citizens United*—along with *Dred Scott*, *Minor*, and *Plessy*—as one of the most infamous decisions, adverse to individual rights, ever rendered by the Supreme Court.

Copyright © 2011 John Marshall Law School; Atiba R. Ellis

Notes

(1) Since several years have passed since *Citizens United* was decided, is Professor Ellis accurate in predicting that this decision could go down as one of the most infamous decisions adverse to individual rights "ever rendered by the Supreme Court"? Is it too early to tell?

(2) Are corporations dominating political electioneering in the ways predicted in the articles above?

3. CEO Primacy—The Power of the CEO

In the article below, Professor Steven Ramirez argues that corporate law has been evolving rapidly to a place where the power and prominence of the Chief Executive Officer (CEO) has become supreme and largely unchallenged. Ramirez views this as problematic for a number of reasons, including the neutering of shareholder power and the entrenchment of significant economic might into the hands of a very small group of monolithic corporate leaders. As you read Ramirez's arguments below, consider the question "Should so much power and influence be placed in the hands of so few?" and perhaps even more importantly "Who is being granted so much economic authority?" Consider further what is meant by his "Race to the Bottom" language. Often, the commanding heights of fair corporate governance would be represented by firms that engage in the fairest and most ethical corporate practices. A race to the bottom would indicate that corporate leadership does the least amount possible to comply with necessary laws and regulations and in so doing, plays to the lowest common denominator in making corporate decisions. A race to the bottom is bad business and bad for stakeholders, as targeting profits at all costs and minimizing corporate governance or fairness leads inevitably to short-termism and a race to the bottom.

The Special Interest Race to CEO Primacy and the End of Corporate Governance Law

Steven A. Ramirez
32 DEL. J. CORP. L. 345 (2007)

I. Introduction

Corporate governance law in the United States is deeply flawed. Legendary mutual fund founder John Bogle asserts that a "pathological mutation" has transmogrified corporate governance from "traditional owners' capitalism" to "new managers capitalism." Prominent business commentator Robert J. Samuelson claims that Chief Executive Officers (CEOs) have "contrived" a "moral code that justifies grabbing as much as they can." In late 2006 and early 2007, a widening scandal over backdated options grants had ensnared more than 200 companies in criminal and civil probes (including two that resulted in criminal fraud charges) revolving around whether "incentive" compensation plans were in fact rigged games designed to enrich officers at the expense of shareholders. Meanwhile, CEO compensation at America's leading public corporations continues to soar. This article shows that "CEO primacy" is rooted in certain key legal changes in the 1980s and 1990s that are in turn rooted in special interest influence. The cost of such CEO primacy to the economy and shareholders is huge. This article argues that this CEO primacy as embedded in law is neither economically nor politically sustainable, and will create constant pressure for reform until the current system of corporate federalism is scuttled.

Our system of corporate governance is dysfunctional because the governing legal structure underlying that system is dysfunctional. Essentially, our system is based upon a historically path dependent corporate federalism that yields three pernicious outcomes, each of which are inherent in the structure of the system. First, a very small group of citizens (those residing in the state of Delaware) has autonomy over corporate law that affects the entire economy coast to coast. Second, federal intervention into this system is in response to broad-based political pressure arising from financial crises. Third, in a non-crisis political equilibrium, management interests are sufficiently dense that they may concentrate their resources on corporate governance issues while the public is oblivious; thus, in the ordinary course, management has the greatest political sway over corporate governance. Each of these elements is exacerbated by deep information deficiencies regarding corporate governance outcomes. The result of this system is to maximize the ability of management to reduce constraints, achieve ever increasing levels of compensation, and impose agency costs upon shareholders and the economy as a whole; indeed, the system is devolving towards CEO primacy and the end of shareholder primacy. This article posits that the resolution of these dynamics will require a deep restructuring of the regulatory environment governing the American public corporation.

At least since William Cary's landmark 1974 article, Federalism and Corporate Law: Reflections upon Delaware, there has been a running debate regarding the proper role for the federal government in the area of corporate governance. On one side of this debate are those arguing that state lawmakers seek to enhance their tax revenues from dispensing corporate charters by providing otherwise suboptimal corporate governance standards that are indulgent to managers, who currently make incorporation decisions. On the other side are those claiming that capital markets would punish corporations hobbled by suboptimal corporate governance, and therefore neither states nor managers would pursue such standards; instead, market competition assures that there is a race to the top, whereby states compete to offer ever more optimal corporate governance. This article proffers a diagnosis that is more dependent upon the negative influence of special interests rather than state versus federal law. Essentially, this article argues that corporate governance law is polluted by familiar notions of regulatory capture and public choice. In fact, this article will show empirically that corporate governance standards are suboptimal under both federal and state law.

As such, this article urges to scholars to rethink the system by which corporate governance is promulgated at both the federal and state level. Getting regulatory incentives right is just as important as getting private incentives right, and in the field of corporate governance, there is compelling evidence that incentives are distorted. To the extent there are manifest deficiencies in our integrated system of corporate governance (arising from state incorporation laws and federal regulation of public companies), there is a need for optimal regulatory structures that can operate to move our system toward an optimal system of corporate governance.

Corporate governance law as presently constructed is not likely to survive. The current system yields inferior substantive outcomes and there is no stable regulatory authority capable of remedying this. Ultimately, superior models of regulating corporate governance will emerge (in the U.S. or elsewhere) that will yield economically superior outcomes for corporate governance standards.

II. Race to the Top or Race to the Bottom?

Historically, the issue of U.S. corporate governance has been left to the states, and Delaware has appropriated the role of providing corporate governance standards for about half of American publicly held companies. However, in specific contexts, the federal government has intervened in corporate governance when investor confidence has eroded to such a level that macroeconomic instability results or is threatened. Irrespective of such episodic, even chaotic, interventions, the system of corporate governance (often termed "corporate federalism") in the U.S. has both the look and feel of regulatory dysfunction-specifically, it appears that management itself dominates the regulatory apparatus that governs its duties and obligations at both the state and federal level, except when a crisis emerges. The corporate corruption crisis that commenced with the failure of Enron in late 2001, and climaxed with the hurried passage of the [Sarbanes-Oxley Act of 2002 (SOX or Act)] in mid-2002, did nothing to shake this view of special interest domination accompanied by transient exceptions. Indeed, events following the enactment of the SOX served only to reinforce this view, as special interest influence operated in the wake of the Act to blunt much of its sting. Thus, leading investor advocates now believe that the American public corporation is a "dictatorship" of the CEO.

The race to the top/race to the bottom debate has evolved in the backdrop of this federal regulatory dynamic. Few have tied the two together as part of a singular special interest dynamic. Yet there is no logical basis for segregating the activity at the state level of corporate governance from the activity at the federal level. Directors and officers are more interested in the substance of law and regulations governing their conduct, rather than the source of such standards. It is true that there is a greater wealth of empirical analysis regarding the race to the bottom/race to the top debate from the perspective of state law. But if managers use special interest influence in one arena to dilute their duties, it is only logical that they would seek to do so in the other. Thus, an integrated view of the evidence, and its manifestations in law, as well as capital markets and economic and financial performance, seems to be a more efficacious method of assessing the optimality of the current corporate governance regime. This integrated view of all the evidence inescapably leads to the conclusion that whatever competitive force may exist to move corporate governance in any direction, both the state and federal systems are subject to dangerous special interest raids that compromise the regulatory infra-structure, which defines and channels corporate activity and has moved our system of corporate governance towards a CEO primacy model.

Some commentators have suggested that federal standards should be expanded or that federal incorporation should displace the operation of state corporate governance standards for publicly held companies, to varying degrees. Federal intervention has thus far been episodic and sporadic rather than comprehensively preemptive. The federal regulatory framework itself, however, has recently been marked by special interest "raids," particularly when the public gaze is diverted from issues of financial regulation—which is to say almost always. The SEC, the primary federal regulatory authority in the area of capital market regulation for corporations issuing securities, has a spotty record, at best, of resisting special interest influence. Thus, vesting comprehensive power over corporate governance for publicly held companies in the SEC (as currently structured at least) is not likely to be successful. Merely calling for federalization of corporate governance misses this point.

On some levels, the corporate corruption crisis of late 2001 and 2002 settled the debate regarding whether the system of corporate federalism in the U.S. leads to excessive laxity in corporate governance standards, or results in competitive pressure for states to formulate even more ideal standards. For example, to the extent the race to the bottom supports more extensive federal intervention into the internal affairs of the publicly held corporation, the spectacular corporate failures of 2001 and 2002 led directly to the SOX—the most invasive federal regulation of corporate governance in history. The SOX excluded management from control over the audit function by requiring an independent audit committee. Therefore, it created an entirely new regulator for auditors of public companies. It also imposed new federal rules of professional responsibility for attorneys "appearing or practicing before the Commission" on behalf of public companies. The Act also enhanced the need for independent directors. Federal intervention is therefore an increasing reality in corporate governance for publicly traded companies; indeed, future meltdowns in investor confidence are likely to lead to ever more intrusive federal regulation, ultimately culminating in some system of federal incorporation.

On another fundamental level, the corporate corruption crisis of 2001 and 2002 seems to have steam-rolled the idea that corporate federalism in the U.S. has resulted in an optimal corporate governance regime. Nevertheless, it is worthwhile to review the empirical record to date with respect to corporate federalism in order to assess the possibility that markets can still be used to continuously move corporate governance in a more ideal direction. The major problem with any argument that markets will move states toward more optimal corporate governance law is that no study has been able to find any evidence that investors make decisions based upon the state of incorporation. Thus, the evidence that Delaware corporations are valued more highly by capital markets is inconclusive at best. Instead, investors seem far more concerned about actual corporate governance practices at firms than which state provides the substantive law framework for corporate governance. There is simply no strong empirical basis that state corporate governance law is impounded into stock market price in a way that will create market pressure for more optimal corporate governance standards.

The most recent empirical analyses of the operation of corporate federalism do not show that there is any race to the top spurred by corporate federalism. In 2003, Professor Lucian Bebchuk and Alma Cohen demonstrated that a major factor driving incorporation decisions is the strength of a given state's antitakeover legislation. Because antitakeover legislation entrenches management and shields them from competitive pressures of the market for corporate control, it is impossible to square this finding with a race to the top. Thus, any empirical foundation for any supposed race to the top has essentially crumbled.

Any uncertainty remaining from the empirical record must be viewed in light of lawmaking that is consistent only with the race to the bottom thesis: increasingly relieving management of legal duties and responsibilities. The so-called duty of care illustrates the race to the bottom quite well. In 1985, the Delaware Supreme Court held a board liable for a breach of the duty of care in *Smith v. Van Gorkom*. The facts of *Van Gorkom* could hardly be more compelling because the outside directors assumed a joint defense with the CEO—and the CEO signed the agreement to sell the public company without reading it and without showing it to an attorney. Nevertheless, shortly after the decision to hold the directors liable for gross negligence was issued, the Delaware legislature enacted a statute that allowed directors to obliterate the duty of care through a provision in the corporation's charter. By 1988, 40 states had enacted director-insulating statutes. The managers of the vast majority of public companies were subsequently able to use their control over the proxy machinery to eliminate their own duty of care. It is difficult to argue that the story of the duty of care in American corporate law is consistent with anything other than a race to the bottom.

Nor is the death of the duty of care the sole outlet for the efforts of management to limit their duties and obligations. Dean Seligman highlights the restriction of shareholder suffrage rights, the decline of tender offers as a source of discipline, and the decline in the ability of shareholders to pursue litigation. Others focus upon the lax standards governing compensation decisions as a problem. Each of the foregoing reflects accelerating laxity in the duties of managers during the 1980s and 1990s, under state law. This laxity is certainly consistent with the race to the bottom thesis. However, a similar dynamic was transpiring simultaneously at the federal level, where the focus has traditionally been on disclosure duties to shareholders.

In late 1995, Congress passed the Private Securities Litigation Reform Act (PSLRA). The PSLRA imposed a new, more stringent pleading standard on plaintiffs seeking relief under the federal securities laws; imposed a new sanctions provision, approaching a loser pays rule on such plaintiffs; created a safe harbor for forward-looking frauds; restricted the ability of plaintiffs to seek class action relief under the federal securities laws; imposed a stricter statutory causation standard for private securities litigants; and restricted the availability of joint and several liability for such claimants. In 1998, Congress followed up with the Securities Litigation Uniform Standards Act (SLUSA), which eliminated state class actions in securities disputes involving public companies. The dual effect of the PSLRA and the SLUSA is to dilute the penalties and enforcement available to deter securities fraud. Thus, laxity is not limited to state law, nor is it the result solely of any state competition for corporate franchise revenues.

Unnecessary or excessive regulation could amount to a tax on innovation or a tax on companies seeking access to the public capital markets. However, there is zero evidence that the private enforcement of the federal securities laws was not needed either at the time of the passage of the PSLRA and the SLUSA, or today. First, there was near unanimity that investor confidence required supporting regulation and that private litigation was essential to enforcing the federal securities laws. Second, the late 1980s and early 1990s were hardly emblematic of a high degree of corporate integrity and honesty in our capital markets. Finally, lax conduct quickly followed the diminution of private enforcement, and empirical evidence demonstrates that auditors, in particular, responded to the PSLRA and the SLUSA in predictable fashion: they allowed the spoliation of audit quality so that CEOs could increase current income and thus their own compensation. As such, it appears that the PSLRA and the SLUSA led directly to the spate of accounting-driven securities frauds that plagued our capital markets in the 1990s and thereafter. For the first time ever, federal law restricted investor rights under state law, turning the federal securities laws on their head.

The end of private securities litigation as a constraint on management is not the only element of federal law favoring the prerogatives of the CEO. CEOs of public companies have the unique privilege of picking their own nominal supervisors—the board of directors. Under the federal proxy rules (applicable to all publicly traded corporations), only management (i.e., the CEO) has the power to use corporate funds to solicit proxy votes for its slate of director candidates. If a mere shareholder wishes to place a person on the board, the shareholder must absorb the printing costs, postage costs, and legal costs of mounting a full-blown proxy solicitation, and these costs can amount to millions of dollars. Thus, there is typically only one candidate for board positions in public corporations, and that candidate is selected by management. This means that the CEO may stack the board with cultural and social clones in order to maximize compensation. Shareholder democracy is a myth in the U.S., and management interests have worked to keep it a myth.

The reductions in investor rights and protections are not limited to legislative and regulatory promiscuity towards management, as the United States Supreme Court has also turned hostile to private claims under the federal securities laws. Beginning in the early 1990s, the Court began to seriously prune the private rights of action available under the federal securities laws. In 1991, the Court narrowed the statute of limitations applicable to federal securities fraud cases. Three years later, the Court eliminated liability for aiding and abetting securities fraud. Then in 1995, the Court limited investor remedies under the Securities Act of 1933. One commentator has noted that: "In forty federal securities law decisions, the Court decided thirty-two cases in favor of defendants, and in almost every one, significantly narrowed the reach of the federal securities laws." Simply put, the Court's approach to private securities litigation evinces deep hostility to investor rights.

Predictably, all of these pro-management outcomes led to a crisis in corporate confidence-culminating in a parade of corporate corruption scandals in 2001 and 2002. The public's gaze focused on corporate governance deficiencies. With elections looming, Congress rushed through the SOX "reforms" that passed the Senate by a vote of 97–0. Almost immediately scholars voiced concerns about the efficacy of the SOX. And, literally on the day the SOX was signed, reactionary forces began to cut back on its reforms. This pattern continued, and ultimately short-circuited the SEC's proxy reform initiative. Many of the SOX reforms seemed to codify practices that were employed by Enron and others; thus, it was known such reforms would not prevent future Enrons. Meanwhile, reforms that enjoyed empirical support languished. Thus, the SOX reforms have been largely ineffective in stopping corporate abuses. Perhaps the most compelling indictment of the SOX reforms is to follow the money; CEO power seems to have been largely unaffected as compensation for senior executives continues to soar.

Recent events illustrate just how weak American corporate governance standards have become. In the summer of 2006, it became clear that thousands of public corporations were backdating options grants to past dates when their stock was trading lower, to maximize payoffs to their senior executives. While backdating may not be illegal if it is both appropriately disclosed and in accordance with tax law, by the end of the summer two criminal cases had been filed against executives at Brocade Communications and Comverse Technology. Moreover, by 2007, over 200 companies (including Apple, Inc.) disclosed that their options practices were under investigation. Rigging options grants to maximize payoff to executives by picking some low price point in the past as a fantasy and fraudulent grant date is like "stealing money from the company and shareholders." It appears that this occurred systematically over a period of ten years throughout corporate America. Such practices seem more about the crass enrichment of executives than creating any incentive for performance; indeed, one company backdated options grants to enrich a dead executive. The mere fact that this kind of scam was occurring at publicly traded companies at all, suggests that corporate governance is not operating to reduce CEO autonomy (and thus agency costs) to acceptable levels.

CEO primacy is a direct outcome of the system of corporate governance law that devolved in the 1980s and 1990s into a dictatorship of management, by management, and for management. At both the state and federal level, corporate governance in the 1980s and 1990s became a parade of managerial indulgences. At every turn, legislators, judges, and regulators eliminated or diluted constraints on the power of management. One must believe that the best means of controlling agency costs is to grant the agent unfettered discretion in order to believe that corporate federalism yields optimal outcomes. Traditionally, some level of judicial deference to management was manifest in the business judgment rule; recently, that concept has succumbed to a new, more promiscuous paradigm of CEO power unencumbered by virtually any civil liability. The fact that this occurred at both the state and federal level suggests that the problem transcends corporate federalism and any debate about the race to the bottom versus the race to the top.

III. The Emerging Science of Corporate Governance

At the same time, there is an emerging science of corporate governance that exists independently of any debate regarding special interest influence or any race either way at the state level. Instead, this body of evidence empirically tests the outcomes of competing systems of corporate governance or specific elements of corporate governance. The studies test the impact of corporate governance on macroeconomic performance across nations, or the impact of specific innovations on corporate financial performance. This emerging interdisciplinary science of corporate governance means that there is an emerging vision of optimal corporate governance. This emerging science serves a dual purpose: not only does it provide aspirational guidance, it also serves as a test of the current system's ability to deliver appropriate corporate governance standards. Instead of theorizing or speculating about sound corporate governance, corporate governance is now studied in terms of actual outcomes, across disciplines. These empirical analyses have covered a wide range of corporate governance issues.

For example, given the centrality of information to the functioning of markets, one may be tempted to conclude that any disclosure of corporate information is beneficial to the functioning of financial markets and the corporation as an institution. However, empirical studies suggest this theoretical supposition is flawed. Instead, corporations providing frequent earnings guidance seem inclined to forgo expenditures that yield long-term profits in order to inflate earnings over the short term. Thus, in one recent study, companies that provided frequent earnings guidance were found to have spent less on research and development than those companies that provided less guidance, and therefore to have suffered stunted financial performance over the long term. It appears that the flawed system of American corporate governance gives CEOs the opportunity to forgo long-term financial performance in favor of short-term profitability (and presumably higher CEO pay).

Corporate governance should operate to limit CEO autonomy and to protect investors; this will lead to superior outcomes, because if investors are confident that their reasonable expectations will be secured by law, they will invest at a lower cost to entrepreneurs. Thus, investor protection is associated with higher economic growth. One study found that companies with superior corporate governance measures enjoyed superior stock market valuations. This is consistent with other studies linking various indices of shareholder rights to financial performance. Weak investor protection leads to a shift in the corporate balance of power in favor of management, which will increase self-dealing and lead to higher compensation for executives. If executive compensation is the "canary in the coal mine" signaling pervasively weak corporate governance, then there is cause for serious concern in the U.S., where CEO compensation relative to earnings has doubled over the past ten years. In the long run, securing the reasonable expectations of investors through legal protection serves the economy in general and entrepreneurs in particular, while also operating to limit agency costs.

Investor protection entails mandatory disclosure of material information to the investing public—such as that required under the federal securities laws in the U.S. To the extent investors have access to reliable investment information, they should theoretically be more willing to invest, meaning entrepreneurs and businesses will enjoy a lower cost of capital. While one may expect private contracts to be the most effective way to assure an efficient means of securing appropriate information flows, in fact, such contracting appears prohibitively costly. Moreover, management is likely to be more focused on shareholder maximization if they are required to disclose financial information periodically. Empirical evidence now supports these theoretical conclusions.

Given that investor protection is essential to securing the appropriate economic and financial operation of the public corporation, it would be natural to consider private enforcement and private rights of action as necessary components of an investor protection regime. In fact, empirical evidence now demonstrates that "standards of liability facilitating investor recovery of losses are associated with larger stock markets." Importantly, "the results suggest that giving aggrieved shareholders the standing to sue, access to information to identify self-dealing, and a low burden of proof would deter self-dealing and promote stock market development." Thus, it appears that facilitating private rights of action in favor of investors is a key element of sound corporate governance.

An additional issue that has been studied in depth is the effect of board diversity upon corporate financial performance. In general, diversity at the board level is associated with superior corporate governance and better financial performance. Diversity has been shown to enhance cognitive functioning of groups and to disrupt groupthink, a dynamic characterized by mindless adherence to group norms and assumptions. Left to their own discretion, it appears that CEOs specifically engage in homosocial reproduction to stock boards with individuals friendly to the CEO's interests in order to enhance their compensation. This natural tendency is also demonstrated through CEO exploitation of board interlocks (where networks of CEOs serve on each other's boards) in a way that enhances their compensation. There is, therefore, powerful evidence suggesting that board diversity leads to superior outcomes in terms of corporate performance and corporate governance, by disrupting the CEO's ability to exploit social dynamics such as groupthink and homosocial reproduction.

A further area of inquiry involves antitakeover protections, which typically operate at the state level to insulate current management from the pressures of competitive corporate control markets. Such protections make it difficult to oust incumbent managers from control, which serves to enhance their power and increase agency costs in the form of higher executive compensation. Another study found that antitakeover legislation also weakened management incentives to negotiate lower labor costs generally, as CEOs apparently utilized their enhanced power to favor co-employees over more distant and less visible shareholders. Indeed, it appears that in general such laws are associated with more lethargic management as the enhanced entrenchment leads to diminished investment in plants and lower productivity and profitability. These facts are consistent with a slew of studies that demonstrate enhanced CEO power is closely associated with higher CEO pay, although not enhanced performance. In all, it appears that antitakeover protections serve to enhance management power and compromise performance.

Board composition has also commanded significant attention from corporate governance scholars. For example, a staggered board may be a powerful antitakeover device that operates to frustrate the ability of outsiders to seize control of a corporation. There is robust evidence that a board that is independent of the CEO enhances corporate valuation. Moreover, boards selected without input from the CEO are more independent, and the corporation achieves a higher market valuation. Yet evidence of the efficacy of so-called outside directors (those who are not otherwise employees of the corporation) is mixed, at best. On the other hand, there is powerful evidence that the separation of CEO and chairman of the board into two positions reduces agency costs and enhances firm value. Similarly, there is evidence that an independent nominating committee for the selection of directors is associated with superior performance. As elsewhere, endogeniety problems plague research in this area, and it is difficult to discern if board composition drives performance, or performance drives board composition. Nevertheless, it does appear that board composition that reduces CEO autonomy is associated with superior outcomes, based upon the best corporate governance science available.

Thus, state legislatures and courts are guilty of the same obliviousness to empirical evidence as Congress.

There is likely a dearth of institutional capabilities within any of these law-making organs to integrate financial, economic, and accounting studies into their deliberative process. Legislators and judges are not required to have advanced degrees in these areas, nor should they be. They have jurisdiction over a wide variety of legal issues and have neither the time nor the expertise for such specialized knowledge. It is hard to imagine a productive debate in the halls of legislatures or the courthouses of America regarding the appropriate weight to give to the emerging science of corporate governance in making corporate governance law. Even an institution with the resources of the United States Supreme Court seems unlikely to rest its opinions on the state of empirical data. Institutionally, neither legislators nor judges are well suited to interpreting and integrating the best academic information on corporate governance into law.

Neither federal nor state authorities have exhibited any sensitivity to the emerging science of corporate governance. Many corporate governance initiatives have not become law despite enjoying empirical support. There is an intolerable chasm between the teachings of corporate governance science and corporate governance law.

Beyond that, however, deficiencies are manifest across corporate governance issues. The current system of corporate governance law looks nothing like emerging corporate governance science. There is no restriction on management's earnings guidance. There is no standard for encouraging more diverse boards to disrupt homosocial reproduction. Antitakeover protections serve to entrench management across the nation. Congress and the United States Supreme Court have gutted private securities claims, even though investor protection is crucial to sound corporate governance. Courts and legislatures aggressively reduced private remedies over the last 20 years. These results are precisely in accordance with the predictions of public choice and other theories of legislation and lawmaking. Moreover, there are quite often footprints of management interests surrounding diluted shareholder protections and compromised investor rights. The science of corporate governance shows that there is no market pressure for optimal corporate governance; there is only market pressure for indulgent pro-management corporate governance law.

IV. CEO Primacy as a Special Interest Outcome

The idea that a "faction" of citizens can subvert government for their own ends at the expense of the "aggregate interests" of society dates at least to the founding of the nation. The solution to this problem animates the antidemocratic structures embedded in the United States Constitution, particularly as initially ratified. The Founders specifically contemplated some form of depoliticized lawmaking to protect against factions. The result, which endures today, is a vision of democratic accountability rather than democratic decision making. Thus, there is little new in considering the pernicious potential of special interest influence, nor the proper political structures for controlling such influence.

The idea that regulation and law are subject to special interest influence exercised by well-organized groups with economic resources has recently been extended to financial markets generally. Financial markets are a key engine of growth and innovation. The corporation is the central economic institution underlying modern finance as limited liability permits financial diversification, driving down the cost of capital and expanding the pool of financial capital. Nevertheless, "[t]he economically powerful are concerned about the institutions underpinning free markets because they treat people equally, making power redundant." Moreover, "[t]hey are a source of competition, forcing the powerful to prove their competence again and again." Thus, the powerful will seek to entrench their control and position, rather than expose themselves to a truly competitive environment. They will do this, if necessary, through well-organized groups that sacrifice competitive markets for legal indulgences. This is why today there is broad support across the political spectrum for the proposition that left unchecked, capitalism "easily degenerates into a system of incumbents, by incumbents and for incumbents."

There are few incumbents more powerful than the incumbent CEOs of public corporations. CEOs have been able to double their share of corporate profits just in the past few years. Soaring executive compensation has substantially contributed to rising economic inequality in the United States. CEOs enjoy almost unfettered discretion over the composition of the central governing organ of American corporations—the board of directors. Short of intentional wrongdoing, neither CEOs nor their nominal supervisors—directors—face any real risk of legal liability, specifically as a result of relatively recent legislative victories. CEOs of public companies are the primary stewards of vast stores of wealth, as the combined market capitalization of the approximately 5000 public companies in the U.S. exceeds $16 trillion.

With tremendous economic resources and relatively small numbers, CEOs face few constraints in organizing politically. One organization, the Business Roundtable, consists largely of CEOs of major public corporations. It litigates and lobbies with the specific intent of minimizing constraints on the power of CEOs. Another organization, the U.S. Chamber of Commerce, represents big business generally, and also operates to free CEOs of legal constraints. Each of these organizations has a long and successful history of achieving pro-CEO outcomes in law and regulation. Other trade associations, such as the American Institute of Certified Public Accountants, also pursue vigorous lobbying efforts that invariably coincide with the interests of their corporate masters, which are operated under the authority of the CEO. In addition, each individual corporation frequently has its own legions of lobbyists that are controlled by CEOs. CEOs also have the ear of elected politicians through their control of campaign contributions, including control over the corporation's own political action committee.

Against this array of CEO power, shareholders hold little sway. Shareholders, unlike CEOs, have no authority to disburse corporate funds to influence law and regulation. The large number of shareholders means that any lobby group formed to pursue their interests generally would face serious collective action problems. Consequently, there is no organization that lobbies in favor of public shareholders. "They are the most overlooked and underrepresented interest group in America." Thus, any political contest between shareholders and managers is a mismatch to say the least.

It would be pleasant to believe that somehow financial markets could remedy this mismatch. Unfortunately, there is little evidence to support such faith in markets. The first problem with such faith is that all markets suffer from imperfect information, and financial markets are no exception. On the contrary, financial markets could not exist if there was perfect information. One manifest imperfection is that capital markets fail to impound information regarding corporate governance issues. For example, there is little credible evidence that incorporation in Delaware adds financial value. As previously shown, corporate governance is manifestly suboptimal in the United States, and seems to permit excessive agency costs. [T]here is no market force in favor of optimal—or even acceptable—corporate governance standards. While corporate governance can be material in certain transient contexts, the markets often seem impervious to its financial consequences. In short, there is little reason to think that the current political structure governing corporate governance generally is likely to ever be efficacious at impounding the best empirical learning regarding corporate governance. In the backwater of the markets' neglect, special interests will hold sway over both state corporate governance law and federal corporate governance law.

Special interest influence can often be difficult to trace. On the other hand it is often quite manifest, in the use of money and influence, and the outcomes that seem otherwise inexplicable, but operate to benefit those with power and influence. For example, Congress has used federal power to eviscerate securities litigation based upon "anecdotal evidence and unproven theories." The PSLRA was driven more by "money and influence peddling" than by any evidence of securities litigation abuses. Similarly, Delaware has long been influenced by corporate management and the corporate bar more than the influence of sound policy. Thus, the evisceration of the duty of care is associated not only with interests of management, but with interests of the insurance industry as well, even though the insurance industry was the only actor that left its fingerprints on the Delaware legislation. In sum, while the outlines of special interest power may be clear, inferences must sometimes be used to explain otherwise highly indulgent outcomes that in context seem best explained by special interest influence.

This means that any proposed improvements to corporate governance in America that do not reckon with the reality of special interest influence are unlikely to lead to durable reform. For example, those arguing that the status quo is acceptable, or that it should be extended to some sort of competitive federalism for securities regulation, fail to acknowledge how collective action distorts markets for law and regulation. Those arguing in favor of an expanded role for the federal government fail to acknowledge that federal law can fall prey to special interest influence as much as state law. By ignoring special interest influence, both approaches, although seemingly at polar opposites, essentially leave the basic collective action and public choice dynamics in place. Both, therefore, to the same extent, are bound to leave corporate governance subject to a continued cycle of chaotic evolution untethered to policy and vulnerable to special interest raids. This is not optimal.

On this latter point, there is broad agreement: both sides to the race to the bottom debate claim that, as currently structured, corporate governance yields suboptimal results. This is also in accord with the empirical evidence to date. This suboptimality is not likely to improve. Many voices in fact concur that creeping federalization in response to repeated corporate governance crises is likely. The federal response has been a mixed bag at best. There is little reason to think state law evolution will be superior. Indeed, at both levels one constant seems true: CEOs seemingly always accrue more power subject to fewer constraints. In fact, the pattern is likely to reinforce itself: economists predict that growing inequality would naturally lead to legal system outcomes that favor the rich and powerful. Until the system is depoliticized to some extent, suboptimal results will continue and perhaps even deepen.

In a related work, I have proposed an optimal depoliticized regulatory structure for public companies that would be charged with articulating corporate governance standards based upon the best empirical data available. Shareholders directly would be empowered to select the federal corporate governance regime. This would create immediate competitive pressure to adhere to the best learning regarding corporate governance for all jurisdictions. The market would react to the pro-nouncements of an agency with recognized expertise and a depoliticized regulatory structure on par with the Federal Reserve Board. This approach would directly seek to impound the best empirical data available into the nation's corporate governance regime.

Earlier, I proposed that senior officers and directors of public companies be subject to a federal professional regulation regime, subject to the supervision of a regulatory agency. There is reason to believe that such a regime could well operate to depoliticize governance standards, as it has to an extent so operated in the securities industry, or with respect to accountants and attorneys. In each instance, professional self-regulation has produced a stable regulatory outcome, without any major crisis. Professional self-regulation of senior officers and directors (under the supervision of an administrative agency) may thus hold the promise of depoliticizing corporate governance.

The same cannot be said of the current corporate governance regime. Academic voices are increasingly recognizing that the current system is not stable in the sense that it yields standards that are not tethered to sound policy, and that the crux of the problem is politics. So long as political considerations dominate the motives of both federal and state policymakers, corporate governance will not be based upon the best empirical learning. Ultimately, there will be constant economic pressure for reform. To this extent, the current regime is inherently non-sustainable. Foreign regimes will adopt superior regimes yielding superior economic outcomes and/or the U.S. will be plagued by serial financial crises until durable reform takes hold.

IV. Conclusion

Corporate governance in the United States suffers from a flawed legal structure that yields suboptimal results. The SEC is subject to the distortions implicit in a politicized regulatory agency. State legislatures show little concern over achieving optimal corporate governance standards. Courts seem to guess at the best corporate governance outcomes rather than rely upon the best financial and economic science available. In short, the reason why corporate governance in the U.S. diverges from the optimal corporate governance emerging from economic and financial science is because there is no mechanism at present to assure that optimal corporate governance standards prevail.

There is little evidence that any market for corporate governance is operating to move standards toward optimal outcomes. Investors seem not to impound material corporate governance law into their investment decisions. Our history of corporate federalism is packed with instances of special interest influence holding decisive power, and not any concept of optimality. More importantly, it is now clear that capital markets are yielding unsatisfactory outcomes in terms of corporate governance. Indeed, permitting unbridled CEO power to reign in corporate America, as it does today, is inconsistent with any principled economic view of how corporate governance should function.

Instead, it appears the only market functioning to define corporate governance is the market predicted by public choice enthusiasts with respect to regulation and legislative action generally. CEOs have superior resources and organizational capabilities. They have incentives to undertake collective action designed to assure that their interests prevail over the general public interest. Lawmakers are beholden to the views of the powerful and the organized, and there is neither an effective investors lobby nor any general economic growth lobby. Outcomes are decisively in favor of CEO power, with little legal constraint. At both the federal and state level, corporate governance outcomes seem best explained by special interest influence.

Thus, solutions to the patent suboptimality of corporate governance in the U.S. must account for the need to create legal structures that can resist the power of special interest influence. The emerging science of corporate governance lights the way for formulating more powerful corporate governance standards. It is up to lawyers to articulate legal and political structures that can make that vision a reality. Either crises or international competition is likely to create pressure for more optimal corporate governance mechanisms. The long-standing system of corporate federalism in the U.S. seems rigged for self-destruction.

Notes

(1) The power and influence of CEOs has grown exponentially in the past two decades. What has been the impetus for such expansion of power?

(2) As CEO power has grown, the influence of the shareholder has arguably decreased. What impact has this had on the corporate governance of many corporations?

(3) Many argue that executive compensation has run amok. How does executive compensation influence the behavior of CEOs?

(4) If Professor Ramirez is correct that "corporate governance outcomes seem best explained by special interest influence" and that as a nation we have permitted "unbridled CEO power to reign in corporate America," what might be an expected outcome when contemplating *Citizens United* and the ability of corporations to make unfettered campaign contributions from general treasury funds?

Now that the rights, responsibilities and powers of corporations have been clearly outlined, and now that the duties and responsibilities of corporate leaders have been laid out, the reader is prepared to engage in a role play exercise that tests the ability of students to exercise decisionmaking authority in the context of a board member sitting on the board of a corporation. The following exercise should prepare a student to experience the pressure and responsibility of strategically planning for the future when tasked with leading a corporation toward greater effectiveness, efficiency and profitability.

D. Private Prison Board Exercise

Assume that you are member of the Board of Directors for the Corrections Corporation of North Carolina (CCNC), a corporation specializing in the management and operation of private prisons. In your capacity as a board member, you must set the long term strategic business plan and goals for CCNC. You will also determine how CCNC will allocate its current spending budget. You must make these decisions in keeping with the duties and responsibilities of board members as discussed in this course thus far. To assist you in making this determination, you will find a set of facts for your use below. Use this information to make informed decisions for the benefit of your corporation. The strategic plan must include which spending priorities you select and an explanation as to why the group allocated each respective expenditure.

Corporate Financial Considerations

- Annual Gross Revenue of CCNC: $50 million
- Annual Net Profit of CCNC: $5 million
- 100,000 shares outstanding
- A majority of shareholders are calling for significant dividends to be paid based on the record profits of the firm.
- Executive employment contracts allow, but do not mandate, lucrative bonuses to be paid to executives and board members based on profits in excess of $3 million per year.
- Paying bonuses to executives and board members incentivizes creativity and hard work amongst a corporation's leadership.
- Private prison companies have been harshly criticized in the popular press for declining care standards for prisoners, including poor food choices and reduced security. This criticism chills investor enthusiasm for purchasing shares in private prison corporations.
- Paying dividends signals to the broader corporate community that CCNC is financially successful and attracts increased investors which improves value in the long term.
- The market for highly skilled and qualified private prison executives is incredibly competitive and keeping executives is centrally important to the long-term vitality of any successful prison corporation.
- Relative to other private prison companies, the CCNC board of directors is underpaid, particularly after such a successful year.

- In the upcoming hotly contested gubernatorial election, the incumbent Governor is stepping down and two fresh faces are vying for the opens seat. As such, campaign contributions will be of vital importance to the race.
- Candidate Jones strongly supports North Carolina privatizing its prison system.
- Candidate Wilson is openly opposed to the War on Drugs and believes that rehabilitating prisoners will reduce the prison population, thereby decreasing cost to the state and allowing increased funding in education.

Prison Statistics

- According to the North Carolina Department of Corrections, the State's inmate population totals 100,000. This figure represents a 5% increase from 2011, a 20% increase over the past five years, and a 40% increase over the past decade.
- It costs the State $20,000 annually to care for each prisoner, nearly $50 per day.
- The total cost to the State to operate its prison system is $2 billion.
- For every dollar spent on prisons by the State, 90 cents is allocated for prisoner housing and care whereas 10 cents is allocated to prisoner rehabilitation.
- According to the Bureau of Justice Statistics, more than 12% of all federally sentenced offenders and about 6% of state prisoners are currently managed by private corrections companies, and these figures are growing.
- It is argued that privatization will save between 10% and 15% of a state's budget, annually.
- Increased spending on rehabilitation, such as drug treatment and job training, reduces recidivism and has proven to be successful in reducing the prison population.
- Nationally, the number of incarcerated persons in the United States has increased over 335% since 1980.
- Nationally, the prison population based on drug sentencing has increased over 1000% since 1980.
- An increase in illegal immigrant prisoners will increase job opportunities for American citizens, particularly in low paying service industries including landscaping, agricultural harvesting, domestic labor, etc.
- Increased spending on recreational activities reduces aggression in prisoners and the number of assaults on prison guards and other inmates.
- Increased spending on food services ensures that prisoners have more healthy dietary options which reduces health-related diseases and overall health costs in prisons.

Spending Options

- Pay a dividend to shareholders
- Pay bonuses to executives and board members
- Make a charitable contribution to Improve Prison Healthcare, Inc., a non-profit organization that works to improve mental health and general health alternatives for prisoners
- Make a charitable contribution to ALEC, a non-profit organization that works with legislators and for-profit corporations to draft model legislation that will expand the reach of private prisons

- Hire lobbying firms to lobby politicians and legislators for objectives that increase profit opportunities. The following firms are available for hire:
    - ◦ Sentencing LLC: A lobbying firm that specializes in lobbying Congress and state legislatures for stronger sentencing regimes aimed at keeping communities safer by keeping criminals imprisoned longer ($1 million per year)
    - ◦ Privatization LLC: A lobbying firm that focuses on lobbying states to privatize state owned prison facilities by selling them to private prison companies and then paying the private facility to house the prisoners (cost $1 million per year)
    - ◦ New Crimes LLC: A lobbying firm that drafts new legislation criminalizing previously non-criminal activity seeking to persuade Congress and state legislators to introduce draft legislation ($1 million per year)
    - ◦ Imprisoning Illegals LLC: A lobbying firm that focuses its efforts on enacting legislation that imprisons illegal immigrants in states with illegal immigration problems ($1 million per year)
- Make a campaign contribution to Governor candidate Jones
- Make a campaign contribution to Governor candidate Wilson
- Invest in rehabilitation programs run by non-profits
- Increase spending on current operations including building improvement, surveillance technology, and prison security and staff
- Allocate funds to build new prisons
- Increase spending for recreational activities for inmates, including library facilities, basketball courts and weightlifting
- Improve food service options by increasing spending on fresh fruits and vegetables

Your responsibility as a corporate board is to draft a mission statement and then determine a coherent plan to best allocate the $5 million net profit that CCNC realized last fiscal year. This $5 million will serve as your spending budget. On each spending priority, you must spend a minimum of $1,000,000. Your entire spending plan must remain within the $5 million budget. For each allocation in your budget please provide a short explanation supporting your decision.

Chapter Four

The Prison Industrial Complex and Corporate Social Responsibility

A. The Prison Industrial Complex

Students are unlikely to encounter the following materials in any corporate textbook in the country. As such, one may speculate why our book, whose main objective is to focus on a conception of corporate justice, provides any discussion about the prison industrial complex. In light of a potential perception that this information could be viewed as irrelevant in the context of a discussion about corporate law, we have included the materials for the following reasons.

First, as professors who teach the intricate details of corporate organization, operation, finance and power, we recognize that students sometimes have difficulty truly understanding the role that corporations play in modern society. More specifically, many students fail to realize that many of the decisions that are made by board members and corporate officers have a palatable effect on the way that every day citizens live their lives. For example, some private prisons, through aggressive lobbying efforts, have influenced government officials to criminalize certain conduct to increase prison populations, thereby increasing corporate profit margins. Our incorporation of these materials will hopefully allow you to appreciate the power of the corporation to influence social policy without losing sight of such power in a labyrinth of complex financial terminology.

Second, we have included these materials because they also highlight the ability of the corporate entity to engage in activities that were traditionally and historically left to the government via the democratic process. Throughout American history, the operation of the prison system was solely a governmental function. This was largely because profiting from incarceration was viewed as morally reprehensible. Today, corporations assume this activity, along with other governmental functions like managing public education, without truly representing the American constituency and while operating primarily for the sole purpose of maximizing profit at any cost.

Finally, we hope to continue to remind our students that injustice still occurs in America and that issues of racial and gender inequality still permeate. It is our hope that these materials will help our readers to see that injustice in the corporate decision-making process leads to unjust results in our communities.

As the board assignment in Chapter Three is meant to illustrate, the morality of a private prison corporation and the perverse incentives incumbent in such a profit maximizing organization seems to us dubious. The existence of a corporation which derives its profits from incarceration and the warehousing of human beings begs the following questions: Are there particular areas of business in which private profit maximizing behavior should not be permitted? Are there particular arenas where the supposed benefits of free-market forces should not be allowed and instead should be left to the government? As detailed below, the rise of the for-profit private prison corporation is a relatively recent development as the Corrections Corporation of America was founded in the early 1980s in Tennessee.

Mass incarceration in the United States has become an "extremely profitable enterprise." In 1983, a group of businessmen conceptualized the idea of a private prison corporation which would run Tennessee state prisons for profit and ostensibly more cheaply and more efficiently than a state government or municipality could. Before the rise of the private prison corporation, the companies that supplied and catered to prisons were already engaging in very profitable enterprises. The "Prison Industrial Complex" (PIC) refers to the myriad and diverse ways that corporations and governments profit off of incarcerating United States citizens and residents, including through the use of prison labor for corporate benefit. As you read the article below, consider the benefits and drawbacks of allowing private industry into the business of carceral policy.

"All Eyez on Me": America's War on Drugs and the Prison-Industrial Complex

andré douglas pond cummings

15 Iowa J. of Gender, Race and Justice 417 (2012)

I. Introduction

"[T]he deprivation of liberty has become an extremely profitable enterprise."

In 1971, President Richard Nixon named drug abuse "public enemy number one" in the United States. Since that time, an explicit "War on Drugs" has dominated the political imagination of the United States. Since declaring a War on Drugs, domestic incarceration rates have exploded, particularly in the African-American and Latino populations. Politicians such as Nixon, Barry Goldwater, and Nelson Rockefeller advocated for harsh drug laws and severe criminal sanctions because they argued that a strong correlation existed between drug addiction and crime. These claims have dominated legislative enactments since the 1970s, virtually ignoring those who argue that drug addiction should be viewed as a public health issue rather than a criminal enterprise. When President Ronald Reagan signed the Anti-Drug Abuse Act in 1986, he effectively criminalized drug addiction; this led to the mass and disproportionate incarceration of primarily non-violent drug offenders from disadvantaged minority populations—over sixty-five percent of whom are African-American and Latino. Since declaring this War on Drugs, U.S. taxpayers have paid more than $2.5 trillion to fund this "war."

Curiously, despite the escalation of mass incarceration rates of minorities for soft drug crimes since the 1970s, violent crime rates have steadily decreased in the United States over the past several decades. No country in the world incarcerates more of its citizens than does the United States. The "tough on crime" political posturing and War on Drugs rhetoric have further led to an eruption in prison profiteering, in what has come to be known as the "prison-industrial complex."

"[T]he prison-industrial complex [describes] an interweaving of private business and government interests" in connection with incarcerating U.S. citizens. This self-perpetuating machine extracts vast profits from free or cheap prison labor and from lucrative private and public prison contracts. Prisons "play a direct role in capital accumulation since their operation generates profit for corporations engaged in building, equipping and operating them as well as those employing prisoners as cheap labour." The perceived political benefits of reduced unemployment rates, additional police funding, and tough rhetoric from elected politicians, judges, and prosecutors—ultimately leading to skewed policies—ensure an "endless supply" of criminal justice "clients." When combining the potential for enormous corporate profit with a politician's need to be reelected, a toxic foundation is laid that portends legislative initiatives sponsored by representatives who use "tough on crime" campaign rhetoric, while simultaneously accepting lucrative contributions from a private prison lobby intent on increasing the stream of U.S. prisoners. From this toxic mix emerges a client stream of disproportionately African-American and Latino drug offenders.

With prisons literally teeming with minority prisoners, some have argued that current U.S. incarceration practices are similar to the impact of slavery upon early American society, as the "focused machinery of the 'war on drugs'" and its disparate impact on African-American prisoners "fracture[] families[,] ... destroy[] individual lives[,] and destabilize[] whole communities." To wit, "current drug policies and regulations have direct and devastating impacts on family structure and particularly impact women and children." While the impact of the prison-industrial complex on urban communities has yet to be fully quantitatively assessed, there are obvious detrimental effects including difficult economic burdens, structural poverty, and lack of consistent familial structure—all of which can lead to a host of negative consequences on minority communities. "In this way, the prison system is a means of violence that serves to oppress and punish an ever-increasing number of African American women, and the 'war on drugs' remains a war on the black community, family and the female body."

Despite the prison-industrial complex's devastating impact on communities of color, the increasing number of imprisoned Americans energizes corporate interests. For example, one prison profiteer recently claimed that the consistent yearly increase in the prison population, "from a business model perspective, [is] clearly good news." Corporate benefits of the prison-industrial complex are manifest because "[g]overnment contracts to build prisons have bolstered the construction industry." Additionally, "[p]rison construction bonds are one of the many sources of profitable investment for leading financiers such as Merrill Lynch" and Wall Street investment firms. These same Wall Street firms are often characterized as divorced from the U.S. punishment regime; however, they profit significantly from prison-construction bonds and by providing financing services at inflated prices. Estimates of the sale of tax-exempt bonds to underwrite U.S. prison construction exceed $2.3 billion annually. Further, corporations that produce products that U.S. citizens consume view prison labor as a profitable enterprise, similar to "third world labor power exploited by U.S.-based global corporations." Notable multi-national corporations that use prison labor are IBM, Compaq, Microsoft, and Boeing, as well as non-high-tech industrial leaders such as J.C. Penney and Victoria's Secret. Corporate use of prison labor makes business sense for these enterprises because they can compensate prisoners at a rate far below that of minimum wage and can therefore be extremely profitable. Some studies indicate that prisoners' compensation ranges from $0 to $1.50 per hour, with the average rate at $.40 per hour.

The political will to normalize criminal sanctions in the United States by bringing in-carceration rates back into line with appropriate violent behavior appears to be non-

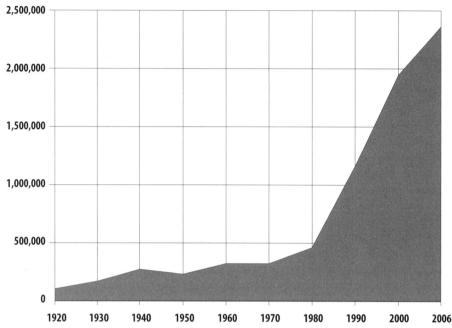

Figure 4.1 Incarcerated Americans 1920–2006

Source: Justice Policy Institute Report: The Punishing Decade, & U.S. Bureau of Justice Statistics Bulletin NCJ 219416 — Prisoners in 2006

existent because the War on Drugs has become an entrenched piece of the criminal fabric in the United States, and the prison-industrial complex relies upon an ever-increasing stream of "criminals" to maximize profit flow. Perhaps this weak political will persists because, as research indicates, global governments that seek to free their capital markets from regulation and oversight also contemporaneously imprison their poor and disenfranchised at massive rates. In seeking to "free" market organization, policy-makers marry harsh incarceration policies with free market fundamentalism in ways that are politically expedient to both politicians and the wealthy elite.

II. Mass Incarceration in the United States

Since 1980, the rate of incarcerated Americans has skyrocketed. As indicated in Figure 4.1, the United States has increased its incarceration rate in the last thirty years by more than an astonishing 335%. The United States now imprisons more of its citizens than any other nation on Earth. "The United States has less than 5% of the world's population. But, it has almost 25% of the world's prisoners."

The vast majority of the prisoner increase in the United States has come from African-American and Latino citizen drug arrests. "The United States imprisons a larger percentage of its black population than South Africa did at the height of apartheid." Given the explosion in incarceration rates as indicated above, one might believe that a simultaneous upsurge in violent crime rates must have also occurred, particularly in urban communities, but this is not so. While the U.S. prison population has increased remarkably in the last three decades, the violent crime rates in the United States over approximately the same period have decreased, and in some cases dramatically. As shown in Figure 4.2, violent crime rates in the United

Figure 4.2 Four Measures of Serious Violent Crime

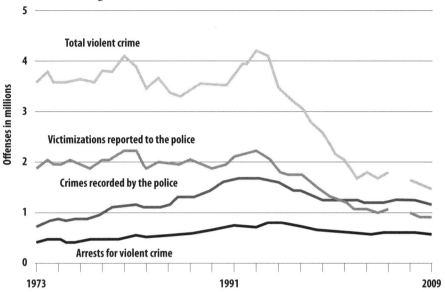

States have decreased markedly since 1990. Serious violent crimes dramatically decreased, while arrests for violent crimes remained static for nearly twenty-five years.

This distortion, incarceration increasing in the face of decreasing violent crime, begs a fundamental question: what underlies this seeming anomaly? Professor Michelle Alexander, author of *The New Jim Crow: Mass Incarceration in the Age of Colorblindness*, endeavors to answer this question by examining America's continuing subordination of its black and brown citizens. Alexander boldly traces the "Southern Strategy" of the President Nixon Era to the racial coding of the President Reagan and President George H.W. Bush Era, through President Bill Clinton's "New Democrat" Era, and concludes that these eras of divisive racial politics and "tough on crime" rhetoric led to a new era of subordination just as nefarious as slavery and Jim Crow. The War on Drugs allows for racial subordination without explicitly naming race: The New Jim Crow. Mass incarceration of African-Americans and Latinos based almost entirely upon drug crimes allows the United States to deprive minority citizens—men in particular—of their constitutional and God-given rights, while appearing race neutral.

When President Reagan successfully federalized drug crime, through incentivizing local and state pursuit of the War on Drugs with federal funding and military-style weaponry made available to local law enforcement, a genuine "war" was unleashed upon the public, in particular upon the United States's inner cities. Local urban law enforcement evolved into paramilitary style units that began using battering rams, tank-like vehicles, and Special Weapons and Tactics (SWAT) teams in our inner-city communities, while adopting a military mentality toward drug users and sellers. Thus, the underrecognized connection between politicians tasked with establishing prison-sentencing policy entering into tacit partnerships with newly militarized local police became a War on Drugs that was to be waged in urban communities and against poor people of color. The following description of local-level law enforcements' "siege mentality" and subsequent Jordan Miles narrative illustrate the real-world implications and devastating consequences visited upon regular citizens when an internal, focused "war" is declared, resulting in mass incarceration.

A. Siege Mentality

"The traditional form of police operations is known as the 'professional' model. The purpose of this model is to develop a paramilitary team of officers able to respond with speed and force to quell criminal disturbances in the community. The philosophy behind this type of policing is simply to put away the bad guys."

This traditional type of policing model, which is employed in Los Angeles, Philadelphia, and many other cities nationwide, develops a "siege mentality" in its officers. This "siege mentality" exists on an "us versus them" plane and incubates a dehumanizing idea toward criminals or "the enemy." It is far easier to violate an individual when he or she is dehumanized in the mind of the violator. This "siege" model focuses an officer's attention on crime control rather than crime prevention, and it isolates the police from the people and the communities in which they serve.

The Christopher Commission employed in Los Angeles to evaluate the L.A. riots found that "the police culture created by the professional model was responsible, in part, for the Los Angeles Police Department's (LAPD) systemic racism and rising brutality." Further, the Commission determined that the "siege mentality" of the officers was grounded in military-style thinking. This is a kind of thinking that allows officers armed with military weaponry to debase citizens based on assumptions and profiles.

Therefore, a significant cause of police abuse and brutality in the United States is directly attributable to the militarization of police forces. The LAPD, for example, began "emphasizing military-style tactics in waging the war on drugs, gangs, and crime. From battering rams to massive displays of force in street sweeps in South Central Los Angeles, the police have relied on paramilitary tactics to police the streets of Los Angeles." Presidents Reagan and George H.W. Bush pervasively initiated the militarized War on Drugs at the federal level. In fact, during the Reagan-Bush Era, "[p]olice brutality became ... an acceptable cost of the 'wars' against crime, drugs, and gangs in urban America."

Furthering this siege mentality, many of the individuals who apply to be, and eventually become, law enforcement agents have served in a branch of the U.S. Armed Forces. These officers can easily visualize the enemy being the "bad" citizens who must be stopped no matter what the cost. When the victims of this ideology have become dehumanized, and war is what the officers are engaged in, it is not difficult to conceptualize how law enforcement officers deprive U.S. citizens of their basic human rights daily, often acting like "gangster cops." One such example occurred on a winter night in Pittsburgh as a slight, symphony student left his mother's house to visit his grandmother, with nothing more than a soda in his pocket.

B. Jordan Miles

When young Jordan Miles, a highly accomplished African-American teen violist enrolled at Pittsburgh's prestigious Creative and Performing Arts High School, stepped out of his mother's house on his way to visit his grandmother on the evening of January 12, 2010, little did he realize that he was about to learn in no uncertain terms what it means to be a young black man in the United States. Moments after he began the routine walk to his grandmother's home, Jordan, who stood 5'6" and weighed 150 pounds, was startled to see three white men, dressed in plain clothes, leap from a dark, unmarked car, and sprint toward him. Jordan, in a panic and thinking the men were about to assault him, ran. Without identifying themselves as undercover police officers, the three white men chased Jordan down, and when he fell on the icy sidewalk, they pounced upon the slight teenager, tased him, beat him with closed fists, kneed him in the face, and tore several dreadlocks from his scalp. Fearing for his life, Jordan attempted to utter the Lord's Prayer during the beating, but the officers repeatedly told him to shut his mouth, shoved his face into the snow and ice on the sidewalk, and asked him over and over where he had stashed his gun, drugs, and money.

Jordan Miles's white assailants were undercover police officers Michael Saldutte, David Sisak, and Richard Ewing. Following the brutal beatdown of Jordan, these three men stated in an affidavit that they believed Jordan had been carrying a gun underneath his winter parka. Jordan, who had no criminal history and not a single arrest on his record had actually carried a Mountain Dew soda in his pocket, which the officers claimed they believed was a gun. Jordan still suffers from facial nerve damage and night terrors, as a result of the profiling and savage beating officers Saldutte, Sisak, and Ewing administered. The Pittsburgh Police Department demoted the three officers from undercover work and reassigned them to uniform patrol, but this occurred only after public outcry and protests forced the hand of the Pittsburgh Police Department's brass.

While many might argue that police brutality and racial profiling are relics of a distant past, the Jordan Miles experience offers stark rebuttal. When law enforcement agents—charged with serving the public and protecting the innocents—see an innocent child, a young teenager with a quiet manner and a talent for orchestral instruments, solely as a gangster drug dealer merely because of his race and class coupled with their police training, then our nation's racial disconnect must be as chasm-like as it has ever been. At bottom, these officers were motivated, even incentivized, to destroy young Jordan, based on their training, the War on Drugs, their preconceived biases, and their suspicion that this young orchestra student was carrying or trafficking drugs. Further, the savagery of the beating that the officers inflicted upon Miles indicates a racial hatred that continues to permeate law enforcement in the United States. When three large white men easily subdue a 5'6" boy, with a Mountain Dew in his pocket, and the boy shows up at the police station having been tasered, kneed in the face, beaten with closed fists repeatedly, and with dreadlocks ripped from his scalp, this signals more than simply subduing a suspected criminal. It represents a drug war gone awry and a deep-seated animosity that belies the most avid post-racial sensibility.

Although the Jordan Miles affair may seem shocking to the uninitiated, the truth is that scenarios like this occur routinely throughout the United States. The War on Drugs has woven into the American fabric a police presence and culture of police abuse that our nation's founders not only never imagined, but also summarily attempted to protect against. The Jordan Miles experience is just one of thousands of urban injustices that law enforcement officers perpetrate consistently upon minority U.S. citizens in the name of the War on Drugs.

C. Twisted Conflicts

As the Jordan Miles affair demonstrates, the War on Drugs literally endangers the lives of innocent minority citizens living in urban communities. With ample evidence that violent crime has diminished nationwide, the paramilitary presence of police in U.S. city centers has not concomitantly diminished. In fact, U.S. government officials never intended for this paramilitary presence to diminish.

Siege mentality and police abuse are both a byproduct of and a necessary prerequisite to the prison-industrial complex. The same political powers that manage the police and concurrently encourage and enable the burgeoning prison system also sanction paramilitary policing. As will be demonstrated below, the prison-industrial complex as a system is dependent on nefarious political conflicts of interest. Politicians who set prison and sentencing policy also incentivize and manage federal, state, and local law enforcement through the federalized War on Drugs. Simultaneously, these politicians accept campaign contributions and take regular counsel from private corporations that lobby the politicians aggressively while profiting greatly from the very prison system these conflicted politicians manufacture.

U.S. politicians and police forces, motivated by corporate profiteers, have incarcerated many more of our citizens for non-violent drug crimes in an era where evidence indicates that our society has become safer and less violent. Why?

III. Motivating Factors Behind the Prison-Industrial Complex

To answer the "Why?" question regarding the motivations behind the massive increase in incarcerated Americans, while crime rates are dropping precipitously, one must examine the underlying policies, structures, conflicts, and institutions that support the prison system in the United States. This analysis suggests that several constituencies benefit significantly from mass incarceration. One constituency consists of those who profit handsomely from an increase in American imprisonment. Another constituency includes those who gain power or electoral advantage from massively incarcerating Americans.

A. Corporate Profiteering

A foundational tenet in U.S. corporate law is that a corporation exists primarily to maximize the profits of its shareholders. Leaders of a corporation who fail to effectively enrich its shareholders might be held to violate management duties and responsibilities, and they may be court-ordered to increase profit payout to stakeholders.

With this basic principle in mind, it is critical to acknowledge that what was once a purely public responsibility, the incarceration of criminals in the United States, has given way to the corporatization and privatization trend of the U.S. prison regime. Privatizing imprisonment has proven to be enormously problematic in several "under-the-radar" ways.

First, the Board of Directors of a prison-building corporation is highly-motivated to seek ways to increase its profit streams. One of the ways that a prison construction company can increase its profits is to win government contracts to build more and more prisons. Increasing incarceration rates in the United States have therefore become a corporate profit objective through the privatization of the prison system. In a recent annual filing, a publicly traded prison company, the Corrections Corporation of America (CCA) unabashedly described the climate and outlook for prison business going forward and provided a blueprint for increasing shareholder profit:

> The significant expansion of the prison population in the United States has led to overcrowding in the federal and state prison systems, providing us with opportunities for growth.... We believe the long-term growth opportunities of our business remain very attractive as insufficient bed development by our customers should result in a return to the supply and demand imbalance that has been benefiting the private prison industry.

This CCA forward-looking projection came from management, who filed the annual statement with the Securities and Exchange Commission and then delivered it to shareholders. Seeing forward-looking profit statements in annual reports to shareholders from public companies that manufacture products or provide consumer services is a straightforward proposition. However, reading profit statements to shareholders from private prison construction and management companies like the one above, which must necessarily base their entire potential profit regime on a steady stream of "clients" (i.e., U.S. citizens sentenced to hard prison time), is an altogether different construction. The law incentivizes private prison company management to maximize profits for shareholders, and a private prison corporation's most direct way to increase shareholder profit is to ensure that "demand" for its services (prison beds) increases. To expand profit, corporate management of private prison companies must hope for, even work for, an increase in the number of human beings incarcerated in the United States. Indeed, this work has been handsomely rewarded in recent years; reports issued in 2011 indicate that the two largest private prison companies, CCA and GEO Group, together profited more than $2.9 billion in 2010.

To increase profits at the rate indicated, private prison corporations hire lobbyists to increase prison populations and prison construction. Lobbying to increase the stream of prisoners and lobbying for untethered, harsher sentencing regimes is not just unseemly, but inhumane, which leads to another hidden problem of prison privatization.

Second, for the CEO who heads a private prison company, one seemingly appropriate action to increase profit for shareholders is to lobby state and federal legislatures to increase prison construction and, by implication, increase the flow of clients—prisoners—into the prison system. The amount of private prison company money spent on lobbying efforts has become dizzying. The largest U.S. private prison companies together have spent dozens of millions of dollars lobbying both state and federal legislators since the origin of the U.S. private prison corporation.

Private prison lobbyists advocate on behalf of harsh legislative initiatives that would increase the number of individuals sentenced to prison. Because "private prisons make money from putting people behind bars, their lobbying efforts focus on bills that affect incarceration and law enforcement, such as appropriations for corrections and detention." In addition, prison lobbyists battle for greater appropriations in expenditures in law enforcement and Homeland Security, stricter immigration laws, and increased immigration detention. They also peddle influence with lawmakers who will implement draconian incarceration policies like the recent Arizona immigration legislation, titled "The Support Our Law Enforcement and Safe Neighborhoods Act" (SB 1070). Emerging reports indicate that private prison lobbyists literally drafted the legislation that became SB 1070, as the legislation introduced into the Arizona legislature was identical to the proposed bill language that emerged from prison lobby meetings with Arizona elected representatives.

Further, private corporations are free to make campaign contributions, and the private prison lobby contributes generously. In light of *Citizens United v. Federal Election Commission*, the private prison corporation's campaign contributions can now be made directly and in an unfettered manner, straight from the private prison company coffers into the hands of the federal and state legislators whom they hope to influence. The private prison companies allocate millions of dollars in campaign contributions to mostly incumbent politicians, seeking to garner influence in the legislative process, to continue privatizing the prison regime in the United States, and to receive favorable contracts for private prison construction.

Third, Wall Street banks and investors profit dramatically from the prison-industrial complex. Prison-construction bonds, often offered as revenue bonds, are one of the many sources of profitable investment for leading Wall Street financiers such as Merrill Lynch and Goldman Sachs. Tax-exempt bonds sold to underwrite new prison construction bring more than $2.3 billion in profit to Wall Street investment banks. *Forbes* magazine touts prison bonds as a smart and safe investment for investors looking for long-term financial security and excellent profit potential.

The corporatization of the prison system in the United States has perversely incentivized public corporations and Wall Street to work *for* mass incarceration and *against* prison reform and rehabilitation. The prison-industrial complex has simply become a cash cow for private prison corporations and Wall Street investment banks. Thirty years ago, investing in private prison companies was not an option. Additionally, Wall Street banks were not in a position to profit massively from prison construction. In the intervening decades, imprisoning U.S. citizens has morphed into a significant growth industry and profit stream.

The U.S. prison-industrial complex is reliant first and foremost on political decisions to address drug abuse from a criminal sanctions perspective rather than a health and addiction perspective. In order to control political and economic power, legislators turn drug use and abuse in the United States into an oligarchy of labor power wherein whites (corporate executives and shareholders) gain wealth while the system not only marginalizes minorities, but also indentures them as prison labor. As Alexander so deftly notes in *The New Jim Crow*, even when African-American and Latino inmates are released from prison, they are so far removed from the "legitimate" labor market that they are almost driven back into the drug markets or "illegitimate" labor markets and returned nearly inevitably to prison, through parole violations or new drug crimes. Our current prison regime in the United States therefore maintains political and economic control by keeping black and brown men powerless while simultaneously allowing prison corporations to maintain a steady "client" base and consequently to increase profit margins.

B. Political Expediency

Professor Bernard Harcourt, in his *The Illusion of Free Markets: Punishment and the Myth of Natural Order*, elegantly describes the political expediency in massively incarcerating poor individuals and the subtle connection between free-market advocacy and mass incarceration. Extrapolating from Harcourt, the War on Drugs is nothing more than a policy that fits seamlessly into a long global tradition of governments harshly imprisoning individuals while simultaneously freeing economic markets from regulation. Harcourt's *The Illusion of Free Markets* disabuses the notion that markets are "free," as he demonstrates that capital markets require a significant degree of state and federal assistance—a fact that free-market fundamentalists conveniently ignore. Historically, across the world, nations that have emphasized unfettered markets, through working to preserve them or free them from regulation and oversight, have concurrently imposed upon their citizens harsh punishment regimes that increase imprisonment rates exponentially. It is as if the governing elite acknowledge that unfettered markets work to enrich the entrenched, while government-imposed incarceration both imprisons the society drag, and at the same time diverts the public attention away from the enriched entrenched and focuses it upon the incarcerated masses.

Harcourt's thesis is that governing elites rely upon notions of natural order in advocating for free markets while simultaneously using the construct of natural order to propound mass incarceration. If this is accurate, then the U.S. electoral and drug policy that began in the 1970s fits perfectly into this thesis Alexander described in *The New Jim Crow*. As incarceration rates exploded over the past two decades, politicians vigorously pursued efforts to deregulate the U.S. capital markets.

In the 1970s, Richard Nixon and his staff settled upon the "Southern Strategy" as an avenue to win elections and to perpetuate the United States's "sordid racial past," including slavery and Jim Crow. By politically dividing blacks and poor southern whites purposely, Nixon began to forge a new Republican strategy that perseveres today. The division, coming upon the heels of the Civil Rights Act of 1964, began to use racial coding to subordinate African-American interests rather than the racist construction used in the Jim Crow era.

> Racial coding has a long tradition in the United States. That it persists in the purportedly post-racial Obama era belies the very positioning of post-racialism and post-racialists. Racial coding entails engaging issues "such as crime and welfare are now widely viewed as 'coded' issues" that play upon race—or more centrally, upon white Americans' negative views of black Americans—without explicitly raising the race card. By embracing coded issues, politicians and pundits are able to exploit white American's racial animosity and resentment toward minority Americans while diminishing the appearance of race hatred or race baiting.

Thus, in this new era of racial coding, politicians continue to paint African-Americans as undeserving recipients of welfare (the welfare queen), undeserving of mercy (Willie Horton ad), undeserving of education (backlash against affirmative action), undeserving of the right to vote (felon disenfranchisement and voting discrimination against the poor), and *more* deserving of prison than freedom (the crack epidemic and mandatory sentencing). This racial coding captured America's imagination and became the dominant political fascination of the country. Political figureheads primarily perpetuated these nefarious concepts, particularly Presidents Reagan, Bush, and Clinton, each of whom were intent on winning elections and simultaneously freeing the capital markets.

Fitting exactly into Harcourt's thesis and dating back to when legislatures punished crack cocaine offenses one hundred times more than powder cocaine, U.S. politicians have scrambled to "win" the title of "toughest on crime." Meanwhile, these politicians voted often and repeatedly to deregulate the U.S. capital markets. When political power and entrenchment become intertwined with mass incarceration, the outcome is an increasing stream of prisoners, with little consideration given to reform or rehabilitation.

Conflict theory, or more accurately, conflict criminology as expanded in the 1970s by sociologists Austin Turk and William Chambliss among others, provides context for Harcourt's historical observations. Turk and Chambliss argue that those in power work diligently to maintain and increase their power by creating laws and policies that criminalize the powerless in order to ensure that the disaffected are unable to gain power. Alexander theorizes that the federalization and criminalization of the drug war was simply an instinctive response from the powerfully entrenched to the political gains that people of color made through the Civil Rights Movement in the 1960s. Harcourt theorizes that when elites in power work to maintain their influence and wealth (through rigged capital markets), the instinctive corollary is to develop ways to criminalize the powerless, all in order to maintain wealth, influence, and position. Simply stated, the War on Drugs perpetuates subordination of minority Americans, while it simultaneously enriches and protects the power of the elite.

IV. Conclusion

With the deeply entrenched profit-driven corporatization of the prison system in the United States now secure, it is difficult to imagine the political will emerging to unravel the mass incarceration regime of American citizens. Prison reform, needed desperately in the United States, would require the dismantling of a carefully orchestrated privatization and the increasingly lucrative business of warehousing American criminals. "Unless the number of people who are labeled felons is dramatically reduced, and unless the laws and policies that keep ex-offenders marginalized from mainstream society and economy are eliminated, the system will continue to create and maintain an enormous underclass."

Will the United States sit idly by while a system of continued racial subordination is perpetuated against the minority poor in our country? The first step in defeating the War on Drugs and mass incarceration must be recognizing the perverse set of incentives and outcomes that this war perpetuates. Once recognized, the second step in reversing mass incarceration requires eliminating these perverse incentives that literally motivate corporate players to seek increased incarceration rates of American citizens.

While a profound corporate backlash would likely occur, the United States could seriously contemplate eliminating most prison time for all drug use. After all, hope in ending the drug war in the United States exists in that recent "data showing that the war on drugs has failed are not in dispute; Obama Administration officials do not even use the phrase." Further, the Fair Sentencing Act was adopted in July 2010 bringing the crack/powder cocaine sentencing disparity from the previous 100-to-1 disparity to a more tenable 18-to-1. Still, "[i]t is common in the U.S. to judge drug addiction morally rather than medically, and most policy flows from that approach."

Dismantling the prison-industrial complex is a moral imperative. If we as a nation are going to make significant strides in ending the racially biased sentencing regime in the United States, we must face down corporate profiteers who have come to rely on the current perverse prison system for incredible profits and the conflicted politicians that enable the perversion.

Notes

(1) What are the primary "perverse" incentives that motivate the leaders of the private prison corporations?

(2) Why do we as a society accept profit motivations in the context of imprisoning our nation's citizens? There is no developed country that exhibits the levels of inequality and poverty that exists in the United States. French economist Thomas Piketty demonstrates the never-before-seen depths of inequality that exists in the United States today based on wealth disparities and opportunity inequalities in his book *Capital in the 21st Century*. Additionally, the Pew Research Center has released wealth gap information for decades and since the Great Recession of 2008 has found that wealth inequality in the U.S. is sharply divided along racial lines. White households significantly outpace Latino and African American households when it comes to median net worth. As recently as 2013, white households averaged $141,900 in net worth while Latino households averaged $13,900 and African American households averaged $11,000. Essentially, white family net worth is 13× greater than that of black families and 10× greater than that of Hispanic families. This disparity is the largest gap since Pew began tracking wealth and net worth. What accounts for this massive disparity in household wealth in the United States?

(3) Why does our nation accept grinding poverty and hopelessness for so many of our urban and rural poor? Nobel winning economist Paul Krugman has an answer and

it is not pretty. In the *New York Times*, Krugman argues in 2015 that "Slavery's Long Shadow" continues to influence and motivate policies and laws that enable staggering inequality and poverty to exist in the United States. "Yet racial hatred is still a potent force in our society, as we've been reminded to our horror. And I'm sorry to say this, but the racial divide is still a defining feature in our political economy, the reason America is unique among advanced nations in its harsh treatment of the less fortunate and its willingness to tolerate unnecessary suffering among its citizens." After acknowledging that racism continues relentlessly in the U.S., Krugman describes the "Southern Strategy" used by Richard Nixon and Ronald Reagan to divide the South along racial lines, and instructs that of the twenty-two states that have refused Obamacare for its citizens, more than 80% of those states are former slave states located in the south. Poverty has been racialized in the U.S. and welfare policy has been racially constructed based on who is viewed as "deserving."

(4) The next obvious question then, is why is our nation's carceral policy so inhumane? While crime and prison policy has always been constructed from the top down, and those at the bottom merely feel the weight of the policies rather than influence how they are made, getting locked up in the U.S. is a disaster. As described in Michelle Alexander's *The New Jim Crow*, cited in the article above, a prison bid can literally crush an individual's future. As you read the article below, consider the following: Who decides what is "criminal" and who decides what a "jailable" offense is in our country?

(5) Why have we allowed private interests to influence carceral policy in the U.S.? Is the private prison machine too powerful? Or can it be effectively ended?

(6) In the 2015 article "Toward a Critical Corporate Law Pedagogy and Scholarship,"[1] Professor Cheryl Wade argues that managing public education is an additional historical governmental function that has inexplicably been turned over in some instances to private for-profit market forces. She describes how, on total, the mixed evidence demonstrates, just as it does in the private prison context, that privatization has not improved the performance of these institutions.

(7) The Jordan Miles incident described in the article above most likely sounded hauntingly familiar to those paying attention to the national news in 2014 and 2015. Police abuse and police killing of unarmed African American men seemingly increased as social media and improved technology allowed the capture of abusive and deadly police conduct on cell phones, body cams, and dashboard cams. These deadly encounters proliferated across the nation and world through emerging social media outlets. While Jordan Miles escaped his traumatizing police encounter with his life, the same cannot be said for Walter Scott, Eric Garner, Tamir Rice, Freddie Gray, Michael Brown, Oscar Grant, and Samuel DuBose, amongst others, each killed by law enforcement officers. Perhaps most chilling, is that the original offenses that led to the police encounter for each of the deceased men above ranged from driving with a broken taillight to selling loose cigarettes to playing with a pellet gun in the park to looking "crazy" at the police to jaywalking to loitering to having no front license plate.

---

1. andré douglas pond cummings, Steven Ramirez & Cheryl Wade, *Toward a Critical Corporate Law Pedagogy and Scholarship*, 92 Wash U. L. Rev. 397 (2015) (describing the failing for-profit privatization efforts of public school systems in New York and across the United States).

Why would engaging in such minor illegal behavior lead to the death of each of these African American citizens?

Banking on Bondage:
Private Prisons and Mass Incarceration
American Civil Liberties Union

EXECUTIVE SUMMARY

The imprisonment of human beings at record levels is both a moral failure and an economic one—especially at a time when more and more Americans are struggling to make ends meet and when state governments confront enormous fiscal crises. This report finds, however, that mass incarceration provides a gigantic windfall for one special interest group—the private prison industry—even as current incarceration levels harm the country as a whole. While the nation's unprecedented rate of imprisonment deprives individuals of freedom, wrests loved ones from their families, and drains the resources of governments, communities, and taxpayers, the private prison industry reaps lucrative rewards. As the public good suffers from mass incarceration, private prison companies obtain more and more government dollars, and private prison executives at the leading companies rake in enormous compensation packages, in some cases totaling millions of dollars.

The Spoils of Mass Incarceration

As incarceration rates skyrocket, the private prison industry expands at exponential rates, holding ever more people in its prisons and jails, and generating massive profits. Private prisons for adults were virtually non-existent until the early 1980s, but the number of prisoners in private prisons increased by approximately 1600% between 1990 and 2009. Today, for-profit companies are responsible for approximately 6% of state prisoners, 16% of federal prisoners, and, according to one report, nearly half of all immigrants detained by the federal government. In 2010, the two largest private prison companies alone received nearly $3 billion dollars in revenue, and their top executives, according to one source, each received annual compensation packages worth well over $3 million.

A Danger to State Finances

While supporters of privatization tout the idea that governments can save money through private facilities, the evidence for supposed cost savings is mixed at best. As state governments across the nation confront deep fiscal deficits, the assertion that private prisons demonstrably reduce the costs of incarceration can be dangerous and irresponsible. Such claims may lure states into building private prisons or privatizing existing ones rather than reducing incarceration rates and limiting corrections spending through serious criminal justice reform.

This year, advocates of for-profit prisons trotted out privatization schemes as a supposed answer to budgetary woes in numerous states:

> **Arizona** has announced plans to award 5,000 additional prison beds to private contractors, despite a recent statement by the Arizona Auditor General that for-profit imprisonment in Arizona may cost *more* than incarceration in publicly-operated facilities. Arizona's Department of Corrections is the only large agency in that state not subject to a budget cut in fiscal year 2012—in fact, the Department's budget increased by $10 million. According to a news report, private prison

employees and corporate officers contributed money to Governor Jan Brewer's reelection campaign, and high-ranking Brewer Administration officials previously worked as private prison lobbyists.

Ohio recently announced that it will become, on December 31, 2011, the first state in the nation to sell a publicly operated prison, Lake Erie Correctional Facility, to a private company, CCA. Notably, the head of Ohio's corrections department had served as a managing director of CCA.

The federal government is in the midst of a private prison expansion spree, driven primarily by Immigration and Customs Enforcement (ICE), an agency that locks up roughly 400,000 immigrants each year and spends over $1.9 billion annually on custody operations. ICE now intends to create a new network of massive immigration detention centers, managed largely by private companies, in states including **New Jersey, Texas, Florida, California and Illinois.** According to a news report, in August 2011, ICE's plans to send 1,250 immigration detainees to Essex County, New Jersey threatened to unravel amid allegations that a private prison company seeking the contract, whose executives enjoyed close ties to Governor Chris Christie, received "special treatment" from the county.

Atrocious Conditions

While evidence is mixed, certain empirical studies show a heightened level of violence against prisoners in private institutions. This may reflect in part the higher rate of staff turnover in private prisons, which can result in inexperienced guards walking the tiers. After an infamous escape from an Arizona private prison in 2010, for example, the Arizona Department of Corrections reported that at the prison, "[s]taff are fairly 'green' across all shifts," "are not proficient with weapons," and habitually ignore sounding alarms. Private facilities have also been linked to atrocious conditions. In a juvenile facility in Texas, for example, auditors reported, "[c]ells were filthy, smelled of feces and urine."

Shrewd Tactics

Certain private prison companies employ shrewd tactics to obtain more and more government contracts to incarcerate prisoners. In February 2011, for example, a jury convicted former Luzerene County, Pennsylvania Judge Mark Ciavarella of racketeering, racketeering conspiracy, and money laundering conspiracy in connection with payments received from a private prison developer. Tactics employed by some private prison companies, or individuals associated with the private prison industry, to gain influence or acquire more contracts or inmates include: use of questionable financial incentives; benefitting from the "revolving door" between public and private corrections; extensive lobbying; lavish campaign contributions; and efforts to control information.

PART I: THE PRIVATE PRISON EXPLOSION

Mass incarceration strains state budgets and deprives individuals of liberty in record numbers. But the social ill of mass incarceration is a bonanza for the private prison industry, which has extracted more and more taxpayer dollars from state budgets as governments dispatch prisoners to private facilities in ever-increasing numbers.

Today, private companies imprison roughly 130,000 prisoners and, according to one group, 16,000 civil immigration detainees in the United States at any given time. As states send more and more people to prison, they funnel ever greater amounts of taxpayer money to private prison operators. By 2010, annual revenues of the two top private prison companies alone stood at nearly $3 billion.

Terminology Used in This Report

The terms "private prison operator" and "private prison company" are used to describe companies that own and/or operate for-profit facilities that incarcerate people — including facilities such as prisons, jails, and immigration detention centers.

The term "private prison industry" is a somewhat broader category. In addition to private prison operators and private prison companies, "the private prison industry" may also include other companies or individuals that profit from private prisons, such as companies that provide consulting services in connection with private prison construction.

A statement in this report that private prison companies, private prison operators, or the private prison industry made a certain claim, engaged in a certain practice, or exhibited a certain feature is not meant to imply that the same statement applies to all private prison companies or operators, or that all members of the private prison industry did the same.

Early Experiments in For-Profit Imprisonment

Early forms of prison privatization yielded horrific results. In eighteenth-century England, private "keepers" ran prisons, making their living by extracting lodging fees from those they incarcerated — and by operating coffee shops and beer taps for affluent prisoners. The rich may have lived well even behind bars, but private jailers had little stake in the well-being of poor prisoners, who were "gouged for fees, cheated on their provisions, loaded with irons, [and] exposed to disease." Fortunately, a movement to improve prison order and establish public control began to gather force in England in the late Eighteenth Century.

In the years following the Civil War, the United States also experimented with a form of privatization. The convict lease system — which has been called a "substitute for slavery" — took hold in the South. Under this system, state and local governments managed the prisons, but prisoners were leased out to work for private companies or individuals. Like the private "keepers" in England, these contractors had little incentive to treat prisoners humanely. According to Professor Michelle Alexander, "Death rates were shockingly high, for the private contractors had no interest in the health and well-being of their laborers, unlike the earlier slave-owners who needed their slaves, at minimum, to be healthy enough to survive hard labor."

Toward the end of the Nineteenth Century, states began to outlaw convict leasing, and Congress forbade the leasing of federal prisoners in 1887. By 1900, virtually all governments around the world had assumed responsibility for management of their own prisons.

The Exponential Growth of Private Prisons

At the beginning of the 1980s, private prisons for adults did not exist in the United States, but recent years have witnessed a reemergence and dramatic expansion of this form of incarceration. The private prison explosion went hand-in-hand with a massive increase in incarceration rates. Since President Richard Nixon first announced the "war on drugs" forty years ago, the United States has adopted "tough on crime" laws that have given it the dubious distinction of having the highest incarceration rate in the world. These laws include:

> *Mandatory minimum sentencing laws*: Such laws impose long sentences and prevent judges from exercising discretion to impose more lenient punishments, where appropriate, based on the circumstances of the crime and the defendant's individual characteristics.

Truth in sentencing laws: Such laws sharply curtail probation and parole eligibility, requiring inmates to remain in prison long after they have been rehabilitated.

Three strikes laws: Such laws subject defendants convicted of three crimes to extremely long sentences. In one case heard by the U.S. Supreme Court, a man charged with stealing golf clubs received a sentence of 25 years to life under a three strikes law.

Mass incarceration has further weakened depressed communities by depopulating them and stripping even nonviolent former prisoners of opportunities to find employment and meaningfully reenter society. And while public safety requires the incarceration of certain criminals, current rates of incarceration are so anomalous that they provide little, if any, public safety benefit.

Between 1970 and 2005, the number of people incarcerated in the United States grew by 700%. Today, the United States incarcerates approximately 2.3 million people. According to the Congressional Research Service, the United States has only 5% of the world's population but a full 25% of its prisoners.

Even compared to this breathtaking rate of overall growth in incarceration, the rate of expansion of for-profit imprisonment far outpaced the field, accounting for a disproportionate increase in the number of people locked up. In 1980, private adult prisons did not exist on American soil, but by 1990 private prison companies had established a firm foothold, boasting 67 for-profit facilities and an average daily population of roughly 7,000 prisoners. During the next twenty years (from 1990 to 2009) the number of people incarcerated in private prisons *increased by more than 1600%*, growing from approximately 7,000 to approximately 129,000 inmates.

Increasing incarceration rates fueled this massive expansion of private corrections. CCA—the largest private prison company in the United States—admits that current sentencing laws increase the company's profits by swelling prison populations, whereas policies aimed at reducing incarceration rates create financial risks for the corporation. Specifically, in a 2010 Annual Report submitted to the Securities and Exchange Commission (SEC), CCA stated, under the heading "Risks Related to Our Business and Industry":

> Our ability to secure new contracts to develop and manage correctional and detention facilities depends on many factors outside our control. Our growth is generally dependent upon our ability to obtain new contracts to develop and manage new correctional and detention facilities. This possible growth depends on a number of factors we cannot control, including crime rates and sentencing patterns in various jurisdictions and acceptance of privatization. The demand for our facilities and services could be adversely affected by the relaxation of enforcement efforts, leniency in conviction or parole standards and sentencing practices or through the decriminalization of certain activities that are currently proscribed by our criminal laws. For instance, any changes with respect to drugs and controlled substances or illegal immigration could affect the number of persons arrested, convicted, and sentenced, thereby potentially reducing demand for correctional facilities to house them. Legislation has been proposed in numerous jurisdictions that could lower minimum sentences for some nonviolent crimes and make more inmates eligible for early release based on good behavior. Also, sentencing alternatives under consideration could put some offenders on probation with electronic monitoring who would otherwise be incarcerated. Similarly, reductions in crime rates or resources dedicated to prevent

and enforce crime could lead to reductions in arrests, convictions and sentences requiring incarceration at correctional facilities.

The GEO Group, the second largest private prison operator, identified similar "Risks Related to Our Business and Industry" in SEC filings:

> Our growth depends on our ability to secure contracts to develop and manage new correctional, detention and mental health facilities, the demand for which is outside our control.... [A]ny changes with respect to the decriminalization of drugs and controlled substances could affect the number of persons arrested, convicted, sentenced and incarcerated, thereby potentially reducing demand for correctional facilities to house them. Similarly, reductions in crime rates could lead to reductions in arrests, convictions and sentences requiring incarceration at correctional facilities. Immigration reform laws which are currently a focus for legislators and politicians at the federal, state and local level also could materially adversely impact us.

Enormous Profits for the Private Prison Industry

The incarceration explosion over the past several decades produced very few winners. Mass imprisonment broke state budgets, tore families and communities apart, and failed to promote public safety in any significant way. But as mass incarceration led to disastrous effects for the nation as a whole, one special interest group—the private prison industry—emerged as a clear winner. A massive transfer of taxpayer dollars to the private prison industry accompanied the unprecedented increase in incarceration and the rapid ascent of for-profit imprisonment.

In the early 1980s, private prisons barely existed in the United States, but that decade would witness the founding of the two companies that dominate the industry today— Corrections Corporation of America (CCA) and the GEO Group (then called Wackenhut Corrections Corporation). By 2010, annual revenues for these two companies alone had grown to nearly $3 billion.

Government contracts (state, local, and federal) provide the dominant source of private prison revenue. Therefore, these astronomical revenue figures demonstrate that private prison companies receive massive amounts of taxpayer dollars.

The ability of private prison companies to capture taxpayer dollars results in handsome rewards for their top executives. According to one source, in 2010, CCA's President and CEO received more than $3.2 million in executive compensation, and GEO's Chairman and CEO received nearly $3.5 million.

Private Prisons, Mass Incarceration, and the American Legislative Exchange Council

CCA, the leading private prison company, has long provided major support to, and had close ties with, the American Legislative Exchange Council (ALEC)—an organization of state legislators that has advocated harsh sentencing and detention laws, such as mandatory minimum sentencing statutes. ALEC provides state legislators with model legislation, and each year, ALEC members introduce hundreds of these model bills in statehouses across the country.

ALEC operates by hosting lavish retreats that bring together state legislators and corporate executives. Almost 2,000 state legislators belong to the organization. According to National Public Radio, at ALEC annual conferences, "companies get to sit around a table and write 'model bills' with the state legislators, who then take them home to their states." Legislators, it has been reported, pay nominal fees to attend the meetings ($50 for an annual membership), while the corporate participants pay thousands of dollars in membership dues.

Top Private Prison Companies

1. Corrections Corporation of America (CCA)

   2010 Revenue: $1,700,000,000

   Prisoner Capacity: 90,037

   Year Founded: 1983

   Headquarters: Nashville, Tennessee

   Head: Damon Hininger (President and CEO)

   Executive Compensation: $3,266,387 compensation package for Hininger in 2010 (according to Morningstar)

2. The GEO Group

   2010 Revenue: $1,269,968,000

   Prisoner Capacity: 81,000

   Year Founded: 1984 (founded as Wackenhut Corrections Corporation)

   Headquarters: Boca Raton, Florida

   Head: George Zoley (Chairman, CEO, Founder)

   Executive Compensation: $3,484,807 compensation package for Zoley in 2010 (according to Morningstar)

As one ALEC member allegedly stated in the late 1990s: "The organization is supported by money from the corporate sector, and, by paying to be members, corporations are allowed the opportunity to sit down at the table and discuss the issues that they have an interest in." After ALEC meetings, legislators return to their home states with ALEC model legislation.

ALEC has pushed legislation that benefits private prison companies by promoting policies that result in mass incarceration. In the 1990s, ALEC championed—and, according to one report by an advocacy group, succeeded in enacting in 27 states—"truth in sentencing" and "three strikes" legislation. Such laws were certain to increase prison populations (whether public or private) and the amount of taxpayer money funneled into prisons.

In the 1990s, ALEC's mass incarceration legislation met with overwhelming success.

While private prison companies deny taking steps to affirmatively support legislation that promotes mass incarceration, and although CCA left ALEC in 2010, according to a recent news report, "for the past two decades, a CCA executive has been a member of the council's [task force that] produced more than 85 model bills and resolutions that required tougher criminal sentencing, expanded immigration enforcement and promoted prison privatization ... CCA's senior director of business development was the private-sector chair of the task force in the mid- to late 90s when it produced a series of model bills promoting tough-on-crime measures that would send more people to prison for a longer time." According to one report by a non-profit organization, "[i]n 1999, CCA made the

[ALEC] President's List for contributions to ALEC's States and National Policy Summit; Wackenhut also sponsored the conference."

Even as ALEC has recently pushed certain piecemeal reforms for low-risk prisoners, the organization continues to trumpet harsh mandatory minimums, stating on its website:

> Each year, close to 1,000 bills, based at least in part on ALEC Model Legislation, are introduced in the states. Of these, an average of 20 percent become law.... Since its founding, ALEC has amassed an unmatched record of achieving ground-breaking changes in public policy. Policies such as *mandatory minimum sentencing* for violent criminals represent just a handful of ALEC's victories in the states.

ALEC has not only done work that helped increase the amount of taxpayer money spent on corrections generally but has also supported policies likely to increase the proportion of corrections spending funneled to private corporations. According to a report by an advocacy group, ALEC's Criminal Justice Task Force at one point reported that prison privatization was a "major issue" on which it was focusing, and according to a recent news report, "[s]tarting in the 1990s, [an] ALEC task force ... produced model bills directly promoting prison privatization. These included bills to let private prisons house inmates from other states without permission of local governments, require privatization of prisons and correctional services and encourage contracting for prison labor."

Immigration Detention and Private Prison Expansion

In recent years, private prisons have profited not only from harsh sentencing policies but also from an unprecedented increase in the number of detained immigrants—a group incarcerated pursuant to civil detention authority but housed in prison-like conditions. According to one group, facilities operated by private prison companies currently house nearly 50% of the more than 30,000 immigrants detained by Immigration and Customs Enforcement (ICE) at any given time.

Like imprisonment, immigration detention has expanded dramatically in recent years. In 1994, the average daily population of detained immigrants stood at 6,785. In 1996, Congress passed the Illegal Immigrant Reform and Immigrant Responsibility Act (IIRIRA), which massively expanded the detention of immigrants. By 2001, the number of immigrants detained at any given time had more than tripled, to 20,429.

Yet even that number would continue to grow, as the September 11, 2001 attacks further fueled the reliance on immigration detention, in turn bringing new business for the private prison industry

The past decade has borne out the prediction that 9/11 would be good business for private prisons. By 2010, the average daily population of immigration detainees stood at 31,020, more than a 50% increase over the 2001 level (and an increase of roughly 450% over the 1994 level).

Recently, ALEC leaders have been involved with discriminatory immigration laws that carry potential benefits for private prisons. On April 23, 2010, Arizona Governor Jan Brewer signed into law Senate Bill 1070, a statute that requires police officers in Arizona to ask people for their papers during law enforcement stops based only on an undefined "reasonable suspicion" that they are in the country unlawfully. Senate Bill 1070, and similar "copycat" laws since enacted in several other states, have the potential to further increase the number of immigrants detained, thereby adding to pressure to build more immigration detention centers.

While mass incarceration injures the nation as a whole, private prison companies enjoy a massive windfall, extracting ever-greater amounts of taxpayer dollars from the public fisc.

PART II: THE FALSE PROMISE OF PRIVATE PRISONS

Although mass incarceration strains state budgets while rewarding for-profit companies, certain private prison supporters and policymakers have put forth privatization as part of a *solution* to budgetary crises confronting states across the nation. Similarly, leading private prison companies promise to provide cost-effective alternatives to governmentally operated prisons. CCA asserts on its website, "[w]ith state and federal budgets stretched and public needs always competing with limited dollars, legislators are faced with critical choices on where to spend scarce resources. Creating a partnership with CCA to construct, manage and maintain their prisons allows governments to care for hardworking taxpayer dollars, while protecting critical priorities like education and health care." Other private prison companies assert that privatization saves money, or is otherwise cost-effective. GEO, for example, claims to provide "20% to 30% cost savings" in facility development, and "10% to 20% cost savings" in facility management.

The view that private prisons save taxpayer money, fuel local economies, and adequately protect the safety of prisoners helps to feed mass incarceration by making privatization appear to be an attractive alternative to reducing prison populations. But the evidence for such benefits is mixed at best. Not only may privatization fail to save taxpayer money, but private prison companies, as for-profit institutions, are strongly incentivized to cut corners and thereby maximize profits, which may come at the expense of public safety and the well-being of prisoners.

Inflated hopes about the supposed benefits of privatization are especially dangerous now, as several states, spurred by fiscal necessity, have begun the difficult work of reducing mass incarceration. Such progress threatens the private prison industry.

The danger currently posed by the private prison industry is that legislators, operating under the highly questionable view that private prisons save money, will turn to privatization as a fiscal solution, rather than cutting corrections spending by reducing the number of people behind bars. For example, despite a recent statement by the Arizona Auditor General that for-profit imprisonment in Arizona may cost *more* than incarceration in publicly-operated facilities, Arizona has announced plans to contract out an additional 5,000 prison "beds." Accordingly, an analysis of the key benefits supposedly associated with private prisons—that for-profit prisons save money, stimulate economic growth, and adequately ensure the well-being of prisoners—is especially relevant in the present moment.

Supposed Cost Savings

Evidence that private prisons save public money is mixed at best. While some research supports such a view, numerous other studies and reports have indicated that private prisons do not save money, cannot be demonstrated to save money in meaningful amounts, or may even cost *more* than governmentally operated prisons. For example:

> In 2010, the **Arizona** Auditor General stated that analysis by the Arizona Department of Corrections "indicated that it may be more costly to house inmates in private prisons" than public institutions.

> In 2010, the **Hawaii** State Auditor issued a scathing report which found that the state's Department of Public Safety "repeatedly misled policymakers and the public by reporting inaccurate incarceration costs." In justifying the decision to send prisoners to CCA prisons in the continental United States, rather than

publicly operated prisons in Hawaii, the Department used a "flawed methodology," "provide[d] artificial inmate costs," and engaged in "skewed cost reporting."

In 2010, a Legal Review Committee, established by Monmouth County, **New Jersey**, to study the legal implications of privatizing the Monmouth County Correctional Institution, reported: "Many studies have been done regarding prison privatization, most of which conclude that the legal implications associated therewith make privatization unattractive. Specifically, increased liability to the public entity, increased reported escapes, private prison guards who are not trained to the level of law enforcement officers, increased number of lawsuits and increased violence and disturbances at correction facilities ... Most objective cost studies show little or no cost savings to taxpayers coupled with an increased safety risk ... [P]rivatization does not appear to be a viable option for Monmouth County's maximum security facility due to the potential increased risk of liability and safety risks without proof of cost savings."

In 2007, the Government Accountability Office (GAO) reported that the **Federal Bureau of Prisons** failed to collect adequate data to determine whether private federal prisons were more or less expensive than publicly operated federal prisons.

A 2007 meta-analysis of previous privatization studies by **University of Utah** researchers found: "Cost savings from privatization are not guaranteed and quality of services is not improved. Across the board effect sizes were small, so small that the value of moving to a privately managed system is questionable."

While a judicial decision does not constitute a study, it is noteworthy that on September 30, 2011, a **Florida** court enjoined the Florida Department of Corrections from implementing the privatization of prisons in 18 counties, finding that the planned privatization failed to comply with procedures mandated by state law, including provisions regarding cost effectiveness.

Scant Economic Benefit for Local Communities

Aside from supposed cost benefits, the leading for-profit private prison companies assert that private prisons spur economic growth for local communities. The GEO Group's website, for example, claims that GEO prisons provide local communities with an "influx of capital [that] has the ability to stimulate the economic makeup of a community through consumer spending, new business enterprises, and capital improvements." Similarly, CCA promises that "[o]ur presence means more revenue for counties, towns, cities and states. Our facilities mean more local jobs for hardworking residents."

The view that prisons substantially promote economic development is highly questionable. According to certain studies, new prisons appear to bring few, if any, economic benefits. A 2010 study by researchers at Washington State University and Ohio State University examined data on "all existing and new prisons in the United States since 1960," reporting findings that "cast doubt on claims that prison building is worth the investment for struggling rural communities." A 2005 nationwide study reported similar results. Yet another empirical study, which was conducted by an advocacy organization and which focused on rural counties in New York State, found that although new prisons create jobs, "these benefits do not aid the host county to any substantial degree since local residents are not necessarily in a position to be hired for these jobs." While it should be noted that these studies did not differentiate between governmental and private prisons, the evidence contained in such studies supports the view that opening new prisons provides scant benefit to local communities.

Furthermore, private prisons can impose costs on local communities by obtaining subsidies, enjoying property tax exemptions, and receiving municipal services (such as water and sewer services) that cost taxpayer money. In 2001, a report by one advocacy group stated that nearly three quarters of large private prisons received development subsidies from the government.

Meanwhile, the benefit to counties where private prisons are built and operated can be quite scant—some receive less than $2 per prisoner per day from the private prison operator. The private prison companies themselves receive a far greater payoff from the government entity (such as a state corrections department) whose prisoners the company incarcerates. For example, private prison operators in Arizona were paid $63.52 per medium security prisoner per day in 2009, and as early as 2000, the federal government agreed to pay CCA almost $90 per day for each detained immigrant at a San Diego facility.

Furthermore, in some cases, local communities eager to build private prisons have set up financial arrangements that ultimately damage their fiscal standing.

Limited Incentives to Curb Recidivism and Prison Violence

Leading private prison companies assert that for-profit facilities protect the safety of prisoners. GEO asserts, "We are committed to establishing and maintaining a workplace that is safe, secure and humane, not only for our trained and experienced professionals, but for the offenders entrusted in our care." CCA states: "On the frontline level, being a member of the security team at CCA means more than performing routine checks on a shift; it means being an ambassador of safety and security for inmates, the surrounding community and fellow staff."

As detailed below, however, certain research suggests that for-profit prisons may be associated with heightened levels of violence toward prisoners. The perverse incentives to maximize profits and cut corners—even at the expense of safety and decent conditions—may contribute to an unacceptable level of danger in private prisons.

Violence in Private Prisons

Although there is some evidence to the contrary, several studies suggest that prisoners in private facilities may face greater threats to safety than those in governmentally operated prisons. One study concluded that "the private sector is a more dangerous place to be incarcerated," and reported, based upon an analysis of national data, that "the private sector experienced more than twice the number of assaults against inmates than did the public sector." Similarly, a United States Department of Justice study, based on a national survey of private prisons, reported that "the privately operated facilities have a much higher rate of inmate-on-inmate and inmate-on-staff assaults and other disturbances" than publicly operated facilities, when institutions of similar security levels are compared. Another study reported: "[T]he survey data presented in this paper show that privately operated prisons ... had much higher escape rates from secure institutions, and much higher random drug hit rates than the Bureau of Prisons."

Another Department of Justice study, which compared a private federal prison, Taft Correctional Institution ("TCI"), with certain other institutions operated by the federal Bureau of Prisons ("BOP"), reported lower levels of violent inmate misconduct at the private prison but also stated that the private prison "contributed to a higher probability that inmates would be involved in overall misconduct for much of the time period than any of the [governmental] comparison prisons."

Flawed Incentives and Private Prison Violence

Dangers in private prisons may reflect, at least in part, financial incentives to minimize costs and thereby maximize profits. Indeed, according to one scholar, "there is a much stronger incentive for private [prison] companies to save costs, not for the public's benefit, but for their own profit." In particular, low pay for private prison staff may result in a higher level of staff turnover. As stated in one study, "private operators are running prisons with workers who are generally paid less than their public-sector counterparts," and "privately operated prisons ... had much higher separation rates for correctional officers."

These shortcuts potentially create grave risks, as pay and turnover may "contribute to the higher levels of violence seen in the private sector." More specifically:

> Privately operated prisons appear to have systemic problems in maintaining secure facilities.... Advocates of prison privatization have argued that private prisons can pay workers less, offer fewer benefits, and still deliver a product that is as good or better than that provided by the public sector. The evidence to date contradicts such an encompassing assertion.

The same study continued: "[t]he data presented here indicate that less costly workers in private prisons have not produced an acceptable level of public safety or inmate care to date."

Private Prisons and Rehabilitation

Private prison operators have limited incentives to reduce future crime. As one scholar notes, "[i]t very well may be that companies operating private prisons ... will be so concerned with cost cutting, profit making, and satisfying their stockholders that some major goals of the institution will be neglected or overlooked. For instance, some aspects of rehabilitation ... may be affected." Numerous religious groups have condemned the perverse incentives inherent in for-profit incarceration—including the absence of incentives to devote resources to rehabilitation.

Not only is there little incentive to spend money on rehabilitation, but crime, at least in one sense, is good for private prisons: the more crimes that are committed, and the more individuals who are sent to prison, the more money private prisons stand to make. Increased recidivism gives private prisons a steady clientele but has negative consequences for the public—more crime, and more money spent re-incarcerating former prisoners.

Although supporters of for-profit prisons contend that such institutions provide an answer to bloated state corrections budgets, these facilities offer no solution—financial or otherwise—to the mass incarceration crisis confronting state governments. The evidence that private prisons provide demonstrable financial savings is mixed at best, and prisons do not appear to provide economic benefits to local communities. Private prisons suffer from flawed incentives and may face heightened levels of violence.

Given these enormous potential drawbacks, why have private prison companies been so successful in persuading policymakers to build more and more private prisons? Much of the answer lies in shrewd—and sometimes cynical—efforts used by some members of the private prison industry to curry political favor.

PART III: THE PRIVATE PRISON PITCH

In order to increase revenue and maximize profit, private prison companies must obtain more and more contracts to lock up increasing numbers of people. Some private prison companies, or individuals associated with these companies, employ a range of aggressive tactics to expand the reach of for-profit imprisonment. This [section] examines such tactics, which include:

Questionable financial incentives

Benefitting from the "revolving door" between public and private corrections

Extensive lobbying

Lavish campaign contributions

Control of information

Not *every* private prison company has been found to engage in each tactic discussed in this chapter, but the tactics used by some companies may pose an especially grave concern at present, as state governments struggle to reduce incarceration costs. Such tactics threaten to undermine real solutions to over-incarceration by encouraging cash-strapped state governments to turn to privatization rather than serious criminal justice reform. The highly questionable view that private prisons provide advantages (financial or otherwise) over governmental facilities may become all the more dangerous when coupled with the influence-peddling strategies discussed [below].

Questionable Financial Incentives

The private prison industry has managed to expand its reach in part because some private prison companies, or individuals associated with those companies, have provided questionable financial incentives to legislators or other government officials.

CASE STUDY: A Travesty of Juvenile Justice in Pennsylvania

In February 2011, a jury convicted former Luzerne County, Pennsylvania Judge Mark Ciavarella of racketeering, money laundering, and conspiracy in connection with his acceptance of nearly one million dollars from the developer of a private juvenile facility. Prosecutors reportedly referred to these activities as a "kids for cash" scheme. Ciavarella was responsible for an enormous share of imprisoned juveniles. Indeed, in the span of five years, Ciavarella's rulings accounted for 22% of decisions to detain children in Pennsylvania — even though Luzerne county accounts for less than 3% of Pennsylvania's population.

According to families with children tried by Ciavarella, the judge would hold trials only minutes long. He allegedly ordered a ten-year-old incarcerated and locked up a high school girl for three months because she mocked a school official on a website. In another reported instance, a twelve-year-old boy took his mother's car and got into an accident. The mother filed a police report, concerned that insurance otherwise would not cover the damage. Ciavarella reportedly jailed the boy for a full two years.

The payments received by Ciavarella from the private prison developer ultimately led not only to Ciavarella's criminal conviction but also to the dismissal, by the Supreme Court of Pennsylvania, of 4,000 juvenile cases handled by Ciavarella. The Court stated:

> Ciavarella admitted under oath that he had received payments from Robert Powell, a co-owner of the [two private facilities], and from Robert K. Mericle, the developer who constructed the juvenile facilities, during the period of time that Ciavarella was presiding over juvenile matters in Luzerne County.... Ciavarella's admission that he received these payments, and that he failed to disclose his financial interests arising from the development of the juvenile facilities, thoroughly undermines the integrity of all juvenile proceedings before Ciavarella.... [T]his Court cannot have any confidence that Ciavarella decided

any Luzerne County juvenile case fairly and impartially while he labored under the specter of his self-interested dealings with the facilities.

The Revolving Door Between Public and Private Corrections

Private prison companies make their money through contracts for prison construction and operation negotiated with public officials. Many in the private prison industry, however, once served in state corrections departments, and numerous state corrections officials formerly worked for private prison companies. In some cases, this revolving door between public corrections and private prisons may contribute to the ability of some companies to win contracts or to avoid sufficient scrutiny from the corrections departments charged with overseeing their operations. A full examination of the numerous instances in which private prison contractors have been hired into and out of government posts could fill an entire report. Select examples include the following:

> Prior to becoming the New Mexico Secretary of Corrections, Joe Williams worked for the GEO Group as a warden. In 2010, the New Mexico Legislative Finance Committee reported that although private prisons, including GEO, failed to maintain prison staffing levels required by contract, the state corrections department—headed by Williams—declined to collect contractual fines. The Committee found that the state might have collected an estimated $18 million from the private prison companies if the corrections department had enforced the contractual rules applicable to private prisons.

> Former BOP Director Harley Lappin, after being arrested for alleged drunk driving, left government service in early 2011. Lappin clearly remained valuable to the private prison industry, and soon began work for CCA, as the company's Chief Corrections Officer.

> According to a letter from the American Federation of Government Employees to Senator Patrick Leahy, during Stacia A. Hylton's tenure as Federal Detention Trustee, GEO obtained contracts to house federal prisoners, including U.S. Marshals Service detainees, that generate more than $80 million in annual revenue for the company. The letter asserts that even before she retired as Federal Detention Trustee, Hylton formed a private consulting company. Shortly after retiring, the letter continues, Hylton accepted $112,500 from the GEO Group, her only client. In 2010, Hylton reentered the federal government, as head of the U.S. Marshals Service.

The following case study further illustrates the problems created by the revolving door between public and private corrections.

CASE STUDY: Former GEO Employees Fail To Report Children Living in Squalor

In 2007, the Texas Youth Commission fired employees responsible for monitoring a West Texas juvenile prison run by GEO because the employees failed to report horrid conditions at the prison. In fact, the employees "not only failed to report substandard conditions but praised the operation. In the monitors' most recent review ... the prison was awarded an overall compliance score of 97.7 percent. In that review, monitors also thanked GEO staff for their positive work with [Texas] youth."

It later came to light that some of the monitors—immediately before commencing their employment as state monitors of GEO's contract performance—had worked *for the GEO Group*. When Texas finally sent independent auditors to the youth facility, the auditors reportedly "got so much fecal matter on their shoes they had to wipe their feet on the grass outside." Findings in the independent report included all of the following:

"The GEO Group does not ensure that the youth are provided with a clean and orderly living environment."

"Cells were filthy, smelled of feces and urine, and were in need of paint."

"[T]here are serious problems with insects throughout the facility and grounds."

"Plumbing chases were not secure at the time of the inspection. Contraband and pests were found in these areas."

"Water leaks are numerous throughout the facility, creating an unsanitary and unsafe environment for all youth and staff."

"There is racial segregation [in] the dorms; Hispanics are not allowed to be cell mates with African Americans."

"Youth sprayed with [Oleoresin Capsicum] pepper spray are not routinely de-contaminated."

The Texas Youth Commission auditors also held focus groups, in which children at the facility reported:

They have "not received church services in over two months."

They are "disciplined for speaking Spanish."

They "are sometimes not allowed to brush their teeth for days at a time."

They "had been forced to urinate or defecate in some container other than a toilet."

The Private Prison Lobby

Certain private prison companies, according to a recent report by Detention Watch Network, spend large sums of money to lobby the House of Representatives, the Senate, and several federal agencies, including the Federal Bureau of Prisons (which incarcerates over 200,000 prisoners at any given time) and the Department of Homeland Security (which detains over 30,000 immigrants at any given time). According to nonprofit groups, CCA alone spent over $18 million on federal lobbying between 1999 and 2009, "often employing five or six firms at the same time," and in 2010, CCA spent another $970,000 lobbying the federal government.

These figures capture only federal government lobbying—but private prison companies also lobby heavily in statehouses across the country. While total expenditures on state lobbying are impossible to calculate because lobbying disclosure requirements vary from state to state, what is clear is that lobbyists for private prisons have fanned out from coast to coast. For example, the Justice Policy Institute recently reported that "[i]n Florida alone, [the three largest private prison companies] utilized 30 lobbyists to advocate for private prison contracts and policies to promote the use of [private] prisons."

Between 2003 and 2011, according to the National Institute on Money in State Politics, CCA hired 199 lobbyists in 32 states. During the same period, GEO hired 72 lobbyists in 17 states.

Campaign Contributions

In addition to lobbying, for-profit prison companies also spend vast sums of money on campaign contributions. Since 2000, the leading private prison companies—CCA, GEO, and Cornell (which has since been absorbed by GEO in a merger)—have contributed over six million dollars to candidates for state office and over $800,000 to candidates for federal office, according to the Justice Policy Institute. The organization further reports

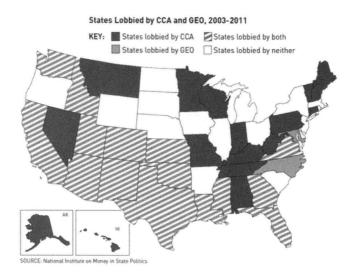

that in 2010 alone, these companies contributed over two million dollars to state political campaigns, with a large fraction of the money funneled to state party committees.

Data maintained by the National Institute on Money in State Politics also reveal the following about private prison campaign contributions: Between 2003 and 2011, CCA contributed to over 600 state candidates, and GEO contributed to over 400. Both corporations have established their own Political Action Committees (PACs). These companies backed a high proportion of candidates who ultimately won elections, which may indicate a strategy of focusing contributions on candidates likely to wield power.

Control of Information

For-profit prison companies go to great lengths, and apparently spend significant funds, to put forth a positive public image. Certain private prison companies offer the public well-manicured websites with extensive press releases and video footage touting their accomplishments, and the industry praises itself in publications such as *Service, Security and Solutions* (published by CCA) and *GEOworld* (published by GEO). Puff pieces on private prison websites cover such topics as the Paws in Prison program (which pairs prisoners with dogs), awards given to the industry, and a charity golf tournament hosted by CCA's chairman.

Private prison companies also funnel money (which, of course, initially comes largely from taxpayers) into communications departments, which churn out positive stories about private prisons.

Meanwhile, according to journalist and policy analyst Tom Barry: "A near-total absence of committed oversight has allowed the prison industry to flourish in the shadows. Requests for the most basic information about the functioning of these prisons and detention centers routinely lead nowhere." A private prison loophole in open records laws contributes to this lack of accountability. Under the Freedom of Information Act (FOIA), members of the public can request documents from federal prisons and immigration detention facilities—but when the federal government sends prisoners to a private prison, the private prison is exempt from FOIA requests. Under many state open records laws, the same asymmetry applies to state prisoners in state institutions and state prisoners in private prisons.

CCA has also blocked efforts by some of its own shareholders to bring greater transparency to the corporation's political contributions. A 2007 stockholder proposal put forward by these groups would have required "an accounting of our Company's funds that are used for political contributions or expenditures" and disclosure of "the internal guidelines or policies, if any, governing our company's political contributions and expenditures." CCA's Board of Directors unanimously recommended that stockholders reject the proposal, and the measure was voted down. More recently, according to a news report, CCA's Board has continued to oppose similar proposals for corporate transparency brought by religious groups that own stock in the company.

A range of aggressive and shrewd tactics drive the expansion of private incarceration. The private prison industry thrives in part by employing effective marketing strategies, rather than offering effective solutions.

CONCLUSION

In America, our criminal justice system should keep us safe, operate fairly, and be cost-effective. Mass incarceration, however, deprives record numbers of individuals of their liberty, has at best a minimal effect on public safety, and cripples state budgets. Meanwhile, the private prison industry rakes in profits by obtaining government money in increasing amounts, by depriving Americans of liberty in ever greater numbers, and potentially by cutting corners at the expense of public safety and prison security.

For-profit prisons are a major contributor to bloated state budgets and mass incarceration—not a part of any viable solution to these urgent problems. In order to reduce corrections spending and mitigate mass incarceration, governments must focus on the hard work of criminal justice reform, and not the false promise of for-profit imprisonment.

Notes

(1) After seeing all of the facts outlined above, why do private prison corporations continue to flourish as profit centers in the United States today?

(2) Recall the "Kids for Cash" scandal in Pennsylvania where two judges took bribes from private prison officials to maintain a steady stream of juvenile offenders into the private prison facility. Why is this case not enough to inspire legislatures to eradicate private prisons and outlaw the warehousing of their state's prisoners in private for-profit facilities?

(3) It is worthwhile to note that "lobbying" is outlawed in most developed countries in the world. Why does the U.S. allow lobbying as a matter-of-course? What are private prison lobbyists seeking when they meet with legislators? Put yourself in the shoes of a private prison lobbyist—what would your "ask" be when golfing or boating with a like-minded legislator? Depending on your "ask," should this type of lobbying be legal?

In the reading that follows, "The Caging of America," *New Yorker* writer Adam Gopnik takes a very real approach to what it might be like to be locked up in an American prison. He traces the purposes and evolution of incarceration and asks whether we really should be locking up large segments of our citizenry for non-violent drug crimes. Ask yourself as you read, why do we incarcerate with such brutality, ferocity and inhumanity in the U.S.?

The Caging of America
Why do we lock up so many people?

By Adam Gopnik*
January 30, 2012

A prison is a trap for catching time. Good reporting appears often about the inner life of the American prison, but the catch is that American prison life is mostly undramatic — the reported stories fail to grab us, because, for the most part, nothing *happens.* It isn't the horror of the time at hand but the unimaginable sameness of the time ahead that makes prisons unendurable for their inmates. The inmates on death row in Texas are called men in "timeless time," because they alone aren't serving time: they aren't waiting out five years or a decade or a lifetime. The basic reality of American prisons is not that of the lock and key but that of the lock and clock.

That's why no one who has been inside a prison, if only for a day, can ever forget the feeling. Time stops. A note of attenuated panic, of watchful paranoia — anxiety and boredom and fear mixed into a kind of enveloping fog, covering the guards as much as the guarded. "Sometimes I think this whole world is one big prison yard, / Some of us are prisoners, some of us are guards," Dylan sings, and while it isn't strictly true — just ask the prisoners — it contains a truth: the guards are doing time, too. As a smart man once wrote after being locked up, the thing about jail is that there are bars on the windows and they won't let you out. This simple truth governs all the others. What prisoners try to convey to the free is how the presence of time as something being done to you, instead of something you do things with, alters the mind at every moment. For American prisoners, huge numbers of whom are serving sentences much longer than those given for similar crimes anywhere else in the civilized world — time becomes in every sense this thing you serve.

For most privileged, professional people, the experience of confinement is a mere brush, encountered after a kid's arrest. For a great many poor people in America, particularly poor black men, prison is a destination that braids through an ordinary life, much as high school and college do for rich white ones. More than half of all black men without a high-school diploma go to prison at some time in their lives. Mass incarceration on a scale almost unexampled in human history is a fundamental fact of our country today — perhaps *the* fundamental fact, as slavery was the fundamental fact of 1850. In truth, there are more black men in the grip of the criminal-justice system — in prison, on probation, or on parole — than were in slavery. That city of the confined and the controlled, Lockuptown, is now the second largest in the United States.

The accelerating rate of incarceration over the past few decades is just as startling as the number of people jailed: in 1980, there were about two hundred and twenty people incarcerated for every hundred thousand Americans; by 2010, the number had more than tripled, to seven hundred and thirty-one. No other country even approaches that. In the past two decades, the money that states spend on prisons has risen at six times the rate of spending on higher education. Ours is, bottom to top, a "carceral state," in the flat verdict of Conrad Black, the former conservative press lord and newly minted reformer, who right now finds himself imprisoned in Florida, thereby adding a new twist to an old

---

    * Adam Gopnik, *The Caging of America*, NEW YORKER, Jan. 30, 2012, http://www.newyorker.com/ arts/critics/atlarge/2012/01/30/120130crat_atlarge_gopnik.

joke: A conservative is a liberal who's been mugged; a liberal is a conservative who's been indicted; and a passionate prison reformer is a conservative who's in one.

The scale and the brutality of our prisons are the moral scandal of American life. Every day, at least fifty thousand men — a full house at Yankee Stadium — wake in solitary confinement, often in "supermax" prisons or prison wings, in which men are locked in small cells, where they see no one, cannot freely read and write, and are allowed out just once a day for an hour's solo "exercise." (Lock yourself in your bathroom and then imagine you have to stay there for the next ten years, and you will have some sense of the experience.) Prison rape is so endemic — more than seventy thousand prisoners are raped each year — that it is routinely held out as a threat, part of the punishment to be expected. The normalization of prison will surely strike our descendants as chillingly sadistic, incomprehensible on the part of people who thought themselves civilized. Though we avoid looking directly at prisons, they seep obliquely into our fashions and manners. Wealthy white teenagers in baggy jeans and laceless shoes and multiple tattoos show, unconsciously, the reality of incarceration that acts as a hidden foundation for the country.

How did we get here? How is it that our civilization, which rejects hanging and flogging and disembowelling, came to believe that caging vast numbers of people for decades is an acceptably humane sanction? There's a fairly large recent scholarly literature on the history and sociology of crime and punishment, and it tends to trace the American zeal for punishment back to the nineteenth century, apportioning blame in two directions. There's an essentially Northern explanation, focusing on the inheritance of the notorious Eastern State Penitentiary, in Philadelphia, and its "reformist" tradition; and a Southern explanation, which sees the prison system as essentially a slave plantation continued by other means. Robert Perkinson, the author of the Southern revisionist tract "Texas Tough: The Rise of America's Prison Empire," traces two ancestral lines, "from the North, the birthplace of rehabilitative penology, to the South, the fountainhead of subjugationist discipline." In other words, there's the scientific taste for reducing men to numbers and the slave owners' urge to reduce blacks to brutes.

William J. Stuntz, a professor at Harvard Law School, is the most forceful advocate for the view that the scandal of our prisons derives from the Enlightenment-era, "procedural" nature of American justice. He runs through the immediate causes of the incarceration epidemic: the growth of post-Rockefeller drug laws, which punished minor drug offenses with major prison time; "zero tolerance" policing, which added to the group; mandatory-sentencing laws, which prevented judges from exercising judgment. But his search for the ultimate cause leads deeper, all the way to the Bill of Rights. In a society where Constitution worship is still a requisite on right and left alike, Stuntz startlingly suggests that the Bill of Rights is a terrible document with which to start a justice system — much inferior to the exactly contemporary French Declaration of the Rights of Man, which Jefferson, he points out, may have helped shape while his protégé Madison was writing ours.

The trouble with the Bill of Rights, he argues, is that it emphasizes process and procedure rather than principles. The Declaration of the Rights of Man says, Be just! The Bill of Rights says, Be fair! Instead of announcing general principles — no one should be accused of something that wasn't a crime when he did it; cruel punishments are always wrong; the goal of justice is, above all, that justice be done — it talks procedurally. You can't search someone without a reason; you can't accuse him without allowing him to see the evidence; and so on. This emphasis, Stuntz thinks, has led to the current mess, where accused criminals get laboriously articulated protection against procedural errors and no protection at all against outrageous and obvious violations of simple justice. You can get off if the cops looked in the wrong car with the wrong warrant when they found your joint, but you have no recourse if owning the joint gets you locked up for life. You may be spared the death penalty if you can show a problem with your appointed defender, but it is much harder if there is merely enormous accumulated evidence that you weren't guilty in the first place and the jury got it wrong. Even clauses that Americans are taught to revere are, Stuntz maintains, unworthy of reverence: the ban on "cruel and unusual punishment" was designed to *protect* cruel punishments—flogging and branding—that were not at that time unusual.

The obsession with due process and the cult of brutal prisons, the argument goes, share an essential impersonality. The more professionalized and procedural a system is, the more insulated we become from its real effects on real people. That's why America is famous both for its process-driven judicial system ("The bastard got off on a technicality," the cop-show detective fumes) and for the harshness and inhumanity of its prisons. Though all industrialized societies started sending more people to prison and fewer to the gallows in the eighteenth century, it was in Enlightenment-inspired America that the taste for long-term, profoundly depersonalized punishment became most aggravated. The inhumanity of American prisons was as much a theme for Dickens, visiting America in 1842, as the cynicism of American lawyers. His shock when he saw the Eastern State Penitentiary, in Philadelphia—a "model" prison, at the time the most expensive public building ever constructed in the country, where every prisoner was kept in silent, separate confinement—still resonates:

> I believe that very few men are capable of estimating the immense amount of torture and agony which this dreadful punishment, prolonged for years, inflicts upon the sufferers.... I hold this slow and daily tampering with the mysteries of the brain, to be immeasurably worse than any torture of the body: and because its ghastly signs and tokens are not so palpable to the eye and sense of touch as scars upon the flesh; because its wounds are not upon the surface, and it extorts few cries that human ears can hear; therefore I the more denounce it, as a secret punishment which slumbering humanity is not roused up to stay.

Not roused up to stay—that was the point. Once the procedure ends, the penalty begins, and, as long as the cruelty is routine, our civil responsibility toward the punished is over. We lock men up and forget about their existence. For Dickens, even the corrupt but communal debtors' prisons of old London were better than *this*. "Don't take it personally!"—that remains the slogan above the gate to the American prison Inferno. Nor is this merely a historian's vision. Conrad Black, at the high end, has a scary and persuasive picture of how his counsel, the judge, and the prosecutors all merrily congratulated each other on their combined professional excellence just before sending him off to the hoosegow for several years. If a millionaire feels that way, imagine how the ordinary culprit must feel.

In place of abstraction, Stuntz argues for the saving grace of humane discretion. Basically, he thinks, we should go into court with an understanding of what a crime is and what justice is like, and then let common sense and compassion and specific circumstance take over. For Stuntz, justice ought to be just the vibe of the thing—not one procedural error caught or one fact worked around. The criminal law should once again be more like the common law, with judges and juries not merely finding fact but making law on the basis of universal principles of fairness, circumstance, and seriousness, and crafting penalties to the exigencies of the crime.

The other argument—the Southern argument—is that this story puts too bright a face on the truth. The reality of American prisons, this argument runs, has nothing to do with the knots of procedural justice or the perversions of Enlightenment-era ideals.

Prisons today operate less in the rehabilitative mode of the Northern reformers "than in a retributive mode that has long been practiced and promoted in the South," Perkinson, an American-studies professor, writes. "American prisons trace their lineage not only back to Pennsylvania penitentiaries but to Texas slave plantations." White supremacy is the real principle, this thesis holds, and racial domination the real end. In response to the apparent triumphs of the sixties, mass imprisonment became a way of reimposing Jim Crow. Blacks are now incarcerated seven times as often as whites. "The system of mass incarceration works to trap African Americans in a virtual (and literal) cage," the legal scholar Michelle Alexander writes. Young black men pass quickly from a period of police harassment into a period of "formal control" (i.e., actual imprisonment) and then are doomed for life to a system of "invisible control." Prevented from voting, legally discriminated against for the rest of their lives, most will cycle back through the prison system. The system, in this view, is not really broken; it is doing what it was designed to do. Alexander's grim conclusion: "If mass incarceration is considered as a system of social control—specifically, racial control—then the system is a fantastic success."

Northern impersonality and Southern revenge converge on a common American theme: a growing number of American prisons are now contracted out as for-profit businesses to for-profit companies. The companies are paid by the state, and their profit depends on spending as little as possible on the prisoners and the prisons. It's hard to imagine any greater disconnect between public good and private profit: the interest of private prisons lies not in the obvious social good of having the minimum necessary number of inmates but in having as many as possible, housed as cheaply as possible. No more chilling document exists in recent American life than the 2005 annual report of the biggest of these firms, the Corrections Corporation of America. Here the company (which spends millions lobbying legislators) is obliged to caution its investors about the risk that somehow, somewhere, someone might turn off the spigot of convicted men:

> Our growth is generally dependent upon our ability to obtain new contracts to develop and manage new correctional and detention facilities.... The demand for our facilities and services could be adversely affected by the relaxation of enforcement efforts, leniency in conviction and sentencing practices or through the decriminalization of certain activities that are currently proscribed by our criminal laws. For instance, any changes with respect to drugs and controlled substances or illegal immigration could affect the number of persons arrested, convicted, and sentenced, thereby potentially reducing demand for correctional facilities to house them.

Brecht could hardly have imagined such a document: a capitalist enterprise that feeds on the misery of man trying as hard as it can to be sure that nothing is done to decrease that misery.

Yet a spectre haunts all these accounts, North and South, whether process gone mad or penal colony writ large. It is that the epidemic of imprisonment seems to track the dramatic decline in crime over the same period. The more bad guys there are in prison, it appears, the less crime there has been in the streets. The real background to the prison boom, which shows up only sporadically in the prison literature, is the crime wave that preceded and overlapped it.

For those too young to recall the big-city crime wave of the sixties and seventies, it may seem like mere bogeyman history. For those whose entire childhood and adolescence were set against it, it is the crucial trauma in recent American life and explains much else that happened in the same period. There really was, as Stuntz himself says, a liberal consensus on crime ("Wherever the line is between a merciful justice system and one that abandons all serious effort at crime control, the nation had crossed it"), and it really did have bad effects.

Yet if, in 1980, someone had predicted that by 2012 New York City would have a crime rate so low that violent crime would have largely disappeared as a subject of conversation, he would have seemed not so much hopeful as crazy. Thirty years ago, crime was supposed to be a permanent feature of the city, produced by an alienated underclass of super-predators; now it isn't. Something good happened to change it, and you might have supposed that the change would be an opportunity for celebration and optimism. Instead, we mostly content ourselves with grudging and sardonic references to the silly side of gentrification, along with a few all-purpose explanations, like broken-window policing. This is a general human truth: things that work interest us less than things that don't.

So what *is* the relation between mass incarceration and the decrease in crime? Certainly, in the nineteen-seventies and eighties, many experts became persuaded that there was no way to make bad people better; all you could do was warehouse them, for longer or shorter periods. The best research seemed to show, depressingly, that nothing works—that re-habilitation was a ruse. Then, in 1983, inmates at the maximum-security federal prison in Marion, Illinois, murdered two guards. Inmates had been (very occasionally) killing guards for a long time, but the timing of the murders, and the fact that they took place in a climate already prepared to believe that even ordinary humanity was wasted on the criminal classes, meant that the entire prison was put on permanent lockdown. A century and a half after absolute solitary first appeared in American prisons, it was reintroduced. Those terrible numbers began to grow.

And then, a decade later, crime started falling: across the country by a standard measure of about forty per cent; in New York City by as much as eighty per cent. By 2010, the crime rate in New York had seen its greatest decline since the Second World War; in 2002, there were fewer murders in Manhattan than there had been in any year since 1900. In social science, a cause sought is usually a muddle found; in life as we experience it, a crisis resolved is causality established. If a pill cures a headache, we do not ask too often if the headache might have gone away by itself.

All this ought to make the publication of Franklin E. Zimring's new book, "The City That Became Safe," a very big event. Zimring, a criminologist at Berkeley Law, has spent years crunching the numbers of what happened in New York in the context of what happened in the rest of America. One thing he teaches us is how little we know. The forty per cent drop across the continent—indeed, there was a decline throughout the Western world—took place for reasons that are as mysterious in suburban Ottawa as they are in the South Bronx. Zimring shows that the usual explanations—including demographic shifts—simply can't account for what must be accounted for. This makes the international decline look slightly eerie. Trends and fashions and fads and pure contingencies happen in other parts of our social existence; it may be that there are fashions and cycles in criminal behavior, too, for reasons that are just as arbitrary.

But the additional forty per cent drop in crime that seems peculiar to New York finally succumbs to Zimring's analysis. The change didn't come from resolving the deep pathologies that the right fixated on—from jailing super predators, driving down the number of unwed mothers, altering welfare culture. Nor were there cures for the underlying causes pointed to by the left: injustice, discrimination, poverty. Nor were there any "Presto!" effects arising from secret patterns of increased abortions or the like. The city didn't get much richer; it didn't get much poorer. There was no significant change in the ethnic makeup or the average wealth or educational levels of New Yorkers as violent crime more or less vanished. "Broken windows" or "turnstile jumping" policing, that is, cracking down on small visible offenses in order to create an atmosphere that refused to license crime, seems to have had a negligible effect; there was, Zimring writes, a great difference between the slogans and the substance of the time. (Arrests for "visible" nonviolent crime—e.g., street prostitution and public gambling—mostly went *down* through the period.)

Instead, small acts of social engineering, designed simply to stop crimes from happening, helped stop crime. In the nineties, the N.Y.P.D. began to control crime not by fighting minor crimes in safe places but by putting lots of cops in places where lots of crimes happened—"hot-spot policing." The cops also began an aggressive, controversial program of "stop and frisk"—"designed to catch the sharks, not the dolphins," as Jack Maple, one of its originators, described it—that involved what's called pejoratively "profiling." This was not so much racial, since in any given neighborhood all the suspects were likely to be of the same race or color, as social, involving the thousand small clues that policemen recognized already. Minority communities, Zimring emphasizes, paid a disproportionate price in kids stopped and frisked, and detained, but they also earned a disproportionate gain in crime reduced. "The poor pay more and get more" is Zimring's way of putting it. He believes that a "light" program of stop-and-frisk could be less alienating and just as effective, and that by bringing down urban crime stop-and-frisk had the net effect of greatly reducing the number of poor minority kids in prison for long stretches.

Zimring insists, plausibly, that he is offering a radical and optimistic rewriting of theories of what crime is and where criminals are, not least because it disconnects crime and minorities. "In 1961, twenty six percent of New York City's population was minority African American or Hispanic. Now, half of New York's population is—and what that does in an enormously hopeful way is to destroy the rude assumptions of supply side criminology," he says. By "supply side criminology," he means the conservative theory of crime that claimed that social circumstances produced a certain net amount of crime waiting to be expressed; if you stopped it here, it broke out there. The only way to stop crime was to lock up all the potential criminals. In truth, criminal activity seems like most other human choices—a question of contingent occasions and opportunity. Crime is not the consequence of a set number of criminals; criminals are the consequence of a set number of opportunities to commit crimes. Close down the open drug market in Washington Square, and it does not automatically migrate to Tompkins Square Park. It just stops, or the dealers go indoors, where dealing goes on but violent crime does not.

And, in a virtuous cycle, the decreased prevalence of crime fuels a decrease in the prevalence of crime. When your friends are no longer doing street robberies, you're less likely to do them. Zimring said, in a recent interview, "Remember, nobody ever made a living mugging. There's no minimum wage in violent crime." In a sense, he argues, it's recreational, part of a life style: "Crime is a routine behavior; it's a thing people do when they get used to doing it." And therein lies its essential fragility. Crime ends as a result of "cyclical forces operating on situational and contingent things rather than from finding deeply motivated essential linkages." Conservatives don't like this view because it shows that being tough doesn't help; liberals don't like it because apparently being nice doesn't help, either. Curbing crime does not depend on reversing social pathologies or alleviating social grievances; it depends on erecting small, annoying barriers to entry.

One fact stands out. While the rest of the country, over the same twenty-year period, saw the growth in incarceration that led to our current astonishing numbers, New York, despite the Rockefeller drug laws, saw a marked decrease in its number of inmates. "New York City, in the midst of a dramatic reduction in crime, is locking up a much smaller number of people, and particularly of young people, than it was at the height of the crime wave," Zimring observes. Whatever happened to make street crime fall, it had nothing to do with putting more men in prison. The logic is self-evident if we just transfer it to the realm of white-collar crime: we easily accept that there is no net sum of white-collar crime waiting to happen, no inscrutable generation of super-predators produced by Dewar's-guzzling dads and scaly M.B.A. profs; if you stop an embezzlement scheme here on Third Avenue, another doesn't naturally start in the next office building. White-collar crime happens through an intersection of pathology and opportunity; getting the S.E.C. busy ending the opportunity is a good way to limit the range of the pathology.

Social trends deeper and less visible to us may appear as future historians analyze what went on. Something other than policing may explain things—just as the coming of cheap credit cards and state lotteries probably did as much to weaken the Mafia's Five Families in New York, who had depended on loan sharking and numbers running, as the F.B.I. could. It is at least possible, for instance, that the coming of the mobile phone helped drive drug dealing indoors, in ways that helped drive down crime. It may be that the real value of hot spot and stop-and-frisk was that it provided a single game plan that the police believed in; as military history reveals, a bad plan is often better than no plan, especially if the people on the other side think it's a good plan. But one thing is sure: social epidemics, of crime or of punishment, can be cured more quickly than we might hope with simpler and more superficial mechanisms than we imagine. Throwing a Band-Aid over a bad wound is actually a decent strategy, if the Band-Aid helps the wound to heal itself.

Which leads, further, to one piece of radical common sense: since prison plays at best a small role in stopping even violent crime, very few people, rich or poor, should be in prison for a nonviolent crime. Neither the streets nor the society is made safer by having marijuana users or peddlers locked up, let alone with the horrific sentences now dispensed so easily. For that matter, no social good is served by having the embezzler or the Ponzi schemer locked in a cage for the rest of his life, rather than having him bankrupt and doing community service in the South Bronx for the next decade or two. Would we actually have more fraud and looting of shareholder value if the perpetrators knew that they would lose their bank accounts and their reputation, and have to do community service seven days a week for five years? It seems likely that anyone for whom those sanctions aren't sufficient is someone for whom no sanctions are ever going to be sufficient. Zimring's research shows clearly that, if crime drops on the street, criminals coming out of prison stop committing crimes. What matters is the incidence of crime in the world, and the continuity of a culture of crime, not some "lesson learned" in prison.

At the same time, the ugly side of stop-and-frisk can be alleviated. To catch sharks and not dolphins, Zimring's work suggests, we need to adjust the size of the holes in the nets—to make crimes that are the occasion for stop-and-frisks *real* crimes, not crimes like marijuana possession. When the New York City police stopped and frisked kids, the main goal was not to jail them for having pot but to get their fingerprints, so that they could be identified if they committed a more serious crime. But all over America the opposite happens: marijuana possession becomes the serious crime. The cost is so enormous, though, in lives ruined and money spent, that the obvious thing to do is not to enforce the law less but to change it now. Dr. Johnson said once that manners make law, and that when manners alter, the law must, too. It's obvious that marijuana is now an almost universally accepted drug in America: it is not only used casually (which has been true for decades) but also talked about casually on television and in the movies (which has not). One need only watch any stoner movie to see that the perceived risks of smoking dope are not that you'll get arrested but that you'll get in trouble with a rival frat or look like an idiot to women. The decriminalization of marijuana would help end the epidemic of imprisonment.

The rate of incarceration in most other rich, free countries, whatever the differences in their histories, is remarkably steady. In countries with Napoleonic justice or common law or some mixture of the two, in countries with adversarial systems and in those with magisterial ones, whether the country once had brutal plantation-style penal colonies, as France did, or was once itself a brutal plantation-style penal colony, like Australia, the natural rate of incarceration seems to hover right around a hundred men per hundred thousand people. (That doesn't mean it doesn't get lower in rich, homogeneous countries — just that it never gets much higher in countries otherwise like our own.) It seems that one man in every thousand once in a while does a truly bad thing. All other things being equal, the point of a justice system should be to identify that thousandth guy, find a way to keep him from harming other people, and give everyone else a break.

Epidemics seldom end with miracle cures. Most of the time in the history of medicine, the best way to end disease was to build a better sewer and get people to wash their hands. "Merely chipping away at the problem around the edges" is usually the very best thing to do with a problem; keep chipping away patiently and, eventually, you get to its heart. To read the literature on crime before it dropped is to see the same kind of dystopian despair we find in the new literature of punishment: we'd have to end poverty, or eradicate the ghettos, or declare war on the broken family, or the like, in order to end the crime wave. The truth is, a series of small actions and events ended up eliminating a problem that seemed to hang over everything. There was no miracle cure, just the intercession of a thousand smaller sanities. Ending sentencing for drug misdemeanors, decriminalizing marijuana, leaving judges free to use common sense (and, where possible, getting judges who are judges rather than politicians) — many small acts are possible that will help end the epidemic of imprisonment as they helped end the plague of crime.

"Oh, I have taken too little care of this!" King Lear cries out on the heath in his moment of vision. "Take physic, pomp; expose thyself to feel what wretches feel." "This" changes; in Shakespeare's time, it was flat-out peasant poverty that starved some and drove others as mad as poor Tom. In Dickens's and Hugo's time, it was the industrial revolution that drove kids to mines. But every society has a poor storm that wretches suffer in, and the attitude is always the same: either that the wretches, already dehumanized by their suffering, deserve no pity or that the oppressed, overwhelmed by injustice, will have to wait for a better world. At every moment, the injustice seems inseparable from the community's life, and in every case the arguments for keeping the system in place were that you would have to revolutionize the entire social order to change it — which then became the argument for revolutionizing the entire social order. In every case, humanity and common sense made the insoluble problem just get up and go away. Prisons are our this. We need take more care.

Notes

(1) What led to the decrease in crime rates in New York City (and the nation)?

(2) Why do we brutalize those we imprison? Why must rape and solitary confinement be a part of imprisonment in the U.S.? Trending in recent years, juvenile offenders

have been subjected to months and even years of solitary confinement. The psychological and emotional damage of solitary confinement has been empirically proven. Why does U.S. carceral policy allow for this type of treatment of children?

(3) Is there a better way to use prisons in the U.S.? Is there a more humane way to warehouse dangerous criminals?

(4) Beginning in 2014, there appears to be a trend toward both decriminalizing and in some states legalizing marijuana. Does this reflect a national appreciation of the fact that the War on Drugs has been a failure? What are we to make of the continuing harsh punishment of marijuana use in some states and the absolute freedom to use marijuana legally in other states?

(5) Professor Stuntz, who argues that the problem with the American criminal justice system is attributable to the Constitution because it incorrectly focuses on procedure rather than principles, avers that a more holistic approach to punishment that focuses on fairness, seriousness and crafting penalties to the exigencies of the crime is likely to result in fewer incarcerations. Is he correct? If race is one of the primary reasons that we observe such a large number of inmates, will a system that gives more power to judges to exercise greater levels of discretion by considering the "equities and fairness" of each set of facts, lead to fewer incarcerations?

When Arizona passed Senate Bill 1070, purportedly the state was intent on getting a handle on the immigration "problem" that was allegedly besetting the state. As the story below reveals, lobbyists and private prison officials were integrally involved in drafting the legislation that was introduced into the Arizona House of Representatives. The story below illustrates what happens when private for-profit prison interests are involved with passing new legislation.

Prison Economics Help Drive Ariz. Immigration Law

By Laura Sullivan*
October 28, 2010

Last year, two men showed up in Benson, Ariz., a small desert town 60 miles from the Mexico border, offering a deal. Glenn Nichols, the Benson city manager, remembers the pitch. "The gentleman that's the main thrust of this thing has a huge turquoise ring on his finger," Nichols said. "He's a great big huge guy and I equated him to a car salesman."

What he was selling was a prison for women and children who were illegal immigrants. "They talk [about] how positive this was going to be for the community," Nichols said, "the amount of money that we would realize from each prisoner on a daily rate." But Nichols wasn't buying. He asked them how would they possibly keep a prison full for years—decades even—with illegal immigrants?

"They talked like they didn't have any doubt they could fill it," Nichols said. That's because prison companies like this one had a plan—a new business model to lock up illegal immigrants. And the plan became Arizona's immigration law.

---

* Laura Sullivan, *Prison Economics Help Drive Ariz. Immigration Law*, NPR (Oct. 28, 2010), http://www.npr.org/2010/10/28/130833741/prison-economics-help-drive-ariz-immigration-law.

Behind-The-Scenes Effort To Draft, Pass The Law

The law is being challenged in the courts. But if it's upheld, it requires police to lock up anyone they stop who cannot show proof they entered the country legally. When it was passed in April, it ignited a firestorm. Protesters chanted about racial profiling. Businesses threatened to boycott the state. Supporters were equally passionate, calling it a bold positive step to curb illegal immigration. But while the debate raged, few people were aware of how the law came about.

NPR spent the past several months analyzing hundreds of pages of campaign finance reports, lobbying documents and corporate records. What they show is a quiet, behind-the-scenes effort to help draft and pass Arizona Senate Bill 1070 by an industry that stands to benefit from it: the private prison industry.

The law could send hundreds of thousands of illegal immigrants to prison in a way never done before. And it could mean hundreds of millions of dollars in profits to private prison companies responsible for housing them.

Arizona state Sen. Russell Pearce says the bill was his idea. He says it's not about prisons. It's about what's best for the country. "Enough is enough," Pearce said in his office, sitting under a banner reading "Let Freedom Reign." "People need to focus on the cost of not enforcing our laws and securing our border. It is the Trojan horse destroying our country and a republic cannot survive as a lawless nation."

But instead of taking his idea to the Arizona statehouse floor, Pearce first took it to a hotel conference room. It was last December at the Grand Hyatt in Washington, D.C. Inside, there was a meeting of a secretive group called the American Legislative Exchange Council. Insiders call it ALEC. It's a membership organization of state legislators and powerful corporations and associations, such as the tobacco company Reynolds American Inc., ExxonMobil and the National Rifle Association. Another member is the billion-dollar Corrections Corporation of America—the largest private prison company in the country.

It was there that Pearce's idea took shape. "I did a presentation," Pearce said. "I went through the facts. I went through the impacts and they said, 'Yeah.'"

Drafting The Bill

The 50 or so people in the room included officials of the Corrections Corporation of America, according to two sources who were there. Pearce and the Corrections Corporation of America have been coming to these meetings for years. Both have seats on one of several of ALEC's boards.

And this bill was an important one for the company. According to Corrections Corporation of America reports reviewed by NPR, executives believe immigrant detention is their next big market. Last year, they wrote that they expect to bring in "a significant portion of our revenues" from Immigration and Customs Enforcement, the agency that detains illegal immigrants. In the conference room, the group decided they would turn the immigration idea into a model bill. They discussed and debated language.

Then, they voted on it.

"There were no 'no' votes," Pearce said. "I never had one person speak up in objection to this model legislation." Four months later, that model legislation became, almost word for word, Arizona's immigration law. They even named it. They called it the "Support Our Law Enforcement and Safe Neighborhoods Act."

"ALEC is the conservative, free-market orientated, limited-government group," said Michael Hough, who was staff director of the meeting. Hough works for ALEC, but he's also running for state delegate in Maryland, and if elected says he plans to support a similar bill to Arizona's law.

Asked if the private companies usually get to write model bills for the legislators, Hough said, "Yeah, that's the way it's set up. It's a public-private partnership. We believe both sides, businesses and lawmakers should be at the same table, together."

Nothing about this is illegal. Pearce's immigration plan became a prospective bill and Pearce took it home to Arizona.

Campaign Donations

Pearce said he is not concerned that it could appear private prison companies have an opportunity to lobby for legislation at the ALEC meetings. "I don't go there to meet with them," he said. "I go there to meet with other legislators." Pearce may go there to meet with other legislators, but 200 private companies pay tens of thousands of dollars to meet with legislators like him.

As soon as Pearce's bill hit the Arizona statehouse floor in January, there were signs of ALEC's influence. Thirty-six co-sponsors jumped on, a number almost unheard of in the capitol. According to records obtained by NPR, two-thirds of them either went to that December meeting or are ALEC members.

That same week, the Corrections Corporation of America hired a powerful new lobbyist to work the capitol. The prison company declined requests for an interview. In a statement, a spokesman said the Corrections Corporation of America, "unequivocally has not at any time lobbied—nor have we had any outside consultants lobby—on immigration law."

At the state Capitol, campaign donations started to appear. Thirty of the 36 co-sponsors received donations over the next six months, from prison lobbyists or prison companies—Corrections Corporation of America, Management and Training Corporation and The Geo Group.

By April, the bill was on Gov. Jan Brewer's desk. Brewer has her own connections to private prison companies. State lobbying records show two of her top advisers—her spokesman Paul Senseman and her campaign manager Chuck Coughlin—are former lobbyists for private prison companies. Brewer signed the bill—with the name of the legislation Pearce, the Corrections Corporation of America and the others in the Hyatt conference room came up with—in four days. Brewer and her spokesman did not respond to requests for comment.

In May, The Geo Group had a conference call with investors. When asked about the bill, company executives made light of it, asking, "Did they have some legislation on immigration?"

After company officials laughed, the company's president, Wayne Calabrese, cut in. "This is Wayne," he said. "I can only believe the opportunities at the federal level are going to continue apace as a result of what's happening. Those people coming across the border and getting caught are going to have to be detained and that for me, at least I think, there's going to be enhanced opportunities for what we do."

Opportunities that prison companies helped create.

Produced by NPR's Anne Hawke.

Clarification Feb. 22, 2012

As we reported, Arizona state Sen. Russell Pearce was the originator of the draft legislation that later became Arizona SB 1070. This story did not mean to suggest that the Corrections Corporation of America was the catalyst behind the law or that it took a corporate position in favor of the legislation.

In our 2010 broadcast piece we said: "Last December Arizona Sen. Russell Pearce sat in a hotel conference room with representatives from the Corrections Corporation of America and several dozen others. Together they drafted model legislation that was introduced into the Arizona Legislature two months later, almost word for word."

Although CCA did have a representative at the ALEC meeting where model legislation similar to 1070 was drafted, we didn't mean to suggest that CCA wrote the language.

Nov. 18, 2011 — In the introduction to the radio version of this story, we said that the legislation that became the Arizona immigration law (SB 1070) was drafted at a meeting of the American Legislative Council, or ALEC. The introduction should have made a clearer distinction between drafting the Arizona bill and ALEC's role in turning it into "model" legislation to be submitted in states across the country.

Notes

(1) Private prison corporations argue that they do not attempt to influence legislation that increases prison sentences or imprisons more citizens. Is this an accurate representation of the business practices of these entities?

(2) If the conservative legislation drafting organization ALEC continues to influence policy and legislative initiatives across the United States, is there a progressive legislation drafting organization to counter the oft-times ruthless policies that come out of ALEC meetings and drafting sessions? If not, why not?

(3) What do you think of the prison lobbyists that approached the city manager of Benson, AZ promising to fill a prison with illegal immigrants that were women and children if he would agree to build a prison in his city?

(4) Review the photo lineups of the members of the Boards of Directors for the two most prominent private prison companies in the United States, Corrections Corporation of America (CCA) and the GEO Group at the following websites:

CCA: https://www.cca.com/board-of-directors;

GEO Group: http://www.geogroup.com/board_of_directors.

Are you able to draw any conclusions from viewing the individuals that are responsible for setting corporate policy and direction for these for-profit prison giants? How do these boards differ from the boards that you participated on during the Prison Role Play assignment from chapter three?

B. Critiquing Corporate Social Responsibility

Recall from the Introduction our definition of Corporate Social Responsibility (CSR). In thinking harder about CSR, do corporations have a responsibility to do more than maximize shareholder profits, particularly in the communities wherein they conduct their business and glean their profits? Much has been written and said recently about a corporation's responsibility to engage in socially responsible behavior. CSR is often defined as a company operating in a manner that respects and accounts for its social and environmental impact on the citizens and communities in which it engages its business. A corporation engaging in CSR will be committed to enacting policies that integrate responsible practices into its daily operations, and with great transparency, reporting these policies and on progress made toward its socially responsible goals.[2] Others define CSR as "the continuing commitment by business to behave ethically and contribute to economic development while improving the quality of life of the workforce and their families as well as of the local community and society at large."[3]

Most would agree that CSR includes a broad commitment by businesses to improve the lives of its employees and improve the conditions of the communities in which they do business. These objectives are most often met by companies adopting fair policies and cultures including governance and ethics, employee hiring, opportunity and training, responsible supply chain and purchasing policies and responsible energy and environmental impacts.[4] Similar to the oft quoted phrase from The History of Epidemics which is a part of the Hippocratic corpus which informs physician responsibility, CSR recommends that corporations "first do no harm," as they seek profit maximizing outcomes. This "do no harm" maxim has been examined above in the context of the private for-profit prison corporation.

In the article that follows, CSR is critiqued from the perspective of efficiency and free markets. While intuitively, CSR makes sense to most, there are critics who argue otherwise. As you read the argument against CSR below, consider whether free markets offer a better solution for how corporations should best interface with its stakeholders.

The Case Against Corporate Social Responsibility

By Aneel Karnani*

August 23, 2010

Can companies do well by doing good? Yes — sometimes.

But the idea that companies have a responsibility to act in the public interest and will profit from doing so is fundamentally flawed.

Large companies now routinely claim that they aren't in business just for the profits, that they're also intent on serving some larger social purpose. They trumpet their efforts to produce healthier foods or more fuel-efficient vehicles, conserve energy and other resources in their operations, or otherwise make the world a better place. Influential institutions like the Academy of Management and the United Nations, among many others, encourage companies to pursue such strategies.

It's not surprising that this idea has won over so many people — it's a very appealing proposition. You can have your cake and eat it too! But it's an illusion, and a potentially dangerous one.

Very simply, in cases where private profits and public interests are aligned, the idea of corporate social responsibility is irrelevant: Companies that simply do everything they can to boost profits will end up increasing social welfare. In circumstances in which profits

---

2. *See supra* Chapter 1.

3. *See id.*

4. *See id.*

* Aneel Karnani, *The Case Against Corporate Social Responsibility*, WALL ST. J., August 22, 2010, http://www.wsj.com/articles/SB10001424052748703338004575230112664504890. Dr. Karnani is an associate professor of strategy at the University of Michigan's Stephen M. Ross School of Business. He can be reached at reports@wsj.com.

and social welfare are in direct opposition, an appeal to corporate social responsibility will almost always be ineffective, because executives are unlikely to act voluntarily in the public interest and against shareholder interests.

Irrelevant or ineffective, take your pick. But it's worse than that. The danger is that a focus on social responsibility will delay or discourage more-effective measures to enhance social welfare in those cases where profits and the public good are at odds. As society looks to companies to address these problems, the real solutions may be ignored.

Well and Good

To get a better fix on the irrelevance or ineffectiveness of corporate social responsibility efforts, let's first look at situations where profits and social welfare are in synch.

Consider the market for healthier food. Fast-food outlets have profited by expanding their offerings to include salads and other options designed to appeal to health-conscious consumers. Other companies have found new sources of revenue in low-fat, whole-grain and other types of foods that have grown in popularity. Social welfare is improved. Everybody wins.

Similarly, auto makers have profited from responding to consumer demand for more fuel-efficient vehicles, a plus for the environment. And many companies have boosted profits while enhancing social welfare by reducing their energy consumption and thus their costs.

But social welfare isn't the driving force behind these trends. Healthier foods and more fuel-efficient vehicles didn't become so common until they became profitable for their makers. Energy conservation didn't become so important to many companies until energy became more costly. These companies are benefiting society while acting in their own interests; social activists urging them to change their ways had little impact. It is the relentless maximization of profits, not a commitment to social responsibility, that has proved to be a boon to the public in these cases.

Unfortunately, not all companies take advantage of such opportunities, and in those cases both social welfare and profits suffer. These companies have one of two problems: Their executives are either incompetent or are putting their own interests ahead of the company's long-term financial interests. For instance, an executive might be averse to any risk, including the development of new products, that might jeopardize the short-term financial performance of the company and thereby affect his compensation, even if taking that risk would improve the company's longer-term prospects.

An appeal to social responsibility won't solve either of those problems. Pressure from shareholders for sustainable growth in profitability can. It can lead to incompetent managers being replaced and to a realignment of incentives for executives, so that their compensation is tied more directly to the company's long-term success.

When There's a Choice

Still, the fact is that while companies sometimes can do well by doing good, more often they can't. Because in most cases, doing what's best for society means sacrificing profits.

This is true for most of society's pervasive and persistent problems; if it weren't, those problems would have been solved long ago by companies seeking to maximize their profits. A prime example is the pollution caused by manufacturing. Reducing that pollution is costly to the manufacturers, and that eats into profits. Poverty is another obvious example. Companies could pay their workers more and charge less for their products, but their profits would suffer.

So now what? Should executives in these situations heed the call for corporate social responsibility even without the allure of profiting from it? You can argue that they should. But you shouldn't expect that they will.

Executives are hired to maximize profits; that is their responsibility to their company's shareholders. Even if executives wanted to forgo some profit to benefit society, they could expect to lose their jobs if they tried—and be replaced by managers who would restore profit as the top priority. The movement for corporate social responsibility is in direct opposition, in such cases, to the movement for better corporate governance, which demands that managers fulfill their fiduciary duty to act in the shareholders' interest or be relieved of their responsibilities. That's one reason so many companies talk a great deal about social responsibility but do nothing—a tactic known as greenwashing.

Managers who sacrifice profit for the common good also are in effect imposing a tax on their shareholders and arbitrarily deciding how that money should be spent. In that sense they are usurping the role of elected government officials, if only on a small scale.

Privately owned companies are a different story. If an owner-operated business chooses to accept diminished profit in order to enhance social welfare, that decision isn't being imposed on shareholders. And, of course, it is admirable and desirable for the leaders of successful public companies to use some of their personal fortune for charitable purposes, as many have throughout history and many do now. But those leaders shouldn't presume to pursue their philanthropic goals with shareholder money. Indeed, many shareholders themselves use significant amounts of the money they make from their investments to help fund charities or otherwise improve social welfare.

This is not to say, of course, that companies should be left free to pursue the greatest possible profits without regard for the social consequences. But, appeals to corporate social responsibility are not an effective way to strike a balance between profits and the public good.

The Power of Regulation

So how can that balance best be struck?

The ultimate solution is government regulation. Its greatest appeal is that it is binding. Government has the power to enforce regulation. No need to rely on anyone's best intentions.

But government regulation isn't perfect, and it can even end up reducing public welfare because of its cost or inefficiency. The government also may lack the resources and competence to design and administer appropriate regulations, particularly for complex industries requiring much specialized knowledge. And industry groups might find ways to influence regulation to the point where it is ineffective or even ends up benefiting the industry at the expense of the general population.

Outright corruption can make the situation even worse. What's more, all the problems of government failure are exacerbated in developing countries with weak and often corrupt governments. Still, with all their faults, governments are a far more effective protector of the public good than any campaign for corporate social responsibility.

Watchdogs and Advocates

Civil society also plays a role in constraining corporate behavior that reduces social welfare, acting as a watchdog and advocate. Various nonprofit organizations and movements provide a voice for a wide variety of social, political, environmental, ethnic, cultural and community interests.

The Rainforest Action Network, for example, is an organization that agitates, often quite effectively, for environmental protection and sustainability. Its website states, "Our campaigns leverage public opinion and consumer pressure to turn the public stigma of environmental destruction into a business nightmare for any American company that refuses to adopt responsible environmental policies." That's quite a different approach from trying to convince executives that they should do what's best for society because it's the right thing to do and won't hurt their bottom line.

Overall, though, such activism has a mixed track record, and it can't be relied on as the primary mechanism for imposing constraints on corporate behavior—especially in most developing countries, where civil society lacks adequate resources to exert much influence and there is insufficient awareness of public issues among the population.

Self-Control

Self-regulation is another alternative, but it suffers from the same drawback as the concept of corporate social responsibility: Companies are unlikely to voluntarily act in the public interest at the expense of shareholder interests.

But self-regulation can be useful. It tends to promote good practices and target specific problems within industries, impose lower compliance costs on businesses than government regulation, and offer quick, low-cost dispute-resolution procedures. Self-regulation can also be more flexible than government regulation, allowing it to respond more effectively to changing circumstances.

The challenge is to design self-regulation in a manner that emphasizes transparency and accountability, consistent with what the public expects from government regulation. It is up to the government to ensure that any self-regulation meets that standard. And the government must be prepared to step in and impose its own regulations if the industry fails to police itself effectively.

Financial Calculation

In the end, social responsibility is a financial calculation for executives, just like any other aspect of their business. The only sure way to influence corporate decision making is to impose an unacceptable cost—regulatory mandates, taxes, punitive fines, public embarrassment—on socially unacceptable behavior.

Pleas for corporate social responsibility will be truly embraced only by those executives who are smart enough to see that doing the right thing is a byproduct of their pursuit of profit. And that renders such pleas pointless.

Notes

(1) Is Dr. Karnani correct in arguing that a company that does everything in its power to boost profits will also benefit society?

(2) When considering the "free market" critique of CSR above as espoused by Karnani, does that critique strike you as realistic and viable? Will the work of corporations flow to the greater good simply because it is good business? Has this "free market" approach been borne out historically, as evidenced by the behavior of corporate actors?

(3) Do corporations have a responsibility to add value and societal benefit to the communities in which they do business? In particular, should corporations benefit the cities and municipalities where they are headquartered?

Chapter Five

Understanding the Financial Crisis

A. The Mortgage Process

To truly understand the financial market crisis, and more importantly, how decision makers in America's corporate board rooms created the crisis and almost destroyed the global financial market system, it is imperative that students have a thorough understanding of the basics. The most important concept to understand is that corporations operate like individual human beings. That means that corporations own things (assets) and will often borrow money (liabilities) to acquire the things that it desires. The law effectively treats corporations as fictional persons.

When a purchaser desires to buy a home, he or she generally does not have the financial capacity to make the purchase with his or her own money. To facilitate the transaction, a buyer will often borrow money from a creditor. Creditors are inclined to assist home buyers because creditors make money when they loan money and charge an interest rate. A creditor determines what interest rate to charge a buyer by analyzing the buyer's risk. This is accomplished by evaluating the buyer's credit score. There are three major agencies (Experian, Equifax, and Trans Union) that evaluate a buyer's credit history after which these agencies will issue each buyer a numerical credit score ranging from 0–850.

A buyer's specific credit score is calculated by analyzing the buyer's credit history. The buyer's credit history is created when a buyer obtains credit to make purchases. For example, a buyer establishes a credit history when s/he applies and obtains a credit card to purchase goods, or obtains a loan to pay for the buyer's education or to purchase an automobile. Once a creditor issues credit to a buyer, the creditor will then notify one or more of the reporting agencies of the obligation. If the buyer fails to pay or if the buyer fails to pay on time, the creditor may report such deficiencies to the credit reporting agencies. The credit reporting agency will then calibrate the degree that the deficiency will affect the buyer's credit score.

Essentially, a buyer's credit score measures the likelihood that a buyer will pay the buyer's obligations when they are due. A buyer with a high credit score is a low risk whereas a buyer with a low credit score is a high risk. Accordingly, banks will charge buyers with high credit scores lower interest rates and buyers with low credit scores higher interest rates.

Credit scores generally fall into two broad categories, subprime and prime. A buyer whose credit score is 620 and below is consider to be a subprime borrower and a borrower above 620 is a prime borrower.

A mortgage is a special type of loan. When a buyer obtains a mortgage, the buyer borrows money from a creditor to purchase a house. The creditor is willing to lend the buyer the money to make the purchase because the creditor retains the right to take back the house (foreclose on the property) if the buyer fails to pay. While the creditor retains the right to foreclose on the home, there is a cost to the lender to go through the process. The typical creditor generally spends approximately 30% of the pre-foreclosure purchase price to foreclose.[1]

While you may intuitively believe that creditors are less willing to lend money to subprime borrowers because they are higher risk and therefore are less likely to repay and because it is rather costly for the creditor to go through the foreclosure process, you would be wrong—especially if you are thinking about the viability of the subprime market as a business strategy prior to the financial crisis! Before the financial crisis, many financial institutions preferred to loan money to subprime borrowers because the creditors could charge higher interest rates to subprime borrowers and as a result, could make more money. In addition, creditors were comforted by a few additional assumptions. First, since land is a limited resource, its scarcity creates inherent value. As a result, over time, land has consistently increased in value. In fact, a study from the Lincoln Institute of Land Policy highlights this reality in substantial detail.[2] The following numbers are in billions of current dollars as of the year 2000.

	Aggregate Market Value of Residential Land	Aggregate Market Value of Homes
1930	17.38704676	113.8
1940	24.88833447	125.5994239
1950	31.15865461	298.7
1960	102.5830967	569.3299999
1970	210.8823138	1058.14
1980	1051.51866	3887.93
1990	3393.05293	8483.379999
2000	5006.507904	13770.04

From the aforementioned table, you should be able to clearly see that the value of land and homes has consistently increased over time. Because of this reality, when bank leaders decided to get involved in the subprime market they were confident that their investment strategy would prove successful. If the buyers did not make good on their mortgage obligations, the banks were confident that they could foreclose on a buyer's home and sell it for enough money to cover both the principal obligation as well as the cost and expenses associated with the foreclosure process, since the banks believed that property values

---

1. According to statistics compiled by the Joint Economic Committee of Congress in 2008, the average total cost to foreclose is approximately $78,000 while it only costs $3,300 to prevent it. "The homeowner has a typical loss of $7,200 which includes loss of equity in the property, moving expenses, and perhaps some legal fees. Those neighbors living in close proximity to the foreclosed house suffer $1,508 in losses from the decrease in the value of their own home as the neighborhood begins to deteriorate. The local government loses $19,227 through diminished taxes and fees and a shrinking tax base as home prices decrease." Glenn Setzer, *Foreclosures Cost Lenders, Homeowners,, the Community Big Bucks*, Mortgage News Daily, June 2, 2008, *available at* http://www.mortgagenewsdaily.com/622008_Foreclosure_Costs.asp.

2. Morris A. Davis & Jonathan Heathcote, *The Price and Quantity of Residential Land in the United States*, 54 Journal of Monetary Economics 2595–2620 (2007) (data located at Land and Property Values in the U.S., Lincoln Institute of Land Policy http://www.lincolninst.edu/resources).

would increase over time. Second, borrowers are most likely to pay their mortgage before paying other financial obligations. This is attributable to the fact that paying a mortgage to some extent is like paying yourself. When a borrower pays a mortgage, the borrower is building equity after each payment. Therefore, the part of the buyer's payment that is allocated to principal is much like taking that same amount of money and placing it in account that can be used by the buyer at a later point.

Because of these two fundamental assumptions, banks disregarded the risk associated with the subprime market and instead focused on chasing the significant profits that it offered. Another point worth noting is that the subprime mortgage market was also attractive because the spreads (difference between the interest rate the bank received from the borrower and the rate at which the bank borrowed the money) was greater and more secure in the context of mortgages. Unlike car loans, student loans, and credit cards, the other major cash generators for bank operations, mortgages offered an additional level of security. The underlying real estate that is secured by the mortgage is an appreciable asset, meaning it increases in value over time.

As you will discover in Dean cummings' article entitled *Racial Coding and the Financial Market Crisis*, discussed below, there is an additional layer to the subprime market that has been left out—predatory lending, the practice of targeting specific groups for abusive and unfair loan terms. ARM - adjustable rate mortgage

B. Collateralized Debt Obligations and Mortgaged Backed Securities

While the subprime market provided banks ample opportunity for large profits, the banks' ability to reap these profits was limited by the duration of the mortgage. Since the typical mortgage term is 30 years, a bank will not recognize its full gain until 30 years from the date at which the mortgage is granted. To remedy this "problem," banks created collateralized debt obligations by issuing mortgage backed securities. A collateralized debt obligation ("CDO") is a financial instrument that aggregates income generating assets into a package. Once the income generating assets are packaged together, the package is broken down into tranches and sold to investors. Tranches are "pieces" or "cuts" of a financial instrument. Tranches allow their owners the right to receive a specific portion of the profits from the CDO. For example, an investor may decide to purchase the first 25% of the revenue generated by the CDO to ensure that the investor is paid before the owners of the other tranches. To put it in another context, assume that your mother has made your favorite dessert and that you have three brothers who are very greedy. The assumption is that a person would want to be first in line in order to receive the first "piece" or "cut" of the dessert. This is the primary purpose of the concept of a tranche.

A mortgage backed security ("MBS") is a type of CDO that is made up of a bundle of mortgages. MBSs were extremely important investment vehicles during the financial crisis. To understand why, think about the limitations on the banks in receiving the benefit of the bargain from the mortgage contract. Again, the banks would not realize the full extent of their bargain until the mortgage was fully paid and that did not typically occur until 30 years after the mortgage contract was entered. As a result, banks got creative. Banks realized that they could "bundle" or package mortgages together into a MBS and then sell tranches in the MBS. This scheme enabled banks to obtain an immediate return by selling the mortgages at slightly discounted rates to other financial institutions that would pay the bank cash "now" in exchange for the right to collect the proceeds from the tranche it purchased. Although the mortgages are sold at a slight discount, banks still made a substantial profit. In addition, having cash "now" enabled banks to fund and expand operations immediately rather than waiting until the money from the mortgage was collected.

C. The Financial Crisis Explained

At this point, you should now have a reasonable understanding of the basics of the United States housing market in the years preceding the financial market crisis. With this understanding, we can now illustrate what happened in the context of the financial crisis through the following example:

FIRST BANK Corporation ("FIRST BANK") creates a subsidiary called 1B Special Purpose Entity, LLC ("1B"). FIRST BANK creates 1B for several reasons. First, creating 1B limits FIRST BANK's exposure in the subprime market because FIRST BANK will cause 1B to purchase mortgaged backed securities ("MBSs") from FIRST BANK. As a result, the risk associated with the MBSs, previously owned by FIRST BANK, are removed from FIRST BANK's balance sheet and moved onto 1B's balance sheet. As such, any liability resulting from the exposure created by the MBSs is effectively shifted to 1B's balance sheet. While the risk of the MBSs has shifted to 1B, FIRST BANK is still exposed to losses experienced by 1B because FIRST BANK has an investor side interest in 1B. If 1B under-performs, FIRST BANK will lose its investment. Second, the creation of 1B allows investors who are unwilling to invest specifically in FIRST BANK to invest in 1B based on the specific purpose for which 1B was created—to take advantage of the high rates of return associated with subprime borrowing. This is an extremely valuable mechanism for enticing investors who do not believe in the long-term or short term viability of FIRST BANK but who are willing to invest in the specific and limited purpose of 1B.

After 1B is in operation, Investor buys a $10,000,000 five year bond from 1B, backed by MBSs 1B purchased from FIRST BANK. The bond gives Investor an annual 10% return ($1,000,000 per year). Because of the risk of default on the 1B bond, Investor purchases a Credit Default Swap ("CDS") from AIG, where the reference entity is 1B. AIG charges 2% per annum on the CDS. As a result, Investor must make regular annual payments to AIG ($200,000 per year for the next five years), much like the premium payment you make every month to remain insured. Thus, the CDS is simply a form of insurance that guarantees that Investor will get paid in the event that 1B does not make good on the bond payment. If 1B defaults on its debt (i.e., misses a coupon payment or does not repay it), Investor will receive a one-time payment ($10,000,000 or the amount that is left) from AIG and the CDS contract is terminated.

If 1B does not default on the bond payment, Investor will receive the following: $1,000,000 per year, every year, for five years from 1B, and at the end of year five, 1B will return Investor's $10,000,000 investment. In exchange for the aforementioned, Investor will make annual payments of $200,000 to AIG for five (5) years for a total cost of $1,000,000.

Based on the scenario above, Investor has earned a net return; investors return after expenses, of $800,000 per year since investor purchased a CDS from AIG and paid $200,000 per year for it to secure Investor's transaction with 1B.

If, however, 1B defaults on the bond in year 3 ($600,000 in payments), Investor will stop making payments to AIG and AIG will return Investor's $10,000,000. Based on this scenario, if Investor had not purchased the CDS, Investor would have lost its original $10,000,000 investment.

In terms of risks, Investor assumes the risk that AIG will not perform its duties under the CDS if required to do so and AIG assumes the risk that 1B will not pay on the bond.

(1) The critical question after reading this illustration is what would make AIG insure Investor's transaction with 1B?

(2) Would you have made the same deal?

(3) Why did Investor buy the bond from 1B?

(4) Why did Investor buy the CDS from AIG?

(5) What would have happened to the financial market system if the federal government had not bailed out AIG? Whose financials would have been impacted?

While the aforementioned narrative provides a useful and general understanding of the financial structure of the mortgage crisis, the investment narrative above was not the only reason that financial institutions fell into grave peril in 2008. To assist in gaining a fuller understanding of the scope of the difficulties that led to the near collapse of global capital markets in 2008, the following material examines several additional contributors to the financial market crisis, including Citibank, AIG, Bank of America, Countrywide, and Goldman Sachs. Each of these entities was near economic collapse before the United States government initiated its bailout plan in 2008 and 2009.

Citibank's "Liquidity Puts"

First, Citibank was exposed to financial liability as a result of entering the MBS and CDS markets to the tune of almost $14 billion dollars based on representations and warranties it made in issuing CDOs it created. To understand this point in greater detail, think back to the aforementioned example. Assume that when FIRST BANK bundled the MBSs into CDOs that FIRST BANK made representations and warranties that it would make good on any devaluation in the CDOs via what is known as a "liquidity put." In summary, the liquidity put allowed Investors to sell back the CDOs to FIRST BANK if the credit markets declined. While it might seem strange that FIRST BANK would provide Investors with this type of guarantee, providing such guarantee increased the potential that an Investor would purchase the CDOs from 1B since Investor knew that its risks were minimized by FIRST BANK's warranty to buy back the CDOs at cost. Moreover, FIRST BANK was willing to offer Investor such an amazing guarantee because FIRST BANK never thought that it would have to buy back the puts. Interestingly, although FIRST BANK included a liquidity put option in the CDOs it created, it did not record the potential exposure of the puts on its balance sheet. Since FIRST BANK sold the CDOs to 1B it considered the risk of the CDOs shifted and too remote to have any impact on its own financials. When the mortgage market collapsed, FIRST BANK had to pay out on the liquidity puts it issued which resulted in approximately $14 billion dollars in exposure.

AIG's Failure to Hedge

AIG's problems were a direct result of its belief that it would never have to make good on the CDSs it issued. With traditional insurance contracts, insurers are legally required to maintain certain cash reserves. Reserves are pools of money that are set aside to guarantee that an insurance company will be able to pay out in the event that it has to make good on the insurance contracts it issues. If an insurance company does not have adequate reserves, it can purchase reinsurance from another insurance company as a means of hedging on the insurance contracts it issues. Essentially, whether an insurance company sets aside reserve funds or purchases reinsurance from another company, it is attempting to ensure that it has sufficient funds to cover any liabilities that it may have to pay in the future. While these requirements are applicable to traditional insurance products, the same rules do not apply to derivatives, resulting in an unregulated market. Since the derivative market was unregulated, and CDSs were categorized as derivatives, AIG was not legally required to maintain any levels of reserves or purchase reinsurance to hedge against the bets made on the CDSs it issued. AIG believed that it could collect the CDS premiums without ever having to pay out because it never believed that the housing market would decline to a position that would require it to make good on its CDS contracts. By refusing the option of hedging, AIG was able to increase its net gain (earning spectacular profits) because it did not have to spend money to insure against its own risk. When the housing market collapsed, AIG was forced to make good on the CDSs it had issued, bringing AIG to the brink of extinction, but for the government's bailout.

Bank of America's Acquisition of Countrywide

In 2008, Bank of America (BOA) was aggressively seeking to expand its operations and its primary mechanism for expansion was through the acquisition of other financial institutions. At the time, Countrywide Financial ("Countrywide") was experiencing substantial difficulty because the housing bubble had just burst. Countrywide was extremely profitable prior to the financial mortgage crisis because it made large sums of money through the issuance of dubious subprime mortgages. In light of Countrywide's early success, the housing bubble popped and Countrywide's financial viability burst right along with it. As a result, Countrywide was hemorrhaging financially. BOA "swooped-in" and acquired Countrywide at what it believed to be a bargain price of "only" 4 billion dollars.[3] BOA's board unanimously approved the acquisition of Countrywide; however, this move proved to be a grave mistake. At the time of the merger, BOA's board did not fully understand the nature of Countrywide's liability exposure due to fraudulent issuance of mortgages. In fact, there is some evidence to suggest that BOA's management did not do enough to fully understand the exposure because management believed that the deal was intrinsically good. According to a 2013 NPR report by Jim Zarroli, BOA's management was blinded by the profits it believed it could make in the market for subprime mortgages and focused more on increasing BOA's size rather than protecting shareholder value. Because of BOA's lack of due diligence, it failed to discover that Countrywide had grossly overstated the value of its mortgage assets and that it had engaged in unethical business practices by issuing mortgages to borrowers it knew could not repay the loans. Countrywide intentionally disregarded any concern for whether a borrower could repay the mortgage and focused only on whether the loan could be packaged and sold effectively moving the risk of failure to repay off of Countrywide's financials and onto investors that were purchasing the packaged mortgages. According to the Justice Department's Statement of Facts, contained in the eventual settlement agreement between the Justice Department and BOA due to Countrywide's fraud, one Countrywide executive wrote:

---

3. The actual price was roughly 2.5 billion because the value of the stock declined before the transaction was finalized.

"My impression since arriving here, is that the company's standard for products and Guidelines has been: 'If we can price it [for sale], then we will offer it.'"

Another Countrywide executive, in a 2007 email, wrote:

"[W]hen credit was easily salable ... [the desk responsible for approving risky loans] was a way to take advantage of the 'salability' and do loans outside guidelines and not let our views of risk get in the way."

These statements clearly reflect Countrywide's conscious disregard for standard business practices in the pursuit of profit. As a result of these practices, BOA is still dealing with the financial fallout from its decision to acquire Countrywide. According to an August 16, 2014 article from *The Charlotte Observer*:

"Since July 1, 2008, when the deal officially closed, the bank's mortgage business has lost $52.7 billion through the first half of this year.... This number ... includes settlements, payments to investors for soured loans, accounting writedowns, and operating losses and profits."[4]

To add additional insult to injury, the losses are still accumulating for BOA. In late August of 2014, the Justice Department reached what it called "the largest civil settlement with a single entity in American history." Pursuant to the terms of the settlement, BOA agreed to pay approximately 17 billion dollars (10 billion dollars to settle State and Federal claims and another 7 billion dollars to assist with consumer relief efforts) all in connection with Countrywide's unethical and fraudulent lending practices.[5]

Goldman Sachs and the ABACUS deal

In 2007, John Paulson retained Goldman Sachs ("Goldman") to create and assist him with selling a CDO that consisted of subprime mortgages. This deal was known as ABACUS 2007-AC1 and Goldman received $15 million dollars for its work in facilitating the transaction. Goldman retained the services of ACA Capital ("ACA"), as an independent third party, to assist with selecting the assets that would make-up the CDO's portfolio. ACA was specifically selected because of its extensive experience in creating CDO's involving subprime mortgages. Once ABACUS was created, Goldman extensively marketed and advertised ACA's involvement in creating the CDO because it knew that potential investors would place a high value on the CDO because of ACA's reputation in the industry.

Fabrice Tourre, the Goldman salesperson responsible for the ABACUS deal, ultimately sold it to IKB Deutsche Industriebank AG ("IKB"). Although Goldman and Tourre consistently held out ACA as the entity that assisted it in creating the CDO, Goldman failed to disclose that Paulson was actively involved with the portfolio selection process purposely selecting the worse mortgages available and those most likely to default. Despite this fact, Tourre specifically represented that Paulson's interests were 100% aligned with IKB's interest. However, Paulson held an interest that was in direct contravention to ACA's interest. Generally, Paulson's involvement would not automatically raise a red flag; however,

---

4. Rick Rothacker, *The Deal That Cost Bank of America $50 Billion—and Counting*, THE CHARLOTTE OBSERVER, Aug. 16, 2014, *available at* http://www.charlotteobserver.com/news/business/banking/article9151889.html.

5. According to Eric Green, a lawyer with the firm that serves as the independent monitor of the settlement, BOA may end up paying substantially less than the 17 billion. Assuming "they do everything right, it will cost them something less than $7 billion." Suzy Khimm, *The Truth Behind the $17 Billion Bank of America Settlement*, MSNBC.COM, Aug. 29, 2014, *available at* http://www.msnbc.com/msnbc/the-truth-behind-the-17-billion-bank-america-settlement (quoting Eric Green).

once ABACUS was created, Paulson "shorted" it and his interest became adverse to IKB's interest. In more simple terms, Paulson bet that ABACUS would fail! Therefore, Paulson was incentivized to select mortgage assets that were toxic and likely to default. In light of Paulson's involvement, and obvious conflict, Goldman never disclosed this information to investors although it also represented IKB. Goldman's intentional misrepresentations and its failure to disclose material information was deceitful and illegal.

Because of Goldman's dereliction of duty, Paulson netted, after taxes and expenses, $1 billion dollars when ABACUS failed while IKB lost roughly $150 million dollars, ACA lost $900 million and Goldman lost $85 million. As a result of Goldman's actions, the SEC assessed the largest penalty it has ever issued against a financial services firm in the amount of $550 million dollars for failing to disclose Paulson's obvious interest in creating an investment vehicle that was likely to fail so he could bet against it and profit.

In settlement papers submitted to the U.S. District Court for the Southern District of New York, Goldman made the following acknowledgement:

> Goldman acknowledges that the marketing materials for the ABACUS 2007-AC1 transaction contained incomplete information. In particular, it was a mistake for the Goldman marketing materials to state that the reference portfolio was "selected by" ACA Management LLC without disclosing the role of Paulson & Co. Inc. in the portfolio selection process and that Paulson's economic interests were adverse to CDO investors. Goldman regrets that the marketing materials did not contain that disclosure.[6]

While the SEC prosecuted Goldman, it failed to bring any claims against Paulson. With the money that Paulson profited from IKB, he gifted 400 million dollars to Harvard's School of Engineering which was renamed the Harvard John Paulson School of Engineering and Applied Sciences.

Notes

(1) What is the common theme that resonates with each of the aforementioned financial crisis narratives?

(2) Who do you think was the most egregious actor? Why?

(3) In each scenario above, corporate leadership enabled and allowed the unethical or fraudulent circumstances to exist and continue. Why? What was motivating corporate executives to turn a blind eye to fraud?

In the following article, "Racial Coding" by Dean cummings, a careful examination of the causes of the Great Recession is undertaken. cummings finds that there were numerous failures that led to the collapse of the U.S. housing market and then subsequently the global marketplace. Despite the corporate governance and government failures identified by cummings, a sinister undercurrent developed that attempted to lay blame at the feet of minority borrowers for causing the crisis. The scapegoating claimed that black and

---

6. Press Release, *Goldman Sachs to Pay Record $550 Million to Settle SEC Charges Related to Subprime Mortgage CDO*, SEC.gov, July 15, 2015, *available at* https://www.sec.gov/news/press/2010/2010-123.htm.

brown borrowers entered the subprime loan market in droves and when these new home-owners could not make payments on their very expensive loans, they defaulted, thereby causing the collapse in MBS investments that were held by nearly all of the Wall Street banks and other investors that were heavily leveraged in housing market securities. As you read the following, consider the reasons that the global economy nearly collapsed, the fact that some countries continue to battle through the consequences of those failures, like Greece, and whether it makes sense to attempt to pin blame on one specific cause or reason.

Racial Coding and the Financial Market Crisis

andré douglas pond cummings

2011 Utah L. Rev. 141

I. Introduction

The financial market crisis of 2008 has plagued the United States and countries around the world. The underlying causes of the 2008 collapse are numerous, intricate, and complex. Academic scholars, investigative reporters, and leading economists are now de-constructing the multiplicity of failures that enabled the breathtaking meltdown that nearly collapsed the global economy. As this thoughtful deconstruction crystallizes, a dis-turbing trend has forcefully surfaced, wherein dozens of writers, scholars, and thinkers, motivated by politics, limelight, and self-indulgence, have attempted to fix a singular or foundational cause as "the" reason for the market crisis of 2008. Attempting to find singular or primary causation by assigning simple blame for the enormous institutional and personal failures that precipitated the financial market crisis is reckless and ultimately counterproductive.

First, it obscures a genuine interrogation of causation and hampers the ability to remedy mistakes and past failures. Second, it allows for misdirection and manipulation of events in a way that confuses and distorts. Third, it camouflages policies and provides cover for policy makers that promoted positions and legislation that enabled the failure. Finally, assigning singular, simplistic blame for political purposes undermines thoughtful and careful introspection that must necessarily be measured when debating and promoting new policy direction and legislation aimed toward prevention of future financial crises.

Perhaps the most startling singular "cause" put forth for the near global meltdown is the "minority borrower" extrapolation that emerged in the very first moments of the Sep-tember 2008 tumult that accompanied the Troubled Asset Relief Program (TARP) debates. During the tensest moments surrounding the mortgage crisis in September and October 2008, as TARP was furiously debated on Capitol Hill, and as doomsday messages were being delivered daily, many pundits on the right named racial "minorities" and lending to "poor minorities" as a root cause for the market collapse.

In an ultimate irony, at precisely the same moment that minority borrowers were being saddled with the responsibility for crashing a global economy, the United States citizenry was preparing to send a minority politician to the White House to take the most powerful seat in the world.

With the financial market crisis as backdrop, President Obama overwhelmingly won the election. Dozens of commentators and millions of Americans then argued that, with the election of Obama as president, the United States officially entered a postracial era.

According to postracialists, America has truly arrived at our colorblind ideal. Racism is a relic of a checkered past that has been affirmatively overcome.

Notwithstanding the attractiveness of the postracial ideology, these arguments were being made at the very same time that a simmering tale was being floated and adopted by many of the very same citizens that were hailing a new postracial America. African American and Latino borrowers were served up as the scapegoat to explain why the global economy was failing. The minority-borrower narrative maintains that because of governmental intrusion into the home lending industry, through the Community Reinvestment Act of 1977 (CRA), Fannie Mae, and Freddie Mac, lenders were forced to provide loans to extremely risky minority borrowers, who themselves were overreaching by trying to purchase homes that they had no business buying. Because lenders had no choice but to provide loans to risky minority borrowers, subprime loans became the avenue of choice for lenders to overreaching minority borrowers and it was because of the then-current failure of black and brown homeowners to pay their mortgages that the subprime mortgage industry collapsed. Thus, as the story purports, the financial market crisis is ultimately traceable to minority Americans and governmental social welfare.

That the minority-borrower narrative would spring up at the onset of this generation's greatest economic ordeal is disappointing. That this narrative would be embraced by so many with so little to support it, with scant questioning or thought, is demoralizing. Critical race theory, however, provides insight into how a twenty-first century dirty little myth can still find traction in the United States.

The dynamism and continuing intensity of American racism is clearly evident in the financial market crisis of 2008.

II. Financial Market Crisis Reality

The neoclassical law and economics theories that drive so much of United States economic policy and legal philosophizing are now being critically interrogated both by longtime critics and surprising new sources. This examination leads many commentators to freshly conclude that the astonishing rise to prominence of law and economic theory in this country has now proven folly as neoclassical economics is intellectually and morally bankrupt. This scrutiny leads other critics to claim that capitalism and the rush to deregulate the U.S. economy in the past two decades have proved a failed exercise.

Two surprising commentators are leading this questioning of laissez-faire capitalism and neoclassical economics and are acknowledging the depths of the failures and the breadth of the negligence. Famed law and economics champion Judge Richard Posner penned A Failure of Capitalism: The Crisis of '08 and the Descent into Depression wherein he admitted, astonishingly to some, that "[t]he [2008 financial market crisis] is a failure of capitalism, or more precisely of a certain kind of capitalism ('laissez-faire' in a loose sense ...), and of capitalism's biggest boosters."

Joining Posner in retrospection and contrition is former Federal Reserve Chair Alan Greenspan, perhaps the fiercest proponent of deregulated free markets. Under 2008 congressional questioning, Greenspan confessed grave error in aggressively advocating that the U.S. derivatives markets be freed from governmental oversight, staking the gravity of his reputation on the fact that large financial institution leaders would never leverage their companies to the point of collapse in pursuit of reckless profit.

Richard Posner and Alan Greenspan conceding significant failure in their foundational economic theories and beliefs should signal to economists, academics, political leaders, and the broader community that there is a striking need to reevaluate the core underpinnings of our current and continuing economic policies. Still, when given the opportunity to truly interrogate capitalism, the way we "do" corporate law, and the pervading neoclassical economic theories in the United States, we as a nation are largely failing that invitation.

Perhaps paralyzed by reelection fear, Congress significantly diluted meaningful regulatory reform—so much so that many argue that it failed to seriously address, in its Dodd-Frank Wall Street Reform and Consumer Protection Act, passed in 2010 in response to the financial market crisis, the necessary reforms that were achingly obvious in the heated aftermath of government bailouts and Wall Street chaos. This has led several prominent economists to predict that a future economic meltdown is a near certainty.

A. Deregulation

A clear deregulatory trend has driven Congress and regulators for the past two to three decades wherein proponents of laissez-faire economics have successfully persuaded leaders and legislatures to adopt positions that hamper oversight and restrict thoughtful regulation of capital markets. Four such examples, which are clearly linked to enabling the market collapse, include deregulatory policies initiated by the Federal Reserve Bank, the Gramm-Leach-Bliley Act, the Commodity Futures Modernization Act, and the Private Securities Litigation Reform Act, amongst a host of other deregulatory legislative and agency enactments.

1. The Federal Reserve Bank

The Board of Governors of the Federal Reserve Bank (Federal Reserve or Fed) played an integral role in the financial market crisis of 2008.

The relaxation of lending standards, the continuing reduction of interest rates, the campaign to free over-the-counter derivatives trading from any oversight, the campaign for repeal of the Glass-Steagall Act, and the catering to the interests of Wall Street investment banks all fell into the deregulatory pattern and agenda that consumed Washington D.C. and the Fed during the 1990s and early part of 2000s. And, as has been well documented, the Fed's immediate response to the financial market crisis was to provide an incredible, unprecedented, and unfettered infusion of bailout capital into the very Wall Street banks whose recklessness brought the economy to its knees.

Reacting to the crisis, the Federal Reserve slashed interest rates on loans and obligations offered to member banks in order to keep the economy afloat. Staring into a potential financial abyss, the Fed hastened to open up new lines of credit to Wall Street investment firms, "creating financial arrangements not unlike deposit insurance, but chillingly devoid of traditional deposit insurance regulatory oversight—without any explicit prior approval from Congress." While the Fed's unprecedented efforts saved Wall Street investment firms and hedge funds from collapse, smaller subprime mortgage loan originators "folded up their tents like the Bedouin—over 100 different subprime mortgage origination companies systematically collapsed."

Thus, TARP bailout funds, approved by Congress to save the economy from catastrophe, were used primarily to prop up Wall Street titans at a cost to U.S. taxpayers of more than $3 trillion dollars. Rather than free up lending, which was a portion of the stated purpose of the infusion of TARP funds, the banks hoarded the capital bestowed upon them from the Fed to improve their balance sheet performance. With that massive infusion of taxpayer capital and huge loans made available to Wall Street firms from the Fed, Wall Street responded almost immediately by paying near record executive compensation bonuses for 2009 "performance" and simultaneously spending hundreds of millions of dollars lobbying fiercely against new financial services regulation.

When news organizations and Congress both appealed to the Fed to provide full disclosure as to the use of TARP bailout funds and massive loans extended to Wall Street investment banks, including a request to see how the funds were dispensed, what tracking mechanisms were in place, and who received what, the Fed stonewalled both news organizations and Congress claiming that the public had no right to see or know what was being done with taxpayer money. The Fed's failure to provide bailout fund disclosure to the public has been challenged in the courts.

The $3 trillion loaned by the Fed to Wall Street banks in order to prop up capitalism and free market fundamentalism is an ironic and disturbing oxymoron. The Federal Reserve gave or loaned taxpayer funds to insulate "capitalism," and Wall Street excess and privilege, sans examination of any sort. Yet, while a specific swath of Americans went very nearly crazy in opposition to passage of Health Care Reform legislation, the vitriol for Wall Street and the complete subjugation of taxpayer rights to corporate interests is largely ignored by these same oppositionists. If government intervention is violently opposed in the health care context, why is government intervention in the form of a Wall Street bailout not opposed in the same manner? Why would those that spit on congresspersons, hurl racial epithets at minority members of Congress, scream homophobic slurs at gay Congressional leaders, and telephone death threats to individuals with the audacity to vote for insurance company reform stand silent in the face of massive taxpayer bailout and the unfettered rescue of an entrenched system of corporate privilege?

2. Gramm-Leach-Bliley

The Gramm-Leach-Bliley Amendment of 1999 is among the most significant injurious deregulatory actions that led to the financial crisis of 2008. Gramm-Leach-Bliley swept away all Glass-Steagall prohibitions against banks entering into the securities and insurance industries. Glass-Steagall was enacted in 1933 to address the regulatory failures that led to the Great Depression. It was designed to stamp out commercial speculation, and most perceived evils that Congress viewed at the time as leading to the Great Depression. Following intense lobbying efforts by the banking industry, the Glass-Steagall firewalls that had been erected between consumer banks and the insurance and securities industries were eliminated by Gramm-Leach-Bliley, essentially brushing away six decades of consumer protection.

Upon passage of Gramm-Leach-Bliley, a frenzy of consolidation, merging, and acquiring ensued wherein the primary banking institutions in the United States became ever larger and more powerful, and simply "too big to fail."

Of course, the Fed possesses the power to regulate commercial banks, which it failed to exercise, particularly following passage of Gramm-Leach-Bliley. Greenspan, believed and preached, as one of his foundational tenets, that private industry was much better situated to police and regulate itself primarily because corporate executives and major financial institution directors would never risk their very existence in reckless or overleveraged positioning.

While Gramm-Leach-Bliley did not necessarily directly impact the actions of Wall Street investment banks Lehman Brothers and Bear Stearns, viewed as the main progenitors of the early reckless trading in the subprime mortgage-backed securities market (the Commodity Futures Modernization Act enabled investment banks to do most of their damage), Gramm-Leach-Bliley perpetuated the environment for commercial banking giants—

Citigroup, Bank of America, Washington Mutual, and Wachovia—to become so large and unwieldy that each faced certain collapse based on their subprime market exposure.

3. Commodity Futures Modernization Act

An additional deregulatory decision that precipitated the market collapse was the 2000 promulgation of the Commodity Futures Modernization Act (CFMA). At a time when financial institutions were combining at a frenzied pace due to the recent enactment of Gramm-Leach-Bliley and as financial innovation in the derivatives trading industry was stressing the parameters of known regulation, Congress, at Greenspan's urging, deregulated the over-the-counter derivatives trading market. Passed as a rider to an omnibus appropriations bill, the CFMA prohibited any type of governmental oversight over the trading of derivative investment vehicles. This legislation, as predicted, proved damaging.

The creation of Collateralized Debt Obligations (CDOs) by Wall Street introduced a nascent industry to the exotic derivatives trading world focused on pooling and packaging home mortgage debt. CDOs offered investors rights to receive periodic payments from the cash flows associated with particularized bundles of home mortgages. The initiation of Credit Default Swaps (CDSs), private insurance-like contracts that act to hedge against the default risk posed by CDOs, introduced an emerging hedging mechanism into the exotic derivatives trading world and evolved into a cottage trading industry. The origination of CDOs and CDSs occurred in the shadows and back alleys fashioned by the CFMA. Both the bundling of CDOs and the hedging of CDO default by insuring against failure through CDSs, were unregulated. In this unregulated environment, investment banks were both creating and trading CDSs, while at the same time underwriting CDOs, essentially creating investment vehicles to sell to clients while simultaneously trading in that same vehicle or selling to other clients often on the other side of the very vehicle they sold to their clients. Both the securitized subprime mortgage investment vehicles and the CDSs that insured against the failure of those securitized subprime vehicles were completely unregulated by any governmental agency or oversight body because the CFMA made it so.

As these unregulated instruments were purchased, traded, passed, sold, and shorted, these large financial institutions were "hedging" by purchasing unregulated insurance contracts, CDSs, which would pay out if the subprime mortgage consumers defaulted and homes were foreclosed upon. In agreeing to the hedge CDS contract, insurance giants like AIG charged hefty premiums to "guarantee" against default of the CDOs, which were bundled, securitized, and sold, all based on an unstable housing bubble and flawed quant modeling. CDOs and CDS contracts were then traded and swapped freely in an unregulated over-the-counter derivatives market wherein a credit default swap contract could end up in the hands of a small hedge fund that had neither the resources nor the wherewithal to pay out its insurance obligation if in fact a CDO default occurred. Further, on these CFMA mandated unregulated markets where CDSs and CDOs were sold, traded, and swapped, they were also short sold, a bet that the underlying instrument would fail. All of the trading, hedging, shorting, and swapping occurred in an atmosphere of recklessness and avarice. Truly, the environment was a recipe for disaster, enabled by Gramm-Leach-Bliley and the CFMA.

4. Private Securities Litigation Reform Act

A further legislative enactment during the deregulation movement that gripped Congress in the 1990s was the Private Securities Litigation Reform Act (PSLRA). The PSLRA made it very difficult for securities fraud plaintiffs to plead fraud in a complaint to such a degree that the pleading would survive a motion to dismiss. Enacted to combat "strike suits" that were purportedly stifling corporate growth and shareholder earnings, the PSLRA changed the securities fraud class action scheme in debilitating ways. Because it was much more difficult for private plaintiffs to get into court following passage of the PSLRA, corporate executives were freed to engage in behavior that they would ultimately not be held accountable for in any recognizable way.

The PSLRA got capital market truism backward: it restricts the private enforcement component of stable, healthy capital markets. Instead, it disincentivizes careful corporate leadership by restricting private shareholders from bringing legitimate enforcement actions.

The deregulatory strategy that descended on Capitol Hill in the 1990s and early 2000s actually took the exact opposite tack of that identified in the healthy capital markets construction outlined above. Successful capital markets require the threat of strong "private lawsuits, combined with common-sense regulation and governmental control...." Nearly every financial market legislation enacted by Congress in the 1990s and early 2000s either weakened the private lawsuit component or scaled back common-sense governmental regulation of the financial services sector—precisely the opposite of what is commonly understood to be the best approach to maintaining the integrity of strong and sustainable capital markets.

While Fed policy, Gramm-Leach-Bliley, the CFMA, and the PSLRA represent destructive deregulatory enactments adopted by Congress in the run up to the 2008 collapse, many other unfortunate enactments contributed, including the Telecommunications Act of 2006, the Securities Litigation Uniform Standards Act of 1998, the Securities and Exchange Commission (SEC) and federal courts' failure to regulate hedge funds, and numerous SEC rules promulgated under its rulemaking authority. The SEC's sins included exempting large Wall Street investment firms from minimum capital requirements, repealing a rule designed to prevent manipulative short selling and limiting shareholders' ability to recover for securities fraud.

Of course, proponents of laissez-faire economics are loathe to embrace any characterization of the financial market crisis that implicates deregulation as a primary progenitor. In the face of overwhelming evidence that neoclassical economic theories of efficiency and private market discipline broke down in newly deregulated markets, market fundamentalists still cling to the notion of completely free markets as the answer. In order to support this unfettered market claim, market fundamentalists must reject deregulation as a cause and instead seek to refocus public attention on causes other than deregulated markets. Market fundamentalists have seized upon governmental intrusion into the housing markets through social steering and the myth of the minority borrower as their base cause of the market failure. Despite this misdirection by market fundamentalists, deregulation cannot be framed as the sole cause of the financial market crisis. The housing bubble and mortgage markets that developed in the early part of the twenty-first century played a major role in the meltdown as well.

B. Housing Bubble

The second conflation of causes of the financial crisis can be explored by deconstructing the "housing bubble" that ballooned and collapsed with its attendant consequences. As Professor Christopher Peterson notes:

> [i]n the past two years, subprime mortgage lending has forced the American economy to the brink of a depression and fundamentally undermined world faith in American consumer financial markets. A host of dubiously underwritten mortgage loans helped inflate a bubble in residential real estate values. As it has

become clear that millions of Americans are not capable of repaying loans crafted for them by commission hungry brokers, the liquidity of securities drawn from those loans froze. Currently about 25% of all subprime home mortgages are delinquent with millions more likely to follow. One rating agency predicts that between 40 and 50% of all subprime mortgages originated since 2006 will eventually end in foreclosure.

Factors contributing to the housing bubble that expanded and then burst, devastating millions of homeowners and investors, included lax oversight over important segments of the lender market, the expansion of predatory lending into minority and poor communities, the growth of predatory borrowing or irresponsible borrowing engaged in by dishonest or greedy borrowers, and housing market cover introduced by governmental policies that protected the growing subprime markets that collapsed under their own weight.

1. Lax Lender Oversight

Before financial deregulation and Gramm-Leach-Bliley, commercial banks wrote mortgages that were primarily based on an individual's demonstrated ability to repay the loan, based upon credit worthiness. Typically, the commercial bank would then hold the mortgage, collecting payments until the mortgage was ultimately paid off by the credit-worthy borrower. Commercial banks were generally careful about how, and to whom, they wrote mortgages, because they held the loan and relied on timely payments to conduct business.

Following the Great Depression, the government became critically involved in the home mortgage business originating government entities to purchase loans and guarantee payment of mortgages in many instances via its initiation of Fannie Mae, Ginnie Mae, and Freddie Mac. Soon thereafter, securitization of home mortgages was initiated by these government-sponsored enterprises (GSEs) allowing investors to purchase mortgage-backed securities that had both liquidity and stability "which generated greater spreads over comparable term treasury obligations than securities of similar risk. Securitization of mortgage loans by [Fannie, Ginnie, and Freddie] allowed the larger capital markets to directly invest in American home ownership at a lower cost than the older depository lending model of business."

When the private sector was finally able to burst through and carve itself out a place in the mortgage loan securitization industry—an evolution that spanned decades—while providing consumers some benefits previously unavailable, it ultimately unleashed a shadow system that eventually spun out of control.

While the GSEs, Fannie, Freddie, and Ginnie, typically invested in mortgages with particular middle-class focused policy objectives in mind, mostly refusing to purchase unusually large ("jumbo") mortgages, home equity loans, variable interest rate mortgages, or most importantly subprime mortgages, purely private institutions recognized these market gaps as potentially lucrative. In the 1970s, as the baby boomers were reaching home buying target ages, the private sector felt the potential benefits of pooling jumbo, variable rate, and subprime home mortgages into mortgage-backed securities and soon began channeling capital into home mortgage lending similarly to the ways the GSEs did with prime mortgages. Unmet demand in the mortgage market segments that was too risky for the GSEs—including variable rate, home equity, and subprime—left enticing and substantial niches for private investors.

The mortgage lending market, once one of careful weighing and balancing and where actual concern for the consumer was clear, transformed into a money grinding market where brokers connected lenders with borrowers, loans were often packaged at the best fee arrangement for the broker and the bank, rather than the consumer, and loans were sold in secondary markets and then packaged as investments, so the risk of return was no longer the concern of one commercial bank, but was spread out over multiple parties. No longer was any party concerned with repayment, default or the consumer's interests because much of the money and fees were paid and collected up front. Once the mortgages were privately securitized and packaged, and once the owner of the securitized mortgage was an investment bank, then very little care or connectivity existed between the mortgage payor and the owner. This unregulated mortgage lending industry led to a confluence of reckless irresponsibility.

First, banks became detached from the credit-worthiness of borrowers as they could immediately resell mortgages in a secondary market. Second, unregulated mortgage brokers made loans to borrowers that were not qualified and often on a predatory basis. Third, many borrowers entered into interest-only loans, many adjustable rate, in order to secure lower monthly payments. When the housing bubble burst and mortgage rates reset at higher levels, many of these homeowners could not pay their mortgage nor sell their homes for a profit, leading to defaults. Fourth, and perhaps most important, mortgages were repackaged as mortgage-backed securities and sold in an unregulated market to investors. When the housing bubble was inflated, the repackaged securities were fine as many investors opted for the high risk bundles of subprime and adjustable rate mortgage-backed securities based on the higher rate of return. When the housing market collapsed, because the unregulated subprime mortgage-backed securities had spread throughout the entire economy, including Wall Street investment banks, national commercial banks, small regional banks, hedge funds, pension funds, and individual investors, the trajectory of the downturn was massive. Further, as hedge funds were left unregulated by the SEC and the buying, selling, and swapping of CDOs and CDSs was conducted in the shadows, banks and hedge funds could engage in highly speculative, outrageously risky trading and betting.

2. Predatory Lending

Unregulated lenders, including unregulated mortgage brokers that engaged in predatory lending, bear significant responsibility for the financial crisis. Predatory lending occurs when a lender deceptively convinces borrowers to agree to unfair and abusive loan terms, or systematically violates terms in ways that are difficult for a borrower to defend against. Subprime loans are those loans most likely to be written through predatory lending practices to borrowers who do not meet prime underwriting borrower guidelines, and are therefore preferred by lenders because profit margins can be significant if a borrower pays out the loan. Subprime mortgages are typically written for borrowers who are adjudged to have very high credit risk, often because they lack a strong credit or work history or have other characteristics that are associated with strong probabilities of default. Subprime loans typically carry much higher interest rates than conventional loans.

During the 1990s, the U.S. witnessed an explosion of a new and aggressive form of "subprime" mortgage lending. Prior to this explosion, "prime" mortgages were generally considered those qualified to be resold to Fannie Mae and Freddie Mac. Both Fannie Mae and Freddie Mac adhered to strict automated underwriting standards, using widely embraced financial modeling that required standardized documentation and pay practices that were similar for all loans purchased by them. These standards led to stable and ho-mogenized prime mortgage loans, thereby permitting secondary markets to treat prime loans like a commodity instead of a tenuous long-term financial association. In contrast to "prime" mortgages, "subprime" mortgages are typically written for borrowers with poor credit histories that did not historically meet the guidelines established by Fannie Mae and Freddie Mac. Further, unlike prime lenders, those lenders that specialize in writing subprime loans typically securitize their own loans and thus have much more freedom to set rates and establish underwriting standards leading to a drastically different set of rates, fees, and guidelines for borrowing depending on which broker or lender a consumer borrows from. The result is that during the housing bubble, unregulated lenders were in a rush to originate new subprime loans in order to securitize and sell them to investors for large profits, often disregarding their own underwriting guidelines when writing the subprime mortgages. "Unlike prime loans, where access to the secondary market is guarded by the play-it-safe GSEs, the secondary subprime market is filled with aggressive investors and businesses looking to maximize their profits by any possible means."

That predatory lending ran amok in the run-up to the financial market crisis is now well established. Mortgage brokers, seeking higher origination fees and profit spreads, fervently sought out borrowers to whom they could sell subprime mortgages. Often, minority communities were targeted for the predatory loans. In 2006, 55% of loans to African Americans were subprime, despite the fact that many of those borrowers qualified for prime loans.

Those that recklessly sold and then bundled predatory subprime loans bear grave responsibility for the financial market crisis.

3. Predatory Borrowing

Deeply embedded in the web of corporate deceit outlined above are the borrowers that are currently defaulting in staggering percentages on their loans, many of them subprime. The role of personal borrower culpability for the financial crisis is one that must be addressed. Despite clear evidence of predatory lending as shown above and below, the mortgage crisis can also be attributed in many respects to "predatory borrowing." In 2006, more than 40% of all subprime loans were written to borrowers that qualified as "affluent" and identified as white. While some subprime borrowers could be characterized as first-time home purchasers, a large group of affluent white borrowers attempted to take easy advantage of lax lending standards by taking out subprime loans in order to purchase second or third homes to flip them for quick profit, or to purchase apartment buildings they could not afford. With easy credit available and a voracious Wall Street appetite for subprime loans for securitization purposes, individual borrowers were more than willing to get in over their heads in order to purchase a home they could not afford or in an attempt to make a swift profit by purchasing and immediately reselling (flipping) based on the ever-increasing housing bubble.

Without doubt, personal borrowers on many levels entered into mortgages that they should not have and many borrowers lied to get approved. That said, the depth of the predatory nature of the origination of subprime loans and the fact that several studies exist that indicate that mortgage brokers, rather than borrowers, actually committed egregious fraud on many loan applications should at least mute those that attempt to place singular blame on borrowers. Still, borrower irresponsibility and overreaching by consumers played a critical role in the economic breakdown.

4. Governmental Cover

Some commentators and think tanks present an interesting view of the underlying cause of the financial market crisis. Many argue that governmental cover remains the primary reason that the appetite for subprime loans grew so voracious.

Mortgage brokers—even predatory ones—cannot create and sell deficient mortgages unless they have willing buyers, and it turns out that their main customers were government agencies or companies and banks required by government regulations to purchase these junk loans.

That the Federal Housing Administration, Fannie Mae, and Freddie Mac held millions of subprime and Alt-A loans indicates the willingness of the private quasi-governmental enterprises to engage in the same risky profiteering that Wall Street investment firms and commercial banks engaged in through the purchase of securitized subprime mortgage-backed instruments.

Although Fannie Mae and Freddie Mac entered the private securitized subprime mortgage-backed market late in the game, they entered that market seeking profit. These GSEs are culpable for buttressing the market and creating additional outlets for purchase of subprime loans and the securitization of those loans. Due to the massive scope of Fannie and Freddie in the mortgage market, their presence in the market, though late, created a significant leveraged position. Further, the GSEs guarantee of many types of subprime loans provided cover for those private bankers that recklessly wrote loans destined to fail knowing that the price on some of those junk loans would be guaranteed by the government through its sponsored entities.

Still, despite attempts favored in some circles to pin singular blame on the government, particularly Fannie Mae and Freddie Mac, for the market crisis, the truth indicates that while Fannie and Freddie did in fact play a role in the financial market crisis, it was not a major one.

Further examples of governmental cover include newspaper reports indicating that the U.S. Department of Housing and Urban Development (HUD) played a role in encouraging Fannie and Freddie's entrée into the subprime mortgage market. HUD, eager to see homeownership more available to low-income families, urged Fannie and Freddie to purchase increasingly more subprime loans by categorizing them as "affordable" through use of an outdated policy allowing the government-chartered firms to count subprime loans as a "public good that would foster affordable housing." Reportedly, between 2004 and 2006, Freddie and Fannie purchased $434 billion in securities backed by subprime loans, thus fostering a greater market for such subprime lending.

During the subprime bubble and breakdown, Fannie and Freddie acted as private firms—private firms with an implicit governmental guarantee of their mortgage buying activity. In a deregulated environment and as private actors, Fannie and Freddie joined their Wall Street brethren in reckless pursuit of profit.

Critics of Fannie and Freddie immediately seized upon their collapse as validation of previous opposition to the housing GSEs. As indicated above, some commentators have gone so far as to actually pin the housing crisis and the severe recession triggered by it on Fannie and Freddie, rather than on foreclosure of privately originated and securitized subprime mortgages or risky speculation in the CDOs and CDS derivatives. While it is true that Fannie and Freddie became involved in the subprime mortgage and securitization market and bear responsibility for contributing to the subprime mortgage crisis, the role of the government-sponsored enterprises was simply one of many causes of the meltdown.

C. Securitization and Derivatives

If deregulation and the housing bubble set the stage for the financial market crisis, the securitization of subprime mortgage loans and the shadow trading of the derivative instruments thrown off by the securitized mortgages overturned the table entirely.

1. Private Securitization of Subprime Mortgages

The profit margins and income streams available from bundling subprime home mortgages into derivative investment vehicles, which were bought and sold in unregulated shadow markets, was too potentially profitable to pass up. Securitization, once a market controlled by GSEs and involving only prime mortgage loans, became unmoored from these places of relative safety in the 1990s. When the private sector seized subprime loans as a securitization vehicle, the frenzied profit pursuit began.

Since the government origination of mortgage securitization in the 1940s and 1950s, the ability to profit on pass-through interest based on homeowner payments that traditionally only default in very small percentages was of keen interest to the private markets. The securitization of subprime mortgages was extremely attractive to the private markets because subprime securitization had been historically avoided by Fannie and Freddie and, despite a higher default rate risk, the interest rates and potential income available (under appropriate risk modeling) were particularly lucrative. Securitizing subprime mortgages typically occurred in the market crisis run-up as follows.

At the outset, a mortgage broker "identifies a potential borrower through a variety of marketing approaches including direct mail, telemarketing, door-to-door solicitation, and television or radio advertising." The borrower is assigned a credit score that plays a significant role in determining the interest rate and other pricing contingencies designated by the broker and originator, who use consumer credit scoring agencies that track outstanding debt, bankruptcies, and prior civil judgments to assign the credit score and determine the interest rates. Once interest rates and pricing terms are set, the consumer formally applies for the mortgage which then typically closes one to two weeks later when the borrower signs all of the necessary paperwork wherein the borrowers become bound to the terms as settled upon.

Quickly thereafter, the loan originator will transfer the mortgage loan to a subsidiary of an investment bank, typically called a securitization sponsor or seller, who then transfers the loan forward into a pool with hundreds of other similarly situated mortgage loans. This pool of mortgage loans will become its own entity, typically called a special purpose vehicle (SPV) which can be organized as a corporation, partnership, limited liability company, or most commonly, a trust. This SPV trust holds no other assets, employs no individuals, and has no function other than owning a pool of mortgage loans. Under the contract that transfers the loans into the pool, the SPV agrees to sell equity pieces, or tranches, of itself to various investors. In the typical securitization arrangement, an underwriter "purchases all of the 'securities'—here meaning derivative income streams drawn from payments on the underlying mortgages—issued by the pool." Thereafter, the underwriters employ placement agents who work on commission to sell the tranched securities to various investors based on portfolio needs and risk tolerance.

Further distancing loan originator from consumer, many sellers of securitized mortgage loans sell the rights to service the loan pool to a separate company that will then be responsible for corresponding with the "consumers, receiving monthly payments, monitoring collateral, and when necessary foreclos[ing] on homes." Occasionally the originator retains the right to service the mortgages, maintaining some connection with homeowners, but typically servicing is outsourced to a company specializing in loan servicing. Additionally, securitization deal sellers and trustees typically hire a document custodian to track the voluminous information and paperwork on loans in a pool. All said, the mortgage loan securitization process described above, including all of the business involved, have created a very powerful and lucrative device for marshaling capital into and from home mortgage loans.

Once the special purpose vehicles have bundled the mortgages into an investment, then credit rating agencies are employed to assign a risk rating to each securitized tranche. That credit rating agencies were misrating the securitized mortgages is now widely understood based on the intimate, conflicted relationship between the underwriting industry and the credit rating agencies that are paid by those the agency is assigned to rate. Once investors made unregulated purchases of the subprime mortgage-backed securities investments, they immediately negotiated credit default swap contracts with insuring firms in order to hedge against the potential loss these investments represented. Of course, the credit default swap contracts were not regulated, so whether or not the insuring firm could even fulfill the terms of the quasi-insurance contract was never queried. Prior to the market collapse, it is now widely accepted that each firm that engaged every step of the subprime securitization process profited handsomely, some would say obscenely.

2. Shadow Trading

Over-the-counter derivatives trading, including CDOs and CDSs, can fairly be described as the straws that nearly broke the camel's economic back. Lehman Brothers and Bear Stearns were deeply involved in purchasing bundled subprime securities, as were dozens of Wall Street titans, such that when the housing market dropped off its heated pace, each deeply entrenched institution was left desperate as borrowers began to default on subprime loans. Each institution that had purchased the securitized subprime mortgage investments had hedged its reckless subprime money grab by entering into credit default swaps contracts primarily purchased through insurers like AIG.

AIG had engaged so recklessly in the shadow CDS market, writing billions of dollars worth of quasi-insurance policies to cover CDOs in the event of default, that it did not have nearly the capital to repay in a situation where any significant number came due. When Bear Stearns and Lehman Brothers needed insurance payouts for defaulted securitized vehicles, AIG had no ability or capital to repay.

Prior to the meltdown, CDSs exploded into the secondary market, where speculative investors, hedge funds, and others similarly situated would buy and sell CDS instruments from the sidelines without having any direct relationship with the underlying investment.

CDSs had been traded and shorted to the point that the CDO holder often had no clue as to where the CDS currently resided or what the underlying firm's capitalization or prospects to pay looked like. So when a default occurred, the insured party or hedged party often had no idea who was responsible for making up the default or whether that end player had the resources to cure the default. The sellers of this CDS insurance were crushed as defaults rose precipitously and the insurers had no ability to pay the CDS contracts it had recklessly written.

3. Credit Rating Agency Capture

The credit rating agencies that provided bond ratings for the subprime mortgage-backed investment market shoulder a significant amount of responsibility for the financial market crisis of 2008. The primary credit rating agencies—Moody's, Standard & Poor's, and Fitch's—began rating investment instruments early in the twentieth century, and continue today, by giving letter grades to debt vehicles in connection with the likelihood of the instrument's default or failure to pay. The ratings typically range in descending order of risk from triple A (Aaa) to C, with Aaa representing the highest quality debt instrument with minimal credit risk and C indicating the lowest rated bond class that would currently be in default with no real prospect for recovery of principal or interest.

As the private securitization of subprime mortgages market ramped up, credit rating agencies stepped in to provide ratings on the various tranches of subprime securitizations that were being structured. The credit rating agency model failed badly. First, the credit rating agencies adopted the "issuer pays" model of compensation for delivering ratings, meaning that gross conflicts occurred when the very parties (investment banks and underwriters) structuring the vehicle and seeking the rating were also the parties paying the fees for the ultimate rating that was delivered. Second, credit rating agencies were not adequately staffed to deal with the securitized subprime market explosion (either staff was not professionally trained or was not provided the time to understand or deconstruct the vehicles). Third, based partially on the breakneck pace that subprime mortgages were being sold and securitized, the credit rating agencies did not adequately document the crucial steps along the way of providing a rating and tracking the substantial participants in the process. Fourth, the credit rating agencies overrelied on outdated risk modeling and dissimilar historical data which negatively impacted the accuracy of the ratings that they provided. Finally, external pressures contributed to flawed rating methodologies, including the concentrated market of subprime mortgage-backed investment originators causing the credit rating agencies to concede on important negotiating positions during the rating process in order to prevent losing an important underwriting client.

These failures and pressures set the table for the ratings disaster that eventuated. Nearly "80 percent of $1.4 trillion in subprime debt issued between 2005–2007 was [wrongly represented as] triple-A rated securities." Investors purchased subprime mortgage-backed bonds that were rated Aaa, indicating an absolutely safe investment vehicle that would have no trouble paying interest or principal, and 80% of those securitized instruments had been assigned a misleading or fraudulent rating. Investors relied upon a rating system that had been captured. Much of the rating malfeasance was driven by greed, pressure, avarice, and flawed modeling.

4. Regulatory Capture

Arthur Levitt, former chair of the SEC, stated, "As an overheated market needed a strong referee to rein in dangerously risky behavior, the commission too often remained on the sidelines." Sean Coffey, a former fraud prosecutor, believes the SEC "neutered the ability of the enforcement staff to be as proactive as they could be. It's hard to square the motto of investor advocate with the way they've performed the last eight years." Not only was there a relaxation of enforcement, there was also a reduction in SEC staff. Coffey asserts that the Bush administration used the argument that loosening up regulations was necessary in order to make it possible for American companies to compete globally.

In light of such regulatory failures, some argue that regulators are too careful not to offend Wall Street giants in order to preserve opportunities to enter the much more lucrative private sector after paying dues on the regulator side for a space. Others argue that regulators are not financially savvy enough to combat creative and bold financial fraud (as many regulators are lawyers, trained in the law, not in economics or corporate finance) thereby allowing obvious financial fraud to go undetected. The financial market crisis minefield is littered with failed regulators, beginning with the SEC and carving a wide swath through the Federal Reserve Bank, the FDIC, the Commodity Futures Trading Commission (CFTC), and the Office of Thrift Supervision.

5. Balance Sheet Fraud

Despite the machinations of the Sarbanes-Oxley Act, criticized at its inception as legislation that was mere "window dressing" and did nothing to meaningfully respond to the Enron, WorldCom, Adelphia, Tyco, Global Crossing accounting scandal era, accounting fraud continues to be perpetrated by some of the nation's most important financial institutions. Sarbanes-Oxley increased accounting oversight, separated accounting and consulting services, increased audit frequency, and significantly increased internal controls, adding incredible new costs, and still, was unable to capture deft accounting fraud engaged by some of Wall Street's most important players.

Further, if not outright fraudulent, recent reports indicate that nearly every investment bank on Wall Street and many national commercial banks engage routinely in balance sheet manipulation in order to mask risk levels and improve leverage levels in mandatory periodic reporting.

6. CEO Primacy

Commentators now argue that corporate law in the United States has evolved to a point where the chief executive officer (CEO) reigns supreme as nearly untouchable in the modern marketplace. The model of shareholder democracy has been ameliorated to the point that the CEO and his pursuit of personal fortune is the primary driver behind most corporate positioning. The CEO dominates American corporations to the extent that he is held to very few standards of responsibility and is able to stave off all shareholder dissent through careful calculation. According to Professor Steven Ramirez, "CEOs of public companies have the unique privilege of picking their own nominal supervisors—the board of directors."

The CEO in the United States has the power to appoint the board of directors that "oversees" his performance, to maneuver board members off of the board if they challenge his decisions, to establish his compensation through the board committee that he appoints, to make reckless decisions that are protected by the business judgment rule, to exercise nearly unfettered power (as the duty of care and duty of loyalty have been judicially emasculated to the point of near nonexistence), and to escape private shareholder lawsuits (as class action securities fraud actions have been congressionally neutered to a near terminal state). CEOs and corporate management have been empowered by U.S. corporate law to generate personal short-term profit and gain at the expense of long-term vitality and shareholder profit maximization in breathtaking ways.

One of the enduring themes of the financial market crisis is that Wall Street executives overleveraged or allowed such reckless overleveraging of their balance sheets that nearly every major firm faced imminent collapse and bankruptcy. The simple reason that these CEOs and other executives allowed their firms to walk to the very edge of the bankruptcy precipice is because they all pursued the fantastic profits that were being kicked off in the securitized subprime mortgage industry. Short-term profit, tied into executive compensation, motivated the audacious decision making and recklessness that forced a federal taxpayer bailout. The reckless pursuit of profit in the above described subprime mortgage-backed securities market is a powerful example of this short-term, personal profit driven vision.

Nearly all the corporate executives that steered their companies into the subprime mortgage morass walked away with bonuses and compensation, not jail time. In the ultimate irony, some of the compensation paid to these reckless executives came from the very TARP bailout funds that were needed to keep the overleveraged firms afloat. While corporate executives that recklessly capsized their firms avoid jail time and any significant consequence for their actions, many minority borrowers, who are underhandedly blamed by some for causing the crisis, find themselves saddled with subprime mortgages that were delivered to them predatorily.

D. Summation

The material above seeks to present an honest picture as to the reality of the financial market collapse of 2008. While not capturing every single piece of the puzzle, the discussion above undertakes to describe most of the principle players in the economic collapse. In light of the many and varied causes carefully described above, the Obama administration, congressional leaders, and market regulators have a critical responsibility to thoughtfully consider ways in which to protect investors from the reckless excess of Wall Street promulgated by its leadership and from its own short-sighted legislative and policy mistakes.

III. Financial Market Crisis Myth

As described by critical race theory, institutional and structural racism has never been appropriately dealt with or eliminated in the United States, and because it has not, continuing manifestations of race hatred simply mutate and find expression in ways that serve to further the interests of the majority. This mutation was on clear display in the days, weeks, and months following the financial market meltdown of 2008, as the minority-borrower narrative spread like a virus throughout the nation. That minority-borrower myth has not subsided in the months that have passed. Today, the minority scapegoating has transmogrified into a racial coding blame game where now rather than pointing specifically at minority borrowers, it is the Community Reinvestment Act, Fannie Mae, and Freddie Mac that are blamed by many, in racial code, for causing the meltdown of 2008.

A. The Dirty Little Myth

In the days following the collapse of Lehman Brothers, and as Congress was intensely debating and posturing in connection with whether to pass TARP, a stunning message began to seep out from particular news sources, various commentators, and Web 2.0. A dirty little myth began to be peddled that essentially blamed the failure of the U.S. capital markets on minority borrowers who were now defaulting on their subprime mortgages, which was the primary factor leading to the collapse of the global economy. Through federal governmental intervention, in the form of the Community Reinvestment Act of 1977 and the securitized subprime loan purchasing activity of Fannie Mae and Freddie Mac, lenders were "forced" to provide undeserving minorities with mortgage loans that never should have been written. Subprime mortgage loans were required to be written, according to the minority-borrower myth, against the will of the lenders.

The dirty little myth seemed absurd to many, but found unbelievable traction. Neal Cavuto on Fox News stated "loaning to minorities and risky folks is a disaster." Ann Coulter, in an article she authored, stated in the headline, "They Gave Your Mortgage to a Less Qualified Minority." Representative Michelle Bachman (R., MN), on the House floor and later on Larry King Live said, "Look at the housing crisis. Government has to take its share of the blame. After all, government was goading these mortgage lenders [saying] 'if you don't give loans out to marginally credit worthy people, we're going to come after you.'" In fact, according to the myth, the overzealous enforcement by the government of the Community Reinvestment Act forced quotas on banks to encourage diversity in the housing market by lending solely "on the basis of race." This is simply false.

While many reputable sources were quick to discredit the claim the myth had been unleashed and it began to creep into households and mindsets across the country. Politicians, pundits, and economists served up minority borrowers and governmental social steering as the primary cause of a near global meltdown.

Economist Thomas Sowell argues that the Community Reinvestment Act was a primary progenitor of the financial market crisis because it required banks to carefully track the loans it was extending to borrowers, including memorializing race, gender, and age. To Sowell and many others, this act of tracing lending according to race, gender, and age allowed federal government regulators to exert enormous pressure on banks that did not appear to lend equally to all potential borrowers. Accordingly, Sowell argues that this act of pressuring banks to loan to all community borrowers where the banks did business had the effect of forcing or mandating that banks lower lending standards in order to increase its lending to minority and low-income borrowers.

Extending the myth of governmental social engineering as a primary cause of the financial market crisis, in 2009, Congress established a commission, styled the Financial Crisis Inquiry Commission (FCIC) that was charged with drilling down into the root causes of the financial market crisis. The FCIC was ordered to conduct an exhaustive investigation, and upon completion, submit a report to Congress that would identify all of the causes and failures that precipitated the meltdown. This bipartisan commission, after conducting hundreds of hours of interviews, began fracturing. In December 2010, the four Republican members of the ten-member FCIC forced a vote in advance of the official report due date where they demanded that the following terms be banned from the final version of the official report: "Wall Street," "shadow banking," and "deregulation." When the Republican committee members' proposal to ban these terms was rejected by the five Democratic members and the one Independent member, the Republican commissioners defected from the FCIC and became determined to issue their own report, called the "Financial Crisis Primer."

The nine-page Republican Financial Crisis Primer, with precious little factual support, bewilderingly ignores Wall Street's role in the financial market crisis, refuses to mention deregulation, credit default swaps, and reckless decision making by Wall Street executives, and instead, focuses fundamentally on the role of Fannie Mae, Freddie Mac, and the goal of homeownership in poor communities as the primary causes of the financial market crisis. No longer is the mythmaking reserved for pundits and an occasional economist— now the Republican commissioners have issued a report that whitewashes Wall Street's role in the crisis, effectively attempting to rewrite history.

B. Nevermind the Truth

Despite the hue and cry that the Community Reinvestment Act forced lenders to extend subprime mortgages to unqualified minority borrowers, the truth is that the CRA was enacted more than thirty years ago, so its evil impact must have laid dormant for more than twenty-five of those years. The CRA requires no quotas or mandatory lending and instead specifies that lenders extend loans in a fair, sound, reasonable, and principled fashion. Additionally, more than 50% of the lenders extending subprime loans during the run-up to the crisis were finance companies that were not required to comply with the CRA. In reality, less than 20% of lenders extending subprime loans were subject to the provisions of the CRA, with some estimates indicating that lenders beholden to the CRA extended just 6% to 7% of the subprime loans subject to default risk during the crisis.

While Thomas Sowell is careful to cabin his criticism of the Community Reinvestment Act by claiming that it only allowed the government to "pressure" banks to loan to poor minorities, many that subscribe to his economic theorizing use his language to argue that the CRA "forced" or "required" banks to write subprime loans to minorities. This is simply untrue. While banks unquestionably have CRA loans on their books that have defaulted during the market crisis, suggesting that some of those loans were extended that likely should not have been, the truth is that the default rates and percentages are significantly lower than the subprime loans written by independent mortgage companies and are in line with typical default percentages expected with CRA subprime loans.

Thus, not only did the CRA play little to no role in the subprime loan abuse, often minority communities were targeted for predatory lending. In 2006, 55% of loans to African Americans were subprime, despite the fact that many of those borrowers qualified for prime loans. Additionally, statistics indicate that 40% of loans to Latinos were subprime; 35% of loans to American Indians were subprime, while just 23% of loans to whites were subprime. Women also received less favorable loan terms across equal presentations of credit worthiness.

Studies indicate that minority borrowers were purposely steered into risky and expensive subprime loans, even when they qualified for better terms. Those lenders that steered minority borrowers into subprime loans were often mortgage brokers that were eager to make a significantly larger profit. For instance, "[i]n two audit studies wherein creditworthy testers approached subprime lenders, whites were more likely to be referred to the lenders' prime borrowing division than were similar black applicants. Further, subprime lenders quoted the black applicants very high rates, fees, and closing costs not correlated with risk." In addition, a classic discrimination study by the Reinvestment Coalition found that black and Latino individuals that posed as borrowers received significantly poorer treatment and were offered costlier, less-attractive loans more often than whites—despite the fact that minority testers had been given more attractive financial profiles, including stronger credit standings and lengthier employment tenures. This study rebuts mortgage companies' claims that lending patterns are determined solely by risk characteristics. "John Taylor, the coalition's president, told a Congressional hearing last year, that minority borrowers were paying a 'race tax.' While lenders are required to report to the federal government such things as race, gender, census tract, amount of loan and income, they omit credit score data." Therefore, in guarding the most important statistic used in making loans, mortgage lenders provide for themselves a ready shield against charges of discrimination and predatory lending.

In further debunking the myth that minority borrowers caused the market crisis and that the CRA was at the root of this failure, nearly 60% of all subprime loans in the 2005 to 2007 period were extended to white borrowers and more than 40% of all subprime loans were extended to white borrowers that qualified as "affluent."

While the mortgage crisis has been recharacterized by some as the fault of minority borrowers and governmental intervention through the Community Reinvestment Act, Fannie, and Freddie, the reality is primarily just the opposite. The financial market crisis has landed heaviest on communities of color. Predatory lending and subprime mortgage abuse is far more responsible for minority involvement in the subprime markets than the CRA. Because minority communities and borrowers were targeted predatorily for subprime loans, foreclosures have devastated urban communities. There are few, if any, facts that support the minority-borrower narrative and governmental social engineering myth. It is just that—a myth. Minority borrowers are no more responsible for the financial market crisis than are Brazilian surfers, Tongan princesses, or Japanese lawyers.

The dirty little myth is unsupportable.

So, why was the myth floated in the face of little evidentiary support? What motivates this blatant misrepresentation that continues to percolate?

IV. Racial Coding

To many, the election of Barack Obama as president signaled a new era for American politics and symbolically represented a coming of age for a country with a tortured racial history. At the very moment that our nation was touted as "coming of age" we regressed into our familiar historical hostility toward our minority citizenry.

A. Code Talk

Racial coding has a long tradition in the United States. That it persists in the purportedly postracial Obama era belies the very positioning of postracialism and postracialists. Racial coding entails engaging issues "such as crime and welfare are now widely viewed as 'coded' issues" that play upon race—or more centrally, upon white Americans' negative views of black Americans—without explicitly raising the race card. By embracing coded issues, politicians and pundits are able to exploit white American's racial animosity and resentment toward minority Americans while diminishing the appearance of race hatred or race baiting.

Classic examples of code talk or racial coding in fairly recent U.S. history include the political invocations of the "welfare queen," the Willie Horton advertisements in the 1988 Bush/Dukakis presidential campaign, and the "Harold, call me" advertisements in the 2006 Harold Ford, Jr., Tennessee Senate campaign, amongst so many others examples.

This racial coding, blaming the minority poor, continues unabated in "postracial" America. The code talk creates subterfuge and massive misdirection in connection with the reality of the meltdown. While capitalism and neoclassical economics should be critically interrogated in light of the colossal failures in the private financial sector that precipitated the crisis, we are instead fervently engaged in propping up these two systems that failed us so spectacularly.

B. Coming of Age?

Postracialism is a deeply loaded term. Taken lightly, postracialism can mean simply that our nation has transcended the "color line" and that truly all people are created equal and treated fairly in this country. Surely, if an African American can become president, race is no longer an issue worthy of discussion. On a much deeper level, postracialism can be used as a tool to perpetuate white privilege and lend additional power to entrenched elites. On a more subtle, contemptible level, racial coding is often used as a mechanism for claiming "colorblindness" as a valued principle but engaging in race baiting and racial fearmongering by playing on the fears of white American's without explicitly mentioning race. When those claiming postracialism are the same parties perpetrating instances of racial coding, a particularly reprehensible plane of racism is on display.

The financial market crisis has laid bare our true place, and it is not postracial. The dirty little myth and its accompanying racial coding indicate that we are not close to becoming a truly postracial America.

V. Conclusion

Very few market players are innocent when it comes to the subprime mortgage industry collapse. Individuals and corporations must be held responsible for their roles, including Wall Street, commercial banks, investment banks, corporate executives, CEOs, regulators, legislators, individual borrowers, lenders, mortgage brokers, credit rating agencies, and governmental entities. All must recognize its role in the meltdown and honestly explore how it needs to change to better protect U.S. shareholders and investors. The parties least culpable for the near global meltdown and least in need of absolution are minority borrowers, particularly minority borrowers that took out loans through the Community Reinvestment Act.

This classic racial coding must be summarily rejected if we ever hope to reach our twin goals of genuinely safeguarding our nation's capital markets and arriving at a truly postracial positioning in America.

Copyright © 2011 Utah Law Review Society; andré douglas pond cummings

Notes

(1) What caused the collapse of the housing market in the United States that led to the great financial crisis of 2008?

(2) What role did minority borrowers play in bringing the global economy to near collapse?

(3) One reason for the financial crisis not discussed by Dean cummings, that many conservatives point to as one of the primary causes of the financial crisis, is the idea of mark-to-market accounting. Pursuant to this generally accepted accounting principal, real estate must be carried on the balance sheet at the lower of cost or fair market value to avoid overstating the value of the business. According to a 2008 article from *Forbes* magazine, several well-known economists articulated that "mark-to-market" accounting was a substantial factor in causing the financial crisis.

According to Chief economist Brian S. Westbury and Bob Stein of First Trust Portfolios of Chicago, approximately 70% of the financial crisis

[was] caused by mark-to-market accounting in an illiquid market. *What's most fascinating is that the Treasury is selling its plan as a way to put a bottom in mortgage pool prices, tipping its hat to the problem of mark-to-market accounting without acknowledging it. It is a real shame that there is so little discussion of this reality.*

William Isaac, chairman of the FDIC in the 1980s under President Reagan, wrote:

During the 1980s, our underlying economic problems were far more serious than the economic problems we're facing this time around.... It could have been much worse. The country's 10 largest banks were loaded up with Third World debt that was valued in the markets at cents on the dollar. If we had marked those loans to market prices, virtually every one of them would have been insolvent.

He further opined that marking down loans to their current fair market value

is contrary to everything we know about bank regulation. When there are temporary impairments of asset values, due to economic and marketplace events, regulators must give institutions an opportunity to survive the temporary impairment. Assets should not be marked to unrealistic fire sale prices. Regulators must evaluate the assets on the basis of their true economic value (a discounted cash flow analysis). If we had followed today's approach during the 1980s, we would have nationalized all of the major banks in the country, and thousands of additional banks and thrifts would have failed. I have little doubt that the country would have gone from a serious recession into a depression.

Additionally, Richard Epstein, the famous law and economics professor from the University of Chicago wrote that mark to market accounting is inefficient. Specifically, he stated that

> Unfortunately, there is no working market to mark this paper down to. To meet their bond covenants and their capital requirements, these firms have to sell their paper at distress prices that don't reflect the upbeat fact that the anticipated income streams from this paper might well keep the firm afloat.[7]

Do you think that the aforementioned conservative scholars are accurate in their assessments about mark-to-market accounting, or is Dean cummings right in his claim that the financial crisis was primarily caused by greed and racism?

(4) According to a report from the "Center for American Progress," Black and Hispanic borrowers were overwhelmingly sold higher priced mortgages. The astonishing point from the report that is highlighted in Figure 5.1 is that Black and Hispanic borrowers, regardless of the income of such borrowers, were placed in higher priced mortgages. In fact, a Black or Hispanic borrower, with a higher income, was almost as likely to get placed in a higher priced mortgage as a Black or Hispanic borrower who did not fit into the higher income borrower category. Conversely, White borrowers that fit into the higher income category were 50% less likely to get placed in a higher priced mortgage.

(5) What do you think accounts for the statistical disparities highlighted by Figure 5.1?

(6) Based on the material presented to this point in the chapter, one would assume, as a prominent Wall Street analyst asserted, that the financial crisis was largely a function of executive greed mixed with a "cavalier disregard for risk."[8] However, such a conclusion would be inaccurate. While executive greed may have been one of the initial narratives for the cause of the financial crisis, along with the blatant misrepresentation that minority borrowers caused it, more recent research and scholarship suggests that the ultimate cause of the financial crisis was fraud. Jamie Galbraith, the Lloyd M. Bentsen Jr. Chair in Government/Business Relations and professor of Government at the Lyndon B. Johnson School of Public Affairs at The University of Texas at Austin, was one of the first scholars to argue that the real cause of the financial crisis was fraud. In a presentation before the Senate Judiciary's Committee's, Subcommittee on Crime, Professor Galbraith highlighted the role that fraud played in the financial crisis.

> Formal analysis tells us that control frauds follow certain patterns. They grow rapidly, reporting high profitability, certified by top accounting firms. They pay exceedingly well. At the same time, they radically lower standards, building new businesses in markets previously considered too risky for honest business. In the financial sector, this takes the form of relaxed—no, gutted— underwriting, combined with the capacity to pass the bad penny to the greater fool. In California in the 1980s, Charles Keating realized that an S&L charter was a "license to steal." In the 2000s, sub-prime mortgage origination was much the same thing. Given a license to steal, thieves get busy. And because their performance seems so good, they quickly come to dominate their markets; the bad players driving out the good.

---

7. Newt Gingrich, *Suspend Mark-to-Market Now!*, Forbes.com, Sept. 29, 2008, *available at* http://www.forbes.com/2008/09/29/mark-to-market-oped-cx_ng_0929gingrich.html.

8. Peter Eavis, *Judge's Ruling Against 2 Banks Finds Misconduct in '08 Crash*, N.Y. Times, May 11, 2015, *available at* http://www.nytimes.com/2015/05/12/business/dealbook/nomura-found-liable-in-us-mortgage-suit-tied-to-financial-crisis.html.

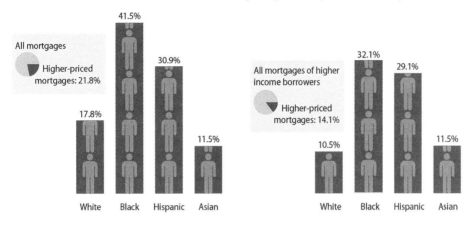

Figure 5.1 Share of mortgages lent in 2006 by 14 major banks and current subsidiaries that were higher-priced, by race/ethnicity

	All borrowers					High-income borrowers only				
	All	White	Black	Hispanic	Asian	All	White	Black	Hispanic	Asian
All	21.8%	17.8%	41.5%	30.9%	11.5%	14.1%	10.5%	32.1%	29.1%	11.5%
Bank of America	15.1%	11.4%	28.1%	21.6%	8.5%	11.1%	8.2%	21.8%	21.2%	9.4%
Wells Fargo	15.5%	13.8%	33.2%	16.4%	5.4%	6.6%	5.6%	17.2%	10.5%	3.8%
JPMorgan Chase	22.0%	16.4%	47.5%	36.6%	12.0%	15.8%	11.0%	44.1%	37.6%	12.1%
Citigroup	55.6%	51.2%	76.6%	71.3%	23.9%	35.7%	27.6%	70.3%	73.5%	22.2%
PNC Financial Services	50.2%	42.6%	67.8%	69.8%	44.7%	45.5%	35.3%	71.9%	74.5%	48.4%
GMAC/Ally Bank	16.1%	13.8%	31.0%	20.5%	9.1%	10.3%	8.2%	18.5%	18.4%	7.8%
SunTrust	6.5%	5.8%	11.4%	9.0%	5.4%	3.8%	3.0%	8.9%	8.3%	4.0%
MetLife (First Tennessee)	9.1%	7.8%	19.0%	13.2%	7.1%	5.9%	5.0%		8.7%	12.4%
Capital One Financial Corp.	20.5%	19.0%	27.0%	21.9%	16.3%	18.0%	15.9%	25.3%	21.3%	16.3%
U.S. Bancorp	15.2%	15.5%	22.4%	13.9%	8.0%	10.3%	10.1%	17.8%	12.6%	8.2%
Regions Financial Corp.	67.7%	59.1%	81.9%	86.3%	77.5%	56.1%	47.0%	73.5%	84.1%	
BB&T	10.8%	10.0%	18.0%	12.3%	3.4%	7.8%	7.5%			
Fifth Third Bancorp	4.6%	4.1%	8.7%	13.7%	2.3%	2.5%	2.4%			
KeyCorp	47.8%	26.2%	45.6%			21.7%	10.3%			

Source: Center for American Progress

The complexity of the mortgage finance sector before the crisis highlights another characteristic marker of fraud. In the system that developed, the original mortgage documents lay buried—where they remain—in the records of the loan originators, many of them since defunct or taken over. Those records, if examined, would reveal the extent of missing documentation, of abusive practices, and of fraud. So far, we have only very limited evidence on this, notably a 2007 Fitch Ratings study of a very small sample of highly-rated RMBS, which found "fraud, abuse or missing documentation in virtually every file." And efforts a year ago by Representative Doggett to persuade

Secretary Geithner to examine and report thoroughly on the extent of fraud in the underlying mortgage records received an epic run-around.

When sub-prime mortgages were bundled and securitized, the ratings agencies failed to examine the underlying loan quality. Instead they substituted statistical models, in order to generate ratings that would make the resulting RMBS acceptable to investors. When one assumes that prices will always rise, it follows that a loan secured by the asset can always be refinanced; therefore the actual condition of the borrower does not matter. That projection is, of course, only as good as the underlying assumption, but in this perversely-designed marketplace those who paid for ratings had no reason to care about the quality of assumptions. Meanwhile, mortgage originators now had a formula for extending loans to the worst borrowers they could find, secure that in this reverse Lake Wobegon no child would be deemed below average even though they all were. Credit quality collapsed because the system was designed for it to collapse.

A third element in the toxic brew was a simulacrum of "insurance," provided by the market in credit default swaps. These are doomsday instruments in a precise sense: they generate cash-flow for the issuer until the credit event occurs. If the event is large enough, the issuer then fails, at which point the government faces blackmail: it must either step in or the system will collapse. CDS spread the consequences of a housing-price downturn through the entire financial sector, across the globe. They also provided the means to short the market in residential mortgage-backed securities, so that the largest players could turn tail and bet against the instruments they had previously been selling, just before the house of cards crashed.

Latter-day financial economics is blind to all of this. It necessarily treats stocks, bonds, options, derivatives and so forth as securities whose properties can be accepted largely at face value, and quantified in terms of return and risk. That quantification permits the calculation of price, using standard formulae. But everything in the formulae depends on the instruments being as they are represented to be. For if they are not, then what formula could possibly apply?

An older strand of institutional economics understood that a security is a contract in law. It can only be as good as the legal system that stands behind it. Some fraud is inevitable, but in a functioning system it must be rare. It must be considered—and rightly—a minor problem. If fraud—or even the perception of fraud—comes to dominate the system, then there is no foundation for a market in the securities. They become trash. And more deeply, so do the institutions responsible for creating, rating and selling them. Including, so long as it fails to respond with appropriate force, the legal system itself.

Control frauds always fail in the end. But the failure of the firm does not mean the fraud fails: the perpetrators often walk away rich. At some point, this requires subverting, suborning or defeating the law. This is where crime and politics intersect. At its heart, therefore, the financial crisis was a breakdown in the rule of law in America.

Ask yourselves: is it possible for mortgage originators, ratings agencies, underwriters, insurers and supervising agencies NOT to have known that the system of housing finance had become infested with fraud? Every statistical indicator of fraudulent practice—growth and profitability—suggests otherwise. Every examination of the record so far suggests otherwise. The very language in use: "liars' loans," "ninja loans," "neutron loans," and "toxic waste," tells you that people knew. I have also heard the expression, "IBG,YBG;" the meaning of that bit of code was: "I'll be gone, you'll be gone."[9]

As further validation of Galbraith's fraud explanation, several defendant banks, including Bank of America Corp, Barclays PLC, BNP Paribas SA, Citigroup Inc, Credit Suisse Group AG, Deutsche Bank AG, Goldman Sachs Group Inc, HSBC Holdings Plc, JPMorgan Chase & Co, Morgan Stanley, Royal Bank of Scotland Group Plc and UBS AG, recently, in September of 2015, reached a $1.865 billion dollar settlement for price fixing of CDSs. Specifically, the suit alleged that the defendant banks engaged in antitrust violations by causing the plaintiffs, including the Los Angeles County Employees Retirement Association and Salix Capital US Incorporated, to pay unfair and unreasonable fees on CDS trades from 2008 until 2013. In addition, the suit alleged that the defendant banks acted to stop the creation of a CDS exchange that would make the buying and selling of CDSs less expensive by uniformly agreeing not to support the exchange and by making it more difficult for the exchange to acquire the necessary licenses to adequately operate the exchange.

(7) Why do you think that the initial narrative of the financial crisis placed blame on everyone other than the decision makers of the financial institutions that caused the problem?

(8) What reasons account for the fact that the initial sentiment regarding the financial crisis was that it was caused by oversight and a disregard for risk rather than blatant fraud?

(9) Does race play into your response to the previous question?

(10) When things like the financial crisis occur, does America generally presume the integrity of white men, which make up most of corporate leadership? If so, why?

(11) Would America have made the same assumptions, that the financial crisis was a function of oversight and a disregard for risk, if the leaders of the financial institutions that caused the financial crisis were women and other racial minorities?

D. Fiduciary Duties in the Context of the Financial Crisis

The following case, *Citigroup*, highlights the difficulty of holding corporate decision makers responsible for their conduct, even when it causes significant harm to the shareholders of the corporation and more importantly, to the fabric of the entire financial market system. Decided by the Chancery Court of Delaware, known to be notoriously corporate friendly, *Citigroup* establishes the standards necessary for holding corporate leaders responsible for actions that severely injure a corporation, a high standard to meet indeed. As you read

---

9. Mark Thoma, *Galbraith: The Role of Fraud in the Financial Crisis*, ECONOMIST'S VIEW, (May 5, 2010, 11:07 am), *available at* http://economistsview.typepad.com/economistsview/2010/05/the-role-of-fraud-in-the-financial-crisis.html.

this case consider the causes of the financial market crisis as outlined above while also pondering whether the director's failures should result in liability or consequence.

In Re Citigroup Inc. Shareholder Derivative Litigation

Civil Action No. 3338-CC (2009)
In the Court of Chancery of the State of Delaware

Opinion

Chandler, Chancellor.

This is a shareholder derivative action brought on behalf of Citigroup Inc. ("Citigroup" or the "Company"), seeking to recover for the Company its losses arising from exposure to the subprime lending market. Plaintiffs, shareholders of Citigroup, brought this action against current and former directors and officers of Citigroup, alleging, in essence, that the defendants breached their fiduciary duties by failing to properly monitor and manage the risks the Company faced from problems in the subprime lending market and for failing to properly disclose Citigroup's exposure to subprime assets. Plaintiffs allege that there were extensive "red flags" that should have given defendants notice of the problems that were brewing in the real estate and credit markets and that defendants ignored these warnings in the pursuit of short term profits and at the expense of the Company's long term viability.

Plaintiffs further allege that certain defendants are liable to the Company for corporate waste for (1) allowing the Company to purchase $2.7 billion in subprime loans from Accredited Home Lenders in March 2007 and from Ameriquest Home Mortgage in September 2007; (2) authorizing and not suspending the Company's share repurchase program in the first quarter of 2007, which allegedly resulted in the Company buying its own shares at "artificially inflated prices;" (3) approving a multi-million dollar payment and benefit package for defendant Charles Prince, whom plaintiffs describe as largely responsible for Citigroup's problems, upon his retirement as Citigroup's CEO in November 2007; and (4) allowing the Company to invest in structured investment vehicles ("SIVs") that were unable to pay off maturing debt.

Pending before the Court is defendants' motion to dismiss the complaint for failure to state a claim under Court of Chancery Rule 12(b)(6) and for failure to properly plead demand futility under Court of Chancery Rule 23.1. The motion to dismiss is denied as to the claim for waste for approval of the November 4, 2007 Prince letter agreement. All other claims are dismissed for failure to adequately plead demand futility pursuant to Rule 23.1.

I. BACKGROUND

A. The Parties

Citigroup is a global financial services company whose businesses provide a broad range of financial services to consumers and businesses. Citigroup was incorporated in Delaware in 1988 and maintains its principal executive offices in New York, New York.

Defendants in this action are current and former directors and officers of Citigroup. The complaint names thirteen members of the Citigroup board of directors on November 9, 2007, when the first of plaintiffs' now-consolidated derivative actions was filed. Plaintiffs allege that a majority of the director defendants were members of the Audit and Risk

Management Committee ("ARM Committee") in 2007 and were considered audit committee financial experts as defined by the Securities and Exchange Commission.

B. Citigroup's Exposure to the Subprime Crisis

Plaintiffs allege that since as early as 2006, defendants have caused and allowed Citigroup to engage in subprime lending that ultimately left the Company exposed to massive losses by late 2007. Beginning in late 2005, house prices, which many believe were artificially inflated by speculation and easily available credit, began to plateau, and then deflate. Adjustable rate mortgages issued earlier in the decade began to reset, leaving many homeowners with significantly increased monthly payments. Defaults and foreclosures increased, and assets backed by income from residential mortgages began to decrease in value. By February 2007, subprime mortgage lenders began filing for bankruptcy and subprime mortgages packaged into securities began experiencing increasing levels of delinquency. In mid-2007, rating agencies downgraded bonds backed by subprime mortgages.

Much of Citigroup's exposure to the subprime lending market arose from its involvement with collateralized debt obligations ("CDOs") — repackaged pools of lower rated securities that Citigroup created by acquiring asset-backed securities, including residential mortgage backed securities ("RMBSs"), and then selling rights to the cash flows from the securities in classes, or tranches, with different levels of risk and return. Included with at least some of the CDOs created by Citigroup was a "liquidity put" — an option that allowed the purchasers of the CDOs to sell them back to Citigroup at original value.

According to plaintiffs, Citigroup's alleged $55 billion subprime exposure was in two areas of the Company's Securities & Banking Unit. The first portion totaled $11.7 billion and included securities tied to subprime loans that were being held until they could be added to debt pools for investors. The second portion included $43 billion of super-senior securities, which are portions of CDOs backed in part by RMBS collateral.

By late 2007, it was apparent that Citigroup faced significant losses on its subprime-related assets.

Plaintiffs also allege that Citigroup was exposed to the subprime mortgage market through its use of SIVs. Banks can create SIVs by borrowing cash (by selling commercial paper) and using the proceeds to purchase loans; in other words, the SIVs sell short term debt and buy longer-term, higher yielding assets. According to plaintiffs, Citigroup's SIVs invested in riskier assets, such as home equity loans, rather than the low-risk assets traditionally used by SIVs.

The problems in the subprime market left Citigroup's SIVs unable to pay their investors. The SIVs held subprime mortgages that had decreased in value, and the normally liquid commercial paper market became illiquid. Because the SIVs could no longer meet their cash needs by attracting new investors, they had to sell assets at allegedly "fire sale" prices.

C. Plaintiffs' Claims

Plaintiffs allege that defendants are liable to the Company for breach of fiduciary duty for failing to adequately oversee and manage Citigroup's exposure to the problems in the subprime mortgage market, even in the face of alleged "red flags" ... As will be more fully explained below, the "red flags" alleged in the eighty-six page Complaint are generally statements from public documents that reflect worsening conditions in the financial markets, including the subprime and credit markets, and the effects those worsening conditions had on market participants, including Citigroup's peers. By way of example only, plaintiffs' "red flags" include the following:

- *May 27, 2005:* Economist Paul Krugman of the *New York Times* said he saw "signs that America's housing market, like the stock market at the end of the last decade, is approaching the final, feverish stages of a speculative bubble."

- *May 2006:* Ameriquest Mortgage, one of the United States' leading wholesale subprime lenders, announced the closing of each of its 229 retail offices and reduction of 3,800 employees.

- *February 12, 2007:* ResMae Mortgage, a subprime lender, filed for bankruptcy. According to *Bloomberg,* in its Chapter 11 filing, ResMae stated that "[t]he subprime mortgage market has recently been crippled and a number of companies stopped originating loans and United States housing sales have slowed and defaults by borrowers have risen."

- *April 18, 2007:* Freddie Mac announced plans to refinance up to $20 billion of loans held by subprime borrowers who would be unable to afford their adjustable-rate mortgages at the reset rate.

- *July 10, 2007:* Standard and Poor's and Moody's downgraded bonds backed by subprime mortgages.

- *August 1, 2007:* Two hedge funds managed by Bear Stearns that invested heavily in subprime mortgages declared bankruptcy.

- *August 9, 2007:* American International Group, one of the largest United States mortgage lenders, warned that mortgage defaults were spreading beyond the subprime sector, with delinquencies becoming more common among borrowers in the category just above subprime.

- *October 18, 2007:* Standard & Poor's cut the credit ratings on $23.35 billion of securities backed by pools of home loans that were offered to borrowers during the first half of the year. The downgrades even hit securities rated AAA, which was the highest of the ten investment-grade ratings and the rating of government debt.

Plaintiffs also allege that the director defendants and certain other defendants are liable to the Company for waste for: (1) allowing the Company to purchase $2.7 billion in subprime loans from Accredited Home Lenders in March 2007 and from Ameriquest Home Mortgage in September 2007; (2) authorizing and not suspending the Company's share repurchase program in the first quarter of 2007, which allegedly resulted in the Company buying its own shares at "artificially inflated prices;" (3) approving a multi-million dollar payment and benefit package for defendant Prince upon his retirement as Citigroup's CEO in November 2007; and (4) allowing the Company to invest in SIVs that were unable to pay off maturing debt.

III. THE MOTION TO DISMISS UNDER RULE 23.1

A. The Legal Standard for Demand Excused

The decision whether to initiate or pursue a lawsuit on behalf of the corporation is generally within the power and responsibility of the board of directors. This follows from the "cardinal precept of the General Corporation Law of the State of Delaware ... that directors, rather than shareholders, manage the business and affairs of the corporation." Accordingly, in order to cause the corporation to pursue litigation, a shareholder must either (1) make a pre-suit demand by presenting the allegations to the corporation's directors, requesting that they bring suit, and showing that they wrongfully refused to do so, or (2) plead facts showing that demand upon the board would have been futile. Where, as here, a plaintiff does not make a pre-suit demand on the board of directors, the complaint must plead with particularity facts showing that a demand on the board would have been futile. The purpose of the demand requirement is not to insulate defendants from liability; rather, the demand requirement and the strict requirements of factual particularity under Rule 23.1 "exist[ ] to preserve the primacy of board decisionmaking regarding legal claims belonging to the corporation."

Under the familiar *Aronson* test, to show demand futility, plaintiffs must provide particularized factual allegations that raise a reasonable doubt that "(1) the directors are disinterested and independent [or] (2) the challenged transaction was otherwise the product of a valid exercise of business judgment." Where, however, plaintiffs complain of board inaction and do not challenge a specific decision of the board, there is no "challenged transaction," and the ordinary *Aronson* analysis does not apply. Instead, to show demand futility where the subject of the derivative suit is not a business decision of the board, a plaintiff must allege particularized facts that "create a reasonable doubt that, as of the time the complaint is filed, the board of directors could have properly exercised its independent and disinterested business judgment in responding to a demand."

In evaluating whether demand is excused the pleadings must comply with "stringent requirements of factual particularity" and set forth "particularized factual statements that are essential to the claim."

Plaintiffs have not alleged that a majority of the board was not independent for purposes of evaluating demand. Rather, as to the claims for waste asserted in Count III, plaintiffs allege that the approval of certain transactions did not constitute a valid exercise of business judgment under the second prong of the *Aronson* test. Plaintiffs allege that demand is futile as to Counts I, II, and IV because the director defendants are not able to exercise disinterested business judgment in responding to a demand because their failure of oversight subjects them to a substantial likelihood of personal liability. According to plaintiffs, the director defendants face a substantial threat of personal liability because their conscious disregard of their duties and lack of proper supervision and oversight caused the Company to be overexposed to risk in the subprime mortgage market.

Demand is not excused solely because the directors would be deciding to sue themselves. Rather, demand will be excused based on a possibility of personal director liability only in the rare case when a plaintiff is able to show director conduct that is "so egregious on its face that board approval cannot meet the test of business judgment, and a substantial likelihood of director liability therefore exists."

B. Demand Futility Regarding Plaintiffs' Fiduciary Duty Claims

Plaintiffs' argument is based on a theory of director liability famously articulated by former-Chancellor Allen in *In re Caremark*. Before *Caremark*, in *Graham v. Allis-Chalmers Manufacturing Company*, the Delaware Supreme Court, in response to a theory that the Allis-Chalmers directors were liable because they should have known about employee violations of federal anti-trust laws, held that "absent cause for suspicion there is no duty upon the directors to install and operate a corporate system of espionage to ferret out wrongdoing which they have no reason to suspect exists." Over thirty years later, in the context of approval of a settlement of a class action, former-Chancellor Allen took the opportunity to revisit the duty to monitor under Delaware law. In *Caremark*, the plaintiffs alleged that the directors were liable because they should have known that certain officers and employees were violating the federal Anti-Referral Payments Law. In analyzing these claims, the Court began, appropriately, by reviewing the duty of care and the protections of the business judgment rule.

With regard to director liability standards, the Court distinguished between (1) "*a board decision* that results in a loss because that decision was ill advised or 'negligent'" and (2) "an *unconsidered failure of the board to act* in circumstances in which due attention would, arguably, have prevented the loss." In the former class of cases, director action is analyzed under the business judgment rule, which prevents judicial second guessing of the decision if the directors employed a rational process and considered all material information reasonably available—a standard measured by concepts of gross negligence. As former-Chancellor Allen explained:

> What should be understood, but may not widely be understood by courts or commentators who are not often required to face such questions, is that compliance with a director's duty of care can never appropriately be judicially determined by reference to *the content of the board decision* that leads to a corporate loss, apart from consideration of the good faith *or* rationality of the process employed. That is, whether a judge or jury considering the matter after the fact, believes a decision substantively wrong, or degrees of wrong extending through "stupid" to "egregious" or "irrational", provides no ground for director liability, so long as the court determines that the process employed was either rational or employed in *a good faith* effort to advance corporate interests. To employ a different rule—one that permitted an "objective" evaluation of the decision—would expose directors to substantive second guessing by ill-equipped judges or juries, which would, in the long-run, be injurious to investor interests. Thus, the business judgment rule is process oriented and informed by a deep respect for all *good faith* board decisions.

In the latter class of cases, where directors are alleged to be liable for a failure to monitor liability creating activities, the *Caremark* Court, in a reassessment of the holding in *Graham*, stated that while directors could be liable for a failure to monitor, "only a sustained or systematic failure of the board to exercise oversight—such as an utter failure to attempt to assure a reasonable information and reporting system exists—will establish the lack of good faith that is a necessary condition to liability."

In *Stone v. Ritter,* the Delaware Supreme Court approved the *Caremark* standard for director oversight liability and made clear that liability was based on the concept of good faith, which the *Stone* Court held was embedded in the fiduciary duty of loyalty and did not constitute a freestanding fiduciary duty that could independently give rise to liability. As the *Stone* Court explained:

> *Caremark* articulates the necessary conditions predicate for director oversight liability: (a) the directors utterly failed to implement any reporting or information system or controls; *or* (b) having implemented such a system or controls, consciously failed to monitor or oversee its operations thus disabling themselves from being informed of risks or problems requiring their attention. In either case, imposition of liability requires a showing that the directors knew that they were not discharging their fiduciary obligations. Where directors fail to act in the face of a known duty to act, thereby demonstrating a conscious disregard for their responsibilities, they breach their duty of loyalty by failing to discharge that fiduciary obligation in good faith.

Thus, to establish oversight liability a plaintiff must show that the directors *knew* they were not discharging their fiduciary obligations or that the directors demonstrated a *conscious* disregard for their responsibilities such as by failing to act in the face of a known duty to act. The test is rooted in concepts of bad faith; indeed, a showing of bad faith is a *necessary condition* to director oversight liability.

1. *Plaintiffs' Caremark Allegations*

Plaintiffs' theory of how the director defendants will face personal liability is a bit of a twist on the traditional *Caremark* claim. In a typical *Caremark* case, plaintiffs argue that the defendants are liable for damages that arise from a failure to properly monitor or oversee employee misconduct or violations of law. For example, in *Caremark* the board allegedly failed to monitor employee actions in violation of the federal Anti-Referral Payments Law; in *Stone,* the directors were charged with a failure of oversight that resulted in liability for the company because of employee violations of the federal Bank Secrecy Act.

In contrast, plaintiffs' *Caremark* claims are based on defendants' alleged failure to properly monitor Citigroup's *business risk,* specifically its exposure to the subprime mortgage market. In their answering brief, plaintiffs allege that the director defendants are personally liable under *Caremark* for failing to "make a good faith attempt to follow the procedures put in place or fail[ing] to assure that adequate and proper corporate information and reporting systems existed that would enable them to be fully informed regarding Citigroup's risk to the subprime mortgage market." Plaintiffs point to so-called "red flags" that should have put defendants on notice of the problems in the subprime mortgage market and further allege that the board should have been especially conscious of these red flags because a majority of the directors (1) served on the Citigroup board during its previous Enron related conduct and (2) were members of the ARM Committee and considered financial experts.

Although these claims are framed by plaintiffs as *Caremark* claims, plaintiffs' theory essentially amounts to a claim that the director defendants should be personally liable to the Company because they failed to fully recognize the risk posed by subprime securities. When one looks past the lofty allegations of duties of oversight and red flags used to dress up these claims, what is left appears to be plaintiff shareholders attempting to hold the director defendants personally liable for making (or allowing to be made) business decisions that, in hindsight, turned out poorly for the Company. Delaware Courts have faced these types of claims many times and have developed doctrines to deal with them—the fiduciary duty of care and the business judgment rule. These doctrines properly focus on the decision-making process rather than on a substantive evaluation of the merits of the decision. This follows from the inadequacy of the Court, due in part to a concept known as hindsight bias, to properly evaluate whether corporate decision-makers made a "right" or "wrong" decision.

The business judgment rule "is a presumption that in making a business decision the directors of a corporation acted on an informed basis, in good faith and in the honest belief that the action taken was in the best interests of the company." The burden is on plaintiffs, the party challenging the directors' decision, to rebut this presumption. Thus, absent an allegation of interestedness or disloyalty to the corporation, the business judgment rule prevents a judge or jury from second guessing director decisions if they were the product of a rational process and the directors availed themselves of all material and reasonably available information. The standard of director liability under the business judgment rule "is predicated upon concepts of gross negligence."

Additionally, Citigroup has adopted a provision in its certificate of incorporation pursuant to 8 *Del. C.* § 102(b)(7) that exculpates directors from personal liability for violations of fiduciary duty, except for, among other things, breaches of the duty of loyalty or actions or omissions not in good faith or that involve intentional misconduct or a knowing violation of law. Because the director defendants are "exculpated from liability for certain conduct, 'then a serious threat of liability may only be found to exist if the plaintiff pleads a *non-exculpated* claim against the directors based on particularized facts.'"

Here, plaintiffs have not alleged that the directors were interested in the transaction and instead root their theory of director personal liability in bad faith.

The Delaware Supreme Court has stated that bad faith conduct may be found where a director "intentionally acts with a purpose other than that of advancing the best interests of the corporation, ... acts with the intent to violate applicable positive law, or ... intentionally fails to act in the face of a known duty to act, demonstrating a conscious disregard for his duties." More recently, the Delaware Supreme Court held that when a plaintiff seeks to show that demand is excused because directors face a substantial likelihood of liability where "directors are exculpated from liability except for claims based on 'fraudulent,' 'illegal' or 'bad faith' conduct, a plaintiff must also plead particularized facts that demonstrate that the directors acted with scienter, *i.e.*, that they had 'actual or constructive knowledge' that their conduct was legally improper." A plaintiff can thus plead bad faith by alleging with particularity that a director *knowingly* violated a fiduciary duty or failed to act in violation of a *known* duty to act, demonstrating a *conscious* disregard for her duties.

Turning now specifically to plaintiffs' *Caremark* claims, one can see a similarity between the standard for assessing oversight liability and the standard for assessing a disinterested director's decision under the duty of care when the company has adopted an exculpatory provision pursuant to § 102(b)(7). In either case, a plaintiff can show that the director defendants will be liable if their acts or omissions constitute bad faith. A plaintiff can show bad faith conduct by, for example, properly alleging particularized facts that show that a director *consciously* disregarded an obligation to be reasonably informed about the business and its risks or *consciously* disregarded the duty to monitor and oversee the business.

The Delaware Supreme Court made clear in *Stone* that directors of Delaware corporations have certain responsibilities to implement and monitor a system of oversight; however, this obligation does not eviscerate the core protections of the business judgment rule— protections designed to allow corporate managers and directors to pursue risky transactions without the specter of being held personally liable if those decisions turn out poorly. Accordingly, the burden required for a plaintiff to rebut the presumption of the business judgment rule by showing gross negligence is a difficult one, and the burden to show bad faith is even higher. Additionally, as former-Chancellor Allen noted in *Caremark,* director liability based on the duty of oversight "is possibly the most difficult theory in corporation law upon which a plaintiff might hope to win a judgment." The presumption of the business judgment rule, the protection of an exculpatory § 102(b)(7) provision, and the difficulty of proving a *Caremark* claim together function to place an extremely high burden on a plaintiff to state a claim for personal director liability for a failure to see the extent of a company's business risk.

To the extent the Court allows shareholder plaintiffs to succeed on a theory that a director is liable for a failure to monitor business risk, the Court risks undermining the well settled policy of Delaware law by inviting Courts to perform a hindsight evaluation of the reasonableness or prudence of directors' business decisions. Risk has been defined as the chance that a return on an investment will be different that expected. The essence of the business judgment of managers and directors is deciding how the company will evaluate the trade-off between risk and return. Businesses—and particularly financial institutions—make returns by taking on risk; a company or investor that is willing to take on more risk can earn a higher return. Thus, in almost any business transaction, the parties go into the deal with the knowledge that, even if they have evaluated the situation correctly, the return could be different than they expected.

It is almost impossible for a court, in hindsight, to determine whether the directors of a company properly evaluated risk and thus made the "right" business decision. In any investment there is a chance that returns will turn out lower than expected, and generally a smaller chance that they will be far lower than expected. When investments turn out poorly, it is possible that the decision-maker evaluated the deal correctly but got "unlucky" in that a huge loss—the probability of which was very small—actually happened. It is also possible that the decision-maker improperly evaluated the risk posed by an investment and that the company suffered large losses as a result.

Business decision-makers must operate in the real world, with imperfect information, limited resources, and an uncertain future. To impose liability on directors for making a "wrong" business decision would cripple their ability to earn returns for investors by taking business risks. Indeed, this kind of judicial second guessing is what the business judgment rule was designed to prevent, and even if a complaint is framed under a *Caremark* theory, this Court will not abandon such bedrock principles of Delaware fiduciary duty law. With these considerations and the difficult standard required to show director oversight liability in mind, I turn to an evaluation of the allegations in the Complaint.

a. The Complaint Does Not Properly Allege Demand Futility for Plaintiffs' Fiduciary Duty Claims

In this case, plaintiffs allege that the defendants are liable for failing to properly monitor the risk that Citigroup faced from subprime securities. While it may be possible for a plaintiff to meet the burden under some set of facts, plaintiffs in this case have failed to state a *Caremark* claim sufficient to excuse demand based on a theory that the directors did not fulfill their oversight obligations by failing to monitor the business risk of the company.

The allegations in the Complaint amount essentially to a claim that Citigroup suffered large losses and that there were certain warning signs that could or should have put defendants on notice of the business risks related to Citigroup's investments in subprime assets. Plaintiffs then conclude that because defendants failed to prevent the Company's losses associated with certain business risks, they must have consciously ignored these warning signs or knowingly failed to monitor the Company's risk in accordance with their fiduciary duties. Such conclusory allegations, however, are not sufficient to state a claim for failure of oversight that would give rise to a substantial likelihood of personal liability, which would require particularized factual allegations demonstrating bad faith by the director defendants.

Plaintiffs do not contest that Citigroup had procedures and controls in place that were designed to monitor risk. Plaintiffs admit that Citigroup established the ARM Committee and in 2004 amended the ARM Committee charter to include the fact that one of the purposes of the ARM Committee was to assist the board in fulfilling its oversight responsibility relating to policy standards and guidelines for risk assessment and risk management.

Plaintiffs nevertheless argue that the director defendants breached their duty of oversight either because the oversight mechanisms were not adequate or because the director defendants did not make a good faith effort to comply with the established oversight procedures. To support this claim, the Complaint alleges numerous facts that plaintiffs argue should have put the director defendants on notice of the impending problems in the subprime mortgage market and Citigroup's exposure thereto. Plaintiffs summarized some of these "red flags" in their answering brief as follows:

- the steady decline of the housing market and the impact the collapsing bubble would have on mortgages and subprime backed securities since as early as 2005;

- December 2005 guidance from the FASB staff—"The FASB staff is aware of loan products whose contractual features may increase the exposure of the originator, holder, investor, guarantor, or servicer to risk of nonpayment or realization.";

- the drastic rise in foreclosure rates starting in 2006;

- several large subprime lenders reporting substantial losses and filing for bankruptcy starting in 2006;

- billions of dollars in losses reported by Citigroup's peers, such as Bear Stearns and Merrill Lynch.

Plaintiffs argue that demand is excused because a majority of the director defendants face a substantial likelihood of personal liability because they were charged with management of Citigroup's risk as members of the ARM Committee and as audit committee financial experts and failed to properly oversee and monitor such risk. As explained above, however, to establish director oversight liability plaintiffs would ultimately have to prove bad faith conduct by the director defendants. Plaintiffs fail to plead any particularized factual allegations that raise a reasonable doubt that the director defendants acted in good faith.

The warning signs alleged by plaintiffs are not evidence that the directors consciously disregarded their duties or otherwise acted in bad faith; at most they evidence that the directors made bad business decisions. Nothing about plaintiffs' "red flags" supports plaintiffs' conclusory allegation that "defendants have not made a good faith attempt to assure that adequate and proper corporate information and reporting systems existed that would enable them to be fully informed regarding Citigroup's risk to the subprime mortgage market." Indeed, plaintiffs' allegations do not even specify how the board's oversight mechanisms were inadequate or how the director defendants knew of these in-adequacies and consciously ignored them. Rather, plaintiffs seem to hope the Court will accept the conclusion that since the Company suffered large losses, and since a properly functioning risk management system would have avoided such losses, the directors must have breached their fiduciary duties in allowing such losses.

The Complaint and plaintiffs' answering brief repeatedly make the conclusory allegation that the defendants have breached their duty of oversight, but nowhere do plaintiffs adequately explain what the director defendants actually did or failed to do that would constitute such a violation. Even while admitting that Citigroup had a risk monitoring system in place, plaintiffs seem to conclude that, because the director defendants (and the ARM Committee members in particular) were charged with monitoring Citigroup's risk, then they must be found liable because Citigroup experienced losses as a result of exposure to the subprime mortgage market. The only factual support plaintiffs provide for this conclusion are "red flags" that actually amount to nothing more than signs of continuing deterioration in the subprime mortgage market. These types of conclusory allegations are exactly the kinds of allegations that do not state a claim for relief under *Caremark*.

To recognize such claims under a theory of director oversight liability would undermine the long established protections of the business judgment rule. It is well established that the mere fact that a company takes on business risk and suffers losses—even catastrophic losses—does not evidence misconduct, and without more, is not a basis for personal director liability. That there were signs in the market that reflected worsening conditions and suggested that conditions may deteriorate even further is not an invitation for this Court to disregard the presumptions of the business judgment rule and conclude that the directors are liable because they did not properly evaluate business risk. What plaintiffs are asking the Court to conclude from the presence of these "red flags" is that the directors failed to see the extent of Citigroup's business risk and therefore made a "wrong" business decision by allowing Citigroup to be exposed to the subprime mortgage market.

This Court's recent decision in *American International Group, Inc. Consolidated Derivative Litigation* demonstrates the stark contrast between the allegations here and allegations that are sufficient to survive a motion to dismiss. In *AIG,* the Court faced a motion to dismiss a complaint that included "well-pled allegations of pervasive, diverse, and substantial financial fraud involving managers at the highest levels of AIG." In concluding that the complaint stated a claim for relief under Rule 12(b)(6), the Court held that the factual allegations in the complaint were sufficient to support an inference that AIG executives running those divisions knew of and approved much of the wrongdoing. The Court reasoned that huge fraudulent schemes were unlikely to be perpetrated without the knowledge of the executive in charge of that division of the company. Unlike the allegations in this case, the defendants in *AIG* allegedly failed to exercise reasonable oversight over pervasive *fraudulent* and *criminal* conduct. Indeed, the Court in *AIG* even stated that the complaint there supported the assertion that top AIG officials were leading a "criminal organization" and that "[t]he diversity, pervasiveness, and materiality of the alleged financial wrongdoing at AIG is extraordinary."

Contrast the *AIG* claims with the claims in this case. Here, plaintiffs argue that the Complaint supports the reasonable conclusion that the director defendants acted in bad faith by failing to see the warning signs of a deterioration in the subprime mortgage market and failing to cause Citigroup to change its investment policy to limit its exposure to the subprime market. Director oversight duties are designed to ensure reasonable reporting and information systems exist that would allow directors to know about and prevent wrongdoing that could cause losses for the Company. There are significant differences between failing to oversee employee fraudulent or criminal conduct and failing to recognize the extent of a Company's business risk. Directors should, indeed must under Delaware law, ensure that reasonable information and reporting systems exist that would put them on notice of fraudulent or criminal conduct within the company. Such oversight programs allow directors to intervene and prevent frauds or other wrongdoing that could expose the company to risk of loss as a result of such conduct. While it may be tempting to say that directors have the same duties to monitor and oversee business risk, imposing *Caremark*-type duties on directors to monitor business risk is fundamentally different. Citigroup was in the business of taking on and managing investment and other business risks. To impose oversight liability on directors for failure to monitor "excessive" risk would involve courts in conducting hindsight evaluations of decisions at the heart of the business judgment of directors. Oversight duties under Delaware law are not designed to subject directors, even expert directors, to *personal liability* for failure to predict the future and to properly evaluate business risk.

Instead of alleging facts that could demonstrate bad faith on the part of the directors, by presenting the Court with the so called "red flags," plaintiffs are inviting the Court to engage in the exact kind of judicial second guessing that is proscribed by the business judgment rule. In any business decision that turns out poorly there will likely be signs that one could point to and argue are evidence that the decision was wrong. Indeed, it is tempting in a case with such staggering losses for one to think that they could have made the "right" decision if they had been in the directors' position. This temptation, however, is one of the reasons for the presumption against an objective review of business decisions by judges, a presumption that is no less applicable when the losses to the Company are large.

C. Demand Futility Allegations Regarding Plaintiffs' Waste Claims

Count III of the Complaint alleges that certain of the defendants are liable for waste for (1) approving the Letter Agreement dated November 4, 2007 between Citigroup and defendant Prince; (2) allowing the Company to purchase over $2.7 billion in subprime loans from Accredited Home Lenders at one of its "fire sales" in March 2007 and from Ameriquest Home Mortgage in September 2007; (3) approving the buyback of over $645 million worth of the Company's shares at artificially inflated prices pursuant to a repurchase program in early 2007; and (4) allowing the Company to invest in SIVs that were unable to pay off maturing debt.

Demand futility is analyzed under *Aronson* when plaintiffs have challenged board action or approval of a transaction. With regard to the claims based on the approval of the Letter Agreement and the repurchase of Citigroup stock, plaintiffs do not argue that a majority of the director defendants were not disinterested and independent. Rather, plaintiffs argue that demand is excused under the second prong of the *Aronson* analysis, which requires that the plaintiffs plead particularized factual allegations that raise a reasonable doubt at to whether "the challenged transaction was otherwise the product of a valid exercise of business judgment."

Delaware law provides stringent requirements for a plaintiff to state a claim for corporate waste, and to excuse demand on grounds of waste the Complaint must allege particularized facts that lead to a reasonable inference that the director defendants authorized "an exchange that is so one sided that no business person of ordinary, sound judgment could conclude that the corporation has received adequate consideration." The test to show corporate waste is difficult for any plaintiff to meet; indeed, "[t]o prevail on a waste claim ... the plaintiff must overcome the general presumption of good faith by showing that the board's decision was so egregious or irrational that it could not have been based on a valid assessment of the corporation's best interests."

1. *Approval of the Stock Repurchase Program*

Plaintiffs' claim for waste for the board's approval of the stock repurchase program falls far short of satisfying the standard for demand futility. Plaintiffs allege that "in spite of its prior buybacks below $50 per share and in spite of the Company's expanding losses and declining stock price, Citigroup repurchased 12.1 million shares during the first quarter of 2007 at an average price of $53.37." Plaintiffs then claim that at the time the buyback of Citigroup stock was halted, the stock was trading at $46 per share. Plaintiffs conclude that the director defendants "authorized and did not suspend the Company's share repurchase program, which resulted in the Company's buying back over $645 million worth of the Company's shares at artificially inflated prices."

Specifically, plaintiffs argue the following:

> As set forth in the Complaint, the Director Defendants recklessly failed to consider and account for the subprime lending crisis, the Company's exposure to falling CDO values by virtue of its liquidity puts, and the collective impact on the Company's billions in warehoused subprime loans. Consequently, the Director Defendants are not entitled to the presumption of business judgment and are liable for waste for approving the buyback of over $645 million worth of the Company's shares at artificially inflated prices pursuant to the repurchase program. Under the circumstances, the repurchase program should have been suspended, and would have saved the Company hundreds of millions of dollars. The magnitude of the Director Defendants' utter failure to properly inform themselves of the

Company's dire straits has only been highlighted by the Company's recent historically low share prices.

To say the least, this argument demonstrates that the Complaint utterly fails to state a claim for waste for the board's approval of the stock repurchase. Plaintiffs seem to completely ignore the standard governing corporate waste under Delaware law—a standard that requires that plaintiffs plead facts overcoming the presumption of good faith by showing "an exchange that is so one sided that no business person of ordinary, sound judgment could conclude that the corporation has received adequate consideration." Plaintiffs attempted to meet this standard by alleging that the director defendants approved a repurchase of Citigroup stock *at the market price.* Other than a conclusory allegation, plaintiffs have alleged nothing that would explain how buying stock at the market price—the price at which presumably ordinary and rational businesspeople were trading the stock—could possibly be so one sided that no reasonable and ordinary business person would consider it adequate consideration. Again, plaintiffs merely allege "red flags" and then conclude that the board is liable for waste because Citigroup repurchased its stock before the stock dropped in price as a result of Citigroup's losses from exposure to the subprime market. Accordingly, plaintiffs have not adequately alleged demand futility as to this claim pursuant to Rule 23.1.

2. *Approval of the Letter Agreement*

Plaintiffs allege that the board's approval of the November 4, 2007 letter agreement constituted corporate waste. Because approval of the letter was board action, demand is evaluated under the *Aronson* standard. Plaintiffs claim that demand is excused under the second prong of *Aronson* because the particularized factual allegations in the Complaint raise a reasonable doubt as to whether the approval was "the product of a valid exercise of business judgment."

The directors of a Delaware corporation have the authority and broad discretion to make executive compensation decisions. The standard under which the Court evaluates a waste claim is whether there was "an exchange of corporate assets for consideration so disproportionately small as to lie beyond the range at which any reasonable person might be willing to trade." It is also well settled in our law, however, that the discretion of directors in setting executive compensation is not unlimited. Indeed, the Delaware Supreme Court was clear when it stated that "there is an outer limit" to the board's discretion to set executive compensation, "at which point a decision of the directors on executive compensation is so disproportionately large as to be unconscionable and constitute waste."

According to plaintiffs' allegations, the November 4, 2007 letter agreement provides that Prince will receive $68 million upon his departure from Citigroup, including bonus, salary, and accumulated stockholdings. Additionally, the letter agreement provides that Prince will receive from Citigroup an office, an administrative assistant, and a car and driver for the lesser of five years or until he commences full time employment with another employer. Plaintiffs allege that this compensation package constituted waste and met the "so one sided" standard because, in part, the Company paid the multi-million dollar compensation package to a departing CEO whose failures as CEO were allegedly responsible, in part, for billions of dollars of losses at Citigroup. In exchange for the multi-million dollar benefits and perquisites package provided for in the letter agreement, the letter agreement contemplated that Prince would sign a non-compete agreement, a non-disparagement agreement, a non-solicitation agreement, and a release of claims against the Company. Even considering the text of the letter agreement, I am left with very little information regarding (1) how much additional compensation Prince actually received as a result of the letter agreement and (2) the real value, if any, of the various promises given by Prince. Without more information and taking, as I am required, plaintiffs' well pleaded allegations as true, there is a reasonable doubt as to whether the letter agreement meets the admittedly stringent "so one sided" standard or whether the letter agreement awarded compensation that is beyond the "outer limit" described by the Delaware Supreme Court. Accordingly, the Complaint has adequately alleged, pursuant to Rule 23.1, that demand is excused with regard to the waste claim based on the board's approval of Prince's compensation under the letter agreement.

D. The Motion to Dismiss under Rule 12(b)(6)

The standard for pleading demand futility under Rule 23.1 is more stringent than the standard under Rule 12(b)(6), and "a complaint that survives a motion to dismiss pursuant to Rule 23.1 will also survive a 12(b)(6) motion to dismiss, assuming that it otherwise contains sufficient facts to state a cognizable claim." Accordingly, for the same reasons stated in the demand futility analysis, the Complaint contains well-pleaded factual allegations regarding the claim for waste for the approval of the Prince letter agreement that make it impossible for me to conclude with reasonable certainty that the plaintiff could prevail on no set of facts that could be reasonably inferred from the allegations in the Complaint.

IV. CONCLUSION

Citigroup has suffered staggering losses, in part, as a result of the recent problems in the United States economy, particularly those in the subprime mortgage market. It is understandable that investors, and others, want to find someone to hold responsible for these losses, and it is often difficult to distinguish between a desire to blame *someone* and a desire to force those responsible to account for their wrongdoing. Our law, fortunately, provides guidance for precisely these situations in the form of doctrines governing the duties owed by officers and directors of Delaware corporations. This law has been refined over hundreds of years, which no doubt included many crises, and we must not let our desire to blame someone for our losses make us lose sight of the purpose of our law. Ultimately, the discretion granted directors and managers allows them to maximize shareholder value in the long term by taking risks without the debilitating fear that they will be held personally liable if the company experiences losses. This doctrine also means, however, that when the company suffers losses, shareholders may not be able to hold the directors personally liable.

For the foregoing reasons, the motion to dismiss or stay in favor of the New York Action is denied. Defendants' motion to dismiss is denied as to the claim in Count III of the Complaint for waste for approval of the November 4, 2007 Prince letter agreement. All other claims in the complaint are dismissed for failure to adequately plead demand futility pursuant to Court of Chancery Rule 23.1.

An Order has been entered consistent with this Opinion.

Notes

(1) In the actual case, Citigroup filed a motion to dismiss or stay the action in Delaware state court in favor of an action pending in New York Federal Court based on the concept of *forum non conveniens*. In deciding to dismiss Citigroup's motion, the Court considered the following six factors:

  • the applicability of Delaware law in the action;

- the relative ease of access to proof;

- the availability of compulsory process for witnesses;

- the pendency or non-pendency of any similar actions in other jurisdictions;

- the possibility of a need to view the premises; and

- all other practical considerations which would serve to make the trial easy, expeditious and inexpensive.

The court ruled that the action was proper in Delaware. Consider each of the afore-mentioned factors and then articulate why the court denied Citigroup's motion.

(2) If Citigroup was incorporated in Delaware, why do you think it wanted to litigate in New York?

(3) Why do you think that Citigroup increased its subprime mortgage portfolio?

(4) In order to get around the § 102(b)(7) limitation of liability provision, what did the shareholders need to prove?

E. Financial Crisis Board Exercise

Now that you have a comprehensive understanding of the financial crisis, its causes, and its affects as well as the legal rules that govern directorial liability for making decisions or failing to act, consider the following exercise.

In the Fall of 1998, the board of Southern California Bank retained you as legal counsel to assist in navigating the details of the promulgation of its next five-year strategic plan. Southern California's board is comprised of fifteen individuals. All of the board members share the same monolithic background in that they are all white males who are Ivy League educated MBA's and JD's.

For the past eight years since 1992, Southern California Bank has experienced minimal growth and investor confidence is declining. Historically, Southern California has always been a conservative bank. For example, its lending division has tended to shy away from higher yielding risky loans and instead has focused primarily on lower risk, lower return loans such as student loans and loans for automobile leases. As a result of this conservative approach, Southern California Bank has continued to remain a strong regional bank, but has been unable to compete with much larger national banks. Because of increasing share-holder hostility towards Southern California's historically conservative approach, there is growing sentiment among the shareholders that change is necessary. As a result, there are grumblings that the controlling shareholders are considering replacing the current board with new directors who have a stronger visionary perspective and who are willing to take advantage of current market opportunities.

Based on these grumblings, the board is now considering adjusting its business mix by accumulating higher-yielding, but riskier, loans—most notably, subprime mortgage loans—in its portfolio of assets. Southern California's primary motivation for this change is attributable to the fact that several of the national banks dealing in subprime loans have substantially increased revenue and profit. Since Southern California Bank has no expertise in the subprime market, it is considering the acquisition of First Franklin Financial, an issuer of subprime mortgages. However prior to making this determination, the board held a lengthy meeting to discuss the issue and thereafter commissioned two separate consulting firms, Wolverine Consulting, LLC and Buckeye Consulting, LLC, to issue a report regarding the viability of an acquisition of First Franklin.

Wolverine's report concluded that an acquisition of First Franklin would result in a substantial windfall. Specifically, it provided that given the current market conditions, within two years, the daily average balance of Southern California Bank's residential real estate loans will more than double, climbing from $15 billion to $30 billion. The report further concluded that it is imperative that Southern California enter the subprime market because "these loans are readily saleable to third parties at a premium over what is paid and also have a much greater lifetime value when held on the balance sheet." Finally, the report concluded that an acquisition of First Financial would resolve any shareholder dissension.

In contrast, Buckeye's report forecast that an acquisition of First Franklin would not hold up because it was far too risky. Moreover, Buckeye opined that the economy was bound to slow down and that Southern California Bank would suffer a major cash crunch if it acquired First Franklin. In addition, Buckeye's report speculated that the primary presumption that real estate will continue to increase in value is fundamental flawed and that such presumption will lead to a historic market collapse. Buckeye's report also cautioned that many of First Franklin Financial's lending practices seemed to prey on unsuspecting minority borrowers. Buckeye further concluded that an acquisition of First Franklin would require a substantial level of monitoring in order to thoroughly explore whether its practices were predatory.

You are counsel to Southern California Bank's board. Help the board navigate this morass of issues. In your response, be sure to analyze the issues as discussed in class. Your answers to the following questions will not necessarily be evaluated on your ultimate conclusions but on recognition of the issues and sub issues presented, and most importantly, your analysis.

(1) How would you advise Southern California Bank about whether or not to acquire First Franklin Financial? You must make an affirmative decision about whether to engage or pass on the opportunity. In answering this question, be sure to explain whether the board will face any liability for breaches of the duty of care based on your planned course of action. Also, pay attention to any other lurking issues that might present issues of liability.

(2) Would you address the lack of diversity on Southern California's board? In answering this question, be sure to explain why you would or would not address the issue. Make sure that you thoroughly detail any difficulties in your chosen action, as well as any legal or moral issues that may be implicated.

Chapter Six

Corporate Board Diversity

A. Homogeneity in America's Corporate Boardrooms

In chapter five we provided a comprehensive breakdown of how the financial crisis began, and more importantly, how the crisis placed the United States and the world in financial peril. We also provided you with the identities of several corporations that were the primary actors in facilitating America's financial collapse. In this chapter, we move into a discussion about how the composition of American's corporate boardrooms is grossly disproportionate to the population of the people in the country. You should understand that the financial crisis burst America's housing bubble, stripped away the equity that millions of Americans had accumulated in their homes via the foreclosure process, substantially limited the amount of available credit as well as heightened credit lending restrictions, lessened the number of available jobs, forced states to cut spending on line items such as education which reduced the overall quality and increased the cost of education, and forced states to eliminate government programs and to lay off state employees who provided services that benefited state residents. After considering the damage inflicted by the financial market crisis of 2008, what role did AIG, Bear Stearns, Countrywide Financial and Lehman Brothers play in the crisis?

Now, to put this into context: In the following images you will be presented with individual pictures and names of the board members who sat on the boards of a couple of the companies that were the primary contributors to the financial crisis. After reviewing the pictures that follow, consider the questions below:

(1) What do these images tell you about America's boardrooms during the financial crisis?

(2) Do you think that these individuals were highly experienced and educated? If so, what about the boardroom setting and the composition led each of these companies into financial ruin?

(3) What is missing from the composition of these boards?

Figure 6.1 AIG Board of Directors 2003

M. Bernard Aidinoff

Ellen V. Futter

Richard C. Holbrooke

Pei-Yuan Chia

Maurice R. Greenberg

Howard I. Smith

Marshall A. Cohen

Carla A. Hills

Martin J. Sullivan

Martin S. Feldstein

Frank J. Hoenemeyer

Edmund S.W. Tse

Jay S. Wintrob

Frank G. Wisner

Frank G. Zarb

Figure 6.2 Countrywide Board of Directors 2001

Angelo R. Mozilo, Chairman

Michael E. Dougherty

Stanford L. Kurland

Jeffrey M. Cunningham

Ben M. Enis, Ph.D.

Oscar P. Robertson

Robert J. Donato

Edwin Heller

Harley W. Snyder

B. Gender, Testosterone, and the Financial Crisis

More recently, a growing body of literature, some of which we will detail below, questions whether the financial crisis could have been prevented with greater corporate boardroom diversity. In thinking about this proposition, consider the following article.

Would Women Leaders Have Prevented the Global Financial Crisis?: Implications for Teaching About Gender, Behavior and Economics

Julie A. Nelson
Professor and Chair, Department of Economics
University of Massachusetts Boston
September 14, 2012

Introduction

In the aftermath of the crisis that shook United States and global financial markets in the fall of 2008, speculation arose about whether it may have been caused, in some sense, by masculinity run amuck. Referring to the bankruptcy of Lehman Brothers investment bank, some asked "whether we would be in the same mess today if Lehman Brothers had been Lehman Sisters" (Kristof 2009; Morris 2009; Lagarde 2010). In Iceland, women were called in to replace high profile male bank leaders and institute a "new culture" (O'Connor 2008). *Time* magazine, having run a laudatory cover featuring Federal Reserve and government economists Alan Greenspan, Larry Summers, and Robert Rubin in February 1999, followed in May 2010 with a similarly-posed cover featuring the regulators Elizabeth Warren, Sheila Blair, and Mary Schapiro. These, *Time* said, were "The women charged with cleaning up the mess."

Would having more women in leadership positions in finance and its regulation naturally lead to a kinder, gentler, and tidier economy? It leads back into long-running debates about the "sameness" or "difference" of the sexes, now with an emphasis on "difference."

This essay argues that there is a gender angle to the financial crisis, but that it is not about "differences" in traits that men and women "bring with them" to their jobs. The first part of this essay discusses how the "difference" view has recently resurged within economics, bolstered by simplistic binary thinking, low quality behavioral research, and media hype. As a case in point, the literature on sex differences in risk aversion will be discussed. Better quality behavioral and neuroscientific research, including important recent research on stereotyping, however, points to a more sophisticated and nuanced understanding. Teaching the skill of noticing both difference and similarity, this essay argues, is essential for developing critical thinking.

The second part of this essay identifies the overwhelmingly more important gender dimension of the financial crisis: The habit of thinking (at least in Western, Post-Enlightenment cultures) of market commerce and finance as stereotypically masculine in nature. Commentators from the left and right alike tend to regard capitalism as characterized in some intrinsic and unavoidable way by masculine-stereotyped qualities such as risk-taking and self-interest, to the exclusion of feminine-stereotyped qualities. This mental image severely distorts what we believe we can and should expect from institutions and leaders (of either sex) in finance, especially in regard to their social and ethical responsibilities. While this false image is largely accepted even by many with ostensibly progressive and feminist sensibilities, it actually helps create and reinforce both cowboy capitalism and sexist oppression. Insights from feminist economics about the biased perceptions underlying the image of the economic "machine" should inform teaching about economies across the board.

Behavioral Research—Friend or Foe?

The fields of behavioral economics (which looks at how people actually make decisions rather than at how a hypothetical "rational actor" would make them) and neuroeconomics (which uses brain scans and such in the study of decision-making), are currently in vogue within (or at least at the close margins of) the economics profession. Such a focus on psychological research has also encouraged a resurgence of "essentialist" views of human sexual difference: Any detectable difference in behavior or brain organization is, once again, being interpreted by some as a hard-and-fast explanation for—and rationalization of—occupational segregation, social hierarchy, and economic inequality.

"Lehman Sisters"

The popular arguments in favor of a "Lehman Sisters" viewpoint are based on the belief that there are fundamental and sizeable differences between males and females in their attitudes towards finance. "Several gender studies have pointed out that women behave and manage differently from men. They tend to be more risk-averse and to focus more on a long-term perspective," writes one French management professor Michel Ferrary (Ferrary 2009), for example. Another management consultant reports that many male executives "feel, from experience, that women tend to be more risk-averse," and that women are "more willing to defend an issue of governance or ethics" (Wittenberg-Cox 2009). Christine Lagarde, France's minister for the economy, industry and employment, has written how "as a woman I am, perhaps, more keenly aware of the damage that the crisis has done" (Lagarde 2010).

Various kinds of evidence suggest that women are more risk-averse (that is, cautious about taking gambles), less prone to overconfidence, less competitive, more sensitive to losses, and more long term-oriented than men. Ferrary, for example, bases his conclusion on a study of the relation of the gender diversity of boards to corporate performance (Ferrary 2009). Myriad researchers have studied gender and risk aversion, or gender and pro-social behavior, by presenting experimental subjects with hypothetical situations or choices concerning lotteries (see reviews in Croson and Gneezy 2009; Nelson 2012), usually in the context of modern economies in the Global North.

While it is sometimes mentioned that such observed differences could be due to differences in socialization (e.g., girls being raised to be less competitive) or created by positional inequalities (e.g., people in weaker positions may have good reason to be more sensitive to losses), biological and evolutionary explanations seem to be currently in vogue. It has been suggested that the levels of testosterone among men working on financial trading floors is related to the ability to make profitable decisions (Coates and Herbert 2008). A large number of popular books (see review in Fine 2010) have argued that men and women are "hard-wired" differently, through the influence, for example, of genetic differences and prenatal hormones. Assertions such as Simon Baron-Cohen's (2003) that men being natural "systematizers" while women are natural "empathizers" have gained audience. The "difference" perspective has influenced the business management literature, where a cooperative and relational approach has been associated with women (Schumpeter 2009). At the extreme, "difference" advocates portray gender differences as large, "Men are from Mars, Women are from Venus" (Gray 1993) dichotomous gulfs between the sexes.

Responses

Feminist writers in the 1970s and 1980s worked hard to discredit biological "proofs" of women's inferiority, and to reveal how an inclination to look for sex "differences" had biased previous research. Many feminists perhaps tend to think of that battle as already having been won. With new generations of readers and a new resurgence of "difference" literature, however, active response is again necessary.

Feminist writers have taken on this task. A few of the major critiques of the essentialist literature—both old and new—may be noted as follows:

- Much of the research on which broad generalizations have been based does not merit confidence. Many studies were based on small samples, offered conclusions and interpretations that were not justified by the data, and/or have since been discredited by later research.

- Studies which find sex differences tend to be considered sexy and publishable, while those that do not are not. This "file drawer effect" will tend to skew reporting towards "difference."

- Meta-analysis (Byrnes, Miller et al. 1999; Hyde 2005) shows that when differences in the behavior of adult men and women have been found, they are not uncommonly quite small. Rather than different planets, it seems that "Men are from North Dakota, Women are from South Dakota" (as Dindia 2006, has quipped).

- Many of the results seem to be highly dependent on context, varying quite widely over types of situations encountered or the nationality or cultural background of the subjects, further shedding doubt on essentialist views. A number of sociologists have pointed out how inequalities in power and access to resources can create the "differences" that are incorrectly attributed to sex (Acker 1990; Kimmel 2000).

- The links from hormones or brain organization to behavior are far from well-established, as the more serious researchers acknowledge. The brain's "plasticity" (Eliot 2009), or responsiveness to experience, makes it particularly hard to attribute behaviors to "nature" alone. The finding of structural differences in the brain also does not—contrary to the popular "difference" literature—point unambiguously to differences in function or ability (Fine 2010, Ch. 13).

None of the abovementioned critics of the "difference" literature claim that males and females are biologically and neurologically identical, only that the essentialist "difference" claims are far overblown.

Economists and the Case of Risk-Aversion

The economics literature on gender and risk-aversion has, unfortunately, been characterized by a "difference" emphasis and a consequent frequent display of some or all of the flaws just mentioned.

But what does the statement that "women are more risk averse than men" actually mean, especially in relation to the question of whether women would "bring something different" to positions of power in the finance industry? It communicates the idea that risk aversion is an intrinsic sex-linked trait: Women are associated with greater risk-aversion, and risk-aversion is in turn equated with womanliness. The presumption is that were a woman or girl not risk averse, she would somehow be denying her own female nature. Many studies hypothesize evolutionary explanations for female risk aversion (e.g., Olsen and Cox 2001; Cross, Copping et al. 2011).

Such an interpretation, however, does not, in fact, correspond at all to any of the research on which the statement is based, due to the empirical importance of intra-sex variability. There is a world of difference between the statements "In this study, women's mean score on the measure of risk-taking is lower than men's" and "women are more risk averse than men." Not all women act the same way, nor do all men. It is rather amazing that in economics and finance—disciplines that pride themselves on their quantitative savvy—that a very basic quantitative question, "How different?" is so rarely asked. A statistically significant finding of "gender difference" (in means) is trumpeted as a "research result," with little or no attention to the substantive size or importance of the difference, or the degree of overlap of the distributions. While favoring of statistical over substantive significance is a common bad habit of economists (Ziliak and McCloskey 2004), it is particularly noticeable in this case because of its divergence from the practice followed in much of the literature on sex differences in psychology (e.g., Byrnes, Miller et al. 1999; Wilkinson and Task Force on Statistical Inference 1999; Hyde 2005; Cross, Copping et al. 2011), in which summary measures of substantive size are reported. Croson and Gneezy's (2009) survey of the sex differences literature for economists, in sharp contrast, states only whether statistically significant differences were or were not found.

A companion paper to this one (Nelson 2012) surveys the economics and finance literature on gender and risk aversion. One finds that not only is information on the substantive size of differences not generally given, but (1) the sorts of statistical information that would allow the reader to analyze the substantive size of the differences is often not presented and (2) the existing literature on sex differences is often mis-cited or selectively cited. In addition, (3) findings of "no sex difference" are systematically underplayed or ignored, and (4) findings that women sometimes act, on average, in a statistically significantly less risk-averse way than men may be explained away in a highly contrived manner. A reasonable conclusion is that the habit in much of economics and finance is to look for difference, and make the empirical results conform to societal preconceptions.

Why might this be? One obvious reason may be that "difference" findings tend to serve the interests of those who want to sustain gender inequalities in economic power (Acker 1990; Barnett and Rivers 2004). Findings that women financial managers have a different "management style" could be used to exclude women from certain realms—for example, to limit women to areas of finance where they are assigned do the hard, unappreciated, and relatively low-paid work of "cleaning up the mess" in bad times, and where they never get the chance to prove that their ability to do more the interesting, creative, and highly compensated work of leading risk-taking organizations in good times (Hall-Taylor 1997; Corrigan 2009; Ibarra, Gratton et al. 2009). The biased presentation of results also bolsters the image of economics as a masculine realm, which might be important for the self-identification of some economists.

In this essay, though, I would like to explore a complementary explanation to that of the preservation of power, which is that a "difference" belief also capitalizes on certain of our cognitive weaknesses. Because this essay is directed towards a scholarly audience, who presumably should be especially concerned with the creation and dissemination of knowledge, and because many of us teach students who may demonstrate these cognitive biases in spades, I will concentrate here on the cognitive aspect.

The Temptations of Simplicity

While behavioral research that exaggerates sex "difference" should be looked on with extreme skepticism by feminist economists, behavioral research on cognitive schema, stereotypes, and confirmation bias are very relevant to examining this tendency towards exaggeration. Cognitive schema are simple mental groupings we use to organize our perceptions. Stereotyping is a process by which individuals are mentally associated with such simple groups. Confirmation bias refers to our human tendency to only take in information that confirms our pre-existing beliefs. The pervasive tendency to draw contrasts between male and female is itself a symptom—researched by some behavioral scientists—of our embodied, evolved, often helpful but sometimes also dysfunctional cognitive habits. The habit of grouping stimuli into categories—the simpler the better—saves on cognitive processing effort. As psychologists use the term, cognitive schemas are the way in which we "organize incoming information and integrate it—through no conscious act of will—into clusters" (Most, Sorber et al. 2007, 287). Stimuli that correspond to an existing schema can be more rapidly processed than stimuli that must be individually sorted and assimilated piece by piece. Research indicates that gender difference is among the organizing principles we use to categorize what we see. We also tend to have a bias towards believing that what is easy is true (Bennett 2010), and what is easier than a simple binary or polar contrast? Binaries such as male/female or up/down (Lakoff and Johnson 1980) seem to be important building blocks for how we perceive, think, and communicate. Because so much of this processing is unconscious, we may not be at all aware of how much influence the attraction to simple binaries has on our perceptions and beliefs.

Thought habits including the overuse of simple binaries and stereotypes can make us stupid. When I teach my undergraduate class on gender and economics, I bring this point home to my students by asking them this decades-old riddle:

A man and his son are in a car accident. The father is killed instantly, and the boy is taken by ambulance to the nearest emergency room. The emergency room surgeon, however, says "I can't operate on him—he's my son!"

How can you explain this?

Being that I teach in Massachusetts where same-sex marriage is now legal, I also tell the students that the answer is not that the boy is being raised by a gay couple. Generally about a third of my students—after discussing the movement of women into non-traditional occupations—hand in answers saying that the surgeon is the boy's stepfather, or the man in the car was the boy's priest, or that the student is simply stumped. Upon hearing the straightforward answer, these students are often incredulous—hitting their foreheads or looking shocked—at their own lack of insight. The word "surgeon" fits so comfortably into the "male" cognitive schema that logical thought is actually blocked.

Beyond Simplicity

Perceptions of gender variation also gravitate towards another simple binary: sameness/difference. For a while, in the 1970s and 1980s, "sameness" was the rage, with much talk of androgyny and a requisite belief, among some feminists, that gender was totally a social construction—that is, that is was entirely the result of "nurture" and power differentials, with no basis in "nature." With "difference" now resurging, observable differences in "nature" such as sex-specific chromosomal and hormonal phenomena are being extrapolated into Mars-versus-Venus disjunctive categories.

Is there no middle ground? Unfortunately, evidence from my own class indicates that—even after explicit coaching in examining the middle ground—the simplistic sameness/difference binary often maintains a great deal of cognitive power. I assigned reading that argues that males and females are both somewhat different from each other and also largely similar to each other. On a true/false quiz I then gave my students, the following were among the questions:

1. Eliot's main point is that men and women are biologically very different from each other. True/False?

2. Eliot's main point is that men and women are really the same. True/False?

In spite of all the students having heard the same lecture, 31% answered that the first statement was true while the second was false, and 23% answered that the first was false while the second was true. Less than half—only 42%—were able to buck dualistic thinking and answer, appropriately, that Eliot made neither argument. Why is it so hard to communicate the simple idea that males and females are both somewhat different from each other and also largely similar to each other?

That is, in a simple world, men and women would be either completely identical or totally different/disjunctive. But in the complex world we live in, the question is not so simple.

Examining and quantifying the degrees of distinctness and alikeness is not, in fact, difficult to do, and could be easily added to economic studies. In Beckmann and Menkoff's "Will Women be Women?" article, for example, one of biggest statistically significant sex differences found is in what the authors refer to as "tournament behavior" among Italian male and female fund managers (2008, 379). The use of professional fund managers as subjects is an improvement over some of the other studies in the literature, in regard to the question of gender and Wall Street, since men and women who self-select into financial occupations may have different characteristics than the general undergraduate student populations who are the subject of many other studies. But is the authors' affirmative answer to their own question actually justified? When asked whether, having a portfolio which has outperformed a benchmark up to that point, the fund manager would "decrease the relative risk level to lock in the performance" 82% of the Italian women managers in this study said they would do so, as compared to 57% of the Italian male managers. 18% of the women managers and 39% of the male managers said they would "not change," while none of the women and 5% of the men said they would "increase risk."

Clearly, in this example, men and women are both similar and different. If avoiding risk is thought of as "womanly," it seems that 57% of Beckmann and Menkoff's male managers "are women." On the other hand, if not decreasing risk is "manly," then 18% of the women managers apparently "are men." In response to the authors' question "Will Women be Women?" the answer actually seems to be that a number of women "are not," while a majority of men "are." Such analysis should shed some doubt on idea that risk-aversion is a sex-linked trait.

Gender and the Social Construction of Wall Street

A more gender-diverse financial industry would be different from the current one, but not because women "bring something different" with them, that men do not possess, when they enter it. As we have just seen many women act "like men" and vice versa, so that one cannot reliably predict behavior from sex. Rather, the important point is that the perspective of any sort of cultural outsider begins to make apparent the particularity of behaviors and values otherwise mistaken as natural, universal, and appropriate within any cultural in-group.

Stereotypes, Masculinity, and Finance

Commerce, in general, has been imagined—at least in the West, and at least since Victorian times—as "masculine," in contrast to the "feminine" sphere of home and family. This cultural ascription of masculinity to the market sphere both makes it seem that only men are the naturally more appropriate participants (thus rationalizing the sexist exclusion of women from positions of financial power), and also makes it seem that only masculine-stereotyped behaviors, values, and skills are natural and appropriate. Participants in commerce are, in particular, assumed to engage in risk-taking and competitive behaviors, to be motivated by individual self-interest, to not pay much attention to social relationships, and to need technical competence to be successful. Note how these are distinctly not the same behaviors and values assumed for women and caring labor, as illustrated in Table

6.1. When caring for family members or working in areas of industry such as child care or nursing, a person is often assumed to be careful, protective, cooperative and altruistic, to express interpersonal warmth, and to possess any requisite abilities simply as part of their (her) "nature." Notice that this dualistic view is just another list of (overly-) simple binaries.

Table 6.1

Masculine Stereotypes and Finance	Feminine Stereotypes and Caring Labor
risk-taking	careful, protective
Competitive	Cooperative
self-interested	Altruistic
Impersonal	Warm
mastery, competence	"naturally" arising

Among areas of commerce, the financial industry seems to have taken the exaggeration of "masculinity" to an extreme. Linda MacDowell in a 1990s study of the City of London (the UK's equivalent to the US's Wall Street) described it as "riven by sexualized and gendered scripts" (McDowell 2010, 652). She described masculine iconic figures of upper class patriarchs and traders, the latter being "embodied as the quintessence of masculine energy … The exuberance, outrageous energy and machismo of traders matched the speed of trading and dealing: shouting, sweating, and screaming …" (McDowell 2010, 653). To these icons we might add the more recent rise of the technocratic masculinity of the mathematical modeler absorbed in complex calculations for valuing financial derivatives (de Goede 2004, 207). Popular writings, social science studies, and legal cases have brought to light unusually the macho and sexualized culture of Wall Street, highlighting virulent sexual harassment and entertainment of clients with prostitutes. Time magazine's choice of the word "sheriffs" to describe Wall Street regulators is an oblique reference to the wild, reckless, undisciplined "cowboy" image of US finance.

The Invention of the Masculine "Nature" of Commerce

This masculine-sex-typed image of what finance is about severely distorts what we believe we can and should expect from its institutions and leaders. Note that while the home is imagined as the realm of virtue and duty, in the masculine image of the marketplace social and ethical responsibilities have no place. Right-leaning commentators will appeal to the free market myth to justify this exclusion: The economy is imagined to be an engine fueled by the energy of self-interest, which when guided by the "invisible hand" of market competition serves the social good. Left-leaning commentators likewise accept the image of the mechanical, self-interest-driven capitalist economy, but decry instead of praise its effects. Both the right and left tend to be dismissive of appeals for corporate responsibility (or any ideas of corporate vision that go beyond profit maximization) because these go against what they believe to be the essential "nature" of market systems. Many feminists have accepted this image of commerce as well. Particularly among feminists in sociology or the humanities, images of a soulless capitalism inherently in league with patriarchy have been popular (e.g., Acker 1990; Orr 2009).

But what if this image of the "nature" of market economies is wrong? The masculine image of economies was, in fact, invented by economists. Historically, it in part goes back to the 18th century work of Adam Smith (Smith 1776 [2001]). Although Smith was a much more complex thinker than his modern legacy would suggest, one part of his thought has had a profound impact on how we think about economics: Smith suggested that economies could be seen as functioning like giant machines, in which the "invisible hand" of markets magically channels the energy of individual self-interest into service of the social good. Smith laid the groundwork for thinking about economies in mechanical, a-social, self-interest-oriented terms.

But the full-fledged notion of "economic man" did not really get developed until the 19th century, when John Stuart Mill (1836) attempted to lay the groundwork for a discipline of economics that would be both fully scientific and carefully demarcated from other endeavors. Mill explicitly peeled off many dimensions of human experience: human bodies were considered to be the topic of the natural sciences; conscience and duty were consigned by Mill to the realm of ethics; life in society was given its own discipline. What was left for economics to deal with was "man [sic] solely as a being who desires to possess wealth, and who is capable of judging of the comparative efficacy of means for obtaining that end" (38). This added an assumption of rationality to the idea of "economic man" as a-social and self-interested.

Why did Mill believe that he had to separate out a very thin slice of human life for analysis by each of the various fields? He believed that this was required by the nature of science. Significantly, his model for science was geometry, and its methodology of reasoning from abstract principles. Mill, to his credit, argued that no economist would ever be "so absurd as to suppose that mankind" is really described by only the parts of human nature selected for study in economics (38). Unfortunately, however, what remained and flourished in later economic thought was not Mill's modesty concerning the ad hoc premises and limited applicability of the geometry-like discipline he proposed, but rather his idea that economics must base itself on an image of autonomous, rational, self-interested beings in order to be "scientific." This approach received a big boost in the late 19th century when "neoclassical" economists found that they could mathematically formalize Mill's idea of desiring the greatest wealth using techniques of calculus.

The inventors of neoclassical economics assumed that individual consumers or workers are rational, self-interested, autonomous agents who maximize a mathematical function that represents their levels of satisfaction or utility. By analogy, firms were seen as rational, autonomous actors who maximize a mathematical function that represents their profits, that is, excess of revenues over costs. These assumptions continue to form the core of mainstream economic analysis today.

Note, then, that the notion of "economic man" is doubly gendered. First, in leaving out all aspects of human life having to do with bodies, emotion, dependence, or other-interest, it highlights only culturally masculine-associated notions of humanity, while blocking out consideration of feminine-associated ones. Not only are the occupations of feeding, cleaning, and nursing bodies (traditionally assigned to women) made invisible, but everyone's experiences of social life in general—and of dependency in childhood, illness, and old age in particular—are denied. "Economic man," in contrast to real humans, neither ever needs care nor has any responsibility or desire to give it. Secondly, the origin of, and continued allegiance to, "economic man" reflects the impact of a gender-biased view of scientific endeavor, which prioritizes mathematical and abstract thinking, and denigrates qualitative analysis or delving into particulars. In attempting to achieve "scientific" status, the discipline of economics has, ironically, instead fallen into dogma. The discipline has been—to use a card [g]ame analogy—playing with only half a deck, both in terms of assumptions about human motivation and in terms of methodology.

Unfortunately, the image of economies as being mechanical, impersonal, a-social, and therefore functioning in a realm beyond the reach of notions of ethics and responsibility has become entirely engrained in most popular and political, as well as academic, discourses.

Many have come to believe—falsely—that a-social, narrow, profit-maximizing behavior is mandated by law or the functioning of markets—a belief that is erroneous (Nelson 2006; Nelson 2011).

The Alternative

Instead of buying into dualisms that contrast men to women, and commercial labor to caring labor, I believe that the best response is to deconstruct the binaries. If we are willing to suspend our belief in the inherent masculinity of commerce, our eyes can be opened to the elements of caring labor that are inherent within commerce (Nelson 2011). Specialists in organizational behavior and the psychological aspects of employment relations have, for example, long known that emotional and social factors play a large role in workplaces (Herzberg 1987). A few behavioral economists (Fehr and Falk 2002) have begun to recognize this as well.

To practice thinking non-dualistically about risk, consider that some amount of bravery and risk-taking is probably a good thing for encouraging innovation and entrepreneurship. The literature risk-taking often hints that those who are not brave enough to take risks are unsuited for leadership roles.

We can get past such trapped thinking by being willing to notice that behaviors do not follow such simple binaries. Being brave and risk-taking does not, in fact, preclude being also careful and protective. Psychologists who see elements of personality as containing many dimensions are already aware of this. Risk-taking without carefulness leads to reck-lessness (as, among other things, we saw in the financial crisis). Carefulness without courage leads to timidity. A recent movie, *127 Hours*, provides a vivid example. It is based on the true story of a young man, Aron Ralston, who lost his arm and nearly lost his life while hiking alone in rugged territory and becoming trapped by a falling rock. The movie makes the point that, had he simply told someone where he was going (as hikers are always advised to do), he would have been rescued. In the epilogue, it is noted that Ralston still goes out on rugged hikes alone, but now tells someone where he is going. That is, Ralston still takes risks, but now also shows an appropriate aversion to being reckless. He is not timid, but he is careful.

To return to the main topic of the present essay, the above analysis implies that a leader in the financial industry or its regulation should be prepared to take risks, but also to do so with proper caution and care. When a one-sidedly "macho" culture of finance developed, however, it became all too easy to denigrate appropriate caution as something sissified and weak, while elevating the reckless behavior associated with aggressive masculinity.

Leaders who are warm and good at managing relationships are often referred to in the management literature as having "soft skills." When such leaders are men, the simultaneous ascription of competence does not seem to be impaired. As Joan Acker has noted "Such qualities [as warmth] are not necessarily the symbolic monopoly of women. For example, the wise and experienced coach is empathetic and supportive to his individual players" (Acker 1990, 153). Psychological research finds, however, that groups that are socially less central tend to be stereotyped as missing in one or the other positive trait (Fiske, Cuddy et al. 2002). For women, this takes the form of the notorious "double bind": If a woman acts competently she is often perceived of as cold and inappropriately unfeminine, while if she is thought of as having good relational skills, she is often assumed to be in-competent in technical domains. Stereotypes of women as being warmer or more careful or altruistic than men may be benevolent stereotypes, but they are stereotypes nonetheless. We should remember this when we are tempted to buy into them.

Neither masculine-stereotyped traits nor feminine-stereotyped traits are, alone, sufficient to make a wise and competent financial leader. In the mechanical economy imaged by neoclassical economics, technical competence in reading financial statements and bravery in pursuing opportunities for innovation might be all that would be necessary for good leadership.

But because the real economy involves real people — and real dangers — relational skill; and due carefulness are also required. We forget this, and allow "cowboy capitalism," at our peril.

Conclusion

The question posed as the title for this paper is badly posed. The idea that women would "bring something different" to finance is dangerous because it (1) exaggerates sex differences in behavior far beyond the degree supported by research (2) stereotypes women (albeit relatively benevolently) as lacking in adventuresomeness and competent only in doing (financial) mopping up, and (3) lets men and markets morally and socially "off the hook" for the consequences of careless and irresponsible actions. On the other hand, were Wall Street firms and regulatory agencies such that they welcomed women and men as equal participants, this might indicate that societal gender stereotypes were breaking down. It might also be likely, then, that certain valuable characteristics and behaviors commonly stereotyped as feminine (such as carefulness) would be encouraged industry-wide, and inappropriate male-locker-room and cowboy-type behaviors frowned upon, to the benefit of the industry and society.

Teaching about gender, economics, and/or finance using the example of the financial crisis, then, can be a prime opportunity to develop students' critical thinking skills. It is worth stressing to students that before one can come up with a good answer, one has to come up with a good question. Being able to recognize a questionable question, and being able to evaluate the empirical (and other sorts of) evidence that can be drawn on to evaluate it, are skills that would serve economics students well in their future studies and future lives.

Notes

(1) What is the primary point of Professor Nelson's article? Is she suggesting that corporations should add more women to the board because women bring qualities that men generally do not possess or is she suggesting that we need to redefine the way that board members are selected and evaluated?

(2) Would Nelson agree with the following statement: "adding more women to the board-room would have prevented the financial crisis because women bring a unique set of viewpoints and methods of thinking that enable them to more effectively balance risk versus reward."

In 2003, Norway's government enacted voluntary legislation, but amended it in 2006, to require that all Norway based corporations comply with specific board member gender requirements by 2008. Based on the size of the corporation, the legislation specifically provided corporations needed to increase female board representation as follows:[1]

---

1. Anne Sweigart, *Women on Board for Change: The Norway Model of Boardroom Quotas As a Tool for Progress in the United States and Canada*, 32 Nw. J. Int'l L. & Bus. 81A (2012), http://scholarly-commons.law.northwestern.edu/cgi/viewcontent.cgi?article=1007&context=njilb

TOTAL # of Directors	TOTAL # of Female Directors Required by Law
2–3	At least 1
4–5	At least 2
6–8	At least 3
9+	At least 40%

Since Norway's groundbreaking legislation, several European countries have followed suit. France, Iceland and Spain set their minimum requirement at 40%, Italy at one-third, Germany and Belgium at 30% and the Netherlands created a non-binding target of 30%.[2]

(3) Why is it that European countries seem to take gender diversity more seriously than American countries?

(4) How would similar legislation be perceived in the United States?

(5) Even if such legislation was approved by Congress, do you think it could survive a constitutional challenge?

(6) Consider the Harvard Implicit Bias test in the context of Corporate Justice and board of director diversity. The well-known Harvard Implicit Bias test measures the implicit biases that we each hold. Individuals that take this test are forced to encounter and acknowledge the subconscious stereotypes that inform their thinking. Gender and racial stereotypes often permeate attitudes about the work one chooses to do and the talent (or lack thereof) that individuals bring to their work. If leaders of U.S. corporations were to take this implicit bias test, what do you think it would uncover? The test can be accessed here: https://implicit.harvard.edu/implicit/takeatest.html.

C. Gender Influence on Market Price and Profitability

In the next article Frank Dobbin and Jiwook Jung explore the value of boardroom diversity based on whether it has any effect on the market price of the stock. To really comprehend the article, it is important to understand that profitability and market price, while somewhat related, are not exactly the same thing. The idea of profitability focuses on the money a business has left over, in a particular period, after subtracting expenses and taxes from the total revenue generated. Market price on the other hand relates to the amount of money a potential investor would pay for a share of a business's stock. While profitability may affect the market price of a share of a business's stock, this is not always true. For example, assume that a company specializing in the sale of widgets, in a particular year, sold an extremely large number of widgets due to a national craze. The financials for the company would reflect that the business was profitable; however, if a newer version of the widget called a zidget, manufactured by the company's competitor, caught the nation's attention, the company's market price would decline. Although the company would appear profitable via its financials, its market price would decline since it is unlikely to continue to experience the same level of profitability in the future.

---

2. Alison Smale & Claire Cain Miller, *Germany Sets Gender Quota in Boardrooms*, N.Y. Times, Mar. 6, 2015, *available at* http://www.nytimes.com/2015/03/07/world/europe/german-law-requires-more-women-on-corporate-boards.html.

Corporate Board Gender Diversity and Stock Performance: The Competence Gap or Institutional Investor Bias?

Frank Dobbin & Jiwook Jung
89 N.C. L. Rev. 809 (2011)

INTRODUCTION

Women have been gaining ground on corporate boards. They held 14.8% of Fortune 500 seats in 2007. Yet the effect of women on corporate performance is a matter of some debate. Studies using data at one or two points in time find that gender diversity on boards is associated with higher stock values and greater profitability.

However, studies using panel data over a number of years, which explore the effects of adding women to boards, generally show no effects or negative effects. This suggests that the association between board diversity and performance identified in cross-sectional studies is spurious—a consequence perhaps of the fact that successful firms appoint women to their boards.

Scholars have assumed that if board diversity affects corporate performance, it is through its influence on group processes in the boardroom. Thus they draw on theories from social psychology about groups. On the positive side, gender and racial diversity may operate as occupational diversity does in small groups, enabling groups to come to better decisions and to come to them more quickly. On the negative side, gender and racial diversity have been found to increase conflict in small groups, and this may inhibit their decision-making capacity.

We explore another mechanism linking board diversity to firm performance. For certain performance outcomes, notably stock price, what goes on in board meetings may be of less importance than what goes on in the equities markets. Boards themselves are attuned to their effects on stock price, and, in the appointment of CEOs, they think long and hard about the signals they want to send to markets. If stock markets react to the appointment of new CEOs, we argue, they may likewise react to the appointment of board members. A study of directors, managers, shareholders, and regulators revealed a widespread belief that board appointments are used to send signals to shareholders and others. A recent study using British data suggested that women on corporate boards have adverse effects on subjectively established measures of corporate performance, such as stock price, which is established through the behavior of stock market participants, but not on objectively established measures, such as profitability, which is established using accounting standards. Our argument builds on that line of thinking. Bias may shape the stock market performance of firms, but it is less likely to shape their profitability.

Our research represents a significant departure, then, from most previous research on board diversity, profitability, and stock performance. We explore how the institutional investor community influences board diversity and stock price. First, we posit that boards are attentive to the demands of institutional investors for greater board diversity. Second, we expect that, paradoxically, investor decision making is influenced by gender bias and that the typical investor will reduce holdings in firms that appoint female directors. Third, we suggest that accountability apprehension will mediate this process, such that visible blockholding institutional fund managers (who hold at least five percent of the stock of a company) and public pension fund managers (who as a group pressed for board diversity) will be less likely to act on gender bias. The behavior of major investors, we suggest, is more likely to be scrutinized by other players in the stock market.

We examine whether board appointments are influenced by institutional investors and whether appointments in turn influence investors. We model these processes by observing year-to-year changes in board diversity, on the one hand, and in corporate performance and institutional investor holdings, on the other, building on the rigorous longitudinal studies that explore whether changes in board diversity lead to changes in performance. We use panel data on more than 400 large U.S. firms for the period 1997 to 2006. To test the hypothesis that institutional investor behavior has promoted board diversity, we examine the effects of shareholder proposals for board diversity spearheaded by institutional investors. Several studies suggest that institutional investors can be effective at shaping corporate social behavior. To test the hypothesis that board diversity activates gender bias on the part of institutional investors, we look at the effects of diversity on stock price and on institutional investor holdings. We rule out the possibility that female directors influence investor holdings by altering board performance and profitability, showing that board diversity has no effect on profits. Finally, to test the hypothesis that accountability apprehension mediates the effect of gender bias on investor behavior, we examine whether blockholding institutional investors and public pension funds are less likely to reduce their holdings in firms that appoint female directors. Both kinds of investors are susceptible to public accountability: blockholders because of the magnitude of their positions in firms, and public pension funds because they were vocal proponents of board diversity.

In this Article, we begin by reviewing social psychological research on group composition and performance that has inspired much of the research on board diversity and performance. In the second section, we discuss previous research findings and detail methodological flaws that may explain the divergence in the results from cross-sectional and panel studies. We then turn to our own theories. We predict that pressure from institutional investors, through shareholder proposals, encourages firms to appoint female board members. But we predict that bias among institutional investors depresses the share prices of firms that appoint female directors without producing a corresponding negative effect on profits. In the data analysis, we follow 432 major U.S. corporations between 1997 and 2006 to examine the effects of shareholder proposals on board diversity and, in turn, the effects of changes in board gender diversity on both share price and profitability. The findings support our central predictions. In the conclusion we discuss further research that could help us to better understand the relationships between boards, profits, and stock price, and we call for institutional investors to scrutinize their own behavior in the face of increasing board diversity.

I. THEORIES OF GROUP COMPOSITION AND EFFICACY

Research in psychology suggests that educational diversity in problem-solving groups improves performance. Put a bunch of MBAs in a room and you'll arrive at inferior solutions, and arrive at them more slowly, than if you mix the MBAs with attorneys, accountants, and engineers. Will these findings about the effects of educational diversity extend to demographic diversity? This is the great promise of workplace diversity: an African American woman and a Latino man on your team will improve its performance.

Studies of board diversity build on these insights—positive or negative—and thus they presume that the effects of board diversity on corporate performance result primarily from changes in board efficacy.

A. Theories Suggesting Advantages of Group Diversity

Research on the diversity of perspectives in decision-making teams suggests that teams with functional (occupational) heterogeneity are more effective at solving problems and implementing change than are homogenous teams. Management researchers first showed that team diversity, in terms of personality, can improve efficacy by expanding perspectives and cognitive resources. Studies indicate that demographic diversity can increase network connections, resources, creativity, and innovation.

Workplace researchers have attempted to explain everything from group conflict to decision making to sales figures with demographic diversity. In most laboratory and field studies, however, the effects of conflict and poor communication appear to dominate. One exception is found in a panel study of the effects of corporate workforce diversity showing that in research-intensive Fortune 1500 companies, adding women to the top management team increased stock price (Tobin's q) in the period 1992 to 2006.

Gender diversity may have positive effects due not to diversity of perspectives, but to a female management style, and this may be the case in particular for research-intensive firms. But the overall effects on boards may not necessarily be positive. Adams and Ferreira find evidence for a kindred argument about corporate board diversity, namely that women pay greater attention to monitoring firms, women board members have better attendance records, women board members improve the attendance of men, and women are more involved in monitoring committees. Adams and Ferreira suggest that while board monitoring has been championed by corporate governance experts, such monitoring may interfere with the efficient management of the firm. They find that increases in the gender diversity of boards lead to decreases in both profits and stock price and suggest that excessive monitoring may be the reason.

B. Theories Suggesting Disadvantages of Group Diversity

Social identity theory, similarity-attraction theory, and social categorization theory suggest that people are drawn to similar others. Mixed gender and racial groups may divide, and diversity may elicit group conflict that interferes with efficacy. Diversity in race, ethnicity, and, to a lesser extent, sex, tends to bring about group conflict, hinder communication, and interfere with cooperation, thereby lowering performance.

Studies show mixed effects of gender diversity on problem-solving efficacy. Compositional theories of "tokenism" and "stereotype threat" suggest that when members of minority groups rise in an occupation, they face expectations that make it difficult to perform to their potential. Kanter argues that when a group has only token representation, members face pressures that may adversely affect their performance. Stereotype threat research suggests that when the status of a minority group is made salient through experimental manipulation, members of that group may underperform because they feel they are being judged as group members rather than as individuals. Majority group members may stigmatize them and underestimate their contributions.

The psychological research thus suggests that we may see either positive or negative effects of board diversity on corporate performance. Boards with women may solve problems more effectively because they hold a wider range of perspectives, but diversity may also thwart problem solving by raising conflict. If diversity is affecting corporate performance by influencing board capacities, we should see effects first on corporate profitability and then on stock returns. A number of studies have shown that investors, and particularly full-time professional fund managers, pay significant attention to board behavior, board structure, and board governance regimes.

II. RESEARCH ON BOARD DIVERSITY AND PERFORMANCE

Analysts have explored the effects of board diversity on both profitability and stock valuation. The overall pattern of findings across the several dozen studies that have been published to date tends to support the view that gender diversity inhibits performance.

The studies that show positive effects use cross-sectional data or observations across very short time periods, and thus are prone to problems of endogeneity; these studies, in short, do not rule out reverse causation. If we examine board diversity and performance cross-sectionally in 2011, we may well see a positive correlation. But has that correlation come about because firms that appoint women experience improvements in performance, or because firms with strong profits and share prices are more likely to appoint women to their boards?

Taken together, these studies are consistent with the idea that firms that are having good runs are more likely to appoint women, but once appointed, women have neutral or negative effects on performance. Several studies addressed this idea directly. Farrell and Hersch examined a sample of 300 Fortune 500 firms between 1990 and 1999, showing that firms with strong profits (ROA) are more likely to appoint female directors but that female directors do not affect subsequent performance. Adams and Ferreira found that Tobin's q, but not ROA, predicts the appointment of female directors, but, as noted, female directors have subsequent negative effects. They concluded: "Although a positive relation between gender diversity in the boardroom and firm performance is often cited in the popular press, it is not robust to any of our methods of addressing the endogeneity of gender diversity." We concur with these recent studies, which suggest that the cross-sectional positive relationship found between board diversity and corporate performance is likely spurious—a consequence of reverse causation. The negative effects found in certain studies may be real, but we suggest a new mechanism to explain this effect: shareholder bias.

III. INSTITUTIONAL INVESTOR ACTIVISM, INSTITUTIONAL INVESTOR BIAS

We build on the growing body of organizational research showing that environmental factors frequently influence organization-level outcomes. Several lines of research have suggested that key players in the equities markets influence both the internal decision processes in large corporations and the pricing of firms. As institutional investors have come to control the lion's share of the stock of large corporations, firms in turn have become more attentive to the desires of institutional investors.

Public pension funds and their associations, notably the Council of Institutional Investors, have actively promoted gender and racial diversity on corporate boards. Indications exist that they have had some success; in large firms, the proportion of female board members has risen, even as boards on average have become smaller. As firms are increasingly attentive to the desires of institutional investors, we predict that firms that receive shareholder proposals in favor of board diversity will increase the representation of women on their boards. Our first prediction, then, is that shareholder proposals favoring board diversity will be followed by increases in gender diversity.

Our theory of the effect of diversity on institutional investor behavior combines elements from bias and accountability theories. First, laboratory and field studies show that gender and racial biases are widespread and that they influence career outcomes. Bias toward members of other racial, ethnic, and gender groups has been widely documented. Social cognition theory in psychology has shown that individuals categorize others automatically and "tend to feel, think, and behave toward that individual in the same way they tend to feel, think, and behave toward members of that social category more generally." They use social categorization to process multitudes of environmental cues rapidly, and they use sex and race as "master statuses." The literature on in-group preference suggests that people generally hold more positive views of people from their own race, ethnic, and gender group. The literature on implicit association goes further, suggesting that even members of a demographic group hold the dominant biases about members of that group; even women associate men with leadership and competence.

We extend this research to suggest that the appointment of women to corporate boards may influence stock performance through investor bias. Institutional investors are the key market makers in equities markets, controlling some eighty percent of the shares of the large firms in our sample. Moreover, because this group tracks changes in corporate strategy and governance, it is cognizant of shifts in board composition. Fund managers can be expected to hold the same implicit associations that the rest of the population holds. Because investors are not accustomed to thinking of women as board members and tend to believe that women lack the human capital and business experience to be board members, we posit that institutional investors may react negatively to firms that appoint women board members. They may be less likely to favor such firms when making buy and sell decisions.

While we expect the average institutional investor to react to the appointment of female board members by lowering, albeit unconsciously, his opinion of the firm, we expect that accountability may attenuate this process. Accountability theory suggests that people who expect others to scrutinize their behavior will self-censor and be less likely to act on their biases. In laboratory settings, subjects who know that someone may review their decisions are most likely to monitor their own actions for evidence of bias and self-correct. This should apply to two groups of institutional investors: blockholders and public pension funds. First, an institutional investor with a large stake attracts attention when she reduces her position in a company.

Second, leading public-sector pension funds have actively promoted diversity on corporate boards through shareholder proposals, and we expect that they will be more careful to behave in accordance with this activism by supporting firms that appoint women to boards. Our third prediction is that blockholding institutional investors and public pension funds will not reduce their holdings in companies that increase the share of women on their boards.

IV. DATA AND METHODS

We conduct three types of analysis. First, we suggest that because large public pension funds have led the charge for greater board diversity, firms that receive shareholder proposals advocating board diversity will see increases in diversity. Thus, we model the log odds of female directors to see if shareholder proposals have an effect.

Second, we expect that bias leads institutional investors to disfavor companies that appoint women directors, and thus we expect that gender diversity will depress stock price. If the presence of women directors depresses stock price without affecting profitability, we will conclude that institutional investor bias is a more likely mechanism than poor board performance. Decreases in board competence should first depress profits, then stock price.

Third, we look at whether increases in board diversity shape institutional investor holdings, to explore the possibility that bias causes investors to decrease their holdings in firms that increase board diversity. We do not expect blockholders or public pension funds to decrease their holdings. Both groups, we suggest, will monitor their own behavior for signs of bias in anticipation of public scrutiny.

A. Sample

The sample is drawn from large U.S. firms that operate in a representative group of industries. The sampling frame is Fortune's list of America's 500 largest companies, supplemented with industry-specific Fortune lists and the Million Dollar Directory for certain industries.

We analyze data on 432 major American corporations for the period 1997 to 2006. We analyze between 2,882 and 3,016 spells, or corporation-years, of data.

V. FINDINGS

We find that institutional investors do promote gender diversity on boards through shareholder proposals favoring diversity. Increases in board gender diversity do not affect subsequent profitability, suggesting that firms that add women to boards do not experience losses in board efficacy, or perhaps confirming what previous studies have implied: boards don't much matter. But an increase in gender diversity on boards is followed by a significant decrease in stock value. The fact that board diversity has no effect on profits, but a negative effect on stock price, lends support to our thesis that institutional investors may sell the stock of firms that appoint women to their boards—not because profits suffer, but because they are biased against women.

Board gender diversity shows a clear pattern of effects on institutional investor holdings that supports our bias and accountability apprehension theses. Non-blockholding institutional investors significantly decrease their positions in firms that increase women directors. This supports our thesis about investor bias. Blockholding investors significantly increase their positions in response to increased gender diversity. When we break down institutional investors into categories, there is a significant positive effect for blockholding public pension funds but no effect for non-blockholding public pensions, whereas the average non-blockholding investor responds negatively to an increase in board diversity. This pattern supports the accountability hypothesis, which suggests that blockholders and public pension funds are most likely to censor their own tendencies to exercise bias.

Our first hypothesis is supported: firms that face shareholder proposals for board diversity do increase gender diversity among directors. Yet shareholder proposals on other issues do not show effects. We find a number of other interesting effects. Financial conditions little affect the appointment of women; profits (ROA), stock value (Tobin's q), and cumulative stock returns show no effects. A reduction in assets increases the likelihood that a firm will see increases in female directorships, which suggests that growing firms are less likely to appoint women. We control for corporate governance characteristics, including independent directors, affiliated directors, number of directors, and CEO/Chair structure. These factors are unrelated to the appointment of female directors. CEO tenure is negatively related to female directorships, likely because recently appointed CEOs champion women directors. As the average tenure of female directors increases, the number of female directors increases. As the average tenure of male directors increases, the number of female directors decreases. Increases in women in management lead to increases in women on the board, but the opposite is true for increases in the total number of female employees.

When it comes to performance, we find that female directors do not affect ROA but have significant negative effects on Tobin's q. This provides some support for the notion that institutional investors do not like to see firms appoint women directors. For both profits (ROA) and stock performance (Tobin's q), most financial variables have the expected effects. For Tobin's q, change in ROA has a positive effect, while changes in systematic risk, dividend yield, and firm size have negative effects. For ROA we see the same effects for these last three variables, and we also see a negative effect of unsystematic risk and a positive effect of firm age. Institutional ownership also has a positive effect, likely because institutional investors buy firms with good prospects or because their activism improves performance. Affiliated directors (those with family or previous employment ties to the firm) have negative effects on ROA, which we may take as support for agency theory's dictum that independent directors are superior board members.

We predicted that institutional investors would shy away from firms that appoint women to their boards, perhaps unwittingly acting on widespread gender biases. We expected this pattern to be moderated, or reversed, among investors who could expect their behavior to be scrutinized by the media and by investors. In particular, we expected anticipation of accountability to cause blockholders and public pension funds to censor their own inclinations to act on biases. Public pension funds spearheaded the call for board diversity, so perhaps they were sensitized by apprehension of accusations of hypocrisy.

Managers of smaller funds and managers of non-blockholding large funds, by contrast, likely do not inspect their own motives for buying or selling stock in a certain company with great care. Reports about financial performance and prospects surely drive their core buying strategies (for nonindexed funds at least), but if their buying and selling decisions are affected at the margins by changes in corporate board diversity, they are less likely than blockholders and public pension funds to self-censor.

While these findings are consistent with our models, we cannot be certain of why institutional investors show this pattern. The positive or neutral reactions of blockholders and public pension funds, contrasted with the negative reactions of other institutional investors, are consistent with our theory. But we cannot entirely rule out other mechanisms. One study found that TIAA-CREF fund managers believe that diverse boards are "less likely to be beholden to management" and thus more likely to behave in the interest of shareholders. If that view were widely held, however, board diversity should lead to increases in institutional investor holdings across the board, as well as stock price, and that was not the pattern we observed. Broome and Krawiec find that firms appoint women and minorities to signal to workers, unions, and investors that they are committed to equality; perhaps institutional investors take this as a signal that firms are no longer focused on maximizing share value.

If that were the sole mechanism at work, we would expect blockholders and public pension fund managers to reduce holdings in firms that appoint women, and that is not the pattern we observe. Finally, it could be that fund managers take the appointment of a woman to be a sign that the board recognizes weaknesses in the firm and is making an effort to bring in new points of view. Again, if that were the sole mechanism, we might expect to see a consistent pattern across different types of investors. Moreover, appointment of a member to broaden the board's perspective might be expected to bolster confidence among fund managers rather than to dampen it.

In our models predicting institutional investor holdings, the financial variables generally have consistent effects across the investor groups. ROA shows a negative effect on blockholding investment, perhaps because blockholders find it more difficult than non-blockholders to exit when a firm is not doing well. But small-holders generally favor firms with strong profits. Systematic risk generally has positive effects, and unsystematic risk shows a pattern of negative effects. Dividend yield shows a pattern of negative effects.

Agency theorists expect that corporate governance will affect profits and will thereby attract investment and drive up stock price. In particular, they advocate for independent directors, small boards, and a split between the CEO and chairman positions. We expect institutional investors to favor companies that follow these prescriptions, and thus expect independent directors to increase institutional shareholding, and affiliated directors (those with work and family ties to the firm), board size, and CEO/Chair combination to reduce institutional shareholding. However, we do not see that pattern.

While firms that follow agency theory's corporate governance prescriptions do not attract significantly more shareholding by institutional investors, changes in the number of female directors do affect holdings. Among all institutional investors, female board members have significant positive effects on holdings by blockholders and significant negative effects on holdings by non-blockholders. When we look at the effects among different types of investors, there are significant positive effects of gender diversity for blockholding public pension funds and investment companies. By contrast, non-blockholding banks and investment companies significantly reduce their shares following increases in female board membership.

This pattern is consistent with our thesis that female directors show adverse effects on stock price in our study and in others, because non-blockholding institutional investors sell shares of companies that appoint women to their boards. While some groups of block-holders buy more shares in response to increases in the number of women on boards, non-blockholders control half of all shares and blockholders control less than a quarter of all shares. The pattern of effects is consistent with bias on the part of non-blockholders, who control most shares.

Our proposition that unconscious bias is at work is reinforced by three other patterns. The first two involve our predictions about accountability apprehension. If bias is the mechanism leading to negative effects on institutional shareholding, we predicted, then accountability apprehension should moderate or reverse the effect for two groups. First, blockholders of shares in the large companies in our sample can be expected to be scrutinized by the market if they sell off shares. On average, blockholders actually increase their holdings in the wake of the appointment of female directors. We interpret this pattern to support the accountability apprehension thesis, and indeed it is consistent with findings from laboratory research showing that subjects favor women in a simulated pay allocation exercise to counter the known tendency to favor men. It could be that blockholders favor women over men as board members, although the preponderance of psychological research suggests that women and men alike expect men to be superior at business activities. Second, public pension funds can expect their behavior to be scrutinized after the appointment of women because those funds spearheaded board diversity shareholder proposals. Blockholding public pension funds increase their shareholdings in firms that add women directors, and non-blockholding public pensions do not significantly change their holdings.

[We suggest] that investors may not be responding to the appointment of women per se, but to the signal that corporate management has moved from a value orientation to a political orientation. If investors respond negatively to firms that adopt a political orientation, we should find that when shareholder proposals for board diversity—which are thought to be motivated by gender politics—are followed by increases in board diversity, institutional investors will be particularly likely to reduce their holdings. Shareholder proposals for board diversity by themselves do not affect investors. In models not reported here, we interacted shareholder proposals for board diversity with female directors. If investors reduce their positions in firms that capitulate to political demands, we should see that when shareholder proposals for board diversity are followed by increases in female directors, investors flee. That is, the interaction of shareholder proposals and female directors should be significant and negative. Instead, the interactions are nonsignificant. This was true for every subgroup of institutional investors and for institutional investors as a whole. The failure of the interaction effect suggests two things: institutional investors do not favor firms that refuse to respond to shareholder proposals, and they do not disfavor firms that respond to shareholder proposals. They disfavor firms that appoint women regardless of whether those firms did so in the face of shareholder pressure. This gives us more confidence that the negative effects of board feminization are the result of institutional investor bias.

CONCLUSION

The effects of board diversity on corporate performance are not well understood, but most research begins with the premise that any effects of gender diversity must result from changes in the efficacy, or monitoring capabilities, of boards. These changes are expected to affect profits directly and stock performance indirectly. Early cross-sectional studies suggested that board gender diversity has positive effects on both profits and stock performance. However, studies using panel data and statistical methods designed to rule out endogeneity suggested that female directors tend to have neutral or negative effects. The big picture seems to be that gender board diversity does not help firms — and it may hurt them.

We offer another theory of the effect of board gender diversity on corporate performance. We suggest that gender diversity may be influencing corporate performance not by shaping the efficacy or monitoring capabilities of boards themselves, but by activating bias on the part of the institutional investors who now control eighty percent of the shares of America's leading companies. We suggest that if institutional fund managers are indeed acting on gender biases and reducing the value of firms that increase female directorships, we should see negative effects of female directors on stock value. We suggest that if female directors are influencing stock price by altering board efficacy, we should see effects on both profits and stock value.

Our findings are consistent with the proposition that bias is affecting stock price. Female directors have negative effects on stock value and no effects on profits. The bias proposition is also supported by the wider pattern of effects of corporate board characteristics, namely, that they do not influence performance when all else is taken into account. Investors are thought to favor companies that create smaller, more agile, boards; that appoint more outside directors; and that separate the chair and CEO roles. These companies are expected to see improvements in profits, increases in stock price, and increases in holdings by professional fund managers. We find that companies that make these changes do not see increases in profits, stock value, or institutional holdings. If these fundamental changes designed to improve board functioning do not shape profits or stock value through improved board efficacy and monitoring, then why would changes in the gender composition of boards affect performance via board efficacy?

As a further test of the bias thesis, we examined the accountability apprehension thesis that investors who could expect their behavior to be scrutinized by outsiders would censor their own bias. We posited that blockholding institutional investors would be more careful than non-blockholders to avoid the appearance of bias against firms that increased the share of women directors. We expected that public pension funds, which as a group led the charge for board diversity, would also take care not to respond negatively to the appointment of women to boards. These patterns were supported by the findings. Blockholders reacted positively to board diversity, and non-blockholding public pension funds did not react negatively.

We suggested that for non-blockholders, accountability should not be so salient, and so natural biases might be unleashed. Because non-blockholding institutional investors controlled half of the shares in the companies in our sample by 2007 and because blockholders control less than a quarter of the shares, the aggregate effect of these two disparate patterns was to reduce the value of firms that appoint women directors.

Students of corporate governance should in future research move beyond the narrow band of theories that has informed research to date. In academic studies of finance, a handful of economic theories, such as agency theory and the efficient markets hypothesis, have dominated. These explanatory frameworks assume fully rational actors making decisions based on careful calculations about a firm's current standing and future prospects. But in the stock market, as in other markets, behavior is shaped in important ways by psychological and sociological factors that these theories neglect. Insights from psychology and from economic sociology promise to enrich our understanding of financial markets.

Notes

(1) Is there a way to reconcile Nelson's point that women should not fit into binary categories of "same" and "different" with Dobbin and Jung's overall point about the influence of diversity in the boardroom?

(2) How would Nelson interpret Dobbin and Jung's findings?

(3) Professors Lisa Fairfax and Doug Branson have conducted extensive research into whether a business case can be made for increasing board diversity.[3] Does increasing diversity at the corporate leadership level lead to greater outcomes, both in profit and efficiency?

(4) When considering the impact of both gender and racial diversity on a corporate board, an argument can be made that women and/or people of color bring palatable positive impact to the boards on which they serve. Emerging evidence seems to indicate that corporations led by female executives get sued less often than corporations helmed by men. According to a forthcoming article by Professors Binay K. Adhikari, Anup Agrawal, and James Malm, currently entitled "Do Women Stay Out of Trouble?: Evidence from Corporate Litigation," corporations with a "higher representation of women in the top management team face fewer lawsuits overall, particularly lawsuits related to product liability, environment, medical liability, labor and contracts." In this article, the authors speculate that this phenomenon may be attributable to three characteristics of female managers. First, they argue that women are more risk adverse and as a result, woman are less likely to engage in high risk — high reward activities.

---

3. *See* Lisa Fairfax, *The Bottom Line on Board Diversity: A Cost-Benefit Analysis of the Business Rationales for Diversity on Corporate Boards*, 2005 Wisconsin L. Rev. 795; *see also* Lisa Fairfax, *Board Diversity Revisited: New Rationale, Same Old Story?*, 89 North Carolina L. Rev. 855 (2011); Douglas Branson, *Women on Boards of Directors: A Global Snapshot*, http://papers.ssrn.com/sol3/papers.cfm?abstract_id=1762615 (Feb. 2011); Douglas Branson, No Seat at the Table — How Governance and Law Keep Women Out of the Boardroom (NYU Press 2007).

Because of their risk aversion, women are less likely to get involved in the type of transactions that lead to law suits. Second, the authors assert that women are less overconfident than their male counterparts. "Higher overconfidence in male executives compared to female executives implies that, even with the same level of risk-aversion, male executives are likely to face more lawsuits because they underestimate the risk of lawsuits." Finally, women are more trustworthy and more likely to comply with rules. Therefore, they are less likely to manipulate or abuse the types of rules and regulations that lead to litigation. The authors further advance another practical benefit of diversity on boards—that corporations with more women board members maintain higher market values because less money is paid from the corporation's coffers to plaintiffs. Specifically, the authors found that "among high litigation risk firms, a firm with a mean fraction of female executives enjoys 7 to 8 cents higher market value per dollar of cash holdings compared to a firm without female executives." Does this emerging research convince you that female leaders improve bottom line corporate performance? How would Professor Nelson respond to the conclusions above?

D. Diversity Doublespeak

If you look at any Fortune 500 company's website, without fail, you will invariably see some reference to a commitment to diversity. These references to diversity appear to suggest that companies truly value and embrace the idea of diversity; however, in the following article, Professor Cheryl Wade challenges this notion.

"We Are an Equal Opportunity Employer": Diversity Doublespeak

Cheryl L. Wade

1 WASH. & LEE L. REV. 1541 (2004)

I. Introduction: Diversity Doublespeak

In January 2004, I attended the Seventh Annual Rainbow/PUSH Wall Street Project Conference in New York City. The mission of the Wall Street Project, founded by Reverend Jesse Jackson, Sr., is to assure "equal opportunity for America's underserved consumers, employees and entrepreneurs. Access to capital, industry and technology continues to be the last stage of today's civil rights movement." Of particular importance to me were two panels entitled "Inclusion Advocates—How Have the Roles of Workforce Diversity Directors, Supplier Diversity Directors and Community Affairs Executives Changed Post 9/11 and Recession?," and "Best Practices: The Steps Multinational Corporations Are Taking to Avoid Diversity Crises." Diversity executives with varying and elaborate titles from several public companies presented on these two panels. Each presenter delivered an adulatory portrayal of their companies' diversity efforts. Each presenter used the same words to describe aspirations of racial equity at their firm—"diversity," "access to opportunity," "inclusion." As I listened to their presentations, I was reminded of a book about a phenomenon called "doublespeak." The book's subtitle was, "How Government, Business, Advertisers, and Others Use Language to Deceive You." The author defined "doublespeak" in the following manner:

> [L]anguage that pretends to communicate but really doesn't. It is language that makes the bad seem good, the negative appear positive, the unpleasant appear

attractive or at least tolerable. Doublespeak is language that avoids or shifts responsibility.... It is language that conceals or prevents thought; rather than extending thought, doublespeak limits it.... Basic to doublespeak is incongruity, the incongruity between what is said or left unsaid, and what really is.

In the three hours and fifteen minutes I spent listening to the presenters on both panels, not one presenter uttered the word "discrimination." None of the panelists spoke of antidiscrimination law and their companies' efforts to monitor compliance with such law. Discrimination, "the D-word," I presumed, was an epithet to be avoided at all costs at gatherings such as these. Implicit in their silence about discrimination and racism was the conclusion that these problems had been resolved within their companies, if they had ever existed at all. Their silence implied that the only remaining issues for corporate managers to address were inclusion of people of color in the wealth generated by public companies, access to equal opportunity, and diversity. This was diversity doublespeak.

I left both panels with unanswered questions. Did the panelists represent the exceptional companies? Have the companies at which the panelists work resolved discrimination problems to the extent that they no longer require discussion? How many people of color were senior managers at their companies? Were people of color, particularly African Americans, promoted at the same rate as whites? Did African Americans earn the same pay as their white counterparts?

Because some of the panels ran concurrently, I could not attend everything. I searched the conference program for a panel, any panel, about the problem of continuing racism and discrimination within public companies. I found only discussions about "inclusion," "access," and "diversity." Yet, to me at least, it seemed clear that race discrimination continues to be a problem for corporate employees, communities, consumers, and suppliers of color. How else can one explain the economic gap between whites and African Americans? In 2002 the average black household income was 64.9% of white household income, and black men earned 73.9% of what white men earned. "Since the stock market bubble burst in March, 2000, black unemployment has soared to nearly 11%, double that of whites. And it's not just less skilled blacks who get hurt. In 2002, the number of employed black managers and professionals fell ... Meanwhile, the number of employed white managers and professionals continued to rise...." Additionally, black male managers and executives earn 23% less than white ones.

There are two possible explanations for the disparities in pay between African Americans and whites and the higher unemployment rate overall for African Americans, including highly educated and professional African Americans. One way to understand this economic gap between whites and African Americans requires acknowledging that discrimination persists among those who serve as corporate agents who make hiring, firing, promotion, and pay decisions. The other explanation, always unspoken (at least in evolved circles), is that African Americans deserve less pay and should be fired first because they are intellectually, or otherwise, inferior to their white counterparts. There seem to be two logical ways to explain why only a painfully small number of senior corporate managers are African-American. Either discrimination is the cause, or African Americans do not have the intellectual acuity to function as senior executives.

Because I do not believe that African Americans are inferior to whites, I believe that race discrimination among corporate actors is one of the primary causes of the economic divide between African Americans and whites. Few would argue with this proposition as a historical fact. For example, within the last ten years, many public companies paid large amounts to settle race discrimination class actions. Most notable among these companies are Texaco and Coca-Cola. Both companies paid historic amounts to settle race discrimination class actions. There are some, however, who seem to believe that discussions about racism and discrimination are no longer relevant in 2004, even though there are many very recent cases where employees of color continue to allege race discrimination in corporate workplaces. I find it interesting that almost all of the companies sued by employees of color within the past ten years, including Texaco and Coca-Cola, engaged in the same kind of diversity cheerleading I heard at the Wall Street Project.

There are two reasons why corporate spokespersons should not talk about diversity while remaining silent about discrimination. First, a company that focuses on diversity alone, without considering discrimination issues, will inevitably and predictably face complaints from, and possibly litigation brought by, employees of color. Diversity efforts, without antidiscrimination efforts, increase the likelihood that the company will engage in litigating and mediating disputes about discrimination. Second, diversity discussions make people of color supplicants, and whites become their benefactors. Employees and suppliers of color must ask for inclusion, equal opportunity, and diversity. As supplicants, people of color risk the possibility that whites will choose not to diversify and include them. White managers of public companies may choose to grant the requests for diversity, access, or inclusion, or they may ignore them. Because of the law prohibiting discrimination, this element of choice does not exist if the focus is on antidiscrimination measures. Corporate officers and employers must comply with antidiscrimination law, and corporate boards owe a duty to monitor such compliance.

Presenters at the 2004 Wall Street Project Conference discussed their companies' diversity, access, and inclusion efforts. For example, they described their companies' programs providing mentors for minority and women employees. Many companies facilitated the formation of "affinity groups." These are separate groups of women, African-American, Asian, and Latino employees who meet periodically to discuss common issues. Companies also established programs for minority public school students to introduce them to the company's business and employees. These are worthy programs, but diversity efforts that focus all corporate energy on such programs while ignoring the issue of compliance with antidiscrimination law, allow workplace discrimination to persist and thrive.

Diversity doublespeak allows companies to avoid responsibility for enduring discrimination within the firm. When managers and boards talk about their diversity efforts while at the same time failing to adequately monitor compliance with antidiscrimination law, their firms' reputations glisten, even while employees of color suffer. Part II of this Article provides an example of diversity doublespeak taken from recent headlines. I also provide a more vivid example of diversity doublespeak in the context of a race discrimination class action brought against Texaco Incorporated. I examine the firm's proxy statements that were drafted and disseminated to shareholders while the discrimination class action was pending. In the proxy materials, Texaco enumerates its affirmative action policies and its policies on diversity, and Texaco also includes a statement from its Corporate Conduct Guidelines. Texaco "believes a work environment which reflects diversity and is free of all forms of discrimination, intimidation and harassment is essential for a productive and efficient work force." Texaco paints a picture of a board of directors that closely monitors compliance with laws prohibiting discrimination.

The discussion of Texaco's doublespeak about compliance in its proxy statements takes me to Part III of this article, which examines the corporate law duty of care. My examination includes consideration of a Delaware Chancery Court settlement opinion describing the monitoring component of the duty of care. It is possible that the opinion merely describes behavior to which directors should aspire and not behavior that should result in a director's personal liability. This observation, however, does not dilute the import of the opinion's description of a board's duty to monitor compliance with the law. It offers a blueprint for corporate self-governance. Whether shareholders file derivative suits claiming directorial care breaches becomes irrelevant. Boards understand that the duty of care is a fundamental part of a firm's "best practices," and the settlement opinion offers important guidance in this regard. Part IV explores ways to make a firm's monitoring obligations meaningful and capable of transforming discriminatory corporate cultures. It is possible that a firm's compliance program, assembled to fulfill care obligations, may be as obfuscating as doublespeak. Some compliance programs are assembled for cosmetic purposes only, and this part of the Article describes one attorney's strategy to make compliance real.

Part V considers the transformative potential of a board that acknowledges discrimination and accepts responsibility for monitoring and compliance failures when discrimination is pervasive and egregious. Acknowledgment and acceptance of responsibility for failing to adequately monitor compliance with antidiscrimination law is helpfully antithetical to the obfuscation that occurs when corporate boards and spokespersons engage in diversity, compliance, and equal opportunity doublespeak.

II. Examples of Diversity Doublespeak

B. Texaco's Proxy Statements

In the 1990s, African-American employees at Texaco and Coca-Cola received the largest amounts ever paid to settle race discrimination litigation. In 1996, Texaco paid over $175 million to settle a race discrimination class action. In 2000, Coca-Cola paid almost $200 million to settle a class action brought against it alleging race discrimination. In addition to the monetary recovery awarded the African-American employees of Texaco and Coca-Cola, both settlements included terms that required the companies to undertake efforts to train employees concerning diversity issues. Both settlements required oversight by a task force composed of members who were not employed by or otherwise affiliated with the companies. This subpart examines statements made by Texaco in its proxy materials during the time between the filing of the discrimination class action and its settlement. These proxy materials provide a graphic illustration of diversity doublespeak.

Even though the Texaco class action litigation was settled years ago, the continued examination of this race discrimination case is important for two reasons. First, Texaco provided an opportunity for other companies to learn how to handle the kind of crisis that Texaco faced. Unfortunately, however, it does not seem that other companies heeded the lessons. Four years after the Texaco settlement, Coca-Cola paid almost $200 million to settle a similar race discrimination class action. Similar allegations of pervasive discrimination have been made at many other companies since the Texaco and Coca-Cola settlements.

In this Part, I use a detailed account of the events that led to the filing of the Texaco race discrimination suit provided in a book written by Bari-Ellen Roberts, one of the lead plaintiffs. I compare Roberts' narrative about race and Texaco to the narrative the company told in its proxy statements. I describe the company's discussion about race and diversity in its proxy statements for 1994, 1995, and 1996 because the discrimination class action was filed in 1994, and it was settled in 1996.

Roberts provides a detailed account of racist harassment at Texaco. Roberts tells disturbing stories of the blatant, overtly racist behavior suffered by many of Texaco's African-American employees. Some employees of color endured "racist taunts" and "physical threats." Texaco's African-American employees complained of racist epithets and jokes. Roberts also writes of subtle discriminatory practices in the way Texaco managers made decisions about hiring, promotion, and pay. African Americans were "passed over for one promotion after another" and were paid less than whites in the same position.

Roberts describes her conversation with an African-American woman in Texaco's human resources department. The human resources employee explained the pervasive nature of racism at Texaco:

> I've talked to lots of blacks who've been working here for years who aren't even being paid the minimum salary for the grade they're in. If they ask for a promotion, they get turned down. The government comes in once in a while and finds violations and Texaco promises to fix them, but absolutely nothing gets done. Most of the blacks are too scared to complain.

Roberts writes of her meeting with Texaco's vice president of human resources about undertaking measures that would enhance racial diversity. She suggested, among other things, that the company start an association for black employees and recruit more at black colleges. He bellowed his reaction to her suggestions: "You people must have lost your minds! ... We'll never do any of these things!"

Not surprisingly, the narrative that Texaco provides in its proxy statements is dramatically different than Roberts's account of race matters within the company. A company's proxy materials provide notice to shareholders of the firm's annual meeting and the matters on the agenda for the meeting. In its proxy statements for 1994, 1995, and 1996 (as in statements before and after this period), Texaco described the credentials of the nominees for election or reelection to its board and asked shareholders to send in their proxies, or votes, for the nominees.

In its proxy statements, Texaco's board seems to take seriously its duty of care, which includes a duty to monitor compliance with the law. Texaco paints a picture of a board of directors that closely monitors compliance with antidiscrimination law. The company states that "Human Resources Committees ... review the development of minorities and women within the company." In the 1996 proxy materials, Texaco made explicit statements about the board's fiduciary obligations and the fact that they include "gathering all the information [the board] deems necessary, from whatever sources, including the officers and managers of the company, outside experts, and others in order to make decisions that are in the best interest of the company and its stockholders." The company claims to monitor "activities of Texaco [that] pose significant risks and ... the company's programs to respond to and contain such risks." In the 1996 proxy materials, Texaco promises its shareholders that "[t]he Board, working with management, has established a series of procedures to assure a flow of information about the company's business."

Texaco's 1996 proxy statement was drafted two years after hundreds of Texaco employees of color alleged pervasive race discrimination within the company, and months before a disgruntled white employee turned over tapes that contained evidence of the blatant racism of some of the firm's managers. (These tapes inspired the company to settle the class action.) In its proxy statements, Texaco's board claims that it gathered information. Did any director or board committee speak to any of Texaco's minority employees? Did the board communicate with the Human Resources vice president who reacted to suggestions from minority employees by saying they had lost their minds? And what about Texaco's Human Resources Committees? The company claimed that these committees monitored minority employees' progress within the company. Did the board or the Human Resources Committees ask why some African-American employees were paid less for the same work? With the monitoring systems that the board described in the proxy materials in place, how could the board not know about some of the problems that Roberts so thoroughly describes in her book? Was the discussion about the board's monitoring and information-gathering systems doublespeak?

Texaco's board also engages in diversity doublespeak. In its 1994 and 1995 statements, Texaco included a shareholder proposal relating to the company's employment practices. The shareholder proponents specifically stated that their goal was to "encourage [Texaco's] Board … and [CEO] to improve [the] corporation's Equal Employment record." In the proxy statements, Texaco's board explained why it recommended that shareholders vote against the proposal. In so doing, the company enumerated its affirmative action policies and its efforts to achieve diversity. The materials described Texaco's "[e]stablishment of … [p]rocedure[s], designed to provide employees with the opportunity to raise and fairly resolve workplace disputes without litigation." Texaco's proxy statement painted a picture of a utopian company. "Texaco is an Equal Opportunity Employer…." The company described its "toll-free telephone line [that] is available to employees to ask any questions about, or to report any violations of" its equal employment opportunity and human resources guidelines.

In the aftermath of the Texaco debacle, a shareholder derivative claim brought by Texaco investors was settled on terms that missed the opportunity to provide meaningful change. Texaco's shareholders filed derivative litigation seeking recovery of corporate losses incurred in the settlement of the race discrimination litigation. According to the court, the shareholders alleged that Texaco directors:

> [B]reached their fiduciary duties to the company and its shareholders, and wasted corporate assets, by intentionally, recklessly, grossly negligently and/or negligently failing to exercise appropriate oversight in connection with Texaco's compliance with federal and state civil rights laws, enforcement of anti-discriminatory practices, conduct within Texaco's human resources department, and particularly in the defense of the [race discrimination class action].

Texaco's shareholders received no monetary recovery in the settlement of the derivative suit. The court-approved settlement of the shareholders' suit allowed for the payment of shareholders' attorney's fees and expenses and gave shareholders the right to request a copy of the public portion of the annual report of the Task Force that was appointed to monitor compliance with antidiscrimination law under the terms of the race discrimination settlement.

Of course, the shareholders were right to pursue their claim that Texaco's board breached the duty of care owed them because of the directors' failure to require adequate information and monitoring systems that would oversee compliance with antidiscrimination law. The court observed that the plaintiffs would have to show reckless indifference by the board to prevail in a claim alleging breach of the board's duty of care and opined that plaintiffs are likely to be unsuccessful in this regard. The court also noted that under Section 102(b)(7), Texaco had severely limited the ability of shareholders to hold directors personally liable for duty of care breaches. There are, however, two problems with the court's discussion.

First, it is a stretch to argue that Texaco's board was not recklessly indifferent to the claims of African-American employees of pervasive race discrimination within the company and the potential effect of those claims on shareholder wealth. Over fifty people contacted a shareholder activist group in a one-year period in the mid-1990s to "complain about discrimination." At least eleven cases were pending with local Human Rights Commissions.

Until the late 1990s, no African American had ever sat on the Texaco board "in the nearly hundred years of the company's existence." The leader of the shareholder activist group described his conversation with top managers at Texaco "about naming some women and blacks" to the Texaco board. Texaco's corporate secretary yelled, "[w]e are simply not seeking skirts or a black face to put on our board!"

"At every level Texaco had far fewer black employees than the industry average and the disparity grew by an alarming degree the higher up the scale you went." And as the African-American plaintiffs worked with lawyers to draft their complaint, they endured "a fresh plague of racial insults." As Roberts and her lawyers added new members to the class action, they gathered alarming stories of racism that included "racist taunts, physical threats, and being passed over for one promotion after another." Several African-American employees were paid significantly less than whites who did the same work. For example, an African-American woman with a "stellar sales record … was … paid $850 a month less than whites who held the same position."

Throughout her book, Roberts describes pervasive, almost ubiquitous discrimination at Texaco. Some of the discriminatory acts were blatant. Others were covert and subtle It is clear that Texaco's vice president of human resources breached the duty of care he owed shareholders to comply with antidiscrimination laws and to monitor the compliance of those supervised to avoid potential litigation costs, settlement fees, and negative publicity that could reduce shareholder wealth. The vice president of human resources and other managers at Texaco were at least "recklessly indifferent" to noncompliance with antidiscrimination law.

The board was indifferent to pay disparities between African-American and white employees and to the lack of African-American directors and senior managers. This indifference to employee interests eventually led to the employees' class action and the attendant negative publicity and large settlement costs that were potentially harmful to shareholders. After the filing of the employee class action, the board remained recklessly indifferent to complaints of discrimination made by hundreds of its African-American employees and to the potential harm that continued discrimination would have on shareholder interests.

The race discrimination suit languished. Even after the Equal Employment Opportunity Commission investigated Texaco and issued a report stating that "[t]here is reasonable cause to believe that [Texaco] failed to promote Blacks … as a class throughout its facilities because of their race," the company "sent out an open letter to all employees that was … full of self-serving distortions about the agency report." What would have happened had Texaco's board and senior managers undertaken a different strategy? Instead of sending a letter to employees denying the claims made by its African-American employees, would the company have avoided the impending crisis if directors and officers had met with the lead plaintiffs in the discrimination suit? What could Texaco's managers and directors have learned from such a meeting? One of the lawyers representing Texaco's employees heard appalling stories about the company's racist climate when she deposed class action members. The plaintiffs described the use of racist epithets and symbols by white Texaco employees and low-level managers, some of whom referred to African-American employees as "nigger," "orangutan," and "porch monkey." The letters "KKK" were painted on an African-American employee's car. One Texaco vice president "dressed up as a black Sambo for a company Halloween party." White managers told racist jokes. Disparaging comments were made about the intellectual acuity of African Americans. The indifference of the board and senior executives to the potential impact of race discrimination on the company and its shareholders converted into action only after a disgruntled employee delivered tapes that contained evidence of discriminatory practices at Texaco. This event occurred, however, only after the large settlement became necessary, and after the company endured a public relations nightmare.

There is a second, and perhaps more important, problem with the court's discussion in the settlement opinion for the shareholder suit against Texaco. The court approved the derivative litigation in part because of the claimed "non-pecuniary ... therapeutic benefits" that the corporation would derive from the settlement's terms. In reaching its decision as to the appropriateness and amount of plaintiff's attorney's fees, the court concluded that there was substantial benefit to the company because the derivative litigation settlement gave shareholders the ability to request the report of the Task Force created pursuant to the settlement of the discrimination litigation.

The terms of the settlement of the Texaco derivative litigation provide a vivid example of the squandered potential for transforming a culture of noncompliance. The settlement terms of the Texaco derivative suit were superfluous and anemic. They duplicated the settlement terms of the race discrimination suit, and they provided for no real transformation of Texaco's racially-toxic climate. Settlements of derivative suits alleging duty of care breaches provide potentially winning outcomes for shareholders. Plaintiffs lose, however, even when their claims are settled because their attorneys fail to negotiate for more substantial settlement terms that may transform corporate cultures. Plaintiffs lose also because courts approve such settlements as fair and reasonable.

IV. Directorial Ignorance Is Directorial Bliss:
In re Caremark International Inc. Derivative Litigation and Cosmetic Monitoring

Years after the enactment of statutes such as Delaware's Section 102(b)(7), Chancellor Allen discussed the duty of care in *In re Caremark International Inc. Derivative Litigation* as though corporate care obligations retained their force and importance. Allen articulated two components of the duty of care. First, directors are obliged to make decisions on behalf of the company in good faith and employ a rational decisionmaking process. Second, directors breach their duty of care when there is "an unconsidered failure of the board to act in circumstances in which due attention would, arguably, have prevented" corporate or shareholder losses.

The best strategy for shareholders claiming harm to their companies resulting from duty of care breaches may be to go to the board and to put directors on notice of compliance problems within the firm. Shareholders who can convince boards to take remedial action to eliminate care, oversight, and monitoring breaches will eliminate the need for derivative litigation in this context. Shareholders who suspect ongoing and pervasive noncompliance with the law within their firms should ask their attorneys to contact boards to inform them about their suspicions. Shareholders—most likely institutional shareholders—or their attorneys should request that boards, in satisfaction of their duty of care, inquire about the suspected noncompliance. Before filing suit, and instead of claiming that demand is excused, shareholders can simply make demand on the board to take corrective action that eliminates duty of care breaches. Shareholders can request that boards take the kind of remedial action that would satisfy their duties to monitor and oversee compliance with law and inquire about compliance when there is a reason to do so.

Advocating an approach such as this seems naively hopeful. Surprisingly, however, the expectation that boards will respond to shareholder demands that they avoid duty of care breaches is not as incredulous as it sounds. Steve Kardell, a Texas attorney, has successfully represented shareholders making such demands on boards. Boards responded favorably, honoring Kardell's requests on behalf of his clients that directors oversee and inquire about claims of employee noncompliance. Shareholders have achieved modest success in eliminating duty of care breaches by simply asking the board to satisfy its care obligations. Kardell's success provides evidence that many directors take duty of care obligations seriously.

Specifically, Kardell has made demand requests on corporate boards on behalf of his shareholder clients requesting that directors fortify corporate codes of conduct and take seriously their compliance obligations. The companies that receive such requests from Kardell may have compliance programs, but the programs "have no muscle." For example, Kardell discovered that even though monitoring and reporting systems are in place, at some companies they may be cosmetic because employees' complaints or reports of corporate noncompliance are implicitly discouraged. In such cases, Kardell's demand contains requests that the board revise its code of conduct or compliance code to include a clause with strong language that clearly prohibits retaliation against employees who blow the whistle.

Kardell was somewhat surprised by the board's response to the demands he made on behalf of his shareholder clients. Kardell expected that his demand requests would be denied. His initial plan was to file suit in response to this anticipated denial claiming that the board's refusal of demand was wrongful. He wanted to get the most serious cases of egregious duty of care breaches before Delaware courts. Kardell, however, in most instances, did not have the opportunity to file on behalf of his clients because the board responded favorably to his clients' demand to take corrective action.

Delaware courts have noted the importance of monitoring compliance with law, but it is clear that specific monitoring obligations are not triggered if directors have no notice of failure to comply with the corporation's legal obligations. Kardell's approach puts "directors on notice of a compliance breakdown. Without notice of deficiencies in the architecture of a corporate code of conduct or compliance program," boards cannot take remedial action. Kardell has used the pre-suit demand process as a mechanism that provides directors with notice that compliance and reporting systems are ineffective. One of Kardell's future strategies in representing shareholders is to demand that boards conduct internal independent audits to determine the effectiveness of their compliance and reporting processes. Another possible strategy is to demand that boards address substantive issues in their codes of conduct. He suggests requiring boards to draft language regarding the company's compliance in specific areas. For example, a company's code of conduct may include language that the company complies with all applicable environmental law.

Directors, especially outside directors who are not involved in the day-to-day operations of the firm, are likely to be unaware of noncompliance within their companies. Shareholders who demand that boards take remedial action may be an important source of information for directors who rely heavily on managers for such information. At times, concerned shareholders may be the only source of information concerning noncompliance because managers have an incentive to withhold information about the company that may create a negative perception concerning their own performance. Perhaps the avoidance of negative publicity serves as an incentive for boards to take remedial action when shareholders describe failures on the part of corporate employees to comply with law and attendant directorial oversight and monitoring breaches.

V. Acknowledgment and/or Apology:
The Potential To Transform Corporate Cultures

Boards are far removed from a company's day-to-day operations, but directors should routinely inquire about all aspects of corporate compliance with the law. Directors should make clear that they expect truthful and complete information. Before corporate cultures can change, the boardroom culture must change. When serious or pervasive noncompliance is uncovered, and this can happen only after meaningful inquiry or monitoring that is intended to uncover violations of law, directors and senior executives should acknowledge the wrongdoing. Acknowledging corporate misconduct that is serious and pervasive is a prerequisite to correcting such conduct. Unlawfulness that is never acknowledged will persist and may worsen.

Of course, the decision about the form that the acknowledgment should take should be left to the board and senior managers. At times, apology for failure to comply with the law is the most appropriate form of acknowledgment. Also up to the board is the decision about when noncompliance should be acknowledged. My suggestion is that acknowledgment is appropriate upon discovery of serious and pervasive noncompliance.

Courts describe a duty to employ rational decisionmaking processes, and obligations to inquire about and monitor conduct that may harm the shareholders or the corporation. Courts do not offer guidance to directors and managers about what they should do when noncompliance is discovered. Without such guidance, directors and managers may do all they can to avoid receiving complete and accurate information about noncompliance. They do not know what to do with such information. They are afraid of the potential lawsuits that may follow if noncompliance is discovered.

The *Caremark* litigation illustrates an important point concerning the issues I raise. Courts, when discussing the duty of care, have failed to discuss fully the "processing" of the information collected, nor have they encouraged boards and officers to draw conclusions, proper or otherwise, from the information they have gathered.

This observation may begin to explain how the duty of care has been rendered meaningless and anachronistic, and why the idea of imposing on boards an obligation to inquire about and to monitor corporate compliance has failed to transform corporate cultures. For it to be meaningful, the board's duty of care should include not only an obligation to inquire and monitor, but also an obligation to adequately analyze the information gathered, to process it carefully, and to acknowledge those instances when failure to comply with the law is discovered. The fear of potential liability would be magnified if directors and managers are asked to acknowledge the failure of their employees to comply with applicable law as I suggest here. So, corporate attorneys must help boards understand that their discovery of corporate unlawfulness is not the worst that can happen. It may mean that the company will be liable to the persons harmed, but it is also likely to mean that the unlawful conduct will not recur. Of course, the decision regarding the type of corrective action taken is entirely up to the board. But corrective action is impossible without acknowledging the need for such action.

Inquiries and monitoring systems are meaningless without a board's desire for receiving complete and accurate information, its willingness to process the information received, and the inclination of directors and senior managers to acknowledge serious pervasive misconduct when discovered. Acknowledging wrongdoing, even apologizing for misconduct, however, will not prevent recurring unlawfulness.

A vital antecedent to taking action that may preclude recurring liability and negative publicity as a result of corporate employees' failure to comply with law is acknowledging the noncompliance. Often, an acknowledgment of noncompliance, accompanied by an apology for harm caused, will go a long way in helping to restore a company's good reputation and minimizing shareholder losses by reducing the likelihood that noncompliance will recur. "Johnson & Johnson is an example of a corporation that used apology successfully and became a role model for handling a crisis during the Tylenol tampering case that killed seven people in 1982." Johnson & Johnson made crucial organizational changes following its apology and reestablished itself as a company deserving public and consumer trust. The company did not avoid liability for injuries resulting from the tampering, but its apology, accompanied by corrective action, may have prevented additional litigation and negative publicity. It is also possible that an appropriate apology may help a company avoid litigation for its misconduct altogether.

Consider the duty of care breaches that occurred at Texaco and Coca-Cola. The non-pecuniary terms of both settlements required steps that would have satisfied fiduciary obligations under the duty of care and should have been taken when pervasive complaints of discrimination were first articulated. Long before the complaints were made, directors, in satisfaction of their duty of care, should have required managers to implement a system that would have alerted the board to potential discrimination. Directors should have been asking questions about compliance routinely. Specifically, directors, or at least a committee of the board, should inquire about employee satisfaction. If directors take seriously this aspect of the monitoring component of the duty of care they owe shareholders, they will ask penetrating questions that will yield truthful answers.

These corporate undertakings are likely to be merely cosmetic without some acknowledgment of pervasive trouble within the workplace. For example, neither Coca-Cola nor Texaco acknowledged the failure of the board and senior managers to adequately monitor compliance with antidiscrimination law.

In the Texaco race discrimination case, African-American employees first complained about discrimination to the vice president of human resources. Before these complaints were made, the absence of the Texaco board's consideration as to whether the company violated antidiscrimination law was appropriate. The approach I advocate, however, would have notified the board that something was amiss at their company when the complaints were made. The board should have asked senior executives whether mid-level managers, such as the vice president of human resources, had received complaints. The board's penetrating questions and expectation of real information from managers would have revealed that some employees were complaining about race discrimination, and this response should have triggered more questions and investigation. All of this may have avoided the negative publicity that led to the settlement. This approach may have been an important step toward transforming a racially-toxic corporate culture, and it may have avoided the large settlement itself.

The Texaco settlement seems to have been inspired by the revelations contained in tapes turned over to the plaintiffs' attorneys by a disgruntled white Texaco manager. The audiotapes contained a conversation of Texaco managers discussing plans to destroy evidence germane to the plaintiff's case. A few days after the tapes became public, Texaco responded to the media's questions about the plaintiffs' allegations. There was no apology in Texaco's initial response after the tapes. There was only diversity doublespeak. The following statement was made in a press release: "The company is committed to providing a work environment which reflects an understanding of diversity, and is free from all forms of discrimination, intimidation, and harassment.... We are dedicated to equal opportunity in all aspects of employment and will not allow any violation of law or company policies."

In a video message to employees, however, Bijur used strong language that came close to an acknowledgment of the obligation of managers to monitor compliance with antidiscrimination law: "We are determined to root out [the employees involved in the] alleged behavior." And in a press release, Bijur apologized:

> With regard to the four individuals involved in the allegations before us, two are active employees. They are both being suspended today.... As to the two retired employees, we believe there is sufficient cause to withdraw benefits.... Fundamentally, we don't believe the statements and actions on the tapes are representative of Texaco.... I want to offer an apology.... I am sorry for this incident; I pledge to you that we will do everything in our power to heal the painful wounds that the reckless behavior of those involved have inflicted on all of us.

Other than his promise that "[w]e are determined to root out" employees involved in the alleged behavior, nowhere in his public comments does Bijur acknowledge that the problem may extend beyond the four employees heard on the tapes. He does not acknowledge that the problem may be structural, systemic, and cultural. In his statements, Bijur apologizes, but he does not accept responsibility for the failure of the board and senior managers to exercise oversight with respect to compliance with antidiscrimination law.

VI. Conclusion

My goal in this Article is to help firms move beyond unthinking repetitions such as "we are an equal opportunity employer" and close the gap between what firms say and what they do when it comes to diversity, discrimination, and compliance issues. In the 1990s, several large publicly-held companies paid huge amounts to settle discrimination litigation. Shareholders have brought derivative suits against corporate boards claiming that directors' fiduciary duty breaches caused the corporate losses incurred when companies settled these discrimination suits for millions of dollars. These settlements, however, have not healed or transformed discriminatory corporate workplaces. In approving the settlements of both the discrimination and derivative suits, courts have allowed boards and senior managers to avoid the very difficult work of frank inquiry into, and meaningful monitoring of, allegations of discrimination caused by racism and sexism. The settlements have no curative power because they do not require companies to acknowledge the problem of discrimination when it exists. Left unacknowledged, the discrimination persists in the face of the kinds of cosmetic organizational changes that corporations have made under the terms of the various settlements.

In this Article, I consider settlement opinions of employment discrimination claims and the resulting shareholder derivative suits that allege that the large amounts paid to settle discrimination litigation cause corporate losses that are the result of the directorial breach of the duty of care. These settlements point out the need to revitalize, clarify, and resurrect the fiduciary duty of care. When employees claim pervasive workplace discrimination, courts should encourage meaningful investigation and corporate acknowledgment of discriminatory practices if discovered.

I suggest nothing drastic in this Article. My modest suggestion is that what is said — whether by corporations or courts — should be taken seriously. There should be no gaping disparity between what companies say — "we are an equal opportunity employer" — and what they do when they fail to acknowledge the tragedy of continuing workplace discrimination. There should be no material gap between what courts say—directors owe a duty of care that includes inquiring about and monitoring compliance with law—and what courts do when they allow anemic settlements of discrimination suits brought by employees and derivative litigation brought by shareholders.

The appeal of the suggestion I make in this Article to revitalize the duty of care to avoid shareholder losses and, more importantly, to achieve racial equity within the corporate workplace is that the duty of care is structural in nature. The duty of care as a structural approach is important in its ability to avoid problems before they harm the corporation, its shareholders, and its employees.

It is interesting that the court that approved the Texaco derivative litigation looked for therapeutic benefits. Therapeutic means to have "healing or curative powers." The goal is to heal, cure, and transform racially-toxic corporate cultures. I do not believe that racism can be eradicated because I agree with Professor Derrick Bell's conclusions about the permanent and indestructible nature of racism. I do believe, however, that corporate cultures can be healed, cured, and transformed. Racist and discriminatory decisionmaking and conduct may persist, but these problems will not thrive in a corporate culture that inquires about such problems, monitors them, and acknowledges the problems when they exist. An unacknowledged disease cannot be healed. It is the acknowledgment of discrimination's existence and harm at Texaco, Coca-Cola, and other companies that is lacking in the settling of discrimination litigation brought by employees and derivative suits brought by shareholders.

Notes

(1) Are the diversity statements that you find on most corporations' websites genuine, or are the statements merely efforts to give the appearance of welcoming a diverse background?

(2) How can institutional and retail shareholders challenge the gap between what companies say about diversity and what they actually do?

(3) Which of the following situations do you believe that a board would be most likely to investigate and resolve: employee theft or allegations of employee discrimination? If your answer is employee theft, what does that say about the way that a board values diversity?

E. Interest Conflict: CEO Primacy versus Diversity

In the following article, that was quoted from in chapter one, Professor Ramirez postulates that diversity in America's corporate boardrooms will not occur in any meaningful capacity until economic, social and political reform dictate such result. Since CEO's, by controlling the proxy statement, control the director selection process, and more importantly, control who determines the fate of the CEO, CEO's are more likely to maintain homogeneity to ensure the continued empowerment of the CEO. Given this inherent conflict, Ramirez argues that increased diversity will not occur unless the interests of America's CEO's align with an appreciation for the value of diversity.

In reading this article, think critically about Professor Ramirez's argument and whether he is correct—will America's boardrooms remain dominated by white males until their interests align with the concept of diversity?

Games CEOs Play and Interest Convergence Theory: Why Diversity Lags in America's Boardrooms and What to Do about It

Steven A. Ramirez

61 Wash. & Lee L. Rev. 1583 (2004)

I. Introduction

At its foundations, critical race theory holds that race in modern America is ubiquitous, that color-blind lawmaking is likely to address only the most blatant racism, and that any progress occurs only when the interests of the powerful converge with the interests of the racially oppressed. Recent events in corporate America illustrate these key points. First, as ever, the bastions of corporate governance remain the nearly exclusive province of white males, with no realistic end in sight. Second, this racial homogeneity exists with little overt racial discrimination and few violations of antidiscrimination law. Indeed, it appears far more likely that board members are chosen based upon cultural proximity to CEOs rather than color. It just so happens that upper class white males are frequently most culturally proximate to upper class white males. Third, any reform is unlikely unless sufficient political and economic pressure is levied upon the people with the power to restructure the law in this specific context. Simply put, this homosocial reproduction will end only when those with sufficient power see it in their interest to end it. In fact, the Sarbanes-Oxley Act of 2002 can only be termed a wasted opportunity to disrupt legally the homosocial reproduction that plagues board selection processes. Reform did not happen because the political calculus governing the reform effort failed to comprehend the racial stakes of the issues at hand.

Implicit in that conclusion is cause for an optimism of sorts. The political calculus could have been different and fundamentally more in favor of a superior outcome in terms of race. Interest convergence theory holds that reform occurs when the interests of the racially oppressed align with the interests of the people who have the power to bring about reform. This process requires that the alignment be fully understood before reform can occur. This in turn underscores the importance of educating and persuading the relevant powers. Competing interests must be overcome. Alliances must be formed—and re-formed—as needed in each specific context. In short, the interest alignment that is fundamental to convergence theory is manipulable.

This Article seeks to demonstrate that convergence theory holds the promise of real and durable reform in the specific context of board selection processes and, by extension, in a host of other areas that may be key to racial progress. Part I of this Article posits that CEOs of many of the largest, most powerful corporations in America have exploited America's racial blind spots to entrench their power and enrich themselves. The Article does not seek to show that any particular CEO has engaged in intentional racial discrimination. Nor does the Article even attempt to argue that any CEO is, or is not, a racist. That is beside the point. The point is that race continues to operate in this specific context to favor whites and disadvantage blacks. Simply stated, CEOs seem highly inclined to take affirmative actions to favor culturally proximate (white) candidates for board membership over (less culturally proximate) candidates of color. They do this for the purpose of rationally maximizing their payoffs in a context ripe for strategic behavior.

Thus, this is yet another context where race matters in our society even in the absence of any intent to discriminate on the basis of race. Part II concludes that CEOs seek to maximize their payoffs by playing the homosocial reproduction game.

Part III of this Article hypothesizes that this dynamic of inadvertent discrimination can be disrupted by law. This type of legal reform could well enjoy broader support among key constituencies, leading to an interest alignment sufficient to support progressive reform. Senior level diversity serves to enhance corporate profitability, and board diversity should serve to quell corporate corruption, thereby further enhancing shareholder wealth. Moreover, there is little doubt that race has imposed billions in macroeconomic costs annually upon our society. Therefore, race operates in the context of board selection to frustrate many broadly defined interests. The sway of race here, as expressed through the operation of the current legal structures governing board selection, only serves the narrow interests of sitting CEOs to maximize their autonomy over corporate wealth and, institutionally, to indulge racial mythology and allow it to impede economic performance. In sum, there is much more pressure for potential reform, and little in favor of the status quo. Part III concludes that the issue of board diversity is one ripe for reform under an interest convergence lens.

The legal issues underlying the homosocial reproduction mechanism have important implications for corporate governance. This Article raises the concern that CEOs will naturally seek boards that are as similar as possible to themselves in all socially relevant characteristics. This Article consequently suggests that real corporate governance reform should focus on neutralizing CEO influence over the board selection process and in the boardroom generally. This may be the only way to assure diversity in the boardroom, as well as sound corporate governance, at least in this lifetime. Perhaps the most important suggestion of this Article, however, transcends mere corporate governance, as salient as that issue has recently become. Specifically, convergence theory is not just a cynical lens for viewing supposed white benevolence; it also reflects a historic truism applicable to all progressive reform. Real and durable reform in America requires the consent and support of the vested interests and political actors with specific political and economic power over any prospective reform. In short, convergence theory not only signals when reformers can seize opportunities, but it also counsels how to proceed: build coalitions of convenience and apply pressure atomistically.

II. Diversity in the Boardroom and the Games CEOs Play

Diversity in the boardroom enhances corporate profitability according to the consensus of scholars of business management, finance, and economics. In addition, diversity seems to add a dimension of abrasion that can serve to mitigate groupthink and thereby heighten the cognitive functioning of the corporate boards. All of this is mainstream management science and is a logical outgrowth of the now established reality of race: race is a function of legal and social construction that leads to cultural diversity, but it has no biological or genetic significance. Due to the cultural moorings of race, diverse board members bring enriched perspectives to the boardroom with no offsetting diminution of merit, defined in accordance with the institutional mission of the business. It is not skin color or other morphological features traditionally associated with race that gives rise to different and valuable experiences and insights; rather it is cultural diversity that leads to cognitive skills that can and do transcend race.

Of course, this being America at the turn of the twenty-first century, many still do believe in race. Because many of these maleducated denizens of our racialized society are shareholders or board members, the pressure to insist upon culturally diverse boards is diluted. Similarly, it is clear that our racialized society fails to invest in the human capital of minority groups at the same rate it invests in whites. Economists also have shown that minority groups generally do not have access to the same social capital—or social networks—that are accessible to whites. Proportionately, this means an artificial shortage of elite people of color throughout our society in general, and for board service in particular. Thus, CEOs may be tempted, under cover of these facts, to avoid any compulsion for diversifying their boards. Instead, studies have demonstrated that executives will seek to fill boards with demographic and cultural reproductions of themselves. This conclusion enjoys empirical support from abroad suggesting that the selection of board members and senior management teams are naturally subject to homosocial reproduction. It is no accident that boards are not diverse.

After all, most people do not get to pick their bosses. Yet in America, even today after much heralded reforms, CEOs of publicly held companies get to pick their bosses—the board of directors. Given this power, it would be natural for a CEO to select a board of directors comprised of the CEO's clones. Instead, CEOs do the next best thing—they select their cultural and demographic clones. This effectively achieves the same outcome: CEO power over board selection leads to enhanced compensation of CEOs. Recent history confirms that American CEOs have received excessive, even outrageous, compensation. Homosocial reproduction is likely a prime cause of this malady.

It is only natural that a CEO would prefer someone that is culturally proximate to himself; nevertheless, it effectively perpetuates yesteryear's tradition of racial apartheid. If directors select CEOs and CEOs select directors, a preexisting apartheid tradition can deteriorate very slowly before giving way to a racially equitable process. Indeed, at today's rate of board diversification, the arrival of racial equity at this level may be measured in centuries rather than decades.

In economic terms, it is increasingly difficult to portray CEOs as rational maximizers fixated on furthering the interest of their corporations in order to further their own self-interest, as the once dominant optimal contracting approach suggested. Under the optimal contracting approach, directors address inherent agency costs that arise from the divergent interests of the shareholders and management by structuring executive compensation packages in a way that minimizes these agency costs. This model supports a generally sanguine view of executive compensation. However, by the summer of 2002, it became clear that pervasive managerial overreaching outstripped examples of optimal contracting. Thus, CEOs can, and often do, exercise power to enhance their compensation at the expense of their corporation. At some firms, it is now clear that optimal contracts do not curb self-serving CEO conduct, and "executives may only be constrained by what they can get away with." The lack of CEO enthusiasm for diversity on the board, notwithstanding the economic rationality of pursuing senior-level cultural diversity in terms of enhancing the financial performance of the corporation, is likely one means of furthering this goal.

Many CEOs, however, stand to gain more from nondiverse boards than they would from diversifying their boards, as demonstrated by studies showing that CEOs of culturally homogenous boards are paid more than CEOs with diverse boards. In fact, there is no reason to think that the issue of diversity will be managed more benevolently than CEO compensation. For example, there are no reports of CEOs being dismissed for mismanaging diversity at the board level, so the threat of dismissal is most likely even smaller than the threat of dismissal for rent extraction in the form of excessive compensation.

In terms of market pressure to diversify, economists, including Nobel laureate Kenneth Arrow, have already shown that race has often exceeded mere economic incentives. From automobile sales to labor markets, economists have now identified the power of race to cause market distortions across the American economy, and there is no evidence that CEO gains from pursuing homosocial reproduction at the board level could somehow be trumped by market forces that have failed to overcome the pursuit of excessive compensation and have failed to trump the power of race in a wide variety of economic contexts. This is not to say that economic doctrine cannot provide some degree of insight to explain why many CEOs refrain from diversifying their boards.

So, will CEOs rationally act to maximize the profitability and value of their businesses by pursuing a diverse board so that the company will have additional profits to share with the CEO as the optimal contracting approach would suggest? I posit they will not always do so. Instead, many will play the homosocial reproduction game, secure in the knowledge that neither shareholders nor capital markets will limit their options. First, each CEO will be able to garner enhanced compensation by creating very homogenous boards complete with other CEOs. Second, any payoffs from enhanced diversity are likely to accrue to the shareholders and not the CEO; such an accrual will occur over a long period that can be measured in years, not quarters. It is much more difficult for a CEO to capture such gains than to obtain excessive compensation. Third, there is the distorting influence of race. There is a growing body of scholarship demonstrating the distortions in market behavior associated with race. When a CEO is selecting board candidates, he is competing in a non-cooperative game with other CEOs in the sense that CEOs will not contract to assure that other CEOs behave in accordance with expectations. Instead, CEOs will attempt to deduce how other CEOs will behave. If enough CEOs succumb to the temptation not to compete in diversifying their boards, then CEOs will face even less market pressure to diversify, just as CEOs appear not to compete in terms of compensation. The central point is this: CEOs will have incentives to engage in strategic behavior to avoid diversification of their board. They will be tempted to play the homosocial reproduction game, and many will succumb.

III. Disrupting the Homosocial Reproduction Game and Converging Interests

All of this suggests an intriguing interest convergence. With all the power that CEOs hold in our managerial corporate state, they are not monarchs that may hold themselves above the law—yet. Very broad constituencies have large economic stakes in the performance of the macroeconomy. To the extent that the full costs of our continued apartheid hangover are fully comprehended, these constituents are a source of potential political and economic power in favor of reform. Corporate capitalists, while clearly on the wane in terms of power over the past several decades, are nevertheless powerful and fundamentally in favor of reducing the power of CEOs. Politicians intuitively fear anti big-business and populist cries for reining in the power of business elites. Combined with advocates for racial reform, whether Latino, African-American, Native-American, white, or Asian-American, these forces would be a formidable political and economic power. Add to this mix the interest of feminists in board diversity, and a convincing convergence of interests in favor of reform emerges.

This Article proposes that those seeking racial reform must be prepared to play the same game by the same rules of all effective reformers throughout American history. Racial reformers must be prepared to forge coalitions with similarly interested parties along the very broad range of issues where race is lurking and to apply pressure to the specific political actors with power over a specific issue.

In my view, the essence of Derrick Bell's convergence theory was well-stated in an entirely different context by Gabriel Kolko in 1963. In The Triumph of Conservatism, Kolko demonstrated that so-called progressive era reforms were "invariably controlled" by business leaders and that, consequently, only reforms they deemed "acceptable or desirable" occurred. Both Bell and Kolko posit that change occurs on terms acceptable to those with power. Kolko rejects any thought that the power establishment is any kind of monolithic, conspiratorial entity. Rather, it is a reflection of the highly diffused nature of political and economic power in the United States. In contrast, Professor Bell thinks the nation is dominated by a white monolith — as it well may have been in the 1960s and 1970s, at least when it came to issues of race. Both Professor Bell and Kolko concur that in the right context progressive reform can operate in accordance with the needs of the "ascendant class" as those needs are shaped and aligned by adept reformers.

The issue, according to Kolko, is one of comprehension; elites will not accept radical reforms that are not in their interests and must be educated with respect to potential reforms that converge with their interests. I posit that racial reformers of the twenty-first century have thus far failed to comprehend fully the opportunities implicit in political capitalism today. Durable racial reform is possible to the extent that it is aligned with the interests of those with political and economic power. The key is to exploit opportunistically events and political pressure to achieve reform that is consistent with racial progress. This is the driving reality of all reform in America. Real and durable change cannot occur in a democracy without the concurrence of those holding political and economic power. While one may bemoan the current distribution of political and economic power, there is little to be gained from dwelling on this point. The end result is merely to burden racial reform with distribution issues that are far more prone to headwinds. A more effective approach is to take the current distribution of economic and political power as a given and find a way to operate within those constraints.

I suggest now that decoupling race from macro-distributional issues can serve to help eliminate one source of oppression, to the extent racial progress is achievable without addressing distributional issues. In all events, law is rarely a source of durable fundamental reform. The ability of the law to alter a distributional outcome that is essentially acceptable to all major sources of political and economic power is dubious at best. On the other hand, there is good reason to think that racial reform is to some degree achievable within the current framework of economic and political power. First, the costs of race in terms of destruction of human capital is staggering, particularly in an era when human capital is increasingly the predominate source of wealth creation. Second, the "ascendant class" is increasingly of color and diverse. Third, compared with any other era of American history, the "ascendant class" realizes the untapped potential of people of color in the United States. Fourth, in contrast to the dark ages of race, when the vast majority of society truly believed in race-based differences that were largely dictated by genetic consequences of racial phenotypes, today's holders of political and economic power are increasingly aware that race is an illusion and that all of its social consequences are the result of its social construction. Finally, in coming years, it will be inescapably clearer that allowing the effects of yesteryear's racial hierarchy to malinger and fester will entail macroeconomic catastrophe. These factors taken together suggest that there will be episodes of opportunity for racial reformers to align their interests with the interests of the "ascendant class," such that breakthroughs like Brown or the Civil Rights Act of 1964 are possible again.

In order to align interests with the current and future holders of power over relevant areas of potential reform, coordinated campaigns of education and persuasion must be undertaken, focusing on the most powerful atomistic interests that can be marshaled in favor of reform. This is precisely what occurred in 1954 when the NAACP convinced nine Supreme Court justices to move boldly away from "separate but equal" to racial integration.

The NAACP coordinated a concerted campaign to persuade nine white males endowed with political power over the specific issue of segregation in public education to fundamentally rewrite American constitutional law.

This is also precisely what could have occurred when Congress and other regulatory authorities imposed the far-reaching Sarbanes-Oxley Act of 2002 and related reform initiatives. A key element of the initiative was to limit CEO power. Restricting CEO power over the director selection process would have been a natural extension of this initiative. Indeed, since the passage of the Act, the SEC has taken affirmative steps to restrict CEO power over director selection. First, the SEC issued rules requiring publicly held companies to disclose information relating to their director selection processes and the function of any nomination committees. Second, the SEC proposed rules broadening the rights of shareholders to nominate directors. Throughout 2002 and 2003, there was significant political and regulatory pressure in favor of trimming CEO prerogatives. In fact, the Sarbanes-Oxley Act passed the Senate by a vote of ninety-seven to zero; it is difficult to imagine a more powerful context for lasting reform of corporate governance at the federal level.

This Article cannot answer these queries: whether the Sarbanes-Oxley reform initiatives could have included provisions weakening CEO prerogatives over board selection (thereby disrupting homosocial reproduction and enhancing diversity within corporate America); or whether the Act could have directly required measures to enhance diversity in the boardroom (thereby weakening CEO prerogatives over board selection). Presumably, however, insulating the CEO from the director selection process—by, for example, requiring an independent nominating committee—would limit homosocial reproduction in three important ways. First, to the extent director-selection power is shifted from the CEO to independent board members, it is shifted to individuals with diminished incentives to indulge in homosocial reproduction because unlike the CEO, the new directors would generally not be setting the compensation package for those who selected them. Second, the selectors—independent directors—would now be a slightly more diverse group than management, and their reduced inclination for homosocial reproduction would be more favorable in terms of diversity. Therefore, any legal mechanism that shifted selection power for new directors to the board and away from the CEO would likely lead to a significant uptick in the presence of diversity in the boardrooms of corporate America as well as an improvement in corporate governance.

Although there were many influential interests in favor of restricting CEO power over the board of directors, the political and regulatory process still defies prediction. There was a wealth of recent scholarship suggesting that diverse boards would enhance board scrutiny of CEO action. In a broad political sense, the environment was ripe for real reform, and there was some recognition that the hold of the CEO over most boardrooms was a root problem of the crisis in investor confidence in the summer of 2002. Moreover, there is constant political pressure for measures that would tend to erase embedded racial inequality within our society. On the other hand, management interests wield considerable power, and recent events suggest there are limits to the degree to which law can rein in this power, at least in a more ordinary environment than that which prevailed in 2002–03. Thus, in the final analysis, the question of whether CEO power over the director nomination process would command sufficient political and economic support to become a durable feature of American corporate law is a question that can only be answered in a nonhypothetical manner after some racial reformer plays the hand that our system of political capitalism deals.

IV. Conclusion

The United States is a capitalist democracy. Consequently, the law in the United States responds to political and economic power. The American legal system is also a highly diffused system. Therefore, reformers must orchestrate political and economic power to bring pressure to bear upon the specific legal actors vested with responsibility over a particular issue if they wish to achieve durable reform. Interest convergence theory is the key to reform and progress in any area of law from race to corporate governance. As Derrick Bell has correctly stated: "Further progress to fulfill the mandate of Brown is possible to the extent that the divergence of racial interests can be avoided or minimized." The converse of Bell's observation is equally true: To the extent interest convergence is maximized, reform opportunities are maximized. This Article seeks to extend interest convergence theory to its logical ends—specifically, to include the possibility that interests can be aligned to further the goal of reform, racial or otherwise. This possibility can come to fruition when individuals seeking specific reforms can convince specific individuals with economic or political power over that specific issue. This is essentially what the NAACP achieved in the Brown decision. This alignment of interests was achieved in the Grutter opinion fifty years later, where it succeeded in securing qualified support for affirmative action from a fundamentally conservative Court. It also explains Richard Painter's efforts to relandscape professional responsibility for attorneys representing publicly held companies. In each case, economic and political power was brought to bear on lawmakers vested with specific power over a specific issue.

The Article also seeks to illustrate these points in the specific context of corporate corruption and the Sarbanes-Oxley Act of 2002. This Act presented an historic opportunity to facilitate more diverse boards. In the end, this reform was forestalled in favor of weaker reforms that will not contribute to the goal of racial reform in any material way. This Article posits that this result flows more from the fact that there was no prime mover striving to forge an interest alignment sufficient to accomplish the specific reforms needed to enhance board diversity than from either the merits of any particular proposal or the support any proposal may have inspired. The lesson to be learned from this reality is the lesson of this Symposium. Race is everywhere; therefore, possibilities for racial reform are similarly ubiquitous. It is even present within issues related to CEO domination of the director selection process. CEOs play the game of homosocial reproduction when selecting directors. Given our apartheid tradition, this means that the upper echelons of corporate America will be essentially the exclusive province of white males far into the future. But, because board diversity can improve corporate governance, racial reformers may find many allies that can serve to facilitate reform in this arena. The challenge is to find economic and political interests that can gain either from enhanced diversity or from improved corporate governance and to educate and mobilize those interests.

Copyright © 2004 by Washington and Lee University School of Law; Steven A. Ramirez

Notes

(1) Why is it that in order to justify diversity one has to show that minorities are somehow more competent than their white male counterparts?

(2) When have white males, who drove the country into financial peril in 2008, had to validate themselves in the same way?

(3) Is it possible to change this paradigm?

(4) Is America's lack of meaningful board diversity attributable to CEO primacy or is it attributable to the idea that there is a lack of qualified minority applicants to serve in America's boardrooms.

(5) Does Ramirez's application of Professor Bell's interest convergence theory align with Karnani's notion about when corporations will make responsible decisions?

Chapter Seven

Realizing Justice

What tools are available to the justice oriented corporate practitioner? Must lawyers merely stand by while status quo notions of corporate supremacy reign supreme? Corporate Justice stands not only for corporate social responsibility and the ideal that corporations do no harm, but also for the proposition that progressive advocates can use the law to assist corporations and their leaders to make decisions that inure to the benefit of communities, employees, and stakeholders while simultaneously rewarding shareholders and executives with increased profitability. This chapter examines and details those tools available to advocates and activists who seek to inspire corporate decisionmakers to do the right thing as they lead the world's most powerful institutions.

We begin with our study of the seminal corporate law case *Zapata v. Maldonado* where we find the Delaware Supreme Court recognizing that in certain rare instances, substituting a Court's judgment for the business judgment of corporate leaders can actually be the right call to make.

A. Retrenchment of Directorial Power: Decreased Deference to Special Litigation Committees

Zapata Corporation v. William Maldonado

430 A.2d 779, 22 A.L.R.4th 1190 (1981)
Supreme Court of Delaware

Before DUFFY, QUILLEN and HORSEY, JJ.

QUILLEN, Justice:

This is an interlocutory appeal from an order entered on April 9, 1980, by the Court of Chancery denying appellant-defendant Zapata Corporation's (Zapata) alternative motions to dismiss the complaint or for summary judgment. The issue to be addressed has reached this Court by way of a rather convoluted path.

In June, 1975, William Maldonado, a stockholder of Zapata, instituted a derivative action in the Court of Chancery on behalf of Zapata against ten officers and/or directors of Zapata, alleging, essentially, breaches of fiduciary duty. Maldonado did not first demand that the board bring this action, stating instead such demand's futility because all directors were named as defendants and allegedly participated in the acts specified. In June, 1977,

Maldonado commenced an action in the United States District Court for the Southern District of New York against the same defendants, save one, alleging federal security law violations as well as the same common law claims made previously in the Court of Chancery.

By June, 1979, four of the defendant-directors were no longer on the board, and the remaining directors appointed two new outside directors to the board. The board then created an "Independent Investigation Committee" (Committee), composed solely of the two new directors, to investigate Maldonado's actions, as well as a similar derivative action then pending in Texas, and to determine whether the corporation should continue any or all of the litigation. The Committee's determination was stated to be "final, ... not ... subject to review by the Board of Directors and ... in all respects ... binding upon the Corporation."

Following an investigation, the Committee concluded, in September, 1979, that each action should "be dismissed forthwith as their continued maintenance is inimical to the Company's best interests...." Consequently, Zapata moved for dismissal or summary judgment in the three derivative actions. On January 24, 1980, the District Court for the Southern District of New York granted Zapata's motion for summary judgment, *Maldonado v. Flynn*, S.D.N.Y., 485 F.Supp. 274 (1980), holding, under its interpretation of Delaware law, that the Committee had the authority, under the "business judgment" rule, to require the termination of the derivative action. Maldonado appealed that decision to the Second Circuit Court of Appeals.

On March 18, 1980, the Court of Chancery, in a reported opinion, the basis for the order of April 9, 1980, denied Zapata's motions, holding that Delaware law does not sanction this means of dismissal. More specifically, it held that the "business judgment" rule is not a grant of authority to dismiss derivative actions and that a stockholder has an individual right to maintain derivative actions in certain instances. *Maldonado v. Flynn*, Del.Ch., 413 A.2d 1251 (1980) (herein *Maldonado*). Pursuant to the provisions of Supreme Court Rule 42, Zapata filed an interlocutory appeal with this Court shortly thereafter. The appeal was accepted by this Court on June 5, 1980.

We begin with an examination of the carefully considered opinion of the Vice Chancellor which states, in part, that the "business judgment" rule does not confer power "to a corporate board of directors to terminate a derivative suit", 413 A.2d at 1257. His conclusion is particularly pertinent because several federal courts, applying Delaware law, have held that the business judgment rule enables boards (or their committees) to terminate derivative suits, decisions now in conflict with the holding below.

As the term is most commonly used, and given the disposition below, we can understand the Vice Chancellor's comment that "the business judgment rule is irrelevant to the question of whether the Committee has the authority to compel the dismissal of this suit". 413 A.2d at 1257. Corporations, existing because of legislative grace, possess authority as granted by the legislature. Directors of Delaware corporations derive their managerial decision making power, which encompasses decisions whether to initiate, or refrain from entering, litigation, from 8 Del.C. § 141(a). This statute is the fount of directorial powers. The "business judgment" rule is a judicial creation that presumes propriety, under certain circumstances, in a board's decision. Viewed defensively, it does not create authority. In this sense the "business judgment" rule is not relevant in corporate decision making until after a decision is made. It is generally used as a defense to an attack on the decision's soundness. The board's managerial decision making power, however, comes from § 141(a). The judicial creation and legislative grant are related because the "business judgment" rule evolved to give recognition and deference to directors' business expertise when exercising their managerial power under § 141(a).

In the case before us, although the corporation's decision to move to dismiss or for summary judgment was, literally, a decision resulting from an exercise of the directors' (as delegated to the Committee) business judgment, the question of "business judgment", in a defensive sense, would not become relevant until and unless the decision to seek termination of the derivative lawsuit was attacked as improper. This question was not reached by the Vice Chancellor because he determined that the stockholder had an individual right to maintain this derivative action.

Thus, the focus in this case is on the power to speak for the corporation as to whether the lawsuit should be continued or terminated. As we see it, this issue in the current appellate posture of this case has three aspects: the conclusions of the Court below concerning the continuing right of a stockholder to maintain a derivative action; the corporate power under Delaware law of an authorized board committee to cause dismissal of litigation instituted for the benefit of the corporation; and the role of the Court of Chancery in resolving conflicts between the stockholder and the committee.

Accordingly, we turn first to the Court of Chancery's conclusions concerning the right of a plaintiff stockholder in a derivative action. We find that its determination that a stockholder, once demand is made and refused, possesses an independent, individual right to continue a derivative suit for breaches of fiduciary duty over objection by the corporation as an absolute rule, is erroneous. The Court of Chancery relied principally upon *Sohland v. Baker*, Del.Supr., 141 A. 277 (1927), for this statement of the Delaware rule. *Sohland* is sound law. But *Sohland* cannot be fairly read as supporting the broad proposition which evolved in the opinion below.

In *Sohland*, the complaining stockholder was allowed to file the derivative action in equity after making demand and after the board refused to bring the lawsuit. But the question before us relates to the power of the corporation by motion to terminate a lawsuit properly commenced by a stockholder without prior demand. No Delaware statute or case cited to us directly determines this new question and we do not think that *Sohland* addresses it by implication.

The precise language only supports the stockholder's right to initiate the lawsuit. It does not support an absolute right to continue to control it.

Moreover, *McKee v. Rogers*, Del.Ch., 156 A. 191 (1931), stated "as a general rule" that "a stockholder cannot be permitted ... to invade the discretionary field committed to the judgment of the directors and sue in the corporation's behalf when the managing body refuses. This rule is a well settled one."

The *McKee* rule, of course, should not be read so broadly that the board's refusal will be determinative in every instance. Board members, owing a well-established fiduciary duty to the corporation, will not be allowed to cause a derivative suit to be dismissed when it would be a breach of their fiduciary duty. Generally disputes pertaining to control of the suit arise in two contexts.

Consistent with the purpose of requiring a demand, a board decision to cause a derivative suit to be dismissed as detrimental to the company, after demand has been made and refused, will be respected unless it was wrongful.* A claim of a wrongful decision

---

* In other words, when stockholders, after making demand and having their suit rejected, attack the board's decision as improper, the board's decision falls under the "business judgment" rule and

not to sue is thus the first exception and the first context of dispute. Absent a wrongful refusal, the stockholder in such a situation simply lacks legal managerial power.

But it cannot be implied that, absent a wrongful board refusal, a stockholder can never have an individual right to initiate an action. For, as is stated in *McKee*, a "well settled" exception exists to the general rule.

"[A] stockholder may sue in equity in his derivative right to assert a cause of action in behalf of the corporation, without prior demand upon the directors to sue, when it is apparent that a demand would be futile, that the officers are under an influence that sterilizes discretion and could not be proper persons to conduct the litigation."

This exception, the second context for dispute, is consistent with the Court of Chancery's statement below, that "[t]he stockholders' individual right to bring the action does not ripen, however, … unless he can show a demand to be futile."

These comments in *McKee* and in the opinion below make obvious sense. A demand, when required and refused (if not wrongful), terminates a stockholder's legal ability to initiate a derivative action. But where demand is properly excused, the stockholder does possess the ability to initiate the action on his corporation's behalf.

These conclusions, however, do not determine the question before us. Rather, they merely bring us to the question to be decided. It is here that we part company with the Court below. Derivative suits enforce corporate rights and any recovery obtained goes to the corporation. "The right of a stockholder to file a bill to litigate corporate rights is, therefore, solely for the purpose of preventing injustice where it is apparent that material corporate rights would not otherwise be protected." *Sohland*, 141 A. at 282. We see no inherent reason why the "two phases" of a derivative suit, the stockholder's suit to compel the corporation to sue and the corporation's suit should automatically result in the placement in the hands of the litigating stockholder sole control of the corporate right throughout the litigation. To the contrary, it seems to us that such an inflexible rule would recognize the interest of one person or group to the exclusion of all others within the corporate entity. Thus, we reject the view of the Vice Chancellor as to the first aspect of the issue on appeal.

The question to be decided becomes: When, if at all, should an authorized board committee be permitted to cause litigation, properly initiated by a derivative stockholder in his own right, to be dismissed? If the board determines that a suit would be detrimental to the company, the board's determination prevails. Even when demand is excusable, circumstances may arise when continuation of the litigation would not be in the corporation's best interests. Our inquiry is whether, under such circumstances, there is a permissible procedure under § 141(a) by which a corporation can rid itself of detrimental litigation. If there is not, a single stockholder in an extreme case might control the destiny of the entire corporation. But, when examining the means, including the committee mechanism examined in this case, potentials for abuse must be recognized. This takes us to the second and third aspects of the issue on appeal.

Before we pass to equitable considerations as to the mechanism at issue here, it must be clear that an independent committee possesses the corporate power to seek the

---

will be respected if the requirements of the rule are met. That situation should be distinguished from the instant case, where demand was not made, and the power of the board to seek a dismissal, due to disqualification, presents a threshold issue.

termination of a derivative suit. Section 141(c) allows a board to delegate all of its authority to a committee. Accordingly, a committee with properly delegated authority would have the power to move for dismissal or summary judgment if the entire board did.

Even though demand was not made in this case and the initial decision of whether to litigate was not placed before the board, Zapata's board, it seems to us, retained all of its corporate power concerning litigation decisions. If Maldonado had made demand on the board in this case, it could have refused to bring suit. Maldonado could then have asserted that the decision not to sue was wrongful and, if correct, would have been allowed to maintain the suit. The board, however, never would have lost its statutory managerial authority. The demand requirement itself evidences that the managerial power is retained by the board. When a derivative plaintiff is allowed to bring suit after a wrongful refusal, the board's authority to choose whether to pursue the litigation is not challenged although its conclusion reached through the exercise of that authority is not respected since it is wrongful. Similarly, Rule 23.1, by excusing demand in certain instances, does not strip the board of its corporate power. It merely saves the plaintiff the expense and delay of making a futile demand resulting in a probable tainted exercise of that authority in a refusal by the board or in giving control of litigation to the opposing side. But the board entity remains empowered under § 141(a) to make decisions regarding corporate litigation. The problem is one of member disqualification, not the absence of power in the board.

The corporate power inquiry then focuses on whether the board, tainted by the self-interest of a majority of its members, can legally delegate its authority to a committee of two disinterested directors. We find our statute clearly requires an affirmative answer to this question. As has been noted, under an express provision of the statute, § 141(c), a committee can exercise all of the authority of the board to the extent provided in the resolution of the board.

We do not think that the interest taint of the board majority is per se a legal bar to the delegation of the board's power to an independent committee composed of disinterested board members. The committee can properly act for the corporation to move to dismiss derivative litigation that is believed to be detrimental to the corporation's best interest.

Our focus now switches to the Court of Chancery which is faced with a stockholder assertion that a derivative suit, properly instituted, should continue for the benefit of the corporation and a corporate assertion, properly made by a board committee acting with board authority, that the same derivative suit should be dismissed as inimical to the best interests of the corporation.

At the risk of stating the obvious, the problem is relatively simple. If, on the one hand, corporations can consistently wrest bona fide derivative actions away from well-meaning derivative plaintiffs through the use of the committee mechanism, the derivative suit will lose much, if not all, of its generally-recognized effectiveness as an intra-corporate means of policing boards of directors. If, on the other hand, corporations are unable to rid themselves of meritless or harmful litigation and strike suits, the derivative action, created to benefit the corporation, will produce the opposite, unintended result. It thus appears desirable to us to find a balancing point where bona fide stockholder power to bring corporate causes of action cannot be unfairly trampled on by the board of directors, but the corporation can rid itself of detrimental litigation.

As we noted, the question has been treated by other courts as one of the "business judgment" of the board committee. If a "committee, composed of independent and dis-interested directors, conducted a proper review of the matters before it, considered a variety of factors and reached, in good faith, a business judgment that (the) action was not in the best interest of (the corporation)," the action must be dismissed. The issues become solely independence, good faith, and reasonable investigation. The ultimate conclusion of the committee, under that view, is not subject to judicial review.

We are not satisfied, however, that acceptance of the "business judgment" rationale at this stage of derivative litigation is a proper balancing point. While we admit an analogy with a normal case respecting board judgment, it seems to us that there is sufficient risk in the realities of a situation like the one presented in this case to justify caution beyond adherence to the theory of business judgment.

The context here is a suit against directors where demand on the board is excused. We think some tribute must be paid to the fact that the lawsuit was properly initiated. It is not a board refusal case. Moreover, this complaint was filed in June of 1975 and, while the parties undoubtedly would take differing views on the degree of litigation activity, we have to be concerned about the creation of an "Independent Investigation Committee" four years later, after the election of two new outside directors. Situations could develop where such motions could be filed after years of vigorous litigation for reasons unconnected with the merits of the lawsuit.

Moreover, notwithstanding our conviction that Delaware law entrusts the corporate power to a properly authorized committee, we must be mindful that directors are passing judgment on fellow directors in the same corporation and fellow directors, in this instance, who designated them to serve both as directors and committee members. The question naturally arises whether a "there but for the grace of God go I" empathy might not play a role. And the further question arises whether inquiry as to independence, good faith and reasonable investigation is sufficient safeguard against abuse, perhaps subconscious abuse.

Whether the Court of Chancery will be persuaded by the exercise of a committee power resulting in a summary motion for dismissal of a derivative action, where a demand has not been initially made, should rest, in our judgment, in the independent discretion of the Court of Chancery. We thus steer a middle course between those cases which yield to the independent business judgment of a board committee and this case as determined below which would yield to unbridled plaintiff stockholder control. We recognize the danger of judicial overreaching but the alternatives seem to us to be outweighed by the fresh view of a judicial outsider. Moreover, if we failed to balance all the interests involved, we would in the name of practicality and judicial economy foreclose a judicial decision on the merits. At this point, we are not convinced that is necessary or desirable.

After an objective and thorough investigation of a derivative suit, an independent committee may cause its corporation to file a pretrial motion to dismiss in the Court of Chancery. The basis of the motion is the best interests of the corporation, as determined by the committee. The motion should include a thorough written record of the investigation and its findings and recommendations. Under appropriate Court supervision, akin to proceedings on summary judgment, each side should have an opportunity to make a record on the motion. As to the limited issues presented by the motion noted below, the moving party should be prepared to meet the normal burden under Rule 56 that there is no genuine issue as to any material fact and that the moving party is entitled to dismiss as a matter of law. The Court should apply a two-step test to the motion.

First, the Court should inquire into the independence and good faith of the committee and the bases supporting its conclusions. Limited discovery may be ordered to facilitate such inquiries. The corporation should have the burden of proving independence, good faith and a reasonable investigation, rather than presuming independence, good faith and reasonableness. If the Court determines either that the committee is not independent or has not shown reasonable bases for its conclusions, or, if the Court is not satisfied for other reasons relating to the process, including but not limited to the good faith of the committee, the Court shall deny the corporation's motion. If, however, the Court is satisfied under Rule 56 standards that the committee was independent and showed reasonable bases for good faith findings and recommendations, the Court may proceed, in its discretion, to the next step.

The second step provides, we believe, the essential key in striking the balance between legitimate corporate claims as expressed in a derivative stockholder suit and a corporation's best interests as expressed by an independent investigating committee. The Court should determine, applying its own independent business judgment, whether the motion should be granted. This means, of course, that instances could arise where a committee can establish its independence and sound bases for its good faith decisions and still have the corporation's motion denied. The second step is intended to thwart instances where corporate actions meet the criteria of step one, but the result does not appear to satisfy its spirit, or where corporate actions would simply prematurely terminate a stockholder grievance deserving of further consideration in the corporation's interest. The Court of Chancery of course must carefully consider and weigh how compelling the corporate interest in dismissal is when faced with a non-frivolous lawsuit. The Court of Chancery should, when appropriate, give special consideration to matters of law and public policy in addition to the corporation's best interests.

If the Court's independent business judgment is satisfied, the Court may proceed to grant the motion, subject, of course, to any equitable terms or conditions the Court finds necessary or desirable.

The interlocutory order of the Court of Chancery is reversed and the cause is remanded for further proceedings consistent with this opinion.

Notes

(1) Given what we have studied thus far about corporate law, are you surprised that the Delaware court is willing to second guess the decisions of a special litigation committee?

(2) Keep in mind that *Zapata* is not implicated until a board appoints a special litigation committee to determine whether a lawsuit is in the best interest of a corporation.

(3) *Zapata* represents one view in regards to the deference that a court should accord to the decision of a special litigation committee. The other highly regarded view is articulated in *Auerbach v. Bennett*, 47 NY2d 619 (1979). In *Auerbach*, shareholders brought a derivative suit against the board of the corporation alleging that the board should be liable because it allowed the corporation to make illegal bribes and/or kickbacks to public officials and/or political parties in foreign countries. A special litigation committee of disinterested and independent board members decided that the suit was not in the best interest of the corporation and filed a motion to dismiss, and in the alternative, a motion for summary judgment. The trial court granted the special litigations committee's motion but the appellate division reversed the trial court. On appeal to New York's highest court, the court reversed the decision of the appellate division. In reaching this holding, the court reasoned as follows:

First, there was the selection of procedures appropriate to the pursuit of its charge, and second, there was the ultimate substantive decision, predicated on the procedures chosen and the data produced thereby, not to pursue the claims advanced in the shareholders' derivative actions. The latter, substantive decision falls squarely within the embrace of the business judgment doctrine, involving as it did the weighing and balancing of legal, ethical, commercial, promotional, public relations, fiscal and other factors familiar to the resolution of many if not most corporate problems. To this extent the conclusion reached by the special litigation committee is outside the scope of our review. Thus, the courts cannot inquire as to which factors were considered by that committee or the relative weight accorded them in reaching that substantive decision — "the reasons for the payments, the advantages or disadvantages accruing to the corporation by reason of the transactions, the extent of the participation or profit by the respondent directors and the loss, if any, of public confidence in the corporation which might be incurred" (64 AD2d, at p 107). Inquiry into such matters would go to the very core of the business judgment made by the committee. To permit judicial probing of such issues would be to emasculate the business judgment doctrine as applied to the actions and determinations of the special litigation committee. Its substantive evaluation of the problems posed and its judgment in their resolution are beyond our reach. *Auerbach*, 47 NY2d at 633–634.

(4) How are the *Zapata* and *Auerbach* approaches different? Which approach gives more deference to the decision of the special litigation committee?

1. Prong One: SLC Independence

The *Zapata* case sets forth the test to be used to determine the independence of a special litigation committee and also gives power to the trial judge to thereafter make an independent determination as to whether in the court's best judgment, the termination of the case as moved for by the defendant is a rational and fair outcome. In the words of *Zapata*:

First, the Court should inquire into the independence and good faith of the committee and the bases supporting its conclusions.... If the Court determines either that the committee is not independent or has not shown reasonable bases for its conclusions, or, if the Court is not satisfied for other reasons relating to the process, including but not limited to the good faith of the committee, the Court shall deny the corporation's motion.... The second step provides, we believe, the essential key in striking the balance between legitimate corporate claims as expressed in a derivative stockholder suit and a corporation's best interests as expressed by an independent investigating committee. The Court should determine, applying its own independent business judgment, whether the motion should be granted.

Therefore, in this very specific instance, a court is allowed to substitute its own business judgment for that of the corporate executives that appointed the special litigation committee. From this two-prong test, we have since seen courts analyze what is required to appoint a truly independent special litigation committee. In the case that follows, *In re Oracle*, we see a trial judge analyze the question as to whether an appointed special litigation committee is in fact, truly independent and able to render an unbiased determination.

As you read the following opinion by Judge Strine, ask yourself whether the Oracle board acted rationally in appointing the two members it did to serve as the special litigation committee to consider whether to motion the court to dismiss a derivative lawsuit.

In re Oracle Corp. Derivative Litigation

824 A.2d 917 (2003)
Court of Chancery of Delaware

OPINION

STRINE, Vice Chancellor.

In this opinion, I address the motion of the special litigation committee ("SLC") of Oracle Corporation to terminate this action, "the Delaware Derivative Action," and other such actions pending in the name of Oracle against certain Oracle directors and officers. These actions allege that these Oracle directors engaged in insider trading while in possession of material, non-public information showing that Oracle would not meet the earnings guidance it gave to the market for the third quarter of Oracle's fiscal year 2001. The SLC bears the burden of persuasion on this motion and must convince me that there is no material issue of fact calling into doubt its independence. This requirement is set forth in *Zapata Corp. v. Maldonado* and its progeny.

The question of independence "turns on whether a director is, for any substantial reason, incapable of making a decision with only the best interests of the corporation in mind." That is, the independence test ultimately "focus[es] on impartiality and objectivity." In this case, the SLC has failed to demonstrate that no material factual question exists regarding its independence.

During discovery, it emerged that the two SLC members—both of whom are professors at Stanford University—are being asked to investigate fellow Oracle directors who have important ties to Stanford, too.

It is no easy task to decide whether to accuse a fellow director of insider trading. For Oracle to compound that difficulty by requiring SLC members to consider accusing a fellow professor and two large benefactors of their university of conduct that is rightly considered a violation of criminal law was unnecessary and inconsistent with the concept of independence recognized by our law. The possibility that these extraneous considerations biased the inquiry of the SLC is too substantial for this court to ignore. I therefore deny the SLC's motion to terminate.

I. Factual Background

A. Summary of the Plaintiffs' Allegations

The Delaware Derivative Complaint centers on alleged insider trading by four members of Oracle's board of directors—Lawrence Ellison, Jeffrey Henley, Donald Lucas, and Michael Boskin (collectively, the "Trading Defendants"). Each of the Trading Defendants had a very different role at Oracle.

Ellison is Oracle's Chairman, Chief Executive Officer, and its largest stockholder, owning nearly twenty-five percent of Oracle's voting shares. By virtue of his ownership position, Ellison is one of the wealthiest men in America. By virtue of his managerial position, Ellison has regular access to a great deal of information about how Oracle is performing on a week-to-week basis.

Henley is Oracle's Chief Financial Officer, Executive Vice President, and a director of the corporation. Like Ellison, Henley has his finger on the pulse of Oracle's performance constantly.

Lucas is a director who chairs Oracle's Executive Committee and its Finance and Audit Committee. Although the plaintiffs allege that Lucas's positions gave him access to material, non-public information about the company, they do so cursorily. On the present record, it appears that Lucas did not receive copies of week-to-week projections or reports of actual results for the quarter to date. Rather, his committees primarily received historical financial data.

Boskin is a director, Chairman of the Compensation Committee, and a member of the Finance and Audit Committee. As with Lucas, Boskin's access to information was limited mostly to historical financials and did not include the week-to-week internal projections and revenue results that Ellison and Henley received.

According to the plaintiffs, each of these Trading Defendants possessed material, non-public information demonstrating that Oracle would fail to meet the earnings and revenue guidance it had provided to the market in December 2000. In that guidance, Henley projected — subject to many disclaimers, including the possibility that a softening economy would hamper Oracle's ability to achieve these results — that Oracle would earn 12 cents per share and generate revenues of over $2.9 billion in the third quarter of its fiscal year 2001 ("3Q FY 2001").

The plaintiffs allege that this guidance was materially misleading and became even more so as early results for the quarter came in. To start with, the plaintiffs assert that the guidance rested on an untenably rosy estimate of the performance of an important new Oracle product, its "Suite 11i" systems integration product that was designed to enable a business to run all of its information systems using a complete, integrated package of software with financial, manufacturing, sales, logistics, and other applications features that were "inter-operable." The reality, the plaintiffs contend, was that Suite 11i was riddled with bugs and not ready for prime time. As a result, Suite 11i was not in a position to make a material contribution to earnings growth.

In addition, the plaintiffs contend more generally that the Trading Defendants received material, non-public information that the sales growth for Oracle's other products was slowing in a significant way, which made the attainment of the earnings and revenue guidance extremely difficult. This information grew in depth as the quarter proceeded, as various sources of information that Oracle's top managers relied upon allegedly began to signal weakness in the company's revenues. These signals supposedly included a slowdown in the "pipeline" of large deals that Oracle hoped to close during the quarter and weak revenue growth in the first month of the quarter.

During the time when these disturbing signals were allegedly being sent, the Trading Defendants engaged in the following trades:

- On January 3, 2001, Lucas sold 150,000 shares of Oracle common stock at $30 per share, reaping proceeds of over $4.6 million. These sales constituted 17% of Lucas's Oracle holdings.

- On January 4, 2001, Henley sold one million shares of Oracle stock at approximately $32 per share, yielding over $32.3 million. These sales represented 7% of Henley's Oracle holdings.

- On January 17, 2001, Boskin sold 150,000 shares of Oracle stock at over $33 per share, generating in excess of $5 million. These sales were 16% of Boskin's Oracle holdings.

- From January 22 to January 31, 2001, Ellison sold over 29 million shares at prices above $30 per share, producing over $894 million. Despite the huge proceeds generated by these sales, they constituted the sale of only 2% of Ellison's Oracle holdings.

Into early to mid-February, Oracle allegedly continued to assure the market that it would meet its December guidance. Then, on March 1, 2001, the company announced that rather than posting 12 cents per share in quarterly earnings and 25% license revenue growth as projected, the company's earnings for the quarter would be 10 cents per share and license revenue growth only 6%. The stock market reacted swiftly and negatively to this news, with Oracle's share price dropping as low as $15.75 before closing at $16.88—a 21% decline in one day. These prices were well below the above $30 per share prices at which the Trading Defendants sold in January 2001.

Oracle, through Ellison and Henley, attributed the adverse results to a general weakening in the economy, which led Oracle's customers to cut back sharply on purchases. Because (the company claimed) most of its sales close in the late days of quarters, the company did not become aware that it would miss its projections until shortly before the quarter closed. The reasons given by Ellison and Henley subjected them to sarcastic rejoinders from analysts, who noted that they had only recently suggested that Oracle was better-positioned than other companies to continue to deliver growth in a weakening economy.

B. The Plaintiffs' Claims in the Delaware Derivative Action

The plaintiffs allege that the Trading Defendants breached their duty of loyalty by mis-appropriating inside information and using it as the basis for trading decisions. This claim rests its legal basis on the venerable case of *Brophy v. Cities Service Co.* Its factual foundation is that the Trading Defendants were aware (or at least possessed information that should have made them aware) that the company would miss its December guidance by a wide margin and used that information to their advantage in selling at artificially inflated prices.

D. The Formation of the Special Litigation Committee

On February 1, 2002, Oracle formed the SLC in order to investigate the Delaware Derivative Action and to determine whether Oracle should press the claims raised by the plaintiffs, settle the case, or terminate it.

The SLC was granted full authority to decide these matters without the need for approval by the other members of the Oracle board.

E. The Members of the Special Litigation Committee

Two Oracle board members were named to the SLC. Both of them joined the Oracle board on October 15, 2001, more than a half a year after Oracle's 3Q FY 2001 closed. The SLC members also share something else: both are tenured professors at Stanford University.

Professor Hector Garcia-Molina is Chairman of the Computer Science Department at Stanford and holds the Leonard Bosack and Sandra Lerner Professorship in the Computer Science and Electrical Engineering Departments at Stanford. A renowned expert in his field, Garcia-Molina was a professor at Princeton before coming to Stanford in 1992.

Garcia-Molina's appointment at Stanford represented a homecoming of some sort, because he obtained both his undergraduate and graduate degrees from Stanford.

The other SLC member, Professor Joseph Grundfest, is the W.A. Franke Professor of Law and Business at Stanford University. He directs the University's well-known Directors' College and the Roberts Program in Law, Business, and Corporate Governance at the Stanford Law School. Grundfest is also the principal investigator for the Law School's Securities Litigation Clearinghouse. Immediately before coming to Stanford, Grundfest served for five years as a Commissioner of the Securities and Exchange Commission. Like Garcia-Molina, Grundfest's appointment at Stanford was a homecoming, because he obtained his law degree and performed significant post-graduate work in economics at Stanford.

As will be discussed more specifically later, Grundfest also serves as a steering committee member and a senior fellow of the Stanford Institute for Economic Policy Research, and releases working papers under the "SIEPR" banner.

For their services, the SLC members were paid $250 an hour, a rate below that which they could command for other activities, such as consulting or expert witness testimony. Nonetheless, during the course of their work, the SLC members became concerned that (arguably scandal-driven) developments in the evolving area of corporate governance might render the amount of their compensation so high as to be an argument against their independence. Therefore, Garcia-Molina and Grundfest agreed to give up any SLC-related compensation if their compensation was deemed by this court to impair their impartiality.

F. The SLC Members Are Recruited to the Board

The SLC members were recruited to the board primarily by defendant Lucas, with help from defendant Boskin. The wooing of them began in the summer of 2001. Before deciding to join the Oracle board, Grundfest, in particular, did a good deal of due diligence. His review included reading publicly available information, among other things, the then-current complaint in the Federal Class Action.

G. The SLC's Advisors

The most important advisors retained by the SLC were its counsel from Simpson Thacher & Bartlett LLP. Simpson Thacher had not performed material amounts of legal work for Oracle or any of the individual defendants before its engagement, and the plaintiffs have not challenged its independence.

H. The SLC's Investigation and Report

The SLC's investigation was, by any objective measure, extensive. The SLC reviewed an enormous amount of paper and electronic records. SLC counsel interviewed seventy witnesses, some of them twice. SLC members participated in several key interviews, including the interviews of the Trading Defendants.

Importantly, the interviewees included all the senior members of Oracle's management most involved in its projection and monitoring of the company's financial performance, including its sales and revenue growth. These interviews combined with a special focus on the documents at the company bearing on these subjects, including e-mail communications.

During the course of the investigation, the SLC met with its counsel thirty-five times for a total of eighty hours. In addition to that, the SLC members, particularly Professor Grundfest, devoted many more hours to the investigation.

In the end, the SLC produced an extremely lengthy Report totaling 1,110 pages (excluding appendices and exhibits) that concluded that Oracle should not pursue the plaintiffs' claims against the Trading Defendants or any of the other Oracle directors serving during the 3Q FY 2001. The bulk of the Report defies easy summarization. I endeavor a rough attempt to capture the essence of the Report in understandable terms, surfacing some implicit premises that I understand to have undergirded the SLC's conclusions. Here goes.

Having absorbed a huge amount of material regarding Oracle's financial condition during the relevant period, the flow of information to top Oracle executives, Oracle's business and its products, and the general condition of the market at that time, the SLC concluded that even a hypothetical Oracle executive who possessed all information regarding the company's performance in December and January of 3Q FY 2001 would not have possessed material, non-public information that the company would fail to meet the earnings and revenue guidance it provided the market in December. Although there were hints of potential weakness in Oracle's revenue growth, especially starting in mid-January 2001, there was no reliable information indicating that the company would fall short of the mark, and certainly not to the extent that it eventually did.

Notably, none of the many e-mails from various Oracle top executives in January 2001 regarding the quarter anticipated that the company would perform as it actually did. Although some of these e-mails noted weakening, all are generally consistent with the proposition that Oracle executives expected to achieve the guidance.

Important to this conclusion is the SLC's finding that Oracle's quarterly earnings are subject to a so-called "hockey stick effect," whereby a large portion of each quarter's earnings comes in right at the end of the quarter. In 3Q FY 2001, the late influx of revenues that had often characterized Oracle's performance during its emergence as one of the companies with the largest market capitalization in the nation did not materialize; indeed, a large amount of product was waiting in Oracle warehouses for shipment for deals that Oracle had anticipated closing but did not close during the quarter.

Thus, taking into account all the relevant information sources, the SLC concluded that even Ellison and Henley—who were obviously the two Trading Defendants with the most access to inside information—did not possess material, non-public information. As to Lucas and Boskin, the SLC noted that they did not receive the weekly updates (of various kinds) that allegedly showed a weakening in Oracle's performance during 3Q FY 2001. As a result, there was even less of a basis to infer wrongdoing on their part.

Moreover, as the SLC Report points out, the idea that the Trading Defendants acted with scienter in trading in January 2001 was problematic in light of several factors. Implicitly the first and foremost is the reality that Oracle is a functioning business with real products of value. Although it is plausible to imagine a scenario where someone of Ellison's wealth would cash out, fearing the imminent collapse of a house of cards he had sold to an unsuspecting market, this is not the situation that Ellison faced in January 2001.

As of that time, Oracle faced no collapse, even if it, like other companies, had to deal with a slowing economy. And, as the SLC points out, Ellison sold only two percent of his holdings. A good deal of these sales were related to options that he had held for over nine years and that had to be exercised by August 2001. In view of Oracle's basic health, Ellison's huge wealth, and his retention of ninety-eight percent of his shares, the SLC concluded that any inference that Ellison acted with scienter and attempted to reap improper trading profits was untenable.

The same reasoning also motivated the SLC's conclusions as to Henley, who sold only seven percent of his stake in Oracle. Both Ellison and Henley stood to expose a great deal of their personal wealth to substantial risk by undertaking a scheme to cash out a small portion of their holdings and risking a greater injury to Oracle, a company in which they retained a far greater stake than they had sold. As important, these executives stood to risk their own personal reputations despite the absence of any personal cash crunch that impelled them to engage in risky, unethical, and illegal behavior.

Although Lucas and Boskin sold somewhat larger proportions of their Oracle holdings—sixteen percent and seventeen percent respectively—these proportions, the SLC concluded, were of the kind that federal courts had found lacking in suspicion. As with Ellison and Henley, the SLC identified no urgent need on either's part to generate cash by trading (illegally) on non-public, material information.

Of course, the amount of the proceeds each of the Trading Defendants generated was extremely large. By selling only two percent of his holdings, Ellison generated nearly a billion dollars, enough to flee to a small island nation with no extradition laws and to live like a Saudi prince. But given Oracle's fundamental health as a company and his retention of ninety-eight percent of his shares, Ellison (the SLC found) had no need to take desperate—or, for that matter, even slightly risky—measures. The same goes for the other Trading Defendants; there was simply nothing special or urgent about their financial circumstances in January 2001 that would have motivated (or did motivate, in the SLC's view) the Trading Defendants to cash out because they believed that Oracle would miss its earnings guidance.

For these and other reasons, the SLC concluded that the plaintiffs' allegations that the Trading Defendants had breached their fiduciary duty of loyalty by using inside information about Oracle to reap illicit trading gains were without merit. The SLC also determined that, consistent with this determination, there was no reason to sue the other members of the Oracle board who were in office as of 3Q FY 2001. Therefore, the SLC determined to seek dismissal of the Delaware Derivative Action and the other derivative actions.

II. The SLC Moves to Terminate

Consistent with its Report, the SLC moved to terminate this litigation. The plaintiffs were granted discovery focusing on three primary topics: the independence of the SLC, the good faith of its investigative efforts, and the reasonableness of the bases for its conclusion that the lawsuit should be terminated. Additionally, the plaintiffs received a large volume of documents comprising the materials that the SLC relied upon in preparing its Report.

III. The Applicable Procedural Standard

In order to prevail on its motion to terminate the Delaware Derivative Action, the SLC must persuade me that: (1) its members were independent; (2) that they acted in good faith; and (3) that they had reasonable bases for their recommendations. If the SLC meets that burden, I am free to grant its motion or may, in my discretion, undertake my own examination of whether Oracle should terminate and permit the suit to proceed if I, in my oxymoronic judicial "business judgment," conclude that procession is in the best interests of the company. This two-step analysis comes, of course, from Zapata.

IV. Is the SLC Independent?

A. The Facts Disclosed in the Report

In its Report, the SLC took the position that its members were independent. In support of that position, the Report noted several factors including:

- the fact that neither Grundfest nor Garcia-Molina received compensation from Oracle other than as directors;

- the fact that neither Grundfest nor Garcia-Molina were on the Oracle board at the time of the alleged wrongdoing;

- the fact that both Grundfest and Garcia-Molina were willing to return their compensation as SLC members if necessary to preserve their status as independent;

- the absence of any other material ties between Oracle, the Trading Defendants, and any of the other defendants, on the one hand, and Grundfest and Garcia-Molina, on the other; and

- the absence of any material ties between Oracle, the Trading Defendants, and any of the other defendants, on the one hand, and the SLC's advisors, on the other.

Noticeably absent from the SLC Report was any disclosure of several significant ties between Oracle or the Trading Defendants and Stanford University, the university that employs both members of the SLC. In the Report, it was only disclosed that:

- defendant Boskin was a Stanford professor;

- the SLC members were aware that Lucas had made certain donations to Stanford; and

- among the contributions was a donation of $50,000 worth of stock that Lucas donated to Stanford Law School after Grundfest delivered a speech to a venture capital fund meeting in response to Lucas's request. It happens that Lucas's son is a partner in the fund and that approximately half the donation was allocated for use by Grundfest in his personal research.

B. The "Stanford" Facts that Emerged During Discovery

In view of the modesty of these disclosed ties, it was with some shock that a series of other ties among Stanford, Oracle, and the Trading Defendants emerged during discovery. Although the plaintiffs have embellished these ties considerably beyond what is reasonable, the plain facts are a striking departure from the picture presented in the Report.

With this question in mind, I begin to discuss the specific ties that allegedly compromise the SLC's independence, beginning with those involving Professor Boskin.

1. Boskin

Defendant Michael J. Boskin is the T.M. Friedman Professor of Economics at Stanford University. During the Administration of President George H.W. Bush, Boskin occupied the coveted and important position of Chairman of the President's Council of Economic Advisors. He returned to Stanford after this government service, continuing a teaching career there that had begun many years earlier.

During the 1970s, Boskin taught Grundfest when Grundfest was a Ph.D. candidate. Although Boskin was not Grundfest's advisor and although they do not socialize, the two have remained in contact over the years, speaking occasionally about matters of public policy.

Furthermore, both Boskin and Grundfest are senior fellows and steering committee members at the Stanford Institute for Economic Policy Research, which was previously defined as "SIEPR." According to the SLC, the title of senior fellow is largely an honorary one. According to SIEPR's own web site, however, "[s]enior fellows actively participate in SIEPR research and participate in its governance."

Likewise, the SLC contends that Grundfest went MIA as a steering committee member, having failed to attend a meeting since 1997. The SIEPR web site, however, identifies its steering committee as having the role of "advising the director [of SIEPR] and guiding [SIEPR] on matters pertaining to research and academics." Because Grundfest allegedly did not attend to these duties, his service alongside Boskin in that capacity is, the SLC contends, not relevant to his independence.

That said, the SLC does not deny that both Boskin and Grundfest publish working papers under the SIEPR rubric and that SIEPR helps to publicize their respective works. Indeed, as I will note later in this opinion, Grundfest, in the same month the SLC was formed, addressed a meeting of some of SIEPR's largest benefactors—the so-called "SIEPR Associates." The SLC just claims that the SIEPR affiliation is one in which SIEPR basks in the glow of Boskin and Grundfest, not the other way around, and that the mutual service of the two as senior fellows and steering committee members is not a collegial tie of any significance.

With these facts in mind, I now set forth the ties that defendant Lucas has to Stanford.

2. Lucas

As noted in the SLC Report, the SLC members admitted knowing that Lucas was a contributor to Stanford. They also acknowledged that he had donated $50,000 to Stanford Law School in appreciation for Grundfest having given a speech at his request. About half of the proceeds were allocated for use by Grundfest in his research.

But Lucas's ties with Stanford are far, far richer than the SLC Report lets on. To begin, Lucas is a Stanford alumnus, having obtained both his undergraduate and graduate degrees there. By any measure, he has been a very loyal alumnus.

In showing that this is so, I start with a matter of some jousting between the SLC and the plaintiffs. Lucas's brother, Richard, died of cancer and by way of his will established a foundation. Lucas became Chairman of the Foundation and serves as a director along with his son, a couple of other family members, and some non-family members. A principal object of the Foundation's beneficence has been Stanford. The Richard M. Lucas Foundation has given $11.7 million to Stanford since its 1981 founding. Among its notable contributions, the Foundation funded the establishment of the Richard M. Lucas Center for Magnetic Resonance Spectroscopy and Imaging at Stanford's Medical School. Donald Lucas was a founding member and lead director of the Center.

The SLC Report did not mention the Richard M. Lucas Foundation or its grants to Stanford. In its briefs on this motion, the SLC has pointed out that Donald Lucas is one of nine directors at the Foundation and does not serve on its Grant Review Committee. Nonetheless, the SLC does not deny that Lucas is Chairman of the board of the Foundation and that the board approves all grants.

Lucas's connections with Stanford as a contributor go beyond the Foundation, however. From his own personal funds, Lucas has contributed $4.1 million to Stanford, a substantial percentage of which has been donated within the last half-decade. Notably, Lucas has, among other things, donated $424,000 to SIEPR and approximately $149,000 to Stanford Law School. Indeed, Lucas is not only a major contributor to SIEPR, he is the Chair of its Advisory Board. At SIEPR's facility at Stanford, the conference center is named the Donald L. Lucas Conference Center.

From these undisputed facts, it is inarguable that Lucas is a very important alumnus of Stanford and a generous contributor to not one, but two, parts of Stanford important to Grundfest: the Law School and SIEPR.

With these facts in mind, it remains to enrich the factual stew further, by considering defendant Ellison's ties to Stanford.

3. Ellison

There can be little doubt that Ellison is a major figure in the community in which Stanford is located. The so-called Silicon Valley has generated many success stories, among the greatest of which is that of Oracle and its leader, Ellison. One of the wealthiest men in America, Ellison is a major figure in the nation's increasingly important information technology industry. Given his wealth, Ellison is also in a position to make—and, in fact, he has made—major charitable contributions.

Some of the largest of these contributions have been made through the Ellison Medical Foundation, which makes grants to universities and laboratories to support biomedical research relating to aging and infectious diseases.

Although it is not represented on the Scientific Advisory Board, Stanford has nonetheless been the beneficiary of grants from the Ellison Medical Foundation—to the tune of nearly $10 million in paid or pledged funds.

During the time Ellison has been CEO of Oracle, the company itself has also made over $300,000 in donations to Stanford. Not only that, when Oracle established a generously endowed educational foundation—the Oracle Help Us Help Foundation—to help further the deployment of educational technology in schools serving disadvantaged populations, it named Stanford as the "appointing authority," which gave Stanford the right to name four of the Foundation's seven directors.

Taken together, these facts suggest that Ellison (when considered as an individual and as the key executive and major stockholder of Oracle) had, at the very least, been involved in several endeavors of value to Stanford.

Beginning in the year 2000 and continuing well into 2001—the same year that Ellison made the trades the plaintiffs contend were suspicious and the same year the SLC members were asked to join the Oracle board—Ellison and Stanford discussed a much more lucrative donation. The idea Stanford proposed for discussion was the creation of an Ellison Scholars Program modeled on the Rhodes Scholarship at Oxford. The proposed budget for Stanford's answer to Oxford: $170 million. The Ellison Scholars were to be drawn from around the world and were to come to Stanford to take a two-year interdisciplinary graduate program in economics, political science, and computer technology. During the summer between the two academic years, participants would work in internships at, among other companies, Oracle.

Given the nature of this case, it is natural that there must be yet another curious fact to add to the mix. This is that Ellison told the *Washington Post* in an October 30, 2000 article that he intended to leave his Woodside, California home—which is worth over $100 million—to Stanford upon his death. In an affidavit, Ellison does not deny making this rather splashy public statement. But, he now (again, rather conveniently) says that he has changed his testamentary intent. Ellison denies having "bequeathed, donated or otherwise conveyed the Woodside property (or any other real property that I own) to Stanford University."

In order to buttress the argument that Stanford did not feel beholden to him, Ellison shared with the court the (otherwise private) fact that one of his children had applied to Stanford in October 2000 and was not admitted. If Stanford felt comfortable rejecting Ellison's child, the SLC contends, why should the SLC members hesitate before recommending that Oracle press insider trading-based fiduciary duty claims against Ellison?

But the fact remains that Ellison was still talking very publicly and seriously about the possibility of endowing a graduate interdisciplinary studies program at Stanford during the summer after his child was rejected from Stanford's undergraduate program.

C. The SLC's Argument

The SLC contends that even together, these facts regarding the ties among Oracle, the Trading Defendants, Stanford, and the SLC members do not impair the SLC's independence. In so arguing, the SLC places great weight on the fact that none of the Trading Defendants have the practical ability to deprive either Grundfest or Garcia-Molina of their current positions at Stanford. Nor, given their tenure, does Stanford itself have any practical ability to punish them for taking action adverse to Boskin, Lucas, or Ellison — each of whom, as we have seen, has contributed (in one way or another) great value to Stanford as an institution. As important, neither Garcia-Molina nor Grundfest are part of the official fundraising apparatus at Stanford; thus, it is not their on-the-job duty to be solicitous of contributors, and fundraising success does not factor into their treatment as professors.

In so arguing, the SLC focuses on the language of previous opinions of this court and the Delaware Supreme Court that indicates that a director is not independent only if he is dominated and controlled by an interested party, such as a Trading Defendant. The SLC also emphasizes that much of our jurisprudence on independence focuses on economically consequential relationships between the allegedly interested party and the directors who allegedly cannot act independently of that director. Put another way, much of our law focuses the bias inquiry on whether there are economically material ties between the interested party and the director whose impartiality is questioned, treating the possible effect on one's personal wealth as the key to the independence inquiry. Putting a point on this, the SLC cites certain decisions of Delaware courts concluding that directors who are personal friends of an interested party were not, by virtue of those personal ties, to be labeled non-independent.

More subtly, the SLC argues that university professors simply are not inhibited types, unwilling to make tough decisions even as to fellow professors and large contributors. What is tenure about if not to provide professors with intellectual freedom, even in non-traditional roles such as special litigation committee members? No less ardently — but with no record evidence that reliably supports its ultimate point   the SLC contends that Garcia-Molina and Grundfest are extremely distinguished in their fields and were not, in fact, influenced by the facts identified heretofore. Indeed, the SLC argues, how could they have been influenced by many of these facts when they did not learn them until the post-Report discovery process? If it boils down to the simple fact that both share with Boskin the status of a Stanford professor, how material can this be when there are 1,700 others who also occupy the same position?

E. The Court's Analysis of the SLC's Independence

I begin with an important reminder: the SLC bears the burden of proving its independence. It must convince me.

But of what? According to the SLC, its members are independent unless they are essentially subservient to the Trading Defendants — i.e., they are under the "domination and control" of the interested parties. If the SLC is correct and this is the central inquiry in the independence determination, they would win. Nothing in the record suggests to me that either Garcia-Molina or Grundfest are dominated and controlled by any of the Trading Defendants, by Oracle, or even by Stanford.

But, in my view, an emphasis on "domination and control" would serve only to fetishize much-parroted language, at the cost of denuding the independence inquiry of its intellectual integrity. Take an easy example. Imagine if two brothers were on a corporate board, each successful in different businesses and not dependent in any way on the other's beneficence in order to be wealthy. The brothers are brothers, they stay in touch and consider each other family, but each is opinionated and strong-willed. A derivative action is filed targeting a transaction involving one of the brothers. The other brother is put on a special litigation committee to investigate the case. If the test is domination and control, then one brother could investigate the other. Does any sensible person think that is our law? I do not think it is.

And it should not be our law. Delaware law should not be based on a reductionist view of human nature that simplifies human motivations on the lines of the least sophisticated notions of the law and economics movement. Homo sapiens is not merely homo economicus. We may be thankful that an array of other motivations exist that influence human behavior; not all are any better than greed or avarice, think of envy, to name just one. But also think of motives like love, friendship, and collegiality, think of those among us who direct their behavior as best they can on a guiding creed or set of moral values.

Nor should our law ignore the social nature of humans. To be direct, corporate directors are generally the sort of people deeply enmeshed in social institutions. Such institutions have norms, expectations that, explicitly and implicitly, influence and channel the behavior of those who participate in their operation. Some things are "just not done," or only at a cost, which might not be so severe as a loss of position, but may involve a loss of standing in the institution. In being appropriately sensitive to this factor, our law also cannot assume — absent some proof of the point — that corporate directors are, as a general matter, persons of unusual social bravery, who operate heedless to the inhibitions that social norms generate for ordinary folk.

This court has previously held that the Delaware Supreme Court's teachings on independence can be summarized thusly:

At bottom, the question of independence turns on whether a director is, for any substantial reason, incapable of making a decision with only the best interests of the corporation in mind. That is, the Supreme Court cases ultimately focus on impartiality and objectivity.

This formulation is wholly consistent with the teaching of *Aronson*, which defines independence as meaning that "a director's decision is based on the corporate merits of the subject before the board rather than extraneous considerations or influences." As noted by Chancellor Chandler recently, a director may be compromised if he is beholden to an interested person. Beholden in this sense does not mean just owing in the financial sense, it can also flow out of "personal or other relationships" to the interested party.

1. The Contextual Nature of the Independence Inquiry Under Delaware Law

In examining whether the SLC has met its burden to demonstrate that there is no material dispute of fact regarding its independence, the court must bear in mind the function of special litigation committees under our jurisprudence. Under Delaware law, the primary means by which corporate defendants may obtain a dismissal of a derivative suit is by showing that the plaintiffs have not met their pleading burden under the test of *Aronson v. Lewis*, or the related standard set forth in *Rales v. Blasband*. In simple terms, these tests permit a corporation to terminate a derivative suit if its board is comprised of directors who can impartially consider a demand.

Special litigation committees are permitted as a last chance for a corporation to control a derivative claim in circumstances when a majority of its directors cannot impartially consider a demand. By vesting the power of the board to determine what to do with the suit in a committee of independent directors, a corporation may retain control over whether the suit will proceed, so long as the committee meets the standard set forth in *Zapata*.

In evaluating the independence of a special litigation committee, this court must take into account the extraordinary importance and difficulty of such a committee's responsibility. It is, I daresay, easier to say no to a friend, relative, colleague, or boss who seeks assent for an act (e.g., a transaction) that has not yet occurred than it would be to cause a corporation to sue that person. This is admittedly a determination of so-called "legislative fact," but one that can be rather safely made. Denying a fellow director the ability to proceed on a matter important to him may not be easy, but it must, as a general matter, be less difficult than finding that there is reason to believe that the fellow director has committed serious wrongdoing and that a derivative suit should proceed against him.

The difficulty of making this decision is compounded in the special litigation committee context because the weight of making the moral judgment necessarily falls on less than the full board. A small number of directors feels the moral gravity—and social pressures—of this duty alone.

For all these reasons, the independence inquiry is critically important if the special litigation committee process is to retain its integrity, a quality that is, in turn, essential to the utility of that process.

Thus, in assessing the independence of the Oracle SLC, I necessarily examine the question of whether the SLC can independently make the difficult decision entrusted to it: to determine whether the Trading Defendants should face suit for insider trading-based allegations of breach of fiduciary duty. An affirmative answer by the SLC to that question would have potentially huge negative consequences for the Trading Defendants, not only by exposing them to the possibility of a large damage award but also by subjecting them to great reputational harm. To have Professors Grundfest and Garcia-Molina declare that Oracle should press insider trading claims against the Trading Defendants would have been, to put it mildly, "news." Relatedly, it is reasonable to think that an SLC determination that the Trading Defendants had likely engaged in insider trading would have been accompanied by a recommendation that they step down as fiduciaries until their ultimate culpability was decided.

The importance and special sensitivity of the SLC's task is also relevant for another obvious reason: investigations do not follow a scientific process like an old-fashioned assembly line. The investigators' mindset and talent influence, for good or ill, the course of an investigation. Just as there are obvious dangers from investigators suffering from too much zeal, so too are dangers posed by investigators who harbor reasons not to pursue the investigation's targets with full vigor.

Delaware law requires courts to consider the independence of directors based on the facts known to the court about them specifically, the so-called "subjective 'actual person' standard." That said, it is inescapable that a court must often apply to the known facts about a specific director a consideration of how a reasonable person similarly situated to that director would behave, given the limited ability of a judge to look into a particular director's heart and mind. This is especially so when a special litigation committee chooses, as was the case here, to eschew any live witness testimony, a decision that is, of course, sensible lest special litigation committee termination motions turn into trials nearly as burdensome as the derivative suit the committee seeks to end. But with that sensible choice came an acceptance of the court's need to infer that the special litigation committee members are persons of typical professional sensibilities.

2. The SLC Has Not Met Its Burden to Demonstrate the Absence of a Material Dispute of Fact About Its Independence

Using the contextual approach I have described, I conclude that the SLC has not met its burden to show the absence of a material factual question about its independence. I find this to be the case because the ties among the SLC, the Trading Defendants, and Stanford are so substantial that they cause reasonable doubt about the SLC's ability to impartially consider whether the Trading Defendants should face suit. The concern that arises from these ties can be stated fairly simply, focusing on defendants Boskin, Lucas, and Ellison in that order, and then collectively.

As SLC members, Grundfest and Garcia-Molina were already being asked to consider whether the company should level extremely serious accusations of wrongdoing against fellow board members. As to Boskin, both SLC members faced another layer of complexity: the determination of whether to have Oracle press insider trading claims against a fellow professor at their university. Even though Boskin was in a different academic department from either SLC member, it is reasonable to assume that the fact that Boskin was also on faculty would — to persons possessing typical sensibilities and institutional loyalty — be a matter of more than trivial concern. Universities are obviously places of at-times intense debate, but they also see themselves as communities. In fact, Stanford refers to itself as a "community of scholars." To accuse a fellow professor — whom one might see at the faculty club or at inter-disciplinary presentations of academic papers — of insider trading cannot be a small thing — even for the most callous of academics.

As to Boskin, Grundfest faced an even more complex challenge than Garcia-Molina. Boskin was a professor who had taught him and with whom he had maintained contact over the years. Their areas of academic interest intersected, putting Grundfest in contact if not directly with Boskin, then regularly with Boskin's colleagues. Moreover, although I am told by the SLC that the title of senior fellow at SIEPR is an honorary one, the fact remains that Grundfest willingly accepted it and was one of a select number of faculty who attained that status. And, they both just happened to also be steering committee members. Having these ties, Grundfest (I infer) would have more difficulty objectively determining whether Boskin engaged in improper insider trading than would a person who was not a fellow professor, had not been a student of Boskin, had not kept in touch with Boskin over the years, and who was not a senior fellow and steering committee member at SIEPR.

In so concluding, I necessarily draw on a general sense of human nature. It may be that Grundfest is a very special person who is capable of putting these kinds of things totally aside. But the SLC has not provided evidence that that is the case. In this respect, it is critical to note that I do not infer that Grundfest would be less likely to recommend suit against Boskin than someone without these ties. Human nature being what it is, it is entirely possible that Grundfest would in fact be tougher on Boskin than he would on someone with whom he did not have such connections. The inference I draw is subtly, but importantly, different. What I infer is that a person in Grundfest's position would find it difficult to assess Boskin's conduct without pondering his own association with Boskin and their mutual affiliations. Although these connections might produce bias in either a tougher or laxer direction, the key inference is that these connections would be on the mind of a person in Grundfest's position, putting him in the position of either causing serious legal action to be brought against a person with whom he shares several connections (an awkward thing) or not doing so (and risking being seen as having engaged in favoritism toward his old professor and SIEPR colleague).

The same concerns also exist as to Lucas. For Grundfest to vote to accuse Lucas of insider trading would require him to accuse SIEPR's Advisory Board Chair and major benefactor of serious wrongdoing—of conduct that violates federal securities laws. Such action would also require Grundfest to make charges against a man who recently donated $50,000 to Stanford Law School after Grundfest made a speech at his request.

And, for both Grundfest and Garcia-Molina, service on the SLC demanded that they consider whether an extremely generous and influential Stanford alumnus should be sued by Oracle for insider trading. Although they were not responsible for fundraising, as sophisticated professors they undoubtedly are aware of how important large contributors are to Stanford, and they share in the benefits that come from serving at a university with a rich endowment. A reasonable professor giving any thought to the matter would obviously consider the effect his decision might have on the University's relationship with Lucas, it being (one hopes) sensible to infer that a professor of reasonable collegiality and loyalty cares about the well-being of the institution he serves.

In so concluding, I give little weight to the SLC's argument that it was unaware of just how substantial Lucas's beneficence to Stanford has been. I do so for two key reasons. Initially, it undermines, rather than inspires, confidence that the SLC did not examine the Trading Defendants' ties to Stanford more closely in preparing its Report. The Report's failure to identify these ties is important because it is the SLC's burden to show independence. In forming the SLC, the Oracle board should have undertaken a thorough consideration of the facts bearing on the independence of the proposed SLC members from the key objects of the investigation.

The purported ignorance of the SLC members about all of Lucas's donations to Stanford is not helpful to them for another reason: there were too many visible manifestations of Lucas's status as a major contributor for me to conclude that Grundfest, at the very least, did not understand Lucas to be an extremely generous benefactor of Stanford. It is improbable that Grundfest was not aware that Lucas was the Chair of SIEPR's Advisory Board, and Grundfest must have known that the Donald L. Lucas Conference Center at SIEPR did not get named that way by coincidence. And, in February 2002—incidentally, the same month the SLC was formed—Grundfest spoke at a meeting of "SIEPR Associates," a group of individuals who had given $5,000 or more to SIEPR. Although it is not clear if Lucas attended that event, he is listed—in the same publication that reported Grundfest's speech at the Associates' meeting—as one of SIEPR's seventy-five "Associates." Combined with the other obvious indicia of Lucas's large contributor status (including the $50,000 donation Lucas made to Stanford Law School to thank Grundfest for giving a speech) and Lucas's obviously keen interest in his alma mater, Grundfest would have had to be extremely insensitive to his own working environment not to have considered Lucas an extremely generous alumni benefactor of Stanford, and at SIEPR and the Law School in particular.

Garcia-Molina is in a somewhat better position to disclaim knowledge of how generous an alumnus Lucas had been. Even so, the scope of Lucas's activities and their easy discoverability gives me doubt that he did not know of the relative magnitude of Lucas's generosity to Stanford. Furthermore, Grundfest comprised half of the SLC and was its most active member. His non-independence is sufficient alone to require a denial of the SLC's motion.

In concluding that the facts regarding Lucas's relationship with Stanford are materially important, I must address a rather odd argument of the SLC's. The argument goes as follows. Stanford has an extremely large endowment. Lucas's contributions, while seemingly large, constitute a very small proportion of Stanford's endowment and annual donations. Therefore, Lucas could not be a materially important contributor to Stanford and the SLC's independence could not be compromised by that factor.

But missing from that syllogism is any acknowledgement of the role that Stanford's solicitude to benefactors like Lucas might play in the overall size of its endowment and campus facilities. Endowments and buildings grow one contribution at a time, and they do not grow by callous indifference to alumni who (personally and through family foundations) have participated in directing contributions of the size Lucas has. Buildings and conference centers are named as they are as a recognition of the high regard universities have for donors (or at least, must feign convincingly). The SLC asks me to believe that what universities like Stanford say in thank you letters and public ceremonies is not in reality true; that, in actuality, their contributors are not materially important to the health of those academic institutions. This is a proposition that the SLC has not convinced me is true, and that seems to contradict common experience.

Nor has the SLC convinced me that tenured faculty are indifferent to large contributors to their institutions, such that a tenured faculty member would not be worried about writing a report finding that a suit by the corporation should proceed against a large contributor and that there was credible evidence that he had engaged in illegal insider trading. The idea that faculty members would not be concerned that action of that kind might offend a large contributor who a university administrator or fellow faculty colleague (e.g., Shoven at SIEPR) had taken the time to cultivate strikes me as implausible and as resting on an narrow-minded understanding of the way that collegiality works in institutional settings.

In view of the ties involving Boskin and Lucas alone, I would conclude that the SLC has failed to meet its burden on the independence question. The tantalizing facts about Ellison merely reinforce this conclusion. The SLC, of course, argues that Ellison is not a large benefactor of Stanford personally, that Stanford has demonstrated its independence of him by rejecting his child for admission, and that, in any event, the SLC was ignorant of any negotiations between Ellison and Stanford about a large contribution. For these reasons, the SLC says, its ability to act independently of Ellison is clear.

I find differently. The notion that anyone in Palo Alto can accuse Ellison of insider trading without harboring some fear of social awkwardness seems a stretch. That being said, I do not mean to imply that the mere fact that Ellison is worth tens of billions of dollars and is the key force behind a very important social institution in Silicon Valley disqualifies all persons who live there from being independent of him. Rather, it is merely an acknowledgement of the simple fact that accusing such a significant person in that community of such serious wrongdoing is no small thing.

Given that general context, Ellison's relationship to Stanford itself contributes to my overall doubt, when heaped on top of the ties involving Boskin and Lucas. During the period when Grundfest and Garcia-Molina were being added to the Oracle board, Ellison was publicly considering making extremely large contributions to Stanford.

Furthermore, the reality is that whether or not Ellison eventually decided not to create that Program and not to bequeath his house to Stanford, Ellison remains a plausible target of Stanford for a large donation. This is especially so in view of Oracle's creation of the

Oracle Help Us Help Foundation with Stanford and Ellison's several public indications of his possible interest in giving to Stanford. And, while I do not give it great weight, the fact remains that Ellison's medical research foundation has been a source of nearly $10 million in funding to Stanford. Ten million dollars, even today, remains real money.

Of course, the SLC says these facts are meaningless because Stanford rejected Ellison's child for admission. I am not sure what to make of this fact, but it surely cannot bear the heavy weight the SLC gives it. The aftermath of denying Ellison's child admission might, after all, as likely manifest itself in a desire on the part of the Stanford community never to offend Ellison again, lest he permanently write off Stanford as a possible object of his charitable aims — as the sort of thing that acts as not one, but two strikes, leading the batter to choke up on the bat so as to be even more careful not to miss the next pitch. Suffice to say that after the rejection took place, it did not keep Ellison from making public statements in Fortune magazine on August 13, 2001 about his consideration of making a huge donation to Stanford, at the same time when the two SLC members were being courted to join the Oracle board.

As an alternative argument, the SLC contends that neither SLC member was aware of Ellison's relationship with Stanford until after the Report was completed. Thus, this relationship, in its various facets, could not have compromised their independence. Again, I find this argument from ignorance to be unavailing. An inquiry into Ellison's connections with Stanford should have been conducted before the SLC was finally formed and, at the very least, should have been undertaken in connection with the Report.

Taken in isolation, the facts about Ellison might well not be enough to compromise the SLC's independence. But that is not the relevant inquiry. The pertinent question is whether, given all the facts, the SLC has met its independence burden.

When viewed in that manner, the facts about Ellison buttress the conclusion that the SLC has not met its burden. Whether the SLC members had precise knowledge of all the facts that have emerged is not essential, what is important is that by any measure this was a social atmosphere painted in too much vivid Stanford Cardinal red for the SLC members to have reasonably ignored it. Summarized fairly, two Stanford professors were recruited to the Oracle board in summer 2001 and soon asked to investigate a fellow professor and two benefactors of the University. On Grundfest's part, the facts are more substantial, because his connections — through his personal experiences, SIEPR, and the Law School — to Boskin and to Lucas run deeper.

It seems to me that the connections outlined in this opinion would weigh on the mind of a reasonable special litigation committee member deciding whether to level the serious charge of insider trading against the Trading Defendants. As indicated before, this does not mean that the SLC would be less inclined to find such charges meritorious, only that the connections identified would be on the mind of the SLC members in a way that generates an unacceptable risk of bias. That is, these connections generate a reasonable doubt about the SLC's impartiality because they suggest that material considerations other than the best interests of Oracle could have influenced the SLC's inquiry and judgments.

Before closing, it is necessary to address two concerns. The first is the undeniable awkwardness of opinions like this one. By finding that there exists too much doubt about the SLC's independence for the SLC to meet its *Zapata* burden, I make no finding about the subjective good faith of the SLC members, both of whom are distinguished academics at one of this nation's most prestigious institutions of higher learning. Nothing in this record leads me to conclude that either of the SLC members acted out of any conscious desire to favor the Trading Defendants or to do anything other than discharge their duties with fidelity. But that is not the purpose of the independence inquiry.

That inquiry recognizes that persons of integrity and reputation can be compromised in their ability to act without bias when they must make a decision adverse to others with whom they share material affiliations. To conclude that the Oracle SLC was not independent is not a conclusion that the two accomplished professors who comprise it are not persons of good faith and moral probity, it is solely to conclude that they were not situated to act with the required degree of impartiality. *Zapata* requires independence to ensure that stockholders do not have to rely upon special litigation committee members who must put aside personal considerations that are ordinarily influential in daily behavior in making the already difficult decision to accuse fellow directors of serious wrongdoing.

Finally, the SLC has made the argument that a ruling against it will chill the ability of corporations to locate qualified independent directors in the academy. This is overwrought. If there are 1,700 professors at Stanford alone, as the SLC says, how many must there be on the west coast of the United States, at institutions without ties to Oracle and the Trading Defendants as substantial as Stanford's? Undoubtedly, a corporation of Oracle's market capitalization could have found prominent academics willing to serve as SLC members, about whom no reasonable question of independence could have been asserted.

Rather than form an SLC whose membership was free from bias-creating relationships, Oracle formed a committee fraught with them. As a result, the SLC has failed to meet its *Zapata* burden, and its motion to terminate must be denied. Because of this reality, I do not burden the reader with an examination of the other *Zapata* factors. In the absence of a finding that the SLC was independent, its subjective good faith and the reasonableness of its conclusions would not be sufficient to justify termination. Without confidence that the SLC was impartial, its findings do not provide the assurance our law requires for the dismissal of a derivative suit without a merits inquiry.

V. Conclusion

The SLC's motion to terminate is DENIED. IT IS SO ORDERED.

Notes

(1) What standards are established by *In re Oracle* to determine whether a special litigation committee is truly independent?

(2) Some would assume prior to *In re Oracle* that the independence of a SLC would be easily established. Why was the Oracle SLC deemed conflicted or not independent?

(3) If Oracle had been genuinely interested in establishing an independent SLC, what should the Board have done to ensure an independent and unbiased inquiry?

(4) Why did Judge Strine not get into the second prong inquiry of *Zapata* by substituting his own business judgment in determining whether the SLCs decision not to pursue litigation against Ellison, Boskin, Lucas and Henry was ultimately fair to Oracle's shareholders and stakeholders?

2. Prong Two: Second Guessing SLC Business Judgment Decisions

For students who have not yet taken Business Associations or Corporations, the facts of the following case may seem convoluted. Despite this reality, we have decided to include it for two reasons. First, it provides a fairly good analysis of the second prong of *Zapata* because it explains how courts substitute their own business judgment for that of a special litigation committee. Second, it provides another example of exactly how difficult it is for shareholders, or anyone else for that matter, to hold directors liable for improper conduct.

In *Primedia*, several minority shareholders brought a derivative action against Primedia's board and Primedia's majority shareholder, KKR, (hereinafter referred to collectively as "the defendants") alleging a *Brophy* action. A Brophy action is a common law action based on Delaware state law for insider trading. Although, most claims for insider trading are brought under federal law (Rule 10(b)) some plaintiffs find that state law is more favorable because of liberal pleading standards and/or because state law allows for full disgorgement of profits. The basis for the *Brophy* action was that the plaintiffs alleged that KKR traded on material non-public information in violation of KKR's fiduciary duty to the corporation. More specifically, the plaintiffs alleged that the defendants had obtained a report that indicated that the corporation's preferred stock was undervalued and that the market value of the preferred stock would increase once the report was made public. Based on this information, the defendants realized that it would be financially beneficial for the corporation to reacquire the preferred stock because the defendants realized that the market price of the preferred shares would increase once the information in the report hit the market (much like corporations can invest in other corporations, corporations can invest in themselves by acquiring their own shares if the corporation believes that the market price will increase). To facilitate the acquisition, the corporation considered redeeming the shares by offering to exchange authorized shares of common stock for the outstanding shares of preferred stock; however, this option was problematic because issuing more common stock would have substantially diluted the market value of the common stock. To avoid wasting the opportunity, the board recommended that KKR purchase the preferred shares. In fact, before the board suggested this option, there was some evidence in the record that KKR had already considered acquiring the preferred shares.

KKR and the board reached an agreement that KKR would acquire the preferred shares and that any acquisition by KKR of the corporation's preferred shares would not constitute a usurpation of a corporate opportunity. As part of the agreement, KKR expressly assented to the inclusion of a "deferral provision," that precluded KKR from continuing to acquire preferred shares if the corporation so requested.

Shortly after KKR began purchasing the shares, the value of the preferred shares increased. In addition, the corporation sold several assets which resulted in an infusion of cash. As a result, the corporation was advised, by its consultant, to redeem the preferred shares that KKR had purchased to eliminate the corporation's obligation to pay KKR dividends because eliminating the mandatory dividend would save the corporation substantial money.

After the corporation redeemed the shares from KKR, KKR made approximately $190 million ($150 million in capital gains and another $40 million from dividends). KKR complied with the preferred stock purchase agreement, with one exception. At one point, the corporation informed KKR that the corporation planned to resume its acquisition of the preferred shares but, KKR, rather than honoring the deferral agreement, purchased 1.5 million dollars' worth of preferred shares.

Based on these events, the plaintiff's brought breach of fiduciary duty claims against the board and KKR alleging a *Brophy* action as well as breaches of the duty of loyalty. The board created a special litigation committee of independent and disinterested committee members that recommended dismissal after conducting a thorough and comprehensive investigation. The court granted the special litigation committee's motion based on *Zapata*. The court easily found that prong one of *Zapata* was met because there was insufficient evidence to suggest that the special litigation committee was not disinterested or independent. The court struggled more with determining whether the special litigation committee met prong two. Nonetheless, the court reasoned that it should accord deference to the business judgment of the special litigation committee under prong two of *Zapata*. Specifically, the court agreed with the special litigation committee that: (1) the statute of limitations for the *Brophy* action had passed; (2) the preferred stock purchase agreement specifically authorized KKR to repurchase the preferred stock so as to eliminate any breach of the duty of loyalty; (3) even if the Brophy action was not time barred, any recovery by the plaintiff's would be limited to 1.5 million not disgorgement of the entire 150 million because KKR was specifically authorized to buy back the preferred shares; (4) the cost to litigate the case would render a 1.5 million dollar recovery unreasonable.

The plaintiffs immediately appealed. While the appeal was pending, the board decided to, and ultimately, merged into another entity, TPR. However, during the valuation process, the board did not consider the total value of the *Brophy* claim ($150 million) in determining the true value of the corporation. As such, the shareholders brought another suit alleging a separate breach of fiduciary duty claim. Essentially, the plaintiffs argued that they should have received more money for their shares but because the merger price of the corporation did not reflect a substantial asset, the value of the pending *Brophy* claim on appeal, they argued that they received inadequate compensation. In response, the defendants moved to dismiss arguing that the plaintiffs no longer had standing since they were no longer shareholders after the merger was approved.

In re Primedia Inc. Shareholders Litigation
67 A.3d 455 (2013)
Court of Chancery of Delaware

OPINION

I. FACTUAL BACKGROUND

The facts are drawn from the Consolidated Amended Class Action Complaint (the "Class Complaint" or "CC") and the documents it incorporates by reference, including the Company's filings with the Securities and Exchange Commission and the Third Amended and Consolidated Derivative Complaint (the "Derivative Complaint" or "DC"), which was the operative complaint at the time of the Merger. I have taken judicial notice of docketed items from the Derivative Action, including a motion to dismiss filed by a Special Litigation Committee formed by the Primedia board (the "SLC") and the SLC's February 19, 2008 report (the "SLC Report"). At this stage of the case, the Class Complaint's allegations are assumed to be true, and the plaintiffs receive the benefit of all reasonable inferences.

A. Primedia, KKR, And The Preferred Stock

In the early 1990s, KKR backed defendant Beverly C. Chell and two other individuals in founding Primedia. Until the Merger, KKR was always Primedia's controlling stockholder. At the time of the Merger, two KKR affiliates—KKR Associates, LP and KKR GP 1996 LLC—served as the general partners for investment funds that owned approximately 58% of Primedia's outstanding common stock. For simplicity, I refer only to KKR. Consistent with its status as Primedia's controlling stockholder, KKR always maintained a significant presence on the Primedia board, although the identity of KKR's representatives changed over time.

During the latter half of the 1990s, Primedia raised capital by issuing multiple series of preferred stock. Three series are pertinent to this case: the Series D Preferred, the Series F Preferred, and the Series H Preferred (collectively, the "Preferred Stock"). The terms of each series contemplated a period during which Primedia would have the option to redeem at a premium, followed by a date on which Primedia was obligated to redeem at a predetermined value. Each series paid annual cash dividends that accrued and were payable in arrears. Each series fixed the annual dividend at a specific amount or as a percentage of the liquidation preference. At the mandatory redemption date, the holders would receive the contractually required redemption payment plus all accumulated and unpaid dividends.

On August 21, 1996, Primedia issued two million shares of Series D Preferred, which carried a liquidation preference of $100 per share and paid annual cash dividends equal to 10% of the liquidation preference. The optional redemption period began on February 1, 2001, but Primedia was obligated to pay an early redemption premium if the stock was redeemed prior to 2006. The mandatory redemption date was February 1, 2008.

On January 16, 1998, Primedia issued 1.25 million shares of Series F Preferred, which carried a liquidation preference of $100 per share and paid annual cash dividends of $9.20 per share. The optional redemption period began on November 1, 2002, but Primedia was obligated to pay an early redemption premium if the stock was redeemed in 2002 or 2003. The mandatory redemption date was November 1, 2009.

On June 10, 1998, Primedia issued 2.5 million shares of Series H Preferred, which carried a liquidation preference of $100 per share and paid annual cash dividends of $8.625 per share. The optional redemption period began on April 1, 2003, but Primedia was obligated to pay an early redemption premium in 2003, 2004, or 2005. The mandatory redemption date was April 1, 2010.

The shares of Preferred Stock were registered under the Securities Act of 1933 and publicly traded. The annual dividends and mandatory redemption date gave the Preferred Stock an investment profile resembling a bond. As long as Primedia had sufficient funds legally available to make the mandatory redemption payment, the returns on the Preferred Stock could be calculated and then adjusted for the possibilities of non-payment or early redemption.

B. The Preferred Stock Exchange Program

In April 2000, Primedia's stock closed at a high of $29.25. But Primedia's value rested largely on its portfolio of internet-related media assets, and with the bursting of the technology bubble, Primedia's shares declined steadily. They reached the low twenties in May 2000, the low teens by February 2001, and the high single digits by September 2001. In March 2002, the stock traded between $2 and $4 per share. By July 2002, it had dipped below $1. The Preferred Stock fell too and traded at a steep discount to face value. The

Series D Preferred, for example, had a face value of $100 per share plus accrued and unpaid dividends but traded in the $20 to $30 range.

During a board meeting on September 21, 2001, Primedia management gave a presentation entitled "Exchange of Preferred for Common." Management anticipated that by issuing shares of common stock in exchange for up to $100 million of Preferred Stock, Primedia could save up to $9 million per year in dividends.

On December 19, 2001, the board authorized Primedia to use shares of common stock to repurchase up to $100 million of Preferred Stock at 50–60% of its face value (the "Exchange Program"). Because the issuance of additional shares of common stock would dilute the existing common holders, the board decided that Primedia would not engage in exchanges at an effective stock price below $5 per share. To derive the effective stock price, Primedia divided the face value of the Preferred Stock by the number of shares of common stock issued in exchange. For example, if Primedia common stock was trading at $2 per share, and if a holder of Preferred Stock exchanged shares with a face value of $1 million for 40 cents on the dollar, then Primedia issued 200,000 shares of common stock in exchange for the Preferred Stock. The effective stock price was derived by dividing the face value of the Preferred Stock ($1,000,000) by the number of common shares issued (200,000), resulting in an effective price of $5 per share.

The first exchanges began in March 2002. On April 8, Primedia issued a press release announcing the Exchange Program. The press release noted that Primedia was authorized to acquire Preferred Stock with a face value of up to $100 million and that Primedia had acquired Preferred Stock with a face value of $62 million as of that point. The lowest effective common stock price in any transaction was $5.16. On April 10, Primedia made a small exchange and continued making exchanges after that date.

On May 16, 2002, the board authorized exchanges for another $100 million in face value of Preferred Stock. Exchanges continued through July 2002.

In total, between March and July 2002, Primedia acquired shares of Series D Preferred with a face value of $23 million, shares of Series F Preferred with a face value of $22.7 million, and shares of Series H Preferred with a face value of $29.8 million. In exchange, Primedia issued 14.4 million shares of common stock.

C. KKR Considers Buying Preferred Stock For Itself.

In early 2002, KKR had four representatives on the Primedia board: Henry R. Kravis, George R. Roberts, Perry Golkin, and Joseph Y. Bae. A fifth member of the board, Dean B. Nelson, was the CEO of a consulting company that provided services exclusively to KKR.

On May 21, 2002, five days after the May 16 meeting at which the Primedia board authorized additional purchases of Preferred Stock, Primedia directors Golkin and Bae coauthored a memo for KKR's Investment Committee and Portfolio Committee (the "May 21 Memo"). Its purpose was to update the KKR committees "on Primedia's performance and revisit the topic of KKR purchasing a portion of Primedia's cash-pay preferred stock." Bae and Golkin told the SLC that KKR previously had discussed possible purchases as early as December 2001.

The May 21 Memo contained nonpublic information about Primedia's performance for both the second quarter of 2002 and the year as a whole. For the second quarter, the May 21 Memo reported that Primedia's EBITDA would be well ahead of publicly disclosed guidance and that the higher EBITDA numbers were nearly assured because of the volume of advertising already sold:

Q2 Estimates

The Company provided 2nd quarter Street guidance for Reported EBITDA of $58–$60 million. The Budget calls for Reported and Cash EBITDA of $66.3 million and $66.1 million, respectively. At this point, most of the second quarter advertising has been sold (with the exception of some weekly publications) and the Company is confident it will meet or exceed Street Guidance.

The May 21 Memo reported that Primedia management projected annual results well above the publicly disclosed figures:

2002 Outlook

The Company's Street guidance for 2002 Reported EBITDA remains at $245–$260 million ($235–$250 million on a Cash basis). This compares to the Company's budgeted Reported and Cash EBITDA of $265 million and $255 million, respectively.

In our recent meetings with the business units, we received a re-forecast for the year of Reported and Cash EBITDA of $271 million and $261 million, respectively, based on first quarter actuals and current business trends. While most business units (with the exception of Enthusiast/EMAP and Haas) have experienced softer market conditions than originally anticipated, the Company's re-forecast is slightly above Budget primarily due to (1) identification and implementation of run-rate cost savings of approximately $60 million ($46 million in 2002), (2) a reversal of $4 million of 2001 bonus accruals and (3) a lower estimate for divested EBITDA, which added $7 million to the new estimates.

The authors of the May 21 Memo concluded that "after our discussions with the business unit heads, we are optimistic that the Company is on track to achieve its targeted cost reductions and deliver its Street guidance of Cash EBITDA of $235–$250 million...."

The authors of the May 21 Memo recommended that KKR purchase shares of Preferred Stock at then-current market prices, before the market became aware of Primedia's improving performance.

Preferred Stock Purchase

On May 8th, Moody's downgraded the Company's senior debt and preferred stock two notches to B3 and Ca, respectively—one notch below S & P—as a consequence of Primedia not yet delivering on its divestiture goal of $250 million. Both Moody's and S & P have Primedia on negative outlook. Although we do not find the Moody's downgrade to be particularly surprising given Primedia's leverage, we believe the downgrade will put downward pressure on the price of the Company's preferred stock. Two days after the downgrade, the Company swapped $2 million par value of preferred stock at 48% of par value for common stock at $2.52 (the equivalent of Primedia issuing stock at $5.25 per share). To date, the Company has completed $65 million par value of swaps at an average price of 60% of preferred par value for common stock at an average price of $3.19 (the equivalent of Primedia issuing stock at $5.28 per share).

Based on (1) our increased comfort level in the Company achieving Street guidance, (2) our optimism for the Company's future prospects and (3) the implications of the Moody's downgrade on the preferred stock price, we continue to believe the Company's outstanding cash-pay preferred stock offers an attractive risk-reward investment opportunity for the 1996 Fund. Primedia currently has $510 million of cash-pay preferred stock outstanding (three separate issues paying dividend of 8.625%–10.00%). We believe it may be possible to buy a sizeable position of the preferred for cash between 45%–55% of par value due to heightened investor concerns about the Company's financial performance, leverage and future liquidity. At these levels, these securities are yielding anywhere between 15%–20% cash-on-cash returns depending on the tranche of preferred. Assuming the preferreds ultimately returned 100% face value in 2004/2005 when Primedia is unwound, the gross IRR on this investment would be between 30%–50% (See Attachment B). We think the 1996 Fund should consider buying up to $50 million of the preferred stock.

We continue to believe that our best chances of acquiring a sizeable block of the preferred stock at a low price will probably be in the next few months before any significant future asset divestitures and/or the Company's business performance improves in 2002/2003.

One reasonably conceivable interpretation of the May 21 Memo, which the Class Complaint embraces, is that Golkin, Bae, and their co-authors recommended that KKR acquire a "sizeable block of the preferred stock" precisely because they had heard presentations from Primedia management during board meetings, talked with the business units, received the Company's internal forecasts, and knew what Moody's and the market did not yet know about Primedia's prospects. The May 21 Memo plainly indicates the advantage KKR would gain by using this information: buying the Preferred Stock at "45%–55% of par value due to heightened investor concerns about the Company's financial performance, leverage, and future liquidity."

Importantly, the authors of the May 21 Memo did not anticipate KKR needing to manufacture an exit from the Preferred Stock position. They simply recognized that KKR could acquire Preferred Stock on the cheap, confident that the Company's contemplated asset sales and positive performance made redemption highly likely.

D. KKR Enters The Market

On May 31, 2002, Primedia acquired additional shares of Preferred Stock in exchange for common stock. On June 19, Primedia engaged in two additional exchanges. By the end of June, however, the price of Primedia's common stock had fallen further, closing on June 27 at $1.61 per share. The decline meant that unless Preferred Stock could be exchanged at less than a third of face value, Primedia would have to issue so many shares of common stock that the effective issuance price would drop below the floor of $5 per share. Primedia's final exchange of 2002 took place on June 27.

KKR was not similarly constrained. On July 3, 2002, KKR formed ABRA III LLC ("ABRA") as a vehicle for purchasing the Preferred Stock. Through affiliates, KKR owned 100% of ABRA.

In an effort to mitigate corporate opportunity concerns, KKR approached Primedia about purchasing the Preferred Stock. In its proposal, KKR undertook to defer to Primedia if Primedia wished to acquire Preferred Stock (the "Deferral Agreement"). On July 2, 2002, Chell emailed a form of written consent to directors Meyer Feldberg, H. John Greenius, and David Bell, with a fax to Bae. The cover memo stated:

> [I]nvestment partnerships managed by KKR are considering the purchase of outstanding shares of Primedia preferred stock for up to $50 million in cash …

> You may be aware that there is a doctrine in corporate law call [sic] "usurpation of a corporate opportunity" …

> The Written Consent states in the first resolution that a cash purchase by Primedia of its outstanding preferred stock would not be in the best interest of Primedia and Primedia waives the opportunity.

The written consent was never executed.

On July 8, 2002, Chell circulated a similar written consent to the full board. The cover memo stated:

> Attached for your consideration is a written consent of the Board of Directors of PRIMEDIA determining that it is not usurping a corporate opportunity for investment partnerships managed by KKR to acquire PRIMEDIA Preferred Stock for cash.

All of the directors executed the written consent, with Feldman's signature page arriving at Primedia on July 12.

ABRA began buying Preferred Stock on July 8, 2002, before the written consent was fully executed. In July, ABRA made thirteen purchases of Preferred Stock, paying a total of $30.5 million for 189,606 shares of Series D Preferred, 216,500 shares of Series F Preferred, and 548,331 shares of Series H Preferred. On July 31, five days after KKR made a large purchase, Primedia announced EBITDA of $65.1 million for the second quarter, exceeding guidance of $58–60 million. Primedia's common stock traded up from $1.00 to $1.30 per share. On August 8, ABRA paid nearly $5 million for an additional 10,750 shares of Series F Preferred and 138,966 shares of Series H Preferred.

E. The American Baby Sale

On September 26, 2002, the board met to approve selling the assets of Primedia's American Baby Group to a third party for $115 million in cash (the "American Baby Sale"). KKR representatives Golkin, Bae, and Kravis participated in the board meeting, as did Nelson, KKR's consultant. Primedia did not announce the sale publicly until November 4.

On September 26, 2002, the same day that the board approved the American Baby Sale, ABRA paid $8.5 million for shares of Preferred Stock with a face value of $22.9 million. On October 7, ABRA paid $30.7 million for Preferred Stock with a face value of $84.9 million.

After the November 4, 2002 public announcement of the American Baby Sale, the trading price of Primedia's common stock rose by 15%. The trading price of the Series D Preferred rose by 38.4%.

On November 5, 2002, a Primedia employee informed Bae that Primedia was resuming its exchanges of common stock for Preferred Stock. Rather than adhering to the Deferral Agreement, KKR purchased 44,000 shares of Series H Preferred for $1.5 million.

In December 2002, with the cash from the American Baby Sale available to fund redemptions, the board authorized the Company to use up to $25 million to buy Preferred Stock. But Primedia could not find willing sellers, in part because KKR had "sucked dry" one of the large holders. During all of 2003, Primedia could only purchase approximately $16 million of Preferred Stock.

In total, through ABRA, KKR acquired 35.8% of the Series D Preferred, 57.9% of the Series F Preferred, and 52.7% of the Series H Preferred. KKR spent $76.4 million for 2,226,197 shares of Preferred Stock with a face value of $222.6 million, paying an average price equal to 32% of face value. KKR's $76 million investment exceeded the $50 million figure referenced in the July 2002 written consent. By contrast, the board authorized Primedia to acquire Preferred Stock with a face value of up to $200 million, yet in the aggregate, Primedia only managed to acquire Preferred Stock with a face value of $75 million.

F. Primedia Redeems The Preferred Stock.

In February 2005, Primedia sold one of its assets, About.com, for approximately $410 million. By this time, the Preferred Stock traded at nearly 100% of face value, and Goldman Sachs advised the board that Primedia should consider redeeming the Preferred Stock because of its relatively high dividend. On March 9, the board approved a plan to redeem all of the outstanding shares of the Series D Preferred and Series F Preferred. These issuances were the most expensive for Primedia because they paid dividends of 10% and 9.2% respectively. On May 11, pursuant to its certificate of designations, Primedia redeemed the Series F Preferred at par plus all accrued dividends. On the same date, also pursuant to its certificate of designations, Primedia redeemed the Series D Preferred at par plus all accrued dividends, plus the contractual early redemption premium.

In 2005, Primedia sold another of its assets in a transaction that generated approximately $385 million in cash. This time, Goldman Sachs recommended redeeming the Series H Preferred. The board approved the plan, and on October 31, Primedia redeemed the Series H Preferred at par plus accrued dividends and paid the contractual early redemption premium.

As a result of the redemptions, KKR realized total proceeds of $222.6 million, representing a capital gain of approximately $150 million on an approximately $76 million investment. In addition, KKR received approximately $40 million in dividends during the time when it held the Preferred Stock, raising its total profits to $190 million.

G. The Filing Of The Derivative Action And The Formation Of The SLC

On November 29, 2005, Kahn filed the first of two derivative complaints on behalf of Primedia. On February 16, 2006, Alan Spiegal filed the second. The actions were consolidated, and the plaintiffs filed an amended complaint in April 2006. The plaintiffs' main theory at the time was that the Primedia directors breached their fiduciary duties by causing Primedia to sell assets and redeem the Preferred Stock prematurely to benefit KKR.

The defendants moved to dismiss the consolidated complaint. In November 2006, Vice Chancellor Lamb denied the motion, holding that the complaint adequately pled that KKR exercised control over Primedia, stood on both sides of the stock redemptions, and received a benefit from those redemptions not shared with other stockholders. *See In re Primedia Inc. Deriv. Litig.*, 910 A.2d 248, 256–61 (Del.Ch.2006) (the "Dismissal Ruling").

On May 23, 2007, the board formed the SLC. Its two members, Daniel T. Ciporin and Kevin J. Smith, were newly appointed independent directors. The litigation was stayed pending the outcome of the SLC's investigation.

In August 2007, the plaintiffs filed their second amended complaint. The new complaint added a claim that by purchasing Preferred Stock between July 8, 2002 and November 5, 2002, KKR usurped corporate opportunities belonging to Primedia.

The SLC thoroughly investigated the redemption claim and the corporate opportunity claim. The SLC and its counsel reviewed some 140,000 documents, conducted twenty-one interviews, and consulted with three experts. During the course of its work, the SLC and its advisors held twenty-three formal meetings and engaged in numerous informal discussions and consultations.

The SLC advised the plaintiffs that it planned to recommend dismissal of the Derivative Action and did not intend to pursue any claims based on the May 21 Memo. The plaintiffs disagreed with the SLC's conclusions and contended that the May 21 Memo supported a strong *Brophy* claim.

The SLC had not previously evaluated a *Brophy* claim. The SLC's counsel understood that the SLC was charged with acting reasonably to maximize the value of the Derivative Action as a corporate asset, but counsel believed the SLC only needed to consider those theories that the plaintiffs explicitly alleged in their complaint based on the limited information that the plaintiffs possessed when they filed their pleading. The SLC's counsel had not viewed the SLC's charge as including a duty to evaluate other reasonably apparent and better supported theories that were revealed during the course of the investigation, even if those theories provided a potential means of maximizing the value of the litigation asset. Of course, the concept of maximizing the value of a derivative action does not necessarily mean litigating every possible claim or insisting on settlement value for it. Maximizing the value of a derivative action for the benefit of the corporation could mean seeking to dismiss claims that an independent SLC reasonably believes, in good faith, after conducting a reasonable investigation, would have a negative risk-adjusted present value for the corporation, taking into account the potential benefits and detriments of pursuing those claims.

After being notified about the *Brophy* claim, the SLC held its final meeting. The SLC did not conduct any additional investigation into the *Brophy* claim, but rather analyzed the claim based on the work it had done to investigate the corporate opportunity theory.

On February 28, 2008, the SLC moved to dismiss the Derivative Action. In support of its motion, the SLC filed a 370-page report and eight volumes of appendices. The report dealt thoroughly and decisively with the redemption claim and the corporate opportunity claim. The report also contained fifteen pages analyzing the *Brophy* claim, concluding primarily that the statute of limitations barred it. The SLC also took the view that there was "no evidence that the inside information was material in light of expert analysis regarding its impact on the market price for Primedia's preferred shares, and no evidence that KKR possessed the requisite scienter given contemporaneous memoranda indicating that KKR planned the purchases months before the inside information was issued."

For the next year and a half, the plaintiffs conducted discovery to test the SLC's disinterestedness and independence, the thoroughness of its investigation, and the reasonableness of its conclusions. In November 2009, the plaintiffs filed their brief in opposition to the SLC's motion and sought leave to file a third amended complaint — the Derivative Complaint — that formally asserted the *Brophy* claim. Leave was granted, and the plaintiffs filed the Derivative Complaint on March 16, 2010.

H. The *Zapata* Hearing

On June 14, 2010, I conducted a hearing on the SLC's motion to dismiss the Derivative Action. *See In re Primedia Deriv. Litig.*, Consol. C.A. No. 1808–VCL (Del. Ch. June 14, 2010) (TRANSCRIPT) [hereinafter *Zapata* Hearing]. Under *Zapata*, a trial court evaluates such a motion under a two-step test. First, the trial court "inquire[s] into the independence and good faith of the committee and the bases supporting its conclusions." *Zapata Corp. v. Maldonado*, 430 A.2d 779, 788 (Del.1981). The SLC has the burden of proving its "independence [and] good faith" and that it conducted "a reasonable investigation." *Id.* If the trial court is satisfied that "the committee was independent and showed reasonable bases for good faith findings and recommendations," the first step is satisfied. At that point, the trial court may proceed "in its discretion, to the next step[,]" under which the trial court "determine[s], applying its own independent business judgment, whether the motion should be granted." "This means, of course, that instances could arise where a committee can establish its independence and sound bases for its good faith decisions and still have the corporation's motion denied."

The Delaware Supreme Court created the second step of the *Zapata* test because it saw "sufficient risk in the realities of a situation like the one presented in this case to justify caution beyond adherence to the theory of business judgment."

> [W]e must be mindful that directors are passing judgment on fellow directors in the same corporation and fellow directors, in this instance, who designated them to serve both as directors and committee members. The question naturally arises whether a "there but for the grace of God go I" empathy might play a role. And the further question arises whether inquiry as to independence, good faith and reasonable investigation is sufficient safeguard against abuse, perhaps subconscious abuse.

In light of these concerns, the second step takes on critical importance:

> The second step provides, we believe, the essential key in striking the balance between legitimate corporate claims as expressed in a derivative stockholder suit and a corporation's best interests as expressed by an independent investigating committee.... The second step is intended to thwart instances where corporate actions meet the criteria of step one, but the result does not appear to satisfy its spirit, or where corporate actions would simply prematurely terminate a stockholder grievance deserving of further consideration in the corporation's interest.

Id. at 789 (footnote omitted). As I understand the decision, the trial court's task in the second step is to determine whether the SLC's recommended result falls within a range of reasonable outcomes that a disinterested and independent decision maker for the corporation, not acting under any compulsion and with the benefit of the information then available, could reasonably accept.

After hearing presentations from counsel, I concluded that the SLC had established that its members were independent, that they had acted in good faith, and that they had conducted a reasonable investigation into the redemption claim and the corporate opportunity claim. I found that the SLC's decision not to conduct an additional factual investigation into the *Brophy* claim was reasonable, because the claim arose from the same factual predicate as the corporate opportunity claim. Having investigated the corporate opportunity claim thoroughly, the SLC possessed an adequate factual record on which to assess the *Brophy* claim. I also found that the evidentiary implications of the contents of the May 21 Memo and the timing of the purchases before the public announcement of the American Baby Sale were sufficiently powerful that it did not require extensive investigation to conclude that a litigable claim existed.

I approved the SLC's recommendations to dismiss the redemption and corporate opportunity claims, finding that they were fully supported by the record and fell within a range of reasonableness. As to the redemption claim, the SLC's investigation established that (i) the asset sales were part of a consistent multi-year business plan to deleverage Primedia's balance sheet, (ii) Primedia sold the assets to third parties on arm's length terms, (iii) the board consistently sought to use the sale proceeds to eliminate the most expensive elements of the Company's capital structure, (iv) Primedia redeemed the Preferred Stock in accordance with the contractual terms in the certificate of designations, (v) the board followed a fair process when making the redemptions, (vi) if evaluated independently of the contract terms, the redemption prices were fair, and (vii) all of Primedia's stockholders benefitted proportionately from the redemptions. Indeed, by the time of the *Zapata* Hearing, the plaintiffs appeared to have abandoned any challenge to the redemptions.

As to the corporate opportunity claim, the SLC recognized that the purchases of the Preferred Stock were a corporate opportunity and that a conflict of interest existed between KKR and Primedia with respect to the purchases. Nevertheless, the SLC's investigation established that (i) until the American Baby Sale, Primedia did not have the capacity to redeem shares of Preferred Stock for cash, (ii) the board and management appropriately limited Primedia's exchanges to transactions with an effective issuance price of not less than $5, and (iii) when KKR was in the market acquiring Preferred Stock, Primedia's stock price had dropped so far that Primedia could not engage in exchanges because of the $5 floor. Primedia therefore did not have the capacity to take advantage of the opportunity, leaving KKR free to exploit it. The SLC's decision not to pursue the corporate opportunity claims therefore fell within a range of reasonableness. The lone exception to the incapacity analysis was KKR's purchase on November 5, 2002, when KKR acquired 44,000 shares of Series H Preferred for $1.5 million. For this purchase, the record indicated that Primedia wanted to reenter the market, Primedia communicated its desire to KKR, and that KKR failed to respond and then bought Preferred Stock for its own account. Nevertheless, in my view, the SLC's decision not to pursue relief for this one purchase did not render its recommendation unreasonable, because the costs, burdens, and distractions of pursuing the litigation easily could outstrip the value to Primedia from the limited potential recovery of the profits on that purchase.

The *Brophy* claim, however, presented difficulties. To succeed on a *Brophy* claim, a plaintiff must show that: "1) the corporate fiduciary possessed material nonpublic company information; and 2) the corporate fiduciary used that information improperly by making trades because she was motivated, in whole or in part, by the substance of that information." *In re Oracle Corp. Deriv. Litig.*, 867 A.2d 904, 934 (Del.Ch.2004), *aff'd*, 872 A.2d 960 (Del.2005). If read in a plaintiff-friendly fashion, the May 21 Memo appeared to be a proverbial smoking gun document. It was co-authored by KKR representatives who were directors of Primedia and who received confidential information about Primedia in a fiduciary capacity. It discussed explicitly that Primedia's EBITDA for the second quarter of 2002 would be well ahead of publicly disclosed guidance and that the higher figures were nearly assured because "[a]t this point, most of the second quarter advertising has been sold (with the exception of some weekly publications) and the Company is confident it will meet or exceed Street Guidance." It then discussed internal information for the year and reported that Primedia management would "achieve its targeted cost reductions and deliver its Street guidance of Cash EBITDA of $235–$250 million...."

The May 21 Memo recognized that the public markets did not have similar information. It noted that nearly two weeks earlier, Moody's had "downgraded the Company's senior debt and preferred stock two notches to B3 and Ca, respectively—one notch below S & P—as a consequence of Primedia not yet delivering on its divestiture goal of $250 million" and that "[b]oth Moody's and S & P have Primedia on negative outlook." The authors of the May 21 Memo then recommended that KKR purchase shares of Preferred Stock at then-current market prices, before the market became aware of Primedia's improving performance:

> Based on (1) our increased comfort level in the Company achieving Street guidance, (2) our optimism for the Company's future prospects and (3) the implications of the Moody's downgrade on the preferred stock price, we continue to believe the Company's outstanding cash-pay preferred stock offers an attractive risk-reward investment opportunity for the 1996 Fund. Primedia currently has $510 million of cash-pay preferred stock outstanding (three separate issues paying

dividend of 8.625%–10.00%). We believe it may be possible to buy a sizeable position of the preferred for cash between 45%–55% of par value due to heightened investor concerns about the Company's financial performance, leverage and future liquidity....

We continue to believe that our best chances of acquiring a sizeable block of the preferred stock at a low price will probably be in the next few months before any significant future asset divestitures and/or the Company's business performance improves in 2002/2003.

The trading that took place after the approval of the American Baby Sale and before the public announcement of the transaction presented a similarly strong case. The May 21 Memo recommended that KKR make its purchases "before any significant future asset divestitures," such as the American Baby Sale. The board approved the sale on September 26, 2002, and three KKR representatives and a KKR consultant participated as directors. Primedia did not publicly announce the transaction until November 4. Between board approval and the public announcement, KKR acquired shares of Preferred Stock with a face value of $107.7 million, paying $39.2 million. After the public announcement of the American Baby Sale, Primedia's common stock traded up 15%, and the Series D Preferred traded up 38.4%.

I determined at the *Zapata* Hearing that a complaint alleging the *Brophy* claim would "blow by" a motion to dismiss. In the eventual appeal, the Delaware Supreme Court expressed uncertainty about this phrase and stated

we are unable to determine whether the Vice Chancellor's comment, "I start from the proposition that there is a *Brophy* claim here that would blow by a motion to dismiss on failure to state a claim," implicitly suggests he thought the information was sufficiently material but dismissed the claim because of his reliance on *Pfeiffer*. Absent a more focused analysis in the record, we must therefore reverse and remand.

Kahn v. Kolberg Kravis Roberts & Co., L.P., 23 A.3d 831, 842 (Del.2011) (footnotes omitted).

My language marked a regrettable lapse into practitioner colloquialism. Defendants often ask their lawyer whether a complaint will "get past" or "get by" a motion to dismiss. When the complaint is quite strong, the practitioner might respond metaphorically that the complaint not only will get past a motion to dismiss, but likely will do so via a judicial decision issued quickly and without much hesitation. In one of our culture's many sports analogies, such a complaint could be said to "blow by" a motion to dismiss. Envision a batsman like the literary Casey. He stands at the plate, representing the defendants. He faces a pitcher, the plaintiff. The pitcher throws his best pitch, the complaint. The batter swings the motion to dismiss bat, hoping to drive the pitch out of the judicial park. But so strong is the complaint that it blows by the motion to dismiss like a 100+ mile per hour fastball. For those whose preferences run to sports with goalies, the metaphor translates easily.

In this admittedly elliptical language, I rejected the SLC's argument that there was "no evidence" to support a *Brophy* claim, finding instead that there was powerful evidence to support such a claim in the form of the May 21 Memo, the timing of the KKR trades, and the market's reaction to disclosure of the information. The information that KKR possessed appeared material, and KKR appeared to have acted with *scienter*. The *Brophy* claim therefore presented "a viable claim" that likely would have required a trial to resolve.

Given that Primedia possessed a valuable asset in the form of a litigable *Brophy* claim, the question under *Zapata* was whether it fell within a range of reasonableness for the

SLC to give up that asset for no consideration. Generally speaking, an unaffiliated third party that possesses a litigable claim will seek to extract something in exchange. Armed with leverage, a third party will use its leverage. The reasonableness of the SLC's decision *not* to attempt to extract anything for the litigable *Brophy* claim turned on what Primedia likely could obtain for the claim and at what cost, with the costs and benefits measured not only in dollars incurred or recovered but also by factors such as the distraction of litigation for management, its consequences for employee and executive morale, whether there would be adverse reactions from customers, suppliers, and capital providers, and the effectiveness of any internal corrective measures or sanctions.

At the time of the *Zapata* Hearing, Court of Chancery decisions conflicted on the continuing viability of *Brophy* and the extent of the recoverable damages. *Brophy* itself was a Chancery decision and thus was subject to further Chancery development. Two members of this Court had questioned the continuing vitality of *Brophy,* noted that the case was decided before the establishment of current remedies for insider trading under the federal securities laws, and expressed concern about duplicative recoveries and potential interference with the federal regime. Other Chancery decisions sought to avoid these problems by limiting *Brophy* to situations in which the corporation itself suffered harm.

In assessing what the SLC potentially could recover on the *Brophy* claim, I relied on *Pfeiffer* and assumed Primedia would not be able to obtain full disgorgement of KKR's profits. To the extent Primedia did not have the ability to acquire Preferred Stock at the time KKR was purchasing, as the SLC reasonably concluded for all of the purchases except for the November 2002 transaction, Primedia was not harmed by those transactions. Primedia's disgorgement recovery therefore appeared limited to profits from the November 2002 purchase, which the SLC's counsel projected might be in the $1.5 to $2 million range. The Delaware Supreme Court's decision in *Thorpe v. CERBCO, Inc.,* 676 A.2d 436 (Del.1996), suggested that KKR also might be held liable for the costs that Primedia was forced to incur because of the breach of the duty of loyalty, such as the costs of the SLC investigation and litigation expenses to defend the stockholder action. The SLC's counsel represented that its investigation cost less than $1.5 million. In total, I estimated that if the case went to trial, the best outcome would be a "mid seven figures damages recovery," discounted for various defenses and reduced by litigation costs. In particular, I saw "litigable arguments going both ways on the statute of limitations" and "a very real possibility that any claim gets stopped right at the outset because of [that] defense."

Because I evaluated the risk-adjusted recovery as "low," it fell within a range of reasonableness for the SLC to recommend dismissing the *Brophy* claim for no consideration, rather than imposing upon Primedia the time, expense, and distraction of litigation. By contrast, if the available remedies included full disgorgement such that the damages could reach $150 million, then the analysis would have been different. The SLC's counsel agreed. ("Obviously, if we're going to say the potential damages are 150 million instead of 1.5 million, it has an impact.") But because of my belief about the available recovery, I granted the SLC's motion to dismiss. Had I understood that full disgorgement was possible, I would have denied the SLC's motion with respect to the *Brophy* claim under the second prong of *Zapata.*

I. The Appeal And The Sale Process

The order dismissing the Derivative Action was entered on June 16, 2010. On July 15, the plaintiffs appealed to the Delaware Supreme Court. They did not challenge the dismissal of the redemption claim. They rather argued that under *Zapata*'s first prong, I erred in finding that the SLC investigated the *Brophy* claim thoroughly and in good faith, and that under *Zapata*'s second prong, I erred in treating full disgorgement as unavailable.

While the appeal was pending, KKR and the Primedia board began considering strategic alternatives. At the time, the board had ten members. Because this board eventually approved the Merger, I refer to it as the "Merger Board." Three directors were associated with or nominated by KKR. A fourth was Primedia's CEO. Another six were outside directors, but several had past ties to KKR or the Company.

For convenience, I refer to the latter six as the "Outside Directors." The Outside Directors were not formally empowered to act as a committee, but they retained their own legal counsel (Gibson Dunn & Crutcher LLP) and financial advisor (Lazard Ltd.).

On January 11, 2011, Primedia announced that it was exploring strategic alternatives. Primedia's financial advisor, Moelis & Company, contacted 117 potential strategic and financial acquirers. Forty-six executed non-disclosure agreements and received access to an electronic data room. On February 25, eleven bidders submitted preliminary, non-binding indications of interest. At a March 1 meeting, the Merger Board decided to allow all but the lowest bidder to continue to the next round of the process. Over the following three weeks, Primedia management met with the ten participants.

J. Oral Argument Before The Delaware Supreme Court

On March 23, 2011, the Delaware Supreme Court sitting *en banc* heard oral argument in the plaintiffs' appeal. The plaintiffs allege that the justices asked questions which suggested that they believed *Brophy* provided for a full disgorgement remedy and would reverse the dismissal of the Derivative Action.

K. The Sale To TPG

Primedia designed its sale process to wrap up in May 2011. On April 20, Primedia's counsel, Simpson Thacher & Bartlett LLP ("Simpson Thacher"), circulated a draft merger agreement to the participants. Moelis instructed them to return a mark-up by May 6 and to provide final bids on May 9.

Three parties submitted bids: On May 13, Bidder X bid to $7.00 per share. On May 14, TPG offered to acquire Primedia for $7.10 per share with a 100% equity commitment. Later on May 15, 2011, the Outside Directors met for thirty minutes with Lazard and Gibson Dunn to consider "the status of the bids and [their] fiduciary duties." Lazard opined that the $7.10 bid was fair.

The full Merger Board then met. At the meeting, Simpson Thacher, a firm with deep and longstanding ties to KKR, advised the Merger Board about the *Brophy* claim. This was allegedly the first time the Derivative Action was discussed in connection with the Merger. The Merger Board concluded that for the reasons discussed in the SLC Report and in light of this Court's dismissal of the Derivative Action (which remained pending on appeal), "the Derivative Action had limited, if any, value to [Primedia]." The Merger Board resolved to accept TPG's bid, adopt the Merger Agreement, and recommend the Merger to its stockholders. After the Merger Agreement was executed, KKR acted by written consent to provide the necessary stockholder approval.

It is undisputed for purposes of this litigation that the Merger Board worked to obtain the best value reasonably available for Primedia's business. The $7.10 per share cash consideration represented a 39% premium over the closing price of Primedia's common stock on January 11, 2011 ($5.10), the date the Company announced that it was exploring strategic alternatives, and a 62% premium over the closing price of Primedia's common stock on May 13 ($4.38), the last business day before the Merger Agreement was executed. The Merger valued the Company's equity at $316 million. It is also undisputed for purposes of this litigation that the Merger Board did not view the Derivative Action as having value to Primedia, did not attempt to extract value for the Derivative Action from TPG, and did not otherwise seek to preserve the value of the Derivative Action for Primedia's stockholders.

L. The Delaware Supreme Court Reverses On *Brophy.*

On June 20, 2011, the Delaware Supreme Court issued an opinion reversing the dismissal of the Derivative Action. In doing so, the senior tribunal made clear that full disgorgement of profits is an available remedy under *Brophy,* regardless of whether the corporation was harmed. Citing *Brophy* itself, the Delaware Supreme Court held that "actual harm to the corporation is not required for a plaintiff to state a claim under *Brophy.*" In the high court's words, "[a]s the court recognized in *Brophy,* it is inequitable to permit the fiduciary to profit from using confidential corporate information. Even if the corporation did not suffer actual harm, equity requires disgorgement of that profit." The Delaware Supreme Court saw "no reasonable public policy ground to restrict the scope of disgorgement remedy in *Brophy* cases—irrespective of arguably parallel remedies grounded in federal securities law." The Delaware Supreme Court remanded the Derivative Action to determine if the broader reading of *Brophy* would alter the balancing under the second prong of *Zapata.*

With full disgorgement available, the potential recovery on the *Brophy* claim ballooned to $190 million, comprising $150 million in capital gains plus $40 million in dividends. From my point of view, this clearly changed the analysis. As I had noted during the original *Zapata* Hearing, it was "pretty obvious," at least to me, that the SLC could not reasonably walk away for nothing from a fairly litigable claim that could result in a recovery of $190 million.

M. Events After The Delaware Supreme Court Decision

On May 23, 2011, the plaintiffs filed actions challenging the Merger in this Court. Other stockholders filed actions in Fulton County, Georgia and Gwinnett County, Georgia, which were stayed pending resolution of this action. On June 3, Kahn filed an amended complaint and moved for a preliminary injunction seeking additional disclosures beyond those in Primedia's preliminary information statement. On June 7, I denied the motion to expedite and declined to schedule a preliminary injunction hearing because the plaintiffs had an adequate post-merger damages remedy.

On June 24, 2011, the Merger Board issued a press release indicating that the SLC had met to discuss the Delaware Supreme Court's decision. The SLC determined that the decision "did not alter the conclusion ... that it was not in the best interests of the Company to pursue the claims asserted in the derivative action." Primedia, Inc., Current Report (Form 8–K) (June 24, 2011). On July 13, the Merger was consummated.

On July 18, 2011, I consolidated the two class actions and established a leadership structure for the plaintiffs. Meanwhile, the closing of the Merger had eliminated plaintiffs' standing to pursue the Derivative Action, which the parties dismissed by stipulation on August 8. *See In re Primedia Inc Deriv. Litig.,* C.A. No. 1808–VCL (Del. Ch. Aug. 8, 2011) (ORDER). The plaintiffs filed the currently operative Class Complaint on December 12.

II. LEGAL ANALYSIS

The defendants have moved to dismiss the Class Complaint pursuant to Rule 12(b)(6) for failure to state a claim on which relief can be granted. In a Delaware state court, the pleading standards under Rule 12(b)(6) "are minimal." The operative test in a Delaware state court thus is one of "reasonable conceivability." This standard asks whether there is a "possibility" of recovery. The test is more lenient than the federal "plausibility" pleading standard, which invites judges to "determin[e] whether a complaint states a plausible claim for relief" and "draw on ... judicial experience and common sense."

A. The Claim Challenging The Fairness Of The Merger

The Class Complaint asserts that the Merger must be reviewed for entire fairness because it conferred a special benefit on KKR, Primedia's controlling stockholder. Through the Merger, the right to assert the *Brophy* claim passed to TPG. The plaintiffs allege that given KKR's stature in the M & A world, it was highly unlikely that any acquirer would sue KKR for insider trading, and particularly so since the acquirers were not being asked to pay any consideration for the *Brophy* claim. It was even more unlikely that a financial buyer like TPG would sue a fellow private equity firm like KKR. But the failure to obtain value for the *Brophy* claim in turn rendered the Merger unfair to Primedia's minority stockholders, because they only received value for their share of Primedia's operating business and not for their share of the Derivative Action.

In *Lewis v. Anderson,* 477 A.2d 1040 (Del.1984), the Delaware Supreme Court held that the right to bring a derivative action passes via merger to the surviving corporation. Where, as here, the surviving corporation is a wholly owned subsidiary of another entity, the litigation asset of the surviving corporation comes under the control of parent. Under those circumstances, the merger extinguishes the former derivative plaintiffs' standing to sue.

What has been less clear under Delaware law is the extent to which stockholders of the acquired corporation can, under limited circumstances, challenge the fairness of the merger by which their standing to sue was extinguished. This Court has considered such claims on multiple occasions and in different procedural contexts.** Conceptually, these claims "embrace the holding of the Supreme Court's decision in *Parnes v. Bally Entertainment Corp.,* which permits a plaintiff to attack a merger directly if the target board agreed to a materially inadequate, and therefore unfair, price because the price did not reflect the value of certain assets—in this case, the Derivative Claims."

As I understand the framework established by *Parnes,* a plaintiff wishing to assert such a claim must first establish standing to sue. If standing exists, then the plaintiff must still plead a viable claim.

1. Standing To Sue Under *Parnes*

A plaintiff claiming standing to challenge a merger directly under *Parnes* because of a board's alleged failure to obtain value for an underlying derivative claim must meet a three part test. First, the plaintiff must plead an underlying derivative claim that has survived a motion to dismiss or otherwise could state a claim on which relief could be

---

** *See Massey Energy,* 2011 WL 2176479, at *2–4 (denying motion for preliminary injunction to block merger that would extinguish derivative standing); *Kohls v. Duthie,* 765 A.2d 1274, 1284–85 (Del.Ch.2000) (same; noting that Court previously denied motion to dismiss the merger challenge); *Merritt v. Colonial Foods, Inc.,* 505 A.2d 757, 763–66 (Del.Ch.1986) (Allen, C.) (granting summary judgment for plaintiffs on claim challenging merger as self-interested transaction designed in part to eliminate risk of derivative action where stockholders did not receive a fair price); *see also Brinckerhoff v. Tex. E. Prods. Pipeline Co., LLC,* 986 A.2d 370, 386–96 (Del.Ch.2010) (assessing strength of derivative claims for which standing was extinguished by merger when evaluating fairness of settlement); *In re Countrywide Corp. S'holders Litig.,* 2009 WL 846019, at *8 (Del.Ch. Mar. 31, 2009) (same), *aff'd,* 996 A.2d 321 (Del.2010).

granted. Second, the value of the derivative claim must be material in the context of the merger. Third, the complaint challenging the merger must support a pleadings-stage inference that the acquirer would not assert the underlying derivative claim and did not provide value for it.

a. Was The Derivative Action Viable?

The first element of the *Parnes* inquiry asks whether the underlying corporate claim has survived a motion to dismiss or otherwise could state a claim on which relief could be granted. If the underlying derivative action is not viable, then there is no litigation asset to value or maintain, and likewise no value to divert to the controlling stockholder or other derivative action defendants.

Although prior cases have not dilated on this issue, it appears to me that Rule 12(b)(6), rather than Rule 23.1, provides the operative standard for judging whether the underlying corporate claim could survive a motion to dismiss. This aspect of the *Parnes* inquiry focuses on whether the corporation possessed a viable claim that the board could have caused the corporation to assert. Rule 23.1 exists for the benefit of the corporation, "not ... for the benefit of defendants." Rule 23.1 does not apply if the corporation asserts the claim or has permitted a stockholder to sue on the corporation's behalf. Consistent with this approach, Chancellor Allen granted summary judgment as to liability in favor of a class of plaintiff stockholders when a controlling stockholder used a squeeze out merger to extinguish meritorious derivative claims. To determine whether the claims were "meritorious," Chancellor Allen referenced the standard from *Chrysler Corp. v. Dann*, 223 A.2d 384 (Del.1996), which established the test for whether a derivative claim is sufficiently meritorious to support a settlement. In *Chrysler*, the Delaware Supreme Court held that

> [a] claim is meritorious within the meaning of the rule if it can withstand a motion to dismiss on the pleadings if, at the same time, the plaintiff possesses knowledge of provable facts which hold out some reasonable likelihood of ultimate success. It is not necessary that factually there be absolute assurance of ultimate success, but only that there be some reasonable hope.

This standard has been equated with Rule 12(b)(6).

During the *Zapata* Hearing, I found that the *Brophy* claim presented "a viable claim" that would "blow by" a motion to dismiss and likely would have required a trial to resolve. Having considered the matter anew in the context of the current motion, I continue to believe that it is reasonably conceivable that the plaintiffs could develop and prove a set of facts that would support a *Brophy* claim.

As noted, to succeed on a *Brophy* claim, a plaintiff must show that: "1) the corporate fiduciary possessed material, nonpublic company information; and 2) the corporate fiduciary used that information improperly by making trades because she was motivated, in whole or in part, by the substance of that information." The following allegations support inferences that KKR possessed inside information through its director representatives, understood its materiality, and acted with *scienter* to trade on the information before it became known to the market.

- On December 19, 2001, the board authorized a program through which the Company would exchange common stock for up to $100 million of Preferred Stock, indicating that the board believed the Preferred Stock was undervalued.

- On March 5, 2002, Primedia began using its common stock to acquire Preferred Stock.

- On May 16, 2002, the board authorized exchanges for up to an additional $100 million of Preferred Stock, demonstrating again that the board believed the Preferred Stock was undervalued.

- Eight days after the Primedia board meeting on May 16, 2002, Primedia directors Golkin, Bae, Nelson, and three other KKR insiders submitted the May 21 Memo to KKR's Investment Committee and Portfolio Committee. The purpose of the May 21 Memo was to provide an update "on Primedia's performance and revisit the topic of KKR purchasing a portion of Primedia's cash-pay preferred stock."

- The May 21 Memo described Primedia management's internal, upward revisions to second quarter EBITDA estimates that went beyond the guidance Primedia provided to analysts. The May 21 Memo reported that achieving the updated estimates was virtually assured because Primedia had already sold "most of the second quarter advertising" even though there was over a month left until the June 30 close of the quarter. When Primedia later issued a press release on July 31, 2002, announcing that it achieved EBITDA of $65.1 million for the second quarter, "exceeding original guidance of $58–60 million," Primedia CEO Thomas S. Rogers described the performance as a "dramatic improvement in EBITDA[.]"

- The May 21 Memo described Primedia management's internal assessment that Primedia would exceed its full year EBITDA estimates by 4% and reported on the KKR representatives' discussions with internal Primedia business heads.

- The May 21 Memo recommended that KKR purchase $50 million of Preferred Stock "before any significant future asset divestitures and/or the Company's business performance improves" in the latter half of 2002 or early 2003.

- The authors of the May 21 Memo made their recommendation "[b]ased on (1) our increased comfort level in the Company achieving Street guidance, (2) our optimism for the Company's future prospects, and (3) the implications of the Moody's downgrade on the preferred stock price." The language of the May 21 Memo indicated that the authors' "increased comfort level" and "optimism" resulted from their internal conversations with Primedia personnel and the information they received about EBITDA for the second quarter and the full year. The reference to the Moody's downgrade and its effect on the "preferred stock price" suggested that the authors recognized that the market did not know what they knew and that KKR should take advantage of that fact.

- Within six weeks of the May 21 Memo, KKR began purchasing Preferred Stock.

- On September 26, 2002, the Primedia board approved the sale of American Baby Group for roughly $115 million in cash, one of the asset divestitures that Primedia had been planning and which the May 21 Memo appears to have anticipated. All directors attended the meeting, including KKR representatives Kravis, Golkin, Nelson, and Bae.

- After the approval of the American Baby Sale, but before the public announcement of the transaction, KKR purchased $39 million of Preferred Stock.

Assuming these allegations are true, as I must at this procedural stage, it does not strike me as inconceivable that KKR breached its duty of loyalty under *Brophy* by misusing material, nonpublic information belonging to Primedia.

The defendants proffer a number of fact-laden arguments about why the foregoing allegations do not support an inference of *scienter* or materiality. First, they observe that

KKR's representatives on the Primedia board appear to have first raised the idea of KKR purchasing Preferred Stock in late 2001, and then made their recommendation again in May 2002. According to the defendants, there is "no evidence that KKR possessed the requisite scienter given contemporaneous memoranda indicating that KKR planned the purchases months before the inside information was issued." I frankly do not follow that reasoning. It is reasonably conceivable to me that thanks to its representatives on the Primedia board, KKR knew in late 2001 that Primedia's business had begun to stabilize and that the Company was working actively on its program of asset divestitures. The market appears not to have known these things, and in particular to have lost confidence in Primedia's divestiture program (leading ultimately to the Moody's downgrade). KKR's representatives readily could have recognized these facts in late 2001, understood that KKR knew information that the market lacked, but decided to forego purchases at that time for any number of reasons. By May 2002, with Primedia's business improving, the risk-return profile for KKR was superior and there appeared to be a limited window in which to act. The May 21 Memo can readily be interpreted as reiterating the basic proposition that KKR had information the market lacked, describing that information in detail, and urging KKR to take advantage of the information before the market learned of the improvement in Primedia's business and its upcoming asset sales. It is undisputed that after receiving the May 21 Memo, KKR made large purchases, precisely as one would expect if KKR were trying to take advantage of a limited trading window, and that KKR made a significant portion of its purchases after the American Baby Sale was approved but before it was announced publicly. At a later stage of the case, the evidence may support a different interpretation, but at the pleadings stage, it is reasonably conceivable that KKR possessed material information and acted with *scienter*.

Second, the defendants argue that the *Brophy* claim fails because the SLC's expert opined that the information in the May 21 Memo was immaterial, citing the apparent lack of a material impact on the trading price of the Preferred Stock. There does not appear to be any dispute that the American Baby Sale was material.

At a later stage of the case, the opinion of the defendants' expert about the information in the May 21 Memo might prove persuasive. It would not be surprising, however, for the plaintiffs to retain an expert of their own, or to develop evidence in discovery or through cross-examination that undermines the opinion of the defendants' expert. For pleading purposes, the language of the May 21 Memo suggests that its authors thought the information in the memo was material. The updated projections were not based on a business model in which the bulk of revenues came in during the last month, or even on the last day of the quarter, but rather rested on Primedia's success in pre-selling advertising. When Primedia disclosed its above-guidance results, its CEO described the performance as a "dramatic improvement in EBITDA[.]" That Primedia would beat Street guidance by nearly 9% seems material, particularly when markets respond disproportionately if a company misses or exceeds earnings guidance by a penny. At the pleadings stage, it is reasonably conceivable that the information in the May 21 Memo was material.

Third, the defendants argue that KKR could not have had the requisite *scienter* in light of expert analysis demonstrating that for every dollar KKR redistributed from the common to the preferred shareholders, KKR lost more than it gained. This argument is another way of pointing out that KKR owned nearly 60% of the common stock, thus if Primedia overpaid for the Preferred Stock, KKR was funding 60 cents of every dollar. But this argument misses the theory of the *Brophy* claim, which does not challenge the price at which Primedia carried out the redemptions. The certificates of designation obligated

Primedia to redeem the Preferred Stock and established the prices at which the redemptions would occur. KKR knew that when the time to redeem arrived, it would be funding its nearly 60% share of the redemptions regardless. The unknown variable was who would own the Preferred Stock and receive the payments, and the question was whether KKR could benefit from being in that position. Because of the information its director-representatives possessed, KKR knew that the market was dramatically undervaluing the Preferred Stock and that KKR could benefit from acquiring the shares before the market understood what KKR knew. Under the *Brophy* theory, KKR used inside information on the purchase, not the sale. The redemption analysis focuses on the wrong point in time for the plaintiffs' claim.

Finally, the defendants argue the *Brophy* claim has no merit because, as the SLC concluded, it was time-barred. I continue to believe that there are "litigable arguments going both ways on the statute of limitations" defense and that there is "a very real possibility that any claim gets stopped right at the outset because of [that] defense." If laches bars the *Brophy* claim, then there is no underlying litigation asset. To date, however, the parties have not briefed the laches defense directly. The defendants have focused on what the SLC believed, and the plaintiffs have argued that the SLC's belief is not controlling. This oblique approach does not provide me with adequate adversarial briefing on the laches issue. Rather than hazarding an opinion on this potentially dispositive defense, I will defer its consideration until a later stage. If the defendants wish, they can present this defense by moving for judgment on the pleadings or for summary judgment.

The *Brophy* claim would survive a motion to dismiss under Rule 12(b)(6). Primedia therefore had a viable corporate asset for purposes of establishing standing to assert a direct challenge to the Merger under *Parnes*.

b. Was The Value Of The *Brophy* Claim Material?

The second element of the *Parnes* inquiry asks whether the value of the derivative claim was material in the context of the merger. In light of the Delaware Supreme Court's re-vitalization of *Brophy* to include full disgorgement of profits, the potentially recoverable damages consist of profits on the redemptions of $150 million plus dividends of approximately $40 million. In addition, an award likely would include interest running on these amounts from the dates on which the shares of Preferred Stock were redeemed and the dividends paid. Given the amount of time that has passed, the interest award could be considerable. Even without interest, a potential recovery of this magnitude would be material in the context of the Merger, which provided Primedia's stockholders with total consideration of $316 million.

The amounts remain material if discounted to reflect the minority stockholders' beneficial interest in the litigation recovery. Primedia's minority stockholders owned 42% of its outstanding stock, so their *pro rata* share of the Merger consideration was $133 million. Their *pro rata* share of a $190 million recovery on the *Brophy* claim would be $80 million.

It is not difficult to calculate the amount of profits and dividends that KKR received, and that amount (plus interest) provides a straightforward measure of the upper bound for the value of the *Brophy* claim. And given its status as a private equity titan, KKR is likely good for the judgment. Clearly there is risk in the litigation, and to succeed, plaintiffs will have to prove materiality and *scienter*. If I assume prevailing on the *Brophy* claim was a toss-up, or even a 1-in-5 proposition, the risk-adjusted, pre-interest recoveries for the minority of $40 million and $16 million, respectively, remain material when compared to their $133 million share of the proceeds from the Merger.

c. Would The Acquirer Assert The Derivative Claim?

The third element of the *Parnes* inquiry asks whether the complaint challenging the merger contains adequate allegations to support pleadings-stage inferences that the acquirer would not assert the underlying derivative claim and did not provide value for it. Without such allegations and the resulting inferences, the merger consideration logically would incorporate value for the litigation, and the merger would not have harmed the sell-side stockholders.

For purposes of *Parnes*, the litigation assets of the acquired corporation can usefully be divided into two categories: (i) claims against third parties, such as contract claims, tort claims, and similar causes of action belonging to the corporation and (ii) claims for breach of duty against sell-side fiduciaries. There is no reason to think either that the acquirer would not determine disinterestedly whether to assert the corporations' claims against third parties or that the value of such claims would not be incorporated into the merger price. By contrast, there is ample reason to think that an acquirer would not assert, and therefore would not pay for, at least some claims for breach of fiduciary duty against sell-side fiduciaries. The acquirer may agree contractually not to sue the sell-side fiduciaries for breach of fiduciary duty.

Even if the acquirer is not prevented from suing, "[a]cquirers buy businesses, not claims." "Merger-related financial analyses focus on the business, not on fiduciary duty litigation." Consequently, "[w]hile the courts may indulge the notion that the [derivative] claims still 'survive' … they usually die as a matter of fact." There are also good reasons to believe that the stock markets do not accurately price derivative claims.

The Class Complaint alleges, and the defendants effectively concede, that the Merger Board did not attribute meaningful value to the *Brophy* claim. The only discussion about the *Brophy* claim came just before the Merger Board approved the Merger and involved all of the KKR representatives. During the discussion, a law firm with longstanding ties to KKR provided the only advice the Merger Board received about the claim. It does not seem likely that TPG or any other party anticipated bringing suit against KKR. They rather bid for Primedia's operating business, planning to treat the Derivative Action "as done" and then "move forward." It is therefore reasonably conceivable that none of the bids, including TPG's, attributed any value to the *Brophy* claim. Indeed, if KKR thought that TPG or any other acquirer actually could and would assert the *Brophy* claim, then KKR made an uncharacteristic financial blunder: Before the Merger, KKR faced potential liability on the *Brophy* claim but would benefit proportionately from its share of any recovery; after the Merger, KKR only would have the liability. Would KKR have sold before the Derivative Action was finally resolved if KKR thought the acquirer would sue?

TPG and Primedia are not exposed to third party claims relating to KKR's dealings in the Preferred Stock, and TPG therefore does not have an incentive to shift a portion of the liability to KKR.

Taking all of these factors together, it is reasonably conceivable that no potential acquirer, including TPG, incorporated the value of the *Brophy* claim into its bid for Primedia. It is reasonably conceivable that like the Merger Board, the bidders attributed no value to the *Brophy* claim and based their bids only on Primedia's operating business. Under the circumstances, it is reasonably conceivable that TPG received a "bargain basement price" for Primedia, representing its value without the *Brophy* claim, that TPG can benefit from owning Primedia "*without* bearing any material costs going forward as a result of [KKR's] prior wrongdoing," and that TPG is therefore "unlikely to pursue those claims."

The plaintiffs have satisfied each of the three elements that *Parnes* and its progeny indicate must be met before a stockholder can maintain a direct claim challenging a merger based on the alleged failure to value a pending derivative claim. It is therefore equitable to allow the selling stockholders to challenge the Merger based on the failure to value the *Brophy* claim.

2. Whether The Challenge To The Fairness Of The Merger States A Claim

The existence of standing to sue does not mean that the Class Complaint necessarily states a claim. The Class Complaint alleges that by approving the Merger at the price TPG offered, without taking any action to preserve the value of the *Brophy* claim, the Merger Board breached its fiduciary duties to Primedia's stockholders. "Any board negotiating the sale of a corporation should attempt to value and get full consideration for all of the corporation's material assets," including litigation assets. The degree to which a court will examine a board's success at this task depends on the standard of review.

When a corporation with a controlling stockholder is sold to a third party, the entire fairness standard applies if the controlling stockholder receives a benefit not shared with the minority. According to the Class Complaint, KKR received a special benefit in the form of a reduction in its exposure to the *Brophy* claim.

In the current case, at the motion to dismiss stage, it is reasonably conceivable that the Merger conferred a unique benefit on KKR. When KKR and the Merger Board elected to sell Primedia, they knew that the plaintiffs in the Derivative Action had pursued the claims tenaciously, including by obtaining the Dismissal Ruling, thoroughly litigating the SLC's dismissal motion, and then taking an appeal. There was no chance that the plaintiffs would simply abandon the field. The outlook would be radically different if KKR could sell Primedia to an entity that purchased the Company for its business operations alone and would be reluctant to antagonize a financial powerhouse like KKR. The prospects would be even better if Primedia ended up in the hands of a fellow private equity firm like TPG, whose principals have business ties to and personal relationships with the principals of KKR.

It is reasonably conceivable that because KKR could be confident that no acquirer would have any interest in pursuing the *Brophy* claim post-Merger, and because the individual defendants acceded to KKR's wishes without extracting any value for or taking steps to preserve the value of the *Brophy* claim, KKR received a unique benefit equal to the minority's share of any potential recovery in the Derivative Action. With numbers ascribed to its components, the benefit works like this. Before the Merger, Primedia owned both its operating business (worth $316 million) and the right to a potential recovery on the *Brophy* claim (worth $190 million). Primedia's minority stockholders owned 42% of its outstanding stock, so their *pro rata* interest in Primedia had an alleged value of $213 million, consisting of one asset worth $133 million (42% of the operating business) and a second asset worth $80 million (42% of the potential recovery on the *Brophy* claim). KKR and its affiliates owned 58% of Primedia's outstanding stock, so their *pro rata* interest had an alleged value of $103 million, consisting of an asset worth $183 million (58% of the operating business), a liability worth $190 million (100% of the judgment in their capacity as defendants), and a related asset worth $110 million (58% of the judgment in their capacity as stockholders in Primedia). In the Merger, the minority stockholders received $133 million, and KKR and its affiliates received $183 million. The Merger effectively diverted the value of the minority stockholders' equitable interest in the *Brophy* claim—$80 million—from the minority to KKR. All figures are exclusive of pre-judgment interest.

Because it is reasonably conceivable that KKR received a unique benefit in the Merger not shared with other stockholders, the standard of review for purposes of evaluating whether the complaint states a claim is entire fairness. The defendants did not implement any protective procedural devices that might alter the standard of review, such as a fully empowered committee, a majority-of-the-minority vote, or both. Entire fairness therefore applies, and I need not consider the plaintiffs' alternative argument that with two directors who were employees of KKR and six others with past ties to KKR, the Merger Board lacked a disinterested and independent majority.

Under the entire fairness standard, the defendants must establish "to the *court's* satisfaction that the transaction was the product of both fair dealing *and* fair price." It is reasonably conceivable that the defendants will not be able to establish that the Merger was both the product of fair dealing and provided a fair price. In a controlling stockholder transaction, the proper "test of fairness" is whether "the minority stockholder shall receive the substantial equivalent in value of what he had before." Before the Merger, Primedia's minority stockholders beneficially owned an asset with an alleged value of $213 million, consisting of $133 million for their share of Primedia's operating business and $80 million for their share of the *Brophy* claim. In the Merger, Primedia's minority stockholders received $133 million, $80 million less than the substantial equivalent of what they held before the Merger.

The defendants offer a number of arguments that amount to reasons why they believed subjectively that the *Brophy* claim had no value and that the Merger was fair. They say, for example, that they believed the Delaware Supreme Court would affirm this Court's dismissal of the *Brophy* claim, that they relied on the SLC's assessment of the merits of the claim, and that they relied on advice from counsel. But when entire fairness applies, "[n]ot even an honest belief that the transaction was entirely fair will be sufficient to establish entire fairness. Rather, the transaction itself must be objectively fair, independent of the board's beliefs." When a merger benefits a controlling stockholder by extinguishing a stockholder plaintiff's standing to pursue derivative claims, the defendants' subjective belief

> affords no ground upon which ... a reviewing court may dependably conclude that the termination of the derivative litigation ... was in the best interest of the corporation and was not simply in the interest of the directors and controlling shareholders who had been charged with wrongdoing. Without the guidance of a truly independent judgment, self-interested directors cannot with confidence know the right course in order to pursue it. In all events, the law, sensitive to the weakness of human nature and alert to the ever-present inclination to rationalize as right that which is merely beneficial, will accord scant weight to the subjective judgment of an interested director concerning the fairness of transactions that benefit him.

Merritt, 505 A.2d at 765

The subjective beliefs of the individual directors and the information on which they relied likely will have significant implications at a later phase of the case. "The entire fairness test is, at its core, an inquiry designed to assess whether a self-dealing transaction should be respected or set aside in equity. It has only a crude and potentially misleading relationship to the liability any particular fiduciary has for involvement in a self-dealing transaction." When a transaction involves self-dealing by one fiduciary but not by others who nevertheless approved the transaction, only the self-dealing fiduciary is "subject to damages liability for the gap between a fair price and the deal price without an inquiry into his subjective state of mind." Self-dealing fiduciaries are liable because they breached their duty of loyalty if the transaction was unfair, regardless of whether they acted in subjective good faith. But as to the other fiduciaries, even ones who might be deemed non-independent because of their status or relationships with the self-dealing fiduciaries, "the presence of the exculpatory charter provision would require an examination of their state of mind, in order to determine whether they breached their duty of loyalty by approving the transaction in bad faith . . . , rather than in a good faith effort to benefit the corporation." If those directors subjectively intended to act loyalty, then "their failure to procure a fair result does not expose them to liability."

If the plaintiffs succeed in proving that the Merger was unfair, only KKR would be liable for self-dealing on that basis alone. The Court would need to conduct a director-by-director analysis of the members of the Merger Board to determine whether they acted with a culpable state of mind. The directors' subjective beliefs about the fairness of the Merger and the viability of the *Brophy* claim would be pertinent to that inquiry. The directors' reliance on counsel's advice and the SLC's determinations also would be relevant to their ability to invoke the protection from liability afforded by Section 141(e) of the Delaware General Corporation Law, which states:

> A member of the board of directors ... shall ... be fully protected in relying in good faith ... upon such information, opinions, reports or statements presented to the corporation by any of the corporation's officers or employees, or committees of the board of directors, or by any other person as to matters the member reasonably believes are within such other person's professional or expert competence and who has been selected with reasonable care by or on behalf of the corporation.

The plaintiffs have therefore stated a claim that the Merger was not entirely fair.

3. Section 102(b)(7)

The individual defendants seek dismissal in light of Section 102(b)(7) of the Delaware General Corporation Law and the exculpatory provision in Primedia's charter. Although those director defendants who are independent and disinterested may ultimately be able to rely upon the charter provision, it is premature to dismiss the claims against them on this basis. When the entire fairness standard of review applies, "the inherently interested nature of those transactions" renders the claims "inextricably intertwined with issues of loyalty." *Emerald P'rs v. Berlin*, 787 A.2d 85, 93 (Del.2001). The Class Complaint contains relatively insubstantial allegations of bad faith against the Outside Directors, but given the standard of review, I cannot dismiss them.

III. CONCLUSION

The motion to dismiss is denied as to the claim for breach of fiduciary duty against KKR and the members of the Merger Board on the grounds that the Merger was not entirely fair in light of the *Brophy* claim. In all other respects, the motion is granted.

Notes

(1) Why would Primedia exchange common shares for preferred shares?

(2) Does a SLC have a duty to consider issues that are not before the SLC in deciding whether to dismiss a derivative suit or is the SLC only required to consider the issues implicated by the plaintiff's complaint? This is interesting considering that this process occurs BEFORE the plaintiff has an opportunity to conduct discovery.

(3) Why do you think that the merger board failed to consider the value of the derivative *Brophy* claim in determining the true value of the corporation? One thing to remember is that the value of a corporation is determined by evaluating the assets of a business. Litigation that a company may pursue against another entity has value and therefore is an asset for purposes of valuing a business.

(4) Why would the right to assert the *Brophy* claim pass to TPG?

(5) For those of you that have taken securities law or that have discussed 10(b)(5), you may know that federal courts have exclusive jurisdiction over insider trading claims pursuant to 10(b)(5). Therefore, claims alleging a violation of 10(b)(5) may only be brought in federal court. Because of this reason, some plaintiffs in Delaware prefer to bring suit under *Brophy* in Delaware state court for two reasons.

First, if federal law applies, the more strenuous pleading standard of Twombly/Iqbal applies under which the plaintiff has to prove plausibility whereas Delaware only requires conceivability. In 2011, the Delaware Supreme Court in *Central Mortgage Company v. Morgan Stanley Mortgage Capital Holdings LLC*, 27 A.3d 531, 535 (Del. 2011) addressed this very issue.

> The pleading standards governing the motion to dismiss stage of a proceeding in Delaware, however, are minimal. When considering a defendant's motion to dismiss, a trial court should accept all well-pleaded factual allegations in the Complaint as true, accept even vague allegations in the Complaint as "well-pleaded" if they provide the defendant notice of the claim, draw all reasonable inferences in favor of the plaintiff, and deny the motion unless the plaintiff could not recover under any reasonably conceivable set of circumstances susceptible of proof. Indeed, it may, as a factual matter, ultimately prove impossible for the plaintiff to prove his claims at a later stage of a proceeding, but that is not the test to survive a motion to dismiss.

> The *Twombly-Iqbal* "plausibility" pleading standard is higher than our governing "conceivability" standard, and it invites judges to "determin[e] whether a complaint states a plausible claim for relief" and "draw on … judicial experience and common sense."

> Since the Supreme Court decided *Twombly* in 2007, various members of the Court of Chancery have cited the *Twombly-Iqbal* "plausibility" standard with approval when adjudicating motions to dismiss. We have not had occasion yet to address the impact, if any, that the United States Supreme Court's holdings in *Twombly* and *Iqbal* should have on the Delaware standard. Indeed, the Vice Chancellor explicitly cited the "plausibility" standard in this very case. We decline to use this case as the vehicle to address whether the *Twombly-Iqbal* holdings affect our governing standard, considering that the parties have not fully and fairly litigated the issue before either the Vice Chancellor or this Court. Instead, we emphasize that, until this Court decides otherwise or a change is duly effected through the Civil Rules process, the governing pleading standard in Delaware to survive a motion to dismiss is reasonable "conceivability."

Second, *Brophy* may allow greater damages than 10(b)(5). In interpreting rule 10(b)(5), courts have limited a plaintiff's recovery to the plaintiffs actual damages. However, under *Brophy* a plaintiff's damages are calculated by full disgorgement. Full disgorgement is measured by the complete benefit that the defendant has retained. For example, assume that a director purchased a share of stock from a plaintiff for $10. At the time of the transaction, the director had inside, material nonpublic information that the stock was undervalued by $30 because the true value of the stock, once the information is made public, will increase to $40. If the director later sells the share to a third party buyer, one year later, for $60, the plaintiff's damages pursuant to rule 10(b) would be $30 based on the market value at the time of the transaction. The $30 represents the actual damage to the shareholder. However under *Brophy*, the plaintiff could recover $50 because that amount represents FULL disgorgement.

B. Limiting Profit Maximization

After carefully examining *Zapata* and the two-prong analysis required by its test, we are now in a position to see that the business judgment of corporate executives is not *always* respected and that a savvy plaintiff's lawyer can bring an action that would allow a judge to substitute her business judgment in the place of bad acting corporate leaders. Is this a valuable tool that can be used by attorneys to challenge the sometimes self-interested decisionmaking by corporate executives? As *Zapata*, *In re Oracle*, and *In re Primedia* teach us, the appointment of SLCs and the investigations they undertake are time-consuming and extraordinarily expensive. Still, the business judgment rule is *not* unassailable. Lawyers can attempt to hold corporate executives responsible for self-serving conduct.

As we continue to examine our toolbox in connection with pursuing corporate justice, we turn to the time-honored concept of profit maximization. As we learned in our study of *Dodge v. Ford*, maximizing profits for shareholders is often cited as the ultimate goal of corporate executives and board members. The business judgment rule did not save Henry Ford when he was sued by the Dodge brothers because Ford stubbornly refused to tie his philanthropic efforts during trial to the long-term health and wealth building of his automobile company. But, is profit maximization the primary goal and objective of a corporation and its leaders? Do members of a board of directors have a duty, a legal duty, to put profit of shareholders first and foremost in their corporate planning? Is profit maximization a sacrosanct, foundational principle of corporate law? Below, please read Professor Lynn Stout's challenge to this principal.

Why We Should Stop Teaching *Dodge v. Ford*

Lynn A. Stout

3 VA. L. & BUS. REV. 163 (2008)

Introduction

What is the purpose of a corporation? To many people, the answer to this question seems obvious: corporations exist to make money for their shareholders. Maximizing shareholder wealth is the corporation's only true concern, its raison d'être. Devoted corporate officers and directors should direct all their efforts toward this goal.

Some find this picture of the corporation as an engine for increasing shareholder wealth to be quite attractive. Nobel Prize-winning economist Milton Friedman famously praised this view of corporate purpose in his 1970 *New York Times* essay, "The Social Responsibility of Business Is to Increase Its Profits." To others, the idea of the corporation as a relentless profit-seeking machine seems less appealing. In 2004, Joel Bakan published The Corporation: The Pathological Pursuit of Profit and Power, a book accompanied by an award-winning documentary film of the same name. Bakan's thesis is that corporations are indeed dedicated to maximizing shareholder wealth, without regard to law, ethics, or the interests of society. Thus, as Bakan argues, corporations are "dangerously psychopathic" entities.

Whether viewed as cause for celebration or for concern, the idea that corporations exist only to make money for shareholders is rarely subject to challenge. Much of the credit, or perhaps more accurately the blame, for this state of affairs can be laid at the door of a single judicial opinion: the 1919 Michigan Supreme Court decision in *Dodge v. Ford Motor Company*.

I. *Dodge v. Ford* on Corporate Purpose

The facts underlying *Dodge v. Ford* are familiar to virtually every student who has taken a course in corporate law. Famed industrialist Henry Ford was the founder and majority shareholder of the Ford Motor Company. Brothers John and Horace Dodge were minority investors in the firm. The Dodge brothers brought a lawsuit against Ford claiming that he was using his control over the company to restrict dividend payouts, even though the company was enormously profitable and could afford to pay large dividends to its shareholders. Ford defended his decision to withhold dividends through the provocative strategy of arguing that he preferred to use the corporation's money to build cheaper, better cars and to pay better wages. The Michigan Supreme Court sided with the Dodge brothers and ordered the Ford Motor Company to pay its shareholders a special dividend.

In the process, the Michigan Supreme Court made an offhand remark that is regularly repeated in corporate law casebooks today:

> There should be no confusion.... A business corporation is organized and carried on primarily for the profit of the stockholders. The powers of the directors are to be employed for that end. The discretion of the directors is to be exercised in the choice of means to attain that end, and does not extend to ... other purposes.

As will be discussed in greater detail below, this was merely judicial dicta, quite unnecessary to reach the court's desired result. Nevertheless, this quotation from *Dodge v. Ford* is cited almost invariably as evidence that corporate law requires corporations to have a "profit maximizing purpose" and that "managers and directors have a legal duty to put shareholders' interests above all others and no legal authority to serve any other interests...." Indeed, *Dodge v. Ford* is routinely employed as the only legal authority for this proposition.

But what if the opinion in *Dodge v. Ford* is incorrect? What if the Michigan Supreme Court's statement of corporate purpose is a misinterpretation of American corporate doctrine? Put bluntly, what if *Dodge v. Ford* is bad law?

This Essay argues that *Dodge v. Ford* is indeed bad law, at least when cited for the proposition that the corporate purpose is, or should be, maximizing shareholder wealth. *Dodge v. Ford* is a mistake, a judicial "sport," a doctrinal oddity largely irrelevant to corporate law and corporate practice. What is more, courts and legislatures alike treat it as irrelevant. In the past thirty years, the Delaware courts have cited *Dodge v. Ford* as authority in only one unpublished case, and then not on the subject of corporate purpose, but on another legal question entirely.

Only laypersons and (more disturbingly) many law professors continue to rely on *Dodge v. Ford*. This Essay argues we should mend our collective ways. Legal instructors and scholars should stop teaching and citing *Dodge v. Ford*. At the least, they should stop teaching and citing *Dodge v. Ford* as anything more than an example of how courts can go seriously astray.

II. *Dodge v. Ford* as Weak Precedent on Corporate Purpose

Let us begin with some of the more obvious reasons why legal experts should hesitate before placing much weight on *Dodge v. Ford*. First, the case is approaching its one hundredth anniversary. Henry Ford, John Dodge, and Horace Dodge have long since died and turned to dust, along with the members of the Michigan Supreme Court who heard their dispute. In fact, *Dodge v. Ford* is the oldest corporate law case selected as an object for study in most corporate law casebooks.

A second odd feature of *Dodge v. Ford* is the court that decided it. The state of Delaware—not Michigan—is far and away the most respected and influential source of corporate case law, a fact that reflects both Delaware's status as the preferred state of incorporation for the nation's largest public companies and the widely recognized expertise of the judges on the Delaware Supreme Court and Delaware Court of Chancery. California and New York have produced their share of influential corporate law cases, as has Massachusetts with regard to close corporations. Michigan, however, is a distant also-ran in the race among the states for influence in corporate law.

Finally, a third limiting aspect of *Dodge v. Ford* as a source of legal authority on the question of corporate purpose is the important fact that the Michigan Supreme Court's statements on the topic were dicta. The actual holding in the case—that Henry Ford had breached his fiduciary duty to the Dodge brothers and that the company should pay a special dividend—was justified on entirely different and far narrower legal grounds. Those grounds were that Henry Ford, as a controlling shareholder, had breached his fiduciary duty of good faith to his minority investors.

As the majority shareholder in the Ford Motor Company, Henry Ford stood to reap a much greater economic benefit from any dividends the company paid than John and Horace Dodge did. Ford had other economic interests, however, directly at odds with those of the Dodge brothers. First, because the Dodge brothers wished to set up their own car company to compete with Ford (as they eventually did), Ford wanted to deprive them of liquid funds for investment. Second, Ford wanted to buy out the Dodge brothers' interest in the Ford Motor Company (as he eventually did) at the lowest price possible. Withholding dividends from the Dodge brothers was an excellent, if underhanded, strategy for accomplishing both objectives.

Thus *Dodge v. Ford* is best viewed as a case that deals not with directors' duties to maximize shareholder wealth, but with controlling shareholders' duties not to oppress minority shareholders.

Finally, not only is the Michigan Supreme Court's statement on corporate purpose in *Dodge v. Ford* dicta, but it is much more mealy-mouthed dicta than is generally appreciated. As Professor Einer Elhauge has emphasized, the Michigan Supreme Court described profit-seeking in *Dodge v. Ford* as the "primary," but not the exclusive, corporate goal. Indeed, elsewhere in the opinion the court noted that corporate directors retain "implied powers to carry on with humanitarian motives such charitable works as are incidental to the main business of the corporation."

III. The Lack Of Authority for *Dodge v. Ford*'s Positive Vision of Corporate Purpose

Dodge v. Ford suffers from several deficiencies as a source of legal precedent on the question of corporate purpose. The case is old, it hails from a state court that plays only a marginal role in the corporate law arena, and it involves a conflict between controlling and minority shareholders that independently justifies the holding in the case while rendering the opinion's discourse on corporate purpose judicial dicta. Nevertheless, one might still defend the continued teaching and citing of *Dodge v. Ford* if the discussion of corporate purpose found in the case were an elegant, early statement of a modern legal principle.

Here we run into a second problem: shareholder wealth maximization is not a modern legal principle. To understand this point, it is important to look at the actual provisions of corporate law. "Corporate law" can itself be broken down into three rough categories: (1) "internal" corporate law (that is, the requirements set out in individual corporations' charters and bylaws); (2) state corporate codes; and (3) corporate case law.

Let us first examine internal corporate law, especially the statements of corporate purpose typically found in corporate charters (also called "articles of incorporation"). Most state codes permit, or even require, incorporators to include a statement in the corporate charter that defines and limits the purpose for which the corporation is being formed. If the corporation's founders so desire, they can easily include in the corporate charter a recitation of the *Dodge v. Ford* view that the corporation in question "is organized and carried on primarily for the profit of the stockholders." In reality, corporate charters virtually never contain this sort of language. Instead, the typical corporate charter defines the corporate purpose as anything "lawful."

What about state corporation codes? Do they perhaps limit the corporate purpose to shareholder wealth maximization? To employ the common saying, the answer is "not just 'no,' but 'hell no.'" A large majority of state codes contain so-called other-constituency provisions that explicitly authorize corporate boards to consider the interests of not just shareholders, but also employees, customers, creditors, and the community, in making business decisions. The Delaware corporate code does not have an explicit other-constituency provision, but it also does not define the corporate purpose as shareholder wealth maximization. Rather, section 101 of the General Corporation Law of Delaware simply provides that corporations can be formed "to conduct or promote any lawful business or purposes."

This leaves case law as the last remaining hope of a *Dodge v. Ford* supporter who wants to argue that, as a positive matter, modern legal authority requires corporate directors to maximize shareholder wealth. On first inspection, corporate case law does provide at least a little hope. Contemporary judges do not cite *Dodge v. Ford*, but some modern cases contain dicta that echo its sentiments. Consider, for example, the Delaware Chancery's statement in the 1986 case of *Katz v. Oak Industries* that "[i]t is the obligation of directors to attempt, within the law, to maximize the long-run interests of the corporation's stockholders...."

This statement is about as *Dodge v. Ford*-like a description of corporate purpose as one can hope to find in contemporary case law. Many other modern cases, however, contain contrary dicta indicating that directors owe duties beyond those owed to shareholders. For example, in *Unocal Corporation v. Mesa Petroleum Company*, the court opined that the corporate board had a "fundamental duty and obligation to protect the corporate enterprise, which includes stockholders," a formulation that clearly implies the two are not identical. The court went on to state that in evaluating the interests of "the corporate enterprise," directors could consider "the impact on 'constituencies' other than shareholders (that is, creditors, customers, employees, and perhaps even the community generally)."

Just as important, even shareholder-oriented dicta on corporate purpose of the *Katz* sort does not actually impose any legal obligation on directors to maximize shareholder wealth. The key to understanding this is the qualifying phrases "attempt" and "long-run."

As a number of corporate scholars have pointed out, courts regularly allow corporate directors to make business decisions that harm shareholders in order to benefit other corporate constituencies. In the rare event that such a decision is challenged on the grounds that the directors failed to look after shareholder interests, courts shield directors from liability under the business judgment rule so long as any plausible connection can be made between the directors' decision and some possible future benefit, however intangible and unlikely, to shareholders. If the directors lack the imagination to offer such a "long-run" rationalization for their decision, courts will invent one.

A classic example of this judicial eagerness to protect directors from claims that they failed to maximize shareholder wealth can be found in the oft-cited case of *Shlensky v. Wrigley*. In *Shlensky*, minority investors sued the directors of the corporation that owned the Chicago Cubs for refusing to install lights that would allow night baseball games to be played at Wrigley Field. The minority investors claimed that offering night games would make the Cubs more profitable. The corporation's directors refused to hold night games, not because they disagreed with this economic assessment, but because they believed night games would harm the quality of life of residents in the neighborhoods surrounding Wrigley Field. The court upheld the directors' decision, reasoning, as the directors themselves had not, that a decline in the quality of life in the local neighborhoods might in the long run hurt property values around Wrigley Field, harming shareholders' economic interests.

Shlensky illustrates how judges routinely refuse to impose any legal obligation on corporate directors to maximize shareholder wealth. Although dicta in some cases suggest directors ought to attempt this (in the "long run," of course), dicta in other cases take a broader view of corporate purpose, and courts never actually sanction directors for failing to maximize shareholder wealth.

There is only one exception to this rule in case law: the Delaware Supreme Court's 1986 opinion in *Revlon, Inc. v. MacAndrews & Forbes Holdings, Inc. Revlon* is a puzzling decision, not least because the Delaware Supreme Court decided the case the same year it handed down its apparently contradictory decision in *Unocal*. In *Revlon*, the board of a public company had decided to take the firm private by selling all of its shares to a controlling shareholder. In choosing between potential bidders, the board considered, along with shareholders' interests, the interests of certain noteholders in the firm. This was a mistake, the Delaware Supreme Court announced; where the company was being "broken up" and shareholders were being forced to sell their interests in the firm to a private buyer, the board had a duty to maximize shareholder wealth by getting the highest possible price for the shares.

Upon first inspection, *Revlon* appears to affirm the notion that maximizing shareholder wealth is the corporation's proper purpose. In the years following the *Revlon* decision, however, the Delaware Supreme Court has systematically cut back on the situations in which *Revlon* supposedly applies, to the point where any board that wants to avoid being subject to *Revlon* duties now can easily do so. The case has become nearly a dead letter. Accordingly, while the Delaware Supreme Court has not explicitly repudiated *Revlon* (at least not yet), for practical purposes the case is largely irrelevant to modern corporate law and practice.

In sum, whether gauged by corporate charters, state corporation codes, or corporate case law, the notion that corporate law as a positive matter "requires" companies to maximize shareholder wealth turns out to be spurious. The offhand remarks on corporate purpose offered by the Michigan Supreme Court in *Dodge v. Ford* lack any foundation in actual corporate law.

IV. The Lack Of Authority for *Dodge v. Ford*'s Normative Vision of Corporate Purpose

Dodge v. Ford usually plays the role of Exhibit A for commentators seeking to argue that American law imposes on corporate directors the legal obligation to maximize profits for shareholders. It is important to recognize, however, that many experts teach and cite *Dodge v. Ford* in a more subtle, and less obviously erroneous, fashion. To these experts, *Dodge v. Ford* is not evidence that corporate law actually requires directors to maximize shareholder wealth. Rather, many observers believe it is evidence that corporate directors ought to maximize shareholder wealth. In other words, many legal instructors teach *Dodge v. Ford* not as a positive description of what corporate law actually is, but as a normative discourse on what many believe the proper purpose of a well-functioning corporation should be.

This is a far more defensible position. Nevertheless, the switch from using *Dodge v. Ford* as a source of positive legal authority to using *Dodge v. Ford* as a source of normative guidance carries its own hazards. Most obviously, it begs the fundamental question of what the proper purpose of the corporation should be.

It is not enough to state that *Dodge v. Ford* represents an important perspective on corporate purpose simply because many people believe it represents an important perspective on corporate purpose. This argument borders on tautology (that is, "*Dodge v. Ford* is influential because people think *Dodge v. Ford* is influential"). Perhaps many people do share the Michigan Supreme Court's view that it is desirable for corporations to pursue only profits for shareholders. But why do they believe this is desirable?

At least until fairly recently, many corporate experts found the answer to this question in economic theory. Not too long ago, it was conventional economic wisdom that the shareholders in a corporation are the sole residual claimants in the firm, meaning shareholders are entitled to all the "residual" profits left over after the firm has met its fixed contractual obligations to employees, customers, and creditors. This assumption suggests that corporations are run best when they are run for shareholders' benefit alone, because if other corporate stakeholders' interests are fixed by their contracts, maximizing the shareholders' residual claim means maximizing the total social value of the firm.

Time has been unkind to this perspective. Advances in economic theory have made clear that shareholders generally are not, and probably cannot be, the sole residual claimants in firms. For example, modern options theory teaches that business risk that increases the expected value of the equity interest in a corporation must simultaneously reduce the supposedly "fixed" value of creditor interests. Another branch of the economic literature focuses on the contracting problems that surround specific investment in "team production," suggesting how a legal rule requiring corporate directors to maximize shareholder wealth ex post might well have the perverse effect of reducing shareholder wealth over time by discouraging non-shareholder groups from making specific investments in corporations ex ante. Yet a third economic concept that undermines the wisdom of shareholder wealth maximization is the idea of externalities: when the pursuit of shareholder profits imposes greater costs on third parties (for instance, customers, employees, or the environment) that are not fully constrained by law, shareholder wealth maximization becomes undesirable, at least from a social perspective.

Finally, it is becoming increasingly well-understood that when a firm has more than one shareholder, the very idea of "shareholder wealth" becomes incoherent. Different shareholders have different investment time frames, different tax concerns, different attitudes toward firm-level risk due to different levels of diversification, different interests in other investments that might be affected by corporate activities, and different views about the extent to which they are willing to sacrifice corporate profits to promote broader social interests, such as a clean environment or good wages for workers. These and other schisms ensure that there is no single, uniform measure of shareholder "wealth" to be "maximized."

Accordingly, most contemporary experts understand that economic theory alone does not permit us to safely assume that corporations are run best when they are run according to the principle of shareholder wealth maximization. Not only is *Dodge v. Ford* bad law from a positive perspective, but it is also bad law from a normative perspective. This gives rise to the question of how to explain *Dodge v. Ford*'s enduring popularity.

V. On the Puzzling Survival of *Dodge v. Ford*

Simple inertia may provide an answer, to some extent. Corporate law casebooks have included excerpts from *Dodge v. Ford* for generations, and it would take a certain degree of boldness to depart from the tradition. But there is more going on here than inertia. Casebooks change, but *Dodge v. Ford* remains. This suggests *Dodge v. Ford* has achieved a privileged position in the legal canon, not because it accurately captures the law (as we have seen, it does not) or because it provides good normative guidance (again, we have seen it does not), but because it serves law professors' needs.

In particular, *Dodge v. Ford* serves professors' pressing need for a simple answer to the question of what corporations do. Law professors' desire for a simple answer to this question can be analogized to that of a parent confronted by a young son or daughter who innocently asks, "Where do babies come from?" The true answer is difficult and complex and can lead to further questions about details of the process that may lie beyond the parent's knowledge or comfort level. It is easy to understand why many parents faced with this situation squirm uncomfortably and default to charming fables of cabbages and storks. Similarly, professors are regularly confronted by eager law students who innocently ask, "What do corporations do?" It is easy to understand why professors are tempted to default to *Dodge v. Ford* and its charming and easily understood fable of shareholder wealth maximization.

After all, explaining the true purpose of corporations is even more challenging and uncertain than explaining reproduction. From a positive perspective, public corporations are extraordinarily intricate institutions that pursue complex, large-scale projects over periods of years or even decades. They have several directors, dozens of executives, hundreds or thousands of employees, thousands or hundreds of thousands of shareholders, and possibly millions of customers. Corporations resemble political nation-states with multiple constituencies that have different and conflicting interests, responsibilities, obligations, and powers. Indeed, the very largest corporations (such as Wal-Mart, ExxonMobil, or Microsoft) have greater economic power than many nation-states do. These are not institutions whose behavior can be accurately captured in a sound bite.

The problem of explaining proper corporate purpose is just as off-putting from a normative perspective. Even the seemingly simple directive to "maximize shareholder wealth" becomes far less simple and perhaps incoherent in a public firm with many shareholders with different investment time frames, tax concerns, outside investments, levels of diversification, and attitudes toward corporate social responsibility. The normative question of what corporations ought to do becomes even more daunting when the answer involves discussions of avoiding externalities, maximizing the value of returns to multiple residual claimants, and encouraging specific investment in team production.

Faced with this reality, it is entirely understandable why a legal instructor or legal scholar called upon to discuss the question of corporate purpose might be tempted to teach or cite *Dodge v. Ford* in reply. Despite its infirmities, *Dodge v. Ford* at least offers an answer to the question of corporate purpose that is simple, easy to understand, and capable of being communicated in less than ten minutes or ten pages. It is this simplicity that has allowed *Dodge v. Ford* to survive over the decades and to keep a place—however undeserved—in the canon of corporate law.

Conclusion

Simplicity is not always a virtue. In particular, simplicity is not a virtue when it leads to misunderstanding and mistake.

Corporations are purely legal creatures, without flesh, blood, or bone. Their existence and behavior is determined by a web of legal rules found in corporate charters and bylaws, state corporate case law and statutes, private contracts, and a host of federal and state regulations. For lawyers, an accurate and detailed understanding of the corporate entity and its purpose is essential to success.

This is why lawyers, and especially law professors, should resist the siren song of *Dodge v. Ford*. We are not in the business of imparting fables, however charming. We are in the business of instructing clients and students in the realities of the corporate form. Corporations seek profits for shareholders, but they seek others things, as well, including specific investment, stakeholder benefits, and their own continued existence. Teaching *Dodge v. Ford* as anything but an example of judicial mistake obstructs understanding of this reality.

Notes

(1) Although Stout opines that *Dodge v. Ford* is no longer good law, is it possible that professors continue to teach this case because of the idea that boards that make decisions to maximize profit are more likely to receive protection of the business judgment rule since a decision based on maximizing profit will be hard for a plaintiff to attack?

(2) In recognition of the idea that a corporation may operate for purposes other than profit maximization, many states have now enacted "shareholder non constituency statutes." These statutes expressly authorize corporate directors to consider the interests of stakeholders other than the corporation's own shareholders. The aim is to allow corporations in a modern society to operate more responsibly. In promulgating these statutes, state legislatures have sought to alter the traditional notion of shareholder primacy—that the directors' single responsibility is to maximize shareholder wealth. As of 2011, shareholder non constituency statutes have been enacted in the following states: "Arizona, Connecticut, Florida, Georgia, Hawaii, Idaho, Illinois, Indiana, Iowa, Kentucky, Louisiana, Maine, Maryland, Massachusetts, Minnesota, Missouri, Nebraska, Nevada, New Jersey, New Mexico, New York, North Dakota, Ohio, Oregon, Pennsylvania, Rhode Island, South Dakota, Tennessee, Vermont, Virginia, Wisconsin, and Wyoming."[1]

---

1. Anthony Bisconti, Note, *The Double Bottom Line: Can Constituency Statutes Protect Socially Responsible Corporations Stuck in Revlon Land?*, 42 Loyola L.A. L. Rev 765, 768 (2009).

Although the specific language of the statutes varies from state to state, the unifying principle common to all constituency statutes is that they enable corporate directors to consider interests other than those of their shareholders when exercising their corporate decision-making authority. Some common provisions include the following:

1. The board of directors of a corporation may consider the interests and effects of any action upon non-shareholders.

2. The relevant non-shareholder groups include employees, suppliers, customers, creditors, and communities.

3. The directors may consider both long-term and short-term interests of the corporation.

4. The directors may consider local and national economies.

5. The directors may consider any other relevant social factors.[2]

While these statutes attempt to empower directors with the authority to act more socially responsible, the common theme in each of the state statutes is that the statutory language is permissive rather than mandatory. Therefore, a board may consider these interests but is not required to do so. In addition, unless state law provides otherwise, pursuant to some specific subset of the duty of care or loyalty, constituents, other than a corporation's own shareholders, are unlikely to have standing to challenge the decision of the board for failure to consider non-constituent interests. Moreover, even if a non-constituent could establish standing, it is highly likely that the board's decision would nonetheless be protected by the business judgment rule.

(3) Does Stout overstate her case in claiming that *Dodge v. Ford* and its profit maximization principle is dead? At the most basic motivational place, what drives the actions of corporate executives?

(4) When engaged at a board meeting planning for the future of a corporation, what is the primary focus of a member of a corporate board? Is it realistic to imagine that corporate board members are contemplating "relevant social factors," or "the interests and effects" of their actions "upon non-shareholders" when planning for the future and determining the budget of the corporation for which they work? Doesn't maximizing shareholder profits as a primary goal ensure longevity for corporate leaders?

C. Shareholder Proposals

While shareholders of a corporation are ostensibly imbued with the power to seat the board of directors by vote, shareholders are often not given power over *who* is placed on the slate for board election. Thus, the ownership power of shareholders is limited and has been neutralized steadily by legislation and the courts for the past twenty years. One power that remains in the hands of an owner/shareholder is the shareholder proposal. If certain prerequisites are met, a nominal shareholder of a corporation can propose that a corporation take specific action and place that proposal in front of all shareholders for a vote. This action is regulated by the Securities and Exchange Act of 1934, and essentially

2. *Id.* at 781–82.

allows a shareholder that owns $2,000 of share value who has held that position for more than one year, to submit a proposal to the board for inclusion in the annual proxy statement for vote so long as the proposal does not implicate certain actions uniquely within the power of the board of directors. To that end, shareholders have the power to bring to light certain corporate actions that are disfavored by the shareholder and positioned for a vote by all of the companies owners/shareholders.

The following examples extrapolated in the *Lovenheim* case and the C. Delores Tucker narrative demonstrate the power of the shareholder proposal as a tool for shareholder activism.

Peter C. Lovenheim v. Iroquois Brands, Ltd.,

618 F.Supp. 554 (1985)
United States District Court, District of Columbia

GASCH, District Judge.

I. BACKGROUND

This matter is now before the Court on plaintiff's motion for preliminary injunction.

Plaintiff Peter C. Lovenheim, owner of two hundred shares of common stock in Iroquois Brands, Ltd. (hereinafter "Iroquois/Delaware"), seeks to bar Iroquois/Delaware from excluding from the proxy materials being sent to all shareholders in preparation for an upcoming shareholder meeting information concerning a proposed resolution he intends to offer at the meeting. Mr. Lovenheim's proposed resolution relates to the procedure used to force-feed geese for production of paté de foie gras in France,* a type of paté imported by Iroquois/Delaware. Specifically, his resolution calls upon the Directors of Iroquois/Delaware to:

> form a committee to study the methods by which its French supplier produces paté de foie gras, and report to the shareholders its findings and opinions, based on expert consultation, on whether this production method causes undue distress, pain or suffering to the animals involved and, if so, whether further distribution of this product should be discontinued until a more humane production method is developed.

Mr. Lovenheim's right to compel Iroquois/Delaware to insert information concerning his proposal in the proxy materials turns on the applicability of section 14(a) of the Securities Exchange Act of 1934, 15 U.S.C. § 78n(a) ("the Exchange Act"), and the shareholder proposal rule promulgated by the Securities and Exchange Commission ("SEC"), Rule 14a–8. That rule states in pertinent part:

> If any security holder of an issuer notifies the issuer of his intention to present a proposal for action at a forthcoming meeting of the issuer's security holders,

---

* Paté de foie gras is made from the liver of geese. According to Mr. Lovenheim's affidavit, force-feeding is frequently used in order to expand the liver and thereby produce a larger quantity of paté. Mr. Lovenheim's affidavit also contains a description of the force-feeding process: Force-feeding usually begins when the geese are four months old. On some farms where feeding is mechanized, the bird's body and wings are placed in a metal brace and its neck is stretched. Through a funnel inserted 10–12 inches down the throat of the goose, a machine pumps up to 400 grams of corn-based mash into its stomach. An elastic band around the goose's throat prevents regurgitation. When feeding is manual, a handler uses a funnel and stick to force the mash down. Plaintiff contends that such force-feeding is a form of cruelty to animals.

the issuer shall set forth the proposal in its proxy statement and identify it in its form of proxy and provide means by which security holders presenting a proposal may present in the proxy statement a statement of not more than 200 words in support of the proposal.

Iroquois/Delaware has refused to allow information concerning Mr. Lovenheim's proposal to be included in proxy materials being sent in connection with the next annual shareholders meeting. In doing so, Iroquois/Delaware relies on an exception to the general requirement of Rule 14a–8, Rule 14a–8(c)(5). That exception provides that an issuer of securities "may omit a proposal and any statement in support thereof" from its proxy statement and form of proxy:

> if the proposal relates to operations which account for less than 5 percent of the issuer's total assets at the end of its most recent fiscal year, and for less than 5 percent of its net earnings and gross sales for its most recent fiscal year, and is not otherwise significantly related to the issuer's business.

II. LIKELIHOOD OF PLAINTIFF PREVAILING ON MERITS

* * *

Applicability of Rule 14a–8(c)(5) Exception

The likelihood of plaintiff's prevailing in this litigation turns primarily on the applicability to plaintiff's proposal of the exception to the shareholder proposal rule contained in Rule 14a–8(c)(5).

Iroquois/Delaware's reliance on the argument that this exception applies is based on the following information contained in the affidavit of its president: Iroquois/Delaware has annual revenues of $141 million with $6 million in annual profits and $78 million in assets. In contrast, its paté de foie gras sales were just $79,000 last year, representing a net loss on paté sales of $3,121. Iroquois/Delaware has only $34,000 in assets related to paté. Thus none of the company's net earnings and less than .05 percent of its assets are implicated by plaintiff's proposal. These levels are obviously far below the five percent threshold set forth in the first portion of the exception claimed by Iroquois/Delaware.

Plaintiff Nevertheless contends that the Rule 14a–8(c)(5) exception is not applicable as it cannot be said that his proposal "is not otherwise significantly related to the issuer's business" as is required by the final portion of that exception. In other words, plaintiff's argument that Rule 14a–8 does not permit omission of his proposal rests on the assertion that the rule and statute on which it is based do not permit omission merely because a proposal is not economically significant where a proposal has "ethical or social significance."**

Iroquois/Delaware views the exception solely in economic terms as permitting omission of any proposals relating to a de minimis share of assets and profits. Iroquois/Delaware asserts that since corporations are economic entities, only an economic test is appropriate.

** The assertion that the proposal is significant in an ethical and social sense relies on plaintiff's argument that "the very availability of a market for products that may be obtained through the inhumane force-feeding of geese cannot help but contribute to the continuation of such treatment." Plaintiff's brief characterizes the humane treatment of animals as among the foundations of western culture. An additional indication of the significance of plaintiff's proposal is the support of such leading organizations in the field of animal care as the American Society for the Prevention of Cruelty to Animals and The Humane Society of the United States for measures aimed at discontinuing use of force-feeding.

The Court would note that the applicability of the Rule 14a–8(c)(5) exception to Mr. Lovenheim's proposal represents a close question given the lack of clarity in the exception itself. In effect, plaintiff relies on the word "otherwise," suggesting that it indicates the drafters of the rule intended that other noneconomic tests of significance be used. Iroquois/Delaware relies on the fact that the rule examines other significance in relation to the issuer's business. Because of the apparent ambiguity of the rule, the Court considers the history of the shareholder proposal rule in determining the proper interpretation of the most recent version of that rule.

Prior to 1983, paragraph 14a–8(c)(5) excluded proposals "not significantly related to the issuer's business" but did not contain an objective economic significance test such as the five percent of sales, assets, and earnings specified in the first part of the current version. Although a series of SEC decisions through 1976 allowing issuers to exclude proposals challenging compliance with the Arab economic boycott of Israel allowed exclusion if the issuer did less than one percent of their business with Arab countries or Israel, the Commission stated later in 1976 that it did "not believe that subparagraph (c)(5) should be hinged solely on the economic relativity of a proposal." Thus the Commission required inclusion "in many situations in which the related business comprised less than one percent" of the company's revenues, profits or assets "where the proposal has raised *policy questions* important enough to be considered 'significantly related' to the issuer's business."

As indicated above, the 1983 revision adopted the five percent test of economic significance in an effort to create a more objective standard. Nevertheless, in adopting this standard, the Commission stated that proposals will be includable notwithstanding their "failure to reach the specified economic thresholds if a significant relationship to the issuer's business is demonstrated on the face of the resolution or supporting statement." Thus it seems clear based on the history of the rule that "the meaning of 'significantly related' is not *limited* to economic significance."

Whether or not the Securities and Exchange Commission could properly adopt such a rule, the Court cannot ignore the history of the rule which reveals no decision by the Commission to limit the determination to the economic criteria relied on by Iroquois/Delaware. The Court therefore holds that in light of the ethical and social significance of plaintiff's proposal and the fact that it implicates significant levels of sales, plaintiff has shown a likelihood of prevailing on the merits with regard to the issue of whether his proposal is "otherwise significantly related" to Iroquois/Delaware's business.

IV. CONCLUSION

For the reasons discussed above, the Court concludes that plaintiff's motion for preliminary injunction should be granted.

ORDERED that plaintiff's application for a preliminary injunction be, and hereby is, granted; and that defendant Iroquois Brands, Ltd., a company organized under the laws of the State of Delaware, be, and hereby is, enjoined from omitting plaintiff's shareholder proposal from its 1985 proxy statement.

Notes

(1) Shareholder proposals are rarely successful once the proposal makes it onto a proxy statement to be voted on by all shareholders. If success is so rare, why do shareholders continue to submit proposals?

(2) What exactly does Lovenheim seek in his shareholder proposal to be placed on the Iroquois proxy statement? If successful in getting his proposal onto the proxy statement, what is Lovenheim's ultimate purpose?

(3) If shareholder proposals are rarely successful, why do corporate leaders try so hard to keep them off of the proxy statement and outside the view of shareholders?

Is the Quest for Corporate Responsibility a Wild Goose Chase? The Story of *Lovenheim v. Iroquois Brands, Ltd.*

D. A. Jeremy Telman
45 AKRON L. REV. 291 (2012)

I. Introduction

In *Lovenheim v. Iroquois Brands, Ltd.*, plaintiff Peter Lovenheim asked the D.C. District Court to enjoin defendant Iroquois Brands, Ltd. (Iroquois) from omitting his shareholder proposal from the proxy materials sent out in advance of its 1985 annual shareholder meeting. The proposal related to a French product, paté de foie gras, which Iroquois distributed in the United States, and which constituted a tiny part of Iroquois' business. Lovenheim, the owner of two hundred shares of Iroquois' common stock, called upon Iroquois to investigate whether the French producer engaged in forced-feeding of the geese, which Lovenheim considered a form of animal cruelty, in producing the paté de foie gras and, if that turned out to be the case, asked Iroquois to consider discontinuing the product until a more humane means of production could be developed.

He decided to submit a shareholder proposal as permitted under SEC rule 14a-8 (the Rule) promulgated pursuant to section 14(a) of the Securities Exchange Act of 1934 (the '34 Act). Those regulations provide that a corporation must include qualifying shareholder proposals in its proxy solicitation materials distributed in advance of annual or special shareholder meetings, along with the shareholder's statement in support of the proposal. A shareholder proposal is any "recommendation or requirement that the company and/or its board of directors take action" that a shareholder intends to present at a shareholder meeting. The District Court granted Lovenheim's motion and preliminarily enjoined Iroquois from sending out its proxy materials without the proposal.

Lovenheim is not only a standard teaching case in corporate law courses, it is routinely cited by the Securities and Exchange Commission (SEC) in response to corporations seeking to exclude shareholder proposals from proxy materials on the ground that the proposals are not significantly related to the corporations' businesses.

II. History of SEC Implementation of Section 14(a) of the Securities Exchange Act of 1934

One might reasonably ask why we permit shareholder proposals in the first place. After all, it is a fundamental premise of corporate governance that managers manage. Shareholders may be the beneficial owners of the corporation, but the separation of ownership and control is one of the key advantages of the corporate form. Although shareholder activism has always been one of the ingredients of U.S. corporate governance, Congress had acted in the early twentieth century to limit the ability of financial institutions to participate in corporate affairs. However, in response to its perception that corporate management was abusing the proxy solicitation process, Congress granted the Securities and Exchange Commission (the SEC) broad power to regulate proxy solicitations in section 14(a) of the '34 Act, and the current form of shareholder activism is a product of an SEC rule first introduced in 1942, the predecessor to the current Rule. The Rule requires management to include in its proxy materials sent out in advance of annual shareholder meetings shareholder proposals to be voted on at those meetings so long as the shareholder meets certain conditions to qualify as a proponent.

A. Implementation of the Rule 1942–1970

In enacting section 14 of the '34 Act, Congress responded to an unpleasant by-product of the separation of ownership and control in the structure of corporations. "[A]s management became divorced from ownership and came under the control of banking groups, men forgot that they were dealing with the savings of men and the making of profits became an impersonal thing." Congress chose to regulate corporate proxies as one mechanism for preventing management from circumventing "fair corporate suffrage."

1. Overview of SEC Regulation of Social Proposals

The SEC's initial regulatory efforts in this area were directed at promoting "full and fair corporate disclosure regarding management proxy materials." In 1942, the SEC took the logical next step by adopting a rule that required management to include in its proxy materials shareholder proposals that constituted a "proper subject for action by security holders." This seemed to offer shareholders an extensive right to provide their input to management, but the SEC immediately saw the danger that shareholders would use the proposal mechanism to raise matters that bore little relationship to company's affairs. In 1945, the Commission issued a release opining that "proposals which deal with general political, social or economic matters" are not proper subjects for shareholder action.

The SEC's approach to shareholder proposals has tended to mirror the times. As one commentator put it, in the 1950s, the SEC "added layers of conditions to the rule and gutted meaningful shareholder access." The SEC relaxed its restrictions during the Vietnam and Watergate eras before again seeking to "squelch access" during the more conservative 1980s.

2. The Rule in the Courts

The first significant court case testing shareholders' ability to challenge management on issues of corporate governance through the mechanism of the shareholder proposal came in SEC v. Transamerica Corp. The main issue in the case was the scope of the "proper subject" for shareholder action referenced in the Rule. Transamerica argued that shareholder proposals must relate to a subject matter on which shareholders were permitted to vote under all legal requirements, including those found in the corporation's charter and by-laws. The SEC took the broader position permitting proposals on any subject matter in which a shareholder had an interest under state law.

The court sided with the SEC, stressing that Transamerica's reading of the Rule would circumvent Congress' intent "to require fair opportunity for the operation of corporate suffrage." Because a corporation must be run for the benefit of its stockholders and not for that of its managers, management could not be permitted to place technical provisions of a corporation's charter or by-laws beyond the reach of the shareholder vote. "The control of great corporations by a very few persons was the abuse at which Congress struck in enacting section 14(a)."

Although it supported shareholder rights in the Transamerica case, between 1948 and 1954, the SEC repeatedly revised the Rule to limit the ability of shareholders to make proposals.

The case law in the two decades following the Transamerica decision was decidedly favorable to the discretion of both corporate management and the SEC, both of which inclined towards excluding proposals, especially social proposals. For example, in *Peck v. Greyhound Corp.*, shareholder Peck brought a proposal calling on the corporation to abolish its segregated seating system in the South. Greyhound sought to exclude the proposal and relied on the 1945 SEC release cited earlier, stating that it was not the intent of the Rule "to permit stockholders to obtain the consensus of other stockholders with respect to matters which are of a general political, social or economic nature." The SEC staff agreed with the corporation's assessment of the propriety of the proposal, finding that it was not on a "proper subject." The Peck court did not go so far as to endorse Greyhound's interpretation of the 1945 SEC Release. However, the court denied Peck's motion to enjoin Greyhound from soliciting proxies and holding its shareholder meeting unless Peck's proposal was included in Greyhound's proxy materials, finding that Peck had failed to exhaust available administrative remedies. In addition, the court noted that considerable deference was due to the SEC's interpretation of its own rules and also found that Peck could not establish that he would be irreparably harmed if his injunction were denied.

Deference to management and the SEC characterized decisions in this area into the late 1960s, when the courts dealt another blow to shareholder activism in *Brooks v. Standard Oil Co.* In that case, plaintiff offered a resolution that called on Standard Oil to intensify its effort to encourage exploration of the world's continental shelves for oil reserves and to encourage the creation of an international regime over undersea mineral resources. Standard Oil notified the SEC that it intended to exclude the proposal, asserting that the proposal could be omitted because it: (1) was not on a proper subject for shareholder action; (2) related to ordinary business matters; and (3) primarily sought to promote a general economic or political cause. Plaintiff, an attorney with expertise in the utilization of underwater mineral resources beyond national jurisdiction, sought a declaratory judgment that his resolution was on a proper subject for action by shareholders.

The SEC issued Standard Oil a no-action letter on the ground that the proposal was not a proper subject for action by shareholders. In so doing, the SEC clearly violated its own rules. The Rule required that, if the corporation claimed a legal ground for the omission of a shareholder proposal, the corporation must include a "supporting opinion of counsel" with its notice of intention to omit. Since Standard Oil provided no such opinion of counsel, it could not possibly have met its burden of production. However, the court concluded that plaintiff was not harmed by the SEC's failure to adhere to its own procedural requirements, as Standard Oil's opinion of counsel would have relied on the same legal arguments as Standard Oil presented in the court case. The court adopted a highly deferential approach to review of SEC no-action letters, accepting the SEC's judgment "unless it can be said that what has been done is without any rational basis on all the elements involved."

Thus, three decades after the SEC first adopted the Rule, the scope of the right of shareholders to bring proposals at annual meetings was narrowly circumscribed in two ways. First, the SEC was granting no-action letters with respect to all proposals except those relating to selection, compensation and accountability of managers. Second, the courts had adopted a highly deferential approach to SEC decisions, even if those decisions were taken at the staff level. This trend was to change dramatically with the D.C. Circuit's decision in Medical Committee for Human Rights v. SEC.

B. The Medical Committee Opinion

The Medical Committee for Human Rights (Medical Committee) obtained by gift, shares in the Dow Chemical Company (Dow). On March 11, 1968, the Medical Committee's national chairman, Dr. Quentin Young, wrote to Dow and enclosed a first version of the Medical Committee's shareholder proposal. The proposal requested the Board of Directors to amend Dow's certificate of incorporation to provide "that napalm shall not be sold to any buyer unless that buyer gives reasonable assurances that the substance will not be used on or against human beings." In the accompanying letter, Dr. Young conceded that its primary motivation was the Medical Committee's concerns for human life, but he also noted that the Medical Committee's investment advisers suggested that napalm production "is also bad for our company's business as it is being used in the Vietnamese War" in part because it was making it "increasingly hard to recruit the highly intelligent, well-motivated, young college men so important for company growth." In addition, the letter noted that the impact on the company for its decision to manufacture napalm was global.

Dr. Young's language, espousing an economic interest in the corporation, was necessary to overcome language in the Rule that permitted a corporation to exclude a proposal "if it clearly appears that the proposal is submitted ... primarily for the purpose of promoting general economic, political, racial, religious, social or similar causes." Still, the original proposal was susceptible to exclusion under another regulation that permitted omission of proposals seeking management action "with respect to a matter relating to the conduct of the ordinary business operations of the issuer."

Acknowledging that "management should be allowed to decide to whom and under what circumstances it will sell its products," the Medical Committee nonetheless urged that "the company's owners have not only the legal power but also the historic and economic obligation to determine what products their company will manufacture."

Dow was unmoved and sent the SEC a memorandum stating its reasons for omitting the proposal. The SEC Division of Corporation Finance granted a no-action letter. The Medical Committee duly appealed, but the full Commission approved the recommendation of its Division of Corporation Finance. The Medical Committee next appealed that decision to the Court of Appeals for the D.C. Circuit.

After an extended discussion, the D.C. Circuit concluded that the SEC determination was reviewable in the Court of Appeals. The court then proceeded to a discussion of the merits of the case.

The court returned to Congress' intentions in passing section 14(a) of the '34 Act, whose "overriding purpose" it was "to assure to corporate shareholders the ability to exercise their right-some would say their duty—to control the important decisions which affect them in their capacity as stockholders and owners of the corporation." In light of this congressional purpose, the court could find no reason why management should be permitted to:

> place obstacles in the path of shareholders who wish to present to their co-owners ... the question of whether they wish to have their assets used in a manner which they believe to be more socially responsible but possibly less profitable than that which is dictated by present company policy.

Not only did the court think that the corporation had not born its burden under the SEC's regulations, it also asserted that the regulations–at least as applied in this case–could not be harmonized with Congress' intent in adopting section 14(a) of the '34 Act.

The case was remanded to the SEC for reconsideration in light of the court's opinion and with instructions that the basis for the SEC's decision must appear in the record "not in conclusory terms but in sufficient detail to permit prompt and effective review." The SEC was sufficiently concerned about the consequences of the decision to appeal to the

U.S. Supreme Court, which granted certiorari. However, before the Court could decide the case, Dow included the proposal in its annual proxy materials, and it received votes from less than 3% of the shares that participated. The facts thus no longer presented an active case or controversy, and the case was dismissed as moot. The status of the D.C. Circuit's opinion was thus unclear.

C. The Effect of Medical Committee

In the aftermath of Medical Committee, the number of shareholder proposals increased dramatically, as did the number of proposals relating to social issues. In addition, the SEC for the first time revised the Rule in a way that restricted the ability of management to exclude such proposals from its proxy materials. In 1972, the SEC revised the portion of the Rule relating to the exclusion of social proposals, permitting the exclusion of proposals only if they were not "significantly related to the business of the issuer or not within its control." In 1976, the SEC again revised the Rule, eliminating all reference to social or political proposals.

III. Fair is Fowl: The Story of Lovenheim v. Iroquois Brands

Peter Lovenheim was something of an amateur investor. When he found out about a company that he liked, he would buy shares. In the fall of 1981, he bought 200 shares of the common stock of Iroquois on the advice of his fiancé, who was a nutritionist, and had recommended the Schiff line of vitamins that Iroquois distributed. Lovenheim also saw potential for Iroquois' stock "because of its involvement in the expanding market for health foods and natural foods." Within a few months of purchasing his Iroquois stock, Lovenheim received proxy materials from which he learned that Iroquois marketed Eduard Artnzer pate de foie gras in the United States. Foie gras is a gourmet food produced from the livers of domesticated geese raised on a carbohydrate-rich diet.

A. What's Good for the Goose: Lovenheim's First Shareholder Proposal

Lovenheim had originally been attracted to Iroquois because the corporation marketed products that promoted healthy lifestyles. He did not think that encouraging the consumption of pate de foie gras was consistent with the rest of Iroquois' product lines, nor did he think that other like-minded shareholders would want Iroquois to be involved in the distribution of pate de foie gras if the production of the product involved significant animal cruelty.

The corporation's view of itself was very different from the way Lovenheim understood it. Although it did market natural foods and vitamins as two of its product lines, those product lines were by no means central to the corporation's mission or identity. Iroquois started out as a brewery and, at the time Lovenheim invested, distributed many diverse product lines, ranging from Champale to Yoohoo, through numerous subsidiaries.

According to Lovenheim, the process of force-feeding usually begins when the birds are four-months old. At farms at which the process has been mechanized, the birds are placed in a metal brace and the neck is stretched so that a funnel may be inserted 10–12 inches down the bird's throat. Four hundred grams of corn mash are then pumped into the birds' stomachs, while an elastic band around its neck prevents regurgitation. Where the process is done by hand, the feeder uses a funnel and a stick to force the mash down the bird's throat. The birds are force fed for between 15 and 28 days, and shortly thereafter they are slaughtered. During the brief period of force-feeding, the geese double their weight, but their livers swell until they account for up to 10% of the bird's total weight. An ordinary goose liver weighs about 120 grams; the liver of a force-fed bird weighs between 800 and 1000 grams. Up to 10% of the birds die before they can be slaughtered as a result of the forced feeding.

On May 10, 1982, Lovenheim wrote to Iroquois' management and requested that it look into the possibility that the pate product that it was distributing was produced through forced-feeding of geese. The corporation did not respond to that letter or to subsequent communications. So, on December 14, 1982, Lovenheim, on his own behalf and on behalf of the Humane Society, wrote a letter to Terence J. Fox, the president of Iroquois, enclosing a shareholder proposal for inclusion in the company's proxy materials for action at the next Iroquois annual shareholder meeting to be held in May 1983. The letter stated that the proposal was prepared in accordance with the relevant regulations promulgated by the Securities and Exchange Commission. Lovenheim also notified the corporation that he intended to attend the annual shareholder meeting.

Under the regulations operative at the time, Lovenheim was eligible to submit a proposal based on his ownership of 200 shares of stock in the corporation for at least one year prior to the shareholder meeting. The proposal asked the corporation to do the following:

> [F]orm a committee to study the methods by which its French supplier produces pate de foie gras, and report to the shareholders its findings, together with its opinion, based on expert consultation, as to whether or not this production method causes undue distress, pain, or suffering to the animals involved and, if so, whether further distribution of this product would risk damaging the good reputation of the Corporation and should therefore be discontinued until a more humane production method is developed.

Presumably, Lovenheim knew or suspected that pate de foie gras is always produced through the force-feeding of geese, and he really wanted Iroquois to stop distributing the product because its distribution encouraged what he considered a form of animal cruelty. But under the SEC rules operative at the time, shareholders could not bring proposals relating to the continuation of a particular product, as control over ordinary business operations was entrusted to management alone. Nor could Lovenheim bring a proposal that simply denounced animal cruelty and demanded that Iroquois adopt a position consistent with his ethical objections to inhumane treatment of animals without running afoul of the SEC regulation intended to prevent the shareholder proposal from being abused as a mechanism of general political protest. As a result, the shareholder proposal has a bit of absurdist theater about it. Proposals must ask the board to form a committee to investigate a matter and make recommendations. That way, the shareholder does not interfere with the conduct of ordinary business operations, as the final decision is left in the discretion of the board.

The corporation included the proposal in the proxy materials distributed in advance of its May 1983 shareholder meeting. It also included its own recommendation that shareholders vote against Lovenheim's proposal.

As he stated he would, Lovenheim appeared at that annual shareholder meeting and presented his proposal. In his presentation, Lovenheim offered a point-by-point refutation of management's arguments. In the ensuing vote, Lovenheim's proposal garnered 50,000 votes, just over 5% of those cast.

B. The Goose Chase: From Proponent to Litigant

Encouraged by this result, Lovenheim offered the same resolution the following year. He wrote well in advance to seek information regarding the date for the upcoming shareholder meeting. To Lovenheim's surprise, the company responded this time by notifying him (through corporate counsel) that Iroquois considered the proposal excludable. During the intervening year, the SEC had again revised its regulations.

The rules now permitted exclusion of proposals relating to business operations accounting for less than 5% of the issuer's total assets and for less than 5% of net earnings and gross sales and not otherwise significantly related to the issuer's business.

However, as Lovenheim pointed out in his responsive memorandum of law, Iroquois thus did nothing more than re-state the purportedly applicable SEC rule. Such a simple assertion was not sufficient to meet the corporation's burden, said Lovenheim, under the applicable federal regulations. In any case, Lovenheim argued, even if it were true that the product at issue did not constitute 5% of Iroquois; assets, earnings or sales, Iroquois could not show that the product was not "otherwise significantly related" to its business.

The Commission recognized that there are many instances in which the matter involved in a proposal is significant to an issuer's business, even though such significance is not apparent from an economic viewpoint.

The SEC sided with Iroquois in a two-paragraph no-action letter. The SEC simply noted that "[t]here appears to be some basis for your opinion that the proposal may be omitted from the Company's proxy material under Rule 14a-8(c)(5)" and concluded that there would be no enforcement action if the Lovenheim proposal were omitted from Iroquois' proxy materials.

Lovenheim appealed the decision of the Division of Corporation Finance to the SEC's five commissioners. The Commission declined review.

Lovenheim attempted to settle his differences with the corporation in advance of the annual shareholder meeting. Iroquois was not receptive to such a settlement.

Lovenheim was undeterred. He prepared his shareholder proposal for a third time. On October 17, 1984, he sent the proposal for inclusion in Iroquois' 1985 proxy statement. Once again, Iroquois responded with a letter to the SEC stating its intention to omit Lovenheim's proposal from its proxy materials. This time, the corporation took the trouble to present some statistics, indicating that the pate at issue accounted for less than 0.05% of the corporation's sales, less than 0.3% of its net earnings and less than 0.09% of its assets for 1982 and 1983, statistics not expected to change significantly in 1984. On January 9, 1985, the SEC's Division of Corporate Finance once again issued a response to Iroquois, stating that it would not recommend any enforcement action if Iroquois were to omit Lovenheim's proposal from its proxy materials.

C. Iroquois' Goose Is Cooked in the D.C. District Court

Lovenheim bypassed an appeal to the SEC commissioners and filed suit in the D.C. District Court seeking an injunction ordering Iroquois to distribute his proposal. This time, he retained Jonathan Eisenberg, an experienced attorney who agreed to work pro bono and to help him on the brief submitted in support of his suit for injunctive relief. Lovenheim's motivation in skipping review by the Commission may have been to save time and resources. It also may have been strategic, since at oral argument in the District Court, his counsel argued that the court owed no deference to a decision by the SEC's staff to issue a no-action letter. It may well have proved harder to persuade the court that it owed no deference to the SEC Commissioners' interpretation of the agency's own rules.

On the law, Eisenberg encouraged the court to consider the relevant regulation, 14a-8(c)(5), as constituting a two-part test, both of which have to be met for the corporation to be permitted to exclude a proposal. Lovenheim did not challenge Iroquois' claim that the economic portion of 14a-8(c)(5) was met, but Eisenberg stressed that in 1976 the SEC rewrote the regulation, removing language that permitted the corporation to omit a proposal "if it is submitted primarily for general political, social ends" and adding language permitting omission of proposals that are not economically significant and "that are not significantly related to the issuer's business."

The effect of the change was, in Eisenberg's view, to eliminate from the SEC's regulation any indication that social proposals "were suspect." Since the 1976 changes, the SEC had required that all social proposals be included so long as the issuer's business was in any way implicated in the proposal.

The requirement that the proposal be significantly related was met here, Eisenberg contended, because Iroquois made $70,000 worth of sales in pate de foie gras. If the issue was significant and the corporation was doing even "one completely outrageous thing a year," Eisenberg maintained, the corporation could not refuse to include a proposal relating to that conduct on the ground that it was not economically significant, in that the conduct did not relate to 5% of the corporation's assets.

Counsel for Iroquois stressed that the connection between the issue raised by the proposal and Iroquois' business was "de minimis," and that the SEC could not possibly have intended to require corporations to include in proxy statements every single social proposal that had any conceivable connection to the corporation's operations.

Iroquois argued, in essence, that the main point of 14a-8(c)(5) was to make certain that proposals relate to significant portions of the issuer's business, even if they raise significant political, social or ethical issues. Corporations are business entities. They and the SEC are primarily interested in economic matters, Iroquois argued, with respect to proxy statements as in all other areas. Medical Committee, as Iroquois understood it, stood only for the proposition that a corporation may not exclude a proposal simply on the ground that it raises ethical and philosophical issues. The opinion did not require the inclusion of proposals that are of no real economic significance to the corporation.

The court sided with Lovenheim on the decisive point. The court recognized the social significance of Lovenheim's proposal and the fact that it "implicate[d] significant levels of sales" for Iroquois. It therefore granted Lovenheim the injunctive relief he sought.

The court's factual findings were significant.

Neither party offered expert testimony on the political, social, or ethical significance of the issue. One is hard pressed to imagine where such expertise would reside or why it should reside in a corporation, in the SEC or in a court. Determining which issues are "important" is not within the institutional competence of any of those bodies.

Leaving significance aside, there was also the question of what constitutes "significantly related" to the business operations of the issuer.

Still, the court's willingness to accept as socially significant any proposal relating to a subject about which some national non-profit organizations had expressed concern, coupled with its willingness to think it significantly related to a business if it accounts for 0.05% of a corporations' assets, suggested that corporations could be obligated to distribute shareholder proposals on nearly any subject that in any way related to their businesses.

There was a great deal of media interest in the case, with articles appearing in The Washington Post, The Los Angeles Times, and The Wall Street Journal, among other newspapers. Given the timing of the opinion, Iroquois had to acquiesce, as there was insufficient time to appeal the decision before the next annual shareholder meeting, which was held just weeks after the District Court's decision.

Lovenheim attended the meeting, as required under the regulations, and he presented his proposal to the shareholders and their proxies. The reception was far from warm. Lovenheim's proposal received less than 8% of the votes cast by Iroquois' shareholders. Despite the court victory and the publicity, ordinary shareholders were unmoved. Or were they? Within months of the shareholder meeting, Iroquois sold the unit responsible for importing pate de foie gras, announcing that it now considered the issue put behind the company.

Lovenheim comes on the tail end of a period in the history of shareholder proposals when individual shareholders were the dominant shareholder activists. His case suggests the difficulties an individual investor might face in trying to put pressure on a corporation through the mechanism of the shareholder proposal and thus illustrates why the transition from individual shareholder activists to institutional activism might have occurred.

D. Lovenheim's Further Adventures in Animal Law

After his experience with Iroquois, Lovenheim, having returned to his native Rochester, began offering his services as a sort of freelance drafter of shareholder proposals for non-profit organizations. He worked with People for the Ethical Treatment of Animals (PETA), and helped them start an ongoing program aimed at bringing animal protection issues to the attention of corporations through shareholder proposals. Lovenheim also teamed up with Henry Spira, a brilliant tactician in the art of "constructive shaming," which involves pressuring corporations into cooperating with advocates for the ethical treatment of animals.

Together, Lovenheim and Spira were able to persuade McDonald's to adopt three basic principles to help assure humane treatment of the animals used in McDonald's products. In the several years Lovenheim worked with Spira, he claims they never had to actually bring a proposal to a vote in a shareholder meeting. Spira had won a reputation for openness to reasonable compromise. He worked with corporations until they agreed to adopt measures that would enhance their reputations for corporate responsibility. The result was almost invariably at least a partial adoption of the substance of the proposals that Spira and Lovenheim brought.

Lovenheim's story thus suggests that shareholder proposals have consequences that go beyond their effects on the corporation to which the proposal originally relates. For a time at least, Peter Lovenheim was transformed by his experience as a proponent into someone who worked with others to promote social change through mechanisms that were not limited to the shareholder proposal mechanism.

IV. Shareholder Proposals and the Separation of Ownership and Control

Lovenheim and *Medical Committee* illustrate the determination and resolve required of any shareholder who wants to get a proposal before the shareholders of a corporation. As the Medical Committee court noted, the SEC's process for reviewing proposals was far from transparent and often resulted in corporations being permitted to omit proposals for reasons that were not effectively communicated to the proponents of those proposals.

For opponents of shareholder proposals, the fact that the proponent in Medical Committee was an organization that promoted social causes and that Lovenheim had close ties with such an organization highlights the problem of shareholder social proposals. Opponents of shareholder proposals view shareholders primarily as passive investors seeking an economic return. So viewed, their only interest in political or social issues ought to be with the effect of such issues on the return on their investment in the corporation. As one critic of the Rule put it: "Stockholder participatory democracy is a myth; investors do not buy stock in public companies with any serious expectation of influencing management. The Wall Street Rule is the only practical rule by which sensible investors are governed. Small investors who do not like management sell their shares." If the issue is essentially an economic one, say the social proposal skeptics, then it ought to be left for corporate managers to decide in the exercise of their business judgment. If the issue is not economic, then it has no business being before any corporate body.

And yet, in the two decades since Lovenheim was decided, neither Congress nor the SEC has taken action to reign in social proposals. On the contrary, the SEC routinely cites to Lovenheim in denying no-action letters to corporations. This final section offers an explanation of why that is the case.

A. The Costs and Benefits of Shareholder Proposals

In connection with its 1984 revisions to Rule 14a-8, the SEC circulated a questionnaire in order to gauge interested parties' attitudes towards shareholder proposals. Nearly three of four respondents agreed or strongly agreed that shareholder proposals are "a waste of management's time and the corporation's money." Most respondents did not agree that proposals are an efficient or effective outlet for concerned shareholders, although the votes were more evenly split on whether the proposals are an "effective way of keeping management aware of shareholder concerns."

Although corporation counsel tends to regard shareholder proposals as a nuisance, the overall costs associated with such proposals do not seem to be that significant. Around the time of the Lovenheim case, the SEC reported that it devoted only 1208 staff hours per year to the review of shareholder proposals and requests for no-action letters, a rough equivalent to the time of one full-time employee. Even the most determined opponents of the proposal concede that its costs both to corporations and to the SEC are not very significant.

As Lovenheim understood at the outset, shareholder proposals can succeed in affecting corporate policy even if they do not come close to winning the shareholder votes necessary for adoption. They thus can be a highly effective way to persuade corporate management to adopt socially responsible positions. From a policy perspective, the costs of shareholder proposals to the SEC and to corporations thus should be balanced against the possible benefits that derive from such proposals. Proponents with ideas about how to improve corporations are a resource to the corporation. If their main recourse is to invest elsewhere, the corporation's resources are dissipated.

One scholar has characterized the Rule as a tax imposed on corporations that pays for a useful mechanism of corporate governance.* Corporations may well regard this "tax" as cheaper and less onerous than government regulation. Shareholder proposals facilitate communication between a corporation's management and its owners in a manner that is more open, clear and specific than any other mechanism for communication between management and shareholders.

B. The Efficacy of Shareholder Proposals

Justifications for the existence of shareholder proposals relating to social issues come in two varieties. One variety focuses on the nature of corporations. It views shareholders

---

* Alan R. Palmiter, The Shareholder Proposal Rule: A Failed Experiment in Merit Regulation, 45 ALA. L. REV. 879, 898 (1994) ("[T]he rule acts as a tax on public companies and their shareholders.").

not as passive investors but as owners who have—and should have—an interest in the social and political impact of a corporation. From this perspective, shareholders have not only a right but a duty to try to influence corporate management to adopt socially responsible policies. In the years following the Medical Committee decision, scholars found ample evidence that corporations were adopting policies on social issues that were either directly or at least apparently stimulated by shareholder proposals.

The other variety is Melvin Eisenberg's safety valve theory; that is, the idea that shareholder proposals provide a useful safety valve in that they permit shareholders to raise their concerns before management and their fellow shareholders in a public forum in which the corporation's leadership must provide some sort of response. As indicated above, the safety valve comes at relatively low cost to the corporation.

But both varieties of defenses of the shareholder proposal process ultimately sound in a theory of the corporation that recognizes that corporations have a role in society that is too large to be reduced to economics. Even those who continue to maintain that corporations exist "primarily to earn a profit for [their] shareholders," acknowledge that the law now recognizes "a greatly enlarged social duty and responsibility of businesses" to care for the "comfort, health and well-being of their employees." In fact, corporations' social duty extends well beyond the well-being of their employees, and there is actually very little support, either in case law or in statutes, for the notion that corporations exist primarily for the benefit of their shareholders. Rather, corporate management is permitted to justify its decisions not only with reference to shareholder interests, but also with reference to the interests of other stakeholders, which may include the interests of creditors, employees, customers, and the industry as a whole or even the community at large.

The law on corporate charitable giving is consistent with this expansive understanding of the purpose of corporations. Corporations are permitted to make charitable donations without any sort of requirement that they justify those donations in economic terms. In the landmark case, A.P. Smith Mfg. Co. v. Barlow, the New Jersey Supreme Court enthusiastically embraced the principle that corporations must supplement their wealth maximizing pursuits with a sense of their social and ethical responsibility to be good corporate citizens.

The Rule and the SEC's permissive approach to social proposals are understandable in light of the broader doctrine of corporate purposes. Corporations do not exist primarily to maximize shareholder wealth. Enjoying as they do the benefits of deference to their business decisions that may be influenced by factors other than wealth-maximization, corporate managers cannot deny shareholders the ability to contribute to the decision-making process through social proposals.

V. Conclusion

Judging by the few court cases that address social proposals, one could easily conclude that cases like *Lovenheim* are akin to nuisance suits that have no impact on corporate governance because the proposals never win anything approaching a majority of the shareholder vote.

Opponents of social proposals tend to view corporations as vehicles for the generation of wealth, and they view shareholders as passive investors concerned only with maximizing the return on their investment. This view of corporations appears to be too narrow. Both courts and legislatures permit corporate boards, in managing their corporations, to consider many factors other than shareholder wealth maximization. The SEC's and the courts' permissive approach to social proposals is thus consistent with other bodies of law that recognize that, because of the increasingly important role of corporations as legal persons within our society, there is a general expectation that corporations will behave responsibly.

While it is difficult to prove that shareholder proposals help them to do so, the cost to corporations and to society of social proposals is minimal. The best evidence that their usefulness outweighs the costs associated with social proposals may be the failure of corporations to mobilize to oppose them. Corporate managers may recognize the value of exchange with their shareholders on social issues, and they may also grudgingly appreciate the consciousness-raising effect that social proposals can have.

Notes

(1) Are shareholder proposals a "nuisance" to be quickly discarded by corporate leaders or are they a useful tool in corporate social policymaking?

(2) After reading of Lovenheim's quest to end the force-feeding of geese by Iroquois, are you convinced that shareholder proposals constitute an effective instrument to shine light on corporate decisions that may injure society at large? If effective, why are shareholder proposals nearly always defeated by a large margin?

D. Shareholder Activism: Protests, Boycotts, Policy Proposals

Peter Lovenheim represents the prototypical shareholder activist. What characteristics define a shareholder activist? In thinking about activism and grass-roots organizing, including picketing, letter-writing campaigns, and boycotts, is using shareholder proposals and derivative lawsuits an effective way to protest? When one considers social engineering and the kinds of protests that have changed United States policy and law, an individual is often drawn to remember the Civil Rights Movement led by Martin Luther King, Jr., and the *Brown v. Board of Education* strategy led by Charles Hamilton Houston and Thurgood Marshall as perhaps the most meaningful protesting and use of legal challenges, that led to the U.S. becoming a more equal country. The Civil Rights Movement was characterized by peaceful protesting, including large marches, demonstrations and boycotts. The *Brown v. Board* legal strategy was characterized by careful planning, strategic filing of lawsuits and seeking out the best plaintiffs to take the most egregious cases to the federal courts.

When one considers effective boycotts, an individual might remember the South African boycotts related to protesting apartheid and the imprisonment of Nelson Mandela. There, the nation of South Africa together with U.S. and international companies that invested or did business in South Africa were targeted as worthy of tourist and consumer boycotts by social activists. Can the concept of shareholder activism be just as effective or important as the famed boycotts and marches of yesteryear? Is the simple act of purchasing shares in a corporation and seeking to place a shareholder proposal on the proxy statement and annual meeting agenda an effective means of social protest? Consider the following case studies as you ponder this query.

Activist C. Delores Tucker Takes On Time Warner Over Gangsta Rap

Civil Rights activist Cynthia Delores Tucker became incensed in the 1980s and 1990s when she listened to gangsta rap music and the messages of misogyny and violence she witnessed. Tucker would wage a campaign against gangsta rap music protesting its content all the way to the Times Warner corporate boardroom. To understand her campaign against violent and counter-culture hip hop, one needs to understand her background. Tucker was born in Pennsylvania in 1927. She was the 10th of 11 children of a minister and a "Christian feminist mother." Tucker played the organ and saxophone from a young age and directed her church choir. She attended Temple University, Pennsylvania State University and the University of Pennsylvania. Tucker became a pivotal figure in the Civil Rights Movement. She raised funds for the NAACP and participated in marches and demonstrations with Dr. Martin Luther King Jr., specifically protesting alongside the minister in Selma, Alabama in 1965. Later, Tucker turned her attention to electoral politics where in Pennsylvania she served on the Democratic Committee and assisted black candidates running for public office. She was well-known as a master fundraiser in her efforts.

In 1971, Tucker was elected Secretary for the Commonwealth of Pennsylvania making her the most powerful African American woman in the state. After unsuccessful bids for lieutenant governor in 1978, U.S. Senator in 1980, and U.S. House in 1992, Tucker continued her political career as chief of the minority caucus of the Democratic National Committee and also chaired the Black Caucus of the DNC for eleven years. Tucker also founded the National Women's Political Caucus and the National Political Congress of Black Women.

In 1993, Tucker was in the spotlight and headlines when she vigorously protested obscenities in rap music. She was arrested several times while picketing in front of music stores that sold gangsta rap music. Tucker viewed gangsta rap as pornographic filth and believed that it constituted a grave disrespect toward black women. Tucker particularly expressed her disdain for the music for the impact that it had on young children stating "eight, ten, and eleven year olds are using drugs because they are told it's cool, ... little boys are calling little girls 'whores' because that's what they hear." Tucker was joined in her 1990s campaign against gangsta rap by civil-rights activists, clergy, and conservatives who pledged their opposition to gangsta rap.

To effect her campaign, Tucker purchased ten shares of stock in Time Warner, the entertainment conglomerate that co-owned Interscope Records, the distributor of Death Row Records owned by Suge Knight containing a roster of artists that included Tupac Shakur, Dr. Dre and other renowned hip hop artists. At the May 1995 Time Warner annual shareholders' meeting in New York City, Tucker was able to gain a speaking opportunity and delivered a blistering seventeen-minute attack on the genre and the company calling Time Warner a "conspirator in the denigration and destruction of the black community." Tucker gained a measure of success in her campaign when in September of 1995 Time Warner announced it would sell off its fifty percent share of Interscope. MCA Records announced it would acquire that fifty percent share of Interscope Records for $200 million. The Canada-based Seagram Co. owned eight percent of MCA Records and thus became the next highly visible target of Tucker and her campaign when Tucker proclaimed "we have discussed programs to begin divestment action against Seagram, as we did against Time Warner, if they profit in any way from this music."

Tucker's campaign against gangsta rap culminated in Congressional hearings which she was able to convene following her successful corporate divestment efforts against Time Warner.

Interscope recording artists and other hip hop stars retaliated against Tucker's campaign. Tupac Shakur recorded "How Do You Want It" where he specifically referred to Tucker and her outrage: "C. Delores Tucker you's a motherfucker; Instead of trying to help a nigga you try to destroy a brother." Tupac again referenced Tucker's campaign against his label and music in "Wonda Why They Call You Bitch" where he raps "Dear Ms. Delores Tucker; Keep stressin' me; Fuckin' with a motherfucking mind; I figured you wanted to know; You know why we call them hoes bitches; And maybe this might help you understand; It ain't personal; Strictly business, baby, strictly business." Other hip hop artists such as KRS-One, The Game, Lil' Wayne, Eminem and Lil' Kim also made reference to Tucker in their music. Following Tupac's death in 1996, Tucker filed a ten million dollar lawsuit against his estate claiming that his lyrics caused her emotional distress, humiliation, shock, fright, and outrage. The case was eventually dismissed. C. Delores Tucker passed away in 2005 in Pennsylvania.

United Methodist Church Divests All Investments From Private For-Profit Prison Corporations

The United Methodist Church ("UMC") is one of the largest denominations in the United States. The church has over 74,000 clergy that participate in the pension investment plan offered by UMC's agency. This agency along with the Board of Trustees came together to evaluate their portfolio holdings and recognized that the pension fund invested in two private for-profit prison companies, the Corrections Corporation of America and the GEO Group. The UMC Board of Trustees elected to sell all of their holdings in the private prison corporations as a matter of good conscience and good fiscal responsibility. Despite the very profitable returns earned by CCA and the GEO Group over the past few decades based largely on the nation's march toward mass incarceration, the board believed that continued investment in companies that profit off of human misery did not fit within their mission as a church and peaceful community.

At the time UMC divested its ownership in the private prison companies, church leadership stated that the request to divest came from the UMC's Interagency Task Force on Immigration. The UMC has a very large Hispanic/Latino population and the Task Force recognized that U.S. mass incarceration disproportionately impacts African-American and Latino citizens. The Task Force further recognized that private prison corporations had begun to focus new incarceration initiatives on detaining unauthorized immigrants, largely Latino, and that the private prisons also often neglected the detainees in their care by failing to provide basic human necessities while they are locked up. The failure of the private prison companies to provide basic health care and reports of harsh and cruel treatment of the detained were further reasons cited by the UMC for divestment of investment dollars from these profit focused private prison corporations. Specifically, the Board of Trustees considered a report that detailed an extraordinarily violent privately run juvenile facility in the state of Mississippi that actually housed some juveniles with adults. Equipped with this information, the UMC board began the divestment immediately.

The UMC Board of Church and Society is responsible for implementing and shepherding the UMC's investment strategies. Similar to other religious organizations, the Social Principles adopted by the Board of Church and Society guides appropriate investment initiatives. Socially responsible investing is a priority for the UMC's Social Principles and the privately run prison corporations ran afoul of those Social Principles which discourages investment in the stock of companies that condone racial discrimination and violates human rights. UMC parishioners expect responsibility in investment strategies, particularly when some corporations engage in inhumane or discriminatory conduct. In divesting, the UMC called upon their membership and others to engage in new practices and treatment of prisoners, including greater rehabilitation efforts and restoration of a person's humanity and dignity rather that stripping prisoners of their humanity.

UK Uncut Uses Social Media to Apply Pressure to Tax Evading Corporations

A common corporate practice is to use tax shelters and government incentives to avoid paying corporate taxes despite reaping enormous profits from the citizens of the nation's that buy the products and pay the salaries of those corporate employees and executives. The term "Corporate Welfare" has been adopted by some to describe the vast benefits some companies gain in tax cuts, tax avoidance, and quid-pro-quo government largesse. A recent movement in Great Britain that has caught fire in the U.S. has begun to hold the feet of some corporate tax dodgers to the fire. UK Uncut, a British social activist organization, devised a social media protest campaign that removed the veil from many leading companies that have not paid corporate taxes in decades.[3] UK Uncut represents itself as a voice for the average working middle class citizen. The goal of UK Uncut is to reveal how many social institutions that rely on government/taxpayer support, could receive generous and appropriate funding if only various corporate players would pay the corporate taxes they are charged with paying. When UK Uncut discovered that several British corporate giants had not paid taxes in years, the organization began to use Twitter and other social media to expose the corporate welfare and to organize sit-ins and boycotts of those corporations who do not pay their fair share.

Vodafone, England's major cell phone provider, was outed by UK Uncut as having failed to pay corporate taxes for many years. Using social media, UK Uncut announced this failure and then organized several sit-ins and a major boycott of Vodafone for its failure to pay any corporate taxes. The first demonstration was a widely attended sit-in of a local London Vodafone retail outlet and set the stage for what became a nationwide movement and boycott of Vodafone nationally. The boycott spread to other cities and protests against Vodafone began to gain traction throughout the country. The media seized on UK Uncut's progress and reported on their actions garnering international attention.

On the heels of UK Uncut's boycotts in England, Warren Buffet in the United States announced publically that his own corporate tax welfare enabled him to pay less in taxes than his personal secretary. When an investing titan like Buffet decries corporate welfare and volunteers to pay his fair share in taxes, the state of corporate welfare comes under the microscope. Social media and greater awareness provides new avenues for activist shareholders and consumers to uncover unfairness and plan 21st century boycotts and protests. Corporate leaders are often sensitive to controversy and pickets and consumer refusal to purchase goods or services can often garner the attention of the corporate boardroom in ways that derivative lawsuits and shareholder proposals cannot.

US Uncut Follows Suit

US Uncut was founded just one month following The Nation's "How to Build a Progressive Tea Party" article was published highlighting UK Uncut's Vodafone protests. US Uncut's founder described his astonishment when he realized that General Electric, ExxonMobil, Citibank and Bank of America had paid $0 in U.S. taxes the year previous to the founding of US Uncut. US Uncut established a website and almost overnight people joined and began planning a national day of action where Bank of America would be protested based on reports that in 2009, Bank of America did not pay a single cent in federal income or corporate tax, while receiving more than twenty million in taxpayer

---

3. Johann Hari, *How to Build a Progressive Tea Party*, THE NATION, Feb 21, 2011, www.thenation.com/article/how-build-progressive-tea-party/.

bailout funds through the Troubled Asset Relief Program (TARP). In Boston, US Uncut organized protests at local BofA branches and "crashed" its Investor Conference that year. US Uncut charged BofA with acting like a corporate parasite, sucking profits out of US consumers while contributing nothing to the community and nation wherein it derives those profits.

US Uncut has also focused its efforts on corporate welfare delivered at the state level. US Uncut highlighted Louisiana Governor Bobby Jindal as providing eleven billion dollars to multi-national corporations in the form of taxpayer subsidies while simultaneously proposing that $300 million be cut from public education by slashing budgets at Louisiana state universities and colleges. The founder of US Uncut seeks to reframe the national debate about how to properly deal with recessions and corporate bailouts, instead forcing corporations to pay income and corporate taxes which he claims will recoup $100 billion per year, rather than aggressively gifting corporate welfare while deeply cutting social programs that benefit U.S. citizens.

Protestors Thwart Private Prison Company GEO Group's Stadium Naming Effort

In February 2013, the GEO Group, one of the world's largest private for-profit prison companies, set out to partner with Florida Atlantic University (FAU) in a $6 million football stadium naming deal. Initially, FAU's President Mary Jane Saunders agreed to accept the deal despite the fact that FAU is a majority minority institution and, as discussed above, minorities are disproportionately represented in U.S. prison populations. The nickname "Owlcatraz" was quickly attached to the FAU Owls football stadium after student protests and faculty opposition, including sit-ins, picketing, and demonstrations, drew national media attention to GEO's record of human rights violations in its private prisons. On April 4, 2013, due to lingering opposition and negative national media attention, GEO Group withdrew its pledged stadium naming donation after CEO Zoley released a self-serving statement blaming "distractions" as the reason the pledge was being pulled. The distractions Zoley spoke of included: (a) student protests challenging FAU to reject the donation as hypocritical, pointing out that GEO Group's profit base is derived almost entirely from human misery and suffering, (b) an overwhelmingly passed faculty resolution calling upon President Saunders to cancel the deal because GEO Group's "business practices do not align with the mission of the university," (c) a sit-in held in President Saunder's office by students, (d) a mocking national spotlight from Stephen Colbert's comedy/news show (suggesting that one of the problems of drawing attention to your business, is that people will pay attention to what your business actually does), and (e) community outrage protesting GEO's intimate affiliation with an institution of higher education.

As discussed in previous chapters, the business model of private prison companies is to profit from human misery, by collecting taxpayer funds from federal and state governments to house prisoners on a per bed, or "per diem," fee basis. Profit maximization is often the driving force behind the GEO Group and all other private prison corporations. Shareholders of GEO Group stock look to the board of directors and executives to return large profits by aggressively imprisoning United States citizens, both directly and indirectly targeting minority populations. They do so by lobbying legislatures to increase sentencing laws, devising new laws and ways to imprison citizens, and engaging indirectly in drafting proposed legislation such as SB 1070 (Arizona's "show me your papers" law) and three-strikes laws. This business model enables taxpayer funds to be funneled into private prison companies coffers (and its executives and shareholders pockets) based on dubious claims that they provide prison services for less cost than government agencies. Aside from taxpayer funds lining the pockets of the GEO Group's executives and shareholders, for no genuinely recognizable good or service, private prison companies such as GEO Group exploit the labor of prisoners by entering into contracts with companies whereby prisoners are employed and paid between $0 and $4 per day for their labor. The fruit of their prison labor is paid to the prison company rather than to the prisoner. Indentured servitude continues in our prisons while GEO Group and other private prison corporations profit from these activities.

The students and faculty at FAU, together with the local community in Boca Raton, Florida successfully used the power of the boycott, demonstrations, picketing, and sit-ins to stymie corporate efforts to propagate harmful corporate endeavors in real time. Drawing attention to the negative impacts of corporate efforts can lead to an appropriate holding of corporations' "feet to the fire" when their records and behaviors harm communities and human beings.

University of California System Divests Investments from Private Prison Corporations

In December 2015, the University of California system announced it would divest itself of all investments that support private for-profit prisons by selling it's nearly $30 million in holdings in all companies that operate private prisons. This announcement came after steady pressure from UC students, faculty, and activist organizations such as the Afrikan Black Coalition. This divestment is both significant and symbolic in that the UC system agreed with its students, faculty and organizations that investing in human misery by supporting private prison corporations is antithetical to the mission of institutions of higher education. Further, this move was precipitated by students and activist groups showcasing the power that committed proponents of social justice and human rights can have on United States campuses and in the greater movement for equality and justice worldwide.

While the UC system's divestment of $30 million of stock it held in the Corrections Corporation of America, The GEO Group, and G4S is relatively minor compared to the system's massive portfolio, divesting these funds sends a powerful message that may provide a model for U.S. and global institutional investors to follow when considering financial practices that have both ethical and social implications. The UC system's divestment follows on the heels of, and may very well have been prompted by, Columbia University's divestment of all of its private prison holdings in June 2015. Cutting off capital investment to private prison corporations is an important step in eradicating the private prison regime that is plagued with perverse incentives that lead to racial and economic inequalities as outlined in the chapters above.

Divestment of UC system's direct private prison holdings will be complete when it sells its $30 million in holdings, but the UC system continues to invest $425 million in Wells Fargo which currently extends a $900 million line of credit to Correction Corporation of America, serves as a trustee to GEO Group's $300 million in corporate debt, and owns one million shares in both CCA and the GEO Group. If the UC system wishes to shed all investment connection to private prison corporations, it must address its investment relationship with Wells Fargo.

Notes

(1) After reading about Delores Tucker, the United Methodist Church, the Uncut movements, the GEO Group's failed stadium naming attempt, and the University of California system, are you convinced that shareholder activism can affect change that results in corporate justice?

(2) Can you imagine a role for recent law school graduates and early career lawyers to impact corporate governance law and changing economic policy in the United States?

(3) Were Delores Tucker's efforts counter-intuitive in any way? How has hip hop generated economic prosperity for young black men who have gained enormous economic benefits from the hip hop hustle? Dr. Dre and Jay-Z are both nearing billionaire status. Would this have been possible if Tucker had been successful in eradicating the kind of music that Dre and Jay-Z have produced over their careers?

(4) What result could be affected if a group of Corporate Justice students banded together, purchased nominal shares in various companies that the group agreed injures U.S. citizens and the economy and literally worked to place shareholder proposals on proxy statements and sought speaking opportunities at annual shareholder meetings? Could this impact corporate policymaking in a socially just way?

(5) Some academics and critics of current corporate law are dubious that shareholder activism and/or demonstrations and boycotts will inspire real change in the behavior of entrenched and elite corporate leaders in the United States. These critics argue that lasting change will only come when shareholders are empowered with an ability to genuinely elect members of boards of directors and wield real power in removing ineffective corporate leaders from office. How can shareholder power be reinvigorated in U.S. corporations? Can a reinvigoration of shareholder power partnered with demonstrations, boycotts and activism change status quo practice in corporate law?

Conclusion

Corporate Justice imagines a world where citizen well-being is more important than corporate wealth and corporate entity well-being. Corporate Justice imagines a world where corporations care more about being good global citizens than they do about making shareholders and corporate executives wealthy. This class and book are an introduction to the ways that ordinary citizens, equipped with knowledge, can begin to seek after a fairer and more just corporate world. Despite the length and breadth of this coursebook, we have not had the opportunity to broach many other subjects that impact Corporate Justice, like executive compensation, shareholder primacy, and other subject of import. We hope to cover these issues in classroom conversation and in future editions of this coursebook.

We believe that good corporate lawyers and attorneys possessed of a social conscience, can impact corporate policymaking and force corporate leaders to become aware of all of the ways that many corporations commit positive injury to the communities in which they derive profit and personal wealth. Our work centers on fairness, equality, and corporate social justice. We invite you to join with us in this movement.

At the end of our class each year, we show a video of Dr. Martin Luther King's speech after the Alabama Church Bombing where four young black girls, who were attending Sunday School at the 16th Street Baptist Church in Birmingham, Alabama, on Sunday, September 15, 1963, were maliciously killed, in a cowardly and despicable act of racial hatred, by members of the Ku Klux Klan. Given that Dr. King's speech occurred directly after one of the most heinous crimes of the Civil Rights Era, one might reasonably expect that he would condemn the actors and those that harbored similar hatred; however, Dr. King focused on a different evil. According to Dr. King, "what murdered these four little girls" was:

> "Every Negro who refuses to go down and vote participated in that act."

> "the apathy and the complacency of many Negros who will sit down on their stools and do nothing and not engage in creative protest to get rid of this evil system."

> "the Negro business and professional individual who's more concerned with his job than he is about freedom and justice."

Instead of solely focusing on external forces, Dr. King reminded his listeners that they also have a responsibility to fight for equality, that they have a responsibility to fight the good fight and to endeavor to seek justice. As you reflect on the material that you engaged with in this book, remember that Corporate Justice is not only focused on the responsibilities of board members and CEOs, but it also focuses on the responsibilities of shareholder/owners and ordinary citizens in advocating for an economically responsible society.

We hope that our book inspires students to accept a similar responsibility. We hope that you help to transition members of disadvantaged communities from a consumer mentality to an owner mentality as shareholders. When citizens learn to build wealth rather than focusing on consumption only, opportunities for future generations are built. We further hope that you use your power as future lawyers to hold corporations accountable that sacrifice people, communities, and social justice for purely self-motivated economic gain. And that you endeavor to represent those persons in business matters that do not have a voice or the sophistication to protect themselves. Most importantly, we hope that you will be motivated, empowered and informed about how to make a difference and to seek Corporate Justice.

Todd J. Clark

andré douglas pond cummings

Index